PEREGRINE BOOKS

A MATTER OF HONOUR

'An important contribution to the study of the British adventure in India; a book rich in detail, compassion and understanding' – Shiva Naipaul in the *New Statesman*

From the time of Clive and the conflict with the French until the blood-soaked days of Partition in 1947, British power in India was guaranteed by an army recruited in large part from the people it held in thrall. Only once was the trust between British and Indian broken: at the brutal, violent explosion of the Indian Mutiny in 1857. But even that apparently lethal fracture was mended, and in 1945 the officers and men of the 'forgotten army' in Burma shared a bond which united peoples of vastly different culture, language, religion and background in a common pursuit of honour.

Dwelling sometimes on a campaign, sometimes on an episode from a battle, sometimes on the story of one regiment or one man, Philip Mason carries forward the story of the army's development in successive scenes of colourful variety. He shows how the Indian and British concepts of honour and duty coincided to produce, against all odds, a highly professional military order which was the equal of any in the world.

'He writes with scrupulous fairness, and with an agreeable and legitimate nostalgia' – C. P. Snow in the *Financial Times*

'Unquestionably a major contribution to India's history from 1746 to 1947' – The Marquess of Anglesey in the *Sunday Telegraph*

Philip Mason spent nearly twenty years in the Indian Civil Service, both in district administration and in the Defence Department of the Government of India. After his retirement from the Indian Civil Service he was for some years Director of the Institute of Race Relations. Under the pseudonym of Philip Woodruff he has published several books, including *Call the Next Witness* and two books on the English rule in India, *The Founders* and *The Guardians*, under the general title of *The Men Who Ruled India*. His latest book is *Kipling: The Glass, The Shadow and the Fire* (1975).

PHILIP MASON

A Matter of Honour

AN ACCOUNT OF THE INDIAN ARMY
ITS OFFICERS AND MEN

PENGUIN BOOKS

Penguin Books Ltd, Harmondsworth, Middlesex, England
Penguin Books, 625 Madison Avenue, New York, New York 10022, U.S.A.
Penguin Books Australia Ltd, Ringwood, Victoria, Australia
Penguin Books Canada Ltd, 41 Steelcase Road West, Markham, Ontario, Canada
Penguin Books (N.Z.) Ltd, 182–190 Wairau Road, Auckland 10, New Zealand

—

First published by Jonathan Cape 1974
Published in Peregrine Books 1976

—

Copyright © Philip Mason, 1974

—

Made and printed in Great Britain by
Fletcher & Son Ltd, Norwich and bound by
Richard Clay (The Chaucer Press) Ltd
Bungay, Suffolk
Set in Monotype Baskerville

Contents

PART II. HIGH NOON OF THE SEPOY ARMY

PART III. THE STORM

Illustrations

Garhwali in action during advance on Maungdaw (*Imperial War Museum, London*)
Sikhs of the 14th Army in the Arakan (*Imperial War Museum, London*)
Two Dogras in forward machine-gun position, Kangaw area (*Imperial War Museum, London*)
Eyre Coote (*India Office Library, London*)
Lord Roberts (*Imperial War Museum, London*)
Auchinleck (*Imperial War Museum, London*)
Slim (*Imperial War Museum, London*)

Maps

Foreword

To write a history of the Indian Army on the scale of Fortescue's *History of the British Army* would be the work of a lifetime. This book has no pretensions to be anything of that kind. It is an attempt to sketch the changing relations of officers and men and to answer certain questions about their behaviour. It is set against the general background of the history of the British in India because the purely military aspects do not make sense in isolation. It is based on well-known standard works, memoirs and regimental histories together with some personal knowledge of Indian peasants at home in their villages, and on friendships with many of their officers. It covers two hundred years and all three Presidency Armies—Bengal, Madras and Bombay—as well as the Indian Army that arose from the reorganization of 1895. No existing book covers this span in one narrative. No one who served in the Indian Army will feel there is enough about his own regiment and I can only say that I too wish there could have been more; I have had to leave out a great deal of what I know and of course there is much more I do not know.

I have tried to judge men's behaviour by the standards of their own day. The frightful increase in human powers of destruction has forced us today to think of war in different terms from the Victorians; ideals of conduct have changed and we question a social structure they took for granted. They should be judged by the standards of honour, duty and service they admired, by what they themselves sought to be. Nor should Indian soldiers be judged in terms of a nationalism of which they had no knowledge. Courage is always a virtue and to forget self and die in the service of others is an act with a value of its own, independent of any analysis of the causes for which men suppose they are fighting. There are many dimensions of thought about human behaviour into which this narrative has not entered but for which it may provide a starting-point.

1974   P.M.

Foreword to the Second Printing

I am glad to take the opportunity of a second edition to deal with some points which correspondents have brought to my notice. Where there was a clear mistake of detail which makes no difference to the argument, I have put it right in the text without comment; for example, the Enfield rifle which was coming into use at the time of the Mutiny was not the Lee-Enfield, which was introduced about forty years later. It is a different case where an opinion expressed in the first edition was based on wrong information. Here it seems fairest to put the right view in a footnote, which draws attention to the mistake and permits an apology. This is what I have done on p. 482.

The most difficult matter to deal with has been the topography of Burma, on which I have been sent a good deal of detailed information. Intelligence about the actual state of roads in Burma was always scanty; maps were sometimes misleading; the classification of poor roads becomes quickly out of date and of course both sides in the war were doing their best to improve their own communications and damage the enemy's. I felt that in a book of this kind detailed maps would be out of place and asked a draftsman to superimpose on the map of Burma a diagram showing the main lines of communication. The result, on p. 489, is oversimplified and is misleading if regarded as a map rather than a diagram. To the West of Mandalay, it suggests that there was a bridge over the Irrawaddy, which is not the case. North of Akyab the track from Chittagong should have stopped about half way; again, the track from Myitkyina to Ledo should stop about half way. In both cases, the text, which refers to 'a way through the mountains', rudimentary when the war began but improved later, is better than the diagram.

One correspondent tells me that there were two good bridle-roads from Kalemyo on the Burma side to Falam in the Chin Hills, and that there was an equally good bridle-road, which could easily have been widened, from Falam to Aijal on the Indian side which led on to rail head. This road was maintained and paid for by India but was apparently unknown to anyone in the Burma military command; General Alexander told my correspondent that he had never heard of this route, which would have made a fourth between India and Burma. It is not shown, even as an unclassified track, on the map attached to Admiral Mountbatten's despatch on Burma (HIND 1096 first edn., November 1944). All this underlines the isolation of Burma and goes to show that I made a considerable underestimate on p. 488 in regretting that not one-tenth of the thought given to the North-West Frontier had gone to Burma. I should have written 'not one hundredth'.

1975   P.M.

I

Introductory: Ruffle of Drums

1. Loyalty, Fidelity, Courage

This is a book about people and how they sometimes behave. In particular, it is about Indian soldiers and about certain virtues — loyalty to comrades, fidelity to an oath, courage under stress. Without these virtues, an army is nothing. In what was to become the Indian Army, they grew slowly and uncertainly, but after a time there was born a most unusual relationship between British officers and Indian men. Their confidence in each other conquered an empire; they established in India a centre of power that extended its influence far over Asia and into the Mediterranean.

Then, after a hundred years, came the crash; regiment after regiment rose; the men murdered their officers, their wives and children. The soldiers had been trusted so completely that, as has often been said, there was not an officer in India who would not happily have sent his family on a journey of a thousand miles with one or two of them as escort. But now confidence was shattered. They no longer believed in the good faith of their officers or of the Government. With terrible savagery on both sides, the Mutiny was repressed; what is most remarkable, a new army was built in the place of the old, a new comradeship grew which cherished some of the old traditions. This new Indian Army, for the rest of the High Victorian period, was one of the main pillars of the Empire and of the Pax Britannica. The Royal Navy policed the seas of the world but would have been ineffective without land forces far larger than Britain was willing to provide from the homeland. It was the Indian Army that made possible control of Asia and the Mediterranean and Cape routes. In the First World War it provided help when help was most needed if the British Army was to survive in France; it held the Suez Canal and the Persian Gulf and eventually defeated the Turks. In the Second World War the revived Indian Army reached its highest point of efficiency and success. Without conscription, two and a half million men came to the colours; it was the largest voluntary army ever raised in the history of the world.

Indian soldiers showed that they could defeat Germans and Japanese. Then, two years after victory, this army was divided between two new sovereign nations and at the same time two hundred years of close co-operation between British and Indian came to an end.

It is a story of many ups and downs, sometimes of victory, sometimes of dogged endurance and defeat; there is much of which both British and Indian may be proud and there are things of which both should be ashamed. But one thread is constant. Weapons, equipment, training —these changed decade by decade. The ability to move quickly and bring force to bear on the enemy at the selected point—this was always needed though the means of achieving it changed. All these were ingredients of victory. But the one unchanging factor, the spirit which makes an army effective, was the confidence in each other of officers and men; this in its turn depends on those three virtues—loyalty, fidelity, courage.

How are they born? What makes a man cling with unbelievable tenacity and in the face of wounds and exhaustion to *honour*—something that will send him out of cover into fire to bring back a wounded com-rade, that will bring him to his feet when he is at the point of death and send him in a last charge to save a piece of coloured silk? Why should *honour* inspire men whose homes are not threatened by invasion, to whom the cause for which they are fighting is remote and unintelligible? Why should they rise sometimes to heroic heights—and why sometimes should they angrily reject their oath, refuse obedience and even kill their officers?

Officers, indeed, have usually had something to fight for. They have belonged to a society which rewards them, if they are successful, with titles, lands or pensions, which, even if they never rise to any great distinction, addresses them in terms of respect, and gives them rank and the means to live in tolerable comfort. But in most periods of history it is hard to see what the men have had to fight for. Think of Nelson's sailors and Wellington's soldiers, often snatched from their homes by the press-gang, or picked up by the recruiting-sergeant because they were in trouble. It was not for money that they fought. Throughout the eighteenth century, the pay of a British soldier was sixpence a day. In 1792 there was a special concession of a bread allowance at 10½d. a week, bringing the total earnings of an infantry private for a week to 4s. 4½d. But he was stopped 3s. a week for food and about 1s. 3d. for cleaning materials, pipeclay, shoes, washing and the like. It did not often happen that he saw sixpence a week in cash. And the conditions of the soldier's life were often frightful; they were subject to harsh discipline and brutal floggings. Yet these men stood fast against the French. 'Whence came the spirit', asks Sir John Fortescue, of the infantry at Albuera, 'which made that handful of battalions ... content to die where they stood rather than give way one inch?' It was not only death they faced but wounds, surgery without anaesthetics, life as a cripple and often as a beggar. Many of them at Albuera realized that their general was 'making a very ill hand of the battle', yet 'when one man in every two, or even two in every three, had fallen, the survivors were still in line by their colours, closing in towards the tattered silk which represented the ark of their covenant.' And, after standing fire and repelling assaults for hours, they were still able to clinch victory with a charge. Sir John's answer is that 'beyond all question' this spirit sprang from 'intense regimental pride'. No doubt — but how is regimental pride born? And surely in their case there was national pride as well?

If these questions need to be asked about British soldiers, how much more force do they carry of Indian! For here were men whose officers were of a different faith and spoke a different language, who *looked* different physically, whose food, drink and everyday habits were remote from those of their men. What made Indian soldiers give their lives for a flag they could hardly call their own? National pride did not play much part till late in their long history. It was only in the Second World War that it appeared and then only occasionally. When it did, it was a two-edged sword: pride in the regiment, in the division, yes, that was something on which everyone could agree, but pride in a nation that was not yet a nation produced very mixed feelings. Officers and men could not share it in the same spirit. Was it then for money that they fought? Certainly their pay, though far from princely, was relatively better than the British soldier's. But it explains nothing to say simply that they were 'mercenary'. Men may come to the colours for pay but it is not for pay that they earn the Victoria Cross. It is an unprofitable servant who does only his duty and there are times when a soldier is expected to do far more. These men often did.

Take, for example, the affair at Koregaum on New Year's Day, 1818. Captain Staunton, of the Bombay Army, received orders on New Year's Eve to bring the troops under his command to reinforce Colonel Burr, 41 miles away, whose two battalions were in danger of being cut off by the larger forces of the Peshwa, the Maratha chief. Staunton marched at eight o'clock that evening. He had some 500 sepoys, that is, privates, of the Bombay Army (the 2nd Battalion of the 1st Bombay Regiment, later the 2nd Battalion, 4th Bombay Grenadiers), 250 newly raised auxiliary horse (who eventually became the Poona Horse), and a party of the Madras Artillery. There were two six-pounder guns with 24 European gunners and some Indian drivers and gun lascars, the whole artillery contingent probably numbering about 100 men, the entire force being less than 900. They marched all night, covering 27 miles, and at about ten in the morning on New Year's Day were preparing to halt for rest during the heat of the day, when they came suddenly in view of the Peshwa's main army. This consisted of about 20,000 horse and 8,000 infantry. The village of Koregaum, with stone-built houses and enclosures, was close at hand, and Staunton at once saw that his best move was to take up a defensive position in the village. But the enemy were equally quick and dispatched three columns of their best Arab troops, each column about a thousand strong, to prevent him.

Neither side was able to occupy the whole village before the other, and there developed a battle, house to house and hand to hand, in the course of which almost every building was taken and retaken. The horse could not be used as cavalry; they fought on foot as infantry. It was thus an infantry and artillery battle, centring on the two guns. The men had eaten nothing since the previous evening and could not reach the well. Attack after attack was launched and driven back. At one point the Arabs captured one of the two guns, killing Lt Chisholm, the only artillery officer, and cutting off his head. But before they could carry his body away or make use of the gun, Lt Pattinson, who had been supposed killed, struggled to his feet from a pile of corpses and called on the Grenadier company of the 2nd/1st to follow him in a charge. They recaptured the gun and he again collapsed, dying later. Towards evening, the enemy called on the British to surrender. Twelve of the British gunners had been killed and eight wounded; the four who were left spoke of asking for terms but Staunton would have none of it and his sepoys were with him; the whole force swore to fight till the last man. They fought on, the seven unwounded gun lascars, not generally reckoned as combatants, working one of the guns when no Europeans survived. About nine o'clock that night, twenty-five hours after their march had begun, Staunton's force cleared the village of the enemy and were able to get water.

When it was light, they found that the whole enemy army was withdrawing, doubtless because they had news of British forces moving up to join Colonel Burr. Staunton's force brought away colours, guns and wounded and marched for the nearest garrison town, where they arrived forty-eight hours after they had left their own station. During that time they had had no food and had been constantly marching or fighting. For nearly twelve hours of fighting they had been without water. The 2nd/1st had lost 50 men killed and 105 wounded out of fewer than 500. Of the 250 auxiliary horse, ninety were killed, wounded or missing. Of nine British officers, only Staunton, one subaltern and the doctor were unwounded; also four gunners out of twenty-four. But, before reaching the town where they might expect rest, they halted to dress their ranks and marched in with drums beating and colours flying.

Many such tales could be told, and the question is still unanswered. Their general wrote, after Koregaum, of the sepoys' 'most noble devotion and most romantic bravery under pressure of thirst and hunger almost beyond human endurance'. Why did they give such service? Was it for a naked oath—the oath of allegiance they swore when they passed out as recruits and were enlisted as soldiers? Was it the personal honour of a man who followed the profession of arms, as his ancestors had done and as his descendants would do after him, and who feared the shame of cowardice? Was it respect—sometimes even affection—for the personal qualities of his officers? Was it fear of an iron discipline? Was there simply a long-instilled habit of endurance? What were the links in the chain of confidence and why did they sometimes snap? They were perhaps harder to forge in the Indian Army than in the British, they were certainly more brittle. Yet how moving, how dazzling to see their strength under a great commander!

None of these questions can be answered by a simple yes or no. If you could answer each of them—and every answer would involve some exception or qualification—you might have some idea of what went to make up the spirit that, at its best, animated this unusual army—or armies, for at first, in a rambling illogical way that is both British and Indian, there were three. In the course of the book some answers to these questions will emerge. In the meantime it is easier to be definite about the results of that spirit. Let us look for a moment, in the broadest of surveys, at what the Indian Army, as an instrument of policy, achieved in the course of two centuries.

2. The First Hundred Years

In the first quarter of the eighteenth century, and indeed well into the second, both the French and the English had some small trading-stations on the coasts of India; they were suppliants to the powerful princes who were nominally Viceroys or Governors on behalf of the Mughal Emperor in Delhi. That distinguished French soldier, the Count de Bussy, wrote:

'Only six years ago, the Nawab of Arcot behaved to the French as a sovereign to his subjects. We never appeared before him but as suppliants, carrying presents which he continually exacted from us. If any even of his inferior officers came towards Pondicherry, formal deputations were sent out to meet him with the greatest marks of respect, and as for the Nizam himself [the Nawab's overlord, the Viceroy of the South], he deigned not to write to any European governor and hardly honoured with a look the rich presents he brought.' This was the position of the English as well as the French.

Within a few years, by the middle of the century, all this was changed. Every power in the south of India was aware that both the French and

English had a military secret which enabled them to triumph over greatly superior forces; this appeared to be a system of drill and training which they could teach others. Alliance with the French or the English was the best way of ensuring success; Indian powers were now competing for their favour. If neither could be persuaded to join a prince as his ally, the next best thing he could do was to persuade a French or British officer to join his service and train his troops. Thus, as early as 1751, the Maratha chief Balaji Baji Rao, the Peshwa, was defeated by troops of the Nizam trained by Bussy. He recognized that he had met something new and tried to induce Bussy to transfer to his army. Bussy was not then prepared to make the change and the best the Peshwa could do was to obtain two Muslim officers whom Bussy had trained.

Thus by the middle of the century there was a new force in the Indian scene. There was a new way of fighting and training troops— more important, and not yet clearly recognized, there was a new approach to war and to the profession of arms. There were two European powers who were supplementing their own very small forces by training Indians in the new methods. At first it seemed as though the French and English might continue, side by side, as pieces on the chessboard of Indian politics, alongside the Emperor in Delhi, the Nizam at Hyderabad, the Nawab of Arcot and the rest; others would learn the new way of fighting, the first advantage of the Europeans would be lost. But this general expectation made no allowance for 'the long, steady, deep-rooted, rational antipathies of the great French and English nations'; one or the other had to be master and neither could suffer the other to remain. And later it gradually became clear that the new method of fighting became fully effective only when it was backed by a new kind of government. It demanded a certain permanence, a continuity in policy, a courteous attitude to the future that was rare in Indian monarchs but essential to the confidence of troops.

In another ten years, by 1760, it was clear that the future lay with the English; the French bid for the empire of India had failed, though it remained a bogy to the English until Waterloo. The British were now strong in Madras and were masters of the rich province of Bengal; Warren Hastings quickly perceived that 'the resources of this country [Bengal] in the hands of a military people...are capable of raising them to the dominion of all India.' This was an outcome that he feared, but which nevertheless came about; before that could be said to have happened, however, the East India Company's armies had to meet three considerable military powers and were to suffer many set-backs.

There were the wars against Hydar Ali and his son Tippoo Sahib, the Tiger of Mysore—both, and particularly Hydar, men of considerable military ability and far more skilled than the British in rapid movement. There were the wars against the Marathas, the great campaigns of Lake and Wellesley and Lord Hastings's vast encircling movement, commonly called the Pindarry War; there was the last great challenge of the Sikhs. Of these, both the Sikhs and the Marathas had shown signs of becoming a nation. But in both cases there had been a falling-off in the national spirit of the army and, when the tug-of-war came, both armies were for the moment past their national peak. There was also the ill-judged and quite unnecessary war with Afghanistan and the disastrous retreat from Kabul. There had been expeditions to Malaya and the Dutch East Indies, to Egypt, Persia, China, Burma and the French islands of the Indian Ocean. By the middle of the century, the whole of India had become, directly or indirectly, subject to British rule, while most of Asia lay under the influence of this new centre of power. In all these wars, the instruments of policy had been soldiers, British and Indian. Sometimes there had been four or five Indian battalions fighting beside one British; sometimes the proportion had been more, sometimes less, but the valour and fidelity of Indian troops had throughout been essential to the enterprise.

3. The Breakdown of Confidence

After the hard-fought battles with the Sikhs, there were no more worlds to conquer. The impetus that had carried the army forward was checked and a kind of dead heaviness began to settle on the land. Financial pedantry was part of it and the sepoy was rewarded for victory by the loss of allowances, but there was much more than this. Regulations grew more strict; there was less room for the kind of officer whose eccentricities had relieved the drabness of the system and inspired his men to follow him 'over the hob of hell'. A narrow humourless intolerance about religion infected many of the British. One of the greatest of the Governors-General put into key positions of power men who saw little good in anything Indian; they were ardent disciples of progress and equality, who looked on the traditional chiefs as no better than brigands. In the Lieutenant-Governor of a province this new spirit might mean hurrying on every reform that seemed, in the cold light of reason, to be dictated by the greatest good of the greatest number; in a newly joined subaltern the same spirit was more likely to mean indifference to his men, reluctance to learn their language, contempt for their customs, a slighting disregard shown every day in word, gesture or expression. Courtesy on one side, respect on the other, still existed but they became more rare. It was in this atmosphere of slighted honour, of failing confidence, that certain sparks fell and the conflagration of the Great Mutiny flared up.

At this stage, two points only need be made. The sepoys of a great part of the Bengal Army had lost confidence in the good will and good faith of their officers and of the Government; how far it was national feeling that moved them is a matter of controversy, but there can be no serious doubt that they were *afraid*—for their religion and way of life, for the esteem in which they were held, for the future of their sons. And their fear was not wholly groundless; much of what they valued really was threatened. Secondly, the loss of confidence was not general throughout India, or throughout the army. Indians played a big part in repressing the Mutiny. The British troops could not move without drivers for guns and baggage, without cooks, water-carriers and sweepers; for every European soldier on the Ridge at Delhi there were ten Indians, exposed to the same hardships and often to the same dangers. But the non-combatants are only one part of the story; Indian troops, too, flowed in to relieve and support the British. Gurkhas of the Sirmoor Battalion (later the 2nd Gurkha Rifles) were on the Ridge at Delhi from the beginning of that long-drawn-out affair. The Guides made a famous march from Hoti-Mardan to Delhi, covering 580 miles in 22 days, coming in with step 'as firm and light as if they had marched only a mile', and turning out to fight on the afternoon of the day they arrived. 'We could not have held our own for a day without help from natives of India.' 'In camp, there is a feeling of confidence in our native troops, Guides, Goorkhas, Coke's Rifles [later 13th Frontier Force Rifles] and Sikhs, all are popular and I think all are smart and useful.'

Those who mutinied came from the Bengal Army and, in general, from the regiments recruited in Oudh. For this there were special reasons, to be discussed later. There were no mutinies in the Madras Army; in the Bombay Army, there were mutinies only in two battalions, and only in certain companies of those. Both the southern armies sent help to the north; the Punjab poured troops to the storm-centres of Delhi and Lucknow. These points must be emphasized here to explain what followed—a great acceleration of the move northward of the army's recruiting-grounds.

4. The Drift to the North

From earliest times, the British had found it necessary to employ natives of the country to guard their factories and warehouses. But at first these were little more than armed watchmen or bands of swash-bucklers, generally hired as a body through some acknowledged leader of their own. They were not soldiers—men recruited direct, trained and sworn in, with known obligations and fixed pay, organized in companies with officers and non-commissioned officers. The first soldiers in this sense were, in Madras, some of them local men, either Hindus or Muslims, while some were adventurers from farther north. The Bombay Army was for long dependent to a more considerable extent on northerners from Rajputana, Oudh and Behar, partly because the territories of Bombay were less extensive than those of the other Presidencies but mainly because for a long time their nearest neighbours — the Marathas — although fine material, were enemies. The Bengal Army, to begin with, took whatever men offered themselves as soldiers. These were seldom if ever Bengalis; they came from 'up the country', which meant from farther up the Ganges, and they were most of them from Behar, with — getting fewer as you went farther — some from Oudh and Rohilkand, some from the Punjab and some from Afghanistan.

In all three armies, officers were concerned about the appearance of their men on parade; they liked to see tall men, and they preferred them to be as fair in complexion as was convenient and to have features of the kind they sometimes called 'Grecian'. Men of fine appearance, of a 'noble' or 'manly' countenance — these are expressions you meet constantly in the military memoirs of the Company's armies. There were always a few officers of the Madras and Bombay Armies to put in a good word for the sepoy who had been born in the south; his fidelity and his courage had been proved again and again. None the less, a preference for men who looked well on parade constantly asserted itself, even in these armies. One example — almost unbelievable because of its ingratitude and stupidity — will be enough to make the point.

For about a century and a half, it was a distinction to be a Grenadier. One company in a battalion, or at some periods in India two companies out of ten, were Grenadiers. They stood on the right of the line on parade; they wore special headgear and 'wings' or epaulettes. They were picked men and had to be above average height; the Grenadier company would be chosen for a task of special danger or difficulty. For a whole battalion to be designated Grenadiers was a very special honour indeed. This honour was conferred on the 2nd/1st Bombay Infantry after Koregaum and the title was still borne in 1947 by the 2nd/4th Bombay Grenadiers. The names of the fifty dead at Koregaum were recorded on a monument; they show that two were Muslims and eight Rajputs, while forty came from the south and of these no less than twenty-two were of very low caste, commonly regarded as untouchable. But since Grenadiers must be tall, the 2nd/1st from then on recruited only Muslims, Rajputs and men from Oudh. The reward of valour was loss of employment.

There was thus a drift to the north, as a recruiting-ground, long before the Mutiny. Until the late 1840s, when still taller men were available from the Punjab, the tendency had been increasingly towards Oudh, and to men of the higher castes. After the Mutiny, the preference for taller and fairer men was reinforced by the fact of solid help from the north in the time of trouble. At the same time, the centre of military attention was on the north-west; Afghanistan and Russia were the possible enemies. In the south there were none; there was nothing left for a soldier but dull cantonment life. The steadfastness of the sepoy from the south was forgotten.

In the years from the Mutiny to the First World War, then, there were more and more Punjabis and Gurkhas; the Oudh sepoys, who had been the backbone of the armies which had defeated Nepal and the Punjab, were now hardly recruited at all. Commanding officers, if left to themselves, usually tended to specialize in a particular class of recruit—a personal liking being reinforced by the convenience of having, at least in one company, men who ate the same kind of food and would eat it together. And the easiest, and in some ways the best, way to recruit was simply to let men go to their villages on leave and bring back their sons and cousins. The result would be a unit closely knit by bonds of blood, region, speech, religion and caste. When the men were well led and contented, it made for valour and fidelity, for pride in the regiment and in its good name. But if the men were badly led or treated in a way that they felt was slighting, it might also mean that they were united in resentment, and, if the worst came to the worst, in mutiny. It made for a close-knit permanent unit, highly professional, in which men made their careers. But it was far from being the ideal basis for an army which in war had to expand to several times its peace-time strength. So there was sometimes a tendency at the centre to press commanding officers to spread their nets wider than their individual preferences might have suggested.

This was one of the points of controversy which developed, but there were many others. In the eighteenth century, in the days of the Company's three armies, there had been controversy, in Europe as well as in India, about the relative advantages of solid mass and extended line, of Prussian discipline against open order and the individual initiative of skilled marksmen. The British had been defeated in America; they had learnt in the American forests what men who knew the woods, and had lived with their weapons since boyhood, could do against regular troops drilled on the parade-ground. On the other hand, their victories in Spain and Portugal showed what a highly disciplined line could do against the Napoleonic columns. But these were not purely tactical arguments; the American sharpshooters were skilled in forest warfare because of the conditions in which they lived; Napoleon made use of columns because conscription put large numbers at his disposal and because, ever since the Revolution, France had to put armies into the field before they could be trained to manœuvre in line. At a deeper level, French revolutionary armies might be ready to die for France — but were they prepared to drill with the exact precision that had been enforced by Frederick the Great? That kind of discipline does not always go with fraternity and equality and an army is the reflection of the State it serves. A certain kind of State is likely to have a certain kind of army. Conversely, the kind of army which a State chooses may transform the State and its whole society, as Sparta's did and Prussia's.

Another controversy peculiar to India, and one which lasted more than a hundred years, concerned the number of British officers appointed to an Indian battalion of infantry. One school argued that everything depended on the British officers and they must supervise everything; there should be at least as many as in a British battalion. The contrary view was that this reduced the responsibility of the Indian officers, who became mere figureheads; it was better to leave internal management to the Indian officers and to run the battalion with as few British as possible. This, of course, appealed to the Government because it was cheaper. It was this kind of argument that led to the widespread use of irregular units, particularly of cavalry. These often had only three British officers: commandant, adjutant and quartermaster; Jacob's Horse (later the 14th Scinde Horse), which was brilliantly led, proved the point admirably. But tempers were not lost on this controversy so often as they were about caste.

In both the Madras and the Bombay Armies, the British had from the first made as little as possible of caste. Men stood in the ranks without any regard for their position in the world outside; to an extent really startling for India, they ate and slept together without regard to these distinctions. 'We put our religion into our knapsacks whenever our colours are unfurled,' said an old subadar of the Madras Army in the 1830s. But this was not at all the case in the Bengal Army. Here only the highest castes were admitted and constant care was taken to avoid any breach of caste restrictions. The historian of the Bombay Army has a tale of an Oudh man of high caste who asked for his discharge from the Bengal Army because a man of a lower caste had been promoted. Having obtained it, he then re-enlisted in the Bombay Army, where much less account was taken of caste and he had to undergo far greater indignities. When asked why he had behaved so strangely, he replied that in Hindustan — that is, in the Bengal Army — it was in their caste that men took pride, but in Bombay it was in the battalion.* Like

---

* It is a very pithy remark in the original: 'Hindustan, *jāt kī ghairat*; Bombay, *paltan kī ghairat*.' *Ghairat* means 'jealousy, care of what is sacred, a nice sense of honour' — very much what Sir John Fortescue meant by 'the ark of their covenant'. *Jāt* here means 'caste', and *paltan* is the English word 'battalion'.

all epigrams, this overstated the point, but there was a good deal in it none the less.

Long before the Mutiny, officers from the two southern armies had constantly criticized the Bengal Army for being too indulgent about caste. It might therefore have been expected that, when the Bengal battalions had mutinied while theirs stood fast, the new army would have been built up on the southern system of putting religion in the knapsack. This was not so. The new army was built on the caste or class *company*. There were notable exceptions – class *battalions* of Sikhs, Marathas, Dogras and Garhwalis – but the most general pattern was the mixed battalion, with one or two companies of Punjabi Muslims, one or two companies of Sikhs, and perhaps a company of Rajputs and one of Dogras, Pathans or Baluchis. Thus the company, not the battalion, became a family affair, and it was in the company that a man hoped his son would find a future. Uniformity in the company made for convenience in administration and recruiting; diversity in the battalion sprang from mistrust after the Mutiny. There could hardly, in such an army, be a widespread conspiracy to restore Muslim rule, such as some had seen in the events of 1857. Yet, paradoxically and unexpectedly, there grew up a comradeship between companies which overrode religious differences.

Behind the reconstruction of the Bengal Army on class lines lay undoubtedly the deep feeling of the late Victorian British about the importance of heredity. Their own startling predominance in wealth, power and prestige seemed to some of them proof that the Almighty was on their side, to others confirmation of the Darwinian view that nature contrived that the fittest and best should reach the top. And no doubt many held both of these inconsistent views at the same time. Either view implied that there were others only less favoured or less fit than themselves. All they saw in India confirmed their opinion; there were hereditary money-lenders, washermen, goldsmiths and scavengers; there were hereditary rulers and soldiers. It was common sense to recognize this and not waste effort trying to turn money-lenders into soldiers. Besides, to recognize the difference was the surest way of enlisting the loyalty of the 'martial races', as they came to be called. The division of the people into 'martial' and 'non-martial' was not an invention of the British; it was the recognition of something already implicit in the Indian social system. But it was extremely convenient to a conqueror.

5. A Modern Army

There were still three armies, with three commanders-in-chief and three lists of officers, long after the Company had ceased to rule. They were amalgamated only in 1895. By that date the Indian Army was—the phrase must be repeated—a highly professional army, the men serving for twenty-one years and both officers and men being more likely than in the British army to have had some experience of active service. It was an army designed to keep the peace in India and to be able to dispatch a temporary force to the Persian Gulf, Malaya, Hong Kong or China; it was strong enough to deal with 'the minor danger'—that is, attack by any Asian power then envisaged—and to provide against the 'major danger' a delaying screen that would give time for reinforcements to come from England. The 'major danger' was defined as a European power, and in the nineteenth century this meant Russia. But the Indian Army at the turn of the century was not designed for contribution to a world war lasting four years. Much of the organization for this had to be improvised while the war was in progress.

Between the First and Second World Wars the first task was to complete the transformation from a professional army designed for a local task into a modern army, capable of rapid expansion in war and of meeting a first-class power. This involved reorganization, rearming, the revision of all training, the substitution of tanks for cavalry, of engines for mules, bullocks, camels and elephants. It meant foreseeing the importance of air power. It cannot be argued that officers at Army Headquarters in India were more far-sighted than those at the War Office in London, and they were much more heavily handicapped than the War Office by lack of funds. At the same time, they were confronted by a second task of a quite different order, a political and social problem of the greatest complexity. They were taking the first steps in turning an army which had established foreign rule over the whole of India into a national army which would be the instrument of an independent State. The higher officers had all been British; clearly, after Independence they would not be, and a somewhat hesitant start was made with training Indian officers to replace them. A really far-sighted and all-powerful statesman would perhaps have seen that this ought to imply training the men to a new outlook as citizens—but British officers had never thought in these kinds of terms, and there was truth in the charge made by Indian leaders that Indian soldiers still thought of themselves as the favoured servants of a foreign power. Almost until the end, there were some British officers who could think of Indian national leaders only as 'disloyal'.

Sir John Fortescue's *History of the British Army* runs to many volumes. A history of the Indian Army on that scale would demand a lifetime's work; perhaps some day such a task will be undertaken. This book, however, is nothing of the kind. It will tell the story in the broadest outline, sketching only some of the major campaigns but pausing now and then to dwell in detail on some incident that illustrates one of the central themes. The first of these is the spirit that animated this army when it was at its best, and the reasons why it sometimes failed. What were the reasons for its victories? How did it differ from the Indian armies of the eighteenth century and before, and why was it able to defeat them? What did it borrow from them as it developed? For it was not simply a British institution transplanted to India; it was the child of two parents, one British, one Indian. Until 1914 many regiments of cavalry were still *silladāri* — that is to say, the regiment was a kind of joint-stock company in which the trooper paid for his horse and equipment when he joined and sold them back when he left. This was directly descended from the practice in the Mughal and Maratha cavalry. In the infantry, the British-trained sepoy before the Mutiny might look a stiff pipeclayed figure beside a matchlock man of a Mughal army or a Maratha horseman — but he came of the same stock, his habits, his food, his religion were theirs, and were utterly foreign to a private of the Dorsets or the Black Watch. He could not be managed as British soldiers were. He might drill much as they did, but when the parade was dismissed he went back to another world. What did his officers think of him and he of them? How did this relationship change in the course of two hundred years? And how did this army fit into the vast empire which it conquered and laid at the feet of the English, attempted to snatch back, and laid at their feet again?

Part I
How It Began

II

French and English

1. A Rabble of Peons

'All Frenchmen', wrote Sir John Fortescue in an age when Englishmen had more self-confidence than they have today, 'had, and still have, a passion for interference with the internal politics of any barbarous or semi-civilized races with which they may be brought into contact.' A French historian might find that remark more just if applied to the English, but he might still concede that it was the French who first saw the military and political opportunities presented to foreigners by the India of the eighteenth century.

Both nations came to trade. Both found it necessary to guard the warehouses in which they stored goods till the arrival of ships from Europe. But the French were quicker to perceive that Indians might be trained and disciplined as soldiers in the same way as Europeans. François Martin had enlisted natives of India as early as 1674, and in 1693, with only thirty-six French and between three and four hundred drilled native troops, he was able to defend Pondicherry for twelve days against a Dutch force of nineteen ships carrying 1,500 Dutch infantry. Again, on the west coast of India, between 1721 and 1729, there was a rehearsal of the later French and English wars on the east coast, and the French speak of 'nos çypayes, soutenus de quelques soldats'. But it was in 1739 that the idea was taken up on a larger scale. In this year, Dumas, the predecessor as Governor of the great Dupleix, 'by a happy inspiration, armed four or five thousand Mahommedan natives and trained and drilled them after the European model. Thus was conceived', wrote Fortescue, 'in danger and emergency the embryo, now grown to such mighty manhood, of a Sepoy Army.'

There was another turning-point which must be scored to the French credit. In 1746 an engineer officer in the French service, M. Paradis, with 230 French soldiers and 700 sepoys, and with no artillery, attacked across a river an Indian force of over 10,000 men, strongly posted and with guns, and drove them headlong from the field. This, the battle of San Thomé, was the first occasion of many which proved that a

resolute attack by properly trained men could usually defeat the
forces of an Indian prince ten times as numerous. From this moment
the French, and a little later the English, ceased to be suppliants;
from now on it was they who were courted.

The English were slower than the French to turn from their ginghams
and mull-mulls, their taffeties and muslins. From their earliest days,
they had employed armed men. This was necessary because, even at
its best, the Mughal Empire was a very loose organization. The
first duties of its local officers were to guard against insurrection and to
collect the revenue. The administration of justice and police-work were
secondary and were often delegated. All over India there were chiefs,
rajas, barons and landowners, who administered a kind of justice
themselves and maintained some degree of order. The Mughal Empire
was a union of these local leaders, in which each was as independent as
the circumstances of the moment permitted him to make himself. As in
feudal Europe, the authorities were of the most varied kind; their
duties and privileges, their rank in regard to each other, were not
exactly defined and would usually depend on the ability and energy
of one man—or sometimes of one woman when the heir was a small boy.
In such a society, anyone who possessed property took steps to protect
it; there is a widespread Indian saying: 'Whoever has the club gets the
buffalo.'* The English Company, wrote the historian of the Madras
Army, 'like a caravan travelling through the desert, carried arms to
protect themselves, and when attacked made use of them'—but as far
as possible they avoided such encounters as bad for trade.

Self-defence, however, was not the whole story. That every landowner
or employer should administer justice was the custom of the country
and it applied even among the servants of a large household. As the
Company grew, and the number of its people increased, it became
inevitable that it should take its place as a part of Indian society—
indeed, of the Empire—like any other chief or landowner. When, to
give one example, the Emperor at Delhi sold to the East India Company
in Bengal the rights of a *zamindar*—who might very roughly be called
lord of the manor—in three villages, they appointed one of their
number to act in this capacity. His duties were twofold. He was the
collector of revenues, but also judge in 'all matters both civil and
criminal, wherein the natives only, subjects of the Mogul, are concerned. He tried in a summary way ...' He was exercising the ordinary
rights of a chief. He was an official of the Empire. This meant he must
have some force at his disposal. And this, in a way they had not always
clearly understood, had been the case with all the foreign settlements
from the beginning.

---

* It is very pithy in the original: '*Jis ki lāthi, us ki bhains.*'

In Bombay, four companies of British troops arrived in 1662; they were ordered in 1668 to ground their arms as the King's men and take them up, if they wished, as the Company's men. This they did and, after a very mixed history of nearly two hundred years, transferred back to the Crown in 1858. They were at that date the First Bombay Fusiliers; their lineal descendants, the 2nd Battalion the Royal Dublin Fusiliers, were disbanded in 1922. In 1684 two companies of Rajputs were entertained, but they do not seem to have had British officers or any regular drill or discipline. In 1704 a new Governor of Bombay complained of the raggedness of the soldiers, who looked 'more like bandits in the woods than military men' — as well they might, for their pay was four years in arrears. In 1706 three companies of 'Gentoos' — which here means 'Hindus'; in Madras it meant 'speakers of Telegu' were disbanded for neglect of duty. There were other ups and downs, but the general pattern seems to have been that there were, up till the middle of the eighteenth century, three kinds of armed men at Bombay. There were always some European troops, usually including a number of 'mestees', or men of mixed Portuguese and Indian origin, some of them often too old for duty; a number of 'topasses', which usually meant Indian Christians with Portuguese names; and some 'sepoys', that is, Hindus or Muslims with no regular uniforms or system of discipline. (The word 'Sepoy' is the way our ancestors spelt *Sipāhi*, from a Persian word *Sipāh*, an army.) None of these sound like a military force liable to inspire confidence in a friend or fear in an enemy. Nor were things better at Madras. As late as February 1747 the native foot soldiers there were still known as peons; there were about 3,000 of them, of whom only 900 had muskets. They were at this time wholly un-disciplined and no British officers had direct command of them.

It was the war with the French that changed all this. In Europe, the French and English were intermittently at war from 1688, when William of Orange became William III, until the final defeat of Napoleon in 1815. The periods of formal war did not, however, always mean hostilities in India, nor did fighting there always end when peace was signed in Europe. For example, from 1740 to 1748 there was war in Europe and open hostilities in India, but when peace came in Europe, fighting continued in India under the pretence of assistance to Indian princes. This was the state of things for nearly ten years, until it was replaced by formal war. By 1763, when the Seven Years' War ended and peace was signed in Europe, the French in India were beaten.

2. The First Round

The French were not only the first to train and drill Indians and the
first to demonstrate the importance of unhesitating attack; they were
also the first to understand that the Mughal Empire was crumbling
and to see how its authority could be used to their advantage. They
could be part of it — and, like the other parts, they could struggle for the
remnants of power. At its best, as I have said, the Empire was a loose
union of chiefs and local governors; often a hereditary chief was also
an official; often an official succeeded in making his office hereditary.
From the death of Aurangzebe in 1707, the actual military strength of
the Emperor was in decline and it was easier for his great officials
to assert their will against him. But his prestige was still immense and to
many chiefs it was still valuable to hold some title from the Emperor.
So Dumas, Governor of all the French stations in India, perceived the
advantage to his masters in France of doing a service to the representatives of the Emperor in the south and of himself holding a title, which
he petitioned should be perpetual to his successors instead of hereditary
to his children.

The background to all that followed, confusing in the extreme if
expressed in detail, is simple enough in essence. There is the Emperor
at Delhi — a shadow, 'a pageant', as the English of the eighteenth
century called him — and his Viceroy of the South, the aged Nizam of
the Deccan, in practice almost independent. But the Nizam's power,
too, is not what it was and his Governor of the coastal regions, the
Nawab of the Carnatic, with his headquarters at Arcot, looks at the
Nizam much as the Nizam looks at the Emperor. The Nawab, too, is
more a hereditary prince than an official and he obeys his overlord
only when it suits him or when he is threatened by overwhelming
force. And the same is true right down the feudal line; the barons of the
south — the *polygars* — pay their revenue when they must. Since they are
frequently protected by thick jungle and steep ravines, or can retire to
an isolated fort on some precipitous rock, there are many occasions
when it is safe to defy the emperor's representative. This is the crumbling
network of the Empire. Even this does not reach to the tip of the
peninsula; in the far south, beyond the jurisdiction of the Nizam or of
the Nawab of the Carnatic, are a group of independent states, of
which the most important are Tanjore and Mysore. Mysore, the last
remnant of a great empire, was soon, for a brief period of two generations, to expand once more and become one of the most formidable
opponents of the British. And to the north and west of the Nizam's
dominions lay the vigorous power of the Marathas — Hindu peasants of
the Deccan and the Western Ghats — whom their great leader Sivaji
had raised in revolt against Aurangzebe and had almost forged into a

nation. They were rebels against the Mughal Empire almost by
definition; their swiftly moving cavalry might erupt at any point and
could often defeat a ponderous Mughal army.

Indeed, this was how Dumas seized his first chance. The Marathas
swept into the Carnatic in 1740 and defeated an army led by the Nawab
of the Carnatic, who was left dead on the field. His widow, with her
children, and with such men and treasure as she could bring from Arcot,
fled for sanctuary to Pondicherry. She was joined by many chiefs and
courtiers. Dumas saw the danger, but also the advantages, of harbouring
them. He calculated that the Marathas were birds of passage, while the
network of the Empire was still strong enough to bring him political,
and eventually commercial, profit. He received the fugitives and
refused to give them up; he showed the Marathas a determined but
friendly front; he took them round his defences, paraded for their
inspection his French troops and his drilled sepoys, sent them away
with a present of 'Nantes cordial', and had the satisfaction of seeing
them withdraw from the Carnatic. The new Nawab rewarded him with
a grant of land, jewels, money and elephants; honours followed from
the Nizam and from the Emperor at Delhi, who made Dumas a
Nawab and a Commander of Four Thousand Five Hundred Horse.

Dupleix succeeded to these splendours in 1742 and made the most of
them. But the resources of the English were greater than his; though
French trade had increased enormously since the beginning of the
century, it was still only half that of the English Company. What was
more immediately to the point, when Dupleix received news of the
outbreak of war, not long after he took charge, he was without any
force at sea. It is one of the cardinal factors in the wars of the French and
English that there were few good harbours on the east coast and that
when the south-east monsoon was blowing neither nation had a safe
anchorage. Madras was particularly dangerous. French naval forces
had frequently to fall back on Mauritius and British on Ceylon;
command of the sea was therefore intermittent, and at the moment the
advantage was with the English. Dupleix therefore suggested that there
should be no war in India, but since the English were expecting a
strong naval squadron, they refused. Dupleix then asked his friend the
Nawab to forbid the English to attack him. This was two years before
M. Paradis's famous victory and the Nawab, confident of his power
over two of his lesser vassals, replied that he would not permit either
English or French to attack each other.

But now the tables were decisively turned. The Governor of
Mauritius, La Bourdonnais, arrived off the Carnatic coast with a
powerful armament of French East Indiamen, assembled and armed at
Mauritius; he fought an action with the British naval commander,
Peyton, which gave no clear victory to either. But Peyton was an

unenterprising commander. He retired to Ceylon to refit and did not attack La Bourdonnais again. This gave Dupleix his chance; La Bourdonnais's fleet attacked Madras, which was in no condition for defence, and was taken on September 21st, 1746. The English had of course appealed to the Nawab to make good his prohibition and he sent a force of about ten thousand men, quite sufficient, he thought, to settle this petty squabble. It was this force that M. Paradis dispersed.

Soon afterwards a British fleet arrived, under Admiral Boscawen; the British now had command of the sea and besieged Pondicherry—unsuccessfully, because they still had inadequate military resources and no commander of talent had yet emerged. When peace was signed, the French gave back Madras in exchange for Cape Breton Island in America, and outwardly everything was the same as it had been. But really things were very different. The French had acquired a military reputation that made them a factor in South Indian affairs and, though the British had not yet done anything to deserve such a reputation themselves, they had at last begun to understand the situation. For more than two years Fort St George at Madras had been in French hands; Fort St David had been the headquarters of the British and this too had been threatened. They now saw the danger they ran and began to raise and train sepoys far more seriously.

3. Veterans of Arcot

The unofficial war which now followed (while in Europe there was peace) makes a very confusing story. The seesaw of victory and defeat is rapid and mainly due to two causes. One is the inability of ships to stay long on the east coast; whoever has command of the sea can move troops up and down the coast and attack the possessions of the other, but he must go away during the monsoon and whenever he needs to refit. The second is that European troops are invincible but perishable—a wasting asset. They can defeat native armies outnumbering them by ten or even twenty to one, but more die of disease than by enemy action, particularly on first arrival. Their numbers are very small; reinforcements of a few hundreds change the scene. It is a war of great distances and neither side has good arrangements for transport or supplies. Further, the country is sprinkled with hill forts, easily defensible by a determined garrison. These affect all the wars that follow; if in the enemy's hands, they are a threat to supplies and so they have to be reduced. But if captured they have to be garrisoned—and so every success reduces the already tiny number available for the main striking force. All these are powerful reasons for training troops who can be recruited locally.

The unofficial war began very soon after the signing of the official peace. The aged Nizam of the Deccan died in 1748. The succession was disputed; one claimant had the support of Dupleix, one that of the British. After two years, and two assassinations, a French candidate, with French help, was created Nizam at Hyderabad. A French contingent under the distinguished Bussy was stationed there and Dupleix was rewarded with grants of land and a vague but magnificent title as Ruler of the South. He was promoted by the Emperor at Delhi to Commander of Seven Thousand—very near the top of the Mughal hierarchy. Meanwhile a disputed succession had also occurred at Arcot, and here too the French candidate—Chanda Sahib—had established himself with Dupleix's help. Thus both the Nizam of the Deccan and the Nawab of the Carnatic were French creations. Dupleix began to build a city that would reflect his glory; it was called Dupleix Fatehabad—'The City of the Victory of Dupleix'.

For the office of Nawab, the British had supported the son of the previous Nawab, Mohammed Ali, who by the late summer of 1751 was besieged by his rival, Chanda Sahib, at Trichinopoly, far away to the south-west. Mohammed Ali had few troops of his own, and the 600 British soldiers who were the backbone of the defence were commanded by a man who did not inspire them with any confidence. 'An officer of proved incapacity' is Fortescue's term for him. The besieging enemy had 900 French infantry, a considerable force of French sepoys, and overwhelming numbers of native troops. It seemed as though Trichinopoly could not hold out much longer, and then there would be really nothing to save the British in south India. There was no fleet on the coast at the moment and there were only 350 British soldiers at Fort St George and Fort St David.

It was now that the courage, vigour and imagination of two men changed the whole scene. It had seemed that we could be saved only by pouring all the strength we could raise into Trichinopoly. Now a young civilian, who had just transferred to the military with a brevet captaincy, put to the Governor a new plan. Robert Clive had judged rightly that nothing could be achieved at Trichinopoly. But both sides had all their strength there; Arcot, the Nawab's capital, was weakly defended. A determined thrust at the heart of his territory would force Chanda Sahib to come to its relief. Clive's brilliant strategy would have been unhesitatingly rejected by most of the early Governors of Madras, but Saunders, who now held office, was a man of rare vision. He let Clive have 200 of his 350 British soldiers. With these and 300 sepoys, and three small field-pieces, Clive set out.

It is a temptation to linger on the story of the three months that followed. The temptation must be resisted, because, though Arcot was decisive for the whole of India for the next two hundred years, the tale has been told many times before and for the purpose of this book it is the results that are important. But the bones of the story are thrilling enough. Clive and his little force surprised Arcot on August 31st and drove out a garrison more than twice their number. He made three vigorous sorties, defeating the enemy troops who were gathering against him, and then set about improving the defences. On September 23rd the place was invested and the siege began. By now those fit for duty were 120 British and 200 Indians; they had to defend a mile of walls. The besieging forces included three thousand of the best troops from Trichinopoly and a French contingent; their total was now about ten thousand. The siege lasted more than fifty days; it was carried on with vigour on both sides, Clive making several sorties, some expensive in life but successful because they filled his men with confidence and impressed his determination on the enemy.

By November 14th a breach had been made in the defences and the French Nawab's son—young Chanda, as Clive called him—who was commanding, determined on an attack; it was the tenth day of Moharram, the climax of the commemoration of the deaths of Hasan and Husain, the grandsons of the Prophet. The garrison were exhausted by the long siege, by heat and thirst, above all by lack of sleep, but they beat off this final assault, although their numbers were now reduced to 80 British and 120 sepoys. British reinforcements arrived; the enemy broke up the siege and withdrew. Clive pursued them, defeating them utterly in a pitched battle at Arni and taking several forts before he returned to Madras. He had inspired his force, British and Indian alike, with a determination which had changed the whole atmosphere in Southern India. 'The feast of Hasan and Hussein may justly be accounted the birthday of our empire in India,' wrote Sir John Fortescue—true, except that it is a fast, not a feast.

The march to Arcot had not only drawn away from Trichinopoly a body of Chanda Sahib's best troops (variously estimated at three or four thousand), but it had persuaded a Maratha force and one from Mysore to join forces with Mohammed Ali, the British Nawab; they had previously been on the point of joining Chanda Sahib. Within a year the tables had been completely turned and Chanda Sahib, with his French allies, surrounded and forced to surrender. A new legend was born. Clive and the veterans of Arcot were invincible.

Through the many battles, the tremendous marching and counter-marching, the fatigue, the heat, the danger, runs this new confidence and pride. It is still taken for granted that there shall be British troops as well as sepoys in any substantial body of men, but increasingly it is taken for granted that both can be relied on to beat the enemy. And more and more often there are examples of the sepoys giving a good account of themselves on their own.

Many of the engagements which followed Arcot have been described as settling the fate of India—but in fact it took several to convince
Dupleix that he was beaten.

When he realized that the tables had been turned at Trichinopoly,
and that now it was the 900 French and 2,000 sepoys who, with the
French Nawab, Chanda Sahib, were surrounded and in danger of
starvation, capture and defeat, Dupleix borrowed Clive's strategy and
struck at his enemy's heart, dispatching for the capture of Madras
a force of 400 French and 2,000 sepoys. Clive went out on February
3rd, 1752, to meet them with a force slightly smaller—380 British and
1,800 sepoys. He learnt that they were at Vendalur, on the road between
Madras and Arcot, able to strike at either. He reached Vendalur at
nine in the evening, having marched 25 miles; learning that the French
had marched for Arcot, he went straight on and by four in the morning
of February 4th reached Conjeveram—a total distance of about 50
miles in less than 20 hours. The French were still making for Arcot but
he had to give his men some rest. He started again at about noon,
and at sunset, some 16 miles farther on, near Kāveripāk, realized that
he had led his weary men into a trap. The French were in concealed
positions on either side of the road and opened fire on him with
artillery and small arms.

It was at such moments that Clive was without rival for the speed and
coolness with which he grasped a situation and took steps to meet it.
His force ought to have been wiped out, but without losing control for a
moment he got his men under such cover as there was and for three
hours fought, by moonlight, a battle on two fronts. Perceiving that
he could not reach a decision on these lines and that his men were too
exhausted to continue much longer as they were, he managed to
withdraw a party, who stole round into the rear of one of the French
positions and there delivered a volley which settled the matter. The
French were routed completely. If Clive had not caught up with them,
they could hardly have failed to retake Arcot, and the tables would
have been turned once more. Kāveripāk was, then, a decisive battle;
it is also an indication of the extraordinary progress the Madras
Army had made in only five years. To march 66 miles in thirty-six
hours and then win a battle that had begun so disastrously argues morale
and discipline of the highest quality. Few men but Clive could have
won such service—but men who could give it deserved such a
commander.

One other small affair deserves mention but not because it was
decisive. As the net closed round the French at Trichinopoly, the
indomitable Dupleix scraped together another force, this time of only
120 French and 800 sepoys, under M. d'Auteuil and sent it with
supplies as a reinforcement. D'Auteuil twice approached the British

lines, but twice fell back when a force moved out against him. He made a third attempt and this time the British decided not merely to drive him off but to pursue him and bring him to action. On May 29th, 1752, near Volconda, the British sepoys, 'veterans of Arcot' (writes Fortescue), outmarched the Europeans and caught up with the enemy; it was decided to attack without waiting for the Europeans and the sepoys 'ran precipitately to attack them ... receiving the fire of the enemy's cannon and musketry, which killed many but did not check the rest from rushing on to the push of bayonet.' D'Auteuil's whole force eventually surrendered. But it is puzzling, at first, to read that there were 600 of these 'veterans of Arcot', while Clive had only 120 sepoys effective on the last day of the siege. The claim to be 'veterans of Arcot' was, however, justified. These men had fought for the French and been driven back from the breach by Clive's men; when the siege was raised they had deserted and begged to be enrolled by the British. Having learnt the words of command in a new language, they were as keen as converts to a new religion; they were confident that while they followed Clive they were invincible.

Again, on March 26th, 1753, the enemy with almost their whole force attacked an advanced battery, manned entirely by sepoys and commanded by Subadar Shaikh Ibrahim; he 'behaved with great bravery and resolution', repelling the enemy with a loss to them of forty killed on the spot and a hundred wounded. Later in the same year it was resolved in Council as follows: 'Mir Mansur, subadar of sepoys, having on many occasions behaved with remarkable bravery and received many desperate wounds, it is agreed that he be presented with a gold chain and medal with on one side the Company's arms and the legend: "The Gift of the Honourable East India Company" and on the reverse his own effigies with a drawn sword in his hand.'

Yet only six years earlier the Indian forces of the Company had been described as a 'rabble of peons'. Now they were becoming a disciplined body with a high morale, co-operating with British troops to defeat the French, as capable as the Europeans of defeating ten times their number of native forces. It was not solely the brilliance and determination of Clive that had made the change, but hard work and organization, on which gallant leadership had set the seal. But before dealing with that period of preparation, let us look at the kind of enemy they had to deal with and the reasons for their success.

III

Elephants and Cavalry: the Indian Model

1. What was the Secret?

Why were French and British troops so startlingly successful against native armies? At the end of the nineteenth century most Englishmen would unhesitatingly have answered this question with some phrase implying that there was an inherent superiority in the European character. Either it was implanted by God and we were now in some strange way the Chosen People, or our climate and situation—the challenge of the hard north-easter balanced by the mild influence of the Gulf Stream, the encircling sea, the abundance of harbours and estuaries, combined with the happy mixture of Teuton and Celt—all these accidents, by natural selection, had produced a people who were manifestly the fittest in the world to conquer and rule.

But, when pressed, any Englishman who knew India would admit that there were Indians whose personal courage could nowhere be surpassed. Nor was it a matter of personal prowess with weapons. All late-Victorian children had heard of Saladin, who had confounded Richard I of England by throwing up a silk cushion and slicing it in two with his scimitar while it was still in the air, a feat quite impossible for the Crusader with his straight ponderous two-handed cleaver of a sword. The tradition continued in India, where horsemen in late Mughal times spent many hours in exact training: swinging their horses in figures-of-eight that grew narrower and narrower till the horse was at such an angle that the rider could pick up a pistol from the ground; burnishing and sharpening swords so far superior to those of the British that English troopers would sometimes dismount and rearm themselves with the weapons of their opponents; exercising their bodies by rhythmic movements, by wrestling, by twanging the steel bow, which developed the muscles of chest, forearm and finger. Man for man, many eighteenth-century writers thought, the Indian trooper, in horsemanship and skill at arms, was the superior, and in personal courage the equal, of the British.

More recently it has been fashionable to ascribe the victories of Europeans to technical superiority. But this—true of course of colonial warfare in Africa at the end of the nineteenth century—does not really apply in India in the eighteenth. Indian armies were using artillery and small arms long before the victory of M. Paradis. It is true that the cannon were ponderous and difficult to move and that their crews regarded it as very creditable if they fired them four times in an hour; but these are not failings in technical skill, if this means, as it is usually taken to mean, ability to construct weapons. The truth was that Indians had not really given thought to the problems of war; no one had really cudgelled his brains as to how to concentrate the maximum possible fire on a given section of the enemy's line; no one had given attention to the point that practice for the crew could turn a gun that fired four rounds an hour into one that fired eight. This greater rapidity of fire was sometimes telling; at a skirmish just before San Thomé the enemy are said to have been extremely disconcerted by the speed with which the French discharged their guns. But this was not the decisive factor. At San Thomé itself Paradis had no artillery, while his enemy had. It cannot truly be said that Europeans had a conclusive superiority in artillery in any of their early battles; Hydar Ali and Tippoo often had far more guns than the British, and, as late as Arthur Wellesley's victory at Assaye in 1803, the enemy had an over-whelming superiority in the number of their cannon—and by this date they were far better served than they had been.

It is true that, at short range, the flintlock musket was a better weapon—because more quickly loaded and fired—than the matchlock, which in the mid eighteenth century was still in general use in India. (The musket threw a heavier ball, but the matchlock had twice the range.) But the advantage did not last long; there was no monopoly of the flintlock and it was soon widely in use. Indeed, as we shall see, by 1763 in Bengal there were Indian-made flintlocks of better quality than the Company's. And it did not take ten times as long to reload a matchlock as a flintlock. Here, too, the advantage lay more in the use made of the weapon than in the weapon itself. Here, too, there was at first a technical advantage with the Europeans, but it was slight, nothing like enough to account for the results.

If then it was neither in personal nor technical superiority that the decisive advantage was to be found, where did it lie? It lay, I believe, in ideas about war, in the nature and organization of armies, and, in the end, in politics and the kinds of government that had grown up in India and to which, so far, all invaders had gradually come to conform.

2. 'Open' War and 'Treacherous' War

Invaders were usually able to defeat Indian armies. The early history of India is one of waves of people coming in from the north-west; it is widely agreed now that the earliest of these people of whom we have any knowledge, the taller, fairer, Aryan-speaking peoples, defeated a people more developed than themselves in what is generally called civilization — people with a highly developed city-life not to be approached again for many centuries. Alexander the Great, more than a thousand years later, marched into the Punjab, where he and his men were impressed by the stature of the inhabitants, whom they thought 'far superior in the art of war to the other nations of Asia'. None the less they inflicted a shattering defeat on a Punjabi army, under a gigantic king whom the Greeks called Poros. They turned back, at a point near what is now the border between India and Pakistan, only because of something like a mutiny among the Greek troops.

The army of Poros was an example of the classical pattern to which Indian armies tended to conform. There was a compact mass of two hundred war elephants in the centre, with chariots, cavalry and infantry. They held a strong defensive position on the left bank of the Hydaspes and Alexander could not cross in the face of such opposition. After some days of feinting at different points, he left the bulk of his army demonstrating an intention to cross, while with only 11,000 of his best troops he made a secret night-march to the north, crossed the river and marched down the left bank. Poros had to change front to meet him but his forces were about four times as strong as those Alexander had with him. The plan of the battle was simple: Alexander engaged the enemy on an extended front and, once they were committed, sent his cavalry on a wide outflanking movement and delivered a crushing charge on Poros's flank and rear. The elephants became unmanageable; Poros was seriously wounded, by no less than nine arrows, and the Indian losses are said to have been two-thirds of their total forces.

Twenty years later, in 303 B.C., Seleukos Nikator, the Conqueror, one of Alexander's generals who had now become King of Western Asia, entered the Punjab, but this time he was defeated by Chandragupta, the first Emperor of the great Maurya line. This is the one occasion when a foreign army of importance was defeated in a full-scale battle. Chandragupta's army seems to have been of the classical type, though no doubt better organized than that of Poros, and it may well be that this victory reinforced a tradition of how an army should be organized and how a battle should be fought which influenced such matters for the next two thousand years. Certainly, after a generation or two, however they had begun, the armies of invaders tended to show curious similarities with the classical Indian army of antiquity.

Most people in Europe know that Machiavelli wrote a guide to statecraft called *The Prince*, which assumed that the motives of every ruler were purely selfish. But many centuries before Machiavelli there was an Indian guide to statecraft written on assumptions even more ruthless and cynical. It is called the *Ārthāshāstrā* and is doubtfully attributed to Chandragupta's minister, Kautilya.

Both in war and peace, intelligence is to Kautilya of the first importance and much use is made of spies. The wise prince will trust no one; there is a list of various ways in which ministers may be tested to prove their fidelity. The prince, for instance, may publicly order a Brahman to teach the sacred books to an untouchable; the Brahman—as arranged—will publicly refuse and will be dismissed with disgrace from his place about the court. Shortly afterwards he will come by night to the house of a minister and suggest to him that a prince who despises religion is not fit to rule; if the minister sends him away indignantly, he has passed that test; but others await him—beautiful women, holy mendicants, noble warriors, ambitious princes. The weakness of all this, of course, is that the minister is more likely than the prince to have read Kautilya.

The whole of two books, and parts of others, are devoted to war. The Commander-in-Chief will have an Inspector-General for each of the four arms—elephants, chariots, cavalry and infantry; the functions of each arm are described, with the circumstances and the kind of country in which they will be found most useful and some indication of the kind of training they need. We need not bother with the chariots, which seem to have disappeared from the Indian scene soon afterwards; they cannot have been much use away from the plains of Northern India. But elephants are of great importance; they are the shock-troops, the tanks, the striking force in attack but also the core of the defence. And they are not only tanks but sappers, useful for crossing rivers and making earthworks; they prepare the roads and camps. They force entrances into impregnable places, quench fires, frighten the enemy. They have one shortly stated but superb function—magnificence! Under this head, they supply what Europe achieves by uniforms, bands, medals and ceremonies. But elephants should not be taken in large numbers into very hot country where the water is scarce or muddy, for if they do not get regular baths, they become 'obstinate'.

Cavalry, too, are important and the Inspector of Cavalry will see that horses are trained to perform difficult feats, including that form of gambade taught at the Spanish School in Vienna in which both forelegs are raised from the ground and horse and rider advance like a kangaroo. This is recommended as a method of attacking elephants; it is laid down that five horsemen trained in this skill are needed for each elephant.

There is a great deal about tactics with which we need not be troubled, though some of it is entertaining enough; the writer strikes one as a trifle bookish, ringing the changes on elephants with armour and elephants without, horses with and horses without, chariots with and chariots without, elephants in the centre and on the wings, an army drawn up as a staff, as a snake or as a circle, and so on. There is, however, one universal rule: to keep in reserve a body of the best troops, hidden from the observation of the enemy. But it is significant that while the functions of elephants in an army take up (in the translation I have used) a page of close print, the functions of infantry take up only one line: 'At all times to carry all weapons to all places and to fight.' These are the duties of infantry proper; the army also includes a body of free labourers to dig, and there is a vast body of camels and bullocks as transport. This attitude to infantry was still strong in the eighteenth century.

Even more to our point is the chapter on 'open fights' as opposed to 'treacherous fights'.* If you are sure that you are overwhelmingly stronger than the enemy, by all means engage in an 'open' fight. But it is implied that the 'treacherous' fight will more often be the object of an experienced general; 'intrigue is better than power,' says Kautilya, and by power he here means numbers. Success in the treacherous fight —as indeed in almost all circumstances—depends on good spies and reliable intelligence. With a sound knowledge of what is going on in the enemy's camp, you may adopt a great variety of ruses. You may bribe some of the enemy's supporters to change sides or you may stir up fighting in the enemy's camp between one faction and another and attack him while this is in progress. Even an untouchable, remarks Kautilya, quoting what sounds like a proverb, can profit by a fight between a dog and a pig. Or you may deceive the enemy into thinking that your army is about to break up from famine or disaffection and thus induce him to leave a strong position and attack you where he is at a disadvantage—and so on. There can be little doubt that in the eighteenth century most Indian generals advanced towards the enemy in this spirit; they were themselves looking for a chance to engage in treacherous war if opportunity offered, and they fully expected it from the enemy. They were usually far from certain of the good faith of large contingents who were supposed to be allies or vassals.

Since a change of allegiance is an essential part of the concept of war, it is important to assess the reliability of your own troops and those of the enemy. In general, 'hereditary troops' will be more reliable than hired, and those the prince has hired himself more reliable than

* These are the words of the translator, and his language is sometimes a little quaint. I am not sure that 'treacherous' is really the right word.

those of an ally who has been bribed or frightened into joining the campaign. The term 'hereditary troops' means of course those from the homeland of a hereditary raja. Clearly the army envisaged by the *Ārthāshāstrā* will be held together by a precarious network of allegiance, all in the end culminating in one man, and Indian history is full of battles which were lost because that one man was killed or wounded — or thought to have been. In the period when Aurangzebe was fighting his brothers for the succession, there were two battles in which the rival to the throne was persuaded, probably by treacherous advice, to dismount from his elephant, whereupon the cry was at once raised that he had been killed and his army dispersed. Here was a problem that was never solved. The prince rides on an elephant so that his troops may see him and know he is there. But the enemy can see him too and once they break into the compact central core of elephants he will clearly be in great danger. The howdah used in war was armour-plated but by tradition had no canopy and its sides were no more than three feet high.

Chandragupta's empire was extremely efficient, and his army is believed to have included a high proportion of troops paid direct by the State and therefore more reliable than those of allies and vassals. In this it was exceptional; it was far more usual for an Indian army to be a loose grouping of chiefs seeking their own advantage. And there are other features described in the *Ārthāshāstrā* which recur for two thousand years: reliance on elephants and cavalry, contempt for infantry, an expectation of the 'fight of treachery'.

3. The Mughal Army

It was in A.D. 1525, eighteen centuries after Chandragupta's victory, that Babur, the founder of the Mughal Empire, swept down from Central Asia and, with no more than 12,000 men, defeated an Indian army of 100,000 at the famous field of Panipat, north of Delhi, where so many battles for India have taken place. It is said that 15,000 of the Indians lay dead after the battle, though all such figures must be treated with reserve. They were defeated by the tactics Alexander had used against Poros: a strong defensive front with which the enemy became heavily involved, and then a swift cavalry movement right round the flank and a charge from the rear.

The Mughals were nomadic horsemen, hardy and swift-moving; they kept a tradition, which lasted as long as the Empire, that the Emperor's sons must be born on a horse-blanket spread on the floor of a tent. The formal wording of a petition to the Emperors had to begin with a reference to 'the exalted stirrup' which the petitioner had succeeded in reaching. The court of the Mughal Emperor was always in theory a camp, and, conversely, whenever the army moved out to war, the whole apparatus of government must go too. In spite of these traditions it was not long before Mughal armies became very like those of Poros and Chandragupta.

There is a description of Aurangzebe's army on the move. He was the sixth generation from Babur, and his death at the end of the seventeenth century took place 178 years after Babur's victory at Panipat. First—according to this account—came camels bearing treasure, one hundred loaded with gold and two hundred with silver; there was the Emperor's hunting establishment, with hawks and cheetahs; there were the official records, which could never be parted from the Emperor, and to carry them were eighty camels, thirty elephants and twenty carts. Fifty camels carried water for the Emperor's kitchen and another fifty the kitchen utensils and provisions; there were fifty milch-cows and a hundred cooks, each a specialist in one dish. Fifty camels and a hundred carts took the Emperor's wardrobe and that of his women; thirty elephants bore the women's jewellery and presents for successful commanders; next came the great mass of the cavalry, the main strength of the army proper; two thousand men with spades went before it to smooth the ground and one thousand after it; then came the elephants of the Emperor and his women. There was a rearguard of infantry.

This cannot always have been the order of march, because when there was an enemy in the neighbourhood, no one would put the treasure at the head of the column. But the picture of Hollywood in the days of Cecil B. de Mille agrees well enough with what other accounts portray and gives one some idea of the ponderous, slow-moving column, a far cry indeed from Babur's hardy swift-moving horsemen. But pomp and luxury had set in much earlier than this. Sir Thomas Roe, ambassador of James I of England to the court of Jahangir, Babur's great-grandson, wrote: 'I took a view of the Mogul's camp, which is one of the greatest wonders I ever beheld (and chiefly for that I saw it set up and finished in less than four hours) it being no less than twenty English miles in compass ... in the middle, where the streets are orderly and tents joined, there are all sorts of shops and so regularly disposed that every man knows whither to go for what he wants.' And in 1750 the Nizam, Nazir Jang, had a camp which exceeded twenty miles in circumference and was thought to include a million human beings.

Behind the visible army lay a complicated system of ranks, rewards and accounts. But it was an artificial system, with little relation, one suspects, to what actually happened. In theory, every official of the empire above the rank of private soldier or servant held army rank. He was a *mansabdār*, holding a *mansab* or office. The lowest was a command of twenty; the highest, for anyone but the Emperor and his immediate family, a command of seven thousand, which was bestowed on Dupleix. Commanders in the higher ranks were of three classes according to the proportion of horsemen. They belonged to the first class if the whole command was of horse, to the second class if more than half, and to the third class if less than half. This must not, however, be supposed to imply that either the men or the horses actually *existed*. 'Lutfullah Khan Sadiq, although he held the rank of Seven Thousand, never entertained seven asses, much less horses or riders on horses.' Dupleix's title *'haft-hazari'*, a seven-thousander, constituted a rank and an entitlement to salary, but again the salary would not, as a rule, be drawn from the treasury. The annual sum was stated in *dāms*—of which 40 make one rupee—presumably in order to make it sound more. This sum would usually be taken as a guide in allotting to the fortunate holder a tract of land which, it was calculated, would yield an annual revenue of that amount, if it could be extracted from the distant and unwilling peasants.

Of course some mansabdars were supposed to be genuine military officers and they seem to have drawn pay which they were supposed to distribute to their men, whom they recruited themselves. From this sum they were allowed to deduct one-twentieth. Thus they had some resemblance to British colonels in the early eighteenth century who expected to make money out of their regiments. As in the British Army, pay was subject to stoppages, but the Mughal accountants seem to have been even more ingenious than those in Whitehall; they stopped one day's pay in the month 'for the rising of the moon'. And it was normal practice to order that pay should be allowed only for ten months or for eight months in the year. It would be surprising if the mansabdars had kept their units always up to strength, but some extreme cases are mentioned; one officer in Bengal in the mid eighteenth century, who was receiving pay for 1,700 men, could not muster more than seventy or eighty. The Indian historian of events in Bengal at that time adds: 'Such are without exception all the armies and all the troops of India'—but he goes on to make exceptions, particularly in the case of Hydar Ali's armies in Mysore. There was in fact a Mughal regulation laying down that a mansabdar should be able at any one time to produce one-third of his troopers when serving in his own province but one-quarter when outside it.

Great care was taken by individual warriors to keep themselves fit. They would go through the physical exercises called the *kasrat* two or three times a day, engage each other with the single-stick, play with the steel bow, which was meant not for war but to develop the muscles; they would practise their horsemanship and burnish their arms. But there was no drill, and the nearest to manœuvres that ever occurred was a kind of hunt in which a large area of forest was surrounded by men who gradually closed in to the centre. The Emperor might occasionally express a wish to see the followers of one of his great officials or tributary rajas, but this was rare, and on such occasions it was unknown for them to carry out any evolution. There was a theoretical pattern to which, with some variations, an army would normally conform in battle; this consisted of three main divisions, the centre, the right wing and the left wing. Each of these had an advance guard, and a screen of skirmishers, and there would be a rearguard to the whole force. But once this formation had been adopted, there was little power to manœuvre or means of communication between the parts.

Chariots had disappeared, the fourth arm being now the artillery. The *Mir Atish* ('Lord of Fire'), the Master Gunner, was an important office-holder in the eighteenth century and was responsible for the manufacture and supply of ordnance as well as being the artillery commander. Gunners, who were called *Golandāz* ('bringer of round-shot', a term used by the British until 1857), were paid directly by the State and for this reason were the most reliable part of the army. But they were extremely slow at loading and firing their guns. These had splendid names, such as 'Tiger Mouth', 'Conqueror of the Army', 'Lord Champion', 'Thunderer', 'Fort-Demolisher', 'Strength of the Throne', but they were very difficult to move; prodigious size was far too highly esteemed. The Raja of Bharatpur was proud of a 48-pounder but had to give up the attempt to move it, to a place only forty miles away, with 500 pair of oxen to pull and four elephants to push. A gun at Agra, exactly measured by an engineer officer in the early nineteenth century, was found to weigh 51 tons, with a bore of 22·5 inches; it was designed to throw a shot weighing 1,497 pounds. *Zam zama*, the 'Thunderer', familiar to readers of *Kim*, had a bore of only 9½ inches. The shot for a gun called *Malik-i-Maidan* ('Master of the Field' or 'Lord of the Battle'), weighed 2,646 pounds. Until well into the nineteenth century the biggest siege-guns used by the British were 24-pounders. Even the smaller guns which marched with the Emperor and went into battle as field-pieces were difficult to move; this was even more so when they were chained together as an obstacle to cavalry. Once the horses were past them they had to be abandoned.

Cavalry made up the bulk of the army. The object of a Mughal commander, if it came to open fighting, was to engage the enemy on an open plain where he could deliver a massed charge of mail-clad warriors. This could be most effective. 'Whosoever has seen a body of ten thousand horse advancing on the full gallop all together will acknowledge with Marshals Villars and Saxe that their appearance is tremendous ' wrote Orme in the eighteenth century, and he is quoted with approval by Colonel Blacker early in the nineteenth century. Yet again and again a few British squadrons would disperse great bodies of horse, although in single combat a European could seldom match an Indian horseman. This was because a vast Mughal army could meet the charge of a British squadron only with that part of its front which covered the same extent and because the shock of a compact body of men riding stirrup to stirrup could cut deep into an undrilled crowd of individuals, however brilliant their personal mastery of sword and horse.

It was the cavalry who enjoyed prestige as warriors, gallant men with swagger and panache. The infantry, on the other hand, were despised as drudges, little more than watchmen to guard the baggage. Horsemanship was highly esteemed and the standard achieved was high, the horse being ridden with a severe bit and a light or loose rein, well in hand. It cannot be mere coincidence that, as in the *Ārthāshāstrā*, they were trained to rise on the hind legs, in the gambade, as a means of attacking elephants. A commander of cavalry would often bring with him his own retainers, mounted at his expense, though sometimes the trooper provided arms and equipment for himself. A man bringing such a troop on his own horses was a *silladār*; a man so mounted was a *bārgir*. Both these terms were used in the British service, and a remnant of the system existed until 1914. Another tradition inherited by the British was recruitment by classes. It was not highly developed among the Mughals, but there were regulations that, for example, an officer from Iran should recruit not more than one-third Mughals; the rest must be Sayyads or Sheikhs. If Afghans were recruited, they should not be more than one-sixth of the force under a given officer, nor must Rajputs be more than one-seventh, except in the case of a Rajput officer, who might take Rajputs only. But it does not seem likely that these rules were strictly observed.

The Mughal army, then, consisted of a number of bands of horsemen, each of which might be linked together by some personal loyalty to the man who had brought them into service, but wholly without any national spirit and with little idea of joint loyalty to Islam; the enemy was often Muslim and there were usually Hindu princes among the Emperor's allies. Nor was there much personal loyalty to the Emperor; the normal occupation of his courtiers was *hasād-wa-fasād* ('jealousy and intrigue') and there was hardly a battle in which some great lord did not stand aside or go over to the enemy. But above all, from top to bottom, there was a sense that nothing was permanent. In the Imperial family, father warred with son and brother with brother; it was common for each new monarch to build himself a new palace or even a new capital to mark his rejection of his father's taste. When the son came to power, his father's favourites usually did well to

hide. The favourite of today was the condemned criminal of tomorrow.*
And the trooper's good fortune was just as hazardous and fleeting as
his commander's. Pay was always in arrears, partly no doubt because
cash was often short but partly as a check on desertion. But desertion
was so common that it was hardly punished. Absconders were allowed
three months' grace to rejoin; if a man who had been on the pay-roll
for some time deserted, and had drawn full pay before disappearing,
a month's pay might be realized from his surety. Military service, in
short, was hardly more binding than work for a building contractor.
There was no provision for widows and orphans. If a man was killed
on service, his widow was entitled to full pay till the date of his death;
if he died of natural causes, to only half his arrears.

Thus it was only with commanders of exceptional powers – born
leaders who were also painstaking administrators – that any sense of
continuity could arise. And such men, rare in any society, in the
Mughal Empire were not only rare but liable to lose their place by
assassination or intrigue. All was fleeting and transitory. Two great
nobles, Sayyad Husain Ali Khan and his brother, virtually became
kingmakers in the early eighteenth century. In 1719 they put Mohammed Shah on the throne; shortly afterwards Sayyad Husain Ali left
Agra, on what was supposed to be the Emperor's business, with as
large an army as any Mughal general ever collected. But he was
assassinated, by the Emperor's orders, and within a few hours his
camp was plundered, his tents were burned and no trace of his mighty
army remained.

Thus the Mughal armies combined almost every military vice.
They were without discipline, they could not move swiftly or manœuvre
in the face of an enemy, their supply arrangements were rapacious
and inadequate, and above all there was neither spirit nor organization
to hold them together. 'They formed a cavalry', wrote Mountstuart
Elphinstone, 'admirably fitted to prance in a procession and not ill-
adapted to a charge in pitched battle, but not capable of any long
exertion and still less of any continuance of fatigue and hardship.'
In a few generations, they had lost the hardiness, the simplicity and
the mobility of the invaders under Babur and had been transformed into
the classical army of India – vast crowds of undisciplined horsemen
surrounding a ponderous assembly of elephants. One function mentioned in the *Ārthāshāstrā* they carried out excellently – magnificence.

* This is a grim but pregnant joke in Persian: 'One dot turns the favourite into a
condemned criminal.' The words are *mahram*, a favourite, and *mujrim*, a condemned
person, and one dot added in the Arabic script changes the first to the second. But
the word for dot can also mean 'a pointed saying' – either a spiteful *mot* of the
favourite or a sentence of death by the Sultan. *Mahram*'s literal meaning is 'a person
so trusted that he is admitted to the harem' – the forbidden place.

And of individual courage and skill at arms they had plenty. All they
needed was military organization and political stability behind it.

4. The Maratha Army

The Maratha army at its best suggested the beginning of the kind of
nation-state that grew up in Europe from Tudor times onward. There
was nothing else like it in India before the rise of the Sikhs under
Ranjit Singh. The Maratha power was swift in its growth because it was
founded on new principles, but these were soon forgotten and both
State and army began to revert to older ways; degeneracy and decay
were well developed while the Maratha empire was still expanding.

Maratha power may really be counted to begin in 1659 when Sivaji
treacherously assassinated a Mughal general and defeated his army.
Sivaji was the son of a petty raja who, before his father's death, had
set up a force of his own as a brigand chief, but one with soaring
ambition: he meant to establish himself against the Mughals as the
independent chief of a Hindu empire based on the Maharashtra
country, that is, the north-western Deccan and the Western Ghats.
It was not exactly nationalism; there were usually some speakers of
the Marathi language fighting against Sivaji, and among his own
followers there were men from other parts of India and some Muslims.
The idea of a nation was still hardly understood in India. But had
Sivaji lived longer and had his principles been followed by his successors,
the Maratha spirit would surely have grown into nationalism. It was
based on the Hindu religion, the Maratha language and the Maharashtra country.

Its beginnings were very small. When Afzal Khan was sent to
suppress Sivaji in 1659, an army of 10,000 was considered sufficient
and Sivaji did not think he was strong enough to meet it by 'open war'.
Although illiterate, he usually acted on the principles of the *Ārthāshāstrā*;
he decided, therefore, on 'treacherous war'. He made proposals to Afzal
Khan for a parley, to which each should come unarmed and with only
two companions; as he greeted Afzal Khan in a ceremonial embrace,
he drove into his body a hidden dagger* and the leaderless army was
then ambushed and destroyed. Ten years later he was able to force a
number of districts, nominally under the rule of Aurangzebe, not

---

* This was the *bāgh-nakh* or 'tiger's claw', a blade with rings fitting over the
fingers so that it lies along the wrist when the hand is closed. I have seen the word
used in English, spelt 'wag-nuck', without explanation, in an eighteenth-century
speech, not about India, as meaning the instrument with which a treacherous stab
in the back is delivered. But I cannot trace the reference.

merely to pay him tribute but to acknowledge that it was due. Sivaji died in 1680 but Maratha power continued to spread for the next century, although Sivaji's principles were increasingly neglected. By the end of the eighteenth century the Maratha cavalry had 'watered their horses in the Indus', Calcutta had found it necessary to construct the Mahratta Ditch as a defence against their raids, they had defeated the Nizam and made him yield half his territory and they had carried their wars to the southern tip of the Indian peninsula. But their achievements were hollow. Eight years after their victory over the Nizam the knell was tolled at Assaye in 1803, but another war was needed before the Maratha empire came to an end in 1819.

Sivaji stands between Akbar and Ranjit Singh as the outstanding leader produced by the sub-continent in two centuries. He saw the weakness of the traditional Indian army and, like Chandragupta, tried to pay as many of his men directly as he could. He never quite eliminated the feudal element—that is to say, the men who came with a personal allegiance to a *silladar*, who had enlisted them, paid them and mounted them. But by the end of his reign, this feudal element was less than a third of the whole, a rare achievement. Two-thirds of his cavalry were by then *bārgirs*, paid by Sivaji, riding his horses.

His attitude to forts was characteristic; the Maratha country abounds in rocky outcrops which when his operations began were usually fortified; his own first step was to seize such a place. Whenever new territory came under his control, he would aim at razing to the ground all forts except those he could keep under his personal control. These were to be garrisoned by his own men; they were to be commanded by three officers, who must be agreed on every step, and of these one must be a Maratha, one a Brahman and one of a third caste. Each of the three must provide a surety or hostage, a son or close relation answerable for his fidelity, who would be kept in Sivaji's camp. At his death he had two hundred and forty forts or castles, not one held by a hereditary nobleman.

Discipline in Sivaji's army was rigid. No women were admitted to his camp, neither wives nor slaves nor dancing-girls, and this rule was enforced. Weight was kept down to the lowest limit possible, the men usually carrying several days' supply of food in their saddle-bags; often there were no tents even for Sivaji himself. Swift movement, surprise, ambush were what he sought to achieve. His men belonged to the fourth great group in the Hindu caste system, the Sudras or manual labourers. In Sivaji's army, little notice was taken of differences between the many Sudra groups—cultivators, shepherds, cowherds and the like. Each of these groups kept separate in the village; each member could marry only within the group. In Sivaji's army they mixed freely, but two hundred years after his death, they were much more particular and only two classes from the Deccan were accepted in the Maratha regiments of the British Army.

Sivaji's men were simple, hardy peasants. He sought to unify them under himself, to reduce the strength of feudal allegiance and caste. His infantry were mountaineers from the Ghats and in his early days there was none of that emphasis on cavalry that later became the rule. But his men had to be paid and it was part of Sivaji's system to pay as many as possible from the State treasury. He disliked the Mughal system of simply allotting a commander rights over a distant district and leaving it to him to collect from the tillers of the soil. Therefore money had to be found, and in cash. That is why the Maratha State became a glorification of the brigand chief; Sivaji and his successors, once the Maratha heartland was consolidated, went to war to get money and on the whole they preferred tribute to loot. Sivaji wanted money paid into the treasury and accounted for, so that he could pay his troops. He disliked indiscriminate looting as bad for discipline and there was great advantage in settling with a raja who would pay his protection-money annually without an expensive military operation to compel him. If he would not be compelled, loot belonged to the State and there were elaborate rules for the division of it. But after Sivaji's death, the brigand element remained, without the discipline.

Sivaji's men were Indians; they were not invaders. Otherwise they were not unlike Babur's invading force: they had the military virtues of discipline and fidelity; they could move fast and manœuvre in the face of the enemy. But a decline began even with his immediate successor and it continued with increasing rapidity. It was easier to let the soldiers pay themselves by loot; it was easier to hire one silladar who brought a thousand men with him than to find a thousand bargirs and mount and pay each one. It was easy to let the Brahmans run the kingdom; they understood accounts and letters and diplomacy. It seemed a great coup when a Brahman minister negotiated with the Mughal Emperor's officials the recognition of the Maratha right to levy tribute on Mughal districts. But the minister needed the support of various great nobles and the stroke did not look so happy when he disbursed three-quarters of the expected receipts to them and virtually set them on the road to independence. Thus the throne was weakened and gradually there was a reversion, both in the army and the State, to that feudalism and disunity that Sivaji had tried to banish.

Strict discipline and simple habits were soon abandoned. Shahu, Sivaji's grandson, moved like a Mughal Emperor of the same period, with a vast train of flags, elephants, guns, women and camp-followers. Four to six miles a day would be the length of a march and, as with the Mughals, the first day would be even less, to enable stragglers to catch up. When Sivaji's degenerate descendants were replaced by their

Brahman minister, the Peshwa, there was some improvement and the line of march became a little 'more military and less processional'; there was an advance guard, the *sadi-fauj** (which the English turned into 'Cherry Fodge'), and no doubt a task-force of cavalry could be detached for rapid movement. But it is a far cry from Sivaji. No march could begin till astrologers had chosen the right day; even then, further delay might be caused because those to whom the commander owed money, including even his troops, would start a *dharna*. The dictionary definition of this word is 'The act of sitting doggedly and fasting'. It is a very ancient Indian practice, revived in a modified form by Mahatma Gandhi, and the convention—which few before the British dared openly to break—was that the person fasted at should observe the same austerities as his creditors. This would continue till the bill was paid. But nobody tried to fast at Sivaji.

By the middle of the eighteenth century, the pay of the army was usually heavily in arrears. The proportion of cavalry paid and mounted by the State had dropped from two-thirds at the death of Sivaji in 1680 to 6,000 out of 38,000 horse—less than one in six—at the third battle of Panipat in 1761. These, the bargirs of the State, were the cream of the cavalry. There were three other classes, the silladars, who brought their own men and horses, the *ekadars*, or 'holders of one', each of whom brought his own horse and equipment, and a fourth class, not included at all in Sivaji's army. They were called by the Marathas *Pendharis,* which the English usually made 'Pindarris'. These might be of any creed, speech or nation, and many were Muslims from the north. They were not paid; on the contrary, they engaged to give the State one-sixth of any booty they might take. They were, in short, licensed robbers and frequently made raids on their own account, but it was to their advantage to have the protection of some more reputable chief, in whose territory they could refit.

The infantry also, by the late eighteenth century, consisted of men of many creeds and tongues. There were Sikhs, Rajputs, Sindis and Baluchis; Arabs, Rohillas, Abyssinians and Portuguese. The Marathas themselves had come to despise the infantry and the old peasant stock was hardly to be found there at all. Mercenaries were paid higher wages, particularly the Arabs, who at one time were paid fifteen rupees a month if they had been born in Arabia, though only ten if born in India, while men from Northern India were paid eight and any who could be found from the Deccan—presumably of low caste—only six. The dream of a Hindu empire based on the Maharashtriyan homeland had been forgotten. Instead the Marathas had made a puppet of the

* I think this is a corruption of the Persian *sar-i-fauj* ('head of the army'), which the Marathas must have borrowed from the Mughals. The Persian words would rhyme, approximately, with 'Surrey' and 'Doge'.

Mughal Emperor and acted in the name not of the Hindu religion but of the Emperor; they had alienated their natural allies the Rajput princes — fellow Hindus — who found them even more rapacious than the Mughals; they had quarrelled hopelessly among themselves. Thus the approach to nationalism which had begun in Sivaji's time had disappeared entirely; it was an army of feudal chiefs and foreign mercenaries, differing little from the Mughal armies.

The Marathas had won battles against the Portuguese and the Mughals and other Indian princes because they were disciplined, mobile, hardy and united. As they grew slower, less disciplined, more luxurious, they perceived the successes of troops trained on the French and English model and resolved to imitate them. They set up drilled infantry battalions, mostly of mercenary troops who were not Marathas, with officers of many nations, with Europeans sometimes as the higher commanders but seldom at the level of company commander. Thus they further reduced their great asset of swift movement. The result was admirably summed up by Sir Thomas Munro: 'By coming forward with regular infantry, they gave us every advantage we could desire. They opposed to us men that never could be made so good as our own, from the want of a national spirit among their officers and of the support of European battalions; and they trusted the success of the war to the event of close engagements.'

5. How It Looked at the Time

The first great advantage of Europeans lay, then, in a stable government with some continuity of policy. Without this, there could be little hope that soldiers would be faithful; far too often, an Indian army was hastily improvised for a campaign and after a defeat the leader would simply disappear, leaving no heir or cause to which soldiers could give their loyalty. Such allegiance as they had was personal to the commander who had recruited them and his case was often worse than theirs; he must fly for his life if his commander was defeated. All followed from this; it was this, as much as Kautilya's teaching in the *Ārthāshāstrā*, that encouraged the tradition of approaching a battle in the spirit of a carpet-seller, manoeuvring less for a strong position in defence or attack than for a good price for defection.

Much that arose from this lack of permanence was apparent to observers at the time. There is a full discussion of the point in Cambridge's *Account of the War in India*, which was published in 1772. He writes:

'It is owing to an entire ignorance of the manners of Asiatics that many people imagine they can never be made soldiers ... Those are greatly mistaken who attribute their dread of firearms and particularly of artillery to a dastardly disposition and an invincible timidity. The true cause lies in the inexperience of their leading men who never understood the advantages of discipline and who have kept their infantry on too low a footing. The Cavalry are not backward to engage with sabres but are extremely unwilling to bring their horses within the reach of our guns, not ... so much through fear for their lives as for their fortunes, which are all laid out in the horse they ride on ...

'Nothing is so ruinous to their military affairs as their false notions in relation to artillery ... they place their chief dependence on the largest pieces, which they know neither how to manage nor how to move ... we march round them with our light field pieces.' He has some remarks on the custom of mounting the commanding officer on an elephant, so that he is 'at once the general and the ensign or standard of that corps' and we can 'end the battle by one discharge of a six-pounder at the Raja's elephant.' Again, an Indian army is hampered by the need to consult astrologers and take omens before any important decision. One form of omen was a fight between wild beasts—but this was not always a fair test of the designs of destiny; it was easy to choose unequal antagonists and give one's own name to the stronger. But superstition—that is, other people's beliefs—might be made an effective instrument of policy; Stringer Lawrence records an occasion when a Brahman in the pay of the enemy came into his camp and persuaded the followers that a sickness which had broken out was due to divine displeasure, whereupon they deserted—a ruse of which Kautilya would certainly have approved. The root of all difficulties, Cambridge concludes, is that their armies are hastily collected and are without discipline.

One feature of war in India was a continual puzzle to English observers. There were many occasions when a fort or some strong place would be resolutely defended and the attackers beaten off. But during the following night the defenders would silently and secretly withdraw; by the morning, they would have disappeared. Why defend the place with such courage if they did not consider it worth keeping? Often no reason could be found that would have influenced a Western commander; they were not covering someone else's retreat nor was the situation changed by the approach of reinforcements for either side. The answer can only be guessed, but it seems possible that the motive was to vindicate honour. 'Let us show them that we are men and that we are not afraid,' they may have said, and, once that was done, withdrawn from a prize that did not seem worth contesting. No one can be sure, but certainly that concern for honour was one of the foundations of the Indian Army that was to come.

IV

Rock-like Infantry: the British Model

1. Winning Battles

While Indian armies until the eighteenth century had tended always to come back to the pattern envisaged in the *Ārthāshāstrā*—a mass of elephants surrounded by a crowd of cavalry—the British firmly pinned their faith on rock-like infantry. That is not to say that cavalry did not carry, with the British as with other people, a social prestige that very few infantry regiments could hope to equal; the tradition of gentlemanly swagger, of elegance in dress, of aristocratic extravagance, has survived till today. And of course both cavalry and artillery played their part in battle. But what was distinctively British in our military tradition was the use of infantry. The tune we knew was 'The British Grenadiers'.

The *Ārthāshāstrā* was by the eighteenth century perhaps some two thousand years old. It had been primarily a manual for running a State; the military part is only about a fifth of the whole. And since the *Ārthāshāstrā* there is little evidence that anyone in India except Sivaji had given serious thought to improving an army. Indians had developed their architecture, their styles of sculpture and painting, while their religious thought had been dynamic and their religious poetry of the highest order. But their social system, one of the most stable the world has known, had been stamped with the seal of religion, not politics. It lasted two and a half thousand years but it had never found any firm political base; it was part of Hinduism. As one surveys that long two thousand years, political chaos is the most frequent condition; empires and States rise and fall, the wars roll to and fro across India, the armies march, but it is hard to see any principle. The issue is usually whether one man shall reign or another; as often as not the battle is between brother and brother or father and son. And since, in all this period, there was little if any thought about the nature of the State, no one gave thought to the best means of providing an army that would protect the State faithfully or to finding a system of tactics that would bring victory.

In Europe, on the other hand, a great deal of thought had been given to military tactics and training, if nothing like so much to paying and feeding soldiers, still less to looking after their families. Writers on the behaviour of animals have recently pointed out that many species, though they often fight others of their own kind, seldom go so far as to kill them. There is an element of ritual in the fighting and a moment comes when the defeated male indicates that he has had enough and the victor then stops. Human warfare, too, sometimes tends to become stylized; for example, in the Netherlands at the end of the seventeenth century, commanders spent six months only in the field and occupied this period in stately marching and counter-marching until they settled down to a siege. But Marlborough disturbed all this, stealing the Dutch army and marching away to threaten a vital enemy interest, forcing the French to follow him and then defeating them in open battle at Blenheim. It might be argued that the history of human war consists of the gradual establishment of such rituals and their periodic shattering by a man of original mind who breaks the rules. He wins battles and is copied, until a new period of ritualism sets in and a new champion arises to destroy it. The Black Prince, Gustavus Adolphus, Frederick the Great of Prussia, Shaka of Zululand have been such men. And the same advantage is obtained by commanders like Cortés— and in India M. Paradis—who introduce the conventions of one continent into the warfare of another.

In Europe, there was constant discussion of the merits of shock as opposed to firepower, and the closely linked question of line versus column. There was controversy about the extended line and the dense line; *l'ordre mince* and *l'ordre profonde* were the technical terms of the eighteenth century. And there were always fanatical believers in the moral value of attack, while others laid stress on the tactical advantage of taking up a carefully prepared defensive position and inducing the enemy to break themselves against it. At Creçy, the English had destroyed a French army which put its faith in attack by a mass of heavily armoured cavalry. This the English had met by dismounted armour in a strong defensive position with bowmen on the flanks, pouring in a swift well-aimed hail of arrows. To this combination of accurate shooting and rock-like infantry they constantly returned—just as the Indians returned to cavalry and elephants. But at Creçy, firepower and the ability to withstand shock were separate; the bowmen, even with the stakes they drove into the ground before them, could not have stood a charge of knights by themselves, while the men-at-arms could not shoot.

From 1346 to 1415, that is, from Creçy to Agincourt, the English were able, without change in their tactics, to defeat far larger French armies who stuck to their faith in armoured knights. Perhaps this was because to change their tactics would have involved a change in the French social system. The absolute distinction between noble and serf left no room for an intelligent infantryman like the English bowman, who was neither a serf nor a noble but quite likely to be the younger son of a yeoman farmer. Then, for a century after Agincourt, warfare on the continent took a new form. The heavy cavalry of the nobles was designed for attack and this represented a political as much as a tactical attitude; the feudal order sought to impose its will on the growing towns. The massed pikemen of the burghers, on the other hand, were designed for defence; they wanted to keep their privileges and liberties. The Swiss invented a moving town, a phalanx of five thousand men massed in an oblong — the walls were of pikes, with a 'tower' at each corner of arquebus men — which was essentially defensive. But improved artillery ended that.

Next came the supremacy of the famous Spanish infantry in the sixteenth and seventeenth centuries. The secret was that firepower and the ability to stand shock were now combined in a marriage of musket and pike; pikemen were combined with musketeers in the same tactical unit, which was ordered in ten ranks. The first rank of musketeers fired and stepped back to reload while the second rank took its place to fire, and so on; the first had reloaded by the time the fifth had fired. The pike was still essential to repel a charge of cavalry; each file of ten men contained pikes of various lengths, the longest being of eighteen feet, managed from the rear rank, so that it was possible to present a stout hedge of bristling points to the enemy. Clearly this closely ordered combination of pike and musket required a very high degree of exact drill and discipline; the musketeer, as he stepped back to reload after firing, had to avoid his comrade coming up to fire and still keep in his file directly behind the pike-heads. This co-ordination could only be achieved by professional troops enlisted for long service, and with such men it was immensely effective against citizen armies, whose enthusiasm had not been schooled by months on the parade-ground. In Alva's campaigns in the Netherlands, his commanders did not hesitate to attack forces of Netherlanders of ten times greater numbers; they were amateurs, filled with patriotic and religious zeal, not trained soldiers. On one occasion Alva claimed to have inflicted losses of over seven thousand on a body of 'rebels' for the loss of only seven 'soldados'. The supremacy of the professional over the amateur was even greater than that of trained troops over native armies in India two centuries later.

Gustavus Adolphus speeded up the process of reloading, and he was therefore able to reduce the number of ranks from ten to six. He adopted a lighter musket and less armour, with a higher proportion of muskets to pikes. About the end of the seventeenth century came the invention

of the flintlock and of the bayonet with a ring, so that the weapon could
be fired and then immediately used as a short pike. In the British Army,
pikes had become obsolete by 1704; fire rather than shock was now all-
important and in Marlborough's wars both French and English had
reduced the ranks to two or three or four, usually three, all musketeers
with bayonets. But while the French still fired by ranks, the British
fired by platoons, all three ranks together, and since they were usually
more highly trained as marksmen, this platoon fire was devastating.
An innovation of Marlborough's was to forbid his cavalry to halt and
fire their pistols, as had been the custom, but to charge the enemy
without stopping, sword in hand, 'at a round trot'.

The drill and tactics of Marlborough's infantry were little changed
for the next half-century. They demanded much time on the parade-
ground and could only be carried out by professional troops enlisted for
long service, with an off-season when no one took the field and recruits
could be trained up to standard. This was the situation when European
methods began to be introduced into India, but, at just that period,
Frederick the Great of Prussia carried the same principles so much
further as to constitute a revolution. He introduced the iron ramrod and
a system of loading in which every movement was so exactly worked out
and so firmly drilled into his men that they could fire five rounds a
minute. They perfected fire by companies, starting from the flanks of a
battalion of ten companies. Company followed company at intervals
of two seconds till the centre was reached. Firing began at two hundred
yards and the men were advancing while it continued. At thirty yards
they charged, but this was only to 'present a cheque for payment';
the battle was already won.

Nor was superiority in firepower the whole story. Frederick's troops
could manoeuvre with the precision of the parade-ground in the face of
the enemy and by rapid and complicated movements could leave one
section of the enemy's army without an opponent while they concentrated on shattering the other wing. His cavalry also could manoeuvre
with exact precision at speed and charge at the gallop, stirrup to stirrup.
For the next twenty years, missions from foreign courts flocked to
Prussia to try to discover the secret of his successes; his methods were
slavishly copied. But after Frederick's death there was deterioration in
the standard of drill and discipline. Then came the Revolution and
Napoleon — and now there was a new urgency about war. The French
were a nation fighting for survival — and, since the lands of Church and
nobles had been distributed, each man was fighting for his own land.
The rest of Europe too was fighting for survival — the survival of the
world they knew, of an ordered society in which every man knew his
place and rank. The issues were too important for the old conventions.
Fighting no longer stopped for six months when the campaigning season

ended; there was no annual interval for training and recruitment. Conscription brought far larger numbers into the field and armies had to fight an enemy before they had been trained to the pitch of the professional infantry of Frederick's day.

Napoleon was forced to fall back on methods that were older, and tactically inferior. His infantry was massed in columns. Campaigns he won by swift movement and strategic daring; he attacked his enemies before they could combine against him. Battles he won by engaging the enemy along his whole front and then bringing shattering artillery fire rapidly to bear on the weakest point and battering a hole into which he poured his reserve infantry. At this stage, the swift movement and concentration of artillery was his greatest single asset. Only the British, protected by the sea, had time to train their infantry to standards of drill and discipline on the Prussian model. They were able to meet the Napoleonic column with the extended line of highly drilled marksmen, concentrating its fire on the head of the column; all through the Peninsular War, they had a tactical advantage over the French which was basically the advantage of Creçy and Agincourt. They also had the advantage that Frederick's army had had, of being able to manœuvre rapidly in the presence of the enemy; no other infantry in Europe at that time could have changed front at the double as the 52nd did at Waterloo.

This is to anticipate; in the middle of the eighteenth century, the methods of the French and British were substantially the same. But enough has been said to show that in Europe much attention had been paid to the theory and practice of winning battles. What is doubtful is whether the sum of human misery produced by the businesslike warfare of Europe was at this time greater than that which resulted from the far more haphazard and chaotic engagements of India; one may hazard the guess that in India there was less slaughter of combatants but an even more wholesale devastation of the countryside.

2. Looking after Men

It is not surprising, then, that when the British began to take more seriously the need to win battles in India they should put their faith in infantry. Their problem was how to make the kind of infantry they wanted out of men who came for hire and who had no national allegiance to the British flag. We have seen the startling change accomplished in the six years from 1747 to 1753, from a rabble of peons to the veterans of Arcot. Most of this change was due to the personal qualities of two men, Clive and Stringer Lawrence. Of Clive we have already caught a glimpse, a man brilliant under the stimulus of danger, calm in crisis, far-seeing as a strategist, often moody and depressed in times of inaction. Stringer Lawrence, who was his life-long friend and has been called the father of the Indian Army, could hardly have been more different in character, for he was a steady, wise, self-effacing man. But he too had that gift of inspiring men to feats of heroism. On October 3rd, 1753, Weycondah, a strong place near Trichinopoly, was assaulted by the sepoys under Lawrence's general command without specific orders from higher authority, and carried, by the resolution of an English sergeant belonging to one of their companies. 'Such was the spirit which Lawrence had infused into them that they emulated the exploits of King Harry's armies after Agincourt,' wrote Fortescue.

Lawrence was the first Commander-in-Chief. He came out to that post as a major in 1748; he was then 51, a tried soldier of varied experience. After two years he returned to England because of ill-health. He was back in 1752, when he superseded Clive, but wholly without friction. Clive had served under him at the capture of Devicottah, when he was still one of the Company's Writers with only a temporary commission. But Lawrence had at this early encounter already perceived that here was a born soldier and leader; on his return in 1752 he fell in with Clive's plans and furthered them in every way he could, giving him when possible an independent command. How rare is the quality of a man who, himself possessed of exceptional powers which have not been acknowledged, will recognize that a man more than twenty-five years his junior has the same kind of powers in a still higher degree and, what is more, will give him every chance to use them! Clive, who cannot have been an easy man to work with, never forgot this consideration and would not accept a sword of honour from the Company unless one were presented to Lawrence too.

But Lawrence should be remembered for other reasons as well as the magnanimity with which he made opportunities for Clive. He himself possessed the power to inspire and his presence as Commander-in-Chief was itself enough to raise the confidence of the sepoys. But there was more than the aura of an outstanding personality. Fortescue had written of Marlborough that he thoroughly understood the British soldier: 'He took care to feed him well, to pay him regularly, to give him plenty of work and to keep him under the strictest discipline — and with all this he cherished a genial feeling for the men which showed itself not only in strict injunctions to watch over their comfort but in acts of personal kindness kindly bestowed.' In all this, of course, British soldiers were no different from any others. All this Lawrence understood; he knew too that the inspiring influence of one leader cannot last for ever; a framework of permanent organization is needed to carry the enthusiasm forward. He worked steadily to build such a permanent framework, but slowly, step by step, under great difficulties. He found the Madras Council more difficult to manage than Marlborough had found Queen Anne.

The first step had been to form the sepoys into companies with a regular establishment and regular pay. It was at first assumed that their ways were so strange and incomprehensible to Europeans that they must be directly commanded by their own officers; it has to be remembered that until about 1747 they had been hired through a leader who had really acted as a contractor. The new companies were quite different—each man knew that he served the Company and was paid by the Company—but it was still felt that they must be commanded by an Indian officer. The establishment changed slightly from time to time, but for about a hundred years the strength of a company was generally a hundred or a hundred and twenty men. The first order prescribing the strength of a company is dated November 1755 and lays down that there should be 1 subadar, 4 jemadars, 8 havildars or sergeants, 8 naiks or corporals, 2 men to carry the colours, 2 drummers, 1 trumpeter, 1 conicopoly* or writer and 84 privates. It would be misleading to call a subadar a captain and a jemadar a lieutenant, but at that time men of these ranks did command the number of men we now regard as the command of a captain or lieutenant. There are earlier muster rolls showing rather larger companies and minor changes followed, but for a long time this was approximately what was meant by a company. It seems reasonable to suppose, from the number of jemadars, that the company was sometimes divided into four platoons but this does not seem to have been a permanent organization. An account speaks of 'troops being told off ... into platoons and firings' before a battle.

In April 1756 there is an order from the President of Fort St George acquainting the Board with his success in persuading the sepoys to wear 'an uniform of Europe cloth'. It had occurred to him that this 'would serve at once to give them a more martial appearance, and take off a considerable quantity of woollen goods'—which, not unnaturally, were not very lively on the Madras market. This step was characteristic in its combination of commercial and military advantages, but it was also significant as one of the first on a road about which there was to be much controversy. British soldiers—and indeed all the British—came to India in a dress which no sensible person could possibly argue was suited to the climate. But they clung to it because from the moment they began on their career of conquest the British felt it essential to distinguish themselves from the apathy and poverty that surrounded them. In the seventeenth century, when they were suppliants, they had been ready to wear loose cotton clothes similar to those worn by Indian

* I am told by a Tamil-speaker that this word is *Kānagu-pillai*—'the accountsfellow'.

Muslims. But once they became rulers, they determined unconsciously that they would not give way to the slack easy ways of the country, so they stuck to thick woollen clothes, high stiff collars, leather stocks, tight breeches. Since the essence of the sepoy was that he had to acquire the rock-like steadiness of British infantry, it was important that he should look like a soldier—that is, a British soldier. So his clothes became, for the first stage of his history, steadily more tight, stiff and uncomfortable.

There could be little permanence about a company and for tactical purposes it was too small a unit. It was resolved to form battalions in 1758, and two were actually raised. In 1759 orders went out for the formation of five battalions (including the two already raised); another was formed later in the year and in 1765 the establishment was fixed at ten battalions. Of these earliest battalions, the senior to survive till 1947 was originally the 3rd Battalion Coast Sepoys, which after various changes became the 1st Battalion, 1st Punjab Regiment. In each battalion, there were nine companies, each of 120 men, one being a Grenadier company. There were fewer company officers now—one subadar, two jemadars and six havildars to each company—a reduction that was presumably to make up for the appointment of battalion officers. To each battalion there were now to be two commissioned officers, both being subalterns (that is, below the rank of captain), three sergeant-majors, and one 'Black Commandant', 'who is to be under the orders of the commissioned officers'. Thus there were five Europeans.

There were also to be three captains, to oversee the whole sepoy establishment. The orders make it clear that the sepoys still came far behind the Company's European troops in the esteem with which they were regarded. The three captains will 'hold their rank and enjoy their companies in the Military'—which means the European battalion. But the subalterns will in most cases be commissioned in the rank of ensign from the sergeants already serving with the companies; they will be 'youngest in the Battalion. But if in length of time they prove themselves worthy of preferment, they may be then allowed rank in the Battalion and succeed there according to seniority.' 'The Battalion' again means the European battalion, which is the only place where a British officer can get promotion.

It is clear too that the British are commanding the sepoys in a remote, supervisory capacity. They are in some ways more like inspectors than commanders. They are urged to infuse the spirit of command into the sepoy officers and 'to make them keep up a good command amongst their sepoys and to support them well in it'. The sergeant-majors are the successors of the sergeants who had drilled the original companies and sometimes, as at Weycondah, led them in battle, perhaps with no very clearly defined legal responsibility. They are now to have the 'immediate direction' of three companies each, and if a detachment of three companies leaves the battalion a sergeant-major is to go with them and have 'a care of their discipline'. The impression given is that they command on the parade-ground or in the field but that the subadar of the company is responsible for most of its internal affairs. The 'Black Commandant' illustrates the point; his title of commandant makes him a good deal more than the subadar-major of a later generation; he is the successor of the old semi-feudal chieftain who had contracted to supply men, and he reflects the feeling that the men's ways are incomprehensible to Europeans.

Perhaps it is because of this feeling that sergeants play so big a part. Since no European can understand the sepoys, it is enough to supply them with drilling-machines, parade-ground automata. At a later stage, when British officers have more direct command, there is a steady growth of the feeling that Indian troops must be commanded by gentlemen, men of education and understanding, who would learn something of their ways and would inspire respect. This was the rational explanation; a deeper influence was the change in the British class-system which followed the French Revolution, an unease in the upper classes at the idea of equality, a sharper insistence on distinction. By Kipling's time, British officers and British other ranks had become so different that they were almost two races. And it was the essence of the Indian Empire that it was ruled by a specially trained class. It was a great comfort to the British in India, as the nineteenth century advanced, to repeat as an article of their social and imperial creed: 'They know at once of course if anyone isn't really a sahib.' Here 'they' means Indians in general and 'sahib' means an officer and a gentleman, born and bred; the sergeant at Weycondah was forgotten.

It is taken for granted by the committee headed by Stringer Lawrence, who recommended the creation of battalions, as well as by the government who passed orders on their proposals, that the 'officers appointed for this duty should have some extraordinary allowance for their trouble.' It is startling to a modern reader to learn how the funds are to be provided; to the eighteenth century, however, it was perfectly normal. The Government found only the pay for so many men; if extra allowances for officers were felt necessary, they must be met from some fund stopped from the men's pay. There was to be a clothing fund, towards which 'each private sepoy is to pay half a rupee per month' or six rupees a year. The havildars and naiks are to pay eight rupees a year, but the higher ranks supply their own uniforms and do not contribute. A sepoy's uniform is to cost $4\frac{1}{2}$ rupees, so there will be $1\frac{1}{2}$ rupees per man available, which from seven battalions will produce rather more than ten thousand rupees a year—two thousand rupees

each for the three captains and three hundred each for the subalterns. Today all this seems shocking—but at least it was legalized and recorded and it was perhaps preferable to the kind of deductions which the old chieftain-contractors had made. There was another fund, for which a stoppage was made from each sepoy of one *fanam* a month, a fanam being one-twelfth of a rupee. This was to make provision for the families of sepoys killed or disabled in the service—an idea quite new for Indian troops.

Let it be added that a sepoy's pay was at this time six rupees a month—about twelve shillings by contemporary reckoning. This was not substantially more than the sum offered by Indian princes; in fact, later in the century the Marathas offered (as we have seen) more than this for men from Northern India. But the Indian princes sometimes paid only for eight months in the year and were usually heavily in arrears; on one occasion in the Maratha Wars a prince, as an inducement to his soldiers to start on a campaign, offered to pay up their arrears on the basis of six annas in the rupee, that is, three-eighths of what he owed them. It has to be assumed, then, that even a net pay of something under five rupees a month, if paid regularly and throughout the year, was worth earning. What is more difficult to discover is what were the expenses of a sepoy. Estimates of what people must spend merely to exist frequently come to more than is available for the purpose and yet people do continue to exist; either they actually get provisions more cheaply than appears, or they manage with less than seems possible, or they have some concealed source of income. What is clear in the case of the Madras sepoy is that he brought his family to live with him—and usually the 'family' included not only wife and children but one or two grandparents or cousins—and fed them, and that he often wished to enlist his son in the service.

There were other steps in setting up a framework of discipline and care for the men. In 1762, when a detachment of the Madras Army was sent to Manila, arrangements were made to pay any who wanted it substantial advances before they left, so that they could provide for their families; also, if they wished, the men could make regular payments to the family in India against their pay. In 1763 Indian officers were given commissions by the Company, though 'given' is not exactly the word since a fee had to be paid which amounted to nearly a week's pay. But perhaps the most important step of all was the reorganization of 1766, which included a code of rules and the form of oath to be sworn when a sepoy was enlisted. There were now ten rather smaller companies to a battalion instead of nine, making still a strength of one thousand to a battalion. Each battalion was to be commanded by a captain, with two subalterns and five sergeant-majors, and a 'Black Commandant', under the orders of the commissioned officers. A captain to command is a big step towards direct command by British officers and a step, if a smaller one, towards the recognition that to command a thousand men demands the same rank, whether the men are British or Indian. The rules also regularize discipline; they provide for courts martial, the courts to be all of sepoys or sepoy officers—that is, no British members; a regimental court martial for example would consist of a subadar, two jemadars, .two havildars, one naik and one colour-man. The colour-man was usually the private next for promotion. Rules are laid down for promotion, the first step to be to 'the most deserving sepoy' and subsequent promotions by service combined with merit.

Another and very striking part of this order is the form of words for the oath on enlistment. When a sepoy is enlisted, 'the company in which he is to serve is to be under arms, the officers at the head of it and the colours advanced six paces in the centre of the front.' The recruit is to stand two paces in front of the colours, and 'with him the person of his religion or caste who is to administer the oath ...' The oath begins with these words:

'I ... A.B. ... do swear to serve the Honourable Company faithfully and truly against all their enemies, while I continue to receive their pay and eat their salt. I do swear to obey all the orders I may receive from my Commanders and Officers, never to forsake my post, abandon my Colours or turn my back to my enemies and that I will in all things behave myself like a good and faithful sepoy in perfect obedience at all times to the rules and customs of war.' The oath goes on to provide that the sepoy will give a month's notice before quitting the service and will in that case return his arms.

No doubt some ceremony of the kind had been used before and this merely regularized an existing custom. It is none the less a vital factor in the development of the army. It would, of course, be possible to make too much of it. Throughout India, the oath taken in a court of law during the British period was treated with no respect at all, but that was a very perfunctory business. 'By my religion I will speak the truth'— that was the brief and unimpressive formula recited in the United Provinces. Further, the whole apparatus of the courts conspired to make a villager feel that he was in the presence of some elaborate mumbo-jumbo whose rules and conventions were utterly incomprehensible. The sepoy's oath was longer and more impressive. It was in itself intelligible; everyone in India knows what is meant by being faithful to the salt one has eaten. It appealed to the personal honour of the man who swore and this concept was often strong among the communities from whom the men came. It was taken in circumstances that were impressive and likely to be remembered; it helped to establish an atmosphere in which fidelity had a meaning. And it bound fidelity to a visible symbol, the colours.

The colours were constantly presented to the men as the emblem of their military honour. There is a Hindu festival at which it is customary to worship the emblems of a man's craft, which in the Hindu system is closely linked with his place in society and his religious duty. In some battalions this festival was made a regimental occasion and the colours were the central object to which veneration was paid. In the immense literature dealing with the Mutiny, it frequently appears that, even when the men were so riddled with suspicion and fear that they had lost all confidence in their officers, they still regarded the colours as *theirs*, the sign of their pride and their loyalty to each other, and in such cases they often marched away with their colours — in one case offering to re-employ their colonel on generous terms as their leader in a new life as a band of mercenaries. But they would still be soldiers, faithful to their comrades and to each other.

Thus by 1766 many steps had been taken to build the permanent framework of an army. This young and rapidly growing institution had been fortunate in its officers, not only in Clive and Stringer Lawrence but in a host of lesser men whose names are forgotten. One of these was Joseph Smith, of whom we first hear as a subaltern under Clive. Later he succeeded Caillaud, who succeeded Stringer Lawrence as Commander-in-Chief of the Madras Army. One of his battles will show how far the sepoy army had progressed in a few years.

3. A Battle and Two Strange Careers

In 1767 there broke out in Southern India a purely Indian war, in which the French had no part. At this time there were four considerable powers in the south. In the greater part of the central plateau, the ruler was the Nizam of Hyderabad, still nominally the Viceroy in the south for the Mughal Emperor, but in practice virtually independent. To his north, there sprawled untidily across the waist of India, from areas near Bombay almost to the east coast, the territories acquired by the five chiefs who formed the Maratha Confederacy. The descendants of Sivaji now had little power; the Peshwa, whose ancestor had been their prime minister, was supposed to preside over the five but in fact they were independent princes who sometimes found it convenient to act together, sometimes not. They were, as we have seen, essentially predatory, and their most obvious prey was the Nizam. But there was another hunter; this was Hydar Ali, a Muslim military adventurer who had seized Mysore from its Hindu rajas and was busily expanding his territories. He was a brave, determined and intelligent man and a fine soldier, but his political morals were exactly those of the

Ārthāshāstrā; a weak neighbour was his enemy. Finally, there was the British Government at Madras.

It would have been difficult to live at permanent peace with either Hydar Ali or the Marathas. A moment came when the Nizam, the Marathas and the British decided that Hydar was a greater threat to each of them than they were to each other, so they formed an alliance against him. Colonel Joseph Smith, with 800 European infantry, 5,000 sepoys in six battalions, rather below strength, and sixteen light guns, marched out to join the Nizam and the Marathas, in the Nizam's territory, above the mountains. But Hydar Ali was formidable in diplomacy as well as in war. He offered inducements which persuaded the Marathas to march home and the Nizam to change sides. Smith, with about six thousand men, found the tables turned completely; he was in enemy territory, with difficult mountains behind him, and confronted by the combined armies of the Nizam and of Hydar Ali, reckoned at 43,000 cavalry and 28,000 infantry with 109 guns, many of far greater calibre than his own. None the less, he successfully withdrew to the Carnatic, the coastal strip below the mountains, suffering some loss to his baggage from the enemy's numerous cavalry but with his main fighting force intact.

He fell back on a place called Changamah, where the Madras Government had assured him that he would find food and reinforcements. There was neither, and Smith had no alternative but to fall back again, to Trinomalee, twenty miles away, where again he hoped to find food. Hydar Ali decided to attack him during this march and chose the point where he would be most vulnerable. A river had to be crossed, after which the road passed close to a village and a series of three hills which commanded the road; then came the entrance to a defile through rocky country. Smith had no cavalry except a detachment supplied by the Nawab of Arcot, on whom he could not rely at all. It was therefore not difficult to surprise him at the dangerous point which Hydar had chosen.

Smith marched from Changamah at noon on September 2nd, 1767. His advance guard under Major Bonjour* had reached the entrance to the defile when, about three in the afternoon, the battalion of sepoys under Captain Cosby, which formed a flank guard on the right of the baggage, was fired on from the village. Cosby and his battalion at once attacked the village and drove the enemy out of it; they fell back on the hills and he followed them, sending word of what was happening to Major Bonjour with the advance guard and to Colonel Smith, who with the main force and the guns was either just crossing or had just crossed the river. Here is Joseph Smith's own account:

---

* Probably a Huguenot like many British officers in the eighteenth century.

'The army immediately faced to the right and as I considered the infinite consequences of dispossessing the enemy of the hills I inclined the army out of the road and ordered the battalions of Cook and Cosby, supported with that of Cowley, to attack them. This was instantly done with the greatest spirit and the enemy's horse drove over the hills. Our troops took possession. The posts were important to both parties; to us, to secure our march, to the enemy to impede it. Hydar Ali soon perceived the mistake of not occupying these hills with his infantry. He would not give up the point so easily. On foot, at the head of his choicest sepoys he attacked the hills with the utmost vigour but every effort was rendered fruitless by the firmness of our sepoys. He was repulsed; his brother-in-law killed and he himself received a wound.'

In the next stage of the battle, Smith attacked along the whole line between the river and the defile, at a right angle to his line of march, bringing into action a battalion formed of the twelve companies of Grenadiers (two from each of six battalions). He drove the enemy back everywhere, but 'it was now between six and seven and night prevented our pursuing further this victory.' He and his men now resumed their march for Trinomalee, which they reached at three the following afternoon, having halted for only an hour and a half and having not only fought a battle against immensely superior forces but marched 'for twenty-seven hours without the least refreshment for man or beast who were never unloaded. In the midst of this fatigue, the troops were chearfull though extenuated ... during the action every corps of sepoys behaved with a regularity scarce to be expected and with as much firmness as could be wished.'

In the same report, Smith says that 'considering the length and obstinacy of this action', losses had not been considerable, but there were men wounded and 'many more sick with violent fatigue. I wish on these occasions of service the hospital was amply provided with Surgeons. We could then afford some succour to the poor and brave sepoy who is wounded and loses a limb in the service. It would be a great encouragement to them to do their duty with spirit.' It seems from this and other references that at this stage there was no medical aid at all for sepoys; later, there was a native *vaid* or *hakim*, that is, a doctor in the ancient Vedic or in the Islamic tradition.

Smith had been told that there would be supplies waiting for him, this time at Trinomalee, and again there were not. Once again, the Nawab of Arcot had sent an official who had procured much of the grain in the countryside but instead of storing it for the army had disposed of it to his own profit. It was some days before Smith could collect grain and march. On September 24th he moved back towards Changamah, where he had camped when he had first retreated below the mountains. He found Hydar Ali and the Nizàm drawn up in a strong position in which 'it was impossible to attack them without evident disadvantage.' He moved a detachment to his left; 'this gave them the alarm, imagining we intended to get round to their rear.' They moved to another position, also a strong one, 'between hills and fortified with redoubts'. Smith moved to confront them, but perceived that he was again at an 'evident disadvantage', as there was swampy ground in his rear through which he could not bring up his guns. He now moved his first line, commanded by Colonel Wood, to the right 'and marched down to gain the left flank of the enemy.' Here he found a more favourable position and ordered three battalions of sepoys to move forward and take from the enemy 'two or three rocks that stood in the plain'. This they did very briskly and a general action now came on; 'the first and second line marched on in good order and soon discovered the enemy's main body drawn up close on a fine rising ground and showing a good countenance ... Their right was secured by a hill and a swamp in front of it. Four large bodies of horse composed the first line with their sepoys in the intervals and in the rear were many rocket men, gingalls,* matchlock men and some pieces of cannon, which played on our right with success ... This did not prevent our men from marching on with a firmness that will ever do them honor, for notwithstanding all efforts from cannon, musketry, rockets and horse, they could not discompose our lines.' Eventually the enemy broke; the Nizam and his men suffered heavy losses, including sixty-four guns, and fled precipitately. Hydar Ali withdrew more cautiously, keeping his force intact, but both left the Carnatic.

Thus Smith and his small force—without any help from cavalry, with inadequate arrangements for supply, and hindered more than helped by his Government—had expelled from the Carnatic an invading force whose total numbers were twelve times his and who had more than six times as many guns. The quality in Smith which made his men follow him comes out in his praise of them and his concern: 'the poor and brave sepoy' 'I never saw men behave with more resolution and intrepidity than those I have had the honour to command' 'We absolutely want rest, for the poor fellows are jaded to death'. From these two linked battles—really one interrupted battle—there emerges a picture not only of the high courage of the sepoys when led by a commander they trusted, and their readiness to endure fatigue and privation, but of their ability to manoeuvre in the face of the enemy. At both battles they had had to change front and carry out complex movements while under fire from cannon and rockets and harassed by

---

* The word is really *janjāl*. It is something between a musket and a light cannon, with a bore of up to two inches in diameter, which could be mounted on an elephant's howdah, on a wall, or fired from a tripod or rest. By Kipling's time it had become a 'jingle'.

enemy horse in great strength. And these battles are noticeable for the very small part played by the Europeans. In many others, it was the Europeans who led the way and suffered losses far out of proportion to their numbers. Here, though the European artillerymen had heavy losses, the main infantry work was done by the sepoys.

But it was still a far cry from the field of Changamah to the high plateau of the Indian Army in Queen Victoria's later years. Two careers, one British and one Indian, neither in the least typical, will illustrate the distance that separated this period of experiment and transition from the settled rules and conventions of a century later. Let us look first at Sir Robert Fletcher, whose career is as different as can be from those of Stringer Lawrence and Joseph Smith, those steady, faithful servants of the Company.

There is no indication of why a man of his wealth and connections should have come to India in the first place, but from his later difficulties it seems a fair guess that he wished to avoid the consequences of some quarrelsome act. He is first heard of in 1760, when, as a lieutenant, he was summarily dismissed for writing an insolent letter to the Government of Madras. He apologized and begged to be reinstated; Eyre Coote spoke on his behalf and his request was granted. During the next five years he did good service in the field and went on expeditions to Mauritius and Manila. But in 1766, having by this time become a lieutenant-colonel, and having been transferred to the Bengal Army, he was tried by court martial and cashiered for fomenting a mutiny among the officers. He returned to England, where he was able to find those with sufficient influence to reinstate him a second time. In 1771 he was back in Madras as a full colonel and a year later he succeeded Joseph Smith as Commander-in-Chief. He was such a nuisance in the Council that his colleagues ordered him to take command of the garrison at Trichinopoly. He pleaded that he was a Member of Parliament and therefore privileged—presumably against undertaking anything so fatiguing—and in any case he thought he ought to return to his legislative duties. His colleagues concurred and he sailed for England. But in 1775 he was back and resumed his office as Commander-in-Chief; he was one of the leaders in the arrest and imprisonment of the Governor, Lord Pigot—but that is another story. In 1776 he went on sick leave and died at sea.

This comic-opera story provides the contrast to the behaviour of men so conscientious and responsible as Joseph Smith and Caillaud and a score of others who patiently and faithfully did their duty and a good deal more, labouring to build up a strong and reliable service. They were the servants of a Government that was frequently torn by faction, jealous of its own soldiers, inclined to meddle in matters of which it had little understanding and short-sighted in its views of policy. And the

Government of Madras was itself only the remote provincial outpost of a commercial company in London. Since it might take eighteen months before it heard London's reactions to what it did or proposed, it often forgot this and behaved as though it was its own master, but its decisions were always liable to be upset. The Company in its turn was subject to continual pressure from the society of eighteenth-century London, a society cynical about profit and patronage, a society coarse, vigorous and magnificent, rich in intellectual and artistic splendours, arrogant as to what was distant and provincial. Yet no picture of that society is complete which forgets that it bred such men as Stringer Lawrence and Joseph Smith.

Experiment and transition are the keynotes. How easy to mis-understand what was happening and slip back into what had been taken for granted twenty years ago! There was, for example, a certain Major Alesieu who threatened to flog any conicopoly (that is, accountant) 'that shall offer to take any account of casualties'. On the contrary, said the Government, a register must be kept and the pay-master promptly informed of any death. But if British officers had lapses—and many did—it was still more difficult for an Indian officer of ambition and ability to see where firm ground lay. Mohammad Yusuf Khan followed a line of conduct which many soldiers of fortune had tried and in which some had been successful, notably Hydar Ali of Mysore—but Yusuf Khan was about thirty years too late.

'Isouf Cawn',* wrote Stringer Lawrence, 'had first a company of sepoys in his own service which were raised by himself. He is an excellent partizan, knows the country well, is brave and resolute, but cool and wary in action. He was never sparing of himself, but out upon all parties, and by his good intelligence brought in provisions to keep us tolerably well supplied. He is born a soldier, and better of his colour I never saw in the country.' In 1754 he was made Commandant of all the Company's sepoys, an office never bestowed on anyone else. In 1755 the Company gave him a gold medal, inscribed ' ... as a reward to courage and to preserve to posterity the name of a brave soldier, a skilful officer and a faithful servant ... ' In 1756 he was sent with a body of sepoys to the two southern districts of Madura and Tinnevelly, where he was stationed for two years. These districts had been placed under the Nawab of Arcot's brother, who, by the common Mughal practice, was expected to pay a fixed rent and recoup himself as best he could. But the Nawab was dissatisfied with him, took the districts from him and gave them, on a short lease of three years, to a contractor—a farmer of taxes. It was Yusuf Khan's task to see that this man was not interfered with and this he did successfully, defeating one minor invasion by Hydar Ali's troops. What else he did is a matter of surmise,

* Contemporaries also call him 'Esoff Cawn'.

but it seems likely that he was quietly feeling his way with local notables, making preparations which might eventually make possible a blow for an independent principality.

In 1759 Yusuf Khan was recalled to Madras and here he continued his good service, but he soon applied for the lease of the two districts himself. The Nawab was already suspicious of Yusuf, and would have refused. 'The will of God had already cast the dice of depravity against that surveyor of the road to rebellion on the very day of the creation of the world,' the Nawab's chronicler later remarked. The same chronicle says that Yusuf had once some time before this, on a sudden opportunity, been about to assassinate the Nawab, but the unexpected presence of Joseph Smith prevented him. He was 'overawed by the majestic appearance of that lion of the forest of war' and dropped the sword from his hand. More prosaically, Captain Caillaud, who had been in the two districts during Yusuf Khan's first stay, had been of the Nawab's opinion and had brought his fears to the notice of the Council. But they persisted in their good opinion of Yusuf and forced the Nawab to grant him the lease. Furthermore, they again sent him to the south with a force of sepoys, this time to defend his own fief. They still took no action when in July 1762 Captain Preston reported that Yusuf Khan's men had been caught trying to bribe sepoys in Trichinopoly to desert to his contingent and that he had collected a force of 6,000 sepoys and 300 horse, all well armed with firelocks supplied by the Dutch and the Danes, and that he had also enlisted both European and African soldiers. Some months later he started a war with the King of Travancore and was reported to be enlisting even more troops; at last he was recalled, but he refused to come and in February 1763 he ran up the French colours.

He was undoubtedly a man of great courage and resolution; he repulsed the first expedition sent against him, negotiated for some months in the following year and eventually refused the best offer Madras would make. No doubt he was hoping for recognition of his independence. Another force was sent against him and he beat off another assault on Madura, his strong place, inflicting heavy casualties. At last, when the place had been blockaded for some months, there was a rising against him in the town; he was arrested and the place surrendered. Yusuf Khan fell into the hands of the Nawab, who immediately hanged him. It was with justice that the Directors in London wrote: 'As you well knew the genius, ambition and abilities of this man, we could wish he had not met with so much indulgence from you.'

It is easy to understand how this model subadar went wrong. It was a period of transition; this was just how Hydar Ali had made himself a king; it was not in principle very different from the foundation of the great state of Hyderabad, where the Mughal's Viceroy had become independent. There is room for suspicion that Yusuf made presents to some of the Councillors; he could hardly be expected to see how stubborn they would suddenly become if he went beyond what they could conveniently ignore. It was a period of experiment; no one was quite clear what belonged to the Nawab and what to the Company and the impropriety of allowing a subadar to farm the revenue of two districts was not so clear then as it would be later. But if the Council were going to behave like a Mughal Viceroy, they should have been more circumspect. If it was not due to corruption, it was mad to send Yusuf with a body of their sepoys to defend his own hopes of profit. It was perhaps a side-effect of this affair that there were to be no more native Commandants of all the Company's sepoys.

V

Crisis Upon Crisis

1. Clive and Plassey

Events in Bengal were more dramatic and more swift even than in Madras. There, the issue between French and English swung to and fro for fifteen years; in Bengal, the French played little direct part and the contest lay between the British and the Nawab of Bengal. And between these two the situation was completely reversed in less than two years. It was of Bengal that Macaulay was thinking when he said that in the course of a few years, a handful of our countrymen subjugated one of the greatest empires in the world. Not only was the reversal of fortunes more complete and more sudden in Bengal but the whole course of events can be seen spread out as a consecutive series, the characters are clearer to the eye, the colours are more vivid, the issues more stark.

Yet — if we can but forget our knowledge of the future — crisis crowds upon crisis and every battle is decisive. The British fled ignominiously from Calcutta in 1756; next year they were back, and after Plassey they were virtually rulers of Bengal. But Plassey did not settle things for ever; their numbers were tiny, and again and again a wrong move would have meant defeat, and defeat would have meant expulsion and perhaps an end to the idea of rule. British Governments were determined to beat the French but they were far from decided about ruling India. By the time Cornwallis came as Governor-General in 1786, Britain was committed to India and would perhaps have rallied at a disastrous defeat and renewed the enterprise; certainly this was so by the time Wellesley came out in 1798. But in those early years, when there were often only a few hundred Englishmen in Bengal, defeat would have cleared the province and it seems quite possible that the English might have come back with instructions that confined them to trade and nothing else.

Traders indeed and nothing more they were till 1756. The wars of the French and English in Madras had passed them by. This was because there was only one Indian authority in Bengal for them to deal with and because, from 1741 till 1756, this authority was in the hands of a wise and able man. The three provinces of Bengal, Behar and Orissa were held by a Viceroy whose suzerain was the Emperor in Delhi; he thus corresponded to the Viceroy of the South, the Nizam, and was no less rich and powerful. But between him and the English in Bengal there was no intermediary, while in Madras the Council had to deal with the Nawab of the Carnatic as well as the Nizam. The Nawab of Bengal, like the Nizam, was by now virtually independent of the Emperor at Delhi; the succession to the viceregal throne had become in effect hereditary, although it was still worth making some effort to obtain confirmation for the succession from Delhi. But Ali Vardi Khan, who became Viceroy in 1741, was a usurper; he had been the Governor of Behar, but, knowing himself more capable than his master, took his place by force. Till his death, he was largely occupied in dealing with Maratha raids, but he was strong enough to forbid English, French or Dutch to improve the fortifications of their headquarters or to make war on each other, and his instructions had on the whole been obeyed.

When Ali Vardi Khan died in 1756 the English at Fort William in Bengal were therefore as unprepared for war or diplomacy as their colleagues at Fort St George had been twenty years earlier. They had virtually no armed forces. As long ago as 1685 it had been determined to maintain, for the whole of India, one thousand European infantry to be divided between the three Presidencies, but this total had never been reached and in 1695 the force at Fort William had been reduced to a guard of two sergeants, two corporals and twenty privates. A private, incidentally, received at that date clothing and rations and a pay of four rupees a month—then about ten shillings. This was the lowest ebb, and before long we hear of 100 or 120 soldiers, though they included Armenians and Portuguese as well as English. By 1752 there were supposed to be five companies of infantry and one of artillery, though they were seldom up to strength.

The artillery company had been formed in 1748 to replace what had long been known as 'the gunroom crew'. It was already considered important that the artillery should be particularly trustworthy; this was not, as is often supposed, a product of the Mutiny, and there was in 1748 a rule that 'no foreigner ... no Indian, black or person of a mixt breed nor any Roman Catholic' should on any pretext set foot in the laboratory, where powder was made, nor should anyone married to a Roman Catholic be admitted to the company of artillery. There were also two companies of militia, formed from the inhabitants of the town, European or Armenian, but they do not sound as though they were of much military value. There were no drilled sepoys, but there were a number of 'topasses, peons and bhaksaris', as messengers, watchmen and the like. They were, however, under no regular discipline and deserted at the first crisis. *Bhaksari*, often spelt 'buxarry', was a word in general use in Bengal at this time to mean any servant, such as a night-watchman or a messenger, who might be expected to use force or engage in much physical exertion; Bhaksar is a district in western Behar, between Patna and Benares. Hardly any natives of Bengal were employed for such work, either by the British or by the Mughals.

This was the position in 1756 when Ali Vardi Khan died. He was succeeded by his grandson, Suraj-ud-Daulah, of whom hardly anyone has ever said a good word — except when he was contrasted with his cousin Miran. 'He made no distinction between vice and virtue,' writes the author of the *Siyyar-al-Muntaqerin*, the contemporary Muslim chronicle, who goes on to say that he soon became 'more detested than Pharaoh'. Whatever his personal life, as a ruler he was impulsive, ignorant and vacillating. He had exaggerated ideas about the wealth of Calcutta and he not unnaturally supposed that a people who had only a few hundred soldiers could be ignored as a military force. 'The Mahometan Governors', wrote Mr Scrafton, a civil servant of the Company, in his narrative of these events, 'look on the growing riches of a subject as boys look on a bird's nest. He eyes their progress with impatience, then comes with a spoiler's hand and ravishes the fruit of their labour.' But the wise old usurper had made an exception of the foreign traders, English, French, Dutch or Danish. When urged to rob their nests, he had replied with a variety of picturesque metaphor but always to the same effect. When bees were making him honey, why overturn the hive and get badly stung? When the land was on fire already — he meant with the Marathas — why set the sea on fire too? Unless he could keep foreigners out altogether, and for that he was not strong enough, it was clearly to his interest that there should be several foreign companies, not one, and that they should not make war with each other in his territory or increase their military strength. He was reasonably successful in carrying out this policy. His grandson, not yet twenty, spoilt and flattered all his short life, could hardly be expected to understand his restraint. He saw no reason why he should not treat them as he treated his rich Hindu subjects and from time to time demand a large cash payment. He waited only for the first occasion — and it came. He had begun to squeeze the Hindu money-lenders and bankers and one of them took refuge in Calcutta. The English would not give him up, and they had broken his grandfather's orders and made some improvements in their fortifications. He marched on Calcutta.

Everyone knows what happened. There were 264 of the Company's regular soldiers present, and 250 militia, both including Portuguese, Armenians and Eurasians; of the 514 men who could be put under arms, 174 were British by birth. They were disgracefully led. The few gestures of defence they made were inept and ignominious. The President of the Council joined in a general panic and fled to the ships lying in the river, without warning the men who were half-heartedly manning the inadequate defences; he was closely followed by the senior military officer. They laid down their arms and Suraj-ud-Daulah marched into Calcutta. He was disappointed to find the Treasury almost empty and reproached Holwell, the senior of those left behind, with hiding the famous wealth of the English. But Suraj-ud-Daulah's behaviour on this occasion was certainly not outrageous; he gave orders that his prisoners' hands should be untied and that they should not be harmed; they should be confined but he did not specify how. What followed became famous as the Black Hole of Calcutta. On a June night, when every stone sullenly throws back the torrid heat of the day, one hundred and forty-six persons were put into the punishment cell of the fort, which can seldom before have held more than half a dozen drunken soldiers. In the morning, twenty-three persons came out alive.* They were released three weeks later. But their sufferings are not part of our story, of which the essential point is that the British had been driven out of Calcutta. They went down the river to Fulta, whence in the middle of July they sent to Madras for help.

The Council at Madras had problems of their own. It is true that they had a military force which, compared with that of Bengal, was considerable—two thousand European soldiers and ten thousand drilled sepoys. But this was 1756; they had been unofficially at war with the French for a decade and everyone knew that very soon an official war was likely to break out again in Europe. Worse, the Council had been warned that at Brest an expedition of 19 ships and 3,000 troops was being prepared for Pondicherry. None the less, with a spirit very different from that lately shown in Bengal, the Council determined to send away a force of nine hundred European soldiers and twelve hundred sepoys, with five naval vessels and some transports. Admiral Watson was in overall command and Clive commanded the land forces; they had orders to get back to Madras as soon as the immediate crisis was past. The Madras Council could hardly foresee that crisis would succeed crisis and that Clive would not come back to Madras till he was on his way home, the conqueror of three provinces.

It was not a large force with which to attack the ruler of so large a domain. There were five companies of the Madras Europeans, but of these two, and many valuable stores, were in ships that were delayed by adverse winds and never reached Bengal. There were also three companies, making about 250 men, of His Majesty's 39th Regiment, who later became the Dorsets and proudly bore the motto *Primus in Indis*.

* For the historical truth of the story, see note on page 117.

But Adlercron, the Colonel of that regiment, who had wanted to command the expedition, had only grudgingly given his consent to sending the detachment and had made the stipulation that they should be used as Marines with the fleet. Once away from Madras, however, this was not very strictly observed, and they were in fact at Plassey and bore that battle honour. The sepoys were not yet organized in battalions—that was to come two years later—but they were drilled and disciplined and they had experience of victory. Above all, they were commanded by Clive, whose power of inspiring Indian troops has seldom been equalled.

Most of the force reached Fulta in December 1756, and in the same month the advance up the river began. It was remarkable mainly for determination, which had been not much in evidence in Bengal that year. Budge-Budge, a fortified place, had to be taken before Calcutta; Clive undertook a march to the far side in order to intercept any retreat, but there were no draught-cattle obtainable and the troops had to pull the guns themselves. After a most exhausting march of fifteen hours, they were surprised at night. Clive, with his usual coolness, extricated his force from a serious difficulty, his Madras sepoys astonishing the enemy by the precision of their movements, their steadiness under fire and their readiness to charge with the bayonet. This was a skirmish, indecisive except for its moral effect, but that must have been considerable; the fort of Budge-Budge was taken shortly afterwards; Calcutta too, and later Hooghly, fell without serious opposition. All three places were on the river and the ships could move quickly into position and make breaches in their fortifications. It was immediately after the taking of Hooghly that we first hear of Eyre Coote, a captain in H.M. 39th, distinguishing himself in independent command; the impression grows that both in the 39th and in the Company's service there were officers with a higher degree of energy, of sense of duty and of courage than any Government can reasonably expect, still less a commercial company.

These three posts taken, there was a short pause, which Clive used to raise the first battalion of sepoys in the Bengal Army. It was raised as a battalion, nearly a year and a half before the Madras companies were formed into battalions, and it went further than the Madras companies had yet done in reproducing the dress, equipment and organization of the British battalions. This first battalion was commanded by a captain—the first being Richard Knox, of the Madras establishment—and it was known at first as the Lāl Paltan, or Red Battalion, because the men wore scarlet uniforms. It became the First Bengal Native Infantry and was later known as Gillis-ka-Paltan, after Captain Primrose Galliez, who commanded it for many years. The men were not Bengalis, but the kind of men the Mughals employed in their army

—adventurers from the north, Pathans, Rohillas, Jats, Rajputs, Brahmans; at first there were more Muslims than Hindus, simply because Muslims had been in the habit of coming for military employment under the Nawab.

When Havelock marched on Cawnpore a hundred years later, he and his men were in a fury—outraged and vindictive. As a tiny minority in control of a vast Empire, the British had come to feel that there was a special sanctity about every drop of white blood. It had to be avenged. It was not in this spirit that Clive and Watson came back; it was not till later that the Black Hole was elevated into a sacred cause. Their objects were more practical; as soon as the three strong places were in their hands they sent envoys to arrange terms for peace. The Nawab temporized, receiving the envoys sometimes with insults and sometimes with flattery, but he continued his slow advance on Calcutta, with an army of 18,000 horse and 15,000 foot, with forty pieces of heavy cannon and fifty field-pieces. There were also 10,000 men to dig trenches and make roads and unnumbered swarms of armed plunderers. It was an army well calculated to make every villager bury his grain and its immediate achievement was to dry up supplies to Calcutta, where it arrived in early February.

Emissaries seeking peace met with the usual evasive replies and they learnt that the Nawab was waiting for the last detachment of his artillery. Clive could not afford delay and he determined on the bold course of attacking this great camp at dawn. He started his march in the small hours, but there was a thick fog and things did not go according to plan; the attack was not a military success. But the moral effect of his audacity was enough; his attack achieved its object. The Nawab decided to negotiate in earnest and, to show his good faith, began to withdraw. On February 9th peace was signed. It restored the English to all the privileges they had previously enjoyed and promised an indemnity for the property that had been seized. They were to be allowed to fortify their possessions, but there was no indemnity for the loss of English life. The Nawab sent dresses of honour to Clive and the Admiral and proposed a further alliance, offensive and defensive, against all enemies. This too was signed.

Now came the test. The new allies had completely divergent aims in view. The Nawab wanted English help, in general against the Marathas, perhaps against his overlord the Emperor, immediately against Afghan invaders, who were close to Delhi. Clive, on the other hand, wanted the Nawab to let him attack the French. French forces in Bengal were too strong to leave behind when Clive went back to Madras, but it was a prime object of the Nawab that neither French nor English should finally master the other; he therefore vacillated, his views fluctuating with the news from Delhi. When he heard that the Afghans were planning a raid on Bengal, he sent Clive the permission he wanted; when things looked better, he withdrew it and sent money, gunpowder and promises to the French. Meanwhile the Council in Calcutta tried to arrange a treaty of neutrality direct with the French.

Clive had seen Madras taken and had been a prisoner of the French; he did not suppose that Pondicherry would agree to neutrality and in any case he was not the man to forgo his present advantage, which might disappear with the arrival of the armament expected from France. He pushed the Council into a half-hearted acquiescence in his own views; he wrote to the Nawab—who at the moment was pressing him for help against the Afghans—that he would move up to meet him as far as Chandarnagar, the French settlement; he induced Watson to send the Nawab a fiery letter. This threatened to 'kindle in his country such a flame as all the waters of the Ganges should not be able to extinguish' unless he complied in full with the terms of the treaty—by which was meant that he should break with the French and allow the British to take Chandarnagar. The Nawab replied in conciliatory language, denied helping the French, and gave what might be interpreted as his consent. Watson had had scruples about attacking the French without consent but he agreed to act on this, and to ignore a second letter, forbidding the attack, which came next day.

The first letter was received on March 13th. By the 23rd Chandarnagar had surrendered; this place too was attacked by the ships from the river. The news infuriated the Nawab, but since he had just received information, which he did not yet know to be false, that the Afghans were marching on Behar, he concealed his feelings as best he could. But he moved his army south of Murshidabad to the village of Plassey. Clive was in camp north of Hooghly; he decided that he could not return to Madras as long as there were other French factories in Bengal and as long as there was a French party at Murshidabad. He urged the Nawab to make a clean break with the French and to allow him to reduce all French factories. The Nawab continued to temporize, and at about this stage there began to mature a conspiracy of the Nawab's own vassals. Two of them approached the British with proposals that a new Nawab should be put on the throne, who would of course be a much more whole-hearted ally. Each proposed himself as the candidate; the British preferred the chief minister, Mir Jafar. He was the Nawab's uncle by marriage; he commanded the Nawab's army and had forces of his own, and he had the support of the rich Hindu bankers. Clive eventually persuaded the other candidate to abandon his own claim and join in the conspiracy.

In plots of this kind, there is always the danger of treacherous betrayal; in this plot, treachery was a very real danger and Clive used the meanest trickery and forgery to prevent it. But that is another story. He continued to send soothing messages to the Nawab until the moment when the plot was ripe. The Nawab, however, while protesting his fidelity to the alliance, was writing to Bussy at Hyderabad and planning with French help to drive the English out of Bengal, so there was little to choose between them, except that Clive was more skilful and much more determined. In the last stage, the Nawab's behaviour was the height of folly; having got wind of the conspiracy and suspecting that Mir Jafar was implicated, he openly proclaimed his intention of destroying him. Mir Jafar shut himself up in his own palace and prepared to defend himself, and at this juncture there arrived from Clive a letter in which he threw off the mask, revealed all he knew of the Nawab's correspondence with the French and announced that he was marching to Murshidabad, where he would submit his complaints to a committee of the Nawab's advisers, headed by Mir Jafar. The Nawab, in terror, humiliated himself before Mir Jafar, begging for his continued support. An apparent reconciliation took place, and on the strength of this the Nawab sent a defiant message to Clive, ordered his army, including Mir Jafar's contingent, to their entrenched position at Plassey, and wrote for help to the French.

This was the background to the famous battle of Plassey, sometimes reckoned one of the decisive battles of the world, though from a military point of view hardly a battle at all. But it was remarkable for the courage involved in the decision to fight. Clive knew of Mir Jafar's reconciliation with the Nawab and guessed that it was a ruse, but he could not be sure. If there was a battle, he could not count on Mir Jafar's help. His 'European' troops were 950 infantry and 150 gunners, but 200 of them were topasses and as many again were French prisoners who had changed sides after Chandarnagar. He had over two thousand sepoys, but these included the Bengal battalion—not yet three months old—as well as his Madras veterans, who were still organized only in companies. He had eight six-pounder guns and two small mortars. The enemy's forces were estimated at fifty thousand foot and eighteen thousand horse with 53 pieces of artillery, mostly of heavy calibre, 18- and 24-pounders and above. At a council of war, all senior officers except Eyre Coote were for withdrawing, Clive himself voting on that side. But after some hours of solitary thought he changed his mind and, against the advice of his council of war, crossed the river. This was a decisive step, because if he were defeated and pursued by hordes of cavalry, it would be impossible to recross without heavy loss.

Plassey was not a hard-fought battle. The Nawab's forces came out to meet Clive with apparent confidence and surrounded him in a vast ring, penning him against the river. Immediately to his front was the main strength of the enemy, including some of the Nawab's best troops and his most faithful general. The encircling troops to Clive's right and right rear were commanded by Mir Jafar and the other conspirators, though Clive could not count with any confidence on how they would behave. Indeed, there is every reason to suppose that the only decision Mir Jafar had taken was that at the end of the day he would be found on the side of the victors. There was a cannonade in which the troops had to stand fast under fire for several hours, but at first there were no serious charges by the enemy's horse. When, some time after noon, an attack did come, it was led with dash and courage by the one faithful general, but he was mortally wounded by a shot from a six-pounder. This, as so often in Indian battles, led to his troops falling back. The Nawab threw his turban at the feet of Mir Jafar and begged him to defend with his life that emblem of his honour and sovereignty; Mir Jafar bowed and withdrew, but the other conspirators advised the wretched Nawab to fly for safety. By the evening, the British forces had possession of his camp and next day Clive greeted Mir Jafar as Nawab of Bengal. Mir Jafar knew, and everyone else knew, that he was on the throne because Clive had put him there.

The battle had been won because a determined leader with a small but disciplined force confronted an irresolute opponent whose supporters were disaffected. The British were now the masters of Bengal but their mastery hung by a thread. They were at war with France and in India were still confronted by an ancient civilization, with many powerful chiefs capable of raising large forces. Their own forces were small, there was no settled habit of discipline and yet all depended on the readiness of the men to follow their officers, of the officers to obey the directions of the Council and of the Council to direct them wisely. In short, the control of these three provinces with their millions of inhabitants rested on something mysterious and intangible, the concentration of human purpose on one course of action. Such a concentration had existed at Plassey; it was common to between three and four thousand men, of whom only a few hundred were of English birth. The enterprise could falter if the commander was lethargic and irresolute — and there was to be such a commander. It could be wrecked if either officers or soldiers withdrew from this cohesion of will in a common purpose. And in the next few years British officers, British troops and Indian troops were all in turn to withdraw their allegiance from that cohesion of will.

2. Crisis with the French

They were astonished; they could not really believe that it was all theirs. And then, almost overnight, they had grown used to it. They took it for granted; it was their right and anyone who interfered with their right was a scoundrel. The years after Plassey are in some ways among the most distasteful in English history. The English had had greatly exaggerated ideas of the wealth of the Nawab, just as he had had of theirs. They exacted from Mir Jafar an immense indemnity as well as substantial presents to each Member of the Council and to the army and the fleet; the terms of the treaty permitted the English to trade duty-free while native traders paid tax. Their agents in their name fleeced the peasants even more outrageously than they did themselves. This is the background to the military development. The greed of the civilians was infectious and spread to the army; it lies behind the instability of the army in these early years; the attempt to reform some of the worst abuses led directly to one of the most dangerous of the continued crises.

Yet somehow the fabric of common intention survived crisis after crisis and held together. There will be no room here to describe many feats of endurance and courage; we cannot tell in any detail of Eyre Coote's march from Murshidabad to the frontier of Oudh in pursuit of the French. In the course of this march, however, there occurred certain events which are turning-points in the growth of the army. The advance guard of two companies of sepoys was commanded by a subadar, Mootan Beg. He arrested a man disguised as a Mahommedan who proved to be a Swiss deserter from the British service; while he was in detention, this man wrote a letter to the French commander giving him the British strength, urging him to turn and attack them, and advising him of the point where he could best do it. The letter was intercepted, the Swiss tried by a court martial of British officers, sentenced to death as a spy and hanged on the spot. There was also a sepoy, one of his guards, who had accepted a bribe to help him to escape. The sepoy was tried by a native court martial of Indian officers; he was sentenced to five hundred lashes and dismissal. This was the first recorded native court martial in the Bengal Army and the first example of what afterwards became a rule, that a man who had been flogged must be dismissed. The frightful penalty was not as frightful—if there can be any degrees beyond a certain point in agony and brutality—as some that were inflicted on British troops at that period, nor is there evidence that Indians were shocked by the cruelty of British punishments. The Mughals used both mutilation and flogging freely. But flogging was a humiliation and it would surely be unwise to employ as a soldier a man who had been so deeply humiliated.

There followed two more incidents which underline the anxiety to enforce discipline and integrity shown by these sentences. The European troops with Eyre Coote, two companies of infantry and an artillery detail, had been loud in complaint for some time about the lack of supplies—particularly of shoes and arrack—and the length of the march; at last they positively refused to go any farther. They were a mixed lot: French deserters, French prisoners, Swiss and German mercenaries as well as British recruits. They said they thought their officers must want to kill them in order to get their share of the prize-money. Coote would not miss his chance of catching the French; he marched on with the sepoys; the lieutenant who was left to bring on the Europeans did eventually get them to Patna, but here they became so disorderly that thirty had to be put in irons. As these had also been ringleaders of the mutiny, Coote tried the thirty by court martial and had them flogged in the presence of the whole detachment. This seems to have ended his trouble with the Europeans, but shortly afterwards the sepoys laid down their arms, those from Madras protesting that they had come far from home and had embarked only for Calcutta, while all complained of privations and fatigue. They were persuaded to think better of this, the officers pointing out the dangers they would run from the surrounding population if they ceased to be a military body, warning them that they would lose their prize-money and no doubt hinting at other consequences. Thus two minor mutinies were smoothed over.

The situation was still very dangerous. There were French prisoners to be guarded, and there were parties of French deserters and free-booters who could be a valuable asset to any hostile leader. And there were plenty of Indian leaders disaffected to the Nawab and hostile to the British. One of Clive's most difficult tasks was to make peace be-tween Mir Jafar, now the Nawab, and one of his chief officers, the Governor of Behar; their mutual distrust was papered over, but Mir Jafar was soon almost as unpopular as Suraj-ud-Daulah had been. One reason for this was the behaviour of his son, the abominable Miran, who seems to have had all the vices of Suraj-ud-Daulah without the grace of manner to conceal them, or even the doubtfully redeeming quality of being too timorous to put some of them into practice. But another reason, just as strong, was that the unfortunate Nawab had to pay such vast sums to the English. On July 6th, 1757, he made a pay-ment in coined silver of over seven million rupees, perhaps seven hundred thousand pounds, and this was not half his debt. He had therefore to squeeze everyone else. Since the English and their agents in the first flush of victory also began to squeeze, Bengal was a most unhappy country. There was a danger that it might break up into a tangle of warring chieftains or that a combination of chiefs might replace Mir Jafar by a new and hostile Nawab.

With the internal situation thus menacing and unstable, the army and navy both displayed greed and dissatisfaction. They quarrelled with each other and among themselves about the prize-money and about seniority. Officers and men were alike affected. The European

soldiers not only grumbled at the insufficiency of their share but
used what they did get to drink themselves to death. When that fine
officer Major Kilpatrick died at Calcutta in October 1757, there were
only five men left alive of the 230 Europeans who had come with him
from Madras little more than a year before. Drink and disease had done
for the rest. The officers did not kill themselves as quickly as the men,
but some set a poor example in other ways. Clive promoted to major
a captain from Bombay whose commission gave him seniority over all
the Bengal captains. In protest, eight captains simultaneously handed
in their resignations. This was perilously near conspiracy to mutiny,
but was not treated as such; Clive maintained that he was right in
making the promotion, as he undoubtedly was, and advised that the
resignations should be accepted, remarking that 'most of the gentlemen
who have been so violent in their remonstrances were grown sufficiently
rich in your service to be desirous of any pretence for quitting it. They
will prove, however, no great loss, as no services can be expected from
men who have so little spirit and gratitude as to resign their commissions at this critical time.'

The time—it was September 1758—was indeed critical. Intrigues
and insurrections against Mir Jafar alternated with plots of his own to
incriminate his ministers in the eyes of the English—and the threatened
French force had arrived off the Coast of Coromandel. There had been
two indecisive naval engagements—and for the English it was a defeat
if they failed to win at sea. Now news arrived that Fort St David had
been taken by the French in June 1758 and that Madras itself was
likely soon to be attacked. The Council of Madras, who had been so
generous a year ago, begged for help. The bad news from Madras
could not of course be kept secret and it had the worst effect in Bengal.
Mir Jafar began to show hostility and there were rumours that the son
of the Emperor at Delhi, with the support of the King of Oudh, was
about to invade Behar. To meet all these threats Clive had about eight
hundred Europeans, the remnants of his Madras veterans, now organized into a battalion under a native commandant, and four battalions
of Bengal sepoys, of which none had been raised two years ago and of
which two were still in the earliest stage.

The French commander, Count Lally de Tollendal—his name before
it was Gallicized was O'Mullally of Tullindally—had summoned
French forces from Hyderabad and from the northern part of the east
coast above Madras. They were all converging on Madras. Clive's
mind turned again to the strategy of Arcot; rather than send more
strength to the centre of the maelstrom, he would hit a vulnerable
point elsewhere and draw the enemy away, breaking up their
concentration. And pat to this plan came an appeal from the raja of a
district on the coast north of Madras; he had just seized the port of

Vizagapatam, confined the French agent there and hoisted the British colours. He would pay any troops sent to help him.

Clive sent much more than half his strength—five hundred Europeans, the Madras battalion of sepoys, the first and second Bengal battalions, six of the best six-pounder field-pieces and a siege-train of four 24-pounders and four 18-pounders. They left by sea on October 12th, 1758, no difficulty about the sea-voyage being raised by the Bengal troops. Perhaps this was because of the preponderance of Muslims at that date; the objection of high-caste Hindus to going by sea was later to play a large part in the history of the Bengal Army. The expedition was under the command of Colonel Forde, one of several remarkable officers from the 39th; he was to find himself diplomat and plenipotentiary as well as general.

One of his difficulties throughout the expedition was money. His 'military chest' contained nothing like enough to pay his troops and provide for other expenses for the time he was bound to be away. This was because the raja had agreed to pay and supply the troops when they arrived. Cash was the more important because of the methods by which Indian armies were fed. There was no army service corps, no issue of army rations. In practice, troops always lived off the country, but by two very distinct methods. One was simply to loot, and this had now—since the days of Sivaji—become traditionally the Maratha method, and was said by British writers to be also the French. The other, practised by the British, and later brought to a high art by Arthur Wellesley, was for the troops to buy their supplies from merchants who came to the camp. In some areas, merchants—*bunnias* or *banyāns*—would come in from neighbouring towns and villages, anxious to sell at a high price to the army. In less developed districts, those who brought food to the troops would be *banjaras* or 'brinjarries'. These were nomad merchants, moving with their wagons or pack-animals, sometimes in vast concourses, buying grain where it was cheap and selling where there was a better market. They were the backbone of Wellesley's campaigns in Southern and Central India. Sometimes the brinjarries worked as independent merchants; at others they were hired by the force commander. Sometimes the force commander bought rice and distributed it; but whether he bought it or whether the men bought it themselves, he always needed cash, and that is why Forde was so seriously dependent on the raja.

Forde landed at Vizagapatam on October 20th. This lies in the Northern Circars, a rich and fertile district which the Nizam had made over to the French, who held it from him as a fief. Its revenue had been collected, under the orders of M. Bussy, who was established at the court of the Nizam in command of a contingent of French troops. At Hyderabad, he was in a position much like that the British Resident would later enjoy. He was the power behind the throne; he had used his power tactfully and his influence was immense. But he had been ordered by Count Lally to march with his contingent to Madras, leaving in the Northern Circars a French brigade under command of the Marquis de Conflans. This officer, who was new to India, had at his disposal for manœuvre forces markedly stronger than Forde's; he had more European soldiers, at least three times as many sepoys and far more artillery.

The raja who had raised the British flag—and thus rebelled against both the French and the Nizam—proved a sad disappointment. He seems to have exhausted all his daring by this one act and his troops are always described as 'a perfect rabble'. What was more serious, he either could not or would not pay the British troops as he had promised. Time was wasted, before Forde could start from Vizagapatam, in trying to bring him to the point. At last, with a treaty signed and more promises but still very little cash, they marched for the south.

On December 3rd, 1758, they came in sight of the Marquis de Conflans. Both commanders waited for some time in a favourable position, each hoping that the other would attack. When both tired of this and when, after some movement, battle was at last joined, Conflans and his men were under two misapprehensions. They believed that Forde had with him only raw troops and they were therefore over-confident. They also believed that red coats were worn only by the Europeans in the British service. This had in fact been the case in Madras until recently. Both sides, as they advanced towards each other, were drawn up in the usual manner of the period—Europeans in the centre, sepoys on the wing. As the clash approached, the Europeans of the British centre were hidden by a belt of maize as high as a man. But the sepoy battalion on the left—the second raised by Clive in Bengal—were in full view, and, taking them for Europeans because of their red coats, the French centre inclined somewhat to their right and attacked them. The Second was a very young corps; it gave way and fell back, the French rushing forward impetuously and in some disorder. Then on their flank appeared from the maize the British centre and poured in rolling volleys of platoon fire. At the same time the British sepoys in front of the French were rallied and began a counter-attack. The French centre began to run and the French sepoys to their right followed their example, though they had hardly been engaged. On the British right, the original Red Battalion—the 1st Bengal Battalion—with some Madras companies had 'stood their ground nobly' against three times their numbers; now the whole French line began to roll back and Forde soon found them in full retreat, with all their guns in his hands. He did not leave it at that, but pursued them as far as he could and captured their whole camp.

This action, generally called the battle of Condore, was a most complete victory, but Forde could not follow it up as he would have liked; he had no cavalry and he was held up by more difficulty with the raja about supplies and cash. This delay gave Conflans time to fall back on Masulipatam, the most important town of the Northern Circars. He was able as he went to pick up the garrisons of various strong places which he abandoned, so that by the time he reached Masulipatam he was stronger than he had been before. The force under his own command still outnumbered Forde's and yet he had been able to detach what he pompously described as the Army of Observation, a force of 200 Europeans and 2,000 sepoys, under M. du Rocher, which had instructions not to come to battle but to move inland, to threaten Forde's communications and keep open for the French the road to Hyderabad. The Marquis de Conflans was drawn up in a position before the town and fort, but when Forde approached he fell back and brought all his men into the fort. This was a very strong place, some way from the town. The southern face was protected by an arm of the sea, while the eastern and western approaches, and part of the northern, were covered by a morass; the surrounding country consisted of rolling sandy dunes, unsuitable for trenches or mines or even gun emplacements. And there was the singular fact that the garrison outnumbered the besiegers. But the hedgehog policy of de Conflans was not necessarily quite so imbecile as it appeared; the French were expecting a reinforcement by sea of 300 French soldiers; du Rocher was keeping open the road to Hyderabad and there were hopes that the Nizam would come to put down the raja's insurrection. There was every chance of surrounding Forde's force and destroying it entirely.

In fact, this almost happened. Things became rapidly worse for Forde. The difficulties of making batteries from which to open fire on the fort were so great that it took from March 7th to March 25th, 1759, to complete them. During this period du Rocher and the Army of Observation moved on to his line of communication with the north, taking the places from which he had hoped to draw supplies; it was confirmed that the Nizam was marching against him with an army of 40,000 men. Cash and supplies dried up, and on March 19th the European troops mutinied; their pay was several months in arrears. Somehow Forde persuaded them that, desperate though the situation was, it would be even worse if they persisted, and they returned to their duty. On March 25th he began his bombardment, but it had little effect and the French were able to repair much of the damage by night. The Nizam and his great army arrived within forty miles; from the north, du Rocher marched to meet him; at the same time, it was reported that ammunition for the batteries was enough for only two days more.

By all reasonable expectations, Forde was lost. If he turned back he was confronted by much stronger forces than his own, well supplied, while he was short of food, cash and ammunition. He would shortly be surrounded. The Marquis was in an almost impregnable fort, expecting reinforcements which would give him twice the British strength. Forde's only hope lay in doing the impossible. He resolved to attack Masulipatam Fort by night from many different points. He had discovered that there was a way through the morass, difficult and little-known, by which a quite unexpected attack might be launched; by this he planned to send Captain Knox and the Red Battalion, with not much hope that they would actually get into the fort, but as a diversion which would help his main attack. He managed to persuade the raja to advance along the causeway from the town to the fort and to create enough noise to keep the eyes of the French on this spot too — and this he did successfully, for a considerable body of French soldiers were by this means kept out of the battle. During the day of April 7th, 1759, the guns delivered the heaviest bombardment yet; it was literally all they had. At midnight Knox began his surprise attack on the south-western corner, and immediately afterwards the raja began his demonstration along the causeway; these diversions were both under way when the real attack was launched on the north-eastern angle. Forde's report to Madras was laconic in the extreme:

'On the night between 7th and 8th instant I attacked Masulipatam, and after a very sharp conflict, had the good fortune to get possession of it. I have taken near 500 European prisoners ... my whole force consisted of 315 rank and file ... I am of opinion this place should be kept in our hands as it is by far the strongest situation in India. My 1,500 sepoys behaved well; with one half of them I made a false attack and joined the other with the Europeans at the real attack; they mounted the ramparts with the Europeans and behaved with great humanity after they got in.' He does not here mention that the troops for the main attack were divided into three divisions, one mixed, one entirely of Europeans and one entirely of sepoys. It was the second of these, the Europeans, who faltered and almost lost the day. The whole force had waded through the morass in the dark and under heavy fire had reached the top of the rampart, the main assault being delivered by the mixed division. They then divided, the European party moving along the rampart to the left, storming the bastions one by one while the other two divisions did the same to the right. The left-hand party had already shown some unwillingness when someone raised the cry of a mine. It was in fact a small magazine for storing powder but nobody stopped to inquire; there was a panic and the men rushed back to the breach. Here they were stopped by their commander, Captain Yorke of the 39th, who with drawn sword threatened to kill the first man to cross the breach and was soon able to rally them and lead them back.

The assault, as has often been said, succeeded because it looked impossible and because it was well planned. It changed the scene in the Northern Circars as completely as Plassey had done in Bengal, though the fact was not so immediately apparent. The reinforcements of three hundred French soldiers were still expected and, if added to the Army of Observation, would once more have given du Rocher a numerical advantage, even without the Nizam. The French ships arrived and the Nizam sent troops to support their landing but Forde marched out of the fort and drove them off; the French ships, finding the fort in British hands and no possibility of an unopposed landing, sailed away with their reinforcements. On that the Nawab offered to treat; he had news of a conspiracy against him in Hyderabad by his brother and he knew that the siege of Madras had been raised. Undoubtedly he was shaken by Forde's determination and his astonishing success. He ceded a large part of the Northern Circars to the British, undertook not to permit French troops in this region or to take them into his own service and finally promised that there should be no reprisals against the raja.

Thus the French had been deprived of an extensive region whose revenues had supported their trade and their military ambition — and part of it had come to the British. French influence at the Nizam's court had been decisively checked; the expedition had helped to raise the siege of Madras; but perhaps most important of all was the demonstration that by resolute courage a British force could extricate itself from desperate circumstances and that the tide was turning against the French. From now on, their successes along the coast were fewer, and fort after fort was captured or recaptured by the British. In January 1760 Eyre Coote, who had returned to Madras as Commander-in-Chief, decisively defeated Lally at Wandewash and for the French that was really the end. They had had too few officers of the quality of Bussy, too many like the Marquis de Conflans, and by now their sepoys were markedly inferior to the British.

Forde's army now marched back to Bengal. They had finished their campaign with complete success; it was, writes Broome in his history of the Bengal Army, 'one of the most successful and important expeditions ever undertaken by this army' — and yet how near it had been to disaster! How narrowly the common purpose had been saved from breaking up! It had been saved by resolute leadership and the growing fidelity and discipline of the sepoys. But the sepoys were still thought of as auxiliaries. 'My whole force', Forde had written, 'consisted of 315 rank and file.' He meant the Europeans, but it was they who had mutinied and who had fallen into panic on the ramparts.

3. Crisis with the Emperor

For the son of one of the later Mughal Emperors, to raise an insurrection was the equivalent of nursing a constituency. It showed ambition,
tested adherents and provided experience; it might clear the way to the
throne. If things went wrong, it could usually be ended by negotiation;
the rising would be aimed at the chief minister, not at the Emperor's
person, and in any case it was hardly possible to increase the suspicion
with which the Emperor regarded his sons. In something of this spirit,
the prince who was eventually to succeed to the throne as Shah Alam
started an insurrection in the spring of 1759, while Forde was before
Masulipatam. Rather than move on Delhi direct, Shah Alam determined to attack Bengal, where Mir Jafar seemed insecure, and there
establish a base from which to return to Delhi. He obtained the support of several chiefs in eastern Oudh and western Behar, and some
ambiguous backing from the Nawab of Oudh, who saw the possibility
of pickings but did not wish to become deeply committed. At the head
of an uneasy confederacy, he began his march. He applied for help to
Clive, addressing him as an official of the Empire and a Commander
of Six Thousand. Clive replied in terms of strict propriety, pointing out
that his duty as an official was to the Emperor not to his son, and that
he was bound by treaty to support Mir Jafar, who was the Emperor's
accredited representative. With that, Clive marched out of Calcutta,
taking all the troops available, and made for Patna; the place was
besieged by Shah Alam, but, with the help of two or three companies
of sepoys, it held out until Clive's advance guard reinforced it; shortly
afterwards Shah Alam's supporters melted away, alarmed by news of
the Nawab of Oudh's successful pickings in their rear. This crisis passed
and must have strengthened the reputation of the Company, though it
left in the mind of Shah Alam no very friendly feelings.

There followed in the autumn of the same year the arrival of a powerful Dutch armament. Holland was not, so far as anyone in Bengal knew,
at war with England, but the Dutch had resented the special privileges
which the English had exacted from the Nawab and this force came
from the Dutch East Indies. Clive continued the bland, and no doubt
extremely irritating, pretence that he was the Emperor's agent; he hoped
for news that there was war in Europe so that he could attack them as
soon as they landed and prevent their influence spreading. There can
be no doubt that Mir Jafar encouraged the Dutch in their invasion;
he wanted to see a powerful counter-weight to the British, and this of
course was just what the British did not mean to allow. There was no
news of war in Europe, but fortunately the Dutch committed the first
act of aggression, whereupon Clive decided that war must have been
declared and that he should behave accordingly. The Dutch land forces

consisted of seven hundred Europeans and eight hundred drilled Malays with an uncertain number of local sepoys. Forde was back in Bengal, fresh from his expedition to the south. He had come back by sea, leaving the First and Second Bengal Battalions to march home. He was sent by Clive to meet the Dutch with all the troops that could be raised — 240 European infantry, 50 volunteers, 80 artillery and 800 sepoys, from the newly raised battalions, the 3rd and 4th. He chose an admirable position but — in view of the oddity of the diplomatic position — wrote to Clive for permission to engage the enemy. 'Dear Forde, Fight them immediately,' wrote Clive. 'I will send you the Order of Council in the morning' — and went on with his rubber of whist. Forde attacked them and won an overwhelming victory, half the Dutch being taken prisoner and nearly half being killed or wounded. The Dutch acknowledged that they were the aggressors, agreed to pay an indemnity and promised that they would not bring troops to Bengal again. That crisis too was concluded.

There followed a brief lull. Clive went to England, leaving as commander in Bengal Major Caillaud of the Madras service. The Directors had refused Forde for this post, in spite of his brilliant record. Now came the death of the Emperor at the hands of his chief minister and Shah Alam immediately proclaimed himself Emperor. He was not the only claimant but he had powerful adherents, including the Nawab of Oudh, and his position was much stronger than before. He went back to his old idea — to secure Bengal first and then march on Delhi. He invaded Behar and moved on Patna for the second time.

The Governor of Behar, Raja Ram Narain, has been mentioned already. Every high official in the Mughal system was a threat to his immediate superior; Ram Narain was an able man and a Hindu, and Clive had already had difficulty in preventing Mir Jafar from destroying him. On the previous invasion of Shah Alam he had at first behaved with great circumspection, welcoming the approaching prince with one stream of messengers while another carried protestations of loyalty to Mir Jafar in the opposite direction. But he had perceived the brittleness of Shah Alam's combination and in the end had defended Patna stoutly. He would hardly be believed if he endeavoured to negotiate with Shah Alam again and he knew that he had no hope of mercy from the Nawab if British supremacy came to an end. Caillaud started for Patna and advised Ram Narain not to come to battle, but to shut himself up in the city and wait for help. But he had some minor successes and was reinforced by troops in whom he had faith; uncharacteristically, he decided to ignore Caillaud's advice, marched out to meet the Emperor, offered battle and was signally defeated. Of the small British force present with Ram Narain, one division of about four companies of sepoys was almost completely destroyed; the other

managed to fight its way back to Patna, of which the second siege now
began. But it did not last long, as Caillaud soon approached with
British troops and with the Nawab's army, commanded by the abominable Miran.

The emperor broke off the siege and moved out to meet Caillaud.
The British forces were much the same as Forde had had against the
Dutch: a few hundred Europeans, the 3rd and 4th Battalions of sepoys
and some field-pieces. They were drawn up as usual with the Europeans
in the centre. It had been understood that Miran's troops would form a
second line, behind the British, but stretching far beyond them on
either flank; in fact, he perversely placed fifteen thousand men in a
dense mass with a two-hundred-yard front on the British right. The
crisis of the battle came when this unwieldy mass began to give way
before repeated cavalry charges. It was crumbling into rout when
Caillaud, taking personal command of the sepoy battalion on the right,
led them to within forty paces of the enemy's flank, whence they poured
in volley after volley of controlled fire and then charged with the
bayonet. This broke the enemy's main thrust, the Nawab's cavalry
rallied, and soon the Emperor's forces were in flight.

This battle, known as Seerpore or Sirpur, was fought on February
22nd, 1760. It should, if Caillaud had had his way, have led to the
Emperor being forced to abandon his hostile invasion. But Miran
would not agree to follow up the victory, and this enabled Shah
Alam, who was by no means a contemptible general, to slip past
Caillaud and Miran and make for Murshidabad, the capital. Caillaud
and Miran had lost the initiative and were forced to follow. There is no
room here to tell the whole story; but Mir Jafar entered into negotia-
tions with the Emperor and prepared to change sides, while at the same
time a considerable force of Marathas approached and offered Shah
Alam an alliance. Things were thus very threatening for the British, but
Shah Alam missed his chances, found things turning against him and
eventually doubled back to Patna, which he again besieged—for the
third time. Here he was joined by a party of French, who had been
operating as free-lances in the country beyond the Ganges to the south
and west of Behar.

Caillaud had lost touch with the Emperor and for some days did not
know in which direction he was heading; he had also to provide
against the Maratha threat and to deal with a rising against Mir
Jafar by the chief of Purnea, a district lying to the north-west of
Murshidabad. He therefore dispatched to the help of Patna Captain
Knox, with his own old battalion, the Red Battalion—back at last from
the south and now commanded by Galliez—and with two hundred
European infantry and some artillerymen with two six-pounders.

Things had begun to look bad at Patna. Several times the besiegers had set foot on the ramparts and though they had so far always been dislodged by gallant attacks of the sepoys, the garrison were disheartened. The enemy's artillery was extremely effective, the troops were fatigued and there were rumours that the chief of Purnea was marching with a large force to join the Emperor. About noon on April 28th, 1760, came a dramatic moment; a cloud of dust indicated that troops were approaching—but were they hostile? Something in the regularity of their line of march seemed to suggest that they were not—and then came glimpses of red coats and the sound of fife and drum. It was Knox with his two hundred Europeans and the Red Battalion, who had marched three hundred miles in thirteen days; they marched into Patna and through the town with drums beating and colours flying and the effect on the spirit of the garrison was electric. 'All said openly that now the English were within their walls the enemy would not dare to come to attack again,' wrote the Muslim chronicler. The very next day, at noon, when the enemy were cooking and resting, Knox made a sortie and captured some guns and stores.

But the rumour about Purnea was true. The chief of that district had gone too far to hope for reconciliation with the Nawab of Bengal; he had raised every penny and every man that he could and was marching along the north bank of the Ganges to join the Emperor with six thousand horse, ten thousand foot and thirty guns. Caillaud and Miran were in pursuit but had no hope of catching him. Caillaud sent a message to Knox, telling him to delay the Purnea force by any means he could. To the astonishment of all, Knox with his thousand men marched boldly out to meet it; none of the Patna troops would accompany him on so absurd an adventure, except one gallant leader of irregular horse, Raja Shitab Roy, with three hundred cavalry. The Purnea army had only to cross the Ganges and then nothing could stop their junction with the Emperor. Knox and the raja planned a night attack, but it miscarried; they lost their way in the dark and had just got back to camp and were preparing to eat and rest when the enemy appeared. Knox carefully chose his position and drew up his force. The enemy surrounded them and then for six hours launched on them charge after charge of cavalry. Once the square was broken, the guns captured and the force about to be overwhelmed, but a bayonet charge by the grenadier company of the Red Battalion drove the enemy back. At length, towards evening, they withdrew; Knox followed them some way, capturing guns and blowing up ammunition tumbrils, and at last marched back to Patna triumphant.

Soon afterwards the larger force under Caillaud and Miran arrived and the third siege of Patna was over. The Purnea force was chased into the foothills of Nepal, the abominable Miran was appropriately struck dead by lightning, and it devolved upon Caillaud to hold together the

Nawab's troops, who were of course several months in arrears with their pay. He succeeded in doing this but was recalled to Calcutta before he could finally deal with the Emperor's invasion of what was nominally his own province. What happened at Calcutta belongs to the next section; here it is enough to say that Caillaud was shortly afterwards appointed Commander-in-Chief in Madras, still the senior post, and was temporarily succeeded in Bengal by Carnac, another officer of the 39th though not of the calibre of Coote and Forde. It was not till early in the following year, 1761, that Carnac was able to return to Behar and engage the Emperor. He was greatly hampered by mutiny, desertion and disorganization in the Nawab's forces, but he induced them to accompany him and on January 15th, 1761, once more confronted the Emperor. His own force consisted of some companies of the Bengal Europeans (later the 1st Bengal Fusiliers and later still Her Majesty's 101st Foot) and three battalions of sepoys, the 1st, 4th and 5th. Early in the battle a lucky shot killed the mahout and wounded the elephant on which Shah Alam was mounted; the beast fled to the rear, hopelessly out of control, and the battle was virtually over. Not long afterwards the Emperor sued for peace. Once again a crisis was averted. More clearly than ever it was shown that, when properly led, Indian troops could be converted into rock-like infantry and win battles in the classic British tradition of long stubborn defence and skilful firepower.

4. Crisis with the Nawab

There were in fact two more crises in the period with which this chapter deals, each of such magnitude that it might have ended British rule. But the first, the crisis with the Nawab, does not reveal anything new from the point of view of the growth and development of corporate spirit in the army. It illustrates the extreme instability of the Bengal political scene and the gallantry of sepoys when led with courage and decision, but of these perhaps we have had enough proof already. The second, however, involved threefold mutinies, of officers, of British rank and file, and of Indian rank and file, and is crucial if we are to understand that spirit.

Nevertheless, we must learn something about the first of these two crises if we are to understand the second. It arose very largely from the greed and factiousness of the Council at Calcutta after Clive left. Mir Jafar, who had been made Nawab after Plassey, had shown, at the Dutch invasion and again at Shah Alam's, that he was ready to side with anyone who would help him to get rid of the British. As at Plassey, he might will the end, but had not the courage to take part in the means. Further, he had not paid up all he had promised. He was thus regarded by the British as treacherous, faithless and inefficient. Nor was he looked on with much more favour by his fellow-countrymen, to whom he was bound to seem rapacious, because of the demands the English made on him, while his timidity and vacillation earned their contempt and distrust. He had alienated most of his former supporters and there was to hand an able and ambitious rival, his son-in-law Mir Kasim. The Council had good grounds for regarding Mir Kasim as likely to make a far better Nawab than Mir Jafar, but no defence is possible of the terms they made for putting him on the throne. These included not only the grant of three districts to the Company but substantial presents in cash to each member of Council and to the army and navy.

Mir Kasim was duly installed, but he proved to be by no means the docile puppet for whom the English had hoped. It is impossible not to feel sympathy with his determined attempt to put Bengal in order, but it was his ill fortune that soon after his accession, the President of the Council, Vansittart, lost several moderate supporters and found himself in a minority to the party of extreme greed. They sent to Patna as their representative a Mr Ellis, who was violent, ill-tempered, intolerant, greedy and bitterly hostile to Mir Kāsim. Ellis committed a number of provocative acts, but there was also in dispute a matter of principle; the English claimed that they had the right to trade duty-free, to which Mir Kasim replied that in that case he would free *all* trade from duty. This the majority on the English Council, with complete blindness to natural justice, regarded as an infringement of their rights. They decided to reinstate Mir Jafar and declared war on Mir Kasim on July 7th, 1763.

One of Mir Kasim's reforms had been of his army, which he had greatly improved. He had reduced the number of his cavalry but increased its efficiency, organizing it in regiments under competent officers and allotting rank and command on a military rather than a purely personal basis. Much of his infantry also was organized in battalions, drilled, wearing uniforms, and officered in imitation of the English sepoy battalions. They were called Telingas, which was the name the English had used of their first Telegu-speaking sepoys in Madras, with whose help Plassey had been won—and here there is a touch of irony, because there were no Telegus among them. Already, even in Madras, the British were turning to other classes, while in Bengal the soldiers on both sides were much the same in speech, religion and caste. They were Muslims from western Behar and Oudh and beyond and a sprinkling of Hindus from the same areas, but, in the case of Hindus, generally men of the higher castes.

The muskets of Mir Kasim's regular battalions were manufactured

in India and trials made later showed that they were superior to the
Company's 'Tower' muskets, which were made in England and
stamped with a representation of the Tower in proof of their quality.*
But Mir Kasim's were of better metal and had better flints. His
artillery too had been greatly improved, the guns smaller and more
manageable, the men trained to fire and load quickly. He had several
European or Armenian officers, among them the notorious Sumroo, an
Alsatian, formerly a butcher, who had come out to India with a party
of Swiss mercenaries in the British service in Madras. He was nick-
named 'Sombre', from his dark complexion and ferocious expression;
this became corrupted to 'Sumroo'. This man commanded a brigade of
Mir Kasim's best troops, four battalions of infantry—'Telingas'—a
regiment of cavalry and a company of artillery. Markar, an Armenian,
commanded a similar brigade. Altogether, Mir Kasim's army in a
short time had become much the most formidable native army which
had so far appeared in India.

What was the first act of war is an arguable point. But certainly one
of the first was taken by Ellis at Patna, who on June 24th, before the
formal declaration, seized the city and its fortifications, except for two
buildings; they had been garrisoned by the Nawab's troops, still
nominally our allies. This was done by surprise, with virtually no
fighting, after which Ellis went home for breakfast, taking no precautions to preserve his prize. This was foolish, because reinforcements
for the Nawab's garrison were expected. In fact, Markar, with his
brigade of regular troops, was distant only a few hours' march. Markar,
in his turn, surprised the city and succeeded in recapturing it. The
British troops—four companies of Europeans, a company of artillery
and three battalions of sepoys, including the Second who had fought at
Condore—were now cooped up in the Company's factory, outside the
walls. After being besieged for four days, they broke out and endeavoured to escape. But they were caught and surrounded; Sumroo's
brigade had now joined Markar's and they were heavily outnumbered.
They repelled the first charges and a moment came when the 3rd
Battalion, Captain Turner's, having used all their ammunition,
charged with the bayonet and drove the enemy back. The European
companies were ordered to support them but, 'worn out by fatigue
and want of nourishment', refused to advance. This was virtually
the end; after considerable losses, the whole force laid down its arms.
The officers, the Company's civilians and the English troops, altogether
about a hundred and fifty men, were taken to Patna as prisoners and
later massacred by Sumroo. Many of the European troops, however,

* Buldeo, the hunter in the Mowgli story called 'Tiger! Tiger!', had a Tower
musket.

were not English, and many of these entered Mir Kasim's service. So did some of the sepoys; the rest, having been stripped of arms, uniforms and equipment, were released.

This total defeat, involving the complete loss of three whole battalions of sepoys—and some of the earliest formed, the 2nd, 3rd and 5th—was a bad start to the war. It is not the purpose of this book to discuss the justice of the wars in which the troops took part unless it appears to have affected their morale. In this case, the action of the British against Mir Kasim is indefensible, and there can be little doubt that the purpose of Mir Kasim was to drive the British out of Bengal and reassert the reality of Mughal rule. But there is no evidence that this made much difference to the spirit of the British sepoys. It was one conqueror against another, and it would be misleading to look on the war in the light of a later spirit of nationalism. Of all the early wars, however, it was the most direct confrontation between the Mughals and the British and it was much the hardest fought.

From a purely military point of view, the bad start was redeemed by a most brilliant campaign. The commander was Major John Adams, who left Calcutta on July 5th, 1763, with less than 850 Europeans, and three weak battalions of sepoys, making only 1,500 Indian troops; he had only ten thousand rupees in his military chest, but it was hoped that he would be joined by various small detachments. One of these, under Lieutenant Glenn, was marching to join Adams with £20,000 in silver, between five and six hundred sepoys and six guns; he was attacked on July 17th by 17,000 irregular troops, mostly cavalry, and for four hours stood charge after charge. Three times the guns and treasure were taken and three times retaken by bayonet charges. Glenn's losses were heavy, most of his European sergeants and gunners being killed, but when the enemy at last withdrew he resumed his march and that same evening boldly attacked and captured a small fort. Next day he joined Adams, bringing a useful supply of grain and bullocks captured in the fort, as well as his guns and treasure.

This was the prelude to the first of the three pitched battles fought by Adams. It was a most desperate affair, far more serious than Plassey. The enemy were commanded by Muhammad Taki Khan— 'Mahommed Tuckee' our ancestors called him—a Muslim officer of skill, energy and courage. The force defeated by Glenn held aloof, from jealousy of Muhammad Taki, but in spite of this he came near to victory. At a crucial moment, he saw a wavering on the British right and led in person a charge of picked Afghan horse against the point of weakness. But Adams had expected this and had posted a company of sepoys in a concealed position who were able to burst from their ambush and deliver volleys of musket fire into the flank of this attack;

Muhammad Taki was killed and this decided the day. This was the battle of Katwa.

Adams now reached Murshidabad, reinstalled Mir Jafar as Nawab and marched on towards Patna with augmented forces. There is no point in telling in detail of the battles that followed or of the storming of the lines of Oodwanullah, although Fortescue describes this as 'a marvellous feat of arms, a feat which has hardly a peer in our military history'. Let us simply hear Fortescue's conclusion on this campaign.

'Starting at the height of the hot season, with a handful of British veterans and little more than a handful of sepoys ... with deficient transport and an empty treasury, Adams marched against the most powerful force in India, trained and partly commanded by European officers, well appointed, well equipped, full of courage and spirit. He ... left his enemy no peace till he had forced him back, step by step, 400 miles and finally driven him from his country ... beat him in three pitched battles, forced him from an entrenched position of stupendous strength and captured two fortified cities. Had Napoleon ... added such a campaign in India to his exploits in Europe, the whole world would still ring with it, yet the conquest of Mir Kasim by a simple English Major of Foot is forgotten.'

In a similar spirit, Broome, the historian of the Bengal Army, compares Adams's achievement with Alexander the Great's—and greatly to Adams's advantage. But the simple Major of Foot could have done nothing without the sepoys—heroes whose exploits were even more thoroughly forgotten than his own.

5. Crisis with the Army

There followed a lull during which external dangers seemed to have receded. Mir Kasim with remnants of his beaten army had been driven into Oudh; here the possibility of his return in alliance with the Nawab of Oudh was a threat, but for the moment a dormant threat. Adams, his health ruined, handed over command to Knox, but he too was worn out with the fatigues he had undergone. Knox too took leave, but neither of these gallant and determined officers reached England; both died at Calcutta. The command of the expedition fell upon Captain Jennings of the Artillery. He had with him, encamped between Patna and the Oudh frontier, something approaching a thousand European soldiers, including two French companies—men captured at Pondicherry who had taken service with the Company— and six battalions of sepoys.

It is said that emissaries from Mir Kasim's force on the other side of the river were at work among the men, offering them inducements to go over. Whether that was so or not, on January 30th, 1764, the European battalion refused to obey the word of command when under arms on parade. Jennings asked for an explanation and was told that they had been promised a distribution of money for putting Mir Jafar on the throne for the second time, that they had carried out their part of the bargain and that they would serve no more till payment had been made. Jennings, not being sure how the sepoys would take this and conscious that they had just the same grievance, decided to handle the situation gently; he remonstrated with the men, promised that he would at once address the Council and that they would be given a dividend as soon as money arrived. They appeared to accept his arguments and resumed their obedience, the parade ending as usual. Jennings then took the wise precaution of detaching the two Grenadier companies of Europeans and two battalions of sepoys from the main body. These he sent to a point near the actual frontier with Oudh.

This was the prelude. On February 11th the assembly was heard beaten without orders and the officers, hurrying to the parade-ground, found the European troops drawn up, with muskets loaded and bayonets fixed, under the command of one of themselves, a man called Straw, whom they had elected major. They said they would wait no longer but would march to Calcutta to make their grievances known, but first they would go to the Oudh border to pick up the Grenadiers. One of the French soldiers soon afterwards told an officer secretly that their real intention was not to go to Calcutta but to cross the river into Oudh, join the forces of Mir Kasim and 'make themselves masters of the whole country'. No one can now be certain, but it seems probable that this had from the start been the intention of some at least of the French and that a good many of the English had been misled. This was the belief of their officers. But at the moment none of this was clear and Jennings took it that the prize-money was the genuine source of the trouble for all the men alike. He tried to reason with them but they would not listen; he tried to arrest Straw but the men advanced on him with fixed bayonets and forced him to give up the attempt. Straw then ordered them to march and they moved off towards the camp on the frontier where the Grenadiers had been sent.

Jennings now showed great decision and presence of mind. He galloped out of camp by a different route and arrived before the mutineers. He at once got the Grenadier companies under arms and sent them back, making sure that they did not go by the road the mutineers were following; he paraded the sepoys and two field-pieces. But he appears to have learnt that though the sepoys were not likely to join the Europeans they were unwilling to fire on them. He was confident—or professed confidence—that the men would listen to reason if refreshed with 'a dram and a biscuit'; he could not believe that Englishmen would desert to the enemy. But it was pointed out to him that less than a third were in fact English and it was at this point that he received news of their true intentions.

Jennings met the mutineers and again addressed them. He persuaded them to accept his panacea of 'a dram and a biscuit', promised them pardon and attention to their grievances if they would return to their duty and pointed out the consequences if they would not. And he now revealed to the English the true plans of the French, appealing to their national pride not to be led astray into treason by their ancient enemies. Straw and many of the English listened to this appeal but the French and a few others of the more desperate continued to cry 'Forward' and finally, in what must have been a scene of great confusion, moved away towards the river. Many of the sepoys went with them, and the straggling column was followed by officers, both of the European and of the sepoy battalions, arguing, pleading and begging. About seventy more of the Europeans turned back that evening and about eighty the next day, mostly Germans; the sepoys too began to change their minds, and eventually the party who joined the forces of Mir Kasim or the Nawab of Oudh consisted of about 150 French and 100 sepoys.

Those who had turned back were not only pardoned but received an immediate distribution of money, this being an instalment of the present promised by Mir Jafar, who had sent a hundred thousand rupees to Jennings for the purpose. Jennings and other officers increased the amount by loans from their own pockets and it was announced on February 12th that it would be divided as follows:

Sergeants of foot and corporals of artillery	Rs. 80
Corporals of foot and gunners	Rs. 60
Privates of foot	Rs. 40
Havildars	Rs. 12
Naiks	Rs. 9
Sepoys	Rs. 6

The Europeans were jubilant, but now it was the turn of the sepoys to be discontented. They refused to accept their share, and following the example of the Europeans decided to appeal 'rather to the fears than to the liberality of the Government'. On February 13th they in their turn beat the assembly and fell in without orders.

Accounts of the scene that followed are confusing and it is not easy to visualize exactly what happened. But it is clear that the Europeans also were on parade and drawn up with two battalions of sepoys on either flank. I can only assume that, although not in the plot, the Europeans responded to the beating of the assembly and that the whole force fell in on parade in its usual formation. It is also clear that the Europeans were enraged that the sepoys should have dared to follow their example and their officers had difficulty in restraining them from attacking them at once. But Jennings kept control, insisting that violence should not be used unless the sepoys attacked the Europeans. There was a moment of critical tension when the sepoy battalion on the extreme left raised a shout, broke ranks and began to stream away to the right, actually passing, it is said, through the ranks of the Europeans. But their arms were shouldered and Jennings judged, rightly as it turned out, that their intentions were not aggressive; they wanted to join the battalion on the extreme right, these two being apparently the most active in discontent. It was touch and go; once Jennings snatched the match from the hands of a subaltern who was about to fire a six-pounder loaded with grape. In fact, not a shot was fired; the two most discontented battalions marched away but did not go far. They were followed by their officers, who told them that Jennings had agreed to increase their share of the prize-money; a havildar would get half the pay of a sergeant, a sepoy half that of a private, and so on. Eventually, they came back to duty—and no more seems to have been said about this mutiny either.

Thus both the Europeans and sepoys had got their way by refusing obedience, the sepoys having distinctly more justification than the Europeans, but both grievances arising from the disgraceful behaviour of the Council in accepting presents for dethroning the Nawab, both for themselves and for the army. Broome, an officer of the Bengal Artillery, whose history, admirable though it is, does display an anxiety to do full justice to his own arm of the service, has nothing but praise for Jennings, also an artillery officer. He argues that by preventing violence Jennings preserved the Bengal Army from utter destruction, which would have resulted had there been a general affray between European and Indian troops. Certainly, his courage, calmness and humanity are to be applauded—but was it right to smooth over both affairs so completely? Jennings was a captain, holding a general's command temporarily, and he cannot be blamed for getting out of his difficulties as best he could at the moment. But troops whose allegiance swings to and fro with flights of oratory, like the Roman crowds in *Julius Caesar* and *Coriolanus*, present a depressing spectacle. Nor can officers have felt much confidence in men whom they had to follow, pleading with them to return to duty. The unpleasant truth is that the greed of the Council and the short-sightedness of accepting French deserters had produced a situation which threatened the very essence of British power. Again and again we have seen that one of the greatest assets of the English lay in a greater fixity of purpose, in a higher degree of common will, than was usually to be found among those who had grown up on the fluid political situation of eighteenth-century India. They won battles partly because they had given thought to tactics, to drill, to training, but also because they had instilled into their troops the habit of unquestioning obedience. The weakness of their enemies again and again had been uncertainty as to which side a chief would take when battle was joined, the readiness of troops to change sides or abandon the struggle if a leader was killed. A terrible precedent had now been set. Had Jennings remained in command and led his men to victory, it might have been obliterated. But his command was temporary and he did not have the opportunity to put things right in his own way. Instead, things grew worse, until, in a shocking scene of deliberate bloodshed, the precedent was reversed and the principle that absolute fidelity is the first duty of a soldier was harshly asserted.

But much was to happen in the few months before that. Already, in February 1764, as these mutinies died away, rumours were afloat that Mir Kasim was about to cross the border again and that he would have the support of the Nawab-Vizier of Oudh and of the Emperor, Shah Alam. Bargaining and intrigue between the three had been in progress for some time. Each was giving presents to the advisers of the other two. Shah Alam sought the support of the Nawab-Vizier for his return to Delhi, where his rival was still in possession; the Nawab-Vizier, in his more ambitious dreams, pictured an Emperor whom he had installed on his throne, while Bengal and Behar were ruled by a Nawab who was also his creation and his creature. Both Shah Alam and the Nawab-Vizier were in correspondence with Mir Jafar as well as with Mir Kasim; both hesitated between the two. Mir Kasim's object was return to power at any price; his great asset was that his troops were better drilled and disciplined than any possessed by the other two. On the other hand, he would not long have the means of paying them. To display their prowess, he offered to suppress a rebellion in Bandelkhand, the country south of the Ganges lying between Oudh and Central India. This he did successfully and the Nawab-Vizier now at last consented to move on Behar. The three armies now began what for Shah Alam was the third invasion of Behar, Mir Kasim having promised tribute, presents and an alliance to each of the other two when he should be restored to power. This was at the beginning of March 1764, less than a month after the mutinies.

Now there befell the English a misfortune from which they had been spared since Clive's arrival in Bengal—a lethargic and irresolute commander. Major Carnac, formerly of the 39th, now in the Company's service, took over the command from Jennings. He had previously had a brief spell in command of the forces in Bengal, before the arrival of his senior, Eyre Coote, and he had then won a battle and had shown no very marked lack of initiative. Since then he had played some part in the discreditable politics of Calcutta, opposing Vansittart and siding with the party of extreme greed. On taking over command from Jennings, he addressed the troops in language which appears to have braced and exhilarated them; the prospect of action, danger and prize-money was often enough to banish discontent, particularly among the Europeans. But after his speech he did nothing; discontent and grumbling began again and there were minor acts of an insubordinate kind. During the next four months a stream of letters from Calcutta urged him, and sometimes positively instructed him, to take the offensive, which had so often been the key to success. He now commanded a much larger force than Adams had had; the three leaders opposed to him were highly suspicious of each other, and the most efficient army of the three had recently been driven out of the country by Adams. A brisk and energetic campaign would not only have divided and disconcerted the enemy but restored the limping morale of the Company's army—as the Council repeatedly pointed out to him. But Carnac kept on the defensive when he could; in spite of an allowance for intelligence purposes far larger than Adams had had, he appears to have been ill-informed of the enemy's movements, and was once surprised and almost captured 'when playing whist with his staff after breakfast'. (Breakfast, let it be said in fairness, was a meal which the British in India usually took after a march which had begun long before dawn.) On another occasion, he made a plan for a raid on the enemy's camp to be followed by a planned retreat leading to an ambush; he changed his mind overnight and countermanded the order for the ambush but did not inform the raiding party of the change. They carefully fell back to an ambush which was not there and had great difficulty in extricating themselves. This is not the kind of behaviour which endears a commander to his troops.

Carnac retreated without giving battle to Patna, where with a total force of about a thousand Europeans, eight battalions of sepoys, and twelve thousand of the Nawab's troops, he allowed himself to be surrounded and contained in an entrenched position by a force no larger than Adams had beaten with half his strength. On May 3rd the Nawab-Vizier attacked this position, showing great courage and skill, but he was not supported by Mir Kasim and was repulsed again and again, after much hard fighting, by the gallantry and discipline of the British troops. When at last the enemy fell back, the whole line wanted to turn the repulse into a victory, but Carnac would not permit an advance, ordered back commanding officers who had moved their troops forward, and would not follow up the success which his men had given him in spite of himself. He thereafter remained on virtually the same ground in front of Patna, until the enemy decided to retire at the approach of the rains. Thus ended a campaign which had achieved nothing. It can hardly be doubted that such forces under the command of Knox or Adams would have again driven the enemy back into Oudh and concluded an advantageous treaty. Nor can there be much doubt that troops who had so recently mutinied but who had welcomed the prospect of battle and victory would be thoroughly disgruntled by such leadership.

Carnac, at this point, was dismissed from the Company's service, not for this campaign but for his factious opposition to Vansittart, the President of the Council, in the previous year; news still took six to nine months to percolate to or from London. He left the army in June and Major Hector Munro took over command on August 13th. On the very next day he inspected the main body of the army and issued a general order in which he said that 'regular discipline and strict obedience to orders is the only superiority Europeans possess in this country over the natives.' He followed this up by a 'long and well-digested code of orders', enjoining far more strict attention to duty by the officers. Among other points, the Articles of War, forming the code of military discipline, were to be read at the head of each corps once a fortnight.

His orders, the manner in which they were expressed and the steps he took to enforce them, seem to have carried immediate conviction to the Europeans, who recognized that he meant what he said. But to the sepoys, used to the often meaningless hyperbole of the Nawab's proclamations, they must have seemed mere bluster. Their officers were few in proportion to the men—still only three to a battalion of a thousand—and since eighteen battalions had been raised as new units within seven years and there had been many transfers, few officers can have known their men well. They do not seem to have been able to convince them that from now onward the soldier's duty of fidelity and obedience would be treated as something rigid and inviolable. There were murmurs and grumblings among the sepoys, cases of minor insubordination; it does not seem that they had any single grievance on which to pin a complaint, but rather that they had become used to a happy-go-lucky approach to the everyday routine of a soldier's life. They found Munro's insistence on the letter of the law irksome. He issued another order on August 24th, which was to be read to all the sepoys of the army and explained to them. This order announced his 'firm resolution to treat the sepoys in every respect as soldiers, to give them all their just rights when they behave well and their just punishment when they behave scandalously'. He went on to say that the money given by the Nawab had now been distributed and there could be no alteration in that. He was sorry it had been given at all, because of the 'licentious, mercenary and unsoldierlike behaviour' it had caused, and therefore 'no such indulgence will ever be permitted' again. Any grievance they might feel should be put to their officers 'in a decent and obedient manner, which will be the surest way of obtaining what they desire'. He hoped he would in future have no occasion for anything but praise and thanks, as they would soon be taking the field against the enemy.

Unfortunately, the troops had recently got what they wanted, not by putting their grievances in a decent and obedient manner, but by refusing duty. Why should it not happen again? A number of incidents occurred in several battalions which showed that discontent was still active. But the officers were able to prevent any open outbreak until September 8th, when there was a mutiny of the oldest battalion, Knox's original Red Battalion. This was at an isolated station where there were no other troops. The men assembled without orders, and said they would serve no longer as promises had been broken; it was never made clear what promises. They did not lay down their arms but used them to imprison their officers and sergeants. Next day, however, they released them and let them go. They did not march away as a body, or disperse to their homes, and perhaps imagined that their officers would come and plead with them as before, and that they would then extort some further prize-money. But their demands were never presented and may not even have been formulated.

Their officers made for Chapra, the nearest station where there were troops. A detachment of Marines and a battalion of sepoys, later the 10th Bengal Native Infantry, started at once and found the Red Battalion encamped in a mango grove. There is no doubt that the native officers had at least acquiesced in their behaviour but no leader had emerged with any clear plan and no one now led them. They were taken by surprise and surrendered; they were deprived of their arms, made prisoners and marched back to Chapra. This place they reached on the morning of September 13th. Major Munro was there and had the entire garrison drawn up to meet them. He ordered the commanding officer of the mutinous corps to pick fifty ringleaders. This was done. Then, from those fifty, twenty-four were selected as the worst. They were tried, at once and on the spot, by a drumhead court martial of the native officers of two other battalions, one being the battalion which had arrested them. Munro addressed the officers of the court, explaining the nature of the offence and the penalties under the Articles of War, and also pointed out the consequences of such offences for the whole service. The twenty-four men were found guilty by the court of desertion and mutiny and sentenced to be put to death by being blown away from guns.

Of this frightful punishment, it was said later by Mountstuart

Elphinstone, one of the most humane, kindly and far-sighted men ever to hold a post of responsibility in India, that it combined the maximum effect on the beholders with the least pain for the offenders, being absolutely instantaneous. It was commonly used by the Mughals and borrowed, for military purposes, by both the French and the British. In the Great Mutiny, there were many cases of men begging to be blown from the guns or shot, a soldier's death, but not to be hanged—the death of a dog. It was not, then, the manner, but the fact, of death that was shocking to the condemned. They had been leaders in what they must have looked on as a trade-union dispute, a process of bargaining that had traditionally been part of the profession of arms. They had listened to the Articles of War as at best a piece of ritual, rhetoric that would never be put into practice. Suddenly they were faced by the realization that a code of conduct quite foreign to their past experience was to be exactly enforced. They met the shock with moving composure.

There were four six-pounders present on the parade. On receiving the verdicts and sentences, Major Munro confirmed them on the spot and gave orders that four of the condemned should be bound to the guns for immediate execution. They were tied with their bodies over the muzzles of the guns. But before they could be fired four others of the condemned stepped forward. They were grenadiers, they said; it had been their privilege to stand on the right of the line and to lead the forlorn hope in the assault on the breach; as grenadiers they claimed the privilege to lead in death as they had in life. Major Munro accepted their plea; the four men from companies of the line were untied and the four grenadiers took their place. At a signal from the commander, the matches were put to the touch-holes and the four guns were fired, scattering fragments of their bodies over the plain.

A thrill of horror ran through the ranks. It is said by those present that there was 'not a dry eye amongst the Europeans', though many of them had been used to 'hard service and fearful spectacles' and two had been on the firing-party which shot Admiral Byng. There was a murmur among the sepoys, and their commanding officer now came forward and brought to Major Munro's notice that their men 'would not allow' the executions to go further. Hector Munro, however, was not a man to whom such language could be used. He told them that the future of the army and indeed of the Government depended on his carrying out a 'high and sacred duty'. He loaded the guns with grape and turned them towards the sepoys; he drew up the Marines and the European Grenadiers on either side of himself. He then sent the commanding officers back to the head of their battalions and ordered the sepoys to ground their arms. The order was obeyed. He then moved them away from their arms and directed the executions to proceed. Sixteen more men were blown away, four at a time. Four were reserved to suffer the same fate in the presence of other battalions who had shown signs of insubordination.

After this display of severity, Munro did not pause long before taking the field. On October 9th, not a month after the executions at Chapra, he marched against the Nawab-Vizier, who was still encamped near Buxar, in Behar territory. The three allies were now virtually reduced to one; the Emperor, Shah Alam, feeling himself powerless in the hands of his formidable vassal, was holding aloof and sending messages to the British; Mir Kasim, in whose name the invasion had been begun, having run out of funds, had seen his famous brigades desert him for the Nawab-Vizier and was himself a prisoner. Thus there was one command, and the Nawab-Vizier had shown himself a bold and skilful commander. But he had been 'taught by the conduct of Major Carnac to undervalue the British'.

Munro, on the contrary, moved towards him with circumspection, taking care when he crossed a river that the crossing should be covered in strength and giving careful instruction to all sections of his army as to the action to be taken if attacked by cavalry. The formation to be adopted—and which was actually employed at the coming battle—was an oblong, two lines of men and guns, of which the rear was prepared to face about if need be; at each end of the front line, a half-battalion understood that its duty might be to move back to fill the gaps at the ends of the oblong and face outward; similarly, a half-battalion in the rear line would move forward. Each line consisted of a central body of three or four hundred Europeans with two battalions of sepoys on either flank.

The army came into sight of the Nawab-Vizier's camp on October 22nd and Munro decided that they should rest on the 23rd and attack him on the 24th. But on October 23rd, 1764, the Nawab-Vizier himself moved out to the attack. The battle followed the now familiar pattern: gallant charges of horsemen against the rigid oblong of infantry. Once again, when the charges of Afghan horse had at last revealed a weakness in the British lines, the commander was able to swing into the exact place where it was needed a well-drilled force which turned the scale. And when at last the enemy began sullenly to fall back, there was this time no hesitation about following them up. The victory was complete. The Nawab-Vizier retreated from Behar and the Emperor, Shah Alam, became positively obsequious in his requests for protection, offering to grant the British not only Bengal, Behar and Orissa but Oudh as well.

This, the battle of Bhaksar, was the last of that series of battles, beginning seven years earlier with Plassey, which were decisive in the sense that at any one of them defeat might have ended British power.

No battles would again be decisive in quite that sense till the Great Mutiny. But a final scene must be drawn. From the 24th till the 27th the army remained at Bhaksar, busily employed in burying the dead and collecting the wounded from both sides. There had been heavy casualties among the camp-followers and there was a great shortage of stretcher-bearers, as well as of surgeons. 'Many poor fellows lay several days upon the field.' Major Munro, however, personally visited the field daily and brought them rice and water. He had showed, throughout the whole campaign, that he was 'a man of remarkably humane and considerate disposition'.

6. Crisis with the Officers

One crisis, however, remained. The mutinies at Bhaksar had their origin in corruption and greed, in lax discipline and a lethargic commander. And now there came further fruit from these seeds; steps towards reform produced a mutiny among officers. The Court of the Company in London were shocked by what they heard of happenings in Bengal and prevailed on Clive to go back to India with instructions to put things right and with powers that overrode those of the President and Council. One of his first steps was to prohibit all servants of the Company — civil and military — from accepting presents; this was naturally unpopular. Soon afterwards he came to the long-standing question of Double Batta.

This was a subject about which grievances arose throughout the history of the Indian Army. *Batta* is defined in the glossary to Cambridge's *Account of the War in India* as 'An extraordinary allowance to the Army when abroad in the field or in any country where garrison provisions are scarce'. In Madras, it had been the custom to allow half batta to soldiers in certain stations where provisions were more expensive than on the coast and full batta when in the field, that is, when in camp or engaged in operations. Batta was payable to officers and to men, and was for fixed amounts, related to pay. After the battle of Plassey, Mir Jafar had made an allowance, to officers, not men, of double batta when in the field, and since the army had been fairly frequently in the field, this made a substantial difference to their emoluments. It made officers of the Bengal Army better off than their colleagues in Bombay and Madras and they had come to think of it as a right. So long as the cost fell on Mir Jafar, the Company raised no objection, but when the three districts of Midnapore, Chittagong and Burdwan were assigned to cover the expense of defending Bengal, the burden became directly theirs. The amount was considerable and far in excess of pay. In 1766, for example, the pay of a lieutenant-colonel was Rs. 248 per month, while single batta in the field was Rs. 620 and double batta Rs. 1,240. Thus, if he had no other allowances, a lieutenant-colonel would draw Rs. 248 a month in Calcutta, in a cantonment away from Calcutta pay plus half batta, that is, Rs. 558, and in the field pay plus double batta, Rs. 1,488—more than five times his pay. For a lieutenant, pay was Rs. 62, batta Rs. 124 and double batta Rs. 248. The disproportion was absurd; either pay was far too low or double batta far too high.*

In fact, of course, pay was far too low. For lieutenants attached to sepoy regiments it was not quite so bad, because they drew an allowance equal to their pay for the attachment. For lieutenants with European battalions, however, pay was quite inadequate and the straightforward remedy would have been to increase pay and reduce batta. Governments, however, are usually more generous over allowances than pay. They feel that pay is permanent and basic, but allowances they may one day be able to reduce; the policy earns a steady harvest in discontent. The company was also influenced by the level of pay in the King's Regiments, but they had no inhibitions about batta. The Court of Directors in London had objected to it some time before this. The Council in Bengal had replied to London urging difficulties; they had temporized, they had held inquiries. They were in a strong position to postpone obedience, because of the time it took to get an answer from London, and they were frightened of the consequences. And well they might be, in the middle of a war, since the cut proposed was generally about two-fifths of emoluments. They held an inquiry into the extra expenses an officer incurred in the field, and received in reply a paper which attempted to show that the extra cost of living in camp for each officer was over Rs. 300 a month—five times the pay of a lieutenant. This included Rs. 71 for the extra cost to each officer of thirty bottles of Madeira, thirty bottles of beer and fifteen bottles of arrack per month. It stated that all servants were paid in camp double the sum they received in garrison, that each officer took his own cook—although five were said to mess together—that each officer had to buy a palanquin as well as a horse, and to keep eight bearers to carry him, with eight bearers for his personal luggage and another eight for the mess equipment. It charged an extra forty rupees a month for 'wearing apparel'.

Altogether, it is not a document that inspires much confidence in its accuracy; it is rather an attempt to support high batta by a series of

* As a young civil officer, nearly two centuries later, I drew travelling allowance when living in tents which came to about a quarter of my pay. But actually I lived more cheaply in camp, mainly because there was no temptation to extravagance. This was an example of a fiction which survived to become true again; for Indian officers it probably *was* more expensive to live in camp, because their families seldom accompanied them.

fictions, when the real remedy was better pay and the provision at
the public expense of what an officer needed in camp. He ought not,
for instance, to have had to buy his own horse; and the custom at this
period of also buying a palanquin would a century later have been
regarded as effeminate. But he could draw a tent from the stores and it
was carried at the public expense. 'It was only', ran one memorial,
'with the assistance of what little an officer could save out of his Full
Batta in the field that he was enabled to subsist decently the rest of the
year in garrison … That if an officer, by the means of great frugality,
and denying himself the comforts of life, in a long course of years had
it in his power to lay by a little money, perhaps to maintain a family or
to enable him to revisit his native country, yet he must pay an extravagant price before he could get a passage home.' But it was a hundred
and fifty years before passages to England were paid by the Government.

The Company, however, continued to harden its heart over the
double batta, and Clive was positively instructed to end it. He took
first some steps to improve the position of officers, particularly senior
officers; he established a fund, charged against the Company's monopoly in certain articles, which provided a considerable addition to the
receipts of field officers—that is, majors and above. He also reorganized
the Bengal Army, providing three brigades—practically divisions in
modern terms—each a self-contained fighting force of one battalion of
European infantry and seven battalions of sepoys, with a company of
gunners and a regiment of irregular horse. This of course meant promotion for a number of officers. Gone were the days when a humble
captain could command an expeditionary force; there were now a
brigadier-general as commander-in-chief, three colonels commanding
brigades, three lieutenant-colonels and an increased number of
majors. And at about this time, Clive also established the fund long
known by his name; Lord Clive's Fund consisted originally of a sum
of half a million rupees, which had been left him by will as a personal
bequest from Mir Jafar. Clive had just laid down that no presents were
to be taken; this was not a present but a legacy, and Mir Jafar died
before the new rule came into force. He might have argued in strict
logic that he could accept it, but, with a delicacy rare at the period—
and in the event singularly fortunate—he put the whole of this sum
into trust for the benefit of officers and men disabled by climate or
wounds.

When Clive had made arrangements to improve officers' prospects,
he published the order which put an end to double batta, except for
troops in Oudh, that is, beyond the boundaries of what was now virtually the Company's territory; within Bengal and Behar there was
also a considerable reduction in the number of places where half

batta could be drawn. All this came into force on January 1st, 1766, and the Council in Calcutta must have heaved sighs of relief when the date passed peacefully. But in fact, the great majority of captains, lieutenants and ensigns were then already entering into a conspiracy. It was talked about in December and the details seem to have been settled in January. The conspirators regarded the order about batta as 'an unworthy attempt to deprive them of the rich advantages for which they had fought and bled'. They therefore agreed to resign their commissions simultaneously, on June 1st, 1766. The commissions were to be handed in advance to a chosen officer in each brigade, who on the appointed day would put them in the hands of commanding officers. The conspirators would, however, continue for fifteen days to do duty without pay. They hoped that during this interval the Council would change its mind and give in to them; they seem also to have thought that if they took no pay for fifteen days they would become exempt from the Articles of War and would have committed no military offence. Soldiers often expect the law to be even more absurd than it is. But in other respects they were business-like; nearly two hundred of them entered into a bond not to reveal their plans or to take back their commissions unless the old double batta was restored. They also contributed to a general fund for the support of anyone who was afterwards punished for his part in the proceedings.

It appeared later that Lt-Col. Sir Robert Fletcher, at whose career we have already glanced and who now commanded the 1st Brigade at Monghyr, had at the end of December or the beginning of January suggested that the captains and subalterns should adopt this course. He was dining with a number of junior officers, mostly on his own staff; he said later that he had done his best to dissuade them from taking part in any such proceedings but that, finding his arguments were disregarded, he decided 'to try to keep in their confidence till they had come to some final resolution and to moderate the rage with which they were actuated'. He had in fact suggested the fifteen days' service without pay simply to prevent their going off in a body. But if that had really been the case, it is hard to see why for four months he did not report to headquarters what he had said and the reactions to it; it was late in April when he first brought the matter to notice and he stands condemned by his own letters and his own statement at his court martial. A strange character! He himself, as a lieutenant-colonel commanding a brigade, drew under the new arrangements a table allowance of Rs. 40 a day, so that he had little personal cause for complaint, and much to lose by his part in the intrigue. But he gives the impression of a man who revelled in intrigue for its own sake.

No other officer of field rank appears to have known anything of the conspiracy until the end of April. A court martial was then convened to investigate the origins of a fire, which in fact was due to a probably rather drunken scuffle, late one night, to which one party was an officer who was unpopular because he had refused to give up his commission. This was in the 3rd Brigade, at Bankipur. The investigation brought to light some suspicious circumstances, and Sir Robert Barker, who commanded the 3rd Brigade, wrote to Fletcher of the 1st, telling him what he had discovered and asking how things were in his command. Fletcher now decided that he could no longer pretend to be ignorant and on April 28th informed Clive of what was threatened, pretending that he had throughout tried to dissuade his officers. At the same time, the conspirators hastily put forward their date from June 1st to May 1st, leaving the brigade at Allahabad, the 2nd, who could not get the news in time, to make their own arrangements for a date as early as they could. No doubt because of the change of date, two officers close to Lord Clive, who might otherwise have been approached more cautiously, received on April 29th anonymous letters asking them to join; these they immediately showed him.

It was the kind of situation in which Clive was at his best. He sent at once to Madras for all the junior officers they could spare, and published the fact that he had done this. He arranged that a resolution should be passed and published that no one who resigned his commission should ever again be employed by the Company; he immediately collected all junior officers at Calcutta and Murshidabad—that is, away from the three brigades—and succeeded in persuading all but five to give up their plans. He wrote to Barker and Fletcher instructing them to put under arrest any officers whose conduct was mutinous and to arrange for courts martial by field officers. He also let it be known that if he could discover the authors of one of the anonymous letters sent to his headquarters' staff, he would have them shot.

This display of firmness did not alter the resolution of the officers of the 1st and 3rd Brigades. Both groups sent in their commissions. Fletcher forwarded those from his brigade; Barker refused to accept those from his. The Council in Calcutta stated their determination to stand fast, reminding the officers that they were better paid than officers in the Royal service and that they would certainly not be re-employed in the latter. Clive started for Monghyr, the station of Fletcher's 1st Brigade. He had sent ahead officers on whom he could personally rely and these arrived at Monghyr to find things far worse than anyone had supposed; the European regiment was in a disorderly state and liable to mutiny. When Clive's fund was mentioned, it came out that none of the officers at Monghyr had heard of it; Fletcher had kept the news of it to himself. Clive's generosity and Fletcher's concealment of it had an immediate effect. Some of the conspirators began to say that Fletcher had been at the bottom of everything and they wished they could see Clive themselves and tell him the whole story.

Next day, May 13th, Captain Smith, one of the faithful officers, heard that the Europeans were on the parade-ground and were refusing to obey orders. He had previously brought up two battalions of sepoys from the camp near by and on this news immediately led them, with bayonets fixed and muskets loaded, to a point where they commanded the parade-ground. Smith told the Europeans he would fire on them unless they went peacefully to their barracks as he instructed them. Fletcher at this moment appeared and harangued them to the same effect; this apparently surprised them, as they said they had thought he would lead them. They did as they were told.

Clive himself arrived on the 14th and spoke first to the Europeans and then to the sepoys. He seems to have been heard respectfully and the parade ended with three hearty cheers. Those officers who had resigned their commissions were encamped near by; Clive ordered them to report to Calcutta at once and sent a battalion of sepoys to conduct them there under guard if necessary. They went peacefully. Clive now went on to Bankipur, where, largely owing to the straightforward behaviour of Sir Robert Barker, who was much respected, things were nothing like so bad. The officers had handed in their commissions but had continued to perform their duty and the European battalion was in perfect order. Most of the officers now submitted and asked for pardon.

The 2nd Brigade was differently placed because there was a considerable force of Marathas threatening an attack. Thus, if not on active service, they were close to it. The sepoy battalions had been moved out of Allahabad to an advanced position towards the Marathas, about a hundred miles away, while the European battalion had been left in cantonments at Allahabad because of the heat. It was hoped that the Maratha threat might have prevented the officers of this brigade from going so far as the others, but this was not the case; indeed, their attitude was more intransigent than the 3rd Brigade's. Colonel Richard Smith, who commanded the brigade and was at the camp, as well as Major Smith, commanding the European regiment at Allahabad, were equally firm. Major Smith's officers were more intemperate in their language than those with the sepoy battalions and he had good reason to suppose they might upset their men. He asked for the help of the 8th Native Infantry, a battalion he had himself commanded; they marched 104 miles in two days and six hours and the very next day were ordered to arm and led by Major Smith to the barracks. Here he arrested all the officers but four, warning them that he would order the sepoys to 'put every one of them to death', if they tried to excite the Europeans to mutiny. He then dictated an apology for the affronts to his authority; they submitted and he then ordered the release of all but six whom he sent away for trial. 'This spirited behaviour' ended the trouble at Allahabad. Colonel Smith, commanding the brigade, did not find it necessary to proceed to these lengths, but he acted in the same spirit, sending away the leaders for trial and accepting the submission of the more moderate. The conspiracy crumbled and fell to pieces before Clive's emissaries from Bankipur arrived; he did not need to go to Allahabad himself.

Now there was general repentance. Most of those sent down to Calcutta petitioned for reinstatement and in most cases this was eventually granted. But Clive would not reinstate them at once and in the interval they lost their pay and allowances as well as seniority, and some were superseded by officers from Madras and Bombay. Others were reinstated with the restriction that they could not be promoted beyond a certain rank. Not till 1776 was there a general amnesty. Those who were pardoned, and all new officers in future, were under covenant to serve for three years at least and in no case to quit the Company's service without giving a year's notice. The leaders, including Sir Robert Fletcher, and the most obstinate were tried by court martial and cashiered. Fletcher pleaded that he should not be tried by his brother-officers, 'whose birth and former lives' had 'given them no opportunity of acquiring an education sufficient to comprehend and judge' such a case as his.

No one, however, was blown away from guns. The officers' mutiny, like the sepoys', was an attempt to apply to their employers the sanctions today freely used by trade unions. In the eighteenth century, even in civil life, a 'combination', whatever its purpose, was a criminal conspiracy under the common law. From 1800 onwards there were Combination Acts more explicit; it was for administering an illegal oath to the members of a Friendly Society that seven Dorset farm labourers—the Tolpuddle martyrs—were sentenced, as late as 1834, to seven years' transportation. These officers were unquestionably guilty of conspiracy and if they did not get their way they meant to go on to mutiny and desertion. There was not much to choose between them and the sepoys, except that the officers ought to have known better. Perhaps all that Madeira and arrack had something to do with it. Yet it can hardly be argued that the threat to the Government was much less in one case than the other; it was in either case a threat involving the total destruction of the system of government. The difference was surely a matter of fellow-feeling; it is easier to harden your heart and blow men to pieces if you do not really know how they think and feel.

It was thanks to the sepoy that the mutinies of the European rank and file and of the officers had been defeated. He was an essential prop of the edifice that was now coming into being, one of the most important.

And yet he was still a mystery, a stranger, even to his own officers, still more of course to men of the Royal army such as Hector Munro.

Note: The Black Hole of Calcutta
There is a vivid account of the Black Hole of Calcutta by J. Z. Hol· well, the senior person present and one of the survivors. No one threw any doubt on this until recently, when it was pointed out that Holwell had been found in some other respects not absolutely reliable as a witness. But that is a long way indeed from proving that the incident did not occur. Nor is it relevant to its historical truth that the incident later became an article of what Dr Spear calls 'imperial hagiology'. There is nothing in Holwell's own account to suggest that Suraj-ud-Daulah committed an act of deliberate cruelty; when he first saw the captives, he ordered their hands to be untied. It is true that he did not take the trouble to see that they were looked after properly—but that was hardly to be expected. His guards were callous, brutal and unimaginative. One hundred and twenty-three people died as a result; we have their names. If Holwell invented the whole thing and persuaded all his contemporaries to believe it, the fate of those 123 becomes a mystery which needs accounting for.

It does not help the cause of truth to rewrite history as though unpleasant incidents had not happened. What is essential is to remember that no one has a monopoly of such incidents; there are plenty of atrocities on the British side to square the account. For example, just one hundred years later, Mr Cooper at Amritsar—in his own words—'repeated the tragedy of Holwell's Black Hole' when he confined for the night two hundred and eighty-two men who had surrendered to him; he dragged out next morning two hundred and thirty-seven, whom he executed on the spot, and found forty-five 'dead from fright, exhaustion, fatigue and partial suffocation'. *He* knew just what he was doing and boasted of it.

Part II
High Noon of the Sepoy Army

VI

An Army in Being

1. Caste and Honour

Some things begin to be clear. The Indian Army began in the rivalry of French and English but in India that issue was virtually settled by the end of the Seven Years' War in 1763. By that date, the sepoys enlisted by the British were generally better than those of the French. 'You would be surprised', wrote Lally de Tollendal as early as February 23rd, 1759, 'at the difference between the black troops of the English and ours; it is greater than that between a Nawab and a cooly. Theirs will even venture to attack white troops, while ours will not even look at their black ones.' And the reasons for this difference begin to be clear—more regular pay, better training and discipline, more confidence in their officers.

To speak of confidence in their officers is to argue in a circle; how confidence arises is the very question we are trying to answer. Both French and English sometimes produced good generals, but something in the social system, the political arrangements and the intellectual atmosphere of England produced a higher proportion of good officers at company and battalion level—men with a strong sense of devotion to their duty and to their men, men who combined personal initiative with a disciplined obedience to a commander. Many seem, incidentally, to have been Huguenots. Almost as important was a greater continuity of policy; with all its faults and difficulties, the English Company was in a much stronger position than the French in relation to the Government; its attention to Indian affairs was continuous, while a European Government's could only be intermittent. And some feeling of permanence, some consistency between past and future, is essential to the confidence a soldier needs; he must feel that what he dies for will not end with his death.

There is another difference between French and English which may be relevant—but this is uncertain ground, a personal opinion about which no one can be sure. The English in India were aloof, and this was not merely a late growth; doubtless we became more aloof as we became more conscious of what began to seem an imperial destiny.

but from the start we did not mix freely or easily with people so different from ourselves. This was to be one of the charges that nationalists were later to level against us, and with much justice — yet aloofness carried with it certain advantages. If the English were more resistant than the French to Indian customs, and if in diplomacy they might therefore sometimes be at a disadvantage as against such a Frenchman as Dupleix, their very rigidity of manners and opinions made them also more insistent on what helped them to win battles. To pay troops regularly was almost unknown in native armies; the French fell into the easy ways of the country more easily than we did and, though our troops were also sometimes in arrears, it was less often and less deeply. And so with the exact minutiæ of drill and clothes and discipline that distinguished the trained soldier from the swashbuckler hired for the campaign. It is the constantly repeated details of drill which make obedience automatic and self-control in the presence of danger a habit. In such matters we were more insistent than the French.

The defeat by John Adams of Mir Kasim's 'Telingas' or drilled battalions foreshadows the later defeat of Scindia's trained soldiers at Assaye and Laswaree, of the Sikhs at Sobraon and Chillianwallah. In those battles of the Sikh and Maratha Wars, enemy forces of great courage, well armed and resolutely led, drilled to European standards by European officers, were defeated by smaller British forces. They were hard-fought battles, very different from Plassey; years later, long after Waterloo, Wellington was asked what was 'the best thing he had ever done in the way of fighting'; he replied with the one word 'Assaye!' And on another occasion he said: 'The battle of Talavera was the hardest-fought in modern times. The fire at Assaye was heavier while it lasted but the battle of Talavera lasted for two days and a night.'

The Sikh battles have often been judged to have been still harder-fought. The reasons for victory are usually more complex than is supposed, but in all these battles the weapons and system of drill were much the same on both sides and there was not much difference in the basic human material, except that the Sikhs had a distinct physical advantage. What was different was the presence of British troops and British officers. On the British side there was fierce competition between European and Indian troops and the leadership was markedly better at company level. The French and Italian commanders of Scindia's and the Sikh troops, like Mir Kasim's foreign officers, were usually at the level of brigadier and above. And Scindia's were not always devoted to his cause.

It has become clear that neither British officers nor European troops nor Indian sepoys had a monopoly of either courage or devotion. All could display unbelievable valour; all could mutiny. European and Indian troops alike might sometimes falter. But, from the point we have

reached till at least the end of the Maratha Wars—that is, for the last
quarter of the eighteenth and the first quarter of the nineteenth centuries—there is a fairly steady growth of confidence between Indian
soldiers and their officers and Government. Individual deserters are
rare and units do not go over to the other side; there are clearly assign-
able causes when a unit refuses its duty and these occasions are not
frequent; fidelity to the colours, to the oath and to the salt a man has
eaten become more and more an accepted habit.

Regiments became institutions; they began to acquire a life of their
own and the men were often linked by personal ties. Braithwaite,
acting as Commander-in-Chief in Madras, wrote in 1793 to protest
against the custom of dividing a regiment by sending away drafts when
a new unit was formed. The argument at headquarters, of course, was
that a battalion consisting entirely of recruits would take much longer
to train. But Braithwaite pointed out:

'In native corps of any standing, the ties of caste and consanguinity
are so strong and numerous, from frequent intermarriages ... that
any separation amongst them must be felt by them as peculiarly dis-
tressful. The inhabitants distributed to different corps [and] severed
from their relations become disgusted with the establishment and from
desertion are frequently lost to it, while their connections in the old
corps, embarrassed in their domestic arrangements and put to much
inconvenience, lose that confidence in the service which they have
been used to have, and that faithful attachment to it for which they have
been so eminently remarkable is greatly weakened.'

Here, for those who have not lived in India, something must be said
about caste, that peculiar institution. Westerners are inclined to think
of it as class, but it is very different, and the reality is obscured by a good
deal of myth and many local complications. But, simplifying enormously, one may say that the Hindus were divided in the nineteenth
century into more than three thousand groups who must not marry
outside the group. The group was divided into subdivisions and usually
it was not permitted to marry *within* the subdivision. The in-marrying
group—in Hindi *jati*—may be compared with a battalion; the subdivision—in Hindi *gotra*—with a company. It is as though a man had
to marry a girl whose father came from the same battalion as himself,
but from a different company. But it is not only marriage. The group
to which a man belongs affects the whole of his outward life; there are
elaborate rules about eating, drinking, smoking and washing. Men
from the higher groups must eat and smoke only with those of their
own group and must not accept food or water from the lower—
though there are almost always exceptions and some kinds of food are
less subject to pollution than others. If these rules are broken, a man
is polluted and may not eat, smoke or drink with his own group, still

less of course with any other. He will be shunned by everyone; he is an outcast, excommunicated. He can only be cleansed, after long penance, by elaborate and expensive ceremonies.

These in-marrying groups cannot be ranked exactly; to arrange them in an order — A is better than B, B than C, and so on — would certainly lead to controversy. There are regional variations and some groups rise or fall in general esteem; sometimes they split or coalesce. But there is some general agreement. Throughout India, the many different in-marrying groups who count as Brahman do come at the top of the tree in the dimension of caste. But they may come quite low in the *social* dimension, being often employed as cooks or office messengers. Ritual esteem does not coincide with social. This is what is so difficult for a Westerner, who is used to thinking in the one dimension of social esteem, to understand. Western observers were also often misled by a myth, in the literal sense of the word. They would be told that at the creation of mankind there were four *orders* of men: Brahmans who sprang from the head of the Creator, Rajputs who sprang from his arms, Banias from his belly and Sudras from his feet. Brahmans were priests and scholars; Rajputs were kings, barons, landowners, soldiers; Banias were traders, bankers, money-lenders. These three orders were 'twice-born', wearing the sacred thread, observing far more restrictions than the others. Broadly speaking, the more abstentions and prohibitions were observed, the higher in the caste system a group was reckoned. Sudras were cultivators, messengers, clerks, artisans, certain domestic servants whose tasks did not pollute, such as those who carried a palanquin, but not scavengers, skinners, sweepers. These, with others, made up a whole range of groups who were outside the caste system and who were generally called 'untouchables'. They too had in-marrying groups and out-marrying subdivisions, precedence among themselves and rules about who might accept water from whom. They were later called 'the scheduled castes' and to treat them as 'untouchable' is today, in independent India, illegal, though it is not the kind of law that can easily be administered.*

* I have used the terms generally used by soldiers in the nineteenth century. It would really be more exact to call the second order, of kings and soldiers, Kshatriyas. But apart from having an odd look to Western eyes, this word was not used by the army. 'Rajput', on the other hand, is confusing because it sometimes means a man belonging to one of the groups ranked as Kshatriya but sometimes it means a Kshatriya from the region of Rajputana. There were caste-groups loosely called Rajputs throughout the plain of the Ganges, in the eastern Punjab and in the Himalayas. 'Bania' is really an occupation and the order should more properly be called Vaish. But nothing in the Indian social and religious system is simple. The Sanskritic word for what I call an 'order' is *varna*; to continue the military metaphor, the order is a higher formation, a grouping of battalions into an army corps. One of the reasons for Western confusion is that we use the one word 'caste' in four different senses: for the whole institution, for the in-marrying group, for the subdivision and for the order.

Caste pervades the atmosphere in India. Though the English often misunderstood it, they were often infected by it. 'I was surprised to find', wrote Honoria Lawrence when she first arrived in India in 1837, 'among Europeans the prejudices of caste and that many of them object to a low-caste native (simply on that ground) as much as a Hindoo would.' And any honest observer who lived in India a hundred years later would confirm her impression. It was to distinguish their soldiers from the surrounding mass but, above all, to give them confidence in themselves that the English insisted on spit and polish, on pipeclay, on appearance. It was easy for them to think that only men of high caste and reasonably good social position — the younger sons of small land-owners and large tenant-farmers — could achieve the confidence and swagger that they wanted. And, as we have seen, they liked to see tall men in the ranks and preferred them to be fair rather than dark. Broadly speaking, the lower castes do tend to be shorter and darker, the higher taller and fairer. And it is generally true that as one goes through India from north to south, and from west to east, the people are more often small and dark.

In the Bengal Army, the victory of caste was complete. In the Madras and Bombay Armies, there was a different tradition and it was always said that in the ranks men were all equal. This was partly because in Madras there are no Rajputs and the Brahmans are even more insis-tent on all that divides them from the rest, with the result that no Madras Brahmans entered the army. But even here the preference for higher caste was constantly cropping up. In 1777 a batch of recruits from Arcot was described as 'low in size, low in caste, and very bad indeed'. In 1794 recruits are to be 'of a proper caste and of sufficient size' and in 1798 General Harris summarized Madras opinion in these words: 'Although men obtained in the Southern countries are much inferior to the Northern recruits in caste, in size and in appearance, they are nevertheless hardy and thrifty and being less subject to local attachments and little encumbered with religious habits and prejudices to interfere with the regular performance of their duty, are found to stand the pressure of military hardships with much fortitude and to manifest at all times a firm adherence to the service.' And in Bombay the same mixture of sentiments was displayed. There were always, and increasingly, more Northerners here. Arthur Wellesley remarked that it was better to use northern troops in detachments to princely states; their physique and caste made them looked up to.

But there was no ambiguity in Bengal. From the earliest days men were recruited not from Bengal, but from Behar and Oudh, and the Hindus were most of them from the two higher orders, Brahmans and Rajputs. It is strange that any Brahman should have entered the army, because there are few Brahman groups which will eat meat or even eggs and many which carefully abstain from taking life—other than human life. It would really be impossible for a Brahman of the higher groups to keep in the army all the rules laid down for his daily life, and, as we have seen, southern Brahmans, who are the most strict, never did enter the army. A Brahman must not touch leather, for example; he must cook every item of his own food; in some groups he must eat alone; the time that he ought to spend in washing and praying would break the heart of any sergeant-major. But the men were tall, fair and self-confident and once they were away from the village could generally be persuaded to compromise on many points. As long as they could cook for themselves food which was ritually clean, as long as their water was drawn by a man of the right grade, as long as they could remove any obnoxious leather before eating, they would curtail the time spent on washing and praying.

So the Bengal Army gave in to caste, the officers paying a scrupulous attention to avoid infringements. Sir Herbert Edwardes has a story in his *Life of Sir Henry Lawrence* of a Brahman subadar of the Bengal Army lying desperately wounded, dying of heat and thirst and loss of blood. A British officer—General Skinner—knelt beside him, raised his head and tried to give him a drink from his water-bottle. But the Brahman would have none of it. 'My caste! My caste!' he groaned. Skinner urged him again to drink; 'No one can see you; no one shall know,' he said. But the Brahman was firm; 'God sees me,' he was just able to say. This was a spirit which, irrational though they thought it, many British officers admired. Pride in caste, pride in family services, pride in the honour of the regiment—these went together and made the spirit of an army. After Assaye, an officer found a party from the 1st/8th Madras Native Infantry burying five brothers. This was a corps which had been with Wellesley so often in so many engagements that they had proudly taken to themselves the title of 'Wellesley's battalion'. On the officer expressing sympathy, he was gently reproved. 'There is no occasion', they said, 'for such feelings or expressions. These men were soldiers; they died in the performance of their duty. The Government they served will protect their children, who will soon fill the ranks they occupied.' Pericles or Lincoln could have said it no better.

Those brothers were Northerners and Muslims. But it is one of the paradoxes of India that Hindu, Muslim and British, bitter though their opposition so often was, shared so much and borrowed so much from each other. The regiment, the colours, were British; destiny and fidelity to salt Muslim; the essential message of the *Bhagavad Gita*, which some regard as the core of Hinduism, is that each man shall perform his proper function. All three understood the concept of honour. The oath at enlistment, the sacredness of the colours, the ceremonial of guard-mounting—these rubbed in the point. There are

two words for 'honour' which are commonly used in Hindustani. A man
has already been mentioned who transferred to the Bombay Army from
Bengal because one gave honour to the regiment, the other to caste, and
his caste had been slighted in the army which honoured caste. He used
the word *ghairat*, for which one of the dictionary meanings is 'a nice
sense of honour' and another 'care of what is sacred'. Most British
officers were more familiar with another word, *izzat*, which means
'glory, honour, reputation'. They are not quite the same; one is reputation in the eyes of the world, the other concern about that reputation
but also something more, respect for one's personal integrity. 'God sees
me!' said the dying subadar. Both meanings come together in the idea
of honour.

Take certain events in the history of one unit. There was a disastrous
affair in 1778, when a force from Bombay was ordered to advance into
Maratha country. But the commander first chosen for the expedition
died, and in their folly the Bombay Government appointed as his successor a 'bedridden invalid' with two members of Council to accompany and support him. It was hardly a recipe for swift and resolute
action—and only resolute action could have made the expedition a
success. The force fell slowly back, pursued by thirty times their number of Maratha troops—disgraceful generalship redeemed by the
courage and skill of superb infantry. The six Grenadier companies of
the three battalions concerned were combined, as was then often the
custom, into one unit as rearguard. It was they who saved the force.
They were, said Scindia, the enemy commander, 'a red wall, no sooner
beaten down than it was built up again'. Later, these companies, with
some others, were combined into a new battalion, the 8th Bombay
Native Infantry, and there was almost a mutiny because this unit was
not from its beginning officially styled a grenadier battalion. It was
soon afterwards besieged in Mangalore by Tippoo's army, reckoned at
150,000; the siege lasted from May 16th, 1783, till January 30th, 1784,
when men were dying of exhaustion at the rate of fifteen a day, while
some were going blind. Campbell, the commander, had 1,900 men
when the siege began, of whom 236 Europeans and 618 Indians were
fit for duty when at last he capitulated with the honours of war. The
British troops were the Black Watch—the 2nd Battalion, 42nd Royal
Highlanders. The 8th Bombay Battalion, their comrades in those nine
heroic months, decided to appoint themselves the 3rd Battalion of the
Black Watch, an unofficial honour seconded by the Black Watch
themselves. Both regiments were awarded the official battle honour
'Mangalore'—one of the very rare occasions when a battle honour was
awarded for a defeat. Further, the 8th Bombay were now granted the
distinction they had coveted of becoming a Grenadier regiment. They
were for long the senior regiment to hold that honour, beating by

thirty-two years the 1st Regiment of Foot Guards—the Grenadier Guards—who were thus distinguished only after Waterloo. This unit, at Independence, was the 1st Battalion, 4th Bombay Grenadiers.

But perhaps nothing makes the point so clearly as the behaviour at Bhurtpore of the 31st Bengal Native Infantry, which later became the 1st Battalion, 7th Rajput Regiment.* They had been with Lake in the amazing campaign in which he defeated Scindia's trained battalions in battle after battle, a campaign for which they received an honorary standard inscribed 'Lake and Victory'. But after six great victories Lake met his match at Bhurtpore. This was a fortress with a circumference of seven miles, the ramparts being of mud, and between 80 and 120 feet in height, surrounded by the moat from which those colossal walls had been dug, a deep and wide ditch with plenty of water. Lake had six thousand infantry and two thousand cavalry, and, by way of a siege-train, only six iron 18-pounders and eight brass mortars. This was quite inadequate; even guns firing 24-pound roundshot could at that time make little impression on massive walls of dried mud, in which they merely buried themselves. He could only have hoped to capture the place if the defenders were taken by surprise—and they were not— or if they were hopelessly treacherous or irresolute. And that they were still less; the raja was himself a Jat and his people were Jats—sturdy, obstinate folk, as stubborn and devoted as any in India.

But Lake was now sure he could do anything and he decided to assault the place even though his guns were inadequate to make a proper breach and he had no ladders long enough for such fortifications. The first assault was made on January 9th, 1805, and was beaten back. After more ineffective cannonading, a second assault was made on January 21st, and again was beaten back. By now a considerable army of Bhurtpore's allies had collected and were threatening, and sometimes harassing, Lake's small force. He went out himself with a detachment which successfully brought in a convoy of bullocks and supplies, and sent off another detachment, which pursued one of these allies, brought him to battle and defeated him—marching 700 miles before it was back at Bhurtpore. While this detachment was away, Lake received some reinforcements from Bombay, but still no siege-train. He could not

* The changes in name are confusing in the extreme. This unit was raised as the 2nd Battalion, 15th Bengal Native Infantry, becoming the 31st just before the second siege of Bhurtpore. It was the 31st in the Mutiny, when we shall hear of it again. It became the 2nd Regiment of Native Light Infantry in 1858, added the title of the Queen's Own in 1877, was later called the Queen's Own Second Rajput Light Infantry, and from 1922 to 1947 was the 1st Battalion, 7th Rajput Regiment. I shall try to stick to the designations for the two longest periods in which there were few changes: 1824 to 1857 and 1922 to 1947. Thus this battalion will be called either the 31st or the 1st/7th.

afford delay, and he ordered a third assault on February 20th. It was badly planned and the leading troops found themselves jammed in a narrow defile with heavy fire concentrated on the head of the column. Three British battalions, His Majesty's 75th and 76th and the Bengal Europeans, later His Majesty's 101st, refused to go farther. They had no confidence in the management of the siege. But two battalions of sepoys and the flank companies of H.M. 22nd were eventually extricated from the jam and 'dashed forward'; they could not get across the ditch at the point where the guns had been directing their fire, but they did get across at another point, they found a bastion that was sufficiently 'ragged' to give a handhold and the 12th Native Infantry planted their colours on the summit. But it was a tiny party, losses had been terrible and they were recalled by their commander, Colonel Don.

Next day, Lake harangued the troops, speaking in terms of 'affectionate regret' of yesterday's failure to live up to their previous high standards; he called for volunteers for a fourth assault. Such was the power of this fierce obstinate old man, matchless in valour and energy, that when he had spoken every man volunteered for the fourth assault. This took place the same day, February 21st, and was directed at the same 'ragged bastion'. Men drove their bayonets into the walls and used the hilts to climb by. But a shower of logs and stones were rolled down on them, and so narrow was the way up that musketry fire could be concentrated on the leaders and as one man fell he brought down those below him. Nearly a thousand men were killed and wounded; the 31st Bengal Native Infantry 'lost 180 men killed and wounded out of about 400 in the short space of two hours'; so runs the official record of their services when they became the Queen's Own in 1877. Once again the attack failed; Lieutenant Templeton of H.M. 76th, who had volunteered to lead the 'forlorn hope', was killed as he neared the summit with the colours in his hands. The 31st, like the 12th the day before, were ordered to fall back. On February 24th Lake marched away and dispersed the menacing hordes that had gathered while he tried to get into Bhurtpore. In April, being left without allies, the Raja of Bhurtpore sued for peace. The fact remained that he had defied the victorious Lake and had cost him 100 officers and 3,100 men.

There are many examples of white-hot courage of the quality shown by the 31st at Bhurtpore. But there is no parallel for what followed. The colours of the 31st had been near the summit, but they had been brought back; they were the symbols of unconsummated valour. They were riddled with shot, tattered, unserviceable; a board of officers sat and orders were passed: they were to be replaced. The new colours arrived; they were to be consecrated next day but until that ceremony took place they were no more than coloured silk. They passed the night of their novitiate in the guardroom, sleeping side by side with the old,

which tomorrow would be cremated. But in the morning nothing remained of the old colours; every fragment had disappeared and no
British officer could learn what had become of them. It was a mystery,
not pursued, soon forgotten.

Almost exactly twenty-one years later, the regiment came back to
Bhurtpore and on January 18th, 1826, the fort was taken. The Commander, Lord Combermere, had an immensely stronger force than
Lake had had—18 battalions of infantry, 8 regiments of cavalry, and a
siege-train of 112 heavy guns, with 50 field guns. Even this armament
could not deal with the mud ramparts of Bhurtpore, but breaches were
made by the explosion of gigantic mines. The troops surged forward to
the assault, through the breaches and into the town, and now it was
discovered that the old colours of the 31st had reappeared. The fragments had been secretly preserved as sacred relics by the men who had
brought them near the summit of the ramparts under Lord Lake; their
sons brought them out into the light and tied them to the new colours,
so that they might redeem by victory the fruitless valour of their fathers.

Bhurtpore, like the colours, had been a symbol. The Company had
been defied and its victorious army, under the Commander-in-Chief
himself, had been forced to march away. It was a reproach to the Company for twenty years. What had happened once might happen again
and to many British minds it had seemed important to restore the
lustre of the Company's arms by a second visit to Bhurtpore. But the
men of that regiment, who had seen their comrades die, who taught
their sons to cherish those pieces of silk, were concerned about something much more intimate than the good name of the Company—the
honour of one regiment, which was theirs; it belonged to them and to
their families more closely than it belonged to their officers and it was
their honour that was sullied until their colours went back to the
breach from which they had been recalled.

2. Drums and Tramplings

The story of the 1st/7th Rajputs at Bhurtpore provoked an Indian
scholar, a historian of more recent events, to say to me sadly: 'You think
this was good but I think it was bad, because Indian was fighting against
Indian.' In the widest sense that all war is evil, of course he was right,
but in a narrower sense he was grieved that the regiment should have
been faithful to the British rather than to a national cause, and here he
was wrong; this was to misunderstand history. The regiment were faithful to their own honour and were more concerned about that than about
the British. Indian nationalism in 1805 was hardly stronger than European nationalism in 1914. Throughout India in 1805, as throughout

Europe in 1914, there was a common culture, much shared religious tradition, memories of moments in history when some degree of political unity had been achieved. But in both there were many languages, bitter religious animosities, regional hostility, few men indeed who would define themselves as first and foremost a European or an Indian. It is only in contrast with some alien force that a feeling of unity grows and in 1805 the British had not been in India long enough to provoke this.

It is not the purpose of this book to recount in any consecutive narrative the tale of wars and battles in which the Indian Army fought. But a certain framework of narrative is essential to an understanding of the discussion: who was the enemy and why were we fighting him? This is a question more likely to puzzle the modern reader than it did the sepoy at the time.

It was in the last quarter of the eighteenth century and the first quarter of the nineteenth, before the clouds began to gather, that the sun of the Company's army stood highest. In one sense, the period of high noon ended with the expedition to Kabul in 1839; in another, the threads of the Great Mutiny run back to the mutiny at Vellore in 1806. The Sikh Wars, though they come after Kabul, really belong to the period of victory and expansion; high noon covers four wars against Mysore and three against the Marathas; these are the main themes. There are two other important episodes, the war with Nepal and the First Burma War, and countless minor expeditions in which there was often fierce fighting, but these were in their nature almost police work, being directed against some feudal chief, either because he refused to pay his dues to his feudal superior—who was sometimes the Company but more often the Company's ally—or because he terrorized his neighbours.

The English by now held extensive territories in Bengal and Madras, some directly, some indirectly through the Nawab of the Carnatic or the Nawab of Bengal. Neither of these princes could any longer be regarded as independent. There was a Governor-General at Calcutta, but his power was at first limited by faction in his Council, while his relations with Madras and Bombay were ill-defined. The strength of the Governor-General grew, until, at the beginning of the century, the Marquess Wellesley was firmly controlling British policy throughout India. But he was himself still subject to control from London and was in fact recalled. This British power—by no means always consistent or united but becoming steadily more so—had at first treated Oudh as a useful buffer state, an ally against more dangerous enemies to the northwest. It had been the policy to preserve it. But at the beginning of the century the Marquess Wellesley, the first Governor-General to aim consciously at expansion, guaranteed the Nawab of Oudh against attack by any outside power, but, in payment for the troops which this guarantee demanded, exacted the cession of certain districts, as a result of which Oudh was entirely surrounded. Oudh ceased to be an independent power; it became a vassal state, but there was no war with Oudh.

In the Punjab, Ranjit Singh was from the beginning of the century consolidating and establishing the Sikh power, but it was his policy to avoid direct collision with the British and his was still a distant frontier State, professing friendship after a wary, guarded fashion of his own. The Emperor at Delhi was no longer a force. He was a symbol of authority whom it was useful to control and for much of this period he was controlled either by Afghan invaders or by the Marathas. The north, except for the disconnected episode of Nepal, was, in this period, and as far as the British were concerned, relatively stable.

As the period begins, the Maratha possessions sprawl across the centre of India, from coast to coast, but they are no longer ruled by one man. The descendants of Sivaji have been reduced to a ceremonial function; the descendants of his great officers of state—the Peshwa, Scindia, Holkar, the Bhonsla and the Gaekwar—are independent princes whose policies increasingly diverge. By definition, the Marathas are rebels against the Mughal Empire; that is how they came into being as a people. Now their ambition is to extend northward at the Emperor's expense, taking Delhi and erupting into Hindustan, and at the same time southward at the expense of his former Viceroy in the south, the Nizam of Hyderabad. They are essentially predators; a main source of their revenue is *Chauth*, literally one-fourth, a tribute levied on their weaker neighbours. And, increasingly, they make use of *pendharis*, or, as the English called them, 'Pindarries', who are simply licensed robbers. They are thus bound to be at enmity—and frequently also at war—with their neighbours, particularly with the Nizam.

South of the Nizam's territories was Mysore, an ancient Hindu kingdom which had fallen into the hands of a Muslim usurper, a military adventurer who rose from the ranks to become a general and took his master's throne. Hydar Ali was a man of considerable ability, both military and administrative, and, from the very nature of his rule, ambitious to expand his territories; for him too, the Nizam was a natural prey. Thus the Emperor's nominal representative in the south, independent in fact, was surrounded by three powers more vigorous than himself, all expanding. It would perhaps have been possible for the English in Madras to keep the peace with Hydar, who recognized their strength and at one time sought an alliance, but it is hard to see how this could have been done except at the expense of the Nizam. The British had really to choose between propping up the Nizam and allowing—or even helping—Hydar and the Marathas to tear him to pieces. Extreme skill, and greater strength than they possessed, would have been necessary to follow any middle course. To let him be destroyed would have run contrary to the basic strategy of European intervention in India, which was to make use of the legal fiction of imperial authority; it would besides have left a very awkward problem when the destruction was complete. This is speculation; the English did not in fact formulate two courses and choose between them but they did, with a good deal of consistency, prop up the Nizam, even though he occasionally bit, or tried to bite, the hand that propped him. To judge that this was on the whole the best course open to them is not to deny that the diplomacy which first made an implacable enemy of Hydar was clumsy. Be that as it may, Mysore, first under Hydar and then under Tippoo his son, was for almost forty years a centre of hostility to the British and an opportunity to the French. There were four Mysore Wars, of which all provide examples of heroism and devotion for which there is no room here. They ended the power of Mysore; they incidentally taught the British in India how to move and organize armies.

Hydar's wars were based on swift movement. He learnt very soon that, unless he had overwhelming strength, he could do very little in a pitched battle against infantry trained and officered by the British. Like all Indian armies of this time, he had vast numbers of cavalry; he possessed also the famous bullocks of Mysore, which 'are to all other bullocks as the horses of Arabia are to all other horses'. His aim therefore was to exhaust British forces by continual marching, to cut their lines of supply, to surround and annihilate detachments, to leave larger armies stranded in deserts from which all grain had been removed, to march round them and strike at their headquarters. In the Second Mysore War, he almost succeeded; he annihilated in succession two isolated British forces, broke into the Carnatic and captured Arcot, overran the whole province. In the end Eyre Coote managed to bring him to battle, and before Haidar's death the tide had turned; Tippoo, his son, made a peace which restored all conquests and left things as they had been.

In the Third War, Tippoo followed his father's general plan, though not quite so consistently and skilfully. But the real difference was that the British had made more careful preparations and could move more decisively, though still slowly. Gone were the days when the Council of Madras would instruct their commander from afar and insist that rice was to be found in a place where there was no rice. Cornwallis, the Governor-General, himself took command and, after two campaigns from which Tippoo extricated himself with great skill, in the third, in 1793, Seringapatam was taken, and terms dictated. But the terms, though they halved Mysore, left it in being and in Tippoo's hands. The power of Napoleon grew and Tippoo, who was far better informed about affairs in Europe than most of his Indian contemporaries, proposed to the Governor of Mauritius a plan for the invasion of Southern India by a force of 5,000 French and 25,000 African troops, to which he would add 60,000 of his own. The Governor of Mauritius, insanely, published a proclamation of these intentions and sealed Tippoo's fate. News of the proclamation reached India on June 18th, 1798. The Marquess Wellesley had only been two months in the country but, within two days, orders went to the Commander-in-Chief to prepare for war with Tippoo. The diplomatic moves were hardly less swift and were speeded in October by the news that Napoleon's troops were in Egypt. What delayed the start of operations was the collection not of men but of bullocks; twenty thousand were said to be required before a move could be made and eighty thousand were eventually employed by the Madras expedition, apart from camels, elephants, horses and mules.

Two armies moved at last, in February 1799, one from Madras and one from Bombay. Tippoo's obvious course was to try to deal with Stewart from Bombay before he could join Harris's much larger force from Madras; in this, he was very nearly successful. Stewart had adopted the unusual arrangement of brigading his European battalions together under Dunlop. Montresor's brigade, consisting of three sepoy battalions, was on March 6th in a detached position at Seedaseer, some miles distant from Dunlop's, when they were attacked by a large force of Tippoo's, said to number 15,000 of his best troops under his personal command. This was exactly the situation which Tippoo sought to achieve; in 1780, in the Second Mysore War, his father had surrounded Baillie with 3,853 men in just this way and had annihilated his force. And later in that war, in 1782, Braithwaite had been surrounded and forced to surrender after twenty-six hours of desperate fighting. But this time the manœuvre failed; the three battalions held out for six hours against charge after charge. Their ammunition had almost given out when Dunlop's brigade came on the scene and attacked Tippoo's rear; Montresor's men now charged with the bayonet and the enemy were scattered. Two of Montresor's battalions survived till Independence as the 1st and 2nd Battalions of the 5th Maratha Light Infantry; 'Seedaseer' was a battle honour especially treasured. The third became the Bombay Pioneers and lost its identity in 1929.

But when that opportunity had failed, Tippoo was doomed, like a bull in the ring; he was forced back to Seringapatam and the place was stormed in May, the Sultan himself being killed fighting in the breach. This time there was to be no repetition; the remnants of the state were returned to the Hindu line, of which the representative was a boy of seven. Mysore became a protected state, losing its independence. There remained the Marathas.

The real reason why peace was impossible with them was, as we have
seen, that they were predators, living at the expense of their neighbours,
but a subsidiary cause was that their internal differences led to occasions
for intervention which it was hard to resist. A dispossessed or defeated
prince would appeal for help to the British, offering large inducements.
This was the origin of the First Maratha War, when, in 1775, the
Bombay Government, at a most inopportune time from every point of
view, involved themselves, and the other Presidencies, in a war for
which they were not strong enough and which settled nothing.

The Second Maratha War was a very different matter. The impossibility of living with the Marathas was now clear; in the north,
they had recovered from their defeat at Panipat by the Afghans in
1761, and Scindia, now master of thirty battalions of regular infantry
drilled by French instructors, was an even more serious threat to
Hindustan than were the other Maratha princes to the southern
presidencies. They had to be dealt with. The Marquess Wellesley
was a man to grasp nettles without hesitation, and an opportunity soon
presented itself. Within the Maratha Confederacy, a struggle between
Holkar and Scindia for control of the Peshwa had given a temporary
advantage to Holkar. He put his puppet on the Peshwa's throne and
the previous Peshwa, Baji Rao, asked for British help. Wellesley agreed
to restore him in return for a treaty—the Treaty of Bassein—which
virtually ended his independence.

The Treaty of Bassein, by establishing a British protected state in the
Maratha homeland, made it almost inevitable that the other Maratha
powers would fight—though Arthur Wellesley, while actively preparing
for war, believed till the last that they would give in. The actual
outbreak of war was advanced by his judgment that the monsoon
period—July, August, September, when rivers were high—was the
most favourable for his operations; he had prepared boats and the
enemy had not. He would therefore allow no procrastination. He had
been given full diplomatic powers by his brother and he insisted that the
Maratha troops should be moved back into peace-time positions
without delay. They were not, and he advanced against them, while
Lake attacked Scindia in the north.

The battles of the next two years were the hardest so far fought in
India. Wellesley's victories at Assaye and Argaum, Lake's successive
blows at Deeg, Aligarh and Laswarree, would perhaps have been
conclusive had it not been for events in Europe. But temporary checks
in India—Bhurtpore and Monson's disastrous retreat—came at a time
of crisis in Europe; the brief Peace of Amiens came to an end in 1804.
The year of Bhurtpore was the year of Austerlitz and Trafalgar. It was
not a time when Britain could afford wars with anyone but the French,
and Wellesley, who stood for rapid expansion and the unification of

India, seemed to ministers in London an unnecessary drain on their strength. And he had not endeared himself to the Directors of the Company, to whom he had often seemed high-handed, arrogant and impatient. He was recalled; peace was made by treaties which undid much that had been achieved. The work of unification was interrupted and, indeed, in many ways, things were worse than before; the Marathas, smashed at Panipat, at Assaye and at Laswarree, could no longer hope for empire; their head was removed, their disunity intensified; more than ever they became predators pure and simple. They relied more and more on contributions paid them by the Pindarries, who issued, says Dr Spear, 'like wild dogs from between the feet of their nominal masters', and laid waste great stretches of countryside. Chaos grew worse in Central India and what had been left unfinished in 1805 was undertaken again in 1817.

This was the Third Maratha War, often called the Pindarry War. The Maratha princes were invited to join in the suppression of the Pindarries. It had been a diplomatic fiction that the princes did not connive at their crimes, but it was hardly to be expected that they would help to bring them to book; they could see very well that this would reduce their power, not to speak of their revenue. But it was not easy for them to choose between acquiescing in their own reduction and war with the British. The tension mounted intolerably; at each of the Maratha capitals the Resident waited for a decision which might easily be announced by an attack on the Residency and his own death.

The design was a vast one; knowing that the Pindarries, though they would not fight, could move with a speed no fighting troops could match, Lord Hastings had decided to surround them by a vast circle of a hundred thousand men, covering some sixteen hundred square miles. It was far the most ambitious enterprise the British had attempted in India; had there been a Hydar Ali inside the ring, it might easily have led to disasters such as Baillie's. But the Marathas were hopelessly disunited. Scindia gave in without a struggle, the Peshwa's army was defeated at Kirkee, the Bhonsla's at Sitabaldi and Holkar at Mahidpur. The net closed inexorably, professionally; one by one the Pindarry bands were hunted down. Marvellous marches through thick jungles, in broken rugged country, daring exploits — of these there were plenty, admirable material for romantic novels in the tradition of Scott. But the Pindarries were gangsters, linked by no ties of blood, caste, religion or any purpose but loot; they were Hindus or Muslims, of all castes, kinds and creeds — any man was welcome to their ranks if he had a horse, a sword and no scruples. Once their protectors would protect them no longer, they had no home-country to fall back on; each chief fled with no ultimate purpose, hoping only to escape for another night, and their followers left them one by one. Chitu, the most famous and daring of all, who had led a gang of five thousand, was reduced to two companions. At last these left him, and he was alone, sleeping in the jungle with his horse's bridle buckled over his arm, when fate caught him and he became 'a tiger's horrid meal'.

It remains only to mention the Nepalese and the First Burmese Wars. In both cases, an isolated kingdom, poorly informed of the extent and nature of British rule in India, provoked war by acts which would probably not have occurred had they understood the full strength of the power they were challenging. The Gurkhas had possessed themselves of Khatmandu only in 1768; in the next forty years they had spread their power east and west over the whole of what is now Nepal, over the Kingdoms of Kumaon and Garhwal and what became later the Simla Hill States. They found further expansion in the hills blocked by the Sikhs, so turned to the plains, swooping down into the Gorakhpur and Basti districts, which were now British. In 1814 a campaign against the Nepalese was organized, four forces advancing simultaneously into the hills. This seems incidentally to have been the first Indian war in which the British were not outnumbered; it was the Gurkhas, with an army of only 12,000, who put up a heroic fight against forces nearly three times stronger than their own. In the first campaign, they drove back three of the four attacks; only Ochterlony in the extreme west made any progress. In 1815, the second campaign, the British did better, but it was not till the third campaign in 1816 that the war was ended. Ochterlony was now in command of the entire operations; he made a rapid advance on Khatmandu, which convinced the Gurkhas that they could no longer resist effectively, and they signed a treaty which lasted till the independence of India. It was one of the few wars which left each side with an increased respect for the other; the recruitment of Gurkhas to the British service began even before peace was signed.

The First Burmese War also began with advances into British territory by a people who had no idea of what they were taking on, but here the resemblance ended. The chief adversaries in Burma were the climate and the nature of the country; fever killed more men than the enemy. Courage was required to assault some of the Burmese stockades but there were no pitched battles. Its chief interest, from the point of view of this book, is in the reactions of Indian troops to service in Burma and to sea voyages. It was this which led to the mutiny at Barrackpore, one of the most shameful events in the history of the British in India.

The period of high noon was far from being a continuous blaze of unrelieved glory. There were disasters — Baillie's, Braithwaite's, Monson's; there were mutinies — at Bolarum, at Vellore, at Barrackpore. Yet steadily, throughout, the army becomes more professional and competent, the sepoy takes it more and more for granted that here is a profession, for himself and his son and his son's son, something permanent, an honourable profession that is likely to bring a pension and respect in the village on retirement, one in which the hardships and dangers are balanced by the glory of constantly recurring victory. But that belief was brittle; in the period that followed, a disastrous war showed that the Company was not after all invincible, while little by little, the men became convinced that their officers, with a few exceptions, no longer respected and cared for them as they had once done, and that their Government was actually planning to betray them. That stage, however, we have not yet reached.

3. Horse, Foot and Guns

THE COMPANY'S EUROPEANS

By the time of the Third Maratha War, the army in India was an army in being, a professional army, consisting of cavalry, artillery, engineers and infantry, with doctors, a veterinary branch, and Government agencies for procuring bullocks, horses and grain. It had assumed the broad outline it was to preserve till the Mutiny and, with some important modifications, for the next hundred and fifty years. But it was still divided into three Presidency Armies. These had resulted from the chances of history, and continued mainly because of sentiment and of a conservative desire for independence—justified, in so far as there was any rational justification, by distance and climate. And there was the division between the King's service and the Company's, both together making the army in India.

First in precedence came the Royal regiments. After the 39th—*Primus in Indis*—a succession of British regiments was posted to India for a spell of duty, of which the length varied at different times, being sometimes for as long as twenty years. They were periodically reinforced by drafts from home, and sent back drafts of 'time-expired men'. When the time came to go, men were frequently offered the chance of transferring to the Company's service, some as soldiers but a few in civil employment on the railways or with the Public Works Department. They came raw and ignorant, officers frequently knowing as little as the men of the country, its ways and its languages. They were often hit very hard by disease; when the 72nd Highlanders landed at Madras in March 1781, they were reduced from 500 to 50 effective men within three weeks. This was partly unavoidable, because only time can give immunity to the dust that everyone in India must breathe—a dust rich in organic matter and very upsetting to unseasoned guts—but partly due to ignorance. The doctors, of course, knew little of infection, and everyone therefore ran risks which today can easily be avoided. But, by trial and error, those who had been longer in the country bought some immunity and had found ways—or so they thought—of avoiding or dealing with certain troubles. Perhaps it was faith, perhaps coincidence. A valuable cure for cholera, which had saved many people, was a mixture of brandy, laudanum (that is, a tincture of opium in alcohol), cayenne pepper and other hot spices.

It was not at first accepted that there should always be a garrison of Royal regiments in India. Indeed, there were none for the fifteen years before 1780. The company might be ready to meet the bill, but men were as hard to come by as money and recruiting was always a problem for the War Office. Regiments at first were sent out for a particular emergency and often stayed longer than had been expected. In 1787 it was decided to raise four new British regiments, two in Scotland and two in England, entirely at the expense of the East India Company and for service in India; these were the 74th and 75th Highlanders, and the 76th and 77th Foot. But gradually it came to be accepted that the army in India should consist of three elements: the Royal regiments, all taking their turn; the Company's Europeans; the Company's Indian troops.

The Company's Europeans had, as we have seen, been originally a force of mixed origins and doubtful value, but by the last quarter of the century they were very different. There were no longer Eurasians, Armenians, Portuguese or French deserters among them in any number; the great majority had transferred from Royal regiments. They were seasoned; they had some degree of immunity to the minor diseases of India; they had most of them decided that this was the life they wanted, perhaps now the only life they could imagine. To contemporary Indians, they presented a strange, indeed a savage, spectacle! All British troops expected to live largely on meat. In the late eighteenth century, at Seringapatam, the daily allowance was one *seer*, or about two pounds, of beef or mutton, with the same of rice, and buttermilk, salt, pepper and firewood. In 1799 it was set at a pound and a half of beef, or an eighth of a sheep, and two drams. In the nineteenth century it was usually one pound of meat in summer, one and a half in winter, with a pound of bread and two drams. A dram was one-fifth of a pint of spirit, at first arrack, later rum, 10 per cent below proof. It was served out after morning parade, before breakfast. Old hands tossed off their two drams at once; others sold it to native dealers, who sold it to those who wanted more. On a campaign, when fresh meat ran short, the beef was salted, and the men would usually get ship's biscuit instead of bread. The third essential was arrack or rum. Altogether, it does not sound a composing diet in tropical heat. It was perhaps of the Company's Europeans in particular that Stocqueler was thinking when he wrote of British soldiers in India as 'walled in and cooped together in a barrack ... checked and controlled at times, next petted and coarsely pampered ... their spirits and strength sinking beneath the climate ... while their passions and excitable energies are the more irritated ... as their moral ones are deteriorating ...` Loose these brave fellows from their confinement ... and at once, like a bull-dog slipped at his victim ... they will dash at him with an instinctive fierceness and alacrity ... [making] almost fiendlike superhuman efforts.'

There were various reorganizations and changes among the European battalions, as indeed in the native infantry; the number of companies in a battalion varied between eight and thirteen. Sometimes battalions were entirely separate, sometimes they were paired or linked together, two to a regiment. Cornwallis proposed in 1794 that all the Company's troops, Europeans and Indians alike, should be transferred to the Crown, the three Presidency Armies being united. But this was much too radical; until 1858 they were still basically divided into Royal regiments, Company's Europeans, Company's native troops — and there were each of these in each of the three Presidencies. During most of the period before 1858 there were two battalions of Company's Europeans in each of the three Presidency Armies; these six battalions became Her Majesty's 101st to 106th when transferred to the Crown.

HORSE

In describing the Second Mysore War, Fortescue had written of Eyre Coote as commanding 'superb infantry' but 'virtually no horse, no transport and no means of getting supplies'. By the end of the century, things were very different. The lack of horse in all the early British campaigns was mainly due to their cost; there was not only the buying and feeding of horses but a trooper was paid considerably more than an infantryman. But there were subsidiary reasons. Apart from the deep-seated British conviction that it was infantry that won battles while cavalry were really a rather flashy extravagance, it was always cavalry that the Nawab of Arcot was anxious to provide as his contribution to the campaign, and it was sometimes argued that if the Nawab's cavalry were disbanded, they would terrorize the countryside. So long as the Nawab was ready to supply cavalry in war and keep it at his own expense in peace, it was hard to convince the Council that they ought to maintain a permanent and expensive force of their own. Perhaps too there was a shade of reluctance on the part of men mainly of middle-class origin to introduce into the society of Madras the essentially aristocratic figure of the cavalry officer who might despise them as traders.

Commanders in the field, however, constantly urged that the Nawab's cavalry were quite unreliable and that British troops were hampered for lack of horse, and at last the Madras Council reluctantly agreed to set up a cavalry arm. In 1769 they increased their troop of Europeans from thirty-eight to one hundred men and added a second troop of the same number of 'foreigners', which meant Germans, Swiss and French deserters, with five hundred native cavalry, organized in four troops each under a jemadar. Two years later the foreign troop was dismounted and two more regiments of native cavalry raised. The European cavalry do not seem to have been regarded as a good investment; they were reduced in 1777, restored in 1778 and finally broken up again in 1779. By 1784 there were, for a few days, nine regiments of native cavalry, each of four troops of 125 men. Four of these, however, had been transferred from the Nawab's service without being consulted; they were heavily in arrears with their pay; they soon mutinied and were disbanded. By 1796 Madras had four native regiments of six troops each.

It was much the same story of half-hearted experiment in the other Presidencies. In Bengal an attempt to form Dragoons and Hussars—one troop of each—from European infantry was a failure; they were too few to be effective, they were expensive, and they weakened the European infantry. But both here and in Bombay troops of 'Mogul horse' were more successful; they were in fact irregular light horse, raised by the Company, and they proved valuable for keeping in touch with the enemy and bringing in information. By 1765 each of Bengal's three brigades had one regiment of regular native cavalry to one battalion of European infantry and seven battalions of sepoys. By the middle of the century Bengal had ten, Madras eight and Bombay three regiments of regular native cavalry, while Bengal and Bombay between them had 38 regiments of irregular cavalry, the successors of the Mogul horse. The Company had no European cavalry.

The early tendency to underrate the value of cavalry was common to all three Presidencies. The British excellence lay in infantry and we had seen hordes of undisciplined horsemen flinging themselves in vain against muskets and bayonets. But eventually it was conceded that, at least for reconnaissance and to follow up a beaten enemy, cavalry had their uses; the last lesson to be learnt was the tactical value of even quite a small force of disciplined horse in battle. The point was made when British cavalry regiments began to reach India; it was proved conclusively at Assaye. There was Lake's victory at Fatehgarh, where he had cavalry and no infantry. If any doubt remained as to the value of Indian cavalry in battle, it was scattered into thin air after Sitabaldi.

The suspense felt at the beginning of the Third Maratha War has already been mentioned. At Poona, the capital of the Peshwa, it has been described with unrivalled clarity by the brilliant pen of Mountstuart Elphinstone: 'After all kinds of warnings of plots against my life and the public peace, I have at last obtained clear and distinct information of intrigues carried on by the Peshwa with our troops ... This is certainly the most embarrassing situation I have ever been placed in and is, of course, accompanied with much anxiety; yet I never wish I were anywhere else.' Elphinstone was the Resident, that is, virtually the Ambassador at the Peshwa's court, but the troops were under his general direction, and since there was no electric telegraph he had to take all decisions himself. He must not precipitate events by moving too soon; if he took any step suggesting that war was inevitable, the Peshwa would almost certainly attack him and the news would bring in Scindia at Gwalior and the Bhonsla at Nagpur. The hope of avoiding war altogether might be faint, but it would be disastrous if war began too soon. But the troops at Poona were in an almost indefensible position, close to the city. Elphinstone had to wait, knowing that he and his men were on the brink of complete destruction, till he had news that all was ready at Scindia's court. Then reinforcements arrived and at last he could move the garrison to a stronger position at Kirkee, four miles away. But he stayed on himself at the Residency for another week, with a small guard of sepoys, leaving, when at last the attack came, at an hour's notice, 'with the clothes on our backs ... The Residency, with all the records and with all my books, journals, letters and manuscripts was soon in a blaze.' He joined the troops at Kirkee and paused to watch the enemy. 'The sight was magnificent as the tide rolled out of Poona ... Everything was hushed except the trampling and neighing of horses and the whole valley was filled with them like a river in flood ... I now ... sent an order to move down at once and attack ... Soon after, his [the Peshwa's] whole mass of cavalry came on at speed in the most splendid style. The rush of horse, the sound of the earth, the waving of flags, the brandishing of spears, were grand beyond description but perfectly ineffectual.'*

Kirkee is memorable because few battles have been described by a writer with so clearly running a pen, such responsibilities and such detachment of outlook, also because in this area it settled the war, which now became a pursuit. But in a military sense, as a battle, it is in no way remarkable; it is the familiar story of spectacular cavalry charges against disciplined infantry, the only point worth noting being that the sepoys were unshakable in spite of the political warfare to which they had been subjected in Poona. Not a man deserted.

But Sitabaldi, though politically parallel, was militarily quite different. Jenkins, the Resident at Nagpur, must have gone through much the same experience as Elphinstone at Poona. His troops too

---

* *Quadripedante putrem sonitu quatit ungula campum* ('The sound of the galloping horses shatters the dust of the plain'). Clearly Elphinstone had this familiar line in mind.

were in an indefensible position. He too held on as long as he could, knowing that a sudden move would precipitate the crisis, still hoping that war might be avoided, looking for news from Gwalior or Poona. Unlike Elphinstone, however, he had little hope of immediate rein- forcement, and there were no British troops at Nagpur or likely to arrive soon. At last he too moved the troops he had away from the city and took up a position on a hill known as Sitabaldi, which was far enough from the city to be defensible and which was close to the Residency. Hopeton Scot, who was in command, had very limited forces, only two battalions of Madras infantry, with the Resident's bodyguard of Bengal sepoys and a detachment of foot artillery with four six-pounders; of cavalry, he had three troops only of the 6th Bengal Cavalry and some men of the Madras Governor's Bodyguard. There were less than fifteen hundred men all told. They were confronted by the Bhonsla's main army, some 12,000 cavalry and 8,000 infantry, of whom 3,500 were Arabs, held in very high esteem.

The battle covered the two days November 26th and 27th, 1817. The enemy's attack developed with increasing ferocity on the main position, persisting for eighteen hours — 'till nature and hope were exhausted.' The cavalry, under Captain Fitzgerald of the 6th Bengal Cavalry, had before the battle been detached from the infantry position, and were posted in the Residency compound; his only orders were to hold his men in reserve and he was soon cut off from Scot. But a moment came when the enemy had actually broken through the defending circle on the crown of the hill, and Fitzgerald saw that the whole force would be destroyed unless some dramatic change could be made. He launched his four troops direct at the enemy's principal mass of cavalry, scattered it 'like a whirlwind' and captured the guns. This 'devoted and generous disobedience' gave Scot the opportunity to summon his infantry to a supreme effort; 'animated by this glorious example,' they poured in a volley, charged with the bayonet, cleared the hill and remained 'masters of the plain'. They were now able to hold on till the arrival of Brigadier Doveton with forces which made up three brigades. Sitabaldi had not been decisive in the same sense as Kirkee, because the numbers available were quite insufficient to follow it up, but it made possible Doveton's decisive victory at Nagpur shortly afterwards and the battle is certainly unusual, and I think unique, in that apart from British officers and a few gunners, only Indian troops were present and the turning-point was a cavalry charge. The Madras Bodyguard bore the battle-honour 'Seetabuldee' at Independence but none of the other units survived.

GUNS

Whatever they thought about cavalry, no one ever doubted the value of artillery. Two points were long disputed, how the guns could best be organized, and whether they should be served entirely by British or by mixed British and Indian gunners. As to organization, the idea of 'private artillery', a section or more of gunners attached to a battalion of infantry or a regiment of cavalry, did not long survive the eighteenth century. The other point was more obstinate. The perpetual shortage of manpower and cash led the authorities in India to raise native artillery units, but the Court of Directors in London periodically forbade this, seeing danger in training Indians in the use of so decisive a weapon. Thus in Madras there were in 1784 two battalions of artillery, each of about 700 men, one European and one native. The European battalion was headed by a lieutenant-colonel and a major, with a captain commanding each company; the company consisted of 20 gunners and 70 matrosses or assistant gunners—a word originally meaning a sailor which came to us through the Dutch. The native battalion of artillery was commanded, as in the infantry, by officers two steps junior in rank to those for the same number of Europeans. A captain commanded the battalion with a captain-lieutenant to help him and three lieutenant-fireworkers. Each company had a sergeant, a subadar and two jemadars; the other ranks were havildars, while the equivalent of private was *golandāz*—the Mughal word for a gunner, literally 'a bringer of roundshot'.

All this was completely changed a year later, the native battalion being broken up and a company of assistant native gunners being attached to each company of European gunners. But before another year had passed, all was changed again. Express orders from the Court of Directors forbade the entertainment of any 'native artillery or golandauz' and directed that the officers and men who were already on the strength should go to the infantry or should be employed as 'lascars' with the European companies. 'None of the natives from the interior of Hindostan shall henceforth be taught the exercise of artillery ... none shall be enlisted as artillery lascars but such as are actually seamen or boatmen.' The fiction that gun lascars, like matrosses, were seamen on shore was a historical survival and seems to have been combined with the traditional English feeling that sailors are always better than soldiers. Fortunately no one in India seems to have taken much notice of this piece of confused thinking. But the Court's distrust was clear and their orders explicit. The European battalion was split into two and the *golandāz* companies broken up. At the same time, each battalion of infantry had attached to it two field-pieces and a detachment to work them, with European gunners and some lascars. The 'lascars' were inferior to golandaz but seem to have done almost everything except aim and fire the guns—and that too they did in emergency, as at Koregaum.

As in other arms, there were continual changes which need not concern us; the term 'gunner', which had once meant a warrant officer and later a non-commissioned officer, came to be applied to the lowest rank, equivalent to private. The gunner's first promotion was now to bombardier, and 'matross' disappeared. The officers—who at one time had been technicians, distinguished by ranks such as lieutenant-fireworker—dropped these appellations and became eligible for high rank, commanding formations of all arms; private artillery was no longer attached to battalions of infantry or regiments of cavalry. There began to be a change in the tactical use of artillery; at the beginning of this period, the guns had been placed in the intervals between companies of infantry, but increasingly they were manœuvred during the battle, and increasingly battles were preceded by an artillery duel in which the object was to silence as many as possible of the enemy's guns before the infantry attack developed; the range of the infantry musket was only two hundred yards and heavy losses would be involved if infantry attacked a position that the enemy had prepared, with earthworks and artillery firing case. This was a parcel of bullets, bound up in a light case which broke up on leaving the muzzle, so that the bullets sprayed out over a widening area.

The orders of the Court of Directors about golandaz were soon forgotten; by 1819 Madras had two European battalions, each of seven companies, and a native battalion of ten companies of golandaz, commanded by a major. Each of the 24 companies—14 European and 10 native—had a company of lascars attached, with light pioneering tools for constructing roads and gun platforms and throwing up protective earthworks before a battery. The lascar companies continued far into the century and did not finally disappear till 1870.

An important development was Horse Artillery. The battalions and companies of the eighteenth century were equipped as a rule with field-pieces, twelve-pounders or six-pounders, which were drawn by bullocks, the men being on foot. Though vastly easier to manœuvre in battle than the huge Indian pieces, they could barely keep up with infantry on the march. As the value of cavalry came to be more appreciated, it became necessary to provide some light artillery which could move with the cavalry; at first, two 'galloper guns' were supplied to each regiment of cavalry, each with a European sergeant and corporal. These were six-pounders, drawn by horses, the crews also being mounted; by the end of the eighteenth century native cavalry regiments usually had two gallopers, though H.M. 8th Royal Irish Hussars refused them on the grounds that they would be a hindrance to their legitimate work. In 1800 an Experimental Brigade was formed in Bengal, with three-pounder and later six-pounder guns, various experiments being made in lightening the carriages without losing strength.

They had to learn to gallop their guns, with their ammunition wagons, across country, pull up, swing round, unlimber, open fire at about five hundred yards range, limber up, and gallop on again. Time for training was short for men who had so recently been foot soldiers, but they seem to have picked up these skills quickly; the Experimental Brigade took part in the Second Maratha War and were with Lake in his famous pursuit of Holkar, with cavalry only, which culminated in an attack by night in which complete surprise was achieved. The Experimental Brigade had proved themselves, and in 1809 they developed into three troops of Horse Artillery.

Officers were lent to the Horse Artillery for short periods; it was a coveted distinction for which there was hot competition. The troops of Horse Artillery were constantly organized and reorganized, but the general pattern—from the point of view of this book—was much the same as for the 'Old Fogs', as the Bengal Horse Artillery profanely called their parents, the Foot Artillery. That is, for some years the Court of Directors insisted that Indians should be employed only in subordinate positions as drivers and lascars. But just before the Third Maratha War, this attitude changed and there was a general reorganization. In Bengal, the three troops of European Horse Artillery were increased by three native troops, which had a high reputation for their ability to move their guns quickly and sustain long marches. There was also a rocket troop mounted on camels, which was mixed, Europeans and native. In 1824 the Horse Artillery was expanded again; five new troops were raised, all European, which, with the rocket troop and the previous six, made a total of twelve troops. They were now organized in three brigades of four troops each, the native troop being numbered 4 in each brigade. The proportion of European to native was thus radically altered. While in the infantry there were usually at least three native units, and often more, to one European, in this arm the proportion was reversed. From now until the Mutiny, though there were various minor changes, Bengal had three brigades of Horse Artillery, one troop out of four in each brigade being Indians and mostly Brahmans and Rajputs from Oudh, while Bombay and Madras had one brigade each. Of foot artillery, on the eve of the Mutiny, Bengal had six European battalions and three Indian; Madras, four European and one Indian; Bombay, two of each. Thus the distrust of the Court of Directors and the passion for economy of the Presidency Governments resulted in a compromise; there were Indian gunners, but they were in a minority compared with European.

SAPPERS

Engineers on the other hand developed on quite different lines; they obstinately refused to give in to the fashions and prejudices of the day, with the result that at Independence, the Madras Sappers and Miners were the oldest corps in the Indian Army who still recruited the kind of men with whom they had begun. They were formed in 1780 as Pioneers; it was their task to dig trenches, and later mines beneath fortifications, and their official designation, which was substituted for Pioneers in 1831, was 'Sappers and Miners'. Experiments with volunteers from the infantry for this work had been unsatisfactory, since they obviously weakened the main force, while civilians hired for the duration of the campaign dropped their tools and fled when the firing began. The Madras Pioneers were at first officered by captains and subalterns seconded from the infantry, with a sprinkling of European sergeants and their own subadars and jemadars; as in other arms, the principle was only gradually established that the rank proper for commanding Indians should be the same as for an equal number of Europeans. By 1830 it was also generally conceded that officers should have special training; cadets for the Engineers now went to Addiscombe, the East India Company's College for gunner and engineer officers, where they received a special education. When they reached India, they were required to pass, within six months of joining the corps, an examination in logarithms, practical geometry, plane trigonometry, the use of chain box, sextant and theodolite, and be able to make a 'route sketch'. Fourteen months from joining, the young officer must be able to show a well-finished plan of a system of fortification drawn by himself, and his knowledge of Vauban's system of fortification would be tested. Engineer officers were long the experts on everything to do with a siege; it was they who drew up for the commanding officer's approval the general plan for reducing a fortress and it was they who pronounced a breach in the fortifications to be 'practicable'.

Recruits for the Madras Pioneers and later for the Madras Sappers and Miners were local and usually of low caste. The officers were throughout adamant that caste must never be pleaded as a reason for not obeying an order. This corps became Queen Victoria's Own in 1877 and their record of services is filled with evidence of their bravery and devotion. Their earliest distinction was for courage under fire when engaged in such tasks as removing hedges—which were often used as a defence like the barbed wire of the twentieth century—and making emplacements for guns and the like. In the Third Mysore War their casualties were higher than in any corps except H.M. 36th. They were noticed for the alacrity with which they volunteered for service in Ceylon, Mauritius and Egypt. By 1810 they included many specialists— stone-cutters, carpenters, bricklayers and the like—but did not lose their original character. Their admirable spirit and coolness in action was specially mentioned in 1818; they distinguished themselves shortly afterwards by marching for fifteen days at an average rate of twenty-five miles a day at the hottest time of the year, and in Burma their 'gallant and indefatigable exertions' were 'acknowledged with peculiar approbation' by the Commander-in-Chief—and so the story goes on. 'Their patient endurance of extraordinary fatigue and privations' and 'the gallant and resolute spirit with which they executed every enterprise' are constant themes; Napier from Sind wrote that he 'never met a more willing or efficient man' than Jemadar Amaraputty of this corps, with his 'sturdy hardworking comrades'. The corps was back from Persia in 1857 after five years' service overseas but immediately volunteered for the relief of Mhow and the attack on Jhansi, operations in the latter part of the Mutiny in which they proved invaluable, and in the course of which Sir Hugh Rose spoke of 'their zeal and intelligence ... which no hardships can abate' and added that 'they lived on the very best of terms with their English comrades.' And it was in similar terms that their officers spoke of them right up till Independence.

What kind of men were these paragons whom no one else would have? They were low-caste Madrassis.

The British in early days did not particularize very carefully, but it does not seem that much change took place in its composition during the whole of the corps' history. In 1877 there were 735 classed as 'Inferior Castes and Native Christians'. Of these, 370 were pariahs and 255 Native Christians, probably of much the same ancestry, the rest being 'chucklers and men of low caste'. 'Pariahs' and 'chucklers' would now be spelt *Parāiya* and *Chakkiliya*. They are both groups which were outside the caste system and were formerly lumped together with various others as 'untouchable'. They removed carcasses of dead animals and used to eat beef; Chakkiliyas worked leather. The touch of either was polluting to a Brahman—and for some Brahmans 'their very approach would pollute the whole neighbourhood'. These seven hundred odd made up more than half the corps, the remaining 550 being classed as 'Tamil' or 'Telegu' with a few Muslims. Tamil and Telegu, of course, indicate language, not caste, and the presumption is that they came from the many caste-groups in the south which are sometimes included under the head 'non-Brahman'; in the eyes of Brahmans, they belong to the fourth order in the caste hierarchy—that is, they are Sudras, servants and cultivators, but not 'untouchable'.

The Abbé Dubois, writing at the end of the eighteenth century about the manners and customs of the Hindus, speaks of the extreme severity with which 'pariahs', 'chucklers' and other untouchables were treated by Brahmans, comparing it with the treatment of Negro slaves on plantations in America and the West Indies. He adds, however, that they 'deserved' to be detested because of their habitual drunkenness and habit of eating not merely beef but carrion. Attempts had been made, wrote the Abbé, by European nations to enlist them in their armies, but, though they were not lacking in courage, it had been found 'difficult to imbue them with military discipline' and 'they are entirely devoid of every principle of honour.' This, however, has been magnificently disproved by the Corps of Sappers and Miners, which suggests that their officers were consistently of very high quality. It was said—and it would be quite in accordance with the Indian caste system if it were true—that men who had served in Queen Victoria's Sappers and who by origin were outcastes made themselves into a new subdivision of their old caste-group, calling themselves 'Quinsap' and marrying their sons only to Quinsap girls. One would expect to find this new caste-group mixing customs learnt in the army with Brahmanical rules which their grandfathers never observed, such as abstaining from beef—but this is speculation.

The Sappers and Miners of the Bombay and Bengal Presidencies had military records equally distinguished, but their history does not illustrate this point about caste; they recruited classes who have their place in other units too. Nor is it necessary to sketch the development of the medical and other departments; enough has been said to indicate the general line of development. This was now a professional army, an army in being, with the different arms and the specialist corps which it needed.

VII
Generals

1. Coote Bahadur

In *War and Peace*, there are a number of passages in which Tolstoy discusses what it is that moves peoples to go to war, to rebel against their leaders or to march across Europe to die in the snow. He is arguing against fashions in history that were current when he wrote. One can agree with him that the great movements of history are seldom due to the free decision of one hero; in such events there are many and complex factors and the courses open to the hero are usually fewer than the onlookers perceive. But Tolstoy goes on to argue that it is an illusion to suppose that any decision is in fact taken by the human will. The idea that a man 'decides' on a course of action is comparable to the belief that we are not in motion as we stand on the surface of the earth. We seem to stand still but in fact we are whirling in circles round the poles of the earth and round the sun, obedient to laws of gravity and physics. And in matters of human behaviour, he believes, we are still waiting for the Copernicus and the Newton who will discover the laws that govern our actions. In particular, he argues that neither Napoleon nor Kutuzov really decided to fight at Borodino or controlled the battle when it began; to fight at that time and place was in the interests of neither. And he strongly suggests that this is true of all battles and all generals, and that the issue is determined not by tactical 'decisions' but by complex and mysterious forces which as yet we do not understand. Napoleon and Kutuzov respond to these earth-currents, Kutuzov being obscurely aware that he is not really in charge, Napoleon, however, being of all men supremely under the illusion that he rules the battle and commands his destiny.

The idea that a general's character and decisions have little to do with the outcome of armed conflict is contradicted by almost every battle in India during the two hundred years with which we are dealing. These battles are not vast struggles like Leipzig or Austerlitz, in which hundreds of thousands were engaged, but nearly all of them illustrate a principle the exact opposite of Tolstoy's—that a commanding officer who is cool and quick-witted in action can save many

casualties and often decide the result of the engagement—and also that
there are some commanders whom men will follow in any enterprise
and others in whom they have no confidence at all.

The tactical point need hardly be stressed. Adams at Katwa in 1763
had foreseen that Muhammad Taki would deliver a cavalry charge
against a particular point in the British line and that this might prove
decisive; he placed a company in position for just that emergency and
it crumpled the charge and determined the issue. Caillaud at Patna,
Forde at Condore, decided the battle by foresight and swift reaction to
a changing situation. This tactical skill depended on an eye for country,
a quick mind that kept cool in the presence of danger, and usually
it meant that there had been painstaking study of many battles in
the past. It depended also on a laboriously acquired technical skill, the
ability by clear orders to manœuvre troops into the position where the
quick mind saw that they could be used with most advantage. But a
general's power to fill his troops with confidence is more mysterious.

Clive had this power, and particularly with Indian troops, and this
was the more remarkable because he spoke no Indian language. The
quality a general needs is not quite what is needed by a company
officer, though one man might have both. Personal courage is essential
if the men are to give their respect, and a general will get the best from
troops only if he puts the defeat of the enemy before his personal convenience. They must feel that he knows what he is about; it is like the
reaction of a horse which at once becomes aware that his rider is
confident and experienced. They must feel that he is a soldier like
themselves. Confident, experienced, determined to beat the enemy,
attentive to detail and to the care of the men under his command—
this is the man they will follow. To all this, he must add *style*—a stamp
of his own on what he says and does, something that comes out in the
stories they tell about him.

Not enough has been said of Eyre Coote. His career was a strange
one. Found guilty of misbehaviour by a court martial and cashiered
before he was twenty, he was three times Commander-in-Chief in
India. His first set-back was due to events for which he could hardly in
fairness be blamed. He carried the colours of a company of the 27th
Foot; this company was overrun at the battle of Falkirk in 1746 by a
confused mass of their own retreating dragoons and of rebel Highlanders in pursuit. The battle had been mismanaged by the general,
who sought a scapegoat, and four officers, including the nineteen-year-
old Eyre Coote, were brought before courts martial. Coote had been
knocked down by the rush of flying men and horses but had held on to
his colours and brought them away safely; he was acquitted of cowardice but found guilty of misbehaviour, though it is hard to see how he
could have prevented the disaster. The incident must have influenced

him; perhaps the memory of this early injustice was one element in the concern for the men under his command that he always displayed.

We have seen him coming to India ten years later, commissioned a second time and now in the 39th, voting for action at Plassey and following the French to the frontiers of Oudh. On his return to England, he was one of the first to give an account of what was known in the eighteenth century as the Revolution in Bengal. He was appointed Colonel of the 84th, a battalion raised specially for service in India, and in March 1759 was appointed Commander-in-Chief in Bengal. This post was still junior to the Madras appointment then held by Stringer Lawrence. But Lawrence was worn out with age and ill-health and left for home just before Coote arrived at Madras in November 1759; Coote took command without going to Bengal and thus for the first time held the senior post in India. The siege of Madras by the French had recently been raised but things still hung very much in the balance. Coote's assumption of command 'seemed to infuse new intelligence and decision into all the operations of the troops ... Daring, valour and cool discretion strove for the mastery in the composition of this great man ... his rigid discipline was tempered with an unaffected kindness and consideration ... which won the affection of the European soldiers and rendered him the idol of the native troops.' Thus wrote Mark Wilks and there can be no question that the tide now turned and success followed success, much of it due to the spirit Coote put into the troops. Three forts were taken from the French, and on January 22nd, 1760, Coote met Lally and Bussy near Wandewash in a pitched battle in which they were totally defeated. It was the classical confrontation of French columns against British line and for the French it was the beginning of the end. Fort after fort fell to Coote's army, the crown of the campaign being the surrender of Pondicherry in January 1761, with 484 guns.

Coote was treated as a hero in England and in 1769 was appointed Commander-in-Chief in India but this time his stay was short. He left within a year, having signally failed to find a way of living with the Madras Council. His third appointment, however, was made when Madras was again in serious danger, at the worst point of the Second Mysore War. Hydar Ali had ravaged the Carnatic almost to the gate of Madras and had surrounded and annihilated Baillie's brigade. Again it fell to Coote to restore the spirit of an army which had lost heart. He fought four pitched battles during the next three and a half years, all decisively victorious, all against forces overwhelmingly stronger than his own. But that is less than half the tale; his enemy was Hydar Ali, a brilliant soldier, much stronger than himself in horse and artillery, determined to avoid a full-dress infantry engagement. Coote had — as has been said before — practically no horse and no commissariat.

He called on his men again and again for forced marches in great heat, often with short rations, and sometimes without food for long periods. They were often many months in arrears with their pay. Yet they always responded to his calls. It was with the war-cry 'Coote Bahadur'* that one of his sepoy regiments charged with the bayonet.

It is hard to get a clear picture of the man as a whole. Only an angel could have avoided quarrelling with the Madras Council, who through nearly the whole period were factious, interfering, pompous and often also corrupt. But Coote, never particularly patient with civilian interference, grew more impatient with failing health and towards the end of his life he was not merely peppery but really difficult. Warren Hastings, a man of unrivalled patience, so much admired him as a soldier that he persuaded him when he was at the point of death to go back to Madras once again as the only means of saving the Presidency. 'I have one foot in the grave and one on the edge of it,' he said as he took ship for the last time. Yet even Hastings, whose support and understanding had been unremitting, wrote of Coote: 'His zeal and spirit are without example ... I am resolved to give him all the support of the Government, though I am certain that he will quarrel with me the moment that we are separated.'

But his touchiness seems to have been reserved for his employers; his concern for his men is mentioned by everyone who wrote about him, and flashes come through in his own words. He wrote to the Government after his first great victory at Wandewash: ' ... the scene is now dreadful to see. Such a multitude of poor objects, and not in my power to give them the least assistance'; and begged the Government to send surgeons. 'Our sepoys are in such a state as renders every attention to them absolutely indispensable.' And on leaving his regiment behind he wrote that his 'situation resembled that of a fond Parent quitting a Family which from their affectionate behaviour and strict observance of their Duty have endeared them to him.' He was never niggardly with praise: 'The good behaviour of the sepoys was more remarkable than anything I could conceive ... I have ordered a gold medal to be made for Bulwansing, a commandant of sepoys, who led the attack the night we took possession of the hill.' It has been said that Sir Charles Napier was the first to mention other ranks than officers in his dispatches, but in fact Sir Eyre Coote mentioned both British and Indian N.C.O.s and privates eighty years before Napier. Most rare in the records of his time, Coote decided after Wandewash that as his troops had received no prize-money, while a number of valuable presents had been made to

* 'Bahadur' in Persian can be an adjective meaning 'bold' or it may mean 'a knight or hero', but in Hindustani it is commonly used after a name as a title or superlative, with an implication of courage.

him, he would make over all he had received to those whose gallantry and good behaviour had made possible his success.

Whatever the secret of the affection the troops felt for him, of the fact there could be no question. In January 1782 a fit of apoplexy struck him down and there was doubt of his survival. 'For nearly two hours, during which little hope was entertained of his life, the despondency painted on every countenance, and particularly on those of the native troops, whose attachment and confidence exceeded the bounds of human veneration, and which could with difficulty be restrained within the limits of decorum to satisfy their anxiety, presented altogether a scene of mournful interest,' wrote Mark Wilks. In September of the same year, when he was again insensible, the sepoys feared that he was dead and that the news was being kept from them. One was deputed to discover the facts and—with just that lack of 'decorum' that Wilks deprecated—approached the litter where the general lay, raised the curtain and inspected his face. 'General Sahib *jita hai*'—'The General is alive!' he cried, and cheers arose from British and Indian alike. Innes Munro, a junior officer who served in this campaign wrote that he was 'the soldier's friend, most dear to the soldiers he commanded for his personal bravery, his great likeability and his affectionate regard for their honour and interests. Other generals have been approved but Sir Eyre Coote was the beloved of the British Army in India.' 'Our old soldier' is the expression constantly used of him by his staff. But the face in the best portrait is not, like for example that of Lord Roberts, one that immediately suggests the soldier; it suggests vision and strong emotions, a leader and a creator, the face of a man who might have designed St Paul's or the Forth Bridge, who would assuredly have inspired love or hate in those he met.

2. Wellesley Bahadur

It was with equal confidence, but on different grounds and with a very different kind of emotion, that men regarded Arthur Wellesley. He was in the first place the child of fortune, the brother of the Governor-General; belonging, like Coote, to the Anglo-Irish ascendancy, but of far more distinguished connections, he seems already booked for success when he first appears on the Indian scene. Let us consider only the six months which culminated in the battle of Assaye in September 1803. We have already glanced at the general situation. The Governor-General, the Marquess Wellesley, known to his staff as 'the glorious little man', had no doubt that the Maratha Confederacy was a threat to the peace and security of the rest of India and must be curbed; he took advantage of war within the confederacy and engaged to restore to his throne the Peshwa, Baji Rao, who had been ousted by one of the other Maratha princes. This was on condition that he signed a treaty which made him a subsidiary of the British. Baji Rao signed; Arthur Wellesley's first duty was to take him back to Poona and put him on the throne, his second to protect him and Hyderabad, the great protected state to the south, against the other Maratha princes.

The first stage of this campaign was a march from Mysore to Poona, about 600 miles, ending with the restoration of the Peshwa. There followed a second period of intense diplomatic activity and military preparation—during which the Peshwa, having got what he wanted, showed himself a very doubtful ally—and finally a series of rapid movements. In these, Wellesley's object was to bring about an infantry battle, in which he was the attacker, while the Marathas, vastly superior both in cavalry and artillery, hoped to cut off his supplies, surround him, hammer him with their guns and, when his army was shattered and exhausted, attack with their trained infantry, repeating on a larger scale Hydar Ali's defeat of Baillie.

As one reads the daily record of Wellesley's letters—to his brother the Governor-General; to the Secretary of State in England; to Stuart, the Commander-in-Chief in Madras; to Colonel Stevenson, who commanded a supporting force under his orders; to the civil officers at the Maratha courts, at Bombay and at Mysore—the outstanding impressions are of immense energy, a staggering attention to detail, a resolute common sense.

Bullocks are the subject of half his letters and no word recurs more frequently. He has to move quickly and his men must be well fed; his force must be self-contained and not live on the country, as the enemy do; they must have light boats and be able to cross rivers, as the enemy cannot. Therefore bullocks are the key to everything, and he writes about bullocks to Bombay, to Seringapatam and to Madras. He had built up a supply of bullocks belonging to the Government before this period began but it was not enough. Now he had to supplement it from other sources. He prefers buying bullocks to hiring, and hiring to the use of 'brinjarries', but he wants as much as he can get by all three methods. 'The brinjarries', he wrote to the Secretary to Government in Bombay, who really ought to have known, 'are a species of dealers who attend the army with grain and other supplies which they sell in the bazaars. In general, they seek for those supplies which are sold at the cheapest rate and they bring them on their bullocks to the armies. Occasionally, however, those supplies have been issued to them from the public stores.' 'Captain Barclay wrote by my orders to the brinjarry gomashta [agent] to desire him to come up from Conjeveram immediately and to inform him that all the brinjarries of the Carnatic, Mysore and the ceded districts would be immediately wanted and that they were to load and join the army.' But it was not simply a matter of saying what he wanted; 'the loads for pack bullocks must be 72 pukka seers [about 144 lb] instead of 60.' If the bags for rice were too small, he might lose 20 seers to a bullock—'which would feed a soldier forty days'. 'The bags for rice must be proper bullock gunny bags, made of the best gunny,' as otherwise the rice may spoil.

Nor was it only rice in which he was interested; detailed instructions pour from his pen about horse-keepers, gram kettles (in which fodder for horses was boiled), the rate of exchange, the daily rations for the wounded, litters for the wounded and bearers to carry them. He sets up a subsidiary depot on the Bombay coast for which he demands 90,000 lb of salt beef for his Europeans and the same of biscuit, the inevitable rice, bullocks for rice, bullocks for guns, kegs for arrack, ten thousand gallons of arrack, musket balls, gram for horses, round baskets covered with waxed cloth, six hundred garees (carts) each to carry 480 pukka seers; there must be 'ghee, turmeric and doll'—'doll' being *dāl*, dried lentils—and it was essential there should be plenty of conicopolies to measure and account for all this mass of provisions. He writes about wheels for the ammunition tumbrils and the width of the metal rim for the wheels of the twelve-pounders; casks for arrack must be repaired and tested and casks for salt beef; the basket boats—an essential part of his plan, borrowed from Caesar—must be covered with two thicknesses of leather, sewed with thongs. So it goes on.

With this attention to detail went strict discipline. A sepoy found guilty of desertion by a court martial was sentenced to death and he directed the sentence to be carried into execution at once and 'other deserters shall be shot also if the Court Martial should sentence that punishment'. But he halts two days to establish a field hospital, 'much wanted on account of deficiency among native corps of carriage for their sick'. His letters suggest that he cares for soldiers as he cares for bullocks, because they are useful: 'I consider nothing in this country so valuable as the life and health of the British soldier and nothing so expensive as soldiers in hospital ... I request ... particular attention to their discipline and regularity and to prevent their getting intoxicating liquors which tend to their destruction.' But he was scrupulously fair in appointments; recommendations from exalted persons are politely refused if there is an officer available with the force whose services have earned promotion.

Thus he forged the instrument he needed—tough, flexible, exactly responsive to his will—a self-contained force that could march. And he was pleased with the result. After the six-hundred-mile march to Poona, at the hottest time of year, 'I never saw the troops look better.' And a few weeks later: 'I never was in such marching trim. I marched the other day twenty-three miles in seven hours and a half and all our marches now are made at the rate of three miles an hour.' This was for an army, with its guns and baggage. Individual marches of detachments were often much longer; after Assaye, he wrote to Munro: 'We marched sixty miles with the infantry in twenty hours.' Before this, the pace of an army in India was often five or seven miles a day and seldom more than twelve. And he wrote on September 8th: 'It is impossible for troops to be in better order than those under my command.'

The battle of Assaye was fought on September 23rd. Stevenson, with a force similar to Wellesley's, was advancing on parallel lines somewhat farther west; they had not united because a larger army would be delayed in narrow defiles and it was essential to catch the enemy. On the morning of the 23rd Wellesley's force arrived after a night march of eighteen miles at a village he knew as Naulnia, where he meant to halt for rest during the heat of the day. Here he received a report that the enemy were close at hand but had already begun to retreat. Since to bring them to battle was Wellesley's great object, and there seemed a chance of catching them on the march, he decided to leave the baggage at Naulnia with a guard of the greater part of a battalion of sepoys, while with the rest he marched forward six miles, without resting his

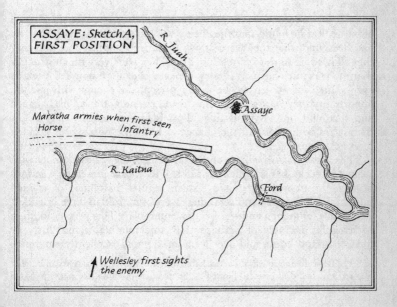

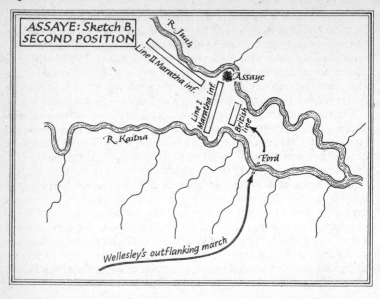

ASSAYE: Sketch B, SECOND POSITION

R. Juah

Line II Maratha inf.

Assaye

Line I Maratha inf.

British line

R. Kaitna

Ford

Wellesley's outflanking march

men. It was a reconnaissance in force, though he hoped for the chance of battle. But he found that the enemy were in greater strength than he had been told, that they were drawn up in a strong position, and that they showed no signs of retreating. Since they were very much stronger than he was in cavalry, Wellesley believed that if he now fell back or even waited for Stevenson, he would present the enemy with just the opportunity they were seeking; they could cut him off from his baggage and surround him. Even if they allowed him to escape, they might themselves withdraw and the chance of battle be missed. He decided to attack them.

The enemy were drawn up on the far bank of the Kaitna, a river with steep and rocky banks which for most of its course presented a serious obstacle to troops. They had sixteen regular battalions of trained infantry with European officers; these were organized in three brigades: Pohlman's, Dupont's and the Begum Sumroo's.* This was in addition to irregular infantry of perhaps the same number, some thirty or forty thousand horse, and over a hundred guns, excellently equipped.

---

* The Begum Sumroo was the remarkable widow of the infamous Alsatian butcher Sumroo who had distinguished himself at the massacre of Patna (see page 98). It is hard to resist the temptation to digress about the Begum Sumroo.

A frontal assault was impossible and the only alternative was to cross the river and attack one of their flanks. Wellesley was assured by the guides that there was no ford across the river. But he noticed that, well to the enemy's left, there were two villages immediately opposite each other and at that point, he reasoned, there must be some means of getting across. He marched right across the enemy's front—'they did not at first perceive my design'—and he crossed the river under distant cannon fire but without infantry opposition. A tributary stream, the Juah, joined the main stream about a mile below the ford. Both armies were now on the tongue of land between these two watercourses, which a mile above the ford narrowed to a width of about a mile. It was here, at the narrowest point, that Wellesley formed his line of battle (see Map A). Meanwhile the enemy, though they had been slow to perceive his 'design', had by now realized that they were about to be attacked from the flank and had re-formed to face him. It was a difficult manœuvre in the crowded space and only well-trained troops could have performed it. Their line along the Kaitna had been abandoned and the infantry, with guns interspersed, now faced Wellesley across the narrowest part of the tongue between the streams (see Map B). On their left, and held by them, was the village of Assaye, packed with guns and infantry, well covered behind strong mud walls. This was impregnable by direct assault without artillery preparation and to a force so small as Wellesley's. Further, from Assaye a fierce enfilading fire could develop on a general advance. He determined therefore to

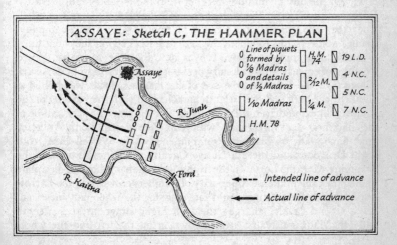

deliver a hammer-blow on the enemy's right, and to leave Assaye well to his own right. His hammer would swing on a pivot of which the hinge was Assaye, but it would not approach the village (see Map C).

His infantry were in two lines, the first line having all its weight on the left. The head of his hammer, on the far left of his first line of infantry, was H.M. 78th Highlanders (later the 2nd Battalion, Seaforth Highlanders). Next to them in line came the 1st Battalion, 10th Madras Infantry and the line continued to the right in much less strength, as a series of picquets, consisting of the 1st Battalion, 8th Madras Infantry and detachments from the 1st Battalion, 2nd Madrassis (the rest of whom were guarding the camp). The second line of infantry, 800 paces behind, provided the handle of the hammer. On the extreme right were H.M. 74th Highlanders (later 2nd Battalion, Highland Light Infantry) with the two other Madras battalions to the left of them. Since Assaye village was so strong, it was to be left till the end; the whole double line, with the hammer-head of the 78th Highlanders and the 1st/10th Madrassis slightly advanced, were to pivot in a wheeling movement, driving the enemy, who were crowded into a narrow space, back upon the Juah river. Then Assaye could be dealt with; during the main advance, the right-hand troops were instructed to keep well away from the village.

Unfortunately, things did not go exactly as planned. The line of picquets diverged to the right, going too near Assaye; the 2nd/12th and 74th followed them, moving directly on the village. The fire from the village was so hot that the advance was stopped on the right and there was a dangerous gap in the centre. The British guns were silenced and could no longer move because the draught-animals had been shot down. Of the fifty men in one picquet from the 1st/2nd Madras Native Infantry (later 1st/1st Punjabis) 21 were killed and 24 were wounded. The 74th were reduced from a battalion to little more than a company, losing 17 officers and 400 men; the 2nd/12th lost 228 but they continued to move as a compact body. It was now that the Marathas loosed a charge of cavalry at the already decimated infantry in front of Assaye village. On the left, the advance of the hammer-head was going as planned; the 74th and the 1st/10th had charged with the bayonet at the Maratha line and driven the infantry from their guns. But the handle of the hammer was threatened with complete destruction. Wellesley must have made up his mind instantaneously. He ordered H.M. 19th Light Dragoons and the 4th Native Cavalry to charge straight at the oncoming Maratha horse. In the frightful shock that followed, discipline told against the immense superiority of numbers crowded in too narrow a space. Now the infantry could move again; the whole advance went on; a second cavalry charge — the 19th Light Dragoons and 4th, 5th and 7th Madras Cavalry — was thrown in on the left and the whole

Maratha line was driven back on the Juah. But horses and men alike were too exhausted to follow a beaten foe.

It was an astonishing victory. Wellesley had 22 cannon, all of small calibre, to more than a hundred, of which 98 were captured; his infantry were outnumbered at least three to one, counting on the enemy side only trained troops with French officers, and they had marched 24 miles before the battle began; his cavalry—at least those used in the battle—were outnumbered by more than ten to one. He was not a man to use superlatives lightly, but he used them often of Assaye. He wrote:

'I cannot write in too strong terms of the conduct of the troops; they advanced in the best order and with the greatest steadiness, under a most destructive fire, against a body of infantry far superior in number, who appeared determined to contend with them till the last.' 'The fire from their cannon was the hottest that has been known in this country.' When the break in the line occurred, the troops 'were exposed to a most terrible cannonade from Assaye', but he would not blame or reprove Colonel Orrock of the 1st/8th Madras Infantry, who had commanded the line of picquets; 'it was not possible for a man to lead a body into a hotter fire than he did.' He wrote to Malcolm (with whom he was as nearly familiar as he was with any man): 'I assure you that the fire was so heavy that I much doubted at one time whether I should be able to prevail upon our troops to advance ... and all agree that the battle was the fiercest that has ever been seen in India. Our troops behaved admirably; the sepoys astonished me.' And to his brother Henry: 'Scindia's French infantry was far better than Tippoo's, his artillery excellent and his ordnance so good and so well equipped that it answers for our service'—that is, we can use the captured guns. 'The bloodiest for the numbers that I ever saw,' he said later; his casualties were a quarter of his strength, and half of them occurred in that tornado before Assaye which would have been avoided if his instructions had been followed.

Assaye has been often described as a general's battle, and so it was; to fight at all was the General's sole decision and the operation was entirely designed by himself. Few indeed have been the commanders who would have ventured on so daring a plan or carried it through with such courage, resolution and dash. But it was also, in another sense, a soldier's battle, illustrating in the highest degree the confidence men feel in a general who knows what he is about. Wellesley made no speeches to his men; he fed them and taught them to march. And by this means he welded British regiments and Madrassis into one instrument. Neither can claim a preponderance in valour. Both cherished the distinction of having followed him. '*We* know him as Wellesley Bahadur,' said an old Indian officer who had been at Assaye, talking many years later to Malcolm, brushing aside as irrelevant the frippery of dukedom and the laurels of Waterloo.

Far away in the north, Lord Lake, the Commander-in-Chief, with a force not much larger, scored victory after victory. He was stronger than Wellesley in cavalry and artillery, but he had only one battalion of British infantry to thirteen of infantry of the Bengal Army. 'Lake and Victory' was the battle honour inscribed on the special colours granted to some of these units, and it was the habit of victory—at least till Bhurtpore—that bound them to him. He was a fierce fighting soldier who never lost a chance to attack, but—again, till Bhurtpore—he was not the man to fling troops headlong at impregnable positions. At Delhi, he brought the enemy by a ruse to attack him in a prepared position, and Laswarree—'as fierce a fight as ever was fought by men,' as Fortescue called it, as dramatic as Assaye and even more decisive— was by no means a 'soldier's battle' but one in which General and soldiers both played their parts.

Contrast Lake's victorious career in the winter of 1803–4 with Monson's disastrous defeat in the late summer of the following year. Monson commanded a force from Lake's army in the north; he advanced southward against Holkar while Murray from the south with Bombay troops came north to meet him. There were obvious dangers in such an advance by two forces from opposite directions, but a moment came when, if either Murray or Monson had been Lake or Wellesley, Holkar might have been destroyed. But they were not; both turned back dispiritedly and, despite the dour courage of their troops, were ignominiously driven from the field. Monson reached Delhi with the loss of all his guns and stores and half his force. Monson's retreat and the repulse before Bhurtpore were remembered as proofs that the Company was not invincible, until they were eclipsed, forty years later, by the greater disaster of Kabul.

NOTE

It is sometimes said that Wellesley employed 4,500 troops at Assaye, but there were about 6,000. The infantry were H.M. 74th and 78th, and the 1st/2nd, 1st/4th, 1st/8th, 1st/10th and 2nd/12th of the Madras Native Infantry. Of these, the 1st/2nd and the 2nd/12th were the ancestors of the 1st/1st and the 10th/1st Punjab Regiment at Independence. His cavalry were H.M. 19th Light Dragoons and the 4th, 5th and 7th Madras Native Cavalry. But he had also some 5,000 cavalry supplied by the Peshwa and the Nizam, allies whose heart was not wholly in the war. They were of some use before he crossed the Kaitna, but did not cross with him and took no part in the battle. Assaye has been often described, but it has not been easy, all the same, to piece together just what happened. Most writers have been writing primarily about Wellesley or British troops and have not been wholly fair to the Madras infantry; both Sir Arthur Bryant and Lady Longford, for example, mention the picquet of 50 men from the 1st/2nd of whom 45 were killed or wounded, but I think a reader would in both cases imagine they belonged to H.M. 74th. Sir Arthur's sketch-map shows H.M. 74th and H.M. 78th but no Madras infantry at all.

VIII
Officers

1. 'Look here, upon this picture, and on this'

'When a young man first arrives in India,' wrote Sir John Shore, 'he will hear philippics against the natives of the country, who are represented as having almost every bad quality; while on the other hand he is overwhelmed with the laudatory expressions adopted whenever the Sepoys are mentioned, whose sense of honour, gratitude and devotion to us, — whose bravery, patience in undergoing fatigue and privations — honesty and various other qualities are described as being beyond all praise.' Shore thought at first that 'the Sepoys' were so different from 'the natives' that they must come from a foreign country. It was in 1769 that he arrived in Calcutta and forty years later that he recalled his surprise at finding that the sepoys were drawn from the 'common peasantry of India', but the point might have been made, with only slight modifications, almost any time before the cataclysm of the Mutiny and again surprisingly soon afterwards.

The reasons for this variety of opinion are not hard to see. Newcomers to a country are often imposed on and do not usually meet the best of the inhabitants; young officers were fair game for everyone from rascally servants to money-lenders, and British troops often saw few civilian Indians except pimps, touts, hawkers and servants of the most degraded kind. Thus they saw a very poor kind of Indian civilian and many formed early impressions which they never corrected. Indian soldiers, on the other hand, particularly in the Bengal Army, were usually from families who owned land and were accustomed to take a leading part in village affairs; they were fine-looking men, proud of their appearance, their personal honour and the honour of their corps. They were also used to dealing with British officers, and understood that they liked a straightforward 'manly' approach rather than the obsequious flattery that was traditional in asking any favour from an Indian superior. So there was a real difference in what the newcomers saw. But, apart from that, it suited conquerors to think poorly of the natives in general; the fact that they were such contemptible creatures justified foreign rule. And, equally, it suited the rulers of this already vast empire to think well of the soldiers on whom they were so largely dependent. If they were to sleep well at night, they must feel secure. It was on the sepoy that their security rested.

The contrast is made again and again in the memoirs of retired officers and in the pamphlets on which they so often laboured in retirement and published at their own expense. One such pamphlet, published in 1849, has a long passage on the fiery valour of Indian troops and the distinguished services of the Indian army, but speaks with dislike of the neighbourhood of Calcutta and Madras, 'where the effeminate and feeble Babus* vegetate'. Here the contrast between Indian soldiers and civilians is beginning to blend with that other contrast, an admiration for the 'martial races' of the north and north-west and a contempt for the peoples of the south and east which became of increasing importance after the Mutiny. But the contrast between attitudes to soldier and civilian is nowhere more clearly expressed than in the memoirs of Captain Albert Hervey of the Madras Army, which were published in 1850.

'Give them the opportunity, [he writes] and they are second to none in the deadly charge, the skirmish or the escalade ... Military ardour and heroic chivalry are ... as bright in the breasts of our noble Sipahees as they were wont to be in the days of Clive ... There is no Army in the whole of Europe in which military discipline is better maintained ... there are no soldiers more faithful, more brave or more strongly attached to their colours and their officers than those of the Madras Army.'

Emotional rhetoric, some would say, but there are many other passages which show that Hervey did admire his men and was genuinely concerned about the welfare of them and their families, that he really tried to help them and was angered by the indifference of some officers. Yet he could write of civilian Indians in general in such terms as this: 'Blacky is indeed as deceitful as his colour is black and as selfish as he is double-faced. Self is visible in all his actions, his thoughts and his schemes.'

Hervey seems unaware of any inconsistency and in this no doubt represents thousands of his countrymen. Emma Roberts had a sharper eye. Her lively notes on what she heard and saw in the course of her travels in India in the early 1830s were published first in Indian newspapers and later in London. She does not make the point so explicitly as Sir John Shore but she comments on the horror of Anglo-Indian

* The word is pronounced 'Bah-boo', with a slight accent on the first syllable. It is a term of respect in Hindi and Hindustani and can mean 'prince' or 'nobleman' as well as 'anyone who can read', but Englishmen used it in a derogatory sense because villagers used it to clerks from whom they were seeking favours.

society at everything 'black', which was so great that a lady coming from England with gold or silver lace on her ball-dress must remove it or risk being called 'a nautch-girl'. Yet she adds that 'the natives of India are disliked and despised only by those who are unacquainted with their language' and she herself is impressed by the general honesty of servants and above all by the fidelity of sepoys, who, if sent in small parties to guard treasure and if attacked by armed robbers, 'will suffer themselves to be cut to pieces to a man rather than desert their posts.'

There is really no end to the testimony as to the good conduct, fidelity and courage of the sepoys. Sleeman, the man who hunted down the Thugs and put an end to that widespread religious fraternity of robbers and murderers, believed that the key to the sepoy's good conduct was the opinion of his family. At least three-quarters of the Bengal infantry came from Oudh, north of the Ganges, and were Rajput, or sometimes Brahman, by caste. They visited their families every two or three years and the 'good feelings of their families continue through the whole period of their service to exercise a salutary influence over their conduct as men and as soldiers.' They know that either misconduct or cowardice will be reported at home, because so many of their comrades come from the same neighbourhood and are often relatives as well; this tends to 'produce a general and uniform propriety of conduct ... hardly to be found among the soldiers of any other army in the world.' It is based on 'a veneration for parents cherished through life'. 'No men can have a higher sense of the duty they owe to the State that employs them or whose salt they eat, nor can any men set less value on life when the service of that State requires that it shall be risked.'

When Sleeman wrote that, he was probably thinking of a dozen cases of such reckless courage. Perhaps he remembered Jemadar 'Burjoor Sing', who, at the second siege of Bhurtpore, when a mine placed in a tunnel below the ramparts failed to explode, 'bravely ran up with a lighted candle and applied it to a part susceptible of instant ignition. The explosion followed and the Jemadar, although much hurt and burnt, escaped with his life.' He was immediately promoted and 'his intrepid and gallant conduct' was mentioned in General Orders. Men have since won the Victoria Cross for less, and it is surely a good deal more than could be expected for a few rupees a month. What today seems even more surprising than this kind of behaviour is that it was so constantly taken for granted.

It is hard for us today to understand the early Victorians. Imperialism had not yet become as brassy, vulgar and self-assertive as it was to be at the time of the Diamond Jubilee, but the certainty that right was on our side was even stronger. Our wars, wrote Stocqueler in *The Old Field Officer*, have been 'almost always for the purpose of extending social improvement and good government ... [and] the blessings of

tranquillity and security of life and property ... [and these] more than
compensate for the rudeness of the process by which amelioration is
usually effected.' This was the view of the Marquess Wellesley and—
until the war of 1839 against Afghanistan—of almost all his countrymen in India. An earlier generation, their roots in the eighteenth
century, had gone forward in the course which opened before them, with
zest and enjoyment, certainly, but with no feeling that their task had
been set them by God—rather with a realistic pessimism as to the
future, sometimes, as with Mountstuart Elphinstone, wryly humorous.

By the 1830s, however, many of the British in India belonged to the
evangelical movement. They were 'serious', a word which became
almost a technical term indicating evangelical convictions. They made
no question that they were in India by the purpose of Divine Providence
—they had an almost Rabbinical scruple about uttering the Divine
Name—but they were often puzzled about their immediate duty. The
best of them, such as James Thomason, the Lieutenant-Governor of the
North-Western Provinces in the 1840s, were convinced that 'in His
own good time' the Lord would convert the whole of India to the
Truth. In the meantime Thomason believed that he must bravely
endure the trial of being surrounded by heathens and unbelievers, and
be scrupulous to exert no compulsion. As an official, he must not
deviate by a hair's-breadth from exact impartiality between all
religions; but in his private life it was a duty to support missionary
endeavour.

This was a height to which few could aspire. Many of the serious
were puzzled that the Lord should be so slow to end the abominations
of the heathen and some wanted to take a more active hand in His work
than the Government would permit. Many were uneasy, and some
were indignant, that the Government should countenance heathen
practices by allowing public holidays on Hindu and Mohammedan
festivals and—worse still—allowing troops to provide guards of
honour when Indian princes attended the ceremonies of their faith.

Sir Peregrine Maitland, for instance, when Commander-in-Chief at
Madras, aimed an indignant memorandum at the Government of
India: 'The Governor-General requires that troops shall still, under the
name of Honorary Escorts, be required to attend, as forming part of the
pageant or ceremony, upon natives of rank when joining in the performance of religious worship, however offensive this duty may be to
their consciences, and it is well-known that it is upon such occasions
that their consciences are most severely wounded.' He resigned half-
way through his normal time in command and perhaps this was one
of the reasons. Many humbler officers felt as he did. Mackinnon, a
captain of H.M. 16th Lancers, arriving in India not long before the
First Afghan War of 1839, was horrified by the Moharram celebrations

at Allahabad; he saw 'scenes of riot and debauchery' which 'have entailed a lasting disgrace on the government of India, which not only tolerates but actually encourages them. Nor has it scrupled to convert the superstitions of the deluded into a substantial accession to the revenues of the country.' Again, Maude, who obtained a cadetship in 1843 and joined the Bombay Army, was distressed to find that a Guard of Honour under a European officer was present when His Highness the Gaekwar of Baroda attended the Dasehra festivities—'but I am thankful to say,' he wrote many years later, 'this countenancing of an idolatrous Hindoo festival has been discontinued.'

Maude was a man who took great trouble to master languages—Hindustani, Marathi and Persian; he went out of his way to visit the site of Babylon, where he meditated on the feast of Belshazzar and the fate of empires as the punishment of imperial arrogance. 'Truly, Babylon has been sorely punished for her iniquities,' he wrote. He visited some places of Muslim pilgrimage, and was dubbed Hajji* by his fellow-officers when he came back to the mess. In Baghdad, he stayed with Armenians. He was in no way an insensitive man or personally intolerant. But his farewell on leaving India for the last time is representative of the way the 'serious' thought. 'May God bless India', he wrote, 'and hasten the time when the people shall throw off the dark cloud of idolatry and superstition which has hung for ages like a pall over the land.'

But of course the serious were a minority, though strongly represented among those who wrote memoirs. Most English officers, and particularly the young, were thoughtless and gay. Life was often short but credit was plentiful. To learn an oriental language really well was hard work; it demanded time which, at a big station, could be better spent in calling on ladies or getting up theatricals, at a small station in shooting or hog-hunting. So for many knowledge of the language was rudimentary and interest in the country negligible. If by any chance a young officer were to open a book on India he would be likely to meet opinions such as those of Charles Grant, a great evangelical and for long Chairman of the Court of Directors of the Company, who wrote in his *Observations on the Asiatic Subjects of Great Britain* that the people of India were 'as a race lamentably degenerate and base'. There were indeed many evils in Indian society—child-marriage, the burning of widows, the vast and murderous conspiracy of the Thugs, the deaths among the pilgrims to the temple of Juggernaut. These loomed large in English eyes but they were not more productive of misery and

---

* *Hajji* is ordinarily used as a title for anyone who has been on the pilgrimage to Mecca. Maude went to Karbala, the scene of the martyrdom of Husain, not to Mecca, and his comrades, very properly, called him Al Hajji Karbalai. But not, perhaps, very often.

degradation than the Slave Trade or conditions in English factories. Grant and his evangelical friends fought these evils in England but they would not on their account have condemned the people of England wholesale, as they often did the people of India. When the thoughtful could see so little that was good in the land they ruled, when their horror at idolatry obscured their perception of fidelity and filial piety, it was hardly surprising that the thoughtless often appeared arrogant and offensive.

Albert Hervey, not one of the least serious, though far from being a 'Blue Light', as British soldiers called the most extreme evangelicals, constantly comes back to the thoughtlessness of young officers. He has a story of a party who 'cruelly and wantonly' shot a monkey at a temple. Monkeys in India are almost as sacred as cows, and doubly so at a temple; the young men were mobbed and were lucky to escape with their lives. Hervey asks whether we should not resent a similar desecration at one of our own places of worship. 'Is this the way to convince the natives that our religion is better than theirs? Idolatry and its blind votaries must and will reign paramount, until professing Christians set a better example by their lives and conversation. We should show our fellow-creatures by precept and example that ours is the only true worship and theirs but the vain image of infatuated ignorance.' But we do nothing of the kind and they look on us as 'immoral, dissipated, depraved and uncharitable'. They conclude that the religion of such people can have no truth or solidarity.

To shoot a monkey in a temple might be no more than thoughtless. But there are also stories in the memoirs that show something worse than thoughtlessness, a temper which seems to have grown as the century went on. Mackinnon, newly arrived, seeing the sights of Delhi, was shown by a Muslim guide the throne of the Mughal Emperors; on this, he said proudly, many a mighty Emperor had sat. '"See then, a man mightier than the present King of the Mogul Empire sit on that throne," exclaimed one of our officers, bringing himself to anchor on the tempting seat.' Mackinnon was not uncritical—his condemnation of the First Afghan War could hardly be more devastating—but he does not condemn this boorish behaviour.

Hervey reports even worse of young officers in the Company's service, who were supposed to be commanding sepoys. He knew of one who would say on parade: 'Dress up, you black brute!' or 'Do you hear me, you nigger?' It is hard to convey to anyone who does not know India how offensive such language would be—and how inconceivable it would have been in the first half of the twentieth century. To men of high caste in Northern India, a light skin meant high caste and high social position: it was socially and sexually desirable. Hervey says this young officer got into very serious trouble, but he caps the story by one even worse. A group of young officers, apparently in their first year in India, were sitting drinking on Christmas morning in the bungalow they shared. The bandmaster, accompanied by the band, who were usually Christians of low caste and despised by the sepoys, came to sing carols; when they had finished, the bandmaster came in to wish the officers a merry Christmas and ask if his men might drink their Honours' health. One told him to go to the devil and wish *him* a merry Christmas; one threw a cup of coffee in the bandmaster's face. Again, the commanding officer took a very serious view of this and the young men would have lost their commissions if they had not been so extremely inexperienced. But the story is evidence of a feeling that was not exceptional. Hervey writes elsewhere:

'I regret much to say that it is too often the case that ... young officers, on first commencing their military career, talk about "those horrible black nigger sepoys" ... they look down on them as brute beasts, and lower themselves even so far as to curse and swear at them ... This is why we hear of misunderstandings, mutinies, courts martial ... Treat the sepoys well; attend to their wants and complaints; be patient and at the same time determined with them; never lose sight of your rank as an officer and consequently a superior ... show that you have confidence in them—lead them well and prove to them that you look upon them as brave men and faithful soldiers—and they will die for you! ... But abuse them; neglect them; place no confidence in them; show an indifference to their wants and comforts—and they are very devils!'

Hervey has a moving story, which he tells at length, of one Mir Imam Ali, of the rifle company, who had been devoted to his company commander. In action in Java this officer was hit by two musket-balls; one was in his shoulder and one had broken his leg. He was helpless on the ground and our troops were retreating. 'Imam Ali came to his rescue, stood over his body, kept the enemy at bay with his rifle ... His unerring aim, his manly bearing ... checked their advance.' His comrades, who had been retreating, were now reinforced; they rallied and drove the enemy back; the company commander was saved. 'The noble Imam Ali' was promoted and the officers gave him a beautiful gold medal. But he was spoilt; everyone made a fuss of him, the brigadier asked him to his house when he had guests to dinner, displayed him and boasted of his courage. There was jealousy among other sepoys and perhaps plots to lead him astray. He took to drugs; he conceived some grudge against the major commanding the battalion. At firing-practice one day he was noticed to be careless and firing indifferently; he was reprimanded, and gave an insolent reply; he was told to appear next morning before the commanding officer. As the parade came to an end and the men marched off, a shot was fired from the ranks which killed the brigadier. It was Imam Ali, who had meant to shoot his commanding officer. Hervey saw him next day in the guardroom; he said he had not known what he was doing and was deeply penitent at having killed a man who had shown him nothing but kindness. 'But we shall meet in Paradise and he will forgive me,' he confidently affirmed. But he broke down when he was visited by the captain whose life he had saved, kissing his feet, sobbing bitterly, begging for his forgiveness. When the time came, he was not afraid to die. 'Put your hand on my heart ... it is absolutely calm and steady,' he said to Hervey, who commanded the guard.

There is something puzzling in the story of Imam Ali. His attachment to the brigadier, to the captain whose life he saved and to Hervey are expressed, but no reason is given for his extreme hostility to the major whom he meant to kill. If it was merely that he was an unsympathetic or bullying character, it is surprising that Hervey does not say so; he does not mention his name and it would have made a point on which he is always insistent. When Victorians are reticent, it is often a sexual scandal they are hiding. It seems possible that the major and Imam Ali had fallen out over a woman; that would be in keeping with his character. It was such men as Imam Ali—men of courage and strong passions, men who were proud and capable of fierce resentment— who were commanded by boys straight from England, often not more than fifteen or sixteen when they arrived. 'I have known such youths (truth obliges me to include myself amongst their number) order about and not unfrequently use harsh and unbecoming language to venerable native officers, whose silver beards and breasts covered with medals spoke of many a campaign and services rendered to the state before, probably, even the stripling's sire was in existence,' wrote Bellew, who came to India before the Pindarry War of 1817. Such youngsters reflected the fashion of Anglo-Indian society. As they grew older, they learnt very often to admire and like soldiers of the kind they knew, if not, as a rule, Indians in general. And they would perhaps say with Hervey: 'Behold the sepoy in the field, or the line of march, in the siege ... How patient under privations! How enduring of fatigue! How meek and submissive under control or correction! How fiery in action! How bold in enterprise! How zealous in the performance of his duty! How faithful of his trust! How devotedly attached to his officers and colours!'

2. The Good Old Days

Although most of the English in India made a sharp distinction between the sepoy, whom they trusted, and the rest of the population, of whom they believed nothing good, there was none the less a continuing deterioration in relations between officers and men. But this was a much more gradual process than has been sometimes supposed. In the eighteenth century the English had been less self-confident than they were later, and with good reason, for again and again it was touch and go; until Assaye and Laswarree it was far from clear who would come out the victors. They were not yet established as superiors and conquerors. Their attitude to the sepoys changed steadily. At first, it was assumed that their ways and thoughts were so completely undecipherable to Europeans that they must be commanded by their own officers. In military dispatches, there is at first a note of surprise when they do well; this gradually disappears until it is accepted without question that, except for the Royal regiments and the Company's Europeans, they are much the best troops in India. Their fidelity is praised to the skies, and if this indicates some awareness of the extent to which we depend on them, that uneasiness is kept well below the surface. Increasingly, they are taken for granted. And confidence increases as danger recedes.

After the Third Maratha War, the frontier had moved up to the Sutlej, and south of the frontier there were no enemies we could not feel confident of beating. With confidence came arrogance. Of this we have seen some examples, deplored by the more sensitive and thoughtful. There began to grow a myth of the good old days, when it had not been like this at all, when British officers had been heroes who lived close to their men, talking round the camp-fire about their affairs, understanding everything they said and always ready to hear their grievances. Each generation of young men from England heard this from their seniors when they arrived; they believed it by the time they were old enough to regard themselves as another generation from the juniors to whom they passed it on.

Like many myths, it contained truth. There was a change, but it was less dramatic than it sometimes seemed to the old major who remembered the glories of his youth. Many factors contributed to the change and one of these was an unforeseen consequence of the reorganization of 1796. This brought to an end the old system of command by native officers; there was now direct command by British officers which covered all aspects of the soldiers' lives. Battalions were now linked in pairs in regiments, the regiment of two battalions having approximately the same number of British officers as one battalion of British troops. Thus, while one of the King's battalions had 44 officers, a battalion of native infantry had 22 or 23, according to where the colonel was listed; there was one full colonel for the two battalions. With minor variations, this lasted till the Mutiny. Each battalion had a lieutenant-colonel and a major, four captains, eleven lieutenants and five ensigns. At this stage, there were eight companies to a battalion and thus there were sixteen officers below field rank, two to a company, and it should normally have been possible for one British officer at least to have been with each company, a captain or one of the senior lieutenants being the company commander, with a subaltern in reserve. There were ten subadars and ten jemadars to a battalion, so normally a company should have one of each. Perhaps it was when this system began that the myth was nearest the truth.

But the change had an effect on the Indian officers which only gradually became apparent. At one time there had been one subadar to four jemadars; the difference in rank had meant a difference in function and the subadar had been a company commander, the jemadar a platoon commander. Now there was little difference in function, but much in pay; the subadar's pay was twice the jemadar's, and, his pension being in proportion, it was the aim of every havildar and jemadar to serve on as long as possible in hopes of the higher rank. Further, whatever the rank, there was a jump in pension at forty years' service. Men stayed on till they had fifty years' service. But to a man of ambition and ability, there was no real increase in responsibility. Since the time of Yusuf Khan, who had commanded all the Company's sepoys in Madras and had tried to set himself up as an independent prince, there had been a steady decline in the prospects for an Indian officer. To meet this, the rank of subadar-major was introduced in 1818, and later, in 1837, the Order of British India, and the Indian Order of Merit with three grades and additions to pension—but this did not alter the fact that an Indian officer was now firmly in place as junior to the youngest of British officers; he could never command more than a company, and that only temporarily. He rose from the ranks, and his education and outlook were usually limited.

In the Bengal Army, it was often argued that the soldier was a natural gentleman, coming from 'yeoman' stock and endued by birth with high status arising from his caste. British ideas about society were thus applied to Indian, and were slightly but subtly misleading. Arguing that it was unnecessary that an Indian officer should know how to read, Sleeman wrote: 'The Rajpoot, the Brahmun and the proud Pythan ... is rated as a gentleman, by his birth, that is caste, and by his deportment in all his relations in life.' On the other hand, Lieutenant-General John Briggs, whose experience had been chiefly in Madras, wrote that to begin with the Indian Army had 'consisted of two classes, of which all armies to be effective must be and always have been composed: one class derived from the better order of society, accustomed to command the services of domestics and underlings; and the other class drawn from the lower grades, who are from infancy habituated to obedience and taught to respect the upper class.' But, in his view, this had been changed when British officers had take direct command; the position of the native officer had been reduced an no more of the old class now entered the service. He makes the familia point about the 'grizzled veteran covered with wounds, who had bee commanding troops with distinction before the stripling now com manding him was born'. When this is all they have to look forward to men of good family will not come into the army. General Brigg argued that the kind of native officer of his day was an expensive luxury and that it would have been better to introduce cadets of good family and education with prospects of promotion to commissioned rank in two years' time—but he was sixty years too soon.

What emerges from all these arguments is that progressively, as the century wore on to the Mutiny, the native officer became less of an ally and more of a foreman—really an overpaid sergeant, as General Briggs had said. The old type of native commandant, whose function disappeared in 1796 and whose loss some bewailed, might have developed into a colleague but he might also have become a rival. The new native officer was a subordinate, if an honoured one. He was emphatically much closer to the men than to the British officers. He was the men's leader, and if officers took the trouble to talk to him and could establish a fairly relaxed relationship, they would have some chance of knowing what the men were thinking and the whole tone of the battalion would be improved. Nothing was more likely to contribute to that kind of understanding than shared recreations, and here too there was a gradual change.

In 1796 an officer who joined the Company's army had not much ground for hoping that he would see his family in England again. Walter Badenach, one of the earliest of those diligent officers who spent their retirement in composing controversial pamphlets, painstakingly compiled tables from the annual returns of the Bengal Army which showed that, between 1796 and 1820, only 201 officers retired to Europe on pension while 1,243 were killed or died on service. As the years passed, the chances of retiring to Europe improved, while furlough became more common. After seven to ten years' service, an officer who could afford it—which was not usually the case if he was married—began to expect the chance of two or three years' absence. Sea-voyages became shorter; in 1790, a voyage to England might take six to nine months, but by the late 'thirties, steamships were coming into use and the overland route was opened; passengers took ship to Alexandria and travelled overland to Suez, halving the distance by sea. By the 'forties the journey to India could take weeks where it had taken months and all mail came by this route. These improvements brought England nearer and changed the outlook, the recreations and the habits of many officers. There were book clubs and magazine clubs in all but the smallest stations; there were ladies to call on, amateur theatricals and balls to take part in. Men could go on leave to 'Simlah, with its romantic scenery, lovely climate, and a thousand gaieties ... where nice young men, decorated and padded ... sport their kid gloves and patent leather before the loveliest of the never-ceasing importations.'

The hookah had been universal; it gave way to the cigar and became the mark of the eccentric old buffer. And this is symbolic of the change of outlook. At the beginning of the century, the 'griffin' — the recent arrival from England — was a stock figure of fun in Anglo-India; he fell off his horse, he shot the wrong birds, he speared domestic pigs, he produced comic situations by using the wrong words in Hindustani and by misunderstanding Indian customs. New arrivals continued to do these things and the joke persisted for a hundred and fifty years, but it became more and more attenuated. The term 'griffin' — which had figured so constantly in the memoirs — fell out of use, together with the expressive adjective 'griffish', applied to the kind of behaviour which the griffin soon sought to avoid. By the 'thirties and 'forties, at any rate in Calcutta and Madras, though to a lesser extent up-country, it became more and more fashionable to admire what came from England and to eschew everything 'black'; increasingly the figure of fun became not the griffin but the peppery colonel with his hookah, his mulligatawny and his Indian mistress.

At the beginning of the century, an officer's eyes were fixed on the Indian scene. He would go on long shooting trips, taking a few men from the regiment with him; he would go out with some local land-owner, hawking, perhaps, or hunting blackbuck with cheetahs. In the station, he would sometimes wrestle with the men or he would fence with them with the single-stick, or there would be cock-fighting or he would pay for a nautch — that is, pay a dancing girl to come and entertain the men. He would sit with his company and find out some-thing of what the songs meant that she sang, or perhaps even learn to interpret the subtle movements of the fingers which are so essential a part of Indian dancing. His recreation, except in Calcutta, was almost bound to have an Indian flavour and was often shared with Indians.

Much of this went on even until 1939. Officers in the 1930s might not play single-stick or wrestle with their men but they took them shooting and might spend an hour or two at a nautch. What had gone, however, was whole-hearted absorption in the Indian scene. It was a gradual process. Regiments would differ; in some, it would be the tradition to spend as much time as possible in shooting, in Indian travel, or in recreations in which the men could take part. In others, there would be little interest in such things, and in every regiment there would be exceptions. But even in those where the old customs were strongest, the chances of uninhibited talk round the camp-fire at night were becoming more remote, and even if an officer's interests were mainly in the scenes around him, it would increasingly be the case that, in the station, the books and magazines which he would see came from England.

At the beginning of the century marriage was the exception, at any rate below the rank of major; senior officers fairly often lived in open concubinage of long standing with Indian women, while the subalterns were perhaps more fickle and various in their attachments. In either case, they were bachelors in the sense that their recreations were largely male. But more and more English women came to India and the moral climate changed. It was not only the 'serious' who regarded liaisons, either permanent or casual, as shocking; the aversion was racial as well as moral. As the 'thirties grew into the 'forties, the fashion in Calcutta, and to a lesser extent in the larger stations up-country, set more and more strongly against everything 'black'. Ladies expressed, says Emma Roberts, an aversion even to 'black' cooks—though they do not seem to have gone so far as actually to do without them. Feminine influence was bound to set the tone in what was called 'Anglo-Indian society' and it is certainly not to be wondered at that Englishwomen regarded with horror any sexual link with Indian women. For once, the 'serious' and the gay were united; the evangelical movements and Victorian propriety joined in condemnation with a strong—if largely unconscious—jealousy of rivals who provided officers with an alternative to matrimony and thus stood in the way of almost the only career open to a lady.

It would be naive to suppose that all contact with Indian women ceased, but it became less and less respectable to cohabit openly with an Indian woman, while casual affairs became less frequent, more casual and less affectionate. The author of *The Blue Pamphlet*, writing in 1857 but drawing on experience in the Bengal artillery which must have gone back to the 'thirties at least, speaks of the necessity of learning Hindustani well and implies that it is usually spoken fluently; a young officer finds it essential for his work, his servants and his sport, while 'his amours are with women not speaking his language'. But in another passage, he takes issue with the 'lamentations' he hears because officers no longer cohabit with native women. 'That they were more respected [when they did] I entirely deny ... no people on earth can better distinguish the gentleman from the sham.' Thus he distinguishes between 'amours' and 'co-habiting', and regards 'co-habiting' as a thing of the past and as, even in the past, the mark of one not 'a gentleman'—one of the most severe of Victorian judgments.

There is an earlier Bengal tradition, mentioned in the memoirs of William Hickey and others, of Indian kept women who were merely servants, who lived in quarters in the compound and were conducted by the principal servant to the master's bed at night. This custom did not improve understanding between the races; not much conversation can have taken place, in Hickey's case at least, since he had very little knowledge of the vernacular. But it was a different matter if a man took an Indian woman to live in his house and scold the servants; it was not marriage, she was not an equal, it might well lead to corruption and favouritism over promotion, but at least he was not aloof, he did talk Hindustani off duty. It was this that was beginning to disappear in the 'thirties under the combined attack of evangelical piety and racial superiority.

This was one more element in the gradual movement of officers apart from their men and towards a more rigid and formal relationship. Another arose directly from the organization of the army and the rapid expansion of the Empire. The army consisted of regiments; every officer below the rank of colonel had his place in a regiment. But from 1800 onwards the army was expanding into special services; officers were required for departmental duties such as collecting rice or bullocks, looking after cantonments and issuing stores. Still more demanding were the calls of the civil administration. More and more districts came under direct British rule; there were nothing like enough covenanted civilians—that is, members of the Honourable East India Company's Civil Service, the parent of the Indian Civil Service; there was besides a feeling that in the first years after annexation, there might be work for which a soldier was better suited. There were also states where a British representative was needed, not only the great ambassadorial posts with the principal states, but many lesser ones. An officer might be sent to some state no bigger than an English county, where the raja was a minor and he must build up an inheritance for the boy to step into, coping as best he could with a jealous mother, ambitious uncles, scheming Brahmans and an oppressed peasantry for whom no one would care if he did not. Meadows Taylor, for example, after very few years of military service went to such a post for the best part of his time. Sir Thomas Munro, one of the great glories of the British in India, eventually Governor of Madras, left his regiment for civil employ before he was thirty; Sir John Malcolm, less illustrious only than Munro, was another who spent almost his whole life in civil posts, ending as Governor of Bombay; Sir Henry Lawrence was another —but the list could go on for pages. In addition, there were what we should now regard as legitimate staff appointments—quartermasters and adjutants to generals commanding brigades and divisions. Men for all these posts were 'on the staff' and stayed on their regimental lists.

Badenach in 1826 calculated that a battalion of native infantry had, on average, only eight or nine out of twenty-three or twenty-four officers present. In 1848 it seems to have risen to about fourteen, but of these some would be sick or on casual leave. Throughout the whole period up to the Mutiny, not less than one-fifth of the officers would be absent on the staff, while if the number on furlough was added, the proportion absent was at least one-third, and it was often much more. Compared with a Royal battalion of the same strength, one of the Company's native battalions had seldom as many as one-third the number of officers. This could only work well if the British officers had been of the highest quality and had been able to delegate much of their work to subadars and jemadars, who were picked for outstanding qualities. But in fact the native officers rose by seniority and as we have seen were far too old when they reached commissioned rank. What was worse, the road for an ambitious British officer led away from the regiment. Political employment was much better paid than regimental, and it was the general view that a man stayed in his regiment only if he had neither the interest nor the ability nor the luck to catch a great man's eye. He was looked on as a failure. If two or three senior men, out of a dozen or less with the regiment, felt they were failures and let things go then there was likely to be apathy and discontent all the way down. What is on the whole surprising is that this was not the case more often.

Thus the myth of the good old days contained an important truth. There was a hardening between officers and men, a loss of sympathy, a loss of zest and of warmth. It was not universal; though there were spots of canker here and there, the tree stood, green leaves grew; affection between individuals survived, pride in the regiment continued. But let us look in more detail at the evidence of one man.

3. The Old Field Officer

One valuable witness is J. H. Stocqueler, whose book, *The Old Field Officer, or The Military and Sporting Adventures of Major Worthington*, professes to be the memoirs of 'the best sportsman, orientalist, billiards-player and cook ... in short, the best *fellow* ... in the Karreebhat Rangers'. In a brief introduction, Worthington persuades his old friend Stocqueler to be his literary executor. This happens some time around 1830, over a dinner in Calcutta, at which 'mango fish' (a kind of smelt) with butter and potatoes are followed by roast kid, cutlets with curry sauce, curried chicken, snipe, ortolans, sweetbread, tarts, jellies and Stilton; the drink is iced champagne, claret and Hodgson's Pale Ale, and the dessert mangoes, Cabul grapes, oranges, almonds and raisins. The name of Worthington's regiment is, incidentally, a joke, because it means the 'Curry and Rice' Rangers. Stocqueller undertakes the task and publishes the memoirs in 1853.

Worthington's adventures begin with his arrival at Calcutta in 1803. He goes through some of the usual experiences of a griffin—in short, is 'properly griffed'—and is soon posted to the cadet establishment at Baraset, a few miles outside Calcutta. This experiment in training cadets was an utter failure, abandoned after a few years. Several hundred cadets, their ages between sixteen and nineteen, were assembled under a commandant, an adjutant and two lieutenants, with one drill sergeant. The idea was to put them through a course of training and study similar to that at the Royal Military College, which had been recently founded in England by the Duke of York and which was to move in 1812 to Sandhurst. At Baraset there were nothing like enough officers or sergeants and it was a fatal mistake to collect in one place young men of that age, 'full of reckless high spirits and with no intention of studying', unless they were going to be kept hard at work under strict discipline. The cadets had little to do and no one seems to have cared to see that they did it; they are described by Worthington as in a continual uproar, blowing coach-horns and bugles, baiting jackals with pariah-dogs, fighting cocks, shooting kites and crows. The great aim is to spend money in Calcutta, but 'debts and extravagance are the least of the evils.' 'Drinking, coarse language, vulgar amusements and gaming' are what the cadets learn; to run up debts is the smart thing and a creditor who comes out from Calcutta to ask for his money is roughly handled and ducked. 'After the ruin of many promising young men and the premature death of not a few', after 'much disgrace and shame, at the bar of the Supreme Court and in debtors' jails', the college was broken up in 1811.

Worthington managed to escape from this nightmare after five months and went to do duty with a regiment at Barrackpore. Here the adjutant and sergeant-major divided the work of the regiment, the other officers spending most of their time on amusements. Parades which all officers had to attend were few, 'yet the men were never in finer order—and such men too!' It was 'quite a sight to observe their fine statures, erect gait, broad and ample chests and well-turned arms' but, nowadays, he adds, there is a gradual deterioration in strength and stature.

Here it may be added that 'the handsome, manly appearance' and 'becoming costume' of sepoys and servants from Northern India is a constant theme with newcomers in the early part of the century. Bellew makes the point as soon as he arrives from Madras, and constantly returns to it; he mentions their 'well-chiselled manly countenances' and speaks of a man whose turban has been knocked off replacing it on 'his noble-looking head'. Emma Roberts speaks of the 'fine, tall, splendid-looking men' she saw in Delhi. It is, of course, still the age of Byron and the newcomer, the artist, and a sprinkling of those who made their lives in India saw the Indian landscape, as well as the Indian countenance, in romantic terms. Landscapes have a Greek or Italian air, whether they are drawn or described in words, and many writers break from time to time into a little set-piece expressing rapturous delight at what is strange and exciting—whether at the hawks and hunting-leopards of feudal retainers in the streets of Delhi, or at flowers and butterflies in the Bengal countryside. But let us go back to the regiment to which Worthington was attached as a cadet.

The commanding officer kept open house. His breakfasts were public; there were few married officers and most of the bachelors attended. There were others—it sounds as though they were captains or senior lieutenants—who took it in turns to act as 'red lions', which meant that they provided open house for those who wished to engage in 'manly amusements—riding, leaping, shooting at a mark, throwing a spear, exercising with the broadsword, both in English and native fashion, racing, hog-hunting'. The hosts acted as instructors to the cadets; they were splendid men—'bold, generous and manly'.

But all this ended when Worthington started up-country for Agra. He travelled by boat, with a party of other griffins, who landed in the evening and explored the countryside, making the usual ludicrous mistakes. They reached Lord Lake's army after the victorious campaign of which Laswarree was the crown, just as the news was coming in of Monson's disastrous retreat. Worthington heard of this from those who had been through it and had just returned; he learnt of the gallantry of the Bengal Native Infantry in retreat, of Monson's personal courage but ineptitude as a general. But there was a lull now in the war and he had time to see the Taj Mahal by moonlight and to visit Fatehpur Sikri—which he 'almost' preferred, for its more masculine austerity. He has indeed a good deal to say about Muslim architecture, but soon comes back to the war. He was in time for the opening of the new campaign as the rains of 1804 came to a close in October.

It is a time of year when the world sparkles every morning with a new freshness; the damp steamy oppression of July and August are finished, a delicious sharpness creeps into the air at night; there is no dust as yet, the first wheat is springing, and there is the certainty that cold nights and dry sunny exhilarating days will succeed each other for months before the heat comes back. 'I was in a delirium of enjoyment,' writes Worthington (or Stocqueler); he was excited by tent life and the coming of the cold weather, by the 'pomp and precision' of newly arriving regiments, and by the tales of old soldiers who remembered war in the Carnatic and Mysore, in Ceylon and Egypt. He is struck by the cordiality between Europeans and natives, officers as well as privates. He recalls an officer of artillery meeting a jemadar of the 8th Bengal Native Infantry, who had once been the 'native adjutant' of a battalion of golandaz. They greeted each other with 'the frankness and good humour of old soldiers'; they were 'on terms of perfect equality, shaking hands, asking after mutual friends'. All this Worthington watched: 'I was engaged in enjoyment but panting with impatience for action.'

At last, the march begins; there is a vast column of elephants, camels, horses and bullocks with the baggage. Worthington is confident that the Marathas, by adopting a European organization for their infantry and artillery, have lost the mobility which was their great strength and cannot equal us in a pitched battle. But their strategy is still to keep us on the move, to raid, to harass, to avoid battle. The army is forced to move in a formation which can quickly be transformed into a vast defensive square, and this slows their movements. In the end, however, the enemy were brought to battle, at Deeg, which, in Worthington's view, of all British battles in India was next to Assaye the most decisive, the best planned and against the biggest odds. All were eager for action, but on the eve of battle one brother-officer contrived to be alone with Worthington, told him where his will was to be found, and added to it the simple codicil: 'You will be kind to the Begum, won't you?'

After Deeg, he is at the first siege of Bhurtpore, where the enemy use shells captured from the British in Monson's retreat, and British gunners call out: 'Thank you, Colonel Monson' whenever a shell bursts near them. He adds that throughout the siege it was 'reckoned a service of danger' to approach Lord Lake. But apart from these engaging touches, he does not add much to what has been told us by the military historians. Soon after the siege comes a chapter on Oriental literature. Worthington argues that 'dunces speak despitefully of Latin and Greek' and so do those who know nothing of Persian, Arabic and Sanskrit; if most of the criticism is due to ignorance, some is also due to religious intolerance. In fact, 'elegance and poetical imagery' pervade these writings, while 'sound moral doctrines and strength of reasoning are also to be met with'. He deplores the use made of Indian languages by the English. 'The tongue is a precious jewel; a thousand pities that it should ever be polluted by abuse ... But the language I frequently hear used by Europeans (and those too in a walk of life that ought to teach them better) towards the natives is filthy ... the only thing which some care to learn of them is scurrility of abuse.' He ends this significant chapter with a long criticism of the prejudice, dislike and injustice to India of which James Mill was guilty. Mill's history of India, conceived in the name of progress and written in the cold light of reason, decried all things Indian as tainted with superstition and degeneracy, and must have contributed almost as heavily as the evangelical attack to the thoughtless fashion of hostility which became prevalent in Anglo-Indian society.

We must not spend too long on the old field officer, but there is a moment in the Pindarry War which is revealing. He is with a small mixed force which is about to attack a fort. The major in command addresses his men before the action. To the British artillerymen he says, gruffly no doubt: 'My lads, you'll do your duty.' To the sepoys he speaks in Hindustani and at greater length: 'Show what the old *jawān-ka-paltan* can do ... and let us teach these *Rajkumar* rascals what the company's sepahees can do!' *Jawān* is a word we shall come back to; it came into general use after the Mutiny in place of sepoy. It is the Latin *juvenis*, and may mean no more than 'young', but often it means a gallant young man, a warrior, a hero — and this battalion had apparently decided that they deserved the title in this special sense. He appealed to regimental pride and also to regional pride; the enemy were from Rajputana, while the company's sepoys, though many of them were Rajputs by caste, came from Oudh. The appeal was entirely successful.

Worthington was no more immune than others from the passion for staff employment; he succeeded in conveying to Lord Hastings the information that he was 'a tolerable hand at a reconnaissance and a sketch' and he was employed for five years on survey work, making the large-scale maps which covered the whole countryside and which became the basis for the peasant's record of rights and the collection of land revenue. But he disapproved of the system which allowed him to do this; it was taken for granted, he says, that everyone wanted to be employed away from his regiment. He felt rather that 'the regiment of an officer should be his home.' This was not at all the case; on the contrary, the system of detaching officers for 'all kinds of staff employ', which, 'being well paid and often conducting to higher honours is greatly coveted', induces men to look on their corps simply as a starting-point. 'None therefore but those who are without interest ... care to cultivate regimental friendships or to study the comfort, tempers and dispositions of the sepoys.'

There is room for only one more of the old field officer's stories. A friend of his was marching through Central India with his company. They had just done a night march of 23 miles and halted for the day. The officer went out with his gun and was attacked and badly mauled by a lion. There was no other British officer; the sepoys did what they could for his wounds and twelve men volunteered to carry him as quickly as possible to the headquarters of the regiment, where there was a doctor. They stripped off their uniforms; these they left, with their weapons and equipment, to be brought on by the rest of the company, who came on by normal stages under the subadar, taking four or five days. The twelve men took turns to carry the wounded officer; they covered 80 miles in nineteen hours, on top of the previous march of 23 miles. The officer's life was saved, but ten of the twelve became seriously ill. When they recovered, the commanding officer thanked them publicly on parade and spoke to all the officers, begging them never to forget this devotion, which would, surely, induce them to esteem and care for their men.

The old field officer retired in 1839. His regiment was ordered to take part in the First Afghan War and he was again excited at the prospect of action and promotion. But one of the objects of the expedition was to relieve Herat, which was besieged by the Persians; they abandoned the siege and the force was accordingly reduced. Worthington's regiment was disappointed and he decided to 'take what the boys would offer him for the step' and retire. It is clear that his memoirs are lightly disguised autobiography; the string of narrative holding his memories together need not be taken too seriously but the episodes and memories have the ring of truth. He is perhaps slightly idealized; Worthington is what 'every man in arms should wish to be'—the ideal officer of his day. And he is very different from his successors of a century later. Few of them would be recommended as the best orientalist or the best cook in the regiment. One is left with a picture of a genial, slightly sentimental bon viveur, a romantic through and through, not in the least ashamed of enthusiasm, inquisitive about many aspects of life. His own memories and tales about his friends are interspersed with tales of a quite different kind, rather like those gloomy stories of dying drunkards collected by Mr Pickwick and almost as incongruous in their surroundings. These too harp on remorse and deathbeds and include some poor verse with a Byronic and Wordsworthian ancestry. But he had a real interest in people and their customs; he spent, for instance, some time, out of friendliness and curiosity, in the company of a clerk, the son of a British officer and a Begum, who became engaged to a very dark Portuguese girl of thirteen and married her in a ceremony lasting a week, a medley of Hindu and Roman Catholic ritual, in which kitchen Hindustani alternated with pidgin English and Portuguese that was probably just as corrupt. He makes fun of poor Jeffery's pretensions, but a later generation would hardly have spoken to him outside the office.

One of Worthington's enthusiasms, shared by most of his contemporaries, has become extremely distasteful in the 1970s; on leave in Ceylon, he killed 87 elephants in five days, merely cutting off the tails as trophies. Bad weather interrupted the slaughter but he got 18 more before he left. And one other custom a later generation will be glad they are spared; men sang songs of their own composition after dinner—and the tone, though sometimes in the light melancholy vein of Thomas Moore, is often bellicose. A young staff officer, before the departure of an expedition to Persia, sings in the mess:

> Once more the trumpet clangs to war! That blast is widely heard!
> And from its brief repose in peace is the martial spirit stirred;
> The British soldier hears the sound and rises in his might;
> The Sepoy feels the thrill of joy and girds him for the fight!

And before the Afghan War, a young officer sings 'The Song of the Subadar', which begins:

> The valour of our Sepoy sires lives in us o'er again
> The British banner in our keep has never met with stain—
> And as we stood by stout old Lake, hurrah! we'll stand by Fane!

'Impossible', he writes before that disastrous campaign, 'that a large body of troops could take the field with more patriotic fervour or more thorough dependence upon the invincible character of an army knit together by the invisible bonds of brotherhood.' But they were destined for the crows and jackals.

4. Mulls and Ducks, King's and Company's

Some points recur again and again in memoirs and pamphlets. The men who wrote them resemble each other too closely to be written off as freaks; there is a groundwork of common belief. But they are none the less exceptions from the general run of regimental officers, by the mere fact that they survived and because they felt strongly enough to put their thoughts on paper. Bevan, who came to the Madras Army in 1808 and retired in 1839, wrote in his foreword that he 'felt it impossible to reside so long in India without becoming the friend of India.' He mastered several languages, including at least Urdu and Kanarese, and recounts stories he heard sepoys telling each other when they did not suspect that he knew the language well enough to understand; he once disguised himself as an Indian woman and went to watch a play, a satirical farce in which a young English officer was being defrauded by his servants. He spent several periods in civil employ, and when engaged in survey work would invite 'the more intelligent' villagers to his tent after dinner, where he would discuss local affairs and history and sometimes entertain them by paying for a nautch—which he found 'innocent and graceful; there was far more to condemn in one Italian ballet than in all the nautches I ever witnessed'. He would send them away after politely distributing betel nut. He eventually developed very advanced ideas, wanting an Indian House of Commons and an Indian House of Lords of mixed Indian and British membership; he did not want to see India directly under the House of Commons in London, for who would arrange the courses Honourable Members would need in the Hindu Laws of Manu and in Muslim theology? And who would attend them? There were no alternatives but Company rule or native rule.

Such tastes and views were certainly not representative but what he notices of his fellow-countrymen reinforces what we have heard already. 'A great error committed by young officers on first joining the Indian Army is to affect contempt for the soldiers whom they are to command, calling them black fellows, niggers, etc.' On this he is more optimistic than some: 'a few months at a station up-country soon clears the head of all that nonsense.' At Madras, however, 'strict formality and etiquette' are the rule and 'the aristocratic feelings of the English repel all attempts at intimacy.' We hear from him once again of the 'incorruptible fidelity' of the Madras sepoys, of their 'devotion to the service and to their officers', particularly when they have been 'conciliated by a mild, firm and consistent line of conduct.' Their pride in their corps is often 'displayed by exertions greater than those made by Europeans'; he tells of the death of Lt G.B., who was so much beloved that the whole of the Grenadier company to which he belonged begged permission to attend his funeral, though it was twenty miles from where they were stationed. As his coffin was lowered into the grave, many burst into tears; they said they had lost a friend whose like they would never see again. But the affection of the sepoys for individual officers has lately been greatly weakened, by orders which reduce Europeans in their estimation, by innovation and by ill-judged economy. All this we have heard before.

Bevan, like Worthington, belongs to a tolerant generation with its roots in the eighteenth century. He is sceptical about the prospects of converting either Hindus or Muslims, who have an ancient faith of their own; he approves of the old custom of British officers contributing to processions and festivals, Hindu or Muslim; the habit is condemned by many on conscientious grounds but he thinks it innocent, and 'required by the plainest considerations of political and personal expediency'. He notes that officers begin to discontinue the old custom of piling their weapons round the altar at the Hindu festival of Dasehra, to be blessed with their men's by the Brahmans. He went on furlough for the first time after twenty-four years and when he came back, after at least two years' absence, he found things changed much for the worse; 'a knot of very scrupulous individuals had established a species of moral tyranny which could only be propitiated by an occasional sacrifice.' He was distressed at the influence of 'persons who seemed to suppose that a noisy zeal for religion precluded the need for exercising Christian charity'; this new temper had led to harsh sentences on officers whose lapses might have been excused, lowering all officers in the eyes of their men, and contributing to the general loss of affection and good will.

Bellew came to Bengal a few years later than Bevan, just before the Pindarry War. He speaks in the same terms as the others of the language used by young officers and has a vivid sketch of his slightly older friend, Tom Rattleton, acting in command of the company. Rattleton sits smoking with his feet on the table, while the subadar of the company and a naik make a report he does not understand. 'Very good,' he says, between puffs at his cigar, and for some time this satisfies them, but at last the naik enters on a long explanation of some dispute on which it seems that a decision will be needed. 'Orders later,' he says, imperturbably.

The Colonel of Bellew's first regiment has a native mistress. 'That little Delilah makes half the promotions in the regiment.' But 'by all accounts these are the men who square best with Jack Sepoy's notions of a proper commander; these are the men whom they would go to the devil to serve; who know how to treat them in their own way and not your pipeclay rigid disciplinarians, who would utterly extinguish the native in the soldier ... It is splendid to hear the colonel talk to the Jacks ... he can make them roar with laughter or shake in their shoes as he pleases.' Hervey's Colonel at one time always sent an N.C.O. ahead, when on the march, to find the best chess-players in the village nearest his camping-ground. They would be brought to play chess with him and be rewarded generously if they beat him, but received only abuse if they lost. In cantonments, he had in his pay a native whose sole duty was to play chess with him. Bellew has a picture of another colonel who would 'abuse the men till they trembled with rage and indignation' and then lead them across country 'in a steeple-chase style' and once marched them straight into the Jumna. Such colonels at the beginning of the century were, in the eyes of the sepoy, the sole source of promotion and punishment, but step by step their powers were reduced; uniformity seemed important at headquarters and some zealous reformer, pained by the haphazard and untidy variousness he discerned, would decide that centralization was the answer. This might mean that a sentence could not be carried out till the offence was forgotten; men could appeal against the colonel's decision and if a trouble-maker was successful in an appeal there would be little peace in that regiment till he was gone.

The reduction in the colonel's powers is a widespread complaint by the 'fifties. Bellew is supposed to be telling us the story of his early days only; his book is called *Memoirs of a Griffin*. But he published in 1843 some thirty years after his first arrival, and many of his remarks date from his retirement. He compares British and Indian troops: 'Our countryman, the British soldier, possesses an unrivalled energy and bull-dog courage, which certainly, when the tug-of-war comes must, as it ever has done, bear all before it. But justice demands the admission that in many other respects the sepoy contrasts most favourably with him — temperate, respectful, patient, subordinate and faithful — one of his highest principles being fidelity to his salt, to which he adds no ordinary degree of courage and every other requisite of a good soldier.' But we must not take them for granted: 'We may bind them to us by the double link of affection and interest, if we study their feelings — but if inexperienced innovators trifle with their customs, we may find that they shake us off like dew-drops from the lion's mane.'

Another theme which recurs is the difference between the three Presidency Armies. Bellew's griffin, on the voyage from England, meets a Captain Marpeet, of the Bengal Army; they stop at Madras and have an opportunity of seeing various drills and reviews by the Madras Army. Captain Marpeet considered the Mulls very inferior to the Qui-Hyes,* 'by whom they were beaten by chalks.' This needs explanation: the captain's name, in the first place, is a joke, of a special early Victorian Anglo-Indian brand; it means 'assault and battery, a punch-up, an affray'. The 'Mulls' were the Madras Army, from mulmull, a kind of muslin in which the Company once traded, or perhaps from mulligatawny soup. 'Qui-hyes' were the Bengal Army, from the custom of shouting 'Koi hai?' meaning 'Is anyone there?' to summon a servant. The Bombay Army were the 'Ducks', from Bombay duck, a kind of dried fish sometimes scattered over curry.

Of the three Armies, the Bengal soon became the largest; by the 'fifties it had 74 regiments of Native Infantry to 52 in Madras and 29 in Bombay, other arms being in proportion. To the Qui-hyes, it was self-evident that in every way they beat the others by chalks. Their men were taller, of higher caste and of higher social status; the Ducks and the Mulls were glad to get from Bengal recruiting-grounds anyone the Qui-hyes did not want. Qui-hye officers were a little more likely to have private means and distinctly more likely to get into debt. They lived more extravagantly; there were more stations with big cantonments and several regiments; there were more likely to be amusements in the station to attract young officers, who would be a little less likely to settle into a life in which shooting was the only recreation. There was more likelihood for the Qui-hyes of catching the Commander-in-Chief's eye and getting a staff appointment.

Neither the Mulls nor the Ducks accepted this view. Their men might not be so tall but they were hardier under privation and much easier to deal with because the Bengal sepoys had such 'nonsensical

* Accent on the second syllable; it rhymes, more or less, with 'the pie'.

whims and prejudices and fancied grievances', and in Burma (noted Hervey) were far more liable to sickness, largely brought on by starvation, because they would only eat an 'unwholesome mixture of raw flour and sugar and parched rice'. The Bombay Army prided themselves on travelling light, for which they were specially commended by Wellesley. And Sir Charles Napier said: 'I feel fearless of an enemy at the head of Bombay troops. With the Bombay soldier of Meeanee and Hyderabad, I could walk through all lands. They are active, daring, hardy chaps, worthy of Sivaji himself.' Mountstuart Elphinstone, accustomed to the ways of Bombay, wrote when he first met the Madras Army that they 'have neither the comforts of the Bengal Army nor do they rough it like the Ducks.' Hervey, incidentally, mentions that, travelling as a subaltern with his Madras régiment on the march, he is accompanied by his own servants and their hangers-on to the number of twenty-five souls—but in Bengal an ensign would have twice as many.

Bombay also pride themselves on the fidelity of their men. During the French wars, many prisoners went over and enlisted in the French service—Irish recruits, some British sailors, Bengal and Madras sepoys. But when Bombay sepoys were shown captured Bengal and Madras sepoys in French uniform, enjoying luxuries which they could have if they would do the same, they 'answered by abusing the traitors who had forgotten their military oath and deserted their colours and such effect had their noble example on these men that, overcome with shame, a large body of them threw down their arms and quitted the ranks.' And the Mulls were proud of the eagerness with which their men volunteered for service overseas.

'The armies of Madras and Bombay are equal in the field to those of Bengal—so say those of the King's service who have served in all—but the Bengal sepoy has the advantage of a finer person and a more military air,' wrote Emma Roberts. Altogether there was healthy rivalry between the three armies—but Bengal's grounds for superiority were social, while Bombay and Madras prided themselves on hardiness, fidelity and courage. There was a similar rivalry between King's and Company's officers. In this too there was a social element, but originally Company's officers had had serious grievances to complain of. At first a King's officer took precedence over every Company's officer of the same rank and, as promotion was often quicker in the King's service, this might have disastrous results. A captain just promoted and newly arrived in India would be senior to a man who had been ten years a captain and who had had twenty-five years' experience of Indian war. And, since small expeditions with only a few companies continued to be common, he might take command over the more experienced man and lead the force into difficulties the other would have foreseen. One case is quoted of a lieutenant in the King's service only fourteen years *old* who took rank before a Company's officer with fourteen years' *service* and at a critical moment was put in charge of a picket consisting chiefly of Indian troops. For long also there was nothing like a fair share for Company's officers of senior appointments, that is of colonels, brigadiers and above.

Gradually these differences were smoothed out, but an underlying jealousy remained. Even as good-tempered a man as Worthington remarks of Lake—a King's officer, generally much admired—that he had an 'indifferent idea of the degree of military talent to be found in any service but his own' and says tartly that Monson, a King's officer, of course, '*had* to command' that disastrous expedition in the late summer of 1804. Thirty years later Hervey says airily that feeling between Royal and Company's officers is now quite out of date—'such thoughtless boyish nonsense scarcely exists nowadays'—but a few pages later he describes the anxiety of his Madras regiment to impress the officers of a Royal regiment whom they entertain when their paths cross on the march. There can be little doubt that they are conscious of being the poor relations; how, indeed, could it be otherwise? The number of officers present in their mess is usually about one third of those in a Royal regiment and it is more difficult to entertain on the same scale. And though they may try to console themselves with the thought of how uncommon brown a King's officer does sometimes get done by the wily native, their own superior knowledge of the country does not go far with men who have recently been in London, who have British orderlies to wait on them in the mess, perhaps more private means, more of that ability to put a social inferior in his place without being openly offensive at which the British so often excel. It may be done by casual reference to the right place to buy riding boots, to a tailor, to a club, to a country house or a shooting-lunch or a day's hunting; there is no answer to it, but it firmly establishes precedence of one kind between individuals, between regiments, between arms of the service. Cavalry did it to infantry and more fashionable regiments to less.

But there were other standards of preference than social rank and from early days there were young men who chose the Company's service because it gave responsibility at so early an age. The Company's junior officers were 'habituated to act in an emergency with a facility that few subordinate officers in Europe have a prospect of obtaining. Before an officer attains the rank of Captain, he must unavoidably have been in command of parties on distant marches, in the conveyance of stores, in the guard of posts and strongholds, in the business of collecting and menacing refractory chiefs ... and in every other species of duty which can occur.' He might when still a boy command a company sent to bring treasure from a remote district to headquarters; his party might be attacked on the way. Thus he was far less likely to spend long years without any chance of showing what he could do—but he might have to wait longer for rank and pay. It was a pernicious dogma of the financial authorities that young officers should be paid less than a living wage; anything more would encourage them to be extravagant. 'They will only spend it,' they must have argued among themselves. How little they understood young men! Once debt has begun, the feeling that a little more or less makes no difference is irresistible. And in a country where credit was so easy, debt was almost forced on subalterns and even captains, unless they spent a great deal of their time in places where they could draw batta.

We have already seen one occasion in Lord Clive's time when officers were so discontented over batta that they formed a combination which would have been called mutiny if it had occurred among other ranks. There was another in Bengal in 1796, of which the officers thought better and submitted before it had gone very far, and a third, almost as serious as the combination of Clive's time, in Madras in 1809. This was partly about tent allowance, but need never have reached such a pitch had it not been for the impolitic behaviour of the Governor, Sir George Barlow, a man who seems to have aroused universal dislike; he was 'despotic in official matters and displayed cold and repulsive manners in private life'. 'I do not believe he had a single friend in the world,' William Hickey had said of him. At one time, there were whole battalions without officers, and for years there was ill-feeling in the Madras Army over this affair.

Apart from these mutinous combinations, there was always some discontent among officers about batta and half batta. It was far too high in relation to pay and there was bound to be injustice about it because it was supposed to be a compensation for the high cost of provisions and wages in some places, but it was out of proportion to the real difference. A committee which reported in 1831 found that a subaltern on arrival had to find from Rs. 1,500 to 1,800 for equipment and uniform, and unless his guardians had provided him with such a sum he must borrow. He must also insure his life as security for the debt, which increased his outgoings, and with the strictest economy his debt was likely to have doubled before he was a captain. Most subalterns owed six or seven thousand rupees. A man might prevent the debt getting worse while he was a captain, but he had little chance of paying off the principal until he became a major. Much depended on where a man was stationed; expenses increased with the distance from Calcutta but in very few was full batta paid. Everywhere else, it was claimed, a man must live beyond his means, quite apart from the initial debt for equipment. In 1837 the Directors agreed that full batta should be paid everywhere beyond the range of two hundred miles.

from Calcutta, and half batta within that distance. This lasted till the Mutiny, and improved things a little. But it was obviously wrong in principle; the Company should have paid an outfit allowance, raised the pay of junior officers and then cut batta to a more realistic level.

To read the memorials presented in Leadenhall Street would lead one to suppose that all the officers of all three Presidencies were seething with discontent. This is, broadly, the conclusion reached by a most painstaking modern Indian historian, Amiya Barat, who would argue that this discontent must have affected the men and their relations with the officers. But the memoirs do not leave one with the same impression. No doubt debt was general; no doubt everyone signed the memorials and representations; no doubt every one grumbled over his Madeira or his brandy and water. But credit was easy, life was short, men were young and full of animal spirits. Most of them seem to have taken it for granted that pay would be inadequate and debt would mount. If they lived to be majors, they would pay it back—but that was far away. No one can be sure, but the impression that reaches me is that very few brooded over these grievances—though no doubt everyone agreed that they ought to have far better treatment. 'Fun and gaiety to most of us was the apparent object of life,' wrote Hugh Gough, posted to the 3rd Cavalry at Meerut in 1854.

5. Trust, Fear and Interest

Men are inconsistent creatures and their impulses and beliefs contradict each other and themselves. We are trying to discover something about the relationship between officers and men in the old armies of the East India Company. We have been looking, so far in this chapter, at the often superficial comments of men who achieved no great distinction and in this at least represent their brother-officers better than those who did. Let us now turn to the considered forebodings of some of the greatest men of the period. But there is a point to be repeated: in general, the sepoy was taken for granted. You can often read a hundred pages of military and sporting adventures without a hint that the sepoy existed; unusual bag of snipe, a magnificent tiger, the Taj Mahal by moonlight, strange encounter with a bear, horrid murder of a traveller —these are the subjects likely to be enumerated in tiny print at the head of a chapter. And the overall note is one of security: 'there can scarcely be a prettier sight', wrote Emma Roberts, 'than a group of fair children ... seated in the centre of their dark-browed attendants and listening with eager countenances to one of those marvellous legends of which Indian story-tellers possess so numerous a catalogue.'

Contrast that picture, symbol of trust and affection, with the thoughts of some of the best and wisest of soldiers in India. 'We are trying an experiment never yet tried in the world, maintaining a foreign dominion by means of a native army.' 'We delude ourselves if we believe that gratitude for the protection they have received, or attachment to our mild Government, would induce any considerable body of the people to side with us in a struggle with the native army.' 'Two important points should always be kept in view ... The first is that our sovereignty should be prolonged to the remotest possible period. The second is that whenever we are obliged to resign it, we should leave the natives so far improved from their connection with us as to be capable of maintaining a free or at least a regular government among themselves.' 'Even if all India could be brought under the British dominion, it is very questionable whether such a change ought to be desired ... the Indian Army, having no longer any war-like neighbours to control, would gradually lose its military habits and discipline and the native troops would have leisure to feel their own strength and for want of other employment, to turn it against their European masters.'

All these are the words of Sir Thomas Munro, taken from two minutes, written one in 1817 and one in 1822. And Sir John Malcolm, following up Munro's thoughts, wrote: 'In an Empire like that of India, we are always in danger.' Sir Charles Metcalfe, ten years later, continued the discussion: 'Some say our Empire in India rests on opinion, others on main force. It in fact depends on both. We could not keep the country by opinion if we had not a considerable force and no force that we could pay would be sufficient if it were not aided by the opinion of our invincibility. Our force does not operate so much by its actual strength as by the impression which it produces and that impression is the opinion by which we hold India.'

Here it is surely necessary to add something which to Metcalfe in the 'thirties perhaps seemed to go without saying. There were at that time two elements in the 'opinion by which we hold India'. One, as he says, was the widespread, though even now by no means universal, impression that we were invincible; it was not universal, because the Sikh empire still stood, and because the first siege of Bhurtpore and Monson's retreat were not forgotten. But it was equally important that to the mass of the peasantry, there was no alternative that they preferred. They might not feel 'gratitude for protection', but few remembered any previous rule that had been so 'mild'. Certainly there were many princes who would have been glad to be rid of the British, but not one who had any strength outside his own dominions. Our enemies had no wide popular support and no rallying-points. The Mughal Emperor was not an inspiring figure to Hindus, while there was no Hindu flag save the Maratha—and to half India that meant rapine and plunder. Nationalism, in short, was not yet born. The peasant, as one of them told Sleeman, was content if he could expect to find the roof still on his hut when he came home from the fields.

But let us go back to Metcalfe; he went on: 'As long as our native army is faithful and we can pay enough for it, we can keep India in order by its instrumentality, but if the instruments should turn against us, where would be the British power? Echo answers, where? It is impossible to support a sufficient army of Europeans to take their place.' He was commenting on a long minute of Lord William Bentinck's, dated March 13th, 1835, not long before Bentinck left India after seven years as Governor-General. The minute may therefore be taken as summarizing his opinions on the present and his views for the future. It is an appreciation of the threats to India and of the forces available to meet them.

Bentinck was not the greatest of Governors-General, but he has good cause to be remembered. He had had the courage to outlaw the burning of widows, from which his predecessors had in turn shrunk; he had started the proceedings which finished the Thugs and their cult of ritual murder; he had abolished flogging in the Indian army. He had by now been right often enough, in causes that were humane and needed courage, to have healed the scar caused by his recall thirty years before when he had been Governor of Madras. Then he had made the wrong decision about the mutiny at Vellore, to which we shall return. He had been wrong again when he was the British representative and commander in Sicily and had tried to start a new war in Italy. His purpose had been to build a free and united Italy fifty years before Garibaldi, instead of helping Arthur Wellesley to win an existing war in Spain and restore the Bourbons, as he had been instructed by his Government. All this had been youthful indiscretion. Now, still courageous, still incurably humane, still a radical, but much more prudent, he recorded his thoughts on the Indian army. He was himself a soldier and he was advised in Metcalfe by one of the wisest of the Company's servants. His minute not only expresses the thought of the first half of the century but introduces the two great themes of the late Victorian period – the threat from the north-west and the belief that southern soldiers were inferior. If it is finally inconclusive, that is perhaps because some of the questions raised were insoluble.

The internal danger, in one sense, Bentinck thought, was slight. 'There no longer exists a single chief, or even a combination of chiefs,' who can be regarded as a threat. He is not, of course, including the Sikhs in this estimate; they were still beyond the frontier. He then reverts to the thoughts of Munro and Malcolm. 'When one hundred millions of people are under the control of a Government which has no hold whatever on their affections, when out of this population is formed that army on the fidelity of which we rely principally for our preservation, when our European troops, of whose support alone we are sure under all circumstances, are so exceedingly limited in number and efficiency as to be of little avail against any extensive plan of insurrection, then indeed,' he concludes, Sir John Malcolm was right and we are always in danger. And the danger increases with peace and idleness, with the spread of education and of discussion in the Press, 'all of which tend to weaken ... the prestige of British superiority.'

Bearing that in mind, he turns to external dangers. To the north, the Gurkhas have no cavalry or artillery and can never be a threat in the plains; to the east, the Burmese may also be disregarded; attack from the sea could produce only an 'insulated debarkation' which could quickly be dealt with. Only the north-west remained. Here the Sikhs were unlikely to risk an attack so long as Ranjit Singh lived, but there was 'no apparent probability' that his wise policy would be 'inherited by his successors'. Trouble would follow his death. The Afghans were rather a loose confederacy than a nation, and presented no cause for alarm. It was to our interest that this State should 'acquire sufficient stability to form an intermediate barrier between India and Persia.' Dost Mohammad, who had recently replaced by a firmer rule the 'feeble guidance' of Shah Suja, might help to build such a buffer. Wise words, indeed, if only they had been borne in mind! But within four years the most inept of all the Governors-General was to try to dispossess Dost Mohammad by force and was to shatter that famous opinion of invincibility on which all depended.

Persia, continued Lord William, could never be a threat by herself. But, with Russian backing, it would be easy to take Herat and advance through Kabul; we might be faced on the Indus by 20,000 Russian troops and 100,000 Afghans and Persians. The Sikhs might join them and could not resist them; they would hold the Punjab. To meet them, we could find in India 103,000 regular Indian infantry—74 Bengal battalions, 52 Madras and 26 Bombay. We had about 20,000 cavalry, more than half irregular. Of Europeans, there were in India of the King's regiments, 20 battalions of infantry and four of cavalry, and four battalions of Company's Europeans, making 18,000 effective rank and file only. Excluding artillery, this is the entire army, and of course not all could be assembled on the frontier.

Bentinck now considered the quality of the Indian army. He had recently received a report that in the Nizam's forces the men from Northern India—Hindustanis and Rohillas, from what is now Uttar Pradesh—were worth ten or twenty of the others. This, of course, was an opinion, hard to prove and no doubt it would have been questioned. The Bengal Army, all of whom come from these areas, average 5′ 7·82″ in height and weigh just over 9 stone. The men from Madras are an inch and a half shorter and a stone lighter. All that Munro said of the virtues of Madras troops may have been true thirty years ago, but now, wrote Bentinck, it was not; 'their physical defects and delicate frame render them very inferior to the Northern Hindostanis.' Could they stand up to a Russian enemy? He was afraid they might not, partly from want of physical strength and partly from want of 'moral energy', by which is presumably meant a cause to fight for. 'Proverbial as is the fidelity of the native soldier ... more especially when he is justly and kindly treated, still we cannot be blind to the fact that many of those ties which bind other armies to their allegiance are wholly wanting in this. Here is no patriotism, no community of feeling as to religion or birth-place.' None the less, north Indians, mixed with a 'due proportion' of British troops, might be as good as Portuguese or Neapolitan troops under British or French direction. 'But of the sepoys of the south of India ... I entertain no such hope.'

What is the 'due proportion' of British troops? They should really be not less than one-third of the strength of the Indian troops, but we have at present less than one-sixth — 18,000 to 120,000. He would therefore increase the number of British troops at once — but he illogically asks only for two battalions of infantry and a regiment of cavalry, which would still not bring the British troops up to one-fifth of the Indian. The only other reforms of any consequence which he suggests are two. The Bombay Army should end its separate existence, the Hindustani element coming to Bengal and the rest staying in the Bombay Presidency which would be reduced to the status of a District under a major-general. And throughout the Indian army, he would reduce the number of British officers. 'Opinions differ much,' he wrote, 'but I think things were never better' than when they were only three or four officers with each corps. 'The connection between European and native officers was much closer, their dependence upon each other greater and a more cordial intimacy existed between all ranks.' This is the system in the irregular cavalry, which is 'more what it ought to be than any other arm'. Men of good families, of high caste and of good courage, who will not enter our ranks 'from dislike of our rigid discipline and from the fear of personal disrespect from our young inconsiderate officers' will enter the irregular cavalry. This force should be increased to 20,000 men and it would 'afford us all the advantages, moral and military, which the Russians have derived from the Cossacks'. These conclusions do not go very far and seem strangely tame in the light of his final opinion, delivered at the end of the minute, almost as an after-thought: 'I fearlessly pronounce the Indian army to be the least efficient and the most expensive in the world.'

Perhaps that remark was added in an impulsive moment of reversion to the character which had been such an irritation to the great Duke a quarter of a century earlier. The minute is certainly not a masterpiece; the figures omit artillery altogether and also irregular infantry—which might not much affect the general argument but does spoil the attempt to establish some proportion between British and Indian troops. The contempt for southern troops is not supported by the facts; perhaps the memory of Vellore had not altogether ceased to pain him. Among the pamphleteers, at least, the weight of opinion was against him on the question of reducing the number of British officers. But the main point is inescapable: the utter dependence of this mighty structure on men whose fidelity was taken for granted. Holt Mackenzie, a civilian of 'large and liberal views', who told his civil officers to go out with their guns and bring back information with their game, had expressed the position admirably: 'I do not think the sepoys have any attachment to the English as a nation … [they] have a great deal of attachment to their officers but this rests upon personal character … so long as they are well-paid they will have a strong sense of the duty of being faithful to those who so pay them … [this] is only to be overcome by some powerful cause of discontent and excitement.'

The Empire depends on the fidelity of the sepoy and this in turn depends on the personal character of his officers—and on the absence of some powerful cause of discontent.

IX

Men

---

1. The Aura of Victory

We have been considering how officers looked at the subtle bond between themselves and the men they commanded. What stands out is that those in the positions of highest responsibility saw how much the power of the British in India depended on the fidelity of the sepoy army, but saw also that they could see no certain way of retaining it. Really, it could only be done by good pay and good officers—and good officers meant men who combined kindness and consideration for their men with firmness and a sense of their own distinct position as leaders. So far there had been enough good officers to outweigh the poor and indifferent, with the result that most of the British in India, for nearly all the time, had come to take the sepoy for granted. This in itself was dangerous, and particularly so when new arrivals from England were increasingly likely to have been affected by religious intolerance or by a national arrogance which was sometimes expressed in terms of colour.

It is much harder to see how things looked from the point of view of the men. One difficulty can best be made clear by my own memory of a conversation with a villager in Rohilkand. It took place more than a hundred years after the period we are thinking about, and up to a point it is very like the kind of conversation with native officers and soldiers that Sleeman recorded. But my conversation took a turn impossible in Sleeman's day and thus displays a characteristic Indian attitude to authority which is likely to have been stronger in Sleeman's day than now. It occurred in 1957, ten years after Independence. I stopped my car on the main road, walked half a mile through the fields to a village, chosen at random, and began to talk to a man I found sitting in front of his house. I deliberately gave him a lead. I said that I saw there was electric power in the village now, which would not have been the case ten years ago, and this was surely an improvement; he agreed. I made one or two other points of the same kind and he continued to agree. What about prices, I asked at last, and what about taxes? Well, of course, they were high, but what could anyone do about that? It was the way of the world. Then have you no complaints? No, he was very satisfied with all the Government did — except for one little thing. At the corner down there, water collected in the rains and his bullock-cart always stuck; could I put that right for him? But who do you think I am, I inquired. He did not know — but I must be some kind of Commissioner or Collector or I would not be asking questions like these. I explained that, though I had once been an official, now I lived in England and was just someone who went about the world writing books. His whole manner changed at once; in that case, he said, everything is frightful. What use to me is electric light or a smooth road for motor cars? Taxes and prices are what matter to me and they are much too high — and so on.

Before Independence, no Englishman in India could wholly throw off the official. Even if he was not himself paid by the Government, some faint flavour of officialdom clung to him. He would be told what the speaker thought would please and flatter him. There might well be no deliberate intention to deceive, no more than a wish to propitiate and to be agreeable. Or, as in my conversation, there might be a concentration on one small practical end which could be achieved. Everything else was designed to produce the right mood. Naturally, much of what officers heard from their men in the days before the Mutiny would be of this kind; there was a change after the Mutiny. There are fragments of verbal evidence that are free from this taint — scraps overheard through the canvas of a tent, perhaps — but very little. What men said to their officers can, however, be checked against certain facts. There is also the story of Sita Ram, but that we shall keep for another section.

Certain ideas, generally current in India but formulated rather differently in Europe, are helpful to understanding the men of the Indian army. We have talked already about honour and caste. Two more need to be looked at. The first is represented by the word *iqbāl*, a word of Arabic origin which in Hindustani has the dictionary meanings 'prosperity, good fortune, prestige, auspices' — but none of these quite conveys the full flavour. *Iqbāl* is not only good fortune but *continued* good fortune, due to some happy combination of the stars, and some quality in the person possessing it which comes from heaven. If, after an occasion for anxiety, such as a visit by the Viceroy, one remarked to an Indian subordinate that it all went off very well, he would reply: 'By your Honour's *Iqbāl*'. It was *your* aura of success that had won the day, something in your destiny, your emanation of confident good fortune, not his humble efforts and painstaking organization.

In the first part of the nineteenth century — until the unjust and disastrous war of 1839 — this word is constantly used of the East India

Company. 'By the *Iqbāl* of the Company Bahadur', war after war was brought to a successful conclusion, disaster after disaster was averted. This habit of victory, due to the Company's star, this aura of triumph and success, was what Metcalfe called the opinion of our invincibility. But seen from the Indian angle, it was less an opinion, a matter of calculation, than a matter of destiny and the favour of heaven. It was unquestionably one reason why men came to the colours and stayed faithful to their oath.

With this idea goes another, closely connected, but operating rather for discontent. As the century progressed, more and more often Indian visitors would complain to senior officials that life under the British was humdrum. Something expressed by the Hindustani word *raunaq* had disappeared. Its literal meaning is 'splendour, lustre, brightness'; here, perhaps, it means 'sparkle, change, excitement, romance, pomp and ceremony'. In the old days, your village might be liable to be burnt by brigands; the tax-collector might tear the rings from your ears or pull the nails from your fingers if he thought you were concealing something —and these things did not happen now. But now the tax-collector came with a depressing regularity and apart from his visits not much else did happen. There were no processions; if you saw the Governor he was liable to be 'a man in a black coat in a buggy'; the raja had flashed with silks and jewels, he had worn a plumed aigrette; he had ridden on an elephant caparisoned splendidly in scarlet and cloth of gold. And the uncertainty of the raja's whims had added to life's excitement. In the old days, the stories did sometimes come true: the beggar might be given a robe of honour and made vizier; the favourite might suddenly be condemned to be trampled to death by an elephant. In the army today, it would take forty years to become a subadar with a pension of forty rupees a month—a long wait and a fair reward but you could not carve out a kingdom for yourself nor even dream of it. There was no splendour, no sparkle. No Viceroy scattered gold coins or moved among his people in disguise like Harun-ar-Rashid; no one was impaled for a careless word. All was slow, drab, reasonable and colourless. The sparkle of the past was remembered, the misery forgotten.

Things were done for the sepoy, as the century advanced. Pay had long been seven rupees—say fourteen shillings—a month; in 1834 it was increased by one rupee a month after sixteen years' service and by two rupees after twenty. Against this, there were stoppages for clothes, limited to five rupees a year, and also for washerman, barber and sweeper, shared by the company; they came to less than six annas a month per man. The sepoy could count on six out of his seven rupees. It was the general rule in the Bengal Army to send remittances to the family, whereas in Madras the family followed the soldier and lived with him. Most Bengal men seem to have kept three rupees a month to live on; some managed with less. It is said that a man sometimes had only one and a half rupees in his pocket at the end of the month; in that case he must have sent a remittance to his family of four rupees or more.

How could anyone live on such sums? A man will eat two pounds of grain a day, but grain is of different kinds. Rice is more expensive than wheat in Northern India, where it is regarded as a luxury for the rich. Wheat comes next to rice and then there are the millets, which until lately were the staple food of the peasantry. The millets are like the rye which in eastern Europe was the main food of peasants in the nineteenth century; the value as food is not less than wheat, but it makes a coarse, dark, bitter flour. Men, and for that matter livestock, reject it if they can get wheat. Chapattis—flat unleavened pancakes—made from either of the two common millets taste not unlike rye bread; they are not unpalatable to nibble, but they are coarser in texture than rye. Like the Mediterranean peoples, Northern Indians like a relish to go with their grain—vegetables, spices, and of course salt—and they add pulses for variety. But it is the price of grain that is important; it is nine-tenths of the cost of living.

Let us take it that a Bengal sepoy usually sent home three rupees and kept three. An order of 1847 provided for the Bengal Army a special allowance if the price of 'provisions' rose above a level at which the sepoy's 60 lb of grain for the month would have cost about two and a half rupees. But that price was never reached in the five years that followed, so one can assume that, incredible though it seems, men could live on these sums. Indeed, Sleeman was told that some of them lived on two rupees, in order to send more home, and two rupees was in fact, as late as the twentieth century, the usual pay for a grass-cutter. The price of grain is usually reckoned by the amount which can be bought for a rupee; usually a rupee would buy about fifty per cent more millet than wheat, and generally in the nineteenth century two rupees would buy about sixty pounds of wheat or ninety of millet. As late as the 'twenties and 'thirties of the twentieth century, cultivators in Uttar Pradesh lived mainly on the millets, selling their wheat for cash. All the accounts of military operations in the south hinge on rice, but the Rohillas and men of Oudh—nine-tenths of the Bengal Army—would not have eaten rice. Their staple would be wheat or millet and if they could not afford wheat they would eat millet. They bought their supplies from a regimental shopkeeper who must surely have stocked several kinds of grain.

This matter of food and prices is important because there are two incontrovertible facts which no one can get round. The first is that service in the army was popular; nowhere in the world, Lord William Bentinck thought, could men be recruited 'with such facility and at such trifling expense' as for the Bengal Army. And yet — this is the second fact on which everyone agrees — as the century advanced, soldiers felt more and more that their position had deteriorated, as compared with the golden days of the Pindarry War. Why, in the first place, was the service popular in view of pay which to a modern reader seems incredibly low?

Pay of course is a matter of expectation and it has to be remembered that at this time there were many people, both in Britain and in India, who expected very little. I talked in 1938 to a woman in Berkshire whose husband had never earned more than ten shillings a week, of which one shilling went for the cottage. They never ate 'butcher's meat' except at the harvest supper once a year. In the 'forties and 'fifties of the nineteenth century a British soldier in India after stoppages and deductions was paid at the end of the month less than nine rupees in cash. In Indian villages, it is misleading to talk about 'wages'; landless labourers usually 'belonged' to landowners, not in the sense that they could be sold, but that they, and their fathers before them, were en-titled to protection and food, in return for labour and support. They were retainers, who would plough or hoe or beat for game or carry messages; they saw very little cash. Even as late as the 1930s, when this system was being challenged, in Rohilkand they often received only two rupees in cash every six months, after the harvest was sold.

The sepoys did not belong to the class of retainers; they were Rajputs or Brahmans, the sons of the landowners who kept these retainers. But they too did not use much cash. They lived on what they grew and sold a surplus to pay the land-revenue. So long as they kept out of the law courts, their needs were slight. A remittance of three rupees a month in cash from a soldier son would be very useful. And a pension, even of three rupees, was well worth having. That had been the figure of a sepoy's pension from 1796; he was eligible for it after twenty years' service, if judged unfit for further service. In 1836, on Lord William Bentinck's proposal, the Court of Directors agreed that a sepoy's pension should be four rupees after fifteen years' service; at the other end of the scale, a subadar with forty years' service would get forty rupees a month and a jemadar twenty. Again, during service, soldiers could go on furlough, or long leave, to their homes, and draw pay; a sepoy received five and a half rupees and a subadar fifty-two. When troops went on service overseas, careful provision was made for the payment of allowances to the sepoy's family while he was away and for a pension, if he was killed, to the heir he chose to nominate. This pen-sion was payable for one life to a 'nominated heir'; he might if he wished leave his personal property to someone else. There was a regimental committee supposed to check these nominations quarterly and keep them up to date. Albert Hervey describes in some detail how these arrangements worked in the Madras Army when his regiment embarked for Burma.

All this was quite new to India. The princes of the past had, as we have seen, 'hereditary troops' and hired troops; the former served in recognition of feudal overlordship, the latter were hired for the campaign. Neither had any expectation of a pension. Again, neither the Mughals nor the Marathas paid a man regular monthly pay for the period of his career, nor did they accept any responsibility for him after he left them. The permanence of the Company's service had been a strong point from the first. But like other benefits, it soon came to be taken for granted.

Sleeman describes in 1841 a conversation he had in 1838 with the Subadar-Major of his regiment, a man who had the title of Sirdar Bahadur and had been awarded the Order of British India, who had in short reached the height of his profession. He spoke with enthusiasm of the recent abolition of flogging, and of the extra two rupees for long service. Flogging had been rare in the Indian army; indeed, the conduct of the Bengal Army was in general almost unbelievably good. Thus, from 1825 to 1833, both years included, that is for nine years, among the other ranks of the Bengal infantry, a force of between 50,000 and 60,000 men at any one time, there were only 35 serious cases tried. Of these, 16 were for desertion (not desertion to the enemy, a different offence of which there were no cases), six for mutiny, one for absence, one for embezzlement, one for sleeping on duty and eight for miscellaneous offences. None were for drunkenness or malingering. Flogging was a terrible disgrace; as the Sirdar Bahadur pointed out to Sleeman, once a man had been tied up and flogged, he could no longer perform the anniversary rites in memory of his parents, the distinguishing mark of the head of a family; he was an outcast, deprived of all social and civil rights. Flogging carried dismissal with it, but the double sentence could only be inflicted by a General Court Martial and had to be confirmed by the Major-General commanding the district. A bad soldier had felt he could go a long way before this would happen; now, he could be dismissed by a regimental court martial and dismissal was a punishment much feared. Discipline was the better for the change; the troops had felt the mere possibility of being flogged a terrible degradation.

This was what the Sirdar Bahadur told Sleeman; another old warrior of the same vintage said that now the army had become 'without fear'—and by that he meant without discipline. Perhaps he was talking to an officer known to hold that view. In fact, Commanders-in-Chief had wished for some years to abolish flogging in the native army, and there was much support among Indian army officers for its abolition. Badenach in 1826 had put the arguments strongly; it was not needed, and in many regiments had not been used for three years at a stretch. It degraded individuals and hurt the feelings of the population. But hardly anyone thought British soldiers could be managed without it; it was needed to keep down drunkenness, insubordination and theft. There were therefore many who thought it could not be abolished for Indians, however unnecessary; if British troops were liable to such a penalty, Indians must be too. This was why it was reintroduced by Lord Hardinge ten years later, though used even less frequently; for British troops, it lasted another forty years.

No doubt the Sirdar Bahadur was right in thinking that the abolition of flogging was popular. Nor can there be any question about the extra two rupees for long service. Some men, said the Sirdar, live on the two rupees and send home all the rest; a soldier's pay is at least double that of a day labourer, added Sleeman. Here it should be noted that other writers of the period say with equal firmness that a soldier's pay was no more than a day labourer's and compared unfavourably with a domestic servant's. But neither of these are anything like precise terms; 'day labourer' might mean a man working on the roads and liable to be out of work tomorrow, or it might mean a village labourer, paid in kind, who was more like a Russian serf or a mediaeval retainer; a domestic servant might mean a European officer's cook, who was really a steward as well as chef, who had high pay and made a profit on the shopping too, or it might mean the man who for two rupees a month fetched grass for a horse. In any case, the soldiers were not men who would have worked as day labourers for someone else. The important question was how their earnings compared with the cost of living at home. Since they were able to make remittances and there was no difficulty about recruiting, one must conclude that the pay was not generally inadequate.

But no doubt men became used to the regularity with which their pay came and the continuity of their service and began to grumble. And when the Sirdar Bahadur goes on to tell Sleeman that the army had not asked for the abolition of flogging or for long-service pay and that 'no army in the world had ever masters who cared for them like ours', one begins to wonder how far he is speaking for the men. He goes on to talk about promotion by seniority, which is known, very significantly, as *haq** — right, the legal right to something that is yours. It is 'very cruel and unjust' to depart from 'right' and promote by merit; it leads to ill-feeling, jealousy and unhappiness; it is mere favouritism. Officers are with the regiment too short a time to know what men are really like. Here, one begins to suspect, is the corner

* The word rhymes, more or less, with 'pluck'.

where the Sirdar's bullock-cart sticks in the rains—not that it is a personal point, because he himself has arrived at the top.

Sleeman, as we have seen already, lays great stress on the close family nature of the regiment. A man who behaved badly in the regiment would be disgraced in the eyes of his family and his village; if he neglected his family and sent home insufficient money he would soon be made to feel the contempt of his fellows in the regiment. The Company's army was thus firmly linked to the one abiding element in India—the social system of the village—which had lasted two thousand years and survived the shifting flow of conquest, the consolidation and decay of empires. The link was still young and the question was whether it could be maintained; Sleeman describes the scene in one village in Oudh in 1817 where three generations were native officers, the grandfather, now said to be a hundred years old, having been at Plassey with Clive, while one of his sons, a grey-headed subadar, had been at the taking of Java in 1807. Pensions for old soldiers, family pensions for the heirs of men killed—these, Sleeman thought, 'make British rule grow more and more upon their affections.' The justification for British rule, he continues, rests upon one principle only, that 'it is our wish as it is our interest to give both Hindus and Muslims a liberal share in all the duties of administration ... and to shew the people in general the incalculable advantages of a strong and settled Government ... It is this principle which has made the native army faithful and devoted to its rulers.'

Sleeman in most of this represented many senior officers of his day. He was a man of immense energy, he wrote swiftly and was not always consistent; a genial optimism sometimes overrode dangers which he saw clearly. Other writers point out that the subadar promoted by seniority was too old to be efficient and that his pay was only fifty-two rupees a month, while in civil employment Indians could become civil judges or deputy collectors, with considerable responsibility, earning six or seven times as much. Sleeman mentions, like everyone of this period, the alienation from their men of young officers, who have the 'often very laborious duty' of amusing the ladies by acting, concerts and balls, and who 'betray signs of the greatest impatience while they listen to the reports of their native officers.' He has another point that is new. We employ not one-tenth of the number of soldiers there used to be in the country; no sooner is a native prince who had lived by plunder prevented from preying on his neighbours than his army is reduced to a handful, and there is no equivalent increase in the Company's forces. 'Take this, my brother,' a trooper was heard to say to his horse during the Pindarry War, as he gave the creature a nosebag of gram to crunch, 'take this in the name of Jaswant Rao Holkar, for to him alone thou owest it! Let him be taken and all India will be at peace and there will no longer be any demand either for thy services or mine.' So there were, from the end of that war onward, plenty of men who, the moment they heard a rumour of trouble, began to 'sharpen their knives and twirl their whiskers and mustachios'. What was even more serious, a time came when even the Company's soldiers began to fear that there would soon be no work for them either. This fear was to grow with startling speed after the Sikh Wars.

Almost every British writer up till the Mutiny repeats that Indian soldiers have no sense of nationalism. But that is not to deny that many Indians, Hindu and Muslim, often felt a generalized dislike for all Europeans. At the first siege of Bhurtpore, it was important for the Company's forces to know where, if anywhere, the moat could be crossed without swimming. But reconnaissance was extremely difficult; the garrison were always on the look-out and the whole expanse of water was open to their fire. One morning, the garrison saw three cavalrymen in British uniform spurring wildly towards the fortifications, pursued by a rather undisciplined mob of horsemen, firing in their direction. The three fugitives flung themselves from their horses at the edge of the water and hailed the garrison. 'How do we get across?' they yelled, 'we're escaping from the "bahnshoot Feringhees" — the incestuous Europeans.' The men on the ramparts pointed out the way — and the three horsemen scrambled on their horses and galloped back to be welcomed by their pursuers, whose noisy fire of blanks had now died down. The word 'Feringhee' would apply to a Frenchman as much as an Englishman; 'bahnshoot' implies incest with a sister but is almost as meaningless as the expression used by American troops today attributing incest with a mother. Clearly the men on the rampart thought it natural that the troopers should want to get away from the unspeakable Europeans — and the troopers knew they would. But in fact the pull of the regiment was stronger.

Those three men from the 3rd Cavalry received a reward of five hundred rupees. Undoubtedly in the early days, the hope of prize-money or rewards was a big attraction, to officers as well as to troops, both British and Indian. But in fact prize-money seems almost always to have led to disappointment and discontent. As we have seen, its distribution was one of the causes of the mutinies before Bhaksar in 1764. The theory was that all loot was handed in to a general fund and that it was then distributed in shares according to rank. But there was often great delay in settling the proportions of the distribution and making payment; periods of up to ten years are spoken of. The chances of prize-money grew less and less as the century wore on, because there were fewer fortresses and walled cities to be taken. Further, the proportions in which distribution was made do not seem to have become less unequal. At Seringapatam in 1792 a colonel received prize-money of £297, a subaltern £52 and a British private £3 15s. 9d. a jemadar, by what arithmetic it is not clear, received slightly less than a British private, a subadar twice as much as a jemadar and a sepoy rather less than half. In 1825, after the second siege of Bhurtpore, the Commander-in-Chief received the very useful sum of nearly £60,000, generals about £6,000 and so on down the scale to the subaltern who received about £238, more than four times what he had had at Seringapatam. But the British private had about £4, much the same as at Seringapatam. The officers' share had enormously increased. The sepoy now had rather more than half a British private's share—£2 12s. Here too the officers had improved against the private; a jemadar had £12 and a subadar £28. But a subadar of forty years' service can hardly have felt it right that a lieutenant less than half his age should have eight times his share.

These were irritations. And there was an undercurrent of feeling that in the course of fifty years the status of the sepoy and of the native officers had grown less in his own village. It was not so much economic as a matter of the estimation in which he was held. It arose from changes in the life of the country. From 1796 to 1815—at the height of the golden age—all sepoys of the Company had priority in the Company's judicial courts; their cases would be tried first and it seems not unlikely that they often found that the court was sympathetic to their case. In the dominions of our ally the King of Oudh there was a similar arrangement. This was a great practical benefit to a landowning family and also added to their prestige. Doubtless, after the privilege came formally to an end, memories of it would remain and it would sometimes operate unofficially. In Oudh, there is no doubt that right up till the annexation in 1856, the sepoy had an advantage in the courts and with all officials. A sepoy could go to the British Resident and put his case and if the Resident took it up, the King would be most unlikely to say him no.

But these advantages had been at their highest pitch when the British power was young. As the peasantry came to know more of British ways, they learnt that the sepoy's privileged position as the prop of the Company did not make him certain of the Company's support. His knowledge of foreign ways was increasingly shared by others; he was less feared because it was seen that these conquerors would not permit their soldiers to break the law. Soldiers are seldom held in high honour when peace and the rule of law prevail, and this, from 1817 till 1857, was the case within India. The sepoy was less honoured than he had been but it was still true, as it was not in England, that a man rose in his neighbour's eyes when he went for a soldier.

All would be well so long as officers and men understood each other. There had been occasions, like that at Bhaksar, when unimaginative rigidity on one side or obstinate suspicion on the other had led to something much more than irritation, to a complete breakdown of understanding and then to fear, anger, discontent and blazing mutiny. But these were few and isolated moments; they will be discussed in Part III. For the moment, the fact remained that up till 1839, the Company Bahadur's *iqbāl* was still supreme, and their star in the ascendant; men still flocked to the colours. Let us look at one of them, Sita Ram, the old subadar.

2. The Old Subadar

Sita Ram, the old subadar, was a Brahman of Oudh, from a village in the district of Rae Bareli, near Lucknow. He served 48 years in the Bengal Army, becoming a subadar when he was about 65 years old; he fought in the Nepalese War and the great war against the Pindarris, he was at the second siege of Bhurtpore, he went to Kabul and was there captured and sold as a slave, he was in both the Sikh Wars and the Mutiny. So at least he says in his memoirs. These constitute the only first-hand evidence of the life of a sepoy and it need hardly be said that doubt has been thrown on their authenticity.

The memoirs were published in India in 1873 in an English trans-lation, made by Lt.-Col. J. T. Norgate, who retired in 1880 with the rank of major-general. There was a second edition of this translation in 1880, another in 1911, and a freely edited text came out in 1970. The original manuscript is said to have been written in Hindi, in the Oudh dialect, and finished in 1861. Norgate says that he translated this document into English, with Indian help, and first published it in 'an Indian periodical since defunct' — but this first publication has not been traced, nor has the original manuscript. Norgate says he had some difficulty in persuading the old subadar to put his memories in writing, because he was afraid that his criticisms of the Government might affect his pension, but he yielded at last. In making the translation, Norgate continues, 'I have often been obliged to give the general meanings, rather than adhere to a literal translation of many sentences and ideas, the true idiom of which it is almost impossible to transpose into English.'

Until fairly recent times, it seems to have been taken for granted that these were the genuine memoirs of Sita Ram; they were widely known, because Norgate's English was translated into Urdu and this version was a set book for various examinations. Most British officers of the Indian Government made its acquaintance; they found the subject matter reasonably entertaining and a good introduction to

Indian life as well as language. But was this the genuine work of a subadar, or an ingenious compilation from actual experience, like Morier's book *Hajji Baba of Ispahan*, or Meadows Taylor's *Confessions of a Thug*? Meadows Taylor had played some part in tracking down the Thugs and interrogating them and he thus had a wealth of material at his disposal. With him, 'I breathe when I write' was much the same as 'I write when I breathe', and he threw many stories of ingenious deception and ruthless murder into a novel, which of course reached a far wider audience than the official accounts. He did not pretend it was anything but a romance — but could Sita Ram be the unacknowledged product of many talks with Indian officers linked only by Norgate's imagination?

Of one point one can be tolerably certain. The memoirs show no sign of the spirit which made so many retired officers produce pamphlets proving that what was wrong with the Indian army was too few British officers or too many — or some other panacea. There is no sign of this. If Norgate did perpetrate a deliberate fraud on his readers, it was not to convince them of any special gospel but with the general purpose, which he acknowledges as the reason for his translation, of increasing understanding between officers and men.

The case against authenticity is that there are many inaccuracies about dates and names, that Sita Ram's movements involve too many changes of regiment, that his views on the whole are those a British officer would expect him to hold, and that the whole thing is too good to be true. He rescues a beautiful girl from a Pindarri freebooter who was about to kill her and lives with her happily ever after; he escapes from Afghanistan in disguise; in the Mutiny he commands a firing-party which was ordered to execute his own son; he is in every important war of the half-century except the Burmese.

To me the lapses in memory are arguments in favour of authenticity. I remember another old soldier, fifty years after Sita Ram's death, who came to visit us one evening as we lay on our sleeping-bags in the open, some fifty or sixty miles west of Delhi. I was with two officers from Army Headquarters; we had gone out on Saturday evening to shoot duck and were spending the night near the water to get the evening and morning flights. It was dark; there was only the fire on which we had cooked supper and a hurricane lamp. The glow was just enough to illumine the old man's face; he said he had come because he had spent his life in the army and had heard there were some officers near his village; he wanted to talk of old days. He began gently kneading our calves — a most refreshing Indian attention after a long march. We asked to what regiment he had belonged. He had forgotten the number, but Queen Victoria was their mother. It must have been the 1st Battalion (Queen Victoria's Own), 7th Rajput

Regiment, the same whose colours disappeared after the first siege of
Bhurtpore and reappeared after the second.

Sita Ram, too, hardly ever remembers the number of a sepoy
regiment; the regiments did after all change their whole system of
numbering when he had about ten years' service, but they were
often known to the men by a corruption of the name of an early
commanding officer. Sita Ram names three battalions in this way and
says they were part of the force which marched to Afghanistan by the
frightful southern route through the Bolan Pass. This is wrong, but they
did go to Kabul by the Khyber route and must have been there when
Sita Ram was there; to think they came earlier than they did is just the
kind of mistake that an old man does make. He says that in the
Gurkha War there was a halt till the guns could arrive from Delhi under
Captain 'Hallow' Sahib. This is not the name of the officer who
commanded the artillery train, but it is a version of the name of Hall,
who commanded the detachment of howitzers and mortars; these
came separately from the main train. To remember the officer's name
was not bad after forty-five years. One could give a dozen mistakes of
this kind, which look to me like slight lapses of memory. There are also
occasional remarks to which Norgate draws attention in a footnote as
difficult to understand; for example, Sita Ram refers with approval
to 'true English *sahibs*, not *sahibs* from the hilly island'. Norgate says he
does not know what this means but it suggests to me that Sita Ram
probably thought Ireland was mountainous.

It could of course be argued that Norgate inserted inaccuracies and
mysteries to add an air of verisimilitude. This I find no more convincing
than the argument of Victorian opponents of evolution, that the
Almighty created the world in seven days but put in the fossils to make
it *look* older. As to transfers from one unit to another, these did take
place and a reasonable framework is established if he belonged to three
units before the Mutiny, the 2nd/26th, the 2nd/15th and the 63rd, and
after the Mutiny to the 12th Punjab Infantry. On this assumption,
most of his moves are accounted for; his company may also sometimes
have been on detachment from the regiment. Battalions were sometimes
made up from the flank companies—that is, the picked men, the
Grenadiers or the Light Infantrymen—of four or five battalions, and
in the Gurkha War a company from the 2nd/26th belonged to one of
these. The 2nd/15th was very much under strength after the Gurkha
War and it is possible that one or two entire companies were transferred
to it from the 2nd/26th. Sita Ram's tendency to ramble and digress
seems to me realistic, and, again if this had been fiction, Norgate
would not have found it easy to conceal the truth. Everyone in India
knew everyone else and there would have been men in India in 1873
who had served in the regiments mentioned. Again, his village is named.

To my mind, there is a strong balance of probability that Norgate did persuade Sita Ram to write down what he remembered; no doubt Norgate had heard most of the story beforehand and discussed it, for if that were not so he could hardly have argued with much conviction that it would be safe for the old man to tell the world his thoughts; no doubt, as Norgate says, it is a free translation. If Norgate was really the author, he was something of a literary genius and something of an amateur anthropologist, and it is odd that he never wrote anything else. He does not sound like a writer in his translator's note — but perhaps that too was just his cleverness.

Sita Ram, then, I regard in general as a credible witness. At the very worst, if, as I think unlikely, he never existed, he does at least represent what almost all British officers thought was the way sepoys felt. He describes life in his village in Oudh, where his father cultivated a substantial piece of land through servants, paid in grain. His heart was fired by the stories he heard from his maternal uncle, a jemadar in the 2nd/26th, whose red coat and officer's gold necklace attracted him. His mother was upset; she had wanted him to be a priest and feared he would be polluted and lose his caste in the army. But his father, rather to his surprise, raised no objection; he had a long-standing legal dispute with a neighbour and a soldier son would help. So Sita Ram, laden with advice from the village priest, went off with his uncle. They arrived at Agra, where Sita Ram saw his first English-man and was surprised that he was not seven feet high. He was taken as a recruit in about 1814. He had a rough time with the drill havildar but he passed out from recruit training after eight months, which was well under the average. At last he put on the red coat he had coveted; he found it very tight and uncomfortable, the shako was very heavy and hurt his head; the musket too was heavy and 'the pouch-belt and knapsack were a load for a coolie.'

Here he says what a good many others had said. Indeed, almost everyone who gave thought to the subject agreed that the British infantryman's uniform was bad enough for anyone, anywhere; it was worse in the heat of India than in Europe, and worse for the sepoy than for the British soldier. The weight to be carried was for an Indian almost half his own, while he was used to loose garments of cotton and never felt at ease when strapped tightly into serge. Two broad leather belts, pipeclayed white, crossed his chest from either shoulder. They were held together where they crossed by a brass plate; one carried the bayonet, the other the cartridge box. Brown Bess, the musket, weighed more than nine pounds and threw a ball which weighed nearly an ounce; the cartridge box contained sixty rounds of ammunition. Another belt went round the cross-belts to keep them together — 'tight enough', wrote Albert Hervey, 'to cut the very intestines out of him'.

'The pack', said Fortescue, 'was hard, rigid and quadrangular and so adjusted as to arrest the circulation.' The head-dress or shako was 'a heavy unwieldy thing ... like an inverted fire-bucket', said Hervey; it was bell-shaped, worn with the wide mouth at the top; the frame was of wicker covered with blue cloth and there was a good deal of brass on it. It weighed between two and three pounds, and the *Delhi Gazette* in 1852 remarked, no doubt with some exaggeration, that a native soldier could rarely move without being obliged to raise one hand to keep his cap on. 'But of course it was very smart,' said Sita Ram.

Early in the memoirs there is a long discussion of officers. 'Nearly all our officers had nicknames by which we knew them.' He mentions 'the Wrestler' and 'the Camel'—because he had a long neck—and 'Damn' *sahib*. 'The Wrestler' was a great hero of Sita Ram's—'a real *sahib*, just as I had imagined all *sahibs* to be ... his chest as broad as Hanuman's, the monkey god.' Most of our officers had Indian women living with them. They could speak our language much better than they do now and they mixed more with us. 'The only language they learn now is that of the lower orders ... which is unsuitable to be used in polite conversation.' They often used to give nautches for the regiment and attended all the men's games. They took us with them when they went out hunting—and so on. 'Now many officers only speak to their men when obliged to do so and they ... try to get rid of the sepoys as quickly as possible. One *sahib* told us that he never knew what to say to us. The *sahibs* always knew what to say and how to say it when I was a young soldier. If I am speaking too boldly, Your Honour must forgive me!'

He has something to say too about British other ranks. 'I was always very good friends with the English soldiers and they used to treat the sepoy with great kindness. And why not?* Did we not do all their work? We performed all their duties in the heat. We stood sentry over their rum-casks. We gave them our own food. Well, English soldiers are a different breed nowadays. They are neither as fine nor as tall as they used to be.' He refers to several British regiments with whom he had served who had been 'kind', remembering their numbers correctly. He is always an admirer of the courage of British troops, who are like no other soldiers in the world for their ferocity and determination, but he finds it a little puzzling:

'I hardly know why they love fighting as much as they do, unless it is for grog. They would fight ten battles in succession for one bowl of grog. Their pay is very little so it cannot be for that. They also love looting but I have seen them give a cap full of rupees for one bottle of brandy. I have been told that the English doctors have discovered some kind of essence which is mixed with the soldiers' grog. Great care

* This is a very common expression in Hindi and Urdu. Not that that proves anything.

has to be taken not to mix too much, since otherwise the men would kill themselves in battle by their rashness ... there must be some kind of elixir of life in ration rum; I have seen wounded men, all but dead, come to life after having some rum.'

He was not alone in this idea, for Brasyer, one of the few men of this period to rise from the ranks, reports that when he joined the Company's service as a gunner in 1833, a tot of rum was the barrack-room remedy for everything. He was attacked by cholera; his comrades gave him rum. When that had no effect, he was given a larger dose, 'steaming hot, a fowl, feathers and all having been stewed in it'. Even this did not help, so they sent for the doctor. Brasyer, incidentally, was a quite exceptional man; he recovered from cholera, not to mention the treatment for it, and had a commission within twelve years of reaching India, ending as a colonel and Companion of the Bath. Quite early in his career he 'went to school and sat among the natives' to learn the language of the people and how it was written; he later learnt Punjabi and became an expert in the ways of Sikhs, enlisting the first Sikhs to join the Company's armies and raising Brasyer's Sikhs, who fought with distinction in the Mutiny and became the 1st/11th Sikh Regiment.

To return to rum and the British soldier, during the first part of the century most observers say much the same as Sita Ram and Brasyer. But Laverack, another ranker who was a dedicated Methodist, a 'Blue Light' and a total abstainer, says that there was a great improvement later. Sir Charles Napier and Sir Hugh Rose had each tried when Commander-in-Chief to reduce the amount of spirits drunk and substitute beer. Laverack gives staggering figures of the losses sustained by his regiment, H.M. 98th. In China, where they drank *samshu*, a local spirit, 312 died in six months; in eight and a half years in India, where rum was obtainable in large quantities, they lost 704 by death and 301 invalided home, while in a second spell in India of about the same duration, under the new policy of restricting spirits, they lost only 175 of all ranks by death and 294 invalided. But there were, of course, other influences at work too.

Others besides Sita Ram mention friendliness between British soldiers and sepoys, but they give a slight impression that it is an exception. In the Coorg War of 1833–4 Hervey speaks of a sepoy whose bravery was so marked that the European soldiers carried him before the general and begged for his promotion on the spot. Later in the campaign the rifle company of this man's regiment marched forty-five miles at a stretch without halting and on arrival insisted on relieving the skirmishers of an Irish regiment who were in action. They came up at the double, 'only stopping when the Irish insisted on shaking hands and saying: "How are ye, my bhoy, Jack Sapay ... "' Hervey also comments on the long line of stragglers who often followed a

European regiment on the march; some had been left behind through drunkenness, some through disagreement with bullock-cart drivers, with whom they had a bad reputation for overloading the cattle and ill-treating their owners. He had seen soldiers who had been left behind begging and trying to sell their boots; on one occasion, the men of his company raised five rupees for an Irish soldier and his family who were destitute and two days' march behind the regiment. Albert Hervey was an amiable man who liked to record amiable qualities, particularly on the part of the sepoys. Sleeman, making the point that active service together made for friendliness, tells of a battalion of sepoys who had served in Lord Lake's campaign alongside H.M. 76th. When peace was established, the sepoys invited the 76th to a party they wished to give them. The 76th accepted, on condition that they should be taken home. They came, got 'gloriously drunk, and woke up next morning each on his own cot in barracks,' though with no recollection of how they got there. They had been carried home by the sepoys—who were surely most unusual in their tolerance of a vice they not only did not share themselves but regarded in the case of an Indian as a mark of the lowest of outcasts.

Many of Sita Ram's adventures would be out of place here—his rescue of the beautiful Rajput girl, his escape from Afghanistan, the two occasions on which his family had to pay the Brahmans large sums to restore his caste. We shall come back to his evidence for the Afghan War and the Mutiny. But the note of tolerance for the unintelligible and even the unkind runs through all that Sita Ram says. An officer of the Royal army had called him 'a damned black pig'; he knew well enough what this meant. But 'it can largely be attributed to hastiness of temper and who can struggle against fate?' He is equally resigned about the one occasion on which he faced a court martial. He became pay havildar. Most of the sepoys in the company kept their savings with him and he used to lend it at good interest, sometimes to officers, all of whom were in debt. All pay havildars did this and everyone knew. But he made a miscalculation. The captain of his company lost all his property when a boat sank in a river; Sita Ram lent him five hundred rupees but the time of furlough came round, there was a run on the bank and Sita Ram could not find all he should have had. He was found guilty of disobedience and deprived of his appointment. 'How incomprehensible are the laws of the English for us Hindus! I was found guilty by a number of Indian officers of my own regiment, not one of whom thought I had done anything wrong ... [but] they thought the Colonel desired me to be punished.' Something else he found incomprehensible was the English readiness to spare a wounded enemy and sometimes to restore his property to one who had been defeated. 'I have seen an officer spare the life of a wounded man who shot him in the back as he turned away. I saw another *sahib* spare the life of a wounded Afghan and even offer him water to drink, but the man cut at him with his curved sword and lamed him for life. "The wounded snake can kill as long as life remains" says the proverb and if your enemy is not worth killing, surely he is not worth fighting against?' He comes back to this point several times and he thought that the Gurkha War was prolonged because we released the Gurkha general, Amar Thapa, when he surrendered. And the Second Sikh War need never have happened if we had not been lenient after the First.

The last words of old Sita Ram are sad. The Company's rule did indeed come to an end a hundred years after Plassey, as prophets had foretold.

'But they did not tell us (says Sita Ram) that another kind of English rule would take its place. This rule was far harder and much harsher. The Company Bahadur and its officers were much kinder to the people of India ... My lord, sepoys will not fight well for those they do not like or for a Government which is not kind to them. They used to be treated kindly but then they turned against their master. They will never find so good a master again ... If your Lordship, when you return to your own country, will always remember that the old subadar Sita Ram was a true and faithful servant, it will be enough for me.'

To the latest edition of his memoirs, his editor has added after the title-page a jingle of two lines from a marching-song of the Bombay Army, and this seems admirably to express the views of Sita Ram. It runs:

> Kabhi sukh aur kabhi dukh
> Angrez ka naukar

It means:

> Sometimes bliss and sometimes woe,
> Servant of the English!

High noon is past. We turn now to the events which led up to the great Mutiny and glance back at several lesser mutinies which might have served as warnings. In the present century, a writer of great distinction, E. M. Forster, made the discovery that Indians need constant kindness. It was a discovery made in the days of the Company by almost every officer who put pen to paper, and in the period I have called high noon a surprising number really did feel a liking and a kindness for the men they commanded. When that liking and kindness began to fail, a terrible storm burst. It destroyed the army Sita Ram had known; he detested the soldiers of the new army and saw no good in it. But different though it was, the new army was a remarkable achievement in which eventually a new liking and respect were born.

Part III
The Storm

X

Gathering Darkness

1. The Fall of the Company's Star

We have seen how important to the soldier's confidence and loyalty was a belief in the *iqbāl* of the Company Bahadur. But in 1839 there began a war, perhaps the most impolitic, unjust and mismanaged in our long history. This led in 1842 to complete disaster—utter defeat. One man was allowed to escape, apparently so that he could tell the tale of horror and prevent his fellow-countrymen from returning. They did return, they won the last battle, but then demonstrated the futility of the entire proceedings by abandoning everything for which the war had been fought. But the tale of the first disaster had swept through India. The star of the Company had fallen. The foreigners could be beaten.

The First Afghan War makes a tale of frightful suffering and misery, some of it due to the obstinacy of the political officer in charge and some to the vacillation of the military commander. General Elphinstone was too old and too sick for such responsibility but surely he can never have been a man capable of decisive action. He changed his mind with everyone he spoke to and no sooner ventured on an order than it was countermanded. But the prime responsibility rests with George Eden, Lord Auckland, the Governor-General who succeeded Lord William Bentinck.

Lord William, in his minute on the defence of India, had reached the conclusion that the main threat was from Russia. He thought that Afghanistan had so far been little more than a confederation of chiefs, but that there was some hope of greater stability now that Dost Mohammad had taken power and expelled his feeble predecessor, Shah Suja. A strong Afghanistan seemed to Bentinck and his wise advisers to be in the British interest as a buffer against Moscow. There would be a triple buffer—Persia at the Russian end, Afghanistan in the middle and, at the Indian end, the Sikh empire of Ranjit Singh, linked by alliance with the Company.

It has been argued that not Auckland but his advisers were to blame, or alternatively that he was the slave of Palmerston's foreign policy, of which it was a cardinal point to support Turkey against Russia and to make the Russians uneasy by an aggressive attitude in the Middle East. But a man need not listen to his advisers and he can resign if given intolerable instructions. Auckland was faced with a sudden sharpening of the Afghan problem. Herat, four hundred miles west of Kabul, was besieged by a Persian army with some Russian support. Herat was the headquarters of a chief who usually admitted some degree of affiliation, if not of allegiance, to Kabul. Were the British to let it fall? Auckland recorded a minute in which he outlined the three courses open to him, and presumably he thought they all fell within his instructions. He rejected the first course, of 'confining our defensive measures to the line of the Indus', and the second, of 'granting succour to the existing chieftainships of Caubul and Candahar', which was much the most sensible. The one he preferred was to 'permit or encourage the advance of Ranjit Singh's armies upon Caubul' and 'to organize an expedition headed by Shah Suja', who would replace Dost Mohammad, and who was clearly expected to behave obediently as a British puppet.

This was a piece of supreme folly, based on two assumptions quite without foundation. The first was that Ranjit Singh would dispatch an army into Afghanistan for no purpose of his own but to please the British; the second was that the people of Afghanistan were longing to replace Dost Mohammad by Shah Suja, whom they had banished thirty years before. But Ranjit Singh was a much more astute and determined diplomat than Auckland and he had a far more realistic understanding of the military difficulties of invading Afghanistan, not to mention the still greater political difficulties of imposing a settlement on the Afghans. He was not such a fool as to do what Auckland wanted. And the popularity of Shah Suja was a mere figment; almost every British officer who has left a record of his impressions in Kabul came within a few weeks to the conclusion that the Afghans preferred Dost Mohammad. Mackinnon, a captain in H.M. 16th Lancers and not long in Asia, heard the answer given by Dost Mohammad's representative to the terms offered him: exile in India on a pension of £10,000 a year. 'On what plea can you found the right of dethroning a monarch, the choice of his country, and placing on the throne yonder despised puppet, whom I spit at?' 'I have rarely heard a speech more to the purpose and never one more difficult to answer,' wrote Mackinnon. 'After the King [i.e. Shah Suja] had been a short time in Kandahar, I knew that the people did not care in the least about him, and their anger grew when they saw that the English were not returning to Hindustan,' said Sita Ram. But the British envoy would not admit what was so plain to everyone else.

Ranjit Singh had pretended to agree to Auckland's plan but made no

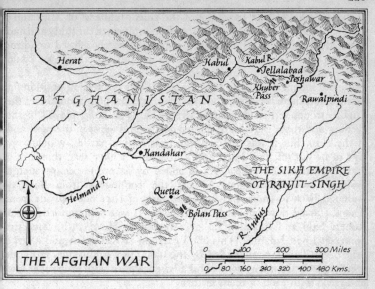

THE AFGHAN WAR

move to carry it out; further, he insisted that Shah Suja's expedition should march round through Sind and Baluchistan and not through his territories. This force included a British cavalry brigade and three British infantry brigades as well as a force specially raised for Shah Suja. This had British officers and many British sepoys, including Sita Ram, who transferred to Shah Suja's service after his trouble as pay havildar. There were about 21,000 fighting men. They met little opposition, the Afghans being much divided, and after great suffering from drought, disease, sunstroke, bad water, bad supplies and mismanagement, the force reached Kandahar and eventually Kabul. Dost Mohammad bolted, was caught and marched off to India; Shah Suja entered Kabul in great pomp, covered with jewels and riding a splendid white horse—but in a sullen and hostile silence. And now came the problem—dare we leave him?

The occasion for the whole expedition had been the siege of Herat—but the Persian army had raised the siege and fallen back before Shah Suja left India. All we had done was to replace by a worthless puppet an able, energetic chief who, far from being unfriendly, saw his interest in terms that could have agreed with ours; he had wanted an independent Afghanistan which could rely on some British support to keep out the Persians and Russians. Macnaghten, the envoy in charge of the expedition, had been one of the chief architects of Auckland's policy; he had worked out his solution of the problem in the study and had elevated his conclusion into a dogma. He obstinately refused to admit that he had been wrong, though even he did not think we could safely leave Shah Suja unprotected.

A cantonment was set up near Kabul. It was not a good position for defence, but there was room for a racecourse and a polo-ground and the English troops settled down to garrison life. The band played in the evening and there were balls, dinner-parties and whist in the mess and at the club. But it was unsafe to go on shooting-parties, which were 'apt to be cut off, murdered and mutilated'. 'I have seen things in a man's mouth which were never intended by nature to occupy such a position,' said Mackinnon. At last the contingent from Bombay marched back to India and in the autumn of 1841 one brigade from Bengal started down towards the Khyber. It was commanded by Sir Robert Sale and included his own regiment, H.M. 13th, later the Somerset Light Infantry. This left a garrison at Kandahar and a large brigade at Kabul, commanded by the unhappy Elphinstone. His gout grew worse in the snow, none of his advisers agreed with each other and he agreed with each of them in turn.

There seemed no reason why the occupation should ever end. But it was very expensive and the authorities in India felt they must economize; they thought that a good beginning might be made by withdrawing the allowances paid to the chiefs of the tribes round the Khyber. These were virtually payments for not cutting our communications. The allowances were stopped, communications were immediately disrupted, and the smouldering discontent and anger of the whole country flared into revolt. Soon the British force at Kabul was virtually besieged; Sale was just able to get into the fortress of Jallalabad, about half-way between Kabul and the Frontier; here he too was to be shut up for many months.

Sale was a fighting leader in whom his troops had confidence; in a sortie his men could always drive the Afghans before them and this was so till the siege was raised. The same was true of Nott at Kandahar, who said: 'I would at any time lead one thousand Bengal sepoys against five thousand Afghans.' The same *had* been true of the troops at Kabul, European and sepoy alike; their confidence had been supreme and the Afghans could not meet them in battle. The walled fortress of Ghazni was stormed by H.M. 13th and the 36th Bengal Native Infantry, before they reached Kabul, a fierce piece of fighting after which the 13th insisted on shaking hands all round with the 36th; there had been nothing to choose between them in valour. But after Sale's departure things went downhill quickly; orders were countermanded so often, the incompetence and irresolution of the leaders was so obvious, that both officers and men lost heart. And now physical conditions became severe. 'The sepoys suffered terribly,' said Sita Ram; 'they lost the use of their limbs and the blood froze in their veins ... Provisions were very expensive. We Hindus never dared to bathe, since it was almost certain death. We had no comfort or ease.' The European troops did not suffer so intensely from the cold, but poor food and half-rations told on them more seriously and they lost the will to fight. Officers grumbled and foretold disaster; 'much reprehensible croaking', says Lady Sale, who had been left behind when her husband's brigade marched, and who would clearly have made a far better commander than Elphinstone. She has a tale of an outlying fort with an upper room which served as a kind of guardroom; here there were some soldiers of H.M. 44th and some of the 37th Bengal Native Infantry. The Afghans climbed up the wall with the help of 'crooked sticks which served them as scaling ladders', picked out the mud which stopped the only window and broke in. 'A child with a stick might have repulsed them. The Europeans had their belts and accoutrements off, the Sipahees the same. They all ran away as fast as they could! ... there was not a pin to choose—all cowards alike.'

Helplessness and irresolution continued. 'The poor General's mind is distracted by the diversity of opinions offered; and the great bodily ailments he sustains are daily enfeebling the powers of his mind,' continued Lady Sale. The British envoy, Macnaghten, was invited to a conference by Akbar Khan, the son of Dost Mohammad; Akbar Khan stabbed him less than a mile from the British cantonment; his head and limbs were cut off and paraded through the town, his body exposed in the Kabul bazaar. Not a bayonet moved; the episode was ignored. At last, on assurances of friendship and protection by that same Akbar Khan, it was agreed that the whole force should retire to India. On Thursday, January 6th, the march from Kabul began; there were about 4,500 fighting men and 12,000 followers. 'The day was clear and frosty; the snow nearly a foot deep on the ground.'

As usual, all was muddle and it took two and a half hours to cover the first mile. The followers were hardly out of cantonments before they were fired on and much baggage was abandoned the first day. The men had been on half-rations for many weeks and for long periods without firewood; both men and draught animals were exhausted, half-starved and bemused with the cold. The leaders, doomed to destruction, behaved as though demented. They were short of food and it was imperative to press on as fast as they could while any remained; the men were as likely to die in the snow at a halt as on the march, yet on the 7th they halted at midday, because Akbar Khan wanted time to clear the passes. This was the man who had stabbed the envoy and was believed by everyone but the political leaders to have

said that not one of the army should return to India, but that he would
set up on the road one headless body as a warning to its countrymen.

The first night should have been enough to show them what was
coming. There were no tents, except two or three small *pals* — a small
single-fly light canvas tent used by servants. Lady Sale wrote:

'All scraped away the snow as best they might to make a place to lie
down on ... there was no food for man or beast procurable ... At
daylight, we found several men frozen to death, amongst whom was Mr
Conductor Macgregor ... numbers of men, women and children are
left on the roadside to perish ... The men were half-frozen; having
bivouacked all night in the snow, without a particle of food or bedding
or wood to light a fire ... Discipline was clearly at an end ... having
no cover for officers or men, they are perfectly paralysed with the cold ...
Numbers of unfortunates have dropped, benumbed with the cold, to be
massacred by the enemy: yet so bigoted are our rulers that we are still
told that ... Akbar Khan is our friend!'

At sunrise on January 8th, 'the confusion was fearful ... every man
paralysed with cold ... many frozen corpses on the ground ... The
enemy soon assembled in great numbers ... Bullets kept whizzing by us
as we sat on our horses for hours ... I felt very grateful for a tumbler
of sherry which at any other time would have made me very unladylike
but now merely warmed me ...' A little later in this same day, Lady
Sale's party was heavily fired on. Her daughter's pony was twice hit; 'I
had fortunately only one ball in my arm; three others passed through
my poshteen near my shoulder without doing me any injury.' But her
son-in-law was severely wounded and died after lingering for two days
in great pain.

It is with plain good sense and indomitable courage that Lady Sale
tells her story. Next day the surgeon who came to see her son-in-law
'kindly cut the ball out of my wrist and dressed both my wounds.' It is to
illustrate the hardships of those who were pregnant (including her
daughter) or who had small children that she mentions that it was
many days before her own wet habit was thawed. The next night was
spent in a sepoy's *pal* which some officers pitched for the ladies; there
were 'nearly thirty packed together without room to turn. Many poor
wretches died round the tent in the night.' Next day it was agreed that
the ladies should go back as captives. They went back along the road to
Kabul, and 'It would be impossible for me to describe the feelings with
which we pursued our way through the dreadful scenes that awaited
us. The road covered with awfully mangled bodies, all naked; fifty-
eight Europeans were counted ... the natives innumerable ... Numbers
of camp followers still alive, frost-bitten and starving; some perfectly
out of their senses and idiotic.' She mentions two officers whose bodies
were recognized and continues: 'The sight was dreadful; the smell of

the blood sickening; and the corpses lay so thick it was impossible to look from them as it required care to guide my horse so as not to tread upon the bodies: but it is unnecessary to dwell on such a distressing and revolting subject.'

Lady Sale went back to Afghanistan and for many months was a prisoner; she, her daughter and the grandson born in captivity were safe in September when her husband and the 13th marched up from Jallalabad; 'happiness so long delayed was actually painful and accompanied by a choking sensation which could not obtain the relief of tears ... But when the men of the 13th pressed forward to welcome us ... each in his own style ... my highly-wrought feelings found the desired relief ... and I could scarcely speak to thank the soldiers for their sympathy.' But we must leave Lady Sale, to knit socks, as she says, for her grandchildren. After she left them, the column stumbled on for a few more days till, at Jagdalak, the remnants of H.M. 44th fought to the last man. As everyone knows, one man reached Jallalabad, and this surely must have been permitted in order to fulfil that thought of Akbar Khan's that one should serve as a warning to his countrymen.

It remains to tell that in April Shah Suja was assassinated. Nott at Kandahar endured throughout the summer; Sale and his illustrious garrison held Jallalabad. At last Sale was relieved by General Pollock and together they marched back to meet Nott at Kabul. It was now felt that enough had been done to show that the British always won the last battle. Afghanistan was abandoned, Dost Mohammad restored, and the utter futility of the whole episode revealed.

But all was not the same as before. Fifteen years later, when British power in India hung trembling in the balance, Edwardes at Peshawar said: 'Men remembered Kabul.' And that phrase tolls like a bell through the intervening years. Men remembered Kabul; they knew now that the Company did not always get its way. Its star had fallen. It was no longer invincible.

2. Sind and Lost Allowances

There followed two wars which for the officers confirmed the certainty that in the end victory was always to the British. But to the sepoy they carried another lesson, confirming him in a sense of injustice and of being taken for granted. The reasons for the annexation of Sind are admirably expressed in two sayings. In England, Mountstuart Elphinstone, long retired, wrote that we had taken the country in the mood of 'a bully who has been kicked in the street and goes home to beat his wife in revenge'. And Charles Napier, the conqueror of Sind – not a man

to underestimate his own achievements — said it was 'a very advantageous, useful humane piece of rascality'. The country was grossly
misgoverned by a loose confederation of amirs and it was in their
misgovernment and the prospect of an improvement under the British
that the humanity lay. Most Victorians believed that the benefits of
British rule justified any interference with existing rights, particularly
the rights of aristocrats whom they regarded as decadent and effete.
But such men as Henry Lawrence and James Outram did not share this
view. Both felt that the amirs had been unjustly dispossessed of hereditary
rights. And throughout India there was hardly a chief or landowner
who gave any thought to the future without a pang of apprehension.

  This sense of injustice and the fear that it aroused affected the
sepoys indirectly. More immediately, they felt that they were one step
nearer the day when all India would be British and the sepoys would
be needed no more — or, rather more sensibly, would be needed in
Turkey, in Egypt or in Russia. If that were so, the rules of caste would
be more and more inconvenient to their rulers, who might therefore
be expected to try to upset them. Sita Ram had felt great apprehension
at crossing the Indus; it was not permitted to a Brahman to set foot in
that unclean land. When he got there, he saw why, for many of his
comrades were eaten by jackals and vultures and he himself, though
he had survived, had lived as a slave to Muslims and had for the second
time had to pay for elaborate and expensive ceremonies to cleanse
himself from pollution. Sind lay astride the Indus and sepoys from
Oudh hated it. *Ab-o-hawa* — 'water and air' — are the Persian words
generally used in Hindustani to describe climate, and in Sind both were
detestable. The air was full of dust, the water often stinking or brackish,
the malaria of a specially malignant species. Upper Sind is notorious
for its heat, temperatures of 130° in the shade being often reached.
Yet, when this country had been annexed, it became part of India
and — with incontrovertible logic — the financiers decreed that foreign
allowance or batta would be discontinued. 'I suppose there will next be
an order joining London to Calcutta,' a sepoy is said to have remarked.

  The war in Sind was remarkable mainly for the character of Sir
Charles Napier, a general who certainly had style and vitality.
Immensely vigorous and quite without fear, he had a gift of trenchant
epigram which ensured that what he said was repeated in every mess
and barracks. His prejudices were fierce, his scruples few. He won the
hearts of many, though he made enemies of those who were not
prepared to give him their whole-hearted allegiance. But the fiery and
romantic imagination which enhanced his appeal to the troops also
persuaded him, after the event, that he had always been right; he was
peacock as well as eagle and his testimony is not always to be relied on.
The armies he met in Sind were quite undisciplined and his dash, his

vigour and the enthusiasm he engendered in his troops carried the day —
but his great victory at Meeanee almost ended in disaster. He was
generous in his praise of the Bombay sepoys, as we have seen. But it was
the Bengal soldiers who so detested Sind and who were so discontented
at finding that the reward of victory was the loss of allowances.

There was a crop of minor mutinies, troops refusing to go to Sind
unless batta continued to be paid as it had been during the war. They
must be seen against the general background; Ranjit Singh was dead
and his wise policy of establishing strength and avoiding conflict was
doomed. No one who gave the matter thought could fail to see the
danger of war with the Sikhs. Some authorities felt that this danger
called for the ruthless suppression of any signs of indiscipline, while
others felt that in such a situation discontent in the army should be
treated with sympathy and understanding. Indeed, the central
authorities themselves alternated between the two points of view. The
tale of one battalion will make the point and serve for several.

The 64th Bengal Native Infantry had a good record. It had served
with credit in the second Afghan campaign, and had been to Kabul and
back. But when ordered to Sind in 1844, the men presented petitions
couched in such strong language as to come near threatening mutiny.
They wanted the batta they had had in Afghanistan. An experienced
and sympathetic senior officer of the Company's service discussed
the matter with the native officers, all of whom assured him that there
was no intention of refusing orders; the regiment started its march to
the Indus. At this point, things seemed to have been settled so satisfactorily that the Commander-in-Chief ordered the dispatch of a letter
promising various minor concessions and awards and that the battalion
should not stay in Sind more than a year. But before this letter arrived,
the 64th had actually refused to obey orders, this time on the trivial
ground that they preferred another route. Their Colonel, on receiving
the Commander-in-Chief's letter — meant to be a reward for past good
conduct — decided to use it rather as a bribe for future good behaviour
and to read it out, concealing from headquarters the incident about the
route. This was bad enough, but he made it far worse by misreading
the letter, admittedly very loosely worded, and telling the men it
meant they were to get 'General Pollock's batta', that is, what they had
had in Afghanistan — twelve rupees a month, instead of eight. Of course,
this was received with acclamation; it was complete victory, all they
had wanted. But this was not what the letter meant and the truth came
to light on pay-day. It was not surprising that the 64th refused their pay.
Their Colonel had lied to them. Once again, a senior officer, George
Hunter, a fine old brigadier much loved by all, came to harangue them
and attempted to pay them himself. He found them on parade 'as fine-
looking and steady a body of men as he could wish to see'. But they

were irritated by the presence of their own officers, who they believed
had deceived them, and attempts to pay them broke up in disorder;
for twenty-four hours they refused to take up their piled arms and
return to duty. At last Hunter himself, their officers being away,
persuaded them to obey orders and to march with him to a place
where there were British troops to overawe them. Here he pardoned all
but the ringleaders. Thirty-nine were brought to trial, six executed.
Moseley, the commanding officer, was cashiered.

Two infantry regiments from Madras, under orders for Burma,
were diverted to Sind. Burma was then not India, so they would have
drawn there the full foreign service batta and on this understanding
had allotted their basic pay for the support of their families. They
meant to live on their batta alone. Their officers, to whom the ways of
the finance officials were unknown territory, assured them confidently
that they would get the same allowances in Sind—but when their
voyage ended and pay-day came it was found that some men had
nothing at all and others owed the paymaster a rupee. The Sixth
Madras Cavalry also refused to march from Jubbulpore to Sind.
In the Bengal Army, the 7th Cavalry and the 34th Infantry refused
duty; the 34th were disbanded and their number struck from the Army
List. The 4th and the 69th also refused to go to Sind but were eventually
—after the disbandment of the 34th—coaxed into a return to duty and
proceeded. The crisis was solved by making Sind a part of the Bombay
Presidency and garrisoning it from Bombay. But another step had been
taken along the road of distrust and loss of confidence. And the Bengal
men had had a just grievance, had refused duty, and in the end had
won their point.

3. The Sikhs

It had been the policy of that wise ruler Ranjit Singh to muster
sufficient military strength to make the English respect him but to
avoid either direct conflict or spineless subservience. In this he had
been singularly successful, but his policy needed a resolute will, a
firm hand and a realistic understanding of the reserves of British
power. When he died, in 1839, at the beginning of the Afghan War,
the firm hand was lost and it was easy for Sikh leaders to overestimate
the strength of the Sikh military machine. This began to usurp control of
the State. To those who had inherited the remains of Ranjit Singh's
authority, it must have seemed that it would be safer if employed in
external war. To prove it in battle might heal internal differences.

It was a formidable machine. Ranjit Singh had gone much further
than any other Indian leader in adopting European methods; he had

borrowed both from the French and the British, perhaps more from the French. 'The interior economy of his regiments, battalions and batteries was almost wholly European,' writes the Sikh historian of the Sikh military system, Fauja Singh Bajwa. In training, weapons, organization, tactics, clothing, system of pay, layout of camps, order of march, regular units of the Sikh army resembled their opponents as closely as they could; indeed, in battle, it was possible to tell the scarlet-coated sepoy of the Bengal Army from the scarlet-coated Sikh only by the colour of his belts. The soldiers of the Sikh State were not all Sikhs; they included both Muslims and Hindus—Rajputs, Jats and Dogras—but most of them were Sikhs, particularly in the infantry, and these men added to a fine physique a feeling that they were 'co-sharers in the glory' of the Sikh empire. They were the army of the *Khalsa*—'the pure'—a military fraternity, linked by a faith in a reforming religion, that was simple, powerful, easy to understand. They had something of the spirit of Cromwell's New Model Army; religious faith bound them together, and they also shared an element of something not far from nationalism. It was not an *Indian* nationalism, for their scorn and dislike for the Easterners* of the Bengal Army was intense. It was the dawn of a nationalism of the Punjab, but essentially a Punjab ruled by Sikhs. It resembled the dawn of Maratha nationalism under Sivaji, before the Maratha armies became mercenary and cosmopolitan.

Fauja Singh's summary gives pride of place to the infantry, which all agreed was excellent. He says the Sikh guns were still heavy and slow to manœuvre, but most British observers spoke highly of the Sikh artillery, noting that the men worked their guns almost as fast as the British; 'the glory of the Sikh regular army was the artillery,' writes Spear. The cavalry were not so good; there was still a feudal element here, regiments being raised by local landowners, pay, discipline and equipment being therefore far more haphazard. But the regular army, at its best, was, Fauja Singh believes, 'very nearly equal to the well-trained and disciplined army of the English East India Company'. Its strength was about 75,000 men of whom more than half were regulars. After Ranjit Singh's death, there was some falling off, in pay, discipline, supplies. Failure was due to the fact that the army was not sufficiently European. The 'egalitarian nature of the Sikh community ... rendered the growth of healthy traditions of discipline ... a bit difficult' and there was 'a lack of competent and sincere commanders', writes Fauja Singh. At least one important Sikh leader held his forces back from battle at a critical moment, just as English leaders withheld support from Richard III at Bosworth.

The first Sikh War came in 1845, two years after the conquest of

* The word used both by Sikhs and British was *Purbiya*, ('easterner'), from *Purab*, ('the east'). It generally meant Brahmans and Rajputs from Oudh and Behar.

Sind, and it ended in 1846; there followed an uneasy two years during which the sovereignty of the Punjab was still Sikh, not British, when all authority was vested nominally in the boy Maharaja, and executive authority was exercised in his name, mainly by Sikh officials with British guidance. Some had thought the Punjab should have been annexed and the Sikh army abolished, but Lord Hardinge and his advisers hoped they could return to the old policy of maintaining a friendly buffer State.

The period was remarkable for two astonishing episodes. A Sikh army of 10,000 men, accompanied by only two British officers, marched to Kashmir and there enthroned the Maharaja of Jammu—a Hindu, not a Sikh. This was part of the treaty, a concession wrung unwillingly from the Sikhs, yet it was enforced by a Sikh army and by these two men, not in direct command. One of them, it is true, was Henry Lawrence. Another Sikh army, with Herbert Edwardes as its adviser, marched to Bannu, an untamed valley of fierce tribesmen who had never paid tribute to Greek, Afghan or Sikh. Edwardes, alone among the Sikh soldiers, with whom we had been fighting a few months before, imposed on them a strange new discipline. They were not to cut the standing corn for their horses or live themselves on the grain they could loot from the peasantry.

These are two examples of something which now began—a sympathy, a mutual respect, a trust between British officer and Sikh. It was something personal, that was to blossom between one man and another, or between one man and a regiment or half a district, intermittently, here and there, until Independence. Such a beginning was made by Brasyer, who had enlisted as a gunner in the Company's service in 1833 and with less than twelve years' service received a commission. He recruited four hundred Sikhs, former enemies, for the Company's service, and thus, as he said, formed 'the nucleus of the Sikh element in our armies'. He became adjutant, quartermaster, interpreter and second-in-command of the new unit, which eventually he commanded. But, in general, the two years between the two Sikh Wars were unhappy; the Sikh leaders resented the presence of the British and the many checks which the British imposed on their ambition, and often, one must add, their rapacity. It was probable, almost certain, that there would be another war—and war there was. It was really a continuation of the first, one war split into two. In the Second War, as in the First, victory hung for a long time in the balance but at last it was complete and this time there were no half-measures; the Punjab was annexed.

In the two wars, there were seven pitched battles. Sir Hugh Gough, later Lord Gough, was in command throughout. He was a fierce, courageous general, a firm believer in the principle of attack; in the view of some contemporary soldiers, he did not sufficiently appreciate recent developments in tactics, due to the increase in numbers and power of the artillery. The theory of the time demanded an artillery duel while the infantry were still out of range of each other. The purpose of this was to reduce the enemy's guns before hurling infantry at them. Gough attacked the Sikhs in strong prepared positions without artillery preparation and their guns tore holes in his infantry with canister and case. There were heavy losses; at Chillianwallah, in the Second Sikh War, it seems quite possible that Gough walked into a deliberately prepared trap, based on an understanding of his character. Some time after noon he found the Sikhs drawn up in a strong defensive position, much of it masked by scrub woodland; he wisely determined to rest his men and wait till morning. But the enemy were as provocative as they could be; 'two six-pound shot passed over our head and in the direction of the staff and Lord Gough and this got the old man's Irish out,' wrote Sergeant Pearman. Gough claimed later that, if he had not attacked them, the Sikhs would have attacked him and he had no alternative but to attack or withdraw. At any rate, attack he did; he changed his mind and went for them that evening, his troops tired, the position not thoroughly reconnoitred. After very heavy fighting and severe losses, he held his ground, but if the Sikh leaders had been united and had attacked him resolutely next day, it seems possible they would have defeated him completely. In this as in other battles, he was saved by the incredible discipline and valour of his troops. But the final battle of the two wars, Gujrat, was a complete victory. Gough for the first time had more guns than his enemy; this time the Sikhs were in an open plain, a much weaker position than Chillian-wallah; Gough attacked in the morning with fresh troops, pounded the enemy with his artillery for two and a half hours before moving up his infantry, used his horse effectively during the battle to protect his flanks, and after it to pursue the beaten Sikhs. There was no question about who had won Gujrat.

The annexation which followed had immediate consequences for the sepoys from Oudh, who still formed nine-tenths of the Company's Bengal Army. Once again, the reward for victory was loss of pay. The logic, to the Military Auditor General and his staff, was inescapable. A soldier enlisted for pay of seven rupees per month. Batta was payable on active service or when outside the Company's territory. The Punjab had become part of the Company's territories and therefore no more batta should be paid. The Military Auditor General in Calcutta issued an order to this effect on June 9th, 1849; it was to have effect from the previous April 1st, so that in every case one month's batta already drawn was repayable.

If the machine of Government is looked on as it must have seemed to the sepoy—a great impersonal 'they', not composed of individuals who marry and sleep and eat—it seems so stupid as to beggar belief that the mistakes of only five years ago should be repeated so soon. It is less surprising to anyone with experience of how readily men segregate themselves in little worlds of their own. Perhaps everyone on the staff of the Auditor General had changed; perhaps no one had ever told them that the last time they had followed their inexorable logic a regiment had been disbanded, men had been sentenced to long terms of imprisonment, officers had been cashiered in disgrace. Perhaps no one in the Auditor General's office knew that last time they had only been able to get out of the impasse by garrisoning Sind from Bombay and thus virtually climbing down. But even if one of these improbable suppositions is correct, surely someone might have pointed out that it was both impolitic and unjust to make a reduction retrospective and require men to refund what they had drawn, not only in good faith but in accordance with the orders as they then stood.

The orders took some time to reach the Punjab. It was at Rawalpindi, on July 24th, 1849, that Brigadier Sir Colin Campbell learnt that the 13th and the 22nd Bengal Native Infantry had refused to accept their pay. It seems likely that this was pay for June, less batta and that the batta already drawn for April and May was to be deducted. As family allowances would also have been sent to the men's homes, not much can have been left for the sepoy. There was a further complication; three companies of the 22nd, owing to carelessness, had received pay at the old rate without deductions. The men did not behave violently and were eventually induced to accept the reduced pay; later they were given the same as the men of the three companies who had been wrongly paid.

What could be worse? An unjust order provokes mutiny and the grievance in the end is acknowledged, at least in part. What could the sepoy think but that no one considered him unless he refused duty? He had—or so it seemed to him—conquered the Punjab and his reward was to serve without extra pay farther from his home, in a climate and among a people he disliked. The discontent was not confined to two battalions. It was reported in December that the 32nd at Wazirabad were in a sullen and unhappy mood, saying that the allowances now ordered would not fill their bellies. Another anomaly now came to light: two other battalions in the same station, the 53rd and the 60th, had elected to keep themselves in constant readiness for service, and by subscribing to this formula had satisfied the Auditor General and continued to draw batta up till the end of 1849. Whether the officers of the 32nd had failed to discover this loophole or had never put it to their men is not apparent; the men cannot have refused it, for that is not urged against them. Hearsey, the Brigade Commander, simply reported that it must 'appear hard to the sepoys of the 32nd regiment that, as serving at the same station, they should get inferior allowances.'

Sir Charles Napier was now Commander-in-Chief; he ordered that the 32nd should be assembled and pay disbursed in the usual way, anyone refusing to be immediately arrested and tried for mutiny. A havildar and three privates refused and were arrested; the others, after an address by Hearsey, took their pay. The four were convicted and sentenced to fourteen years hard labour, but Napier revised the sentence. They were sentenced to death, which he then commuted to transportation for life. 'In eternal exile,' said Napier, who never understated his case, they would 'expiate their crimes. For ever separated from their country and their relations, in a strange land beyond the seas,' they would 'linger out their miserable lives.' This was in a general order to the troops.

In February 1850 the 66th, who had just arrived from Lucknow at Govindgarh, in the Punjab, let their officers know of their discontent. The officers remonstrated, reminding them that they had enlisted for seven rupees a month and that there was provision for extra money if wheat went above fifteen seers to the rupee. But one company refused to take off their accoutrements and go to their lines; eventually they petitioned to be discharged. Next day the grenadier company took their arms without permission and refused to surrender them until they had seen the major commanding the battalion. Eventually, 95 men were tried for mutiny, 4 being sentenced to 14 years hard labour, 28 to 10 years, and 8 to 7 years. Six were acquitted and 47 dismissed. The 66th was disbanded; their colours and number were given to Gurkhas, the Nusseree (Rifle) Battalion, who now became the 66th Regiment of Native Infantry (Goorkhas), later the 1st King George V's Own Gurkha Rifles.

That was the end of the crop of incidents arising directly from the annexation of the Punjab. But discontent had been far more widespread than these incidents alone would suggest; no less than twenty-four battalions had shown signs of refusing their pay. And these events were not forgotten; the sepoys knew nothing of the Military Auditor General and could hardly be expected to be understanding about his pathetic isolation in a world of paper and figures. They were puzzled and unhappy. They felt deserted. 'Half a sheet of paper ought to show every soldier his rate of pay, by sea, by land, on leave, on the staff, in hospital, on duty, etc.,' wrote Sir Henry Lawrence. 'There ought to be no doubt on the matter. At present there is great doubt, though there are volumes of Pay and Audit regulations.' To the sepoys, it seemed that their officers no longer had any power to help them, while the Company, the Government, once their father and mother, cared for them no longer.

There were indirect results to this affair as well. Sir Charles Napier had been strict, indeed fierce, with the men of the 32nd. None the less, he must have had some sympathy with their grievance. The price of food was higher in the Punjab than in the old provinces. The proviso of extra money if the price of wheat flour rose above 15 seers (30 lb) for a rupee had recently been changed to one more complicated and in practice less favourable to the sepoy. Dalhousie, the Governor-General, was at sea; without waiting for his return, Napier gave orders to return to the old regulation. He was right in common sense and justice, hopelessly wrong in exceeding his powers. And of course Napier was a firebrand, compounded of superlatives. He did nothing by halves and his opinions were always extreme. He justified his action in vivid rhetorical language; the whole army was on the point of mutiny, the Empire in danger. Now of all the Governors-General in the long line from Warren Hastings to Mountbatten, there were three—Wellesley, Dalhousie and Curzon—who seem born for the purple, autocrats by nature, Tsars incapable of brooking the least breach of prerogative. 'I cannot sufficiently express the astonishment with which I read [the Commander-in-Chief's opinions],' wrote Dalhousie on his return, in a lengthy minute. 'I desire to record my entire dissent … from the statement that the army has been in mutiny and the Empire in danger.' The style is perhaps a shade less magisterial than Wellesley's, less brilliant and less acid than Curzon's, but any one of the three might have written most of it and in his conviction that he was right, Dalhousie is the equal of either. Yet in fact, when allowance has been made for Napier's extravagance of expression, he was nearer right than Dalhousie. There *was* danger and this controversy added to it. 'The strife between Dalhousie and Napier was proclaimed, almost as it were by beat of drum, in all the Lines and Bazaars of the country,' wrote Kaye, 'and all men knew that the English, who used so to cling to one another, that it seemed that they thought with one strong brain and struck with one strong arm, were now wasting their vigour by warring among themselves and in their disunion ceasing to be formidable.'

Napier resigned and went to England; the supremacy of the Governor-General, and incidentally of the Military Auditor General, was firmly asserted. The Punjab was now a British province, ruled with a minimum of red tape and regulations, by a band of picked men, many of them soldiers, who would have been remarkable in any age. Their achievement is partly relevant to the story of the Indian Army, because only nine years after the battle of Gujrat, when the sepoy army of Bengal rose against its officers, the defeated Sikhs came to our help and after the Mutiny formed an essential girder in the new structure. Why should this have been? A brave and disciplined army, held together by ties of discipline and the beginnings of a Punjab nationalism, had been defeated in 1845 and had risen, to be defeated a second time, in 1848.

Nine years later, in 1857, when British power seemed to hang in the balance, when indeed it must have seemed that one more push would drive us into the sea, would not any detached observer have expected the Sikhs to seize the opportunity and attack us? Why did they not?

It is not difficult to see some reasons. But first let us be clear as to what happened. The Sikhs did not flock to the colours to help their beloved conquerors the moment the Mutiny broke out. With a few exceptions, those already in the Company's service stood firm; Brasyer's Sikhs competed with the 78th Highlanders in the storming of the Shah Najif building at the first relief of Lucknow. Some Sikhs had been recruited into the regiments of the Bengal line, where they mixed oddly with the Brahmans and Rajputs from Oudh. Sometimes, but not always, they stood fast when the Oudh sepoys mutinied. And when the decision was taken to raise fresh regiments in the Punjab, there was no difficulty in finding recruits.

This would not have been so if the whole countryside had been sullen with hatred. It was not. The administrators of the Punjab were exceptional men, intensely vigorous, imbued with a strong sense of mission, determined that their rule should make the Punjab a better place than it had been. The important things for a peasant are peace, low taxes, the right to inherit land, someone to hear his troubles. In all these respects, there was improvement in those first years of British rule; the new administrators started with a clean slate, fixed their own rates of revenue and made sure that they were not excessive. They were always on horseback, always in camp, listening to the villager. They checked the rapacity of the great nobles and it is not to be supposed that such men felt much affection for British rule. But for the Sikh peasantry the yoke was light and often the district officer did inspire a trust based on mutual respect. There was not, perhaps, a positive enthusiasm for the British flag but there was no hostility to contend with and there were plenty of men who felt that soldiering was their profession, who were ready to take up arms for pay and who saw good prospects of loot.

But the evidence suggests that there was also an element of something more positive than this. The Sikhs under Ranjit Singh had been proud of their army; they had been beaten by an army of which less than a third was of British stock and the rest Purbiyas from Oudh and Bihar, a people between whom and themselves there was mutual dislike and contempt. The Sikh did not observe the minute and scrupulous rules of personal cleanliness and the ritual about food which were so important to a Hindu of high caste. To the Brahmans of Oudh, he seemed dirty, uncouth and a barbarian, but also robust, bullying and aggressive. There was fear mixed with their contempt. Everywhere else in India the Bengal sepoy off duty could walk in the bazaar with a swagger; in the Punjab, if he ventured to swagger, it was with some trepidation.

'The sepoys dreaded the Sikhs as they were very strong men,' said Sita Ram. The Sikhs returned the contempt without the fear; they were sure they could have beaten the Easterners man for man. They resented the presence of Eastern troops in the Punjab; their embryo nationalism had been Punjabi, not Indian, and they were eager to take any chance of getting their own back on the Bengal sepoy, this time with the British on their side.

That is to go forward in the story. For the moment, we have the Punjab garrisoned with Bengal sepoys as well as with British troops. The sepoys were unhappy; they were far from home, food was expensive and water and air, if not so detestable as in Sind, were still harsh and unpleasing. There were no extra allowances and they were surrounded by large coarse men who did not even know how uncivilized they were. What was also borne in on them was that, within India, there were no more worlds to conquer. If the Company continued to need them, it would be for foreign countries where their caste was liable to be broken. And already the Company was beginning to look for new sources of recruitment. The colours of the 66th had been given to Gurkhas; Sikhs were being enlisted in sepoy regiments. 'This annoyed the sepoys exceedingly,' says Sita Ram, because they were unclean. 'They were never as smart as we were on parade and their practice of using curds to clean their long hair gave them an extremely disagreeable odour.' The sepoy of Oudh had once believed that the Company Bahadur was his father and mother, but he had also believed that he was the Company's sole prop and support. Neither belief seemed justified any longer.

4. The Pattern of Mutiny

Some twenty years ago, when I was looking at the doings of the British in India from another angle, it seemed to me that whenever there was a mutiny in the Indian army, from first to last, there were three elements to be found. There was usually something from outside, perhaps news of a bad crop at home in the village and of no remission in the land tax, perhaps active efforts by someone deliberately trying to cause trouble, spreading some rumour about forcible conversion to Christianity or the return of some ancient Indian hero. None of this would matter if there were good officers who knew their men and in whom the men had faith, but if all the good officers were away on the staff, if the Colonel was old and spent the day looking forward to his brandy and water, if the young men were straight from England, knew nothing of 'the black fellows' and thought only of dancing or shooting—well, then the men would believe the wildest things. So much about the

English was incomprehensible in any case that nothing seemed too absurd. They did, just before the Great Mutiny, believe rumours that the English might plot to destroy their caste by mixing the ground bones of cows with the flour they bought in the bazaar, or that they would be assembled on the parade-ground in order to be destroyed by a mine that would explode beneath them.

Clearly they would never have believed such stories as that unless the whole atmosphere was poisoned by a deep distrust, and in that there must surely have been present almost always these two elements— something from outside the regiment and a failure by the officers to maintain confidence. The third element—one without which the other two never seemed to catch fire—was a purely military grievance, something to do with pay or clothing or food. The simple and obvious answer to a grievance for which no hearing can be obtained is to refuse service. In the armies of the princes of India, it had been common practice to refuse to march until arrears of pay had been dealt with. To the English, this was, in a soldier, mutiny, a terrible crime, punishable with death. But to Indians it seemed part of the normal process of bargaining with an employer. The word commonly used in Hindustani for 'mutiny' does not convey the same meaning as the English word; the idea was foreign and no special term for this heinous military offence existed. The word used—*ghadr**—has for its first meaning 'faithlessness', or 'ingratitude'. So long as the Colonel was the father and mother of his regiment and had power to deal with most grievances, this was what mutiny was—but as the Colonel's power diminished, as the decisions which mattered to the sepoy were more and more often taken by people at a distance whom he had never seen, the word came less and less to represent what the sepoy felt he was doing. Even if his officers listened, no one at headquarters seemed to take much notice; it must sometimes have seemed that if he was to get anyone to pay attention, his only course was to refuse duty. He learnt in the army that in this, as in so many other things, the English had strange ideas and as a rule he remembered to behave as they expected. But the lesson was foreign and sometimes he forgot it.

VELLORE

There were many small mutinies between that day of horror when Hector Munro had blown away the grenadiers at Bhaksar and the crop of mutinies arising from financial pedantry and the annexation of Sind. Let us look at two of the most serious of these incidents of the past, either of which might have thrown a good deal of light on the situation

* This word is impossible to transliterate phonetically in a way that is intelligible to an English reader who has no special knowledge; it rhymes, more or less, with 'rudder' and the initial letter is a guttural as much like a French *r* as like a *g*.

in the 1850s. There was what was known as the massacre at Vellore in 1806. During the stirring times which led up to Wellesley's victories in 1803 at Assaye and Argaum, there had been no time to stop and think about anything but fighting, but now, when there was peace in India, officers began to consider what they could do to improve the sepoy, by which they meant to make him look more English on parade. In November 1805 the Commander-in-Chief of the Madras Army, General Sir John Cradock, issued a change in regulations by which the troops were to wear a round hat instead of a turban; it would have a feather in it and a leather cockade; they must also wear leather stocks, they must display no painted marks on the face and no 'joys', which meant jewellery such as earrings.

The question of changing the pattern of the soldier's turban had been debated eight years before in 1797 by a Military Board, who gave it 'every consideration which a subject of that delicate and important nature required'. But Sir John Cradock did not think it delicate or important; the order was drafted by a Major Pierce, approved by Colonel Agnew, signed by the Commander-in-Chief and sent out.

This was a time when, the war being over, the reforms of 1796 were first beginning to make themselves felt. Many British officers had retired on pension, there had been many re-postings, many of the officers with a battalion were new. And the native officers were beginning to understand the effect on their prospects of the new system, by which there were 22 or 23 British officers to a battalion. It was not a good time to make unnecessary innovations. To a British officer recently arrived, untrained in such matters, Sir John Cradock's order might seem unimportant, the objections trivial and pointless. But anyone with a knowledge of India would know that a hat is quite different from a turban and that a 'hat-wearer' is the common name used for a native Christian, that leather of any kind is an abomination to a Hindu and regarded with suspicion by a Muslim because it may be pigskin, and that a beard is of special importance to a Muslim as an outward sign of his faith. Not so many would be aware that earrings were often linked with family rites in childhood and worn till death, that the marks on the forehead of many Hindus were not, in fact, as the English called them, caste-marks, but were rather indications of the sect a man followed and of his having recently gone through the ceremonies of his religion. But only a boor would fail to know they had religious meaning and that it was deeply humiliating to have them rubbed off on parade. Altogether, it would be hard to have concocted a more offensive order.

That was the military grievance, and there were a number of battalions in which the officers were not sufficiently known and trusted to deal with the discontent it caused. There is less certainty about the 'something from outside'. In the inquiries that followed the mutiny, military officers laid emphasis on the external influence, while the political officers pooh-poohed it, believing that the order about hats was enough to account for all that happened. This is hardly tenable. There must have been political activity, active attempts to subvert the troops, particularly in Vellore. But the politicals were probably right in thinking that there was nothing like so close-knit, so conscious, so carefully worked out a plot as the soldiers supposed. The plot or agitation hinged on Tippoo Sultan of Mysore, the son of Hydar Ali, who had been killed at the siege of Seringapatam in 1799. The throne of Mysore had been restored to the Hindu family from whom Hydar Ali had usurped it, but Tippoo's wives and sons, with numerous retainers, were pensioners of the East India Company; they lived in a vast palace at Vellore. It was the sons of Tippoo and their retainers who did all they could to encourage a rising of the troops.

It was not difficult. There was discontent and uneasiness about the offensive order and all that was necessary was to emphasize the well-known fact that untouchables converted to Christianity usually adopted a hat as a sign of their new status. And surely it was significant that *cross*-belts were an essential part of the uniform? Every sepoy was marked with the cross. And what was that strange implement suspended from the cross-belts? A turn-screw? That is what they say—but it looks very like a cross. And leather—why must a soldier wear leather round his neck and on his hat? And have you heard that in Ceylon a colonel marched his whole regiment to church and made them sit through the service? And that a shipload of padres has just arrived from England to convert you? And that the English have sprinkled all the salt in the bazaars with the blood of cows and pigs?

These were the questions that were asked. And perhaps, if they had not been asked, Vellore might have been an affair like those on the borders of Sind forty years later, when men refused their duty but did not turn to murder. Questions, insinuations, rumours—these were repeated until, when men's minds were thoroughly unsettled, there came the positive suggestion that the sepoys should kill their officers and the British troops in Vellore. It was hoped that if the sepoys could seize the fort at Vellore and hold it for a week, there would be risings elsewhere and soon throughout the south soldiers everywhere would proclaim the restoration of the house of Tippoo and raise the tiger flag of Mysore. No doubt some of Tippoo's old retainers found their way to the main military stations and whispered their soft poison; they remembered the wealth, splendour and power of Tippoo's empire and they hoped for a return of those days of military glory, of loot and conquest. To attain their ends, they played on religious fears, on hostility to foreign ways—but it would be a misreading to suppose that they expected support from the general population. Tippoo's had been a military empire and his short dynasty was Muslim and foreign; only freebooters and swashbucklers and perhaps a few fanatics for Islam wanted the tiger standard back.

But let us return to the course of events. Cradock's order went out in November 1805. Objections expressed by the 2nd/4th Madras Native Infantry at Vellore were reported, but met with a reply that was absolutely uncompromising; the orders were to be carried out at once. Anyone who showed signs of disobedience was to be tried by court martial. A squadron of H.M. 19th Dragoons was dispatched to Vellore to act as escort to any prisoners who were to be brought to the Presidency for trial. There were 21 prisoners, of whom two were sentenced to 900 lashes and of course dismissal; 19 were sentenced to 500 lashes each, but were pardoned on making a full apology. The 2nd/4th were moved to Madras and their promotion stopped—but they appeared to have given in.

All this was in May 1806; it had taken six months for discontent to swell and break out and throughout India the hot weather is the time for troubles. In the villages, there is little work in the fields; in cantonments, the cold-weather manœuvres are over, garrison life sets in, and between morning parade and evening exercise, officers are in their bungalows, troops on their cots. Rumours go from mouth to mouth; if there *is* a grievance, there is nothing to do but discuss it. And the treatment of the 2nd/4th had neither reassured nor overawed the others. The pot simmered slowly until in July it boiled furiously over. While it cooked, the Commander-in-Chief reported to the Governor the widespread discontent which his order had caused; he was ready to cancel it. But the Governor of Madras, Lord William Bentinck, who at thirty-two years of age had not yet grown into the wisdom he was later to display, believed it would be wrong to climb down and things were left as they were.

In July the troops at Vellore were four companies of British infantry —H.M. 69th—and almost three battalions of Madras infantry—six companies of the 1st/1st, the whole of the 2nd/1st and the 2nd/23rd. What happened was clearly not the result of some momentary panic; it must have been talked about and the first steps fixed in advance. That night, July 10th, the guards on duty in the fort were provided by H.M. 69th and the 1st/1st Madras Native Infantry. Some two hours after midnight the European sentries were shot down, British soldiers in the hospital murdered, and fire was poured in through the windows of the barracks on the rest of H.M. 69th as they lay on their cots. Officers came out of their houses to find out what was going on and were shot down before they knew what was happening. From the palace, retainers of the house of Tippoo poured in to join the troops and the striped tiger standard was hoisted. So far all had gone according to plan—but it does not seem that plans had gone much further. If they had thought about it, the mutineers would have seen that their first tasks were to man the ramparts against any relief force and to put an end to any resistance within the fort. Instead, they gave themselves up to loot. By next morning, everything in the fort was chaos and confusion. And the relief force was not long in coming.

An officer of the 69th, who was outside the fort when the outbreak occurred, had learnt as much as he could of what was happening and had made for nearby Arcot to get help. Here were H.M. 19th Dragoons and some of the Company's Madras cavalry. Rollo Gillespie, commanding the 19th, is said to have been on his way, with one of his troops, within fifteen minutes of getting the news and to have covered the sixteen miles in less than two hours. The rest of the 19th were not far behind, and with them a squadron of the Madras cavalry, who seem to have been as eager as the dragoons to attack the mutinous infantry. With the Madras squadron came the galloper guns—not yet known as horse artillery. If the mutineers had not been at sixes and sevens, it should have been easy for them to defend the fort against cavalry and such light guns as these—and if they had held out for a few days, there might have been risings elsewhere. But, though it was now about nine o'clock in the morning, they had not even shut the main outer gate, and though they had shut the inner gate, they had not effectively manned the ramparts near the entrance. Gillespie left orders for the galloper guns to be used as soon as they arrived to blow in the inner gate and himself attracted the attention of the survivors of the 69th, who pulled him up on a rope. He mustered them for a charge and was able to clear a space round the inner gate until it was burst open by the guns. Then the cavalry poured in, and from that moment there was no doubt of the result. Many of the mutineers were killed on the spot, many escaped over the walls, many were made prisoner.

In the outbreak at Vellore, fourteen British officers were killed, and 115 other ranks of H.M. 69th were killed or died of wounds; many more were wounded. Of the mutineers, about 350 were killed when the fort was taken; after trial, six were blown away from guns, five shot by musketry, eight hanged, five transported; the regiments were disbanded.* The obnoxious orders were then cancelled. Later, Lord William Bentinck and the Commander-in-Chief were recalled to England, also Colonel Agnew and Major Pierce, whose ingenious scheme of improvement had started the trouble. Before the year ended, there were several other alarms in other parts of the Presidency, but in

---

* The 1st/1st, 2nd/1st and 2nd/23rd were disbanded. Regiments with these numbers were re-formed a year later; the 1st/1st eventually became the 1st/1st Pioneers and survived till 1933.

each case timely warning and swift action averted an outbreak. It is
surprising that things settled down as quickly as they did.

BARRACKPORE

Barrackpore is near Calcutta and the mutiny at Barrackpore in 1824
concerned the Bengal Army. It was an affair even more shocking than
Vellore; at Vellore there was loss of life, massacre and murder, reprisals,
public executions; it was tragedy in the deepest sense because it could
have been avoided with imagination and some understanding of how
Indians felt and behaved. But, at Barrackpore, to these same elements
of tragedy was to be added a rigid brutality that was more direct and
odious.

To understand the military cause, it is necessary to go back to the
eighteenth century. The troops of the Bengal Army had then acquired
a settled aversion to movement by sea. Indian troops had at first been
recruited with no thought of doing more than protect the Company's
possessions inside India. But war with France and Spain quickly
widened British interests and requirements; Madras troops had come
to Bengal by sea in 1756 and, as early as 1762, 650 Madras sepoys
went on an expedition to Manila, which was taken on October 6th.
They were described as 'a most necessary corps' and the Commander
asked for 2,000 more. They were volunteers; in several early expeditions, forces were made up of individual volunteers from several units
but later it became customary in Madras to ask a whole unit to volunteer and they seem always to have done so. Indeed the Madras Army
from the earliest days prided themselves on their readiness for overseas
service, and it was to mark this readiness that the group of Madras
regiments which later became the 2nd Punjab Regiment bore a golden
galley as their badge. Their willingness survived some daunting experiences; 300 Madras sepoys sailed from Manila for Madras in the
autumn of 1764, but, owing to contrary winds and the poor condition
of their ship, had to return after several months. Late in 1765 they
embarked a second time in another ship, which eventually sailed in
January 1766 but put back twice. They sailed from Manila for the
fourth and last time on March 12th, 1766, but the captain was more
interested in private trade than in reaching Madras and the officer
commanding the troops had to take over the ship and force the captain
to put in to the nearest possession of the East India Company, Fort
Marlborough in Sumatra. This was in September 1766. Here the
Madras troops waited some time for a passage and at last reached
Madras in August 1767, just under three years from their first embarka-
tion from Manila. A third of them had perished on the journey.

The Bengal sepoys had at first been as ready as the Madras men to
go by sea. In 1758 two battalions were sent to Madras by sea and no

complaints have been recorded; in 1767 three battalions were equally ready. But two later detachments were in great distress by the time they reached Vizagapatam, rather more than half-way to Madras; they were short of food and water; they threatened to take the ships and run them on shore unless allowed to land. From now onward it became a cardinal point of faith with the Bengal sepoy that he could not go by sea. It would break his caste and it was not in his contract. Of course, travel by sea did present difficulties; there had to be separate water-butts for men of high caste, which they had to be assured had been filled by men of the right degree of sanctity and which must not even be approached by the wrong; a Brahman could not go through the elaborate rituals of daily ablution that were prescribed for him. Since it was clearly impossible in wooden ships for every man to have his own fire and cook his own food, Brahmans and Rajputs would have to live during the journey on parched gram or on raw flour and sugar. But these difficulties might perhaps with tact and firmness have been overcome. Once away from the village, men in the army always did make some compromise with strict rule—a burden impossible to bear, as St Paul had said of the Jewish law. It is one of the points about caste that is hard to understand that there *are* flexibilities and that a body of men can be persuaded to waive some points—though others never— provided a precedent is established. And as in other faiths, support can usually be found in the ancient scriptures either for the relaxation of a rule or for some new prohibition. But once it has been decided that caste is vitally involved and that the scriptures prohibit this or that, one might as well argue with the waves of the sea. After 1767 it was estab- lished that the scriptures forbade men of high caste to travel by sea. With the exception of six special battalions for general service, the Bengal Army therefore recruited men for service only in places which they could reach by land. In 1781, when the Carnatic was invaded by Tippoo and Madras was in dire need of help, five thousand Bengal sepoys left Midnapore in January and did not reach Eyre Coote till August. By sea, they need not have taken more than a fortnight.

In 1824 there began the First Burmese War; most of the Indian troops were from Madras, because of this difficulty about movement. But some Bengal battalions were needed and they were usually marched first to Chittagong and thence into Burma, by tracks through the mountains that more than a hundred years later were still slow, difficult and infested with a particularly malignant form of malaria. It was a war of little military interest except to underline the importance of transport, supplies and good medical arrangements. The 47th Bengal Native Infantry were ordered to Burma and as a first stage were marched from Muttra in the North-Western Provinces to Barrackpore. Here they waited till the rains should end and they could start their march;

other units were also waiting for the same purpose and rumours were busy. Those about the climate, the disease and the hardships of Burma were basically true, though no doubt exaggerated. There was also a military set-back at Ramu in Burma, of which the wildest accounts appeared in the native press; these of course were magnified still more by rumour and the talk in the bazaars was that the British had been driven into the sea and the Burmese were advancing on Calcutta. In the bazaars everyone knew that the Burmese had magical powers, that they tortured prisoners and mutilated the dead. In that very year, there had been a reorganization; each old regiment of two battalions had been split into two single separate regiments, the officers being divided strictly by seniority. This had separated many officers from the men who knew them. Altogether, the atmosphere was ideal for anyone who wished to foment a grievance—and a serious grievance presented itself.

Neither bullocks nor drivers could be found. As we have seen, a sepoy on the march, with his knapsack, musket and sixty rounds of ball ammunition, was heavily loaded, and when the regiment was moving it was customary to hire bullocks to carry the men's private possessions. These did not change much in a hundred years; a roll of striped blue and white matting made the outside of the bundle and at night was spread on straw to make a bed; rolled up, it contained brass vessels for cooking and drawing water from a well, of which each man must have his own, and usually a cotton quilt for warmth at night. The men had to pay for the hire of bullocks to carry these bundles and it usually cost them their marching batta of one and a half rupees a month. But now there were no bullocks. Some regiments had marched already and taken the best; no doubt the rumours had caused others to go into hiding. The official agency could find no more and the soldiers of the 47th were told to find their own. At the same time, a rumour went through the bazaars that since there were no bullocks, and they could not march to Burma, they were to be shipped direct to Rangoon. The Colonel commanding the 47th, one Cartwright, offered to buy bullocks from his own pocket for the transport of the men's baggage and at last a collection of miserable creatures was got together. Now the Government belatedly agreed, not to buy them, but to advance money for their purchase. Ten bullocks were allotted to each company and Cartwright made an advance to each man of four rupees. This was on October 31st and the regiment was to march next day. He thought all would now be well.

But by this time the regiment was beyond reason. They refused to bring their knapsacks on parade, saying that they were old and unserviceable, that they had been promised new ones, and that there had been stoppages for knapsacks. They said they would not go to

Burma without double batta and they would not set foot in a boat at any point on the route. Next day they refused to parade, seized the colours of the regiment and threatened violence to the Brigade Commander and Brigade-Major. Finally, they told Cartwright they would march only if the Government would provide the bullocks free and give them double batta, but added a new condition, that the Subadar-Major and Havildar-Major should be put to death. The Subadar-Major was a Muslim and it was alleged that he was a bully, that he had too much influence with the Colonel, and that he had threatened the Hindus that he would force them all to go in a ship. The men were eventually brought to the parade-ground, but again refused to obey Cartwright's orders. They stayed on the parade-ground the whole of November 1st — the day when they should have marched — and all night too.

At midnight the Commander-in-Chief, Sir Edward Paget, arrived. He had ordered to Barrackpore two battalions of British infantry, a company of artillery, a troop of the Governor-General's bodyguard and the 68th Native Infantry. This imposing force arrived early on the morning of November 2nd and was immediately drawn up on the parade-ground covering the 47th, who presented the Commander-in-Chief with a petition. This repeated their fears of being sent by sea; they begged to be discharged in a body and allowed to go home. Sir Edward Paget replied that he understood their objection to going by sea, that he had never ordered any sepoy to go by ship unless he agreed and would listen to them further, but that they must first lay down their arms and surrender unconditionally. But they refused to ground arms and a party seized and destroyed the colours of the 26th, another regiment which was under orders for Burma and was discontented but much less seriously affected. At this, Paget ordered two guns to open fire on the 47th. They were loaded with case or canister. The mutineers broke and fled; they offered no resistance. Indeed, their muskets were not loaded. Few were killed but many wounded; a number were taken prisoner. That day, November 2nd, a native court martial sentenced 41 prisoners to death. Of these, twelve were executed next day; the sentences on the others were commuted to hard labour. The regiment was disbanded and the number erased from the Army List.

A special inquiry was held and reported at length on the causes of the mutiny. There were the special matters already mentioned — rumours about what had happened at Ramu and about conditions in Burma. There was the lack of transport bullocks, and by general agreement this was the prime cause. But there was also a long list of general causes, which would be included in any list of causes of the Great Mutiny of 1857: reorganization, strange officers, the officers' lack of interest in their men, the soldier's feeling that they were now held in lower esteem than before, the expansion of British territory, the rise in prices.

The personalities of two men were all-important. Cartwright was lacking neither in zeal nor sympathy but he seems to have been one of those men who insist on exact and unnecessary detail and who seldom inspire respect. He was said by the men to have been in the pocket of the Subadar-Major, and this is the kind of thing about which the men are usually right; it is clear that he was quite unable to get the men to listen to reason. They had of course a genuine grievance over the transport but a commanding officer with influence would have been able to keep them to that point and prevent the spread of a general distrust and discontent.

Kaye says of Sir Edward Paget that he was 'a hard strict disciplinarian with no knowledge of the native army and a bitter prejudice against it'. It seems beyond doubt that he gave no warning before he ordered the guns to open. The mutineers had not themselves loaded; they were not told the guns were loaded and ready to fire; indeed, Kaye adds that it is doubtful whether they even knew the guns were there, behind the British regiments. The effect throughout the army was bound to be fear and distrust. ' "They are your own men whom you have been destroying," said an old native officer; and he could not trust himself to say more.' Had the General commanding the division been a man with long knowledge of the country and a commanding personality— Malcolm or Ochterlony, Skinner or Hearsey—he could surely have avoided that sudden and brutal act which, like Dyer's at Amritsar a hundred years later, suggests a man using power to vent a deep dislike which had perhaps grown stronger from being long suppressed.

These two cases, Vellore and Barrackpore, set the pattern of mutiny. They were warnings to which few paid attention.

XI

Fear and its Causes

1. The Threat to Property

The sepoy's faith in the star of the invincible Company had been
shaken by the retreat from Kabul; his faith in the Company's care for
its children had received shattering blows when the foreign allowance
had been withdrawn for service in Sind and the Punjab. More and more
often, over the past thirty years, the best officers had left the regiment
for special appointments while those who stayed had lost interest by
the time they were promoted. It had become more and more common
for young officers to be interested in anything but their duties and to be
bored with their men. The Colonel's powers had been reduced; the
whole machine had grown stiff, centralized and impersonal.

None the less, it still worked; the successes of this army had been so
sensational, pride in the regiment had been so strong, the impact of
good officers, of regular pay and pensions had been so marked an improvement on anything soldiers in India had known before, that it held
together. And, as the Mutiny was to show again and again, the personal
link between officer and men was still often strong; not only were there
men who risked their lives to save an officer they loved but there were
many officers who refused to believe in the possibility that *their* men
could go wrong. One of the haunting pictures from the Mutiny which
recurs is of the old colonel, utterly bewildered because his men will not
listen to him, the tears running down his face as he cries out to them:
'My children! My children! Oh, my children!'

There is much that is significant about this scene. '*Mere bābā-log*'
were the words used — *baba-logue* in the spelling of the time. *Baba* in its
first meaning is a term of respect for an old man, but was always used
by Indian servants of white children. This may surprise a European
but it is very Indian; one word means both 'yesterday' and 'tomorrow';
there is another word which means 'the day before yesterday' and 'the
day after tomorrow'. Time stretches in either direction; respect for the
old and for the very young are the same. But there is a nursery flavour
about *bābā-log*; as used by a colonel of his men, it is affectionate but

very paternal. 'My dear little children' is perhaps the nearest we can get. *Log* means 'people' and is simply a nursery plural, as in *bandarlog*, 'the monkey people'. A colonel's relations with his men must always be based on a formal convention; this choice of words suggests a brittle convention with a shallow sentimental background. They were grown men with wives and children of their own and the words suggest that he had forgotten this.

The army held together, but more by the memory of what it had been than by what it was. It was vulnerable to political attack from outside or to the spread of doubts from within. That is the military background. At the same time, throughout India, there was a feeling among the classes who would normally have influence—that is, priests and landowners—that deliberate attacks were developing on both property and religion. This of course was immensely disturbing to the sepoy of the Bengal Army; he was a villager as well as a soldier; he came from the upper section of village society, of which land and religion were the props. The feeling was by no means without grounds. For thirty years now, English administrators had more and more often belonged to one school of thought; they were more and more often 'levellers'. At Haileybury, the training college for the civil servants of the Company, they might have been taught by Malthus; they had learnt 'political economy' and had been influenced by the teachings of Bentham and Mill. They believed in *progress*, perhaps more in abstract progress than in people. They did not often see how disturbing progress might be. They were eager for social improvement, intolerant of all who stood in their way; they made no allowance for the attachment men often feel for old ways, even when they are irrational and even oppressive. Least of all did they understand that their 'progress', their 'improvement', were to most Indians foreign and therefore distasteful. It is after all a good deal easier to see the need for drastic change in a country which one will leave on retirement than in one's own. There were still men like Henry Lawrence, Outram and Bartle Frere, who were warmer of heart than the 'levellers', less sure that they were right, more tolerant of Indian ways. But the levellers grew in power and influence; they were utterly sure that it was their duty to end anomalous privileges as well as customs they considered immoral and degrading. 'The native aristocracy had been for some time an abomination in the eyes of English statesmen in India,' wrote Kaye, the historian of the Mutiny, and of the leveller school it was true.

To understand what the levellers were trying to do about land is quite easy provided one dismisses European ideas and starts from the traditional Indian basis. To begin with, there are cultivators and a sovereign; the sovereign is entitled to a share of the crop and has various rights over waste land and forest. In many parts of India, the cultivators in each village had once constituted a kind of joint-stock company, each cultivating his own fields, which he passed to his children, but jointly having rights in forest and grazing land, and united against outsiders from any other village. Sometimes these share-holders were responsible jointly for paying the King's share of the crop. In some parts of India, notably and perhaps significantly in the Maratha country and the.Sikh country, these village communities could still be found and still sometimes paid the King's share of the crop direct to the King. But in many other parts the village community had been ob-literated by intermediaries between the sovereign and the peasants. Sometimes the sovereign had rewarded an official by granting him the right to collect the King's share of the produce in so many villages, perhaps for a fixed tribute or service. For the Mughal Emperors, this was the standard way of paying an official. Often an official's son contrived to make this personal grant hereditary. Sometimes a petty sovereign had been reduced, becoming tributary to a greater; sometimes a successful robber chief had established himself by force as master of half a county and had there collected the King's share. Over the greater part of India there was a complicated tangle of rights, some going back many generations, some only two or three or less; some had been sold, many had been divided by inheritance. Sometimes there were several intermediaries between the man who ploughed and the sovereign. They ranged from a petty squire whose thirty or forty cultivators did not till two hundred acres between them to one of the Oudh *taluqdars*, who might have the title of Maharaja and pay tribute to the King of Oudh for an estate the size of an English county.

Some of these intermediaries protected their tenants or subjects against everyone else, lent them money for weddings and settled their quarrels. Others did little for them and wrung from them all they could. Perhaps most were oppressive, as the levellers certainly believed; often their agents were more oppressive than themselves. None came up to the standard of the ideal landlord in England, the best of whom were introducing new crops and improving the system of agriculture and the output of their estates. Such landlords as Coke and Townshend in the eighteenth century played the part taken today by agricultural research stations. Landlords of this kind formed part of the picture of an ideal society cherished by most Englishmen. At the end of the eighteenth century Cornwallis as Governor-General had tried to create landlords of this kind in Bengal; half a century later it seemed to the levellers as clear as daylight that his attempt had failed, that the inter-mediaries between sovereign and peasant were generally reactionary parasites. Hence there arose a temper of opinion in which, as Kaye wrote, 'To oust a Taluqdar was held by some young settlement officers to be as great an achievement as to shoot a tiger.' Such young men—

and some of their elders—believed that to restore the old village community and remove all intermediaries between the cultivator and the Crown was the finest thing they could do. And they elevated this belief into a dogma, held with passionate, almost religious, fervour.

Everywhere in the 'thirties, 'forties and 'fifties of the century, work was in progress to establish and record rights in the land and to settle the revenue—the King's share—which had to be paid on it. It was an immense task, involving much detailed work, and it was rightly regarded as of far more importance than merely bringing in revenue, because it would very largely influence the kind of society that would grow up. The levellers examined with jealous care the claims of every landowner or petty chief. The fact that some of the Company's officials were *not* levellers made the whole process even more disturbing than if there had been one uniform system. The case of the Raja of Mainpuri may be cited to illustrate this point. He was a great landowner who supposed his estate to include 189 villages; these he had inherited from his ancestors and from all of them his agents collected the King's share of the crop, as they had for a century. About half the total of this he paid to the Government. But a zealous young settlement officer, having carefully examined such deeds as the raja could produce, found that his claim was valid for only 51 of them—reducing his property at a blow by nearly three-quarters. The Commissioner, a man of the old school who detested the levellers, reversed the young man's decision, but the Board of Revenue, headed by a leveller, restored it; the Lieutenant-Governor agreed with the Commissioner and ordered the Board of Revenue to return his property to the raja. But while the formalities necessary for restitution were still being ponderously ground over, a new Lieutenant-Governor appeared who was the prince of all levellers —and once again the raja was shorn of the greater part of his estate. This kind of thing happened to hundreds of little estates, for which there were often none of the title-deeds that were demanded. In 1852 there was appointed in the southern Maratha country the Inam Commission; it examined the titles of 35,000 estates, of which three-fifths were held to be not good and were therefore confiscated.

Such vicissitudes were unsettling to all men of property. They would clearly make enemies of many great landowners. But it was not only the great who were threatened. Every claim to collect the King's share was scrutinized with the same jealous care—and this meant a threat to thousands who could never be called great nobles. There were endowments all over India for charity and religion, which often meant that a village, or part of a village, paid its dues to the descendant of a priest or schoolmaster who did very little in return. There were still plenty of such sinecures in England in the nineteenth century; they might mean that after providing for the charity intended, there was a comfortable surplus for someone, as there was for the warden of the alms-houses at Barchester. Such endowments might be either Hindu or Muslim; they were property, giving a family consequence in the village—but they had also a sanctity in the eyes of the villagers, embodying the wishes of the pious dead and providing for the continuance of a mosque or a temple, a school for learning the Shastras or the *Qur'an*, a hostelry for pilgrims, or a last home for sick and aged cows. Sometimes a whole village had been dedicated simply to the support of a group of Brahmans. To the levellers all such endowments were anathema, partly because they provided a surplus for which no service was given and partly because they were not Christian—and the levellers, almost to a man, were adherents of a Christianity whose temper was highly intolerant. Tenures of this kind were felt by the levellers to be a scandal and a reproach, and these too were now to be rigorously tested and if possible ended.

What was likely to be the effect on the army? 'The sepoys are almost all landholders, many of them Brahmans, whose families are supported by the charitable foundations which it is now sought to confiscate and destroy,' wrote the *Englishman* on November 2nd, 1838, and the article went on to foresee 'a loss of confidence in British faith and honour' that would mean that 'we shall very soon have to trust for our security to British troops alone.' But perhaps few understood that not only the great nobles were threatened, and not only charitable foundations, but everyone who paid the King's share for land he did not actually plough himself. Landowners and tenants in many parts were much less distinct classes than in England and there were men who tilled one piece of land for themselves and let out another. It might be only a few acres but it gave them consequence and brought in a little cash and such men must have felt themselves threatened.

Even those who were supposed to benefit by the levellers' reforms felt uneasy. They looked with suspicion at anything new, fearing that it might be even worse than the present. For some of the intermediaries—'landlords' is the nearest English word but a little misleading—they had a respect, even an affection. And the system was personal, it did provide some elasticity. After the Mutiny, the English became far more cautious about 'progress' and this was one of the grounds for criticism levelled at them by the National Congress. In Uttar Pradesh (which had once been the North-Western Provinces and later the United Provinces) the Congress Government soon after Independence did very much what the levellers had wanted to do; they ended the rights of intermediaries. In 1957, a hundred years after the Mutiny, I often started a conversation in a village of Rohilkand by mentioning this reform. No more oppressive landlords! Now they paid direct to the Government, their *own* Government. Surely they thought this was a good thing? Not a bit of it. Again and again the answer came that the landlord had been human; he would grant delay if hail had slashed the crop, if locusts or rust or blight had taken their share; he would lend money for a wedding; he would take something on account. But the Government man—you have to pay standing up! No time to sit down and talk it over; no gossip, no bargaining, no allowance for that lawsuit or that long illness.

2. The Threat to the Princes

So the levellers by a well-meaning rigidity made enemies of influential men who might have been friends and spread an unease among all who had any property in land—and apart from silver ornaments and coin buried under the bed, land was the form that savings would usually take. And the spirit which inspired the young settlement officer to abolish, wherever he could, any intermediary rights in land reached to the top of the pyramid. The Governor-General, Lord Dalhousie, whose reign was from 1848 to 1856, backed the levellers everywhere and in his own special sphere of dealing with Indian states he applied just the same principles. He believed passionately that British rule was always for the benefit of the peasant and that the rule of an Indian prince was likely to be oppressive and corrupt. He regarded princely misgovernment as a reproach to the British name and the states as obsolete survivals, standing in the way of the united and progressive India which he pictured. He therefore sincerely regarded it as a duty to annex the territory of a prince wherever grounds for doing so could be found. It is remarkable how closely his policy anticipated that of Congress in 1947.

There were two main grounds for annexation and one on which he laid special stress. It was established Hindu practice to adopt an heir if there was no natural son; indeed, it was a religious duty, since there were funeral rites which must be performed by a son, whether natural or adopted. Dalhousie asserted, and applied whenever possible, the doctrine that since the paramount power might decide a disputed succession in a state, its approval was necessary for *any* succession and, in the case of an adopted heir, might be withheld. In that case, there being no natural heir, the state would lapse to the Paramount Power. Dalhousie did not invent this 'doctrine of lapse' but he revived it, and applied it far more rigorously than ever before. 'When the right to territory by lapse is clear,' Dalhousie wrote, 'the Government is bound to take that which is justly and legally its due, and to extend to that territory the benefits of our sovereignty.' The doctrine did not apply to all states, but only to those 'dependent' on the Paramount Power; this included such a state as Mysore, where the original Hindu royal family had been restored by the British after the defeat of Tippoo; it did not include the ancient states of Rajputana, which had been in existence long before the British landed in India. But this distinction, however clear in the Governor-General's office, was not much understood outside. It was obscured, for the world in general, by Dalhousie's second reason for annexation. It was his policy to assume the government of any state, whether dependent or not, and whether there was an heir or not, where misgovernment had been prolonged and chronic. And finally, wherever there survived a title and a pension to which no duties were attached — something which represented only a memory of past magnificence or the mercy shown to the vanquished by an earlier and more magnanimous generation — then Dalhousie made it a settled policy to abolish or reduce.

During his eight years in office, Lord Dalhousie proposed to annex seven Indian states. In one case, the Directors in England decided against annexation; in two others, the decision was reversed by Lord Canning, who succeeded Dalhousie. But the mere fact of discussion was enough to unsettle the remaining princes. During the same period four hereditary titles and the pensions that went with them were threatened, three being actually extinguished. And finally Oudh was annexed, on grounds not of lapse but of continued misgovernment. Oudh was one of the two great Muslim states that remained and one that had for nearly a hundred years been a faithful ally. Meanwhile the Nizam, the ruler of the other great Muslim state, was ordered to surrender a large stretch of territory in order to pay the cost of the Hyderabad contingent, the force deputed to protect him and incidentally to keep him in order.

That catalogue is enough to make the point. There was uncertainty and fear; every prince was bound to feel that the rule of his house was no longer safe. In addition, some implacable enemies were made. But the mere catalogue does not show the full extent of the threat. To most Indians the policy seemed one of pure greed and injustice. Thus it sapped the foundation of British rule, which was confidence in the permanence of a power that would sustain the social order. It was this confidence that made government possible with a minimum use of force and with staggeringly few foreign officials. Further, the states on whom the blow happened to fall seemed as though chosen to threaten as wide a range of interests as possible. One of the first was Satara; this was undoubtedly 'dependent', in the sense in which the Governor-General's office used the term, having been revived by the British after the last great Maratha War to provide a principality for the descendants of Sivaji. In 1848 the Raja of Satara died, leaving no natural son. Dalhousie decided that no heir by adoption should succeed and thus began the fatal series. Satara was a small state, but the raja was held in special respect by all Marathas. The question asked in every princely state was what he had done to deserve this punishment for his family. He had been guilty of no infidelity against the British, and it occurred to most to contrast the magnanimity of the British in 1818 with their greed in 1848.

That blow to Maratha pride was quickly followed by another. The Bhonsla of Berar, also known as the Raja of Nagpur, died without heir. His had been one of the five great states of the old Maratha Confederacy; it was one of the largest to survive. No doubt his ancestors had fought against the British and been conquered; no one would have been surprised if his territories had been confiscated in 1818. But they had been spared and again the raja, if far from a model ruler, had done no overt wrong. He had postponed the adoption of an heir, but by the custom of his people his widow could do this for him. Dalhousie, however, declared the state annexed and the shock was made worse by the auction of the raja's goods, including his elephants, camels and horses and the jewels of his mother and wives.

Jhansi was a much smaller and less important Maratha state, undoubtedly 'dependent' because it was elevated from a subordinate status as a dukedom or barony; its chief had been a vassal who became a raja at the general settlement of 1818. Further, the last three rajas had been more than usually incapable and degenerate. Its annexation, when the last raja died, would not be remembered if it had not been for the implacable fury it aroused in the Rani of Jhansi, who in 1857 killed every European on whom she could lay her hands, led troops with a spirit and determination no man could have bettered and died in battle, by the sword of a British trooper, fighting mounted, dressed as a man, at the head of her followers.*

Proposals went to London for the annexation of one Rajputana state and, though they were not sanctioned, the fact that this was even discussed must have been known and must have filled with horror every princely bosom. For the Rajput princes were not upstarts like the Marathas; their pedigrees went back to the Sun and the Moon; they were the descendants of the first Aryan invaders who had come over the Himalayas three thousand years before. As if that were not enough,

---

* The Rani of Jhansi sent letters to British officers in the early stages of the Mutiny protesting her continued loyalty, and explaining that she had been forced into what she did. Dr Sen, the Indian historian of the Mutiny, accepts these at their face value, but the facts suggest to me that they were an insurance against an uncertain future, like the letters to the Pretender sent by Marlborough and other nobles at the court of Queen Anne. The Rani has been a heroine of the Indian National movement, and in my view it is more honourable to her name to suppose that she was always at heart a gallant antagonist of a Government which she undoubtedly thought had wronged her.

Dalhousie had proposed to oust from the Red Fort the descendant of Akbar, the Emperor in whose name the Company had governed, by whose grants their first possessions had been held. Up till the 1840s British officers had approached his presence barefooted, made obeisance and presented a ceremonial offering of gold. Now his heir, in return for recognition and a pension, was to give up the imperial title and leave his palace. This proposal was never carried out but an end was made of the title of the Nawab of Arcot (or of the Carnatic, as he was sometimes called) in whose name we had fought those first wars with the French. And the pension promised by Sir John Malcolm to the Peshwa, Baji Rao, was disallowed to his adopted son.

The Peshwa had undoubtedly fought against us and been beaten; he had surrendered to the mercy of the British and he had been treated with generosity. He had been deprived of his territory, his sovereignty and even his title; he had been banished to another part of India, near Cawnpore. But he had been granted a yearly pension of eight lakhs of rupees—about £80,000—for himself and his family. He had enjoyed it for thirty years, living in some state, surrounded by relatives and retainers, but actually saving money, and in all his outward behaviour at least appearing to justify Malcolm's argument that such chivalrous generosity to a beaten foe was an act of wise policy. He executed a will, leaving all he possessed to his adopted son, the Nana Sahib, a young man of twenty-seven, of whom the British in general had approved as 'not at all addicted to any extravagant habits and invariably showing a ready disposition to attend to the advice of the British Commissioner'. That officer recommended that, as an act of grace, some part at least of the former Peshwa's pension should be continued to his heir, so that he might support the family and retainers of his father by adoption. But the Lieutenant-Governor was Mr Thomason, a leader of the levellers, and the Governor-General was Lord Dalhousie. The recommendation was disallowed and the Nana Sahib was told he must live on the capital his father had saved. He sent emissaries to London, as the families of Satara and Nagpur had done; they argued that the case of the Peshwa was like that of the Emperor at Delhi and that the pension had been intended to be perpetual. But they were unable to change the decision. The Directors concurred with the Governor-General. And, though the Nana Sahib did not reveal his feelings till 1857, another enemy had been made, one hardly less implacable than the Rani of Jhansi.

The last and most important was Oudh. It was one of the two great Muslim states, the two substantial survivals of the empire of Akbar and Aurangzebe. The Kings of Oudh had been as famous for the beauty and luxury of their capital as for the corruption and incompetence of their administration. But for eighty years they had been loyal allies and their territory was the main recruiting-ground for the Company's army. Governor-General after Governor-General had warned successive kings that they must mend their ways or be deposed — but again and again it had been decided to spare Oudh, because of the effect on the army, because of its loyalty, and because there were good arguments for retaining native states in general. These had been urged by the wisest of the British in India, from Warren Hastings to Metcalfe and Munro, and they were still supported, even in Dalhousie's reign, by Colonel John Low, who argued the case forcefully to the Governor-General, and by Henry Lawrence, Sleeman and Outram. None of these men disputed that Oudh was so incompetently governed that it had become a scandal; all agreed that intervention was necessary. But they thought it should be temporary; they believed we should intervene to put things in order and then restore the monarchy, that above all we should be seen not to profit by the intervention. But their pleading was in vain and Oudh was annexed in 1856.

The arguments for preserving Indian states in general were of several kinds. The states provided an opportunity for an ambitious Indian that was denied him in British India. In a state, he could be Prime Minister; in a British district, he could be no more than deputy to the District Magistrate. They provided a contrast to our system of government — and in the 'forties and 'fifties almost every Englishman thought that anyone who made the comparison must prefer our rule. Also, they provided a network of allies, none powerful enough to be a threat by themselves and most unlikely to form a powerful combination, yet many of them strong enough to be of some help in case of internal troubles. Without the states, we should be far too dependent on the native army, which in itself was dangerous. And it would be the more dangerous, because the native army, while conscious of its power, would feel that there were no more worlds to conquer, its occupation was gone and its existence threatened. Thus the army was an important element in the arguments of those who still ventured to contest the views of the levellers. There was one more point in their case — perhaps the strongest, but the least likely to appeal to such men as Thomason and Dalhousie. 'In one respect,' wrote John Low, 'the natives of India are exactly like the inhabitants of all parts of the known world; they like their own habits and customs better than those of foreigners.'

The annexation of Oudh was the culminating blow in the attack on property. As we have seen already, it had a special effect on the army, because this was the home of most sepoys in the Bengal Army. It strengthened several feelings already prevalent and growing stronger — that there was no longer any faith to be put in the word of the Company; that over the whole of India there would soon be one uniform foreign rule, deadening the Indian quality of life, levelling and reforming, destroying all that distinguished men of high caste and good family from their inferiors; that for the army there would soon be no occupation except overseas and that thus their caste and the restrictions it imposed would become merely a nuisance to their officers. At the same time, they were immediately aware that they had lost a privileged position; as soldiers of the Company they had been able to get a hearing from the King of Oudh's officers that no one else in the village could hope for. Now they were villagers like anyone else.

There can be no doubt that the levellers were disinterested men of high ideals, concerned—if in a somewhat abstract way—for the good of the peasant. It can be argued that they were far-sighted statesmen, anticipating as they did the kind of reform the Indian National Congress was to take up a hundred years later. But there is a coldness about their approach and a lack of humanity; they did not understand that men like old ways best. There can surely be no doubt that their reforms helped to bring about the unease, the suspicion and the unhappiness which are the background to the Mutiny.

3. The Threat to Religion

Some implacable enemies had been made, there was a general feeling of unease over the threat to property. But the attack on religion seemed to the sepoys more explicit and more terrifying. There were many acts of the Government which contributed to their apprehension, but they could have had no effect if it had not been for the changed attitude of the English to religion, something of which many sepoys had direct evidence. The English of the eighteenth century had believed in God, but they were creatures of the Age of Reason; they were aware of doubts, they were content like Warren Hastings to leave the religious creed of Hindus to 'the Being who has so long endured it and who will in his own time reform it'. But the beliefs of the evangelical school—and this meant many officers, both civil and military—were far more positive and dogmatic. Colonel Wheler, who in 1857 was commanding the 34th Native Infantry at Barrackpore, wrote in that year in a letter to the Government: 'As to the question whether I have endeavoured to convert Sepoys and others to Christianity, I would humbly reply that this has been my object, and I conceive is the aim ... of every Christian ... that the Lord would make him the happy instrument of converting his neighbour to God, or, in other words, of rescuing him from eternal destruction.' For the last twenty years he had been in the habit of speaking on this subject to Indians whom he met in 'the highways, cities, bazaars and villages'. And Wheler was not alone in his missionary zeal. R. T. Tucker, a civil servant of the Company, encouraged a Bengali clergyman, himself a convert to Christianity, to preach the gospel to the prisoners in the district jail. It was Tucker who at his own expense set up columns inscribed with the Ten Commandments in Hindi and Urdu at the entrances to Fatehpur city, while he helped prisoners who had been converted to obtain plots of land and set up as farmers on their release. Village record-keepers or *patwaris* who were to be trained in the Hindi script were sent to the mission school to learn it and each came away with a copy of the New Testament. The memoirs of James Laverack, a Methodist soldier who served both before and after the Mutiny, speak of meetings in public places at which the object was to convert and in which British officers and men sometimes took part. Missionaries preached in bazaars and market-places, denouncing in violent terms the creeds of Hindu and Muslim alike. And it was hard for the sepoy to distinguish between the missionary and the chaplain paid by the Government. The duty of the chaplain was the care of British soldiers and officials; he was as much part of the establishment as the doctor but it was not part of his official duties to convert anyone. The missionary on the other hand brought money from England privately subscribed; his aim was avowedly to convert. But how could the sepoy make such a distinction? They were all padres, they were all white; of course the Government was behind the missionaries.

All this effort to save from damnation was not Government policy, but there was much sympathy for it among the individuals who made up the Government. And the belief grew, not only among the sepoys but among many others, that the Government was only waiting for a favourable moment to come out openly in favour of conversion on a wide scale. In 1855, there occurred what S. N. Sen, the first professional Indian historian of the Mutiny, rightly calls the height of missionary indiscretion. A certain Mr Edmond, writing from Calcutta, apparently on behalf of a number of missionaries, sent a circular letter to many officials of the state and to many 'educated natives', arguing that the time had come for 'all men to embrace the same system of religion'. Railways and the electric telegraph had brought all men closer; all men felt the same hopes and fears; for all, death was the end. 'Has the one God, who made all, appointed different methods of obtaining present and future happiness to different portions of His family? Surely, this cannot be.' And the letter continued with the clear implication that the one religion which rational consideration suggested was that of the superior beings who had brought India the wonders of science. This letter put its finger on a point already sore; railways and telegraphs were felt in themselves to be a threat to religion, partly for the direct reason that on a long journey a Brahman might have to sit near a man of low caste and must either abstain from food altogether or abandon the proper ritual; he might afterwards have to spend money on expensive ceremonial to cleanse himself from pollution. But there was more to it than that; the European's mastery of science could hardly fail to suggest that he had some clues to the nature of the universe which the Brahman priests had missed. There were ancient prophecies of an accursed age, ruled by demons, in which there would be an end to caste and therefore to the whole system of rewards and penalties for acts in a previous incarnation—and thus to all morality. And this was exactly the vision that Edmond's letter suggested. It was widely believed to be inspired by the Government—a kite to try the wind. The Commissioner of Patna reported that 'intelligent natives', especially 'the better class' of Muslims, were 'impressed with a full belief that the Government were immediately about to attempt the forcible conversion of its subjects.' The Lieutenant-Governor of Bengal issued a proclamation denying any such intention, which no doubt confirmed many in the idea that the intention existed, even if it had been postponed. And letters were published answering the proclamation and showing what grounds 'intelligent natives' had for believing that a war on their religion was really threatened.

Behind what to most Indians seemed an open assault lay something subtler, the impact of education and of Western science. Macaulay's famous minute had poked outrageous fun at Persian and Sanskrit literature and all oriental learning; it had turned the scale after long debate and had meant that higher education throughout India should be in English and the subjects taught should be Western. This was bound to be a threat to the priesthood; the system of thought which had led to the discovery of steam-power and to the spread over much of the world of a parliamentary system of government must inevitably clash with a rigid system of outward ceremonial, dogmatic teaching and social hierarchy. This would have been so even if the teachers had been sympathetic to Hinduism. But they were not. Kaye, an excellent historian, liberal in his sympathies, wise and far-seeing in his judgments, wrote: 'Brahminism is the most monstrous system of interference and oppression that the world has ever yet seen and ... it could be maintained only by ignorance and superstition of the grossest kind.' In this view he represented almost every Englishman of his period. He goes on to quote a Hindu writer who says that 'grammar, geography, law, medicine and metaphysics' all form an essential part of Hinduism; to teach any system which had not been handed down for two thousand years was to threaten the whole fabric. Today most Westerners would suppose that even if Sanskrit geography and physics were wide of the mark, there was much wisdom in the philosophy and religion that accompanied them, but in the 1840s neither the Brahmans nor the

English thought on such lines. Both saw only stark opposition. To teach science or Western philosophy was to threaten religion.

The Company had once made it a dogma that there should be no interference with religion. But there was much in the Hinduism of that period that was degenerate; practices unknown in the Vedas had received the sanction of the Brahmans and some of them were repugnant to Europeans. The best-known of these—though there were others equally indefensible—was *sati* or suttee, the practice of burning a widow alive with her husband's corpse. There is a certain barbaric nobility about the Rajput queen who casts herself on to the pyre beside the warrior husband brought back dead from battle; there is as least one account by an eye-witness of a widow rapt in ecstasy who stepped into the flames as though into a bath. But there are many more of frightened women who, in a moment of weakness, when the impact of death was fresh, had given a half-willing consent under pressure, who were tied to the corpse and forced to go through the agony by priests and their own relations. Several of the Governors-General had wished to end the practice but they had shrunk from prohibiting it because they feared the effect it might have on the Brahmans and Rajputs of the Bengal Army. But Lord William Bentinck had the courage to make *sati* murder. His Government congratulated themselves on the success of the measure; there was no outbreak in protest. Indeed, there was much support among enlightened Indians. But to the old-fashioned and orthodox, it was an attack on religion. It was remembered.

Another measure, even more obnoxious in orthodox eyes, became law in 1850; this permitted a son to inherit his father's property even though he had changed his religion. It was regarded by both Hindu and Muslim as designed to encourage the conversion of their children to Christianity. Then again, it was a logical step, if a Hindu widow was not to be burned, to make it possible for her to remarry. An Act was prepared for this purpose; though it had some Hindu support, Hindu orthodoxy argued that wives would now be encouraged to poison their husbands—and that the next step would be the prohibition of polygamy and another blow at the Hindu family. The Act permitting widows to marry was actually passed after Dalhousie had left, under Canning; it took effect in July 1856. The question of checking and regulating, though not actually prohibiting, polygamy was discussed, but for the moment postponed.

Thus the family, the centre of Hinduism, was felt to be under attack. And there was evidence of the Government's secret intentions to be deduced from what they were doing in the gaols. It had been the custom to allow every prisoner to prepare his own food. But this was not only objectionable to a tidy mind; it was administratively inconvenient. A man could spend a long time over his cooking and avoid work. A regulation of 1845 provided that there should be Brahman cooks who would prepare meals for all the prisoners; this, to anyone with a slight acquaintance with the caste-system, would seem innocuous, but in fact Brahmans are divided into many different groups who cannot eat together or eat food cooked by one of the other groups. There is a proverb in mockery of this, to the effect that where there are four Brahmans of one particularly exclusive group there will be six cooking-places. A tactful governor, in a particular prison, might have introduced something of the kind, at least for all but a privileged few—but a Government regulation, in an atmosphere already suspicious, was bound to confirm the idea that the Government meant to break up caste. Then Muslim prisoners were to be shaved. And next an attempt was made to forbid prisoners the use of a brass *lota*; this is a drinking vessel, personal to the user, essential to every Hindu and cherished also by Muslims who have absorbed Hindu ideas. But it can be used as a weapon, and Kaye mentions the case of a British magistrate killed in a gaol near Calcutta by a blow from a brass lota. So it was proposed to substitute earthenware vessels—but earthenware is far more liable to pollution than brass; even fine porcelain cannot, by any amount of washing, be freed from pollution if a Christian has eaten from it. The order about earthenware lotas was worse than an order in a modern gaol that everyone must use the same toothbrush; it was not only physically disgusting, it was sacrilegious. It was regarded as religious persecution; the gaols were being used to destroy caste and interfere with the cycle of rebirth. Townspeople sided with the prisoners; there were riots in at least two places in Bihar. This was in 1855.

The coming of Lord Canning after Lord Dalhousie might, if men had understood his character, have reduced the tension. He was a far less imperious man than Dalhousie, less rigid, more ready to make allowances for the point of view of others. But it was he who gave formal assent to the Act permitting Hindu widows to remarry and to the annexation of Oudh, both measures proposed and worked out by his predecessor. And it was he and his Council who were responsible for the Act which for the sepoys put the final touch to their loss of confidence. This was the General Service Enlistment Act, which went out as an order on July 25th, 1856. It had in fact been discussed in 1852 but the idea had not then been pursued. As we have seen, men of the Bengal Army, except for six battalions out of seventy-two, were enlisted for service only in places to which they could march. This was obviously most inconvenient for the military authorities, particularly after the Second Burmese War of 1852. Burma now had to have a permanent garrison of Indian troops, and it was only reasonable that the Bengal Army should bear part of this burden. Of the six Bengal general service battalions, three were already in Burma and three just back;

three relief battalions were needed at once, and indeed more than three; Madras, with a smaller army, was already providing a bigger contingent than Bengal, because Madras men were enlisted for general service. It was surely against all reason that a Government should have to beg its soldiers to volunteer for garrison duty within its possessions; more than one member of the Council wrote a long minute showing how unreasonable it was. The Bombay Army enlisted for general service and many of their men were Brahmans or Rajputs from Oudh. Even Brahmans from the Bengal Army had been known to volunteer for service beyond the sea—so there could be no rigid rule forbidding it. In fact, the Bengal sepoy would go when it suited him and this was most unsatisfactory. Of course, it was said, we must not break faith with those already in service, but there could be no possible objection to making general service a condition of employment for all recruits in future.

So they reasoned, and perhaps they would have been right if it had been a matter of reason, if the Bengal Army had not been a family affair, and if the atmosphere had not been already full of suspicion. But this general order confirmed all that the sepoys had most feared. Now it was clear that it was beyond the seas that they would be most useful to their foreign masters. The next step would be to apply the act to soldiers already in service. Indeed, the service was ruined already; the army they had known had meant a career for their sons as well as themselves. They would not let their sons come forward now.

This Act more than anything else must be held responsible for the rumours that spread during the next twelve months. Queen Victoria, it was said, had specially chosen Lord Canning and had entrusted him with the duty of converting all her subjects; the English were tired of the high-caste sepoys of Oudh and had already decided to enlist 30,000 Sikhs—those dirty, hairy barbarians. It was only a step from this to believing that the plot to break the caste of the sepoys had already begun. Sir Henry Lawrence in 1857 reported to Lord Canning a conversation he had had with a jemadar of artillery, a man of twenty years' standing, specially mentioned by his commanding officer for intelligence and good service; this man was absolutely convinced that for the last ten years, the British had been trying to spoil men's caste by mixing bone-dust with the flour. 'You want us all to eat what you like that we may be stronger and go everywhere,' he said. He thought we wanted to take Hindus to sea to conquer the world for us. He knew that we could raise men in England—but Hindus were cheaper. It is against such thoughts as these that the business of the greased cartridges must be seen.

4. The Cartridges

When Lord Dalhousie left India in 1856 he recorded in a long farewell minute his views on the questions he thought important. He hardly mentions the native army, in spite of the fact that the Commander-in-Chief had recently resigned because he thought it on the verge of mutiny. His confidence in its fidelity was complete, and on this point Kaye has expressed the feelings of his countrymen admirably. 'The fidelity of the Native Army', he wrote, 'was an established article of our faith ... The British Sepoy had faced death without a fear, and encountered every kind of suffering and privation without a murmur. Commanded by officers whom he trusted and loved, though of another colour and another creed, there was nothing, it was said, which he would not do, there was nothing which he would not endure ... History for a hundred years had sparkled with examples of his noble fidelity.' And in another passage, having suggested that victory and success were the links that bound officer and man, he goes on to speak of personal attachment. 'You might see the sepoy of many fights, watchful and tender as a woman, beside the sick-bed of the English officer, or playing with the pale-faced children beneath the verandah of his captain's bungalow. There was not an English gentlewoman in the country who did not feel measureless security in the thought that a guard of sepoys watched her house or who would not have travelled, under such an escort, across the whole length and breadth of the land.'

This was the surface. This was what the English saw and believed. They had to believe it. If they had tried to look deeper, they might not have slept at night. Consider first numbers. With a population of about 150 million, India had an army of 300,000 men, of whom normally 40,000 were of European stock; in 1856 there were rather fewer, only about 23,000 Queen's troops and between 13,000 and 14,000 Company's Europeans. In many stations there were no European troops at all; there was a heavy concentration of them in the Punjab but in the seven hundred miles between Lucknow and Calcutta only one battalion of British troops.* In a score of cantonments where there were no British troops at all, the sepoys paraded and stood on guard; saluted officers and their ladies, pipeclayed their equipment, cleaned their muskets as usual. But at heart, as we have seen, many were unhappy, apprehensive about the future, frightened and mistrustful, half dreading and half hoping to hear something that would confirm the gnawing suspicion that the Government they had once trusted was

* H.M. 53rd had their headquarters at Calcutta with various outlying detachments. H.M. 10th were at Dinapore, near Patna, about 500 miles away by river. H.M. 32nd had detachments at Cawnpore and Lucknow. There were only two British battalions for the whole of Bengal and Behar.

plotting to destroy what they most valued. It was a sultry explosive atmosphere that waited only for a spark.

There were two small incidents that seem now like a rehearsal of what was to come, one near Calcutta in 1852 over the old question of going by sea to Burma, one in 1855 at Bolarum in South India. Here, by a singular combination of ignorance and inefficiency, the dates of a festival were confused, and a garrison order issued which unintentionally prohibited any procession on the day most important to Muslims. The Nizam's 3rd Cavalry mutinied and killed the Brigadier. They had a commandant who seems to have been afraid of his men and far from straightforward to his superiors; they had a bad record and were 'opium-eaters to a man'. No one thought this had anything more than local significance. But it was not long before there came just the spark that was needed to ignite the whole lowering sulphurous mass of unease and distrust. This was the famous affair of the cartridges. Our worst enemies could not have imagined a better means of harming us.

The smooth-bore musket was still the standard weapon of the British Army. Its range was short and as far back as the American War of Independence—ninety years ago—the value of the rifle had been discovered. By making the bullet spin in its flight, it shot accurately over a longer range than the musket and was therefore better than a musket for sharpshooters—what a later generation was to call snipers—and for skirmishers in extended order. But to reload a muzzle-loading rifle was a slow business. The charge of powder had to be rammed in, as with the musket, and since the bullet must fit the rifling it had to be tapped down the whole length of the barrel with a wooden mallet. From Waterloo to the Crimea, battles were still fought in close order; volleys of musketry fired in rapid succession were decisive. So until someone could invent a quicker way of loading, the musket was preferable for close order and was still the general weapon. H.M. 60th Rifles, however, were in India and many sepoy battalions had a rifle company; both the 60th and these companies were armed with a rifle that had only two grooves. This took a cartridge made up of powder only and a separate bullet which was wrapped in a patch of cloth, smeared with a lubricant, which helped the loader to ram the bullet home. No one had raised any objection to this; in native rifle companies, the lubricant was supposed to be a mixture of wax and vegetable oil.

Experiments had been going on for some time and the authorities in England had decided to rearm the entire army with the Enfield rifle. This was still a muzzle-loader; breech-loading rifles were not introduced to the army till 1867 but the Enfield could be loaded much more quickly than the old pattern of rifle and was accurate at much longer range than the musket. The Enfield had three grooves instead of two and the cartridge was made up with powder and bullet in one package; the paper holding the powder also encircled the cylindrical part of the bullet; it was heavily greased, so that it could be forced down through the rifling. The other end of the cartridge, away from the bullet, had to be broken immediately before loading to enable the charge to ignite. In the standard drill of the time, this had been done with the teeth. It was said that the oil and wax on the bullet for the two-groove rifle became stiff and unserviceable with time; experiments showed that tallow kept its usefulness longer, and the cartridges made in England for the Enfield were greased with tallow. Early in the experimental period — as far back as 1853 — some of these cartridges had been sent to India to see whether this grease would stand the climate; the Military Secretary to the Government had then pointed out that cartridges greased with tallow might be objectionable to Indian troops and suggested that they should be distributed to British troops only. But this was disregarded; the cartridges were given to Indian guards in certain stations, no objection was raised, and it was reported that they were suitable for use in India. Since then, the new rifle had been proved in the Crimean War and was to be used everywhere with the new cartridges; that wise warning of four years before had been quite forgotten. The Ordnance Department started to make up the new cartridges in India and put out a contract for tallow, without any stipulation as to what kind. Had the tallow come exclusively from sheep or goats, it would have been less objectionable. But it was unlikely that it would, unless very strict precautions were taken, because in India mutton costs twice as much as beef and the contractors would naturally supply the cheapest.* There cannot be any reasonable doubt that the tallow used on the new cartridges, whether prepared in England or in India, contained the fat of cows; those from England certainly, and from India probably, contained also the fat of pigs.

But they had not been issued to troops. Three Musketry Depots had been set up, at Dum-Dum near Calcutta, at Ambala and at Sialkot in the Punjab. To all these depots, detachments from battalions had been sent for instruction in the use of the new Enfield rifle, but they were still, at the beginning of 1857, in the early stages, learning to handle it and to use the sights; no ball cartridge had reached them. Meanwhile, in the rifle companies the old two-grooved rifle was still in use and bullets with greased cloth patches were being used, as they always had been.

* Among Hindus, of course, to eat beef is the deepest degradation. Muslims generally prefer mutton, saying that it is less 'heating' than beef. I suspect that this is partly an infection from Hinduism; Muslim villagers have also told me they do not eat peacock because it is heating, but really I think because the peacock is venerated by Hindus.

Early in January 1857 a lascar of low caste employed in the ordnance factory at Dum-Dum had the audacity to ask a high-caste sepoy for a drink of water from his personal lota. The reply was couched in terms that no one has thought fit to record. The lascar replied that caste would soon be ended because the sepoys would be forced to bite the ends off cartridges covered with the fat of pigs and cows. This of course would hit both Muslims and Hindus, since the pig is forbidden to one and the cow is sacred to the other. The effect on men of high caste or from good Muslim families was both sacrilegious and physically disgusting, as though a Catholic were asked at the same time to profane a sacrament and to touch excrement with his lips. The news spread like fire in grass dry after long drought; it spread to all the neighbourhood of Calcutta; it filtered up the roads radiating out to the north and west.

On January 22nd Lieutenant Wright, commanding a detachment of the 70th Native Infantry at Dum-Dum, reported to the Major in command of the Musketry Depot that his troops were seriously upset by what they had heard. General Hearsey, commanding the division, received the information on the 23rd and the same day wrote to head-quarters in Calcutta. He knew that the Commander-in-Chief and the Adjutant-General were away, and asked that the information should be passed at once, without waiting for their views, to the Military Secretary to the Government; he suggested that the sepoys should be allowed to grease their own cartridges with oil and beeswax, as for the bullet and patch for the old rifle. But the 25th was a Sunday and it was not till the 26th that his letter was forwarded to the Military Secretary, who received it on the 27th and acted immediately. On the 28th Hearsey got the permission he wanted and announced it at once. In the normal course of official business, this would be counted good going; Kaye thinks the delay important because on the 27th a native officer asked on parade whether the orders had been received and had to be told they had not. But the atmosphere of suspicion was so acute that it seems doubtful whether much difference would have been made even if Hearsey had sent an A.D.C. on a fast horse to bring the orders back with him. There were men ready to persuade others that once again the Government had postponed their wicked plot because it had been discovered. And the story had excited the men so much that they now looked suspiciously at even the old cartridge that had been used for Brown Bess, the musket. This did not need lubrication; it was put up in paper with a slight glaze, and they began to suspect that this paper was impregnated with some forbidden substance or even that it was not paper at all, but a pig's or a cow's bladder.

Birch, the Military Secretary, had acted with promptitude. He went to Dum-Dum on January 27th, saw the new Enfield cartridges, sent Hearsey the orders he wanted and telegraphed to the Adjutant-

General at Meerut asking that general orders to the same effect should go out to the whole army. The Adjutant-General and his staff hesitated, arguing that the issue of general orders would raise doubts in the minds of the sepoys about the cartridges they had used so long. Here of course they were right, except that the doubt already existed. There was delay, but eventually orders were issued to the whole army that new cartridges made up with grease should go only to British troops, that Indian battalions should make their own arrangements for lubricating the new cartridges with vegetable oil and beeswax and that the drill should be changed, permitting them to break the cartridges with the fingers instead of the teeth.

Thus almost any British officer who gave thought to the matter at all would have said that the danger was past; to have contemplated giving Indian troops cartridges covered with tallow was a piece of ignorant folly, but the ordnance authorities in England could hardly be expected to be well informed about Indian religion, the matter had come to light before any of the new cartridges had been issued to Indian troops and the orders had made everything clear. But in fact nothing *was* clear; the troops in some battalions were so suspicious of an attack on their religion that the orders merely confirmed their belief that something had been intended, and there was no clearness about which cartridges had been covered with the dangerous grease. Indeed, this is far from clear in many later accounts, which speak of troops refusing to accept 'the cartridges' as though they were the Enfield greased cartridges, whereas it was always the old cartridges, or the new ones ungreased.* Conscious of their own good intentions, the British simply could not believe that anyone would credit them with anything so ridiculous as a plot to convert the sepoys by fraud—yet every move they made confirmed the sepoys in this belief. Officers and men alike simply did not understand each other's way of thinking. One British officer, addressing Indian troops, told them that he and his fellow-countrymen were *Protestants*, and it was therefore unthinkable that they would try to

---

* I have gone into some detail because there has been so much confusion, but I am not sure I have not simplified too much on two points. Kaye says positively that all the rifle companies were still using the old two-groove rifle at the beginning of 1857. But there is a reference in an indent in the ordnance department to 'tallow of the purest kind' for the Minié rifle. This was used in the British Army outside India in 1851. It was a four-groove rifle. So there must have been some troops in India using the Minié as well as the 'old two-groove rifle', the Enfield and the musket and thus *four* kinds of cartridge. Further, it seems that tallow was used before 1857 to lubricate the Minié and there are some indications that tallow—supposed to come from sheep or goats—was sometimes used with the patch for the bullet of the two-groove rifle. Most Brahmans are vegetarians and though to touch mutton-fat with the fingers would not contaminate in the same way as beef with the mouth, it is the kind of thing a Brahman would much prefer not to know he had done.

convert anyone by *fraud*; they would accept only converts whose *reason* led them to accept the faith. The sepoys are said to have nodded to show they understood.

Things had not reached the same pitch of mutual incomprehension everywhere. In some battalions, trust in the officer was not yet dead; in some, the habit of discipline was so strong that the men did not show their feelings. But in all the battalions near Calcutta there was fear and unhappiness. There were mysterious fires at night, burning arrows shot into the thatch of bungalows. And there were plenty of enemies, glad to take this heaven-sent chance of tampering with the main prop of British power. The King of Oudh was in exile near Calcutta and he was surrounded by retainers anxious to restore his kingdom. There was a body known as the Dharma Sabha, whose purpose was to preserve orthodox Hinduism. There were both Brahmans and *maulvis* — the religious leaders of Islam — only too eager to fan any flame of religious bigotry.

Much has been written of a mysterious plot which lay behind the outbreak of 1857. That there were plenty of ill-wishers to the British is certain and that they were spreading poison where they could is more than likely but it is a very different matter to suppose that there was a concerted plot. It was natural that immediately after the Mutiny British officers should look for a plot; if some outside agency had misled the poor sepoy, that would partly account for something that was deeply wounding to his officers. The deeper causes were then still obscure. Now that they are clearer, the plot seems an unnecessary supposition; and the firmest adherents to the theory of a plot have to suppose that it broke down.

But through all that follows there runs one thread, the fearful dilemma which in some form always confronts an officer who knows that mutiny is possible. Shall he show his trust and confidence, and walk abroad with a smiling face, hoping that the men will respond to the trust, or at the worst suppose the confidence to mean that help is coming? Or shall he take such precautions as he can, risking the danger that they may provoke the first shot? Meanwhile the men, demented by suspicion, debate whether to wait for what they fear or to strike first.

XII

The Storm Breaks

1. Mutiny in Bengal

There were four native battalions at Barrackpore under Hearsey's command, the 2nd, 34th, 43rd and 70th. Two of these, the 2nd and the 43rd, had been under Nott at Kandahar throughout the Afghan affair; he had called them his 'beautiful sepoy regiments', and when all went wrong at Kabul they had stood fast. But now the 2nd rivalled the 34th as the most suspicious and disaffected — and the whole garrison was unhappy. It so happened that two detachments of the 34th Native Infantry marched on routine business from Barrackpore to Berhampore, about 100 miles to the north, arriving one on February 18th and one on the 25th. Here there was one battalion of native infantry, the 19th, some cavalry and some artillery, no British troops. The 19th had recently been stationed alongside the 34th and knew them well; rumours about cartridges and the British plot to defile the men had already reached the 19th and there is no doubt they discussed the matter with the 34th, who, coming straight from the capital, were expected to know more. On February 28th, there was to be a parade of the 19th in the ordinary course of events, and, as was customary, percussion caps were to be handed out the night before, the cartridges next morning.*

The men were excited and frightened; they had seen the cartridges which were to be distributed next day. They were the ordinary cartridges for muskets, but made up at different times, and the men detected two different kinds of paper. This, they thought, confirmed what they had been told, that even the cartridges for muskets were now tainted with some subtle pollution. They refused to accept the percussion caps. Their commanding officer, Colonel Mitchell, at once went to the lines,

* Until 1842 Brown Bess, the standard musket, was fitted with a powder-pan into which the soldier poured a small charge of powder that was ignited by the flint and in its turn ignited the larger charge inside the musket. In 1842 percussion caps were introduced; these were ignited by the direct blow of the hammer. They made loading quicker and were much more reliable in wet weather. They were encased in thin copper.

where he addressed the native officers angrily, threatening them with various punishments if they persisted in being so unreasonable. They thought he would not have been so angry unless there had been some truth in what they suspected; he was angry because his trick had been found out. He on the other hand went back to his bungalow wondering what he should do if they refused to obey orders next morning. There were no British troops within reach but he thought that the cavalry and artillery were not affected and might overawe the infantry. He sent out orders for a general parade; this meant that all three arms would parade next morning instead of the infantry only. News of this reached the 19th, already greatly excited by their commanding officer's threats and the interpretation they had put on them. They persuaded themselves that next morning greased cartridges were to be forced upon them at the muzzles of the guns. That night, after excited discussion, they beat to arms, rushed to possess themselves of their muskets, took possession of the very cartridges they had feared they would be made to take in the morning, loaded, rushed to the parade-ground. Here they seem to have stood irresolute, not knowing what to do next.

Colonel Mitchell heard the commotion, sent a message ordering the cavalry and artillery at once to the parade-ground and went there himself. He acted resolutely, showing great courage, clearly aware of the extreme danger in which he stood. Behind him were cavalry and artillery who might not obey him; in front were infantry in open mutiny. He summoned the native officers; they came; he again harangued them angrily. They explained that the men were frightened; they knew a general parade had been ordered and were afraid they would be forced to abandon their religion. If the artillery and cavalry were withdrawn, they would return to their duty. Mitchell said they should first lay down their arms and return to duty but the native officers begged him to let them bring the men back without threat. At last he agreed to this — but he would still have a general parade next morning. Again they pleaded with him; the men were frightened and unless the general parade was cancelled, they could not be reassured. At last he gave in to that too. He ordered the cavalry and artillery back to their lines and they moved off; he waited. The native officers went back to their men and at last they too began to move away. Some degree of trust had been restored.

That midnight scene illustrates the knife-edge on which events were balanced. The sepoys, frightened and bewildered, trembled on the edge of killing their officers; perhaps one shot would have been enough to start a volley from the whole battalion. Mitchell, not a cool man, hid his apprehension behind a mask of anger, put a bold face on things and in fact just avoided that one extra step of provocation that would have brought the shot; he contrived also to avoid abject surrender. His morning parade, of the 19th only, took place just as usual. From now onwards the 19th behaved perfectly. But the midnight incident had to be reported to the Government, who resolved that since the whole regiment had unquestionably mutinied, they must be disbanded. But it would not be safe to do this except in the presence of a British battalion—and there was none available, H.M. 53rd being widely scattered in detachments. A steamer was sent to Rangoon to bring H.M. 84th and this battalion arrived on March 20th. The 19th Native Infantry, who had now been in suspense for nearly a month, were ordered to march to Barrackpore. They still did not know their fate, but it was here that the disbandment was to take place. It was fixed for March 31st, which was a Tuesday. They must have guessed that they had something to fear, but they marched steadily on without incident.

Meanwhile, earlier in the month, two sepoys of the 2nd had come to the subadar commanding the guard at Fort William in Calcutta, who on that day came from the 34th, with proposals for seizing the fort and defying the British. The subadar arrested them; they were tried and sentenced to 14 years hard labour each. The authorities began to think that the 34th were less infected than the 2nd. But on Sunday March 29th there occurred the affair of Mangal Pande, spelt by our ancestors 'Mungul Pandy',* often reckoned the first incident of the Mutiny. His name came to be used by the British as a contemptuous term for all mutineers; the Pandies we called them, as we spoke later of the Hun or the Boche. This was two days before the parade at which the 19th were to face their punishment—a matter about which everyone had some inkling, just as everyone knew that H.M. 84th had come from Rangoon to enforce some act which threatened the sepoys. The 19th were at Baraset, eight miles away, waiting for orders; it was common talk that the 2nd and the 34th would join them in resistance to whatever was in store. In this electric atmosphere, Mangal Pande, a private of the 34th, drunk with *bhang*—an infusion of hemp—seized and loaded his musket and went to the quarter-guard, where he marched up and down, calling on his comrades to follow him and resist forcible conversion. It was Sunday evening. The quarter-guard, under the command of a jemadar, Ishwari Pande, did nothing to stop him. The European sergeant-major appeared; Mangal Pande fired at him and missed. Again, no one arrested him. One man rushed to the house of the Adjutant, Lieutenant Baugh, who rode to the quarter-guard, where his horse was brought to the ground by Pande's second shot. There followed

* The first word rhymes with 'bungle'. The second word is a Brahman caste-name; the *a* in this is long, like the *a* in 'harsh'. But our great-grandfathers made Pandy rhyme with 'candy'.

a hand-to-hand encounter with swords, in which Baugh seems to have had the worst of it and been wounded. The sergeant-major, too, was wounded before Pande was overpowered by one Muslim sepoy. This gave the two wounded men time to escape; they were surrounded by a threatening crowd, and, far from helping them, the men of the guard seem to have actually struck them and threatened to shoot the man who intervened. Soon after this, General Hearsey arrived on the scene, and Mangal Pande endeavoured to shoot himself, inflicting a wound that was not fatal.

It is hard to reconstruct exactly what happened, but there can be no doubt that a man had fired on two of his superiors and tried to murder them, with the active sympathy of the guard and others of the regiment. Two nights and a day followed of acute fear and anxiety; on the morning of the 31st all the available troops in the area were drawn up on the parade-ground, with two batteries of field artillery as well as H.M. 84th. General Hearsey rode out to meet the 19th, and came on to the parade-ground at their head. They took up their position facing the guns; the order disbanding the regiment was read out, and they obediently piled their muskets, belts and bayonets. In recognition of their good behaviour since the outbreak in February, they were not further disgraced; they were allowed to take home their uniforms, they received their full pay, they were to be provided with transport to their homes at the public expense and encouraged to visit places of pilgrimage on the way. Many of them are said to have expressed their penitence for what had happened, to have said that all their troubles were due to the 34th and to have wished they might have been allowed to fight it out with them. When they left the parade-ground, they cheered Hearsey and wished him a long and happy life.

Thus March ended—and again officers hoped that perhaps the trouble would blow over. On April 13th the Adjutant-General sent out his final orders to the musketry depots, repeating that the teeth need no longer be used to break the cartridges, and that cartridges were to be greased by the men themselves, using only ingredients of which they approved. Officers were to explain carefully, to reason, but finally to be quite firm and—if men persisted in refusal, which was unlikely—to arrest them. These instructions did, however, indirectly recognize that the men of a detachment at the musketry depot might be faced with an agonizing problem: they might themselves believe what their officers told them and use the cartridges in good faith, but on their return to the regiment they might be outcasted—the worst fate that could befall them. It was all very well for the Adjutant-General to promise punishment for anyone who taunted them; that would not restore their caste.

But it was hard for anyone in high authority to be confident. An anonymous letter sent in March to Major Matthews, commanding the 43rd Regiment at Barrackpore, runs as follows:

'We will not give up our religion. We serve for honour and religion ... You are the masters of the country. The Lord Sahib has given orders, which he has received from the Company, to all commanding officers to destroy the religion of the country. We know this ... The officers in the Salt Department mix up bones with the salt. The officer in charge of ghee mixes up fat with it; this is well known ... the Sahib in charge of sugar burns up bones and mixes them in the syrup the sugar is made of; this is well known ... the senior officers have ordered rajas, noblemen, landowners, money-lenders and peasants all to eat together and English bread has been sent to them; this is well known ... throughout the country, the wives of respectable men, in fact all classes of Hindus, on becoming widows are to be married again; this is known. Therefore we consider ourselves as killed.' The letter goes on to add the cartridges to this catalogue, and emphasizes the unanimity of all sepoys in the station, and of all but two named native officers. Incidents followed which showed that these beliefs were widespread.

2. The Tenth of May

On April 24th a parade was held of the 'skirmishers' of the 3rd Cavalry at Meerut. These were picked men, fifteen from each of the six troops. They were armed with carbines, unrifled, which fired the old cartridge. The purpose of the parade was simply to explain to them that they need no longer bite the cartridge but tear or pinch it with the fingers. But of the ninety men, only five would handle cartridges of the kind they had been using without complaint for years. This was a sad blow to any idea that the affair would blow over. Not only was Meerut one of the most important military stations in the country, but this was the first sign of trouble among the cavalry, where there was a much higher proportion of Muslims than in the infantry. It had been thought that the feeling was mainly among the Hindus. Meerut was full of rumours and scares; the tale of cow's bones in the flour was very strong and there were stories of suspicious travellers spreading sedition among the troops. Both at Army Headquarters and in Meerut it was the view that firm action was needed and after a week of waiting the eighty-five troopers were brought to court martial. Meanwhile, in Lucknow, Sir Henry Lawrence disarmed the 7th Irregular Oudh Battalion; at Barrackpore, seven companies of the 34th were disbanded; Mangal Pande and Ishwari Pande, the jemadar commanding the guard on the day he ran amok, had both been hanged. May 9th dawned and there was a great punishment parade at Meerut, meant to impress the troops.

At this parade, the sentences of the court martial on the eighty-five troopers were read out. There had been no question of their guilt; they had disobeyed military orders. All had been sentenced to ten years imprisonment with hard labour, but in the case of eleven of the youngest the sentence had been reduced to five years. The men were stripped of their uniforms; smiths fastened fetters and manacles on their limbs. It was a long business. At last they were led away, carrying their boots, which some tried to throw at their Colonel. Hugh Gough, son of the Commander-in-Chief in the Sikh Wars, was a subaltern who had recently joined the regiment. He had been, he says, a 'thoughtless young subaltern', like so many others to whom 'fun and gaiety' were 'the apparent object of life'. But he had been proud of his regiment; we 'used to pride ourselves on being steadier on parade than the British cavalry regiment at Meerut.' He went to the civil gaol to settle the pay of the men in his troop, where the scene 'made the strongest impression' on him. The men 'at first were sullen and impassive'; then they began to realize that they really were being discharged from 'the honourable service into which they had been born'. They had been soldiers held in the highest esteem in their villages. They broke down completely; 'old soldiers with many medals … wept bitterly, lamenting their sad fate and imploring their officers to save them … I have seldom if ever in all my life experienced a more touching scene.'

That evening a native officer of Gough's troop came to him 'under pretence of making up the accounts' and warned him that a general mutiny of all the native troops in Meerut would take place next day. Gough went to the Colonel, who 'treated the communication with contempt, reproving me for listening to such idle words.' None the less, Gough did repeat what he had heard to the Brigadier, Archdale Wilson, whom he happened to meet during the evening. He too was incredulous. May 10th was Sunday; the morning passed as usual, there was a church parade; the scorching heat of a May afternoon settled down on Meerut and the English as usual got through it as best they could, sleeping or idly turning the pages of a book. There was an evening church parade for British troops and, about the time when men would be falling in for this, Gough was dressing for duty; he must have been orderly officer that evening. Suddenly, the same native officer with two orderlies arrived at a gallop; the rising had begun. Gough went at once to the Native Infantry lines, 'usually a scene of perfect discipline and neatness, rows of mud barracks neatly thatched, with the quarter-guard ready to turn out and happy contented sepoys lounging about'. But now there was 'a scene of the most wild and awful confusion … huts on fire … sepoys dancing and leaping frantically about, calling and yelling at each other and blazing away in the air … a maddened crowd of fiends and devils.' Gough's companion, the native officer, implored him to go, so at last he did, a volley of shots being fired at him as he left. He went to his own troop, where there was similar disorder, men galloping to and fro, the lines being burnt, men helping themselves to the ammunition they feared to be unclean. His efforts were useless and 'seeing that all was lost and my power as their officer absolutely gone', he gave in to 'the earnest and indeed forceful solicitations of the better disposed' and made for the European lines. He had to go through the bazaar and here there was 'a unanimous outbreak of fanatical and race feeling'. The whole population seemed to be up in arms and we 'had literally to cut our way, pelted with stones, through hundreds of men armed with *tulwars* and *lathies*'—that is, with swords and clubs. 'I never heard again of my friend the native officer ... he said he must go back ... so saluted and left me ... I found his house after the war but no one knew what had become of him ... a braver or more loyal man I have never met ... he risked his life again and again to save mine and I had hardly known him before.'

That is part of the account of one eye-witness. There are many and there is conflict among them over detail. But there is much in common—warnings unheeded or laughed at; the drowsy bungalows in the searing heat of a Sunday afternoon; the leisurely preparations for the evening ride or drive or the evening church service. Then shots, galloping hooves, flames; the blazing thatch of the next bungalow, the mangled body of a comrade lying by the roadside, the gallop to the men's lines—now the stories diverge. There was terrible confusion, a lack of leadership on both sides, incredible folly. Only of the broad outlines of what happened is it possible to speak with any certainty.

The 3rd Cavalry rose first and made for the gaol to release their comrades. This they did successfully. It is typical of the complacency of the commanding officers at Meerut that no special precautions had been taken at the gaol; there was a sepoy guard from the 20th Native Infantry, who, with the other infantry regiment, the 11th, soon joined the cavalry. But there was indecision among the mutineers, irresolution, nothing planned. It was said later that all three regiments were convinced that the punishment of the eighty-five was only a beginning; two thousand sets of fetters were waiting in the civil gaol for those who would not give up their religion. The courtesans in the bazaar had taunted them on the Saturday evening because they had not been men enough to resist the imprisonment of their comrades. And it is said that at this critical moment on the Sunday evening—at the time of church parade—someone raised the cry that the white soldiers were arming and coming to imprison or kill them. All was tense; everywhere there was the feeling of something terrible about to happen.

Men who hoped for trouble, and therefore for loot, were coming in from the neighbouring villages; there crept out from the alleys and backways of the city the ruffians who appear whenever trouble is brewing. If there is to be a Hindu procession and the Muslims have talked of breaking it up—or the other way round—they will sharpen their knives and they will be ready, hanging about in case of trouble, ready to run in when the riot begins, to rob and kill a wounded man, to cut the throat of anyone unprotected and alone, to seize the chance, if things get bad enough, of breaking into shops and making off with whatever they can find. In every tumult, in every great city, in 1857, in 1947—and no doubt for centuries before that—they have been there. Some of these men must have been moving about the city that Saturday night, joining in the jeers of the harlots, hoping for trouble. And, back in their lines, troopers and sepoys talked about the fate they felt sure would overtake them and came back again and again to the thought that they would die rather than endure it.

The warnings pointed to trouble but with no certainty of time or place—and it seems likely that there was no certainty. Once they had galloped to the gaol and released their comrades, the 3rd Cavalry seem to have had no further ideas; some of their troopers, and some sepoys from the two infantry battalions, after that first frenzied burst of senseless activity described by Gough, went in parties to set fire to the bungalows of officers and of the civil magistrates and sometimes to kill their occupants; they were joined by crowds from the city who shared in the atrocities. There was, writes Dr Sen, a mad orgy of arson, pillage and murder.

Throughout India, wherever there were English officers, the name of Mrs Chambers was repeated: she was a young wife, recently arrived from England, and far advanced in pregnancy. She was found hacked to pieces. This was one of the many cases quoted as a reason for indiscriminate reprisals, no quarter and no mercy for the sepoys. But it soon appeared that this was probably the work of a Muslim butcher from the city; he was caught, brought to the spot and hanged for it. That is not to question that sepoys took part in much of what happened. Those most deeply implicated seem to have egged on their companions to go in as deep as themselves; once they had killed an officer or an officer's wife, they knew there could be no mercy and therefore no turning back, no betrayal.

But the whole proceedings of the mutineers at Meerut were aimless and uncoordinated. None of them, for instance, went to the treasury, where there was a guard of sepoys. That guard was found faithfully performing its duty when a detachment of H.M. 60th Rifles arrived and took over without incident. Not a rupee had been touched. At one end of the cantonment, says Kaye, men were smartly saluting their officers while at the other end they were killing them. One troop of the 3rd Cavalry followed Craigie, their troop commander, who managed to get them together. A party of these men went with Craigie's friend Mackenzie to the bungalow they shared. Mackenzie brought out Craigie's wife and his own sister, called the troopers to him and 'commended their lives to their charge ... they threw themselves off their horses and prostrated themselves before the ladies, seizing their feet and placing them on their heads, as they vowed with tears and sobs to protect their lives with their own.' The rest of this troop, under Craigie's command, worked to restore order and end the looting. That troop stayed faithful throughout the Mutiny.

This lack of any concerted plan on the part of the rebels is the only excuse—and a quite insufficient one—for the inactivity of the British. Hewitt, the commanding General, was nearly seventy, a stout easygoing man, 'liked by all and respected by some'. He was the last man for an emergency and seems to have had no positive ideas about what to do. Had his Brigadier been a man of imaginative energy this might not have mattered, but Archdale Wilson, who later for a time commanded at Delhi, was correct, cautious, the kind of man who knows the regulations and sees objections to every course proposed. Carmichael Smyth, who commanded the 3rd Cavalry, is admirably portrayed in Kaye's sentence: 'The unquestionable honesty of his nature was of that querulous irritable cast which makes a man often uncharitable and always unpopular.' That evening he went everywhere but to the lines of his own regiment. The officer commanding the Carabineers formed up his men and proceeded—slowly, formally and inexcusably—to call the roll before moving off. No senior officer seems to have urged the need for a rapid move down the road to Delhi; one man such as Rollo Gillespie, who had galloped to Vellore fifty years before, might have saved many thousands of lives. And yet such historical might-have-beens are pointless. If the mutineers had not taken Delhi and the long agony of that summer had been avoided, how would the bitterness and fear have spent itself? How could the army have been reconstructed?

The 60th Rifles were stopped on the way to church. They marched back and collected their rifles; after some delay a detachment went off to the treasury and another to guard bungalows; the rest, with the Carabineers, marched round the cantonment trying to find a body of rebels they could fight. But no such body was to be found and eventually they bivouacked on the parade ground. Bungalows were blazing, men, women and children were still being murdered, but since there was no organized body to attack they settled down for the night, hoping in the morning to find an enemy. But by morning hardly a rebel sepoy or trooper was left. They were straggling away in small parties, mostly towards Delhi. Even now swift action by the cavalry might have saved Delhi but every difficulty was seen and nothing was done.

If there had been a plot for a national rising in the summer of 1857,

it is inconceivable that any sane man should have chosen Meerut as
the starting-point. There was a big concentration of British troops—
the Carabineers, the 6oth Rifles, the artillery headquarters and a
considerable force of British gunners. To choose Meerut would have
implied a thorough understanding of the characters of Hewitt and
Wilson and a gamble on their inactivity. And it is surely clear that
there was no one in charge of the mutineers on May 10th. After the
Mutiny those who believed that there had been a plot thought it had
been timed for Sunday May 31st and that it exploded three weeks too
soon because of the punishment parade. But had there been any plot
worth the name, surely even three weeks beforehand it would have
been settled that someone should be in command, that the treasury as
well as the gaol should be taken at once and the whole body of troops
marched off towards Delhi as quickly as possible. But it was all far more
haphazard than that. The men were beside themselves with fear and
anger; no doubt there had been talk of a rising as the only way to save
their faith and honour; one spark would be enough. Perhaps it was,
as is said, a cook-boy who came running to say that the 6oth Rifles
were falling in—as they were, without arms, for church. Perhaps it was
one man who shouted: 'To the gaol!' That most of them should make for
Delhi was inevitable. It was only forty miles away, it was a strong
walled city, there were no British troops there, it was the ancient
capital and the seat of the Mughal Emperor. What no reasonable
planning could have foreseen was that mutineers from Meerut would
get there without being brought to battle, without even pursuit. Yet
this happened. They reached Delhi unchallenged, entered the city
without difficulty, told their tale, and soon the sepoys rose in Delhi
too and here too murder, arson and pillage broke out.

Years afterwards Lord Roberts recorded his opinion that it would
have made little difference if the Carabineers had been sent at once
after the mutineers towards Delhi. The whole regiment could not have
gone, as they had many recruits and many unbroken horses. They
might have dispersed the infantry but could not have caught the 3rd
Cavalry. But this judgement is based on his conviction that the whole
Bengal Army had resolved on mutiny, and it does not make allowance
for the psychological effect of complete British inertia.

3. Delhi

The story of the Mutiny is one on which it is hard for an Englishman
to dwell without continuous sorrow, without an alternation of pride
and shame, pity and anger. There is pride not only at the courage, the
tenacity of purpose, the endurance shown by our countrymen but

also that so often Indians risked their lives to show such affection and fidelity. There is shame at the indiscriminate savagery with which vengeance was often wreaked on innocent people for crimes in which they could not possibly have had a hand. There is anger at complacency and treachery, pity for physical sufferings and bereavements and for the bitterness and hatred, the suspicion and the arrogance. It is a story of suspense and excitement which can hardly be rivalled; in every station of Northern India there was tense waiting, gallantry, cowardice, folly, often a dramatic turn of fortune, sometimes trust wisely given and generously repaid.

But this is not a history of the Mutiny and we must leave a hundred stories untold. What I have tried to do so far is to show how the Mutiny came about, the causes of the suicidal panic among the sepoys, their sense of fear and betrayal; what remains to be shown is the outrage and horror on the British side, the fruit this later bore and the extraordinary achievement by which an Indian army was rebuilt in spite of the storm of the Mutiny.

On the morning of Monday May 11th there was a great parade at Delhi. There were six battalions of native infantry, no British troops; they were assembled to hear the proceedings of the court martial which had sentenced Ishwari Pande of the 34th to be hanged, and to hear that the sentence had been carried out. The men in the ranks all, in various degrees, shared the fears about their religion which had possessed the troops at Barrackpore and Meerut; in Delhi, there was an extra element of unrest because the place was the ancient capital and in the Red Fort the descendant of the Mughals still bore the title of Emperor.* Here there was less talk of the bones of cows and more of the prophecy that infidels would rule for a hundred years before the Crescent of Islam was restored. There were tales of a coming Persian invasion, with Afghan help. None the less, the great parade passed without incident, though there were murmurs in the ranks.

But hardly was the parade over before the first troopers of the 3rd Cavalry began to cross the Jumna from Meerut. They had no difficulty in entering the city and here they told of officers killed and their bungalows burnt, an end of the Company's reign. Above all, there had been no pursuit. What had become of the English? They must be cowed by the hand of Heaven, their spirit broken. There were even rumours that they had all been killed. One of the Delhi regiments joined the mutineers at once. The bad men with their knives crept out from the lanes

---

* The English at this period called him the King of Delhi and his Persian title was Padshah or King, not Shahanshah—King of Kings—or Emperor. But in a country full of rulers who aspired to sovereignty, the word 'Emperor' represents exactly what the Mughals had been and Bahadur Shah was still felt to have some power to make the sovereignty of others legitimate.

in the hope of plunder. With one after another of the other regiments, it was the same story; they would answer the call to arms, follow their officers to the point where they met mutinous troops—and then there would come the refusal to fire, and sometimes they would let others shoot their officers, sometimes they would try to save them provided only that they fled. The mutinous infantry from Meerut came in as the day wore on; they swarmed after the cavalry into the Red Fort and virtually took the Emperor prisoner.

That unhappy old man had little choice; he does not seem to have had much desire to risk his allowance from the Company—about £10,000 a month—his easy life without responsibilities, and the polite pretence of his titles and dignities; all this was a heavy weight to set in the scales against the doubtful chance of driving out the English and restoring the glories of the house of Akbar. Bahadur Shah was really much happier as he was, secluded in his palace, making verses about the history of his house, with little to trouble him but the intrigues of his young queen and of his many sons and their retainers, all of whom were anxious about the succession and many of whom did dream of restoring the Emperor's power. But the old man saw the British officers who were in the Fort killed; his own people gave in at once and joined the mutineers. He was powerless. The rebels stabled their horses in his hall of reception; they camped in his courtyard. They treated him with little respect. But they made him their nominal leader and it was in his name that the rebellion was carried on.

On that first day in Delhi, May 11th, there were a few groups of British officers who held out in some building that could temporarily be defended, confident that help would come from Meerut before nightfall. One such party, of three officers and six warrant officers, held the powder magazine, which they determined to defend as long as they could and to blow up if they could hold it no longer and help had not come. But no help came. General Hewitt, although Delhi was within his own district, decided that his first duty was to protect the stores and wounded at Meerut; Archdale Wilson referred to regulations which limited his responsibility to the station he commanded. His advice to the General was to protect what they had and not embark on adventures in pursuit of mutineers of whose movements they had no reliable information. It would be dangerous to divide the forces on which they could count. They stayed where they were. By the evening of that Monday the powder magazine had been blown up by its defenders and the other parties in Delhi had either been killed or had fled; some tried to make their way to Meerut or Agra and some, after stirring adventures and terrible hardships, succeeded. Some fifty were taken prisoner, all but six of them women or children. They were kept in miserable conditions for five days; on the 16th they were taken out and butchered. They were cut to pieces with swords, by whose orders was not discovered with certainty. This massacre has been forgotten; that at Cawnpore became a legend. The reason perhaps is not so much that the numbers at Delhi were smaller as that at Cawnpore British troops arrived on the scene within a few days. Be that as it may, when that day's work was done, no English were left in Delhi.

It will be better to complete the story of Delhi in one place; this means explaining in its barest essence the strategy of the Mutiny considered as a war. Delhi was in the hands of the enemy; it was the ancient capital and the seat of the Emperor and so long as the rebels held Delhi, they had a psychological advantage. The first object in the war was to convince the people of India that the British would not be driven out. Everywhere there were men who waited for the outcome, ready to join the winning side. To recover Delhi would convince such men as nothing else could; every week that Delhi stayed in rebel hands strengthened their doubts.

Delhi then was the first great focal point and incomparably the most important. The second was Lucknow and the third Agra. At Lucknow the troops had mutinied by the end of May and Sir Henry Lawrence was besieged in the Residency; to relieve Lucknow was the next object, second only in importance to the recovery of Delhi. Agra was the capital of the North-Western Provinces; Agra too was besieged, though much less dramatically than Lucknow, and once Delhi was taken the relief of Agra would follow as a matter of course.

The three focal points make a triangle at the heart of the area affected. In the whole of Oudh, and throughout what was later to be called the United Provinces or Uttar Pradesh, in parts of Central India and the Central Provinces, there were military stations in which the troops eventually mutinied. The country surrounding these stations was a chequerboard. One local chief, angered by the policy of the levellers, might come out clearly for the rebels, another might stake his future on British victory; most would wait to see what happened. The villagers took one side or the other according to circumstances, following a chief or a village leader, sometimes joining the mutineers to hunt down and kill, quite as often hiding and feeding fugitives. From the point of view of war, this area had to be thought of as temporarily hostile country.

To get troops to Delhi and Lucknow was the first task. It will be remembered that, except for H.M. 32nd at Lucknow and H.M. 10th at Dinapore near Patna, there were no British troops between Calcutta and Meerut. But there were British troops in the Punjab, and from outside the country troops could be brought to Calcutta or Bombay. From Calcutta, the Ganges made the old lifeline to the north-west; it ran by Patna, Benares and Allahabad to Cawnpore, and from

Cawnpore to Lucknow is only forty miles. But in 1857 there was a quicker route; the railway went as far as Raniganj, about 150 miles from Calcutta. From there the road went on nearly 300 miles to Benares. For Calcutta, the task was to procure British troops from any source possible and push them up the railway, the road or the river. H.M. 84th from Rangoon was already in Calcutta, and another battalion could be summoned from Burma. The Company's Madras Europeans were brought there by sea. There was an expedition on its way to China and it was possible to intercept this at Singapore; and by great good fortune, Lord Elgin, who accompanied it as the political and diplomatic representative of the Queen's Government, saw the urgency of Lord Canning's message and answered his call for help. There was also an expedition in Persia, including six British battalions and some Bombay troops; they finished their war in May and three British battalions were able to start for India; they too came by sea to Calcutta.

There was as yet no communication with London by electric cable and no Suez Canal; the overland route through Egypt was in operation for officers and their families but could not be used for large bodies of troops, and the sea route by the Cape still took months. Substantial help from England did not arrive till the autumn and meanwhile the numbers sent up from Calcutta were pitifully small. From railhead at Raniganj to Benares was five days' journey by horsed vehicles; but enough horses could be found to send only twenty-four men a day. Another hundred could be sent by bullock-cart but would take at least three times as long.* Thus it was at first only a trickle of help which could reach even as far as Benares. Neill, who commanded the Madras Fusiliers, the first reinforcements to start from Calcutta, did not reach Benares himself till June 5th; his men were thereafter coming in at the rate of twenty-four a day. It was not till June 30th that his advance guard, even then consisting of only four hundred Europeans and three hundred Sikhs, started from Allahabad for Cawnpore. It is against these figures and the importance of even so small a trickle that one must see the inaction of the force at Meerut.

Nor was it easy to spare men from the Punjab. As we have seen, there were only 23,000 Royal troops in the whole of India; the Punjab was a recently conquered province with virile and warlike inhabitants, and beyond it was Afghanistan and Central Asia, from which fierce invaders had so often poured into the plains of India. There was no surplus

* As the crow flies, Raniganj to Benares is 275 miles, say 300 on the ground. Sixty miles a day with three relays of ponies a day is possible; it would take about six hundred ponies, on the assumption that the only vehicles available were native tongas or ekkas taking two men each. Ordinary bullocks will not do more than two miles an hour and the fast-trotting bullocks are rare. Bullocks could not keep up twenty miles a day for fifteen days.

even in the Punjab. Further, there was a disgraceful lack of readiness. The regiments who were in the hills near Simla had not twenty rounds of ammunition apiece, no tents, no transport. Two troops of Horse Artillery had no reserve ammunition and their wagons were seven days distant. It had recently been decided not to maintain bullocks and carts permanently but to procure them when war broke out, and this would take time. The doctors emphasized the dangers of exposing British troops to the heat of May in the plains. A siege-train would be needed and it was in any case bound to move slowly; nor were there reliable troops available for its escort. The specialists of the Commissariat department in Simla made careful estimates of the time it would take to muster and provision a mobile force, adding, no doubt, a comfortable margin for safety; they reached conclusions which to John Lawrence at Lahore seemed shocking.

Canning from Calcutta sent long telegrams urging Anson, the Commander-in-Chief, to move quickly on Delhi, 'make short work of the rebels' and dominate the country beyond Delhi before the trouble had time to spread. Lawrence was closer at hand, more detailed and practical, but no less impatient of delay. He thought the force could march with four days' supply of food; there had been a good harvest and his officers would bring in supplies. He did not think the mutineers would offer much serious resistance and the people of Delhi would open their gates to a British force. 'Reflect', he wrote, 'on the history of India. Where have we failed, when we acted vigorously? Where have we succeeded, when guided by timid counsels?'

Goaded by Canning and Lawrence, Anson overruled most of the objections from his specialists and made plans to assemble at Ambala — 120 miles north of Delhi — a force which by June 5th would be at Bāghpat, still some thirty miles from Delhi. Here it would meet the troops which Hewitt had been instructed to send from Meerut. The first part of this plan was accomplished but on May 28th, just outside Ambala, Anson himself died of cholera. He was already in poor health and exhausted by the anxieties of the situation. Sir Henry Barnard, a recent arrival with Crimean experience, took command and moved on without waiting for the heavier guns. He brought from Ambala H.M. 9th Lancers, a squadron of H.M. 4th Lancers, H.M. 75th Foot, both battalions of the Company's Bengal Fusiliers (Europeans), and two troops of horse artillery; from Meerut to join him at Bāghpat came Archdale Wilson, with two squadrons of the Carabineers, six companies of H.M. 60th Rifles, a field battery and a troop of horse artillery. He had fought two battles against the mutineers already and, though his men were terribly punished by the heat, they were full of the confidence of victory and the whole force was burning for vengeance. They met the mutineers near Delhi at the village of Badli-ki-Serai. Barnard's force totalled about 800 British cavalry, 3,000 British infantry, and 500 of the Sirmoor Battalion of Gurkhas (later the 2nd Gurkha Rifles) with a light field battery and three troops of horse artillery. He was heavily outgunned and outnumbered. The sepoys had taken up a strong defensive position and fought with courage but showed no ability to manoeuvre in the field; their officers had no experience of commanding anything bigger than a company and they allowed themselves to be outflanked and enfiladed by the horse artillery. Charges with the bayonet by the British infantry settled the battle. 'The rebels stood well to their guns ... many fought with the courage of desperation and stood to be bayoneted' but they were driven from their position in the end and forced back within the walls of Delhi. The British force took up its position on the Ridge, to the north-west of the city, a long low outcrop of red stone.

At the end of the nineteenth century, two narratives were published which were written by Indian officials who were in Delhi throughout the siege and had kept diaries. Both writers were intelligent men, one Hindu, one Mohammedan. Both record that after Badli-ki-Serai the mutineers were demoralized and disheartened and had made no preparations for a siege. Both thought that if the British had attacked the city that night they would have found the gates open and met with no resistance. But the British troops were utterly exhausted.

There now began what is generally called the siege of Delhi. It was not a siege in the ordinary sense of the word. The British forces lay opposite the north-western face of Delhi; it was a great city, seven miles in circumference, and their front covered only two miles. On the north-eastern side was the Jumna and the whole southern face of the city lay open, a great semicircle four miles long from east to west. Throughout the three months of the siege sepoys were coming in to reinforce the garrison, who greatly outnumbered the so-called besiegers and who were never short of supplies.

On the British side, there was controversy throughout the whole period as to the best course of action. Anson had from the outset seen great difficulties in the recovery of Delhi, which Canning and Lawrence made light of. The idea of attacking a walled city with a force much smaller than the garrison was startling to a soldier not long used to India; the Delhi Field Force had only light artillery and were short of ammunition even for that, while the garrison had heavier guns, five times as many as ours, well served and with plenty of ammunition. Although the powder magazine had been blown up, the ordnance depot at Delhi had contained vast supplies of artillery and munitions, all of which had fallen into the mutineers' hands on May 11th. We could not bring our guns close enough to the walls to be in any way effective; there was no prospect of making a breach. Even if a surprise attack on a gate should enable us to make an entry, we had not the men to take, still less hold, a city the size of Delhi and at the same time guard the camp; the troops would find themselves involved in street fighting in which their losses would be very heavy and they might be driven back or the camp surprised behind them. The effect throughout India of an unsuccessful attack would be disastrous.

Anson would, from a purely military point of view, have preferred to collect a much stronger force and advance on Delhi when his preparations were complete. Delhi was a mustering place to which mutineers were rallying from every direction. Once they were assembled there and decisively defeated, the back of the thing would be broken; a premature attack, even if it was successful, would mean a protracted hunt after much smaller parties. Anson was dead, but the arguments he had used were bound to occur to any soldier who had read his textbooks and whose experience had been mainly in Europe. Indeed, in India too, Lord Lake's repulse at Bhurtpore had never been forgotten. To these arguments the political advisers replied again and again that the moral effect was all-important and that every week that Delhi was in rebel hands added to the number of our enemies.

Barnard, the second commander, won the hearts of all who met him by his kindliness of manner and his devotion to duty. He rode here and there all day in the sun, seeing the troops and looking to their comfort; he was believed never to sleep. He was not convinced of the wisdom of the operation, but he yielded to the strong pressure of his political advisers and the ardour of a group of young Engineer officers, who advised him that although, with no siege artillery, a breach could not be made, a night attack in which a gate was blown in by powder-bags was practicable. This attack was planned for the night of June 12th, four days after Badli-ki-Serai. An accident prevented it; by some extraordinary omission, the brigadier responsible for part of the plan was told nothing about it until shortly before it was due to start. He galloped, just after midnight, to Sir Henry Barnard, in order to put before him the military arguments against the attempt; Sir Henry gave in to him. The surprise attack was postponed.

The Engineers made another plan, dated June 14th; a Council of War met twice and the senior officers were heavily against it. 'I dread success almost as much as failure,' wrote Archdale Wilson in a written opinion. It was decided to wait for reinforcements. The Engineers, within a week, put forward a third plan, urging that reinforcements were pouring in to the enemy and that, with every attack they repulsed, the force on the ridge suffered losses which they could not afford. They might beat back the enemy again and again—as indeed they did—but though they might inflict losses ten times their own, they would still be worse off in proportion because they were so few. This time Barnard was not to be shaken; he was firm in refusal but by the end of June he agreed to what he described as a gamester's throw — a fourth plan, not dissimilar from the others, timed for July 3rd. But news reached him that the enemy had received powerful reinforcements and that they were planning an attack on his camp for that same morning. This attack too was postponed. On July 5th Sir Henry Barnard was dead of cholera; no doubt heat, exhaustion and anxiety had made him less able to resist it. General Reed now assumed command of the Field Force; he assured his subordinates that his health was much improved, though to them he seemed an invalid, but he had to resign the command twelve days later on grounds of ill-health and was succeeded by Archdale Wilson, the fourth to hold the post in less than two months.

During August there was a steady flow of reinforcements from the Punjab, not startling in point of numbers but significant. Quite as significant, the party in favour of action received two remarkable recruits, John Nicholson, who brought in the Mobile Column from the Punjab, and Baird Smith, an Engineer of greater weight and seniority but no less ardour than the indomitable planners of June. Nicholson was one of the Titans of the Punjab, the team gathered by John Lawrence, men of more than human energy and an intense devotion to duty which permitted no relaxation. Revered by those who worked under him, he must have been an uncomfortable colleague to his seniors. On his way to the Ridge, it was represented to him that men were collapsing and must be permitted to rest; he allowed it, but himself remained standing in the burning heat until they were ready to start again. Lord Roberts wrote years later: 'Nicholson impressed me more profoundly than any man I had ever met before or have ever met since.' In the district of Bannu which he ruled, a sect arose who regarded him as a saint and paid him almost divine honours. But he was not an easy companion; on August 7th, the night of his arrival on the Ridge, he dined at the headquarters mess and 'the silent solemnity of his demeanour was unpleasantly apparent to men whose habitual cheerfulness ... had been one of the sustaining influences of Camp Life.' But his presence was a tonic to the rank and file, who burned for action and had begun to feel that nothing would ever happen.

Indeed, soon after he took command, Archdale Wilson had considered retreating from a position in which the tables had by now been turned and the besiegers had become the besieged. The enemy were now much stronger than they had been when Barnard had decided on the gamester's throw; they had made several sorties aimed at getting behind the position on the Ridge and cutting its communications. Perhaps if the Delhi Field Force withdrew from its now merely defensive role it could more usefully take the offensive elsewhere. It was Baird Smith, the Engineer, who persuaded Wilson that such a step would be disastrous. Having given up that idea, Wilson did not seriously return to it though he kept an eye over his shoulder. His letter to Lawrence, begging for reinforcements, is couched in distinctly negative terms: 'Je retiendrai cette position jusqu' à la fin,' he wrote, and added rather inconsistently: 'Si je ne suis pas renforcé vite, je serai forcé de retirer à Kurnaul.' The British often sent messages in French or in Greek script in case they fell into the hands of sepoys.

That was perhaps the worst moment. Soon after his arrival Nicholson decisively defeated a powerful enemy force which was marching from Delhi to get behind the troops on the Ridge. John Lawrence responded nobly to Wilson's appeal and sent him every man the Punjab could raise—more indeed than most of his advisers thought he should have sent. On September 4th the siege-train at last arrived and Baird Smith submitted his plan for setting up batteries and making breaches, and for the final assault. Wilson pointed out the difficulties and dangers and appeared to be about to refuse consent. Nicholson wrote to a friend of 'appealing to the Army', or, in other words, mutiny. He told Roberts, still a subaltern, that he would have proposed that Wilson should be superseded and—since he himself was the next senior—that he would have stood down to serve under Campbell of the 52nd. But in the end Wilson, having set out all his objections in a letter to Lord Canning, reached a strange decision. He wrote: 'I disagree with the Engineers entirely. I foresee great if not insuperable difficulties in the plan they propose; but as I have no other plan myself I yield to the remonstrances of the Chief Engineer.' Thus, with a doubtful and half-hearted commander, preparations began.

Baird Smith achieved something quite remarkable. He had to establish batteries close enough to the walls of Delhi to be effective without giving away all our intentions; the enemy still had a superiority in artillery, but distributed over a wide front. For the concentration of fire he needed, the batteries must be built in places commanded by the enemy's guns; they must therefore be finished with all the speed possible and kept concealed until finished. All the early stages were got through secretly at night; the last stages were completed under fire, much heroism being shown by the gunners, by the supporting infantry— the Kumaon Battalion, later the 3rd Queen Alexandra's Own Gurkha Rifles—and by the nameless pioneers who dug. 'They were merely unarmed pioneers and not meant to be fighting men. With the passive courage so common to Natives, as man after man was knocked over, they would stop a moment, weep a little over their fallen friend, pop his body in a row along with the rest, and then work on as before.' Fire was opened from these batteries on September 11th, within a week of the siege-train's arrival. The enemy had been slow to realize what was happening, but had now started to move their heaviest guns to positions from which they could reply. They were too late; in another forty-eight hours it would have been the attacking force who were too late. Three days were enough; now 'for the first time we were able to fire with metal equal to theirs.' Fire was kept up throughout the 12th and 13th, and by the evening of the 13th breaches were established.

Four columns were to assault four different points; the attack was timed for dawn on September 14th. Nicholson led the first column and had an overall coordinating command of the others; there was no lack of vigour or determination in the assaulting columns. Two went for bastions where breaches had been made; they were held up, because the breaches had been filled during the night by sandbags and chevaux-de-frise, but they got through. The third column was to enter by the Kashmir Gate, which was to be blown in by the powder bag party. This is not the place to tell the tale of that exploit, for which four Victoria Crosses were awarded, but it was in the end successful. The first three columns were in the city; the fourth, on the extreme right, was repulsed and driven back to its starting point. The whole position on the Ridge was in danger of being outflanked but this was prevented by a cavalry counter-attack. Inside the city, the third column made good progress but the other two were held up by just the kind of situation which Wilson and his predecessors had foreseen—heavy musketry fire from house-tops and windows, light field-pieces at street crossings. Nicholson tried to lead his men into a narrow gully which all but he thought impossible and at once fell mortally wounded. By evening a bite had been made into the city, but sixty British officers and eleven hundred men were killed or wounded and all forward movement checked. That night the British troops found liquor put out for them in the streets; the sepoys knew what bait they would find attractive. Soon many were insensible. Wilson seems to have wanted to retire but again Baird Smith persuaded him that it would be disastrous. And, as so often in the Mutiny, the enemy did not counter-attack next morning, when by all accounts they might have won a crushing victory.

All supplies of liquor were destroyed. Sandbags were built up into barricades and on the 16th a house-to-house advance began, a cautious enlargement of the segment so far taken. The dangers that Wilson had feared were seen to be real; British soldiers, of such indomitable courage in the open, hated a war in which they could not see their enemy, in which they might at any moment be struck down by an unseen hand. Both H.M. 75th and H.M. 8th refused orders to advance. Wilson's depression grew stronger. He could not sleep and wrote to a friend that both his body and mind were giving way. He talked again of retiring, withdrawing all troops from Delhi. Nicholson, dying slowly in the camp upon the Ridge, raged with frustration and cried: 'Thank God I have still strength enough to shoot that man.' Once again, Baird Smith persuaded Wilson that he must go on. But the advance con-

The Head of the Advanced Guard of the Mahratta Army coming to join Earl Cornwallis near Seringapatam · May 28th 1791

The Head of the Advanced Guard of the Mahratta Army coming to join Earl Cornwallis near Seringapatam, May 28th, 1791. This gives some idea of the individualist approach to military action in armies of Indian princes. The Marathas were more disciplined than most; this is the Sar-i-Fauj (Cherry Fudge to our ancestors) spearhead of picked troops

Blessing the Colours, c. 1845. A Brahman is blessing the regimental colours of the 35th Regiment of the Bengal Army, who became Light Infantry in 1843. It was an essential feature of the Hindu social and religious system that each man should perform in his appointed station the function to which he was born, and it was an annual custom for each trade or calling to honour the tools of their craft. In early days British officers piled their swords with the men's muskets but this went out of favour in the 1830s with the rise of a narrower evangelical attitude to religion

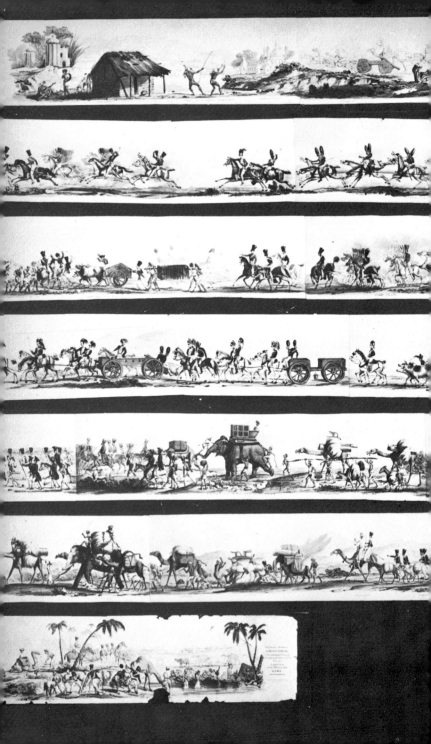

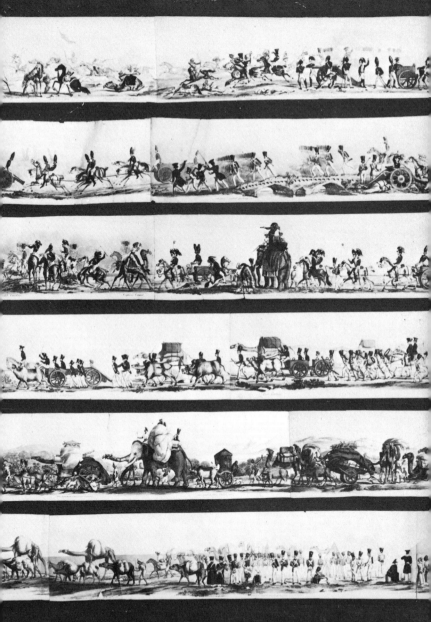

Troops of all arms of the Bengal Army in Scinde, *c.* 1845. One of the achievements of the British in India was to reduce the numbers of followers who accompanied soldiers on a campaign. But the panorama, drawn in loving detail by an unknown officer, shows that they were not altogether eliminated!

Tom Rattleton receiving a report

The Native Court Martial. Both these pictures are from *Memoirs of a Griffin* (Bellow, London, 1843). In the years before the Mutiny young British officers had grown casual and often contemptuous; Indian officers were promoted by seniority and were often too old

Officers of Rifle and Light Infantry Regiments in Full Dress, *c.* 1845

Three veterans of the
Mutiny from the 53rd Sikhs
(later the 3rd/12th Frontier
Force Regiment), 1909

Officers of Probyn's Horse,
c. 1862. In the reconstruction
after the Mutiny great
emphasis was laid on the
value of the Irregular Corps,
with very few British officers
and informal dress. Indian
officers had much more
responsibility in irregular
corps

Pathans attacking a Sangar defended by Sikhs, 1897
Gordon Highlanders carrying down Gurkha wounded, 1897

The Ambuscade: drawing by Vereker Hamilton of Pathans behind a rock waiting for British troops, 1897

The death of Wigram Battye of the Guides

Subadar-Major Santbir Gurung,
Second Gurkha Rifles (who kept the
vigil described in Kipling's story,
In the Presence)

Skinner's Horse

Risaldar-Major, Murray's Horse, later
20th Lancers

The Hon. Major-General His Highness
Sir Pratap Singh Bahadur, G.C.S.I.,
K.C.B., etc., of Jodhpur (all portraits on
this page by Major A. C. Lovett from
The Armies of India, 1911)

The Colonel

The Adjutant

The Risaldar Major

The Soldiers

An Indian Cavalry Regiment, seen by one of themselves. Drawn by Lt.-Col. Frank Wilson, 19th Lancers, in 1947 to illustrate a children's book, *Cecil the Car* in which Queen Victoria appears. But, except for the red coats, not much had changed before the 1930s

Rifleman Darwan Singh Negi, Royal Garhwal Rifles, winning the Victoria Cross
by clearing a German trench, November, 1914
Garhwalis in France, 1914

Soldiers of the Second World War:
Subedar Habib Khan, Punjabi
Muslim, 13th Frontier Force Rifles
Hakim Beg, Sniper, of the Rajput
Regiment

Rifleman Manparsad Pun, Gurkha,
25th Indian Division

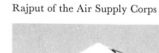

Rajput of the Air Supply Corps

The Western Desert: Sikh Viceroy's Commissioned Officer reporting to Infantry Battalion Headquarters

Nazi flag captured by Indian troops at Sidi Omar

The War in Burma:

Indian troops climbing hill feature during advance of 15 Corps

The War in Burma:
Garhwali in action during advance on
Maungdaw

Sikhs of the 14th Army in the Arakan

Two Dogras, Melu Ram and Deya Ram, in forward light machine-gun position,
Kangaw area

Eyre Coote

Lord Roberts at the time of the March from Kabul to Kandahar, by Charles Furse

Auchinleck

Slim

tinued slowly; on the 19th the Lahore Bastion was taken, a key point in the outer wall which had held out for six days; quite suddenly, on the morning of the 20th, the city was found to be almost abandoned.

Delhi was taken. Nicholson died on September 23rd; Archdale Wilson begged to be relieved of his command by a younger man. He had shown himself quite free from egotism and ambition and had tried to do his duty but he had neither the imaginative fire nor the robustness needed in such a war. A score of younger officers were the real victors, of whom perhaps Baird Smith more than any man deserves the praise. The determination of these leaders and the stubborn valour of the troops had won in the end. Dozens, scores of men deserved the Victoria Cross. But if mention is to be made of any, none deserve it more than Major Reid and the Sirmoor Battalion, later the 2nd Gurkhas, who held the Hindu Rao's House, the post on the extreme right of the British line, for three months and eight days, morning, noon and night. They sustained and defeated 16 separate attacks and lost 327 men killed and wounded out of 490.

Delhi was taken; it had been the symbol of success for the mutineers and its fall was the turning-point. The Emperor Bahadur Shah was made a prisoner on September 21st by Hodson of Hodson's Horse, who next day took the surrender of three of his sons. The courage of this exploit he stained by murder; he ordered them to leave the bullock-cart in which they were travelling and to strip off their outer garments; he then shot them. His later claim that he was threatened by a hostile crowd is hard to reconcile with the facts; they had surrendered to him and his act was deliberate. There can be no doubt that if a subadar and a party of rebel sepoys had taken a British officer prisoner and later killed him in similar circumstances we should have regarded it as treacherous murder.

Delhi was taken; the mutineers had fought with personal courage but they had been badly led. There had been differences between the Emperor's sons and sepoy leaders; the sepoy leaders had no experience of handling large bodies of troops but above all there was no unquestioned authority. The two narratives by Indians reveal a picture of profound confusion. Rumours of all kinds run through the city; everyone in turn is accused of being in touch with the English. There is no money in the treasury and all pay is in arrears. The gentle vacillating old Emperor taunts the soldiers one day with their failure and on the next is persuaded to proclaim that he will lead them in person. And then again he is in a mood of resignation; he announces that he has donned his shroud already and will spend the rest of his life meditating in a garden. There is no one to perceive how exhausted the enemy must be and to summon men to the one more effort that will bring victory. They have set up a military board—but that is no way to run a war.

Delhi was taken; and 'many who had never struck a blow agai
us ... and who had been plundered and buffeted by their own arm
countrymen, were pierced by our bayonets or cloven by our sab
or brained by our muskets.' To most British soldiers, to some office
every sepoy was guilty of the worst crimes that were supposed to ha
been committed by any of them. And often it was assumed that eve
male inhabitant of Delhi had sheltered and abetted the sepoys. No c
will ever know how much innocent blood was shed. Twenty-one m
of the princes, Bahadur Shah's sons, were tried and hanged next da
'some men caught going out of the Kashmir Gate disguised as wom
were caught and hung.' The city was treated as a captured fortr
which the victors were entitled to loot—but if that were so, this wa
war, the Emperor was logically a hostile power and his sons entitl
to be treated as loyal to him rather than as traitors to the Compar
By no code is it a crime to escape from a captured city in disguise. W
it a rebellion or a war? We treated it as both, as suited the mome
But officers and men alike were beyond logic; 'seldom, if ever, sir
War began', wrote Kaye, 'had there been so much to exacerbate a
infuriate an army as then inflamed the brains and fevered the blood
the men who found themselves inside the blood-stained city.'

4. Cawnpore

Everywhere, in their varying circumstances, the English in India,
the news of May 10th reached them, faced the same dilemma—
trust and hope that trust would be repaid, or to take precauti
which would confirm the sepoys' fears and bring the explosion near
   In the Punjab there was little hesitation. This was in part due to
character of John Lawrence—a man always ready to make the ha
choice between two evils—in part to the special circumstances o
recently conquered country. The Punjabis hated the sepoys while th
had acquired a respect, if not an affection, for the British. John La
rence saw—no one more clearly—the importance of retaking De
and he knew that it could be done only if he spared every man he co
from the Punjab. He knew he must pay a price for that effort. He w
even, to the horror of his faithful disciples, ready to give Peshawar to
Afghans if it would release men for Delhi. He did not take long to ma
up his mind that he would not hold back British troops from De
merely to watch sepoy battalions who might mutiny.
   The first disarming in fact took place in his absence and without
knowledge. He was not in Lahore when the news arrived from Mee
and Delhi, only one day behind the events. Montgomery, who h
Lawrence's authority in his absence, and Corbett, the Brigadier, w

both resolute men and were quickly agreed. They knew Lawrence would back them. They had information which they believed reliable that the sepoys, who outnumbered the British troops in Lahore by at least four to one, were 'up to their necks in sedition'. They decided that it must be all or nothing and made careful plans for disarming the entire brigade. Three battalions of infantry and a cavalry regiment suddenly found themselves confronting a line of guns and the loaded muskets of British troops. They piled arms, sullenly but obediently. This was on May 13th; Lawrence approved and it quickly became the general policy to disarm, even before disobedience had occurred.

It was the easier for Lawrence to do this because he had British troops available and because there was no sympathy for the sepoys in the surrounding population. Many of his civil officers had caught from the Punjabi peasants something of their dislike for the Purbiyas — the Easterners — by whom they had been conquered. Many of them had no hesitation about regarding every sepoy as a mutineer and a murderer. It was from military officers that the objections came; again and again, they were confident that *their* men would never mutiny. At one disarming parade, the officers threw their swords and spurs on the piles of sepoys' muskets. John Lawrence was firm; these things had to be done. But he saw the price that had to be paid; he wrote to Edwardes at Peshawar: 'Each step we take for our own security is a blow against the Regular Sepoy. He feels this and on his side takes a further step and so we go on until we disband or destroy them or they mutiny and kill their officers.' There was the dilemma clearly stated; he saw the tragedy, he saw the risk. He took the risk by the throat.

It was a double risk. First, by vigorous action he might drive the sepoys to mutiny that might have been avoided. Secondly, by raising local levies, particularly of Sikhs and Afghans, he might arm and train fresh enemies. There were already some Sikhs in the service of the Company and, though most of them had proved reliable, it was not true of all. But he believed that hostility to the Purbiyas and the chance of loot would be strong attractions and that some Sikhs would see that their hope of a big part in a new India would lie in a military alliance with the British. He took this calculated risk and was proved right.

Not all had his resolution. It will be remembered that between Calcutta and Lucknow there was only one British regiment, H.M. 10th at Dinapore near Patna. Here there were three sepoy regiments, and so long as they were armed, H.M. 10th must stay to watch them. All through May and June and for most of July each side waited and watched; Patna was a turbulent city, with a strong Muslim element. There were signs of defection among local landowners and even civil officials; these were dealt with sternly. No one hesitated in these days to hang a man who planned sedition and some were hanged even for seditious talk. There were spasms of panic, both among the Indian population and among the British indigo-planters, who were always eager for repressive action. But till July 25th waiting and watching was the order of the day. 'Make everybody show a good face,' wrote the Commissioner to his subordinates; 'be plucky and snub any fellows who are impudent. If any people talk sedition, threaten them with a rope.' But in July there arrived in Calcutta H.M. 5th Fusiliers; they were sent up the river at once in flats, towed by steamers. It was still the policy to get every British soldier to Cawnpore and Lucknow as quickly as possible, but Calcutta sent orders to General Lloyd, who commanded at Dinapore, empowering him to disembark the Fusiliers if he wished to disarm the three sepoy regiments. But he must disarm all or none, and on no account must he delay the Fusiliers.

For all those weary weeks, the Calcutta press and the local planters had been clamouring that the sepoys at Dinapore should be disarmed. But the Government had urged patience and the officers had protested that *their* men were loyal. Now it would be easier; the risk involved in the actual operation would be less and the Government had consented. But Lloyd still hesitated to take so irrevocable a step and finally he compromised. He decided to take away the percussion caps, but not the muskets and ammunition; this he felt would be less humiliating. This, in itself a half-measure, was sadly mismanaged. A parade was fixed for July 25th at which there was a show of European strength,* but nothing unusual took place; the sepoys had with them the usual supply of percussion caps as well as cartridges and these were not withdrawn. It had been Lloyd's intention to leave them the fifteen rounds each man carried—which would soon be shot away in practice and drill—but remove further supplies of caps from their regimental magazines under cover of the parade. But things had been sadly mistimed. The parade was dismissed and the men were moving away when they met bullock-carts carrying the percussion caps to the European lines. There were angry demonstrations and it seemed at one time as though the carts would be stopped and the caps seized. No such incident actually occurred, the officers being able to persuade the men to go to their lines. But it was now clear that they were unreliable, particularly the 7th and the 8th. The 40th had resisted the idea of stopping the carts.

General Lloyd now decided to take away the caps in the sepoys' possession. There were to be soothing explanations, pointing out that this would remove temptation to which men might be subjected

---

* H.M. 5th Fusiliers had not in fact been disembarked, but there were two companies of H.M. 37th Foot. This regiment was in Ceylon and the Governor did not feel he could spare more than two companies, but even two companies made a difference. Some companies of H.M. 10th had already gone upstream. The Company's 37th Native Infantry had been at Benares and by this time were disarmed.

by the 'evil machinations of designing scoundrels'. But by now of
course it was much too late for this kind of thing. The sepoys knew they
were not trusted and were afraid that this was the first step before something worse. The 7th and the 8th broke into open mutiny, fired on any
Europeans they could see and, taking their colours and their regimental
treasure, fled from Dinapore. The 40th hesitated, and a party of native
officers and N.C.O.s brought their colours and treasure to the parade-
ground, apparently with the intention of defending them against
mutineers. But they were fired on from the roof of the hospital by a party
from H.M. 10th; they fled and joined the others. Another party of the
40th stayed behind and protested their fidelity to their officers; they
were officially accepted as part of the loyal garrison but a party of
H.M. 10th set upon them at night and bayoneted many of them as they
lay sleeping on their cots.

General Lloyd 'was old and infirm. He was grievously afflicted with
the gout. He could not walk. He could not ride.' He now went on board
a steamboat on the river, from which it does not appear that he was
able to exercise any effective supervision. The mutineers escaped; there
was no serious pursuit. Three battalions made their way to the most
disaffected district in the whole of Bihar. Here they joined themselves
to Kunwar Singh, a Rajput landholder who had good cause for resentment at the Company's rule and who played a leading part in the
operations of the next six months. This day's bungling led to a long
chain of events: the siege of the little house at Arrah, the defeat of the
first force sent to relieve it, and much more for which there is no room
here.

The affair at Dinapore has been told at this point in the story as a
contrast to the disarming at Lahore and to illustrate the dilemma in
which every commanding officer was placed. It can hardly be disputed
that Lloyd was too old, too ill and too irresolute for the post he held.
The disarming was bungled; if it had to be done, it should have been
swift, efficient and ruthless. But that is not to imply that it should have
been done as soon as the news arrived from Meerut. This was not the
Punjab; some of H.M. 10th had already been sent up the river towards
Cawnpore and Lucknow and it would have been difficult, even with
the sepoys at Dinapore disarmed, to send many more, leaving the long
stretch of country to Calcutta even more denuded.

Lord Canning's dilemma was not quite the same as John Lawrence's.
There were no British troops except at Calcutta and Dinapore and to
disarm at those centres would be likely to spark off mutinies at every
smaller station and fill the countryside with disaffected men. In Bengal,
the sepoys were by no means despised by the surrounding population.
They would have been far more dangerous in Bengal and Behar than
among the hostile Sikhs. Here in these great provinces, where there

were more than ten thousand of the native inhabitants to every English soldier, it was essential to play for time. And Canning was clear that time could only be bought by reassuring, not by frightening, the sepoys. 'You talk', he wrote to an officer of irregular horse, 'of the necessity of striking terror into the Sepoys. You are entirely and most dangerously wrong. The one difficulty, which of all others is the most difficult to meet, is that the regiments which have not yet fallen away are mad with fear—fear for their caste and religion, fear of disgrace in the eyes of their comrades, fear that the European troops are being collected to crush and decimate them as well as their already guilty comrades.'

'The one difficulty … ' he wrote, and it was indeed one that it was impossible to meet. The story of the 6th Native Infantry at Allahabad was by this time known to every Englishman. This was a regiment whose officers had a special pride in the care they had taken of their men. They, more than any others, were sure that *their* men at least would never be unfaithful to their salt. And they had proof, for early in June the sepoys of the 6th begged to be led against the rebels at Delhi. Their request was sent by telegraph to Calcutta; the thanks of the Governor-General were flashed back. On June 6th a parade was held to convey this message to the regiment. This parade was held at sunset; the message was read; the men greeted it with loud cheers. The officers of the 6th once more congratulated themselves on the fidelity of their model regiment. But that night at nine o'clock the men rose and killed many of their officers; the Colonel eventually reaching the fort just as his horse fell dead from musket fire. Among those killed were eight boys of sixteen or seventeen years old, straight from England, cadets still unposted to a regiment. Their fate became part of the legend of the Mutiny: 'Remember the poor little griffins!' men said to each other, whetting their appetite for vengeance.

This affair of the 6th seemed to most Englishmen utterly unaccountable, the blackest treachery and ingratitude. Yet it is not, perhaps, so difficult to understand; news had reached Allahabad by telegraph that on June 4th an attempt had been made—with only a very small British force—to disarm the Company's 37th Native Infantry at Benares and that, as the men resisted, the guns had opened fire. It is easy to see how that would be reported in the bazaar. 'It has begun,' they would whisper, 'they have shot down innocent sepoys on the parade-ground at Benares. Soon it will be here.' Another case, not quite a parallel, but in the eyes of British officers and soldiers equally inexplicable, was that of the 41st at Sitapore. This station, barely fifty miles north of Lucknow, was garrisoned by one regular battalion, the 41st Native Infantry, and two irregular battalions, formerly in the service of the King of Oudh. All protested their fidelity. One old native officer, with tears in his eyes, begged his commandant 'not to cast away the confidence and break the bonds of a life of cherished comradeship; and it would have been strange', writes Kaye, 'if such appeals as these had not touched the hearts of Sepoy officers, who, in camp and canton-ment and on hard-fought fields, had shared their dangers and privations and had never known them to murmur.' Birch, Colonel of the 41st, trusted them till the end.

Birch had in fact marched them towards Lucknow and exchanged shots with the mutineers; they had shown no sign of disaffection, and had come back 'covered with honour as loyal soldiers'. But on June 2nd there was a rumour that the flour in the bazaar had been polluted and the sepoys insisted that it should be thrown into the river. This was done. Next day they rose, seized the treasury, shot down Colonel Birch, killed the Commissioner, George Christian, and his wife and child, and many other officers and their families, burning or smashing their houses and all their belongings.

It would be shallow to suppose that all this pent-up hatred was due only to the rumour about the flour. This was Oudh, so recently annexed, and the sepoys, as we have seen, had special reasons for disliking the annexation. Here, more than anywhere, the whole population was disaffected. Here the levellers had been at work with more even than their usual tactlessness and discourtesy; great landholders and small were hostile to a regime which had robbed them of their rights; all the hangers-on of the King of Oudh were dispossessed and bitter; the King of Oudh's troops, transferred wholesale, found they had to be far more assiduous in spit and polish for much the same pay as before —and they had not yet had time to appreciate the advantages of its more regular arrival. Nor had the peasantry, whose interests were so dear to the levellers, had time to see any benefits from their policy. All this was on top of the anger and fear felt by conservative people every-where in India at the threats to religion and property. No one will ever know just how the men of the 41st felt. It can only be guessed that their discontent and suspicion were mounting slowly, like a great weight of water behind a dam of customary obedience and respect for individual officers. When the dam broke, then it would be in a frenzy of hate and despair that they would stamp out all traces of those they had once trusted and now feared and hated.

The English of the mid nineteenth century were less widely ac-quainted than their great-grandchildren with psychological ideas and phraseology. They knew well enough that a son's respect for his father can turn to hate. Their novels are full of it, but they did not link it with the name of Oedipus and it still surprised them. And just as the Vic-torian fathers were astonished at their sons' ingratitude, so were they at the sepoys'. There was almost total lack of understanding on their side but they were outraged that *he* should so misunderstand *them* as to suppose they would put the ground bones of cows in his food. 'My children! My children!' said the old colonel, weeping, and they shot him. It was only in a frenzy of emotion that they could bring themselves to rebel and when they did they must slash and stab again and again.

To the English, it was a shock to their pride, an outrage to all they had believed. They had been so secure in the sepoys' fidelity, they had taken them so much for granted! Yet perhaps, even in the careless, arrogant English, deep below the level of conscious thought, here and there lay buried an ember of fear in the face of a people so much more numerous. That must never be expressed. What could be spoken about, what infuriated them more than even the treachery and ingratitude, was the killing of women.

It was part of the Victorian ideal to put women on a pedestal. No doubt the Victorians often fell below their own ideals; no doubt they exploited women, both sexually and economically, as well as idealizing them. But they set a high value on chastity; they observed an elaborate code of behaviour in regard to women. They did everything they could to exaggerate the difference between the sexes. Women were weak, emotional, lacking in common sense—but they were sacred. An officer must not mention a woman's name in the mess; this was supposed to be because they were so much respected but it surely suggests that most officers knew so little of women that they could regard them only as objects of forbidden desire which they dared not openly discuss. They were frightened of these precious, untouchable creatures. And that those treacherous scoundrels the sepoys—whom the English despised because they were conquered, and, as they say so often, for their colour—should lay beastly hands on *their* women, those fragile symbols of purity and of repressed desire, raised them to a pitch of frenzied rage which has not been equalled in their history. It is significant that they often supposed that sepoys had outraged English ladies before killing them. No one can say this never happened but I have seen no evidence that it did and there is strong evidence that it did not in the massacres of which there is record.* Such a pitch of anger had been roused that the English had to attribute to the sepoy what in themselves they would have regarded as most dreadful. That is why John Nicholson, to the Victorians a hero of heroes, of whom Lord Roberts wrote that 'he was the *beau ideal* of a soldier and a gentleman' was able to write: 'If I had them [the murderers of women and children in Delhi] in my power today and knew that I were to die

---

* At least one girl of Eurasian stock was abducted after Cawnpore by a trooper who meant to make her his mistress. But that is not the same thing. Russell of *The Times* went into this question at great length and concluded that the stories were without foundation; Kaye reached the same conclusion.

tomorrow, I would inflict the most excruciating tortures I could think of on them with a perfectly easy conscience.' That is why so often no distinction was made between innocent and guilty. It is a fact that this was how men felt; it is the reason for their behaviour. It is not a justification.*

But they had provocation enough, without resorting to fantasy about sexual crimes. The story of Cawnpore is too well known to be told here at length, but it provides one more illustration of the dilemma—trust or prepare for the worst—and of all the legends of the Mutiny, it is the core and heart. But it must not be forgotten that rage had reached white heat before Cawnpore. The news of what had happened at Meerut and Delhi was enough and the vengeance taken at Allahabad and on the march upstream was as terrible as anything that happened after Cawnpore. Yet since this book is an account of how men felt and, since Cawnpore came to be the symbol of the crimes they were avenging, this is the place to recall what happened.

General Wheeler, who commanded at Cawnpore, was over seventy, but a far more active and well-preserved man than General Lloyd. He had a brigade of three native infantry battalions and a cavalry regiment—some three thousand men—and of British troops only a few gunners and some details from three different infantry regiments on their way through—less than three hundred men all told. There was a powder magazine in a small fort, which might well have been defended for some time. He was urged to occupy this fort but he judged that to remove the sepoy guard, to order English women and children into the fort and to stock it, as though for a siege, would provoke the explosion he hoped to avoid. Instead, he prepared an entrenchment with a parapet only four feet high of loose earth, and collected in this some stores, enough for a few days only. This indicated distrust without providing safety. The rising came on the night of June 4th; a blaze in the sky told of officers' bungalows on fire; the treasury, the magazine and the gaol were all taken and the mutineers began to march to Delhi. They did not, however, get very far.

The adopted son of the Peshwa, the Nana Sahib, became in British legend the fiend embodying all that they hated most in the Mutiny. The disallowance of his father's pension has already been recounted and it cannot be sensibly supposed that he was imbued with any passionate loyalty for the British. But with characteristic self-assurance they were sure that he was well disposed and after the outbreak at

* The Victorians also attributed to the Rani of Jhansi sexual excesses for which there does not seem to be any sound evidence. Sylvester, an officer at the siege of Jhansi, wrote: 'During the many long hours, we on picket-duty watched and wondered what she said and what she did to those best-favoured among a band of chieftains and imagination ran wild in the fervid heat.'

Meerut had asked him to send some of his retainers to guard the treasury. These men offered no resistance to the mutineers but joined them on their march to Delhi. When they reached the Nana's estate, the whole body turned back to Cawnpore. Whether it was the Nana himself or his advisers who played the principal part, it was in his name that they laid siege to Wheeler's pitiful entrenchment.

The siege began on June 6th; it lasted till June 27th. There was little cover, either from artillery fire or from the sun—and what that means, at that time of year, can scarcely be conveyed to those who have not experienced it. The besiegers, outnumbering the besieged ten to one, had the whole city to draw on and the Cawnpore magazine; their guns were not only far more numerous but much heavier. The besieged were too few to stand regular watches and there was nowhere in the entrenchment where they could be under cover secure against gunfire; they had no rest. The only well was in full view of the enemy and water could be drawn only at night; even then, owing to the creaking of the windlass, it was a service of great hazard. But though the gallantry and the sufferings of those in the entrenchment were extreme, indeed almost beyond belief, it is the end of the siege that became a legend. Provisions ran short, the guns became less effective and ammunition began to run low. Death, wounds and sickness had terribly reduced the defenders; some had gone mad. Yet they were able to repel a full-scale attack mounted against them on June 23rd, the anniversary of Plassey. Two days later a message was brought from the Nana Sahib offering terms. Wheeler was reluctant to surrender, but was persuaded that there was no other way of saving the sick, the women and the children. It was agreed, by emissaries on behalf of the Nana Sahib, that they should be given carts and elephants to take them to the river, where there would be boats that would take the whole garrison downstream.

On June 27th, early in the morning, the move to the boats took place. There were some forty boats assembled, each with a light shelter of thatch against the sun. As the party embarked, the boatmen set fire to the thatch of the boats and fled. A heavy fire was opened from the banks at the same time and a general massacre began. It was at first indiscriminate but, towards the end, word was given that the women and children were not to be killed but taken prisoner. There were about one hundred and twenty-five; other prisoners were later added and the total number rose to about two hundred. They were crowded together in a small house in conditions of extreme misery and humiliation; they were made to grind corn for the Nana Sahib's household. On July 15th, when it was known that Havelock's forces from downstream were at last nearing Cawnpore, the order was given that they should be killed. The sepoys ordered to shoot them from the windows disobeyed orders and fired at the ceiling; butchers were sent for who went into the room with long knives to slaughter them. Next day they were dragged out; not all were dead but the living were soon finished off and all the bodies were thrown into a well.

It was this massacre above all that roused the English to fury. There can be no question that it took place, nor that it was by the orders of someone in the Nana's household. Nor can there be any doubt that the shooting at the riverside was planned and that a signal was given for it to begin. There were guns in place along the river bank. Dr Sen, whose scrupulously careful history of the Mutiny was written after Independence and at the request of the Indian Government, argues that the Nana was not personally responsible; however that may be, the point of importance for this book is that the English thought he was and made him into a fiend more hated than Buonaparte or Kaiser Wilhelm. It is also relevant that the British in the entrenchment had decided early in the siege that they would not take prisoners; if a prisoner was taken, he was shot at once. And terrible things had been done already by the avenging forces at Allahabad and on the way upstream.

When the mutiny of the 6th Native Infantry took place at Allahabad, the tiny trickle of twenty-four British soldiers a day was already beginning to build up at Benares into a force which could march upstream to Allahabad, seventy miles away. Neill, with a small party of his Madras Fusiliers—the Company's Europeans—reached Allahabad on June 11th, five days after the mutiny of the 6th, and next day another hundred of his Fusiliers came in. The fort at Allahabad was still in British hands, largely owing to the tact, energy and power of command of Brasyer of Brasyer's Sikhs, but the city of Allahabad had been for five days given up to loot and murder, directed not only at Europeans, Eurasians and Christians, but also at Bengalis, of whom there was a colony. Neill's men had little difficulty in clearing the city and they took fierce and indiscriminate vengeance. 'Soldiers and civilians alike were holding Bloody Assizes or slaying Natives without any assize at all, regardless of sex or age,' wrote Kaye. And he quotes papers submitted to Parliament by the Governor-General in Council which state that 'the aged, women and children are sacrificed as well as those guilty of rebellion.' More explicitly, the Government reported that 'the indiscriminate hanging not only of persons of all shades of guilt, but of those whose guilt was at the least very doubtful, and the general burning and plunder of villages whereby the innocent as well as the guilty without regard to age or sex were indiscriminately punished ... had deeply exasperated large communities not otherwise hostile to the Government.' Rice Holmes in his *History of the Indian Mutiny* says: 'Old men who had done us no harm, helpless women with sucking infants at their breasts, felt the weight of our vengeance.' Men boasted that they had spared no one. When at last Neill felt strong enough to dispatch a force onwards towards Cawnpore on June 30th—three days after the surrender—his instructions to that force were clear. 'Attack and destroy all places en route close to the road occupied by the enemy but touch no others.' Certain villages are listed as guilty and 'are to be destroyed; all men in them to be slaughtered. All sepoys not giving a good account of themselves are to be hanged at once; all heads of insurgents to be hanged.'

Neill was a fierce indomitable Scot, well read in the Old Testament, convinced that what he did was justified. 'God grant I may have acted with justice,' he wrote in his diary; 'I know I have with severity but under all the circumstances I trust for forgiveness.' He goes on to state the circumstances which justify the severity, in this case the hanging of a sepoy with twenty years' service who had been identified as having joined the insurgents. He speaks by name of three English women, one being Mrs Chambers, who as we know was killed at Meerut on May 10th. Neill says here that it was a butcher, not a sepoy, who had murdered this 'beautiful young girl'. It was surely a strange reason for hanging a sepoy who had never been near Meerut. And is it really more heinous to kill a beautiful girl than a plain one? He also mentions Miss Jennings, who was believed by her own brother to have been dragged naked through the streets, tortured and outraged before being killed at Delhi, but there is good evidence that though she was killed it was in private and at once, without outrage or torture. And, again, the man now hanged had had nothing to do with Miss Jennings or Delhi. When Neill at last reached Cawnpore—and he might have been there sooner if he had not burnt so many villages—he saw the room in which the massacre of the women took place and it was certainly a sight to make any man furious. Major North wrote: 'Tortured by the fierce thought of revenge and penetrated by the sense of their sufferings, strange wild feelings woke within us. Vaunting, eager, maddened, we sped onward to the dreary house of martyrdom, where their blood was outpoured like water; the clotted gore lay ankle deep on the polluted floor and also long tresses of silken hair, fragments of female wearing apparel, hats, books, children's toys were scattered about in terrible confusion.' Neill saw this and his feelings too were strange and wild. But he does not seem to have thought it mattered who was punished so long as punishment was inflicted. His orders were that the room was to be cleaned by those who had taken part in the mutiny. 'Each miscreant after sentence of death is pronounced on him will ... be forced into cleaning up a small portion of the bloodstains; the task will be made as revolting to his feelings as possible and the Provost-Marshal will use the lash in forcing anyone objecting to complete his task. After properly cleaning up his portion, the culprit is to be immediately hanged.' In his own account of what he did, Neill continues that the first culprit was a subadar of the 6th who was made to do the work with a sweeper's brush put in his hand by a sweeper; a Mahommedan officer of the civil court was flogged and made to lick up part of the blood with his tongue. 'I will hold my own', Neill continued, 'with the blessing and help of God. I cannot help seeing that His finger is in all this—we have been false to ourselves so often.'

This was a strange religion, far indeed from the Sermon on the Mount. Kaye believes that Neill thought these men were concerned in the actual slaughter of the women, but what evidence there is—and there is no doubt it is shaky—is that sepoys of the 6th had refused to fire on the women and that the Nana had threatened to blow them from guns for their refusal. In their anger, such stern covenanting men as Neill and Nicholson and many others seem to have thought that everyone who took any part in the Mutiny was responsible for every crime perpetrated by everyone else. No doubt there were others in the ranks of British regiments who were glad of the opportunity to vent their ferocity on a people of whom they had not the least understanding. And no doubt there were others, particularly among the young, in whom a spontaneous high-spirited pugnacity found pleasure in any kind of excitement and to whom the enemy simply did not count as people. These were amongst the feelings on the English side. Both sides were embarked on a mounting spiral of outrage, of revolt and of cruel reprisals.

5. Lucknow and the Last Stages

The high drama of the Mutiny seen as a whole centres on Delhi. Once Delhi had fallen it could no longer be doubted that British rule would in the end be restored. In personal terms, looking at individual lives, Cawnpore and Lucknow are more moving, because against the background of almost incredible hardship and endurance hangs the uncertainty of whether these gallant people will be saved. And in dozens of smaller places, there is a similar uncertainty and tension, acute for the man in charge with decisions to make, agonizing for the man with wife and children. How different for the high-spirited young! 'Here we are, in a jolly state of excitement,' wrote one such from Fyzabad on May 19th; 'we don't know but that Fyzabad may kick up a row and the sepoys join in it any hour they like. I need hardly say how we gallop from one bungalow to another when the post arrives to see who has the latest news ... News just arrived here that we must prepare to make a stand if the worst comes; this is pleasant! ... What a spree!' In every one of those small stations, there is this background of tense excited waiting, culminating in many varied ways in murder or flight.

It was the same pattern at Lucknow. Here as Chief Commissioner was Henry Lawrence, who combined all John's resolute daring and energy with a warmer nature that made him revered and loved as few men have ever been. He came nearer than anyone to solving the dilemma of whether to show trust or take precautions. He contrived to assemble stocks of food and ammunition in the Residency without precipitating the conflict. He disarmed the first irregular regiment which showed signs of disaffection without bringing everything to a head—this at a time when every day gained was important. Among the hundreds of dramatic scenes of 1857, none is more vivid than that of the evening of May 30th, when news that the expected outbreak had occurred reached Henry Lawrence as he sat at dinner with his staff. They went out on to the steps before the Residency. It was clear moonlight; there was the sound of firing in the distance. They stood waiting. The subaltern commanding the sepoy guard on the Residency brought up his thirty men and asked if he should load. ' "Load? Yes, certainly," said Lawrence, "and take care of my property." As the men brought up their muskets in the act of loading, they levelled straight at the little group of officers waiting for their horses on the steps. And perhaps,' wrote Kaye, 'there was not one of them who did not experience a feeling of relief when the men shouldered their arms and marched off to defend the gateway.'

This is not the place to tell once more the story of that heroic siege— though to read of it again is to experience pity and terror to a high degree. There was a month between the rising on May 30th and the moment at the beginning of July when the siege closed down. The main fighting force of the garrison had just suffered a defeat in the field. They had lost in one morning, by enemy action and heat exhaustion, 119 British soldiers, nearly half the total who had marched out that day. For eighty-seven days, under continuous artillery fire, on short rations, in intense heat, that garrison endured not only danger—sometimes more acute, sometimes less, never absent—but the most exhausting toil, burying the remains of men, horses and bullocks killed by gunfire, repairing defences, digging mines and countermines, dripping with sweat in the torrid dark of narrow underground passages. 'There was no spot … throughout the entire defences, where a dying soldier or an ailing woman or child, could feel an instant's security.'

The defenders included many Indians. At the beginning of the siege, on July 1st, the effective strength was 927 Europeans and 765 Indians. On September 25th there were 577 and 402 effective. Some of the Indians were Sikhs but many were sepoys of the regular line, Oudh Brahmans and Rajputs, the faithful remnants of the regiments which had mutinied. They had come to the Residency at the time of the outbreak but had been sent away before the siege proper began. Henry Lawrence was seriously ill and he was at last persuaded to make over affairs to a committee and take some rest. His rest lasted less than three days, but in that brief interval Martin Gubbins, the Financial Commissioner, chairman of the committee, a man of great courage, intelligence and energy but incurably pugnacious and impulsive, sent away to their homes those devoted men. Lawrence rose from his bed and sent messages to recall them; with the addition of some pensioners, they made a force of some 800 infantrymen. Of these men, Brigadier Inglis of the 32nd (the Duke of Cornwall's Light Infantry) who succeeded Lawrence as commander, wrote:

'With respect to the native troops, I am of the opinion that their loyalty has never been surpassed. They were indifferently fed and worse housed. They were exposed, especially the 13th Regiment, under the gallant Lt Aitken, to a most galling fire of roundshot and musketry, which materially decreased their numbers. They were so near the enemy that conversation could be carried on between them; every effort, persuasion, promise and threat was alternately resorted to in vain, to seduce them from their allegiance to the handful of Europeans, who in all probability would have been sacrificed by their desertion.'

The famous eighty-seven days is counted from the beginning of July until September 25th, but that first relief by Havelock was by no means the end of the siege. The trickle of reinforcements that reached Cawnpore had been so thin and the threats to Cawnpore itself had been so powerful that Havelock, determined soldier though he was, had been three times forced to fall back. He simply had not the men to hold Cawnpore, the head of his lifeline to Calcutta, and at the same time provide a force that could cut its way to Lucknow. Three times he had crossed the Ganges from Cawnpore and begun the advance to Lucknow; three times he had made good progress but heavy losses had brought home to him the virtual certainty that, if he went on, Cawnpore would fall before he could get back. When he crossed the river for the fourth time he had more than three thousand men, twice the number he had had on the third attempt. This time he reached the outskirts of Lucknow without much fighting but to get into the Residency cost him over seven hundred men, nearly a quarter of his force, and he was not strong enough to fight his way back with the sick and wounded, the women and children. It was a reinforcement, not an end to the siege.

It was not till November 17th that Sir Colin Campbell, later Lord Clyde, relieved the Residency for the second time, after very heavy fighting, in which there can really be little doubt that if the enemy had had an experienced commander with a good staff, the attacking force would have been in danger of destruction. Highlanders and Sikhs had vied with each other in their determination to get into the great buildings—palaces, forts and mosques—which lie along the river bank. They had stormed them one by one and had made contact with the Residency. But the front on which they had made their advance was very narrow; the enemy still held in overwhelming strength the great square of the Qaisar Bagh and between this and the river was only a narrow defile. Through this the sick and women had to be moved out of the Residency, under fire. It took three days to do it; Campbell had to march back swiftly to Cawnpore and arrived there only just in time to defeat powerful forces which were close to Cawnpore.

Delhi was taken, Agra and Lucknow relieved. The war was far from over, because the whole of Oudh and most of Rohilkand were in enemy hands, while south of the Ganges there were large hostile forces. They were composed of sepoys, mostly from Oudh, but were supposed to be fighting for the restoration of Maratha power. They were better led than any other of the armies of the mutineers, by Tantia Topi and by the Rani of Jhansi. But though these two provided overall direction, in which the rebels were so conspicuously lacking elsewhere, they could not make up for the lack of officers of middle rank, majors, colonels and brigadiers. The operations which cleared up these areas, though they meant hard-fought battles, long marches, skilful movements and startling risks taken, add little, from the point of view of this book, to what we already know. When Sir Colin Campbell finally took Lucknow —the third time British troops had fought their way in—he had 30,000 men and the issue was not seriously in doubt. Sir Hugh Rose's campaign against Tantia Topi in Central India was for much of the time a pursuit. The main object of the mutineers was to avoid action; when it was unavoidable, they fought with a courage that was literally desperate. They had no hope, they were doomed. By the late summer of 1858 they had no armies in the field. Those who were still living had been driven into the jungles of the Himalayan foothills, where most of them perished of malaria or starvation.

The Mutiny was over and we must begin to look to what was to come next, the reconstruction. Clearly, the question would have to be considered of whether there was to be a native army in India at all. That there should be was in fact decided largely on grounds of money and manpower, but it was, none the less, a decision that was to have a profound effect on the future development of India as a nation. Once that was clear, it would have to be settled whether it should be one army or three, how it should be officered, how manned. And it would be safe, to anyone acquainted with British habits of thought, to predict that it would be based, at least as a starting-point, on what existed when the Mutiny was over. Let us look then at what forces existed, and let us then consider, so far as we can, the nature of what had happened

and its effect on the relations of officers and men—which means, basically, of British and Indians.

The two southern armies had hardly been affected. In the Bombay
Army, although of 26,000 men about 7,000 were Brahmans and
Rajputs from Oudh and Behar, there was mutiny in only two battalions, the 26th and the 27th, both recently raised, both with a high
percentage of Purbiyas. And even in these two cases, only part of the
regiment was affected and the Maratha soldiers—of whom there were
about 8,000 in the whole army—stood firm. This is the more surprising
because the Nana claimed that he was the Peshwa and had raised the
famous saffron banner of the Marathas. Throughout the Mutiny,
there was nothing nearer an appeal to national feeling than this.
Perhaps the Marathas disliked the Purbiyas more than the British;
perhaps the Bombay Army's attitude to caste and its stricter discipline
were the reason. Perhaps more Bombay officers stayed with their
regiments and fewer obtained staff posts; perhaps they were what the
Bengal officers would no doubt have called old-fashioned—rather less
European in their outlook, more inclined to smoke a hookah and keep
a native mistress, able to spare time more readily to listen to the men.
Whatever the reason, it was the fact that the Bombay Army did not
mutiny and supplied most of the forces used in Sir Hugh Rose's campaign.

In the Madras Army, there were no exceptions; not one regiment
mutinied. The Madras artillery were of great value at Cawnpore and
in the Oudh campaign; six battalions of native infantry from Madras
were employed in Central India. There would therefore be strong
arguments, when the war was over, for keeping three armies, separately organized, with different traditions. What would be difficult
would be to decide what the Bengal army should be like. It consisted,
by the end of the Mutiny, of faithful remnants from regiments which
had mutinied, like those who had served so staunchly through the
siege of Lucknow; of a few complete line regiments which had stood
fast; of some irregular or specialized corps, such as the Guides; of
improvised corps, the followers of some young and vigorous leader,
such as Hodson's Horse, Mayne's Horse and Meade's Horse, which
last two later combined to make the Central India Horse; of Gurkhas,
also at this stage mostly irregular; and of Punjabis, both Sikhs and
Muslims. Some Punjabis had been enlisted as individuals in the sepoy
regiments before the Mutiny—to the disgust of the high-caste men—
and some of these had been included among the faithful remnants;
many more had been raised during the Mutiny as local levies by John
Lawrence.

The old Bengal Army, Nott's 'beautiful Sepoy Regiments', had been
all of a kind, dressed and drilled and pipeclayed to perfection, in theory

interchangeable. How different was the improvised, heterogeneous collection of units left at the end, each with its own leader, its own young traditions! How strange were the chances that had decided the fate of those who had stood fast! Consider, for instance, the 31st Bengal Native Infantry, who had been at both sieges of Bhurtpore and had kept so jealously the honour of their regiment and the fragments of their tattered colours. At the outbreak of the Mutiny this battalion was at Saugor in the Central Provinces, together with the 42nd, the 3rd Irregular Cavalry* and a company of European gunners. In the middle of June there was some disaffection in the 42nd, and four men were arrested. But there was no general outbreak, and a party, consisting of detachments from all three regiments, was sent out on a special mission, which they carried out successfully, several days' march from Saugor. But they then insisted on dictating to their commanding officer what should be done with the prisoners they had taken. He gave in to them, released the prisoners, and stayed where he was, unable to bring back his guns.

News of this indiscipline reached Saugor, where the Brigadier decided that he could no longer trust any native troops. The 31st were relieved of their duty as guards on the fort, and this was shared between the few Europeans. All officers, their wives and children, were ordered into the fort. The British officers of the 31st begged to be allowed to stay with their men, but the Brigadier would not permit it. But he told the 31st that their British officers would be permitted to stay with them if they handed over any men guilty of sedition. On this, Subadar Bhowani Baksh Tewari volunteered to lead out a party to bring back the disaffected detachment. He found that all the men of the 42nd, and some of the 31st, had deserted, and the officer in charge did not consider it safe to move the guns. The subadar brought back the guns and the faithful remnant but, before he was back, the 42nd and the 3rd Irregular Cavalry had broken into open mutiny and had started looting the deserted bungalows. On July 6th three troopers of the 3rd went to pillage the bungalow of an officer of the 31st, guarded by a sepoy of the regiment. He ordered them to go away but, as they did not obey, he shot one and killed a second with the butt of his musket; the third fled. This infuriated the two mutinous regiments, and the 42nd opened fire on the lines of the 31st. The latter sent a message to the fort, asking for guns and the help of their officers, but the Brigadier would not consent. Next morning the 42nd left Saugor, by the Cawnpore road; the 31st, in spite of the rebuff from the Brigadier, pursued them, caught and defeated them, bringing back their colours and four hundred stand of arms. From now on they were accepted as

* It was not this regiment but the 3rd Light Cavalry, a regular regiment, which began the Mutiny at Meerut.

completely reliable and were employed on detachments against the
mutineers. But what combination of qualities in their officers, British
and Indian, kept them faithful so long? And would it have turned out
differently if that sentry—his name is recorded as Hussos Khan*—had
joined the three troopers? One man's loyalty to his trust produced an
inter-regimental conflict which settled the issue for the 31st, who
survived to become the 1st/7th Rajput Regiment.

Take again the 21st Bengal Native Infantry. They were at Peshawar
at the outbreak of the Mutiny and were then spoken well of—but so
were many others. There were four other battalions of native infantry
in the station; in line with general policy in the Punjab, it was decided to
disarm them. When the disarmament took place on May 22nd the 21st
was spared, on the double grounds that as the senior regiment it had
so far set a good example and that it was 'indispensable to keep one
Native Infantry Corps to carry on the duty of the station'. So the 21st
served on and so much impressed the Lincolnshire Volunteers, who
later reached Peshawar, that they presented them with their regimental
march 'The Lincolnshire Poacher'. At the Proclamation Parade
transferring India to the Crown, 'on the left of a long line of troops, clad
in the loose khaki clothing that is now so familiar, stood a corps that a
twelve-month had made as extinct in Upper India as the dodo. There
stood in its scarlet coatees, its shakos and white cross-belts, a surviving
regular Bengal Battalion, that had alone, of the original Peshawar
garrison, escaped disarmament and avoided mutiny.' It became the
4th Battalion, 1st Punjab Regiment in 1922.

Again, let us look at Brasyer's Sikhs. Brasyer was commissioned in
1846 after the battle of Sobraon, less than twelve years from coming to
India as a gunner in the Company's service. He claims to have recruited the first Sikhs after the Sikh Wars and in 1856 became the
Commandant of the unit that came to be known by his name. On May
7th they were in garrison at Mirzapur when they received orders to
move at once to Allahabad; they entered the fort at daybreak on May
11th, a march of about 60 miles. It will be remembered that on June
6th the 6th Native Infantry at Allahabad fired on their officers and
killed 'the poor little griffins'. There were no regular British troops at
Allahabad, but in the fort by this time there were about fifty of a kind of
Home Guard of European invalids—that is, the Company's European
pensioners—and volunteers. But the regular guards were supplied by
the 6th. As soon as the outbreak occurred, Brasyer's Sikhs disarmed
them. They were burning, Brasyer says, to be led against the enemy. He
allowed them, at about this time, to put on a *lunghi* and a *kurta*—that is,
a turban and a loose shirt-like garment worn outside the trousers—and

* An unusual Muslim name, but it might be Ḥassūs meaning 'separated, set aside
or dedicated'.

wore the same himself, thus making them quite different from the red-coated sepoys and identifying himself with them. But inside the fort, there was much distrust of the Sikhs. One man in particular was an object of suspicion. Brasyer took all his Sikhs out of the fort and then spoke to them. He pointed out that he was alone with four hundred of them, and that he trusted them utterly. He made the accused man his orderly and then led them in some minor operations near the fort, clearing buildings that had been occupied by the enemy, after which he marched back into the fort. They provided the Sikhs who marched with Renaud's advance guard to relieve Cawnpore. They were with Havelock on his attempts to relieve Lucknow, competing eagerly with the 78th Highlanders for each building captured at the first relief. Brasyer says he was the first European of Havelock's force to set foot in the Residency. 'But everyone thought I was a burly Seikh!' It should be added that the Sikhs also competed with British soldiers in their indiscriminate fury against the civil population, were not much less drunken and even more addicted to loot. Brasyer's Sikhs stayed in Lucknow till Colin Campbell's second relief, when they marched away with him. They also played a distinguished part in the final capture of Lucknow in 1858.

But it had been on June 6th, 1857, that they had rendered the most vital service. These were early days and many Sikhs were undecided. But it was not only as an example that Brasyer's Sikhs were so valuable. It was even more important that they held the Fort for the few critical days till Neill and the Madras Fusiliers arrived. Allahabad was a vital link in the chain to Cawnpore and Lucknow; if the mutineers had taken the fort and defended it with any determination, it would have been hard to get them out without a siege-train and the delay might well have meant losing the Lucknow garrison, with incalculable results throughout India. This regiment became the 14th Ferozepur Sikhs and eventually the 1st Battalion the 11th Sikh Regiment.

Mention has already been made of the Sirmoor Battalion of Gurkhas, later the 2nd King Edward's Own Gurkha Rifles, and their gallant defence of the Hindu Rao's House on the Ridge at Delhi. But before the Mutiny broke out this battalion had revealed an attitude that was of great importance in the reconstruction. They had been raised in 1815, one of four battalions formed from the disbanded Nepalese army; they had then been a local corps, who wore 'mountain dress' and had no tents, because with their kukris they could make a hut from brushwood in ten minutes. They performed many useful services but did not command for a long time the general admiration which the British later gave them. When Henry Lawrence was Resident at Khatmandhu between 1843 and 1845, he shows no sign at all of the romantic affection with which the Gurkhas were later regarded. 'A happier peasantry I have nowhere seen,' but he does not entertain the idea that as soldiers they were out of the common. The Sirmoor Battalion, however, distinguished itself in the Sikh Wars, particularly at Aliwal in 1846. Lord Gough said then that they 'vied in ardent courage with Grenadiers of our own nation.' They became a general service corps in 1850. In 1857, when the Lee-Enfield rifle was to be provided to all native troops, they sent a detachment to Ambala for training, just as the regiments of the line did. There were four such Gurkha detachments and they asked to be allowed to pitch their tents with British soldiers, not with 'the black folk'. This was permitted. They next asked if they might have the new cartridges at once and were given the ungreased cartridges which were now standard for all but Indian troops. But they brought these back, saying they were for 'black folk' and they wanted exactly the same as British troops.

No one has ever accused Gurkhas of flattery or guile; like the Sikhs, but to a greater extent, they recognized in British soldiers qualities they admired and they wished to be reckoned with them rather than with the high-caste Hindus of the plains, who despised the Gurkhas as low-caste and dirty barbarians. This sympathy between Gurkhas and British troops persisted and grew, and the officers who served with Gurkha troops came more and more to feel an affection and admiration for their men which led to a desire to emphasize their difference. Part of the Indian Army they might be, but they were not Indian! When the term 'Native Officer' was dropped, their subadars and jemadars became *Gurkha* Officers, not Indian Officers. The fact that they were all Rifle Regiments helped to emphasize the difference. The Gurkha regiments became the extreme example of the separatism that grew up; 'our men are different' was the feeling of every good regimental officer. But to this we shall come back. Other regiments were born at about this time but enough has now been said to illustrate the diversity of the units that were left when the Mutiny was over, the odd way they had grown up, their dependence so often on individual leadership. Let us turn now to the new period of reconstruction.

Part IV
Soldiers of the Queen

XIII

The New Army

1. After the Mutiny

The Mutiny was over. Its roots went back many years, to the disaster of Kabul and even before. The British had used Indian soldiers to conquer India and then had taken them for granted. They had been so sure of the fidelity they had inspired in those early days that they had done nothing to preserve it. They had encouraged officers to stay on in command of troops till they were gout-ridden invalids of seventy; they had allowed a system to develop which drained away from the regiments officers of energy and ambition. These were the failures of the army; in the civil Government, the main mistake had been too hot a zeal for radical reform, an intolerant pressure for an immediate progress that threatened religion and property. On both the civil and military sides, the machinery of government, impersonal and remote, had grown at the expense of the individual initiative of the man on the spot.

As we have seen, there are three ingredients that make mutiny probable. If there is no understanding between officers and men, and if there is also widespread discontent outside the army among people with whom the soldiers are in sympathy, then only one thing more will be needed—a spark to touch off the powder. All these conditions were present in 1857, and in some units they were strong. But above all, and more deeply and obscurely, the sepoys felt slighted and threatened. They had left home, family and village for a new life in the army; their fathers had taken pride in the regiment and had been confident that their officers would look after them. They had trusted their officers with their lives, their honour and their religion. But in many units they felt they had been betrayed by a new generation of officers who did not like them or listen to them, who despised their customs and religion, who made light of their honour. Betrayed and deserted, they turned in savage anger on those they had once trusted.

On the English side, there was complete incomprehension of this fear and sense of betrayal. It was black ingratitude, faithlessness and villainy. How refreshing, in contrast, to turn their eyes to the Sikhs, who had been thoroughly beaten but had taken it in good part, in the true sporting spirit of a side defeated at cricket! In less than ten years they had become so grateful for the benefits of British rule that they were happy to fight for it! They were simple, manly, upright fellows, very different from those sly, intriguing Brahmans. The English — a tiny minority in a vast and incomprehensible population — had often, as we have seen, expressed themselves contemptuously about the great majority of the people of India, but made an exception of the sepoy, whom they had trusted and admired. They despised the people they had conquered but they had also a subconscious sense of the danger of their position; they *had* to trust and rely on someone. They were almost bound to divide the 'natives' into two classes, good or faithful and bad or hostile; they could praise one and vilify the other. When there is not much comprehension, there is not much room for subtle shades of character. Prospero finds no one in his island but Ariel and Caliban. And now that the old kind of sepoy, once Ariel the good native, had shown himself ungrateful, it was time to recognize him as Caliban and look for a new Ariel. From now onwards, it was even more common for officers to divide the people of India sharply into two classes, good and bad, and in the good class fell the peoples of the north who had come to their help during the Mutiny. What had at first been a tendency hardened into a doctrine. These were the martial classes, and only they would make soldiers.

Gurkhas and Sikhs had made more formidable antagonists than most of our other foes in India. It was natural that a commanding officer should want the best men he could get, and it was easy to train Sikhs and Gurkhas for the business of war; they took to it with relish. There were great advantages, from the point of view of regimental recruiting, in getting men whose fathers had served in the regiment and whose village elders valued the honour of the regiment. Nor is it fair to blame the men of 1860 for failing to foresee the World Wars of the twentieth century or the needs of an independent India. They wanted an efficient army for a limited purpose, which they set about providing from the men who came readily to the colours and were the kind of men they wanted. It is not in the least surprising that colonels of regiments in 1860 should not have spent much time in remembering 1760, when their great-grandfathers had shown that men of all kinds and classes could be trained by the right officers to defeat armies ten times as strong as they. That *they* might be charged with ingratitude would hardly have occurred to them.

British officers recruited the men who would make good soldiers quickly and easily. Their preference was in full accord with the ancient traditions of India, whose social order had for so long been based on hereditary specialization. Their preference was reinforced by the subconscious need to separate the men they knew and relied on from the incomprehensible masses, who were contemptible individually, but dangerous because their numbers were so vast and their reactions so irrational.

With this distinction went an ideal, which changed as the century wore on. The dream of the Noble Savage had been widespread in the eighteenth century. It spread from the philosophers to the novelists, and *Rob Roy* and *The Last of the Mohicans* made English-speaking people familiar with the noble but simple figure of the chief who is brave, chivalrous, generous, hospitable, true to his word, cherishing the honour of his people above all things. The British in India had — the best of them — wanted their soldiers to be like this; they had not been content with 'chucklers' and men who were 'low in stature, low in caste and altogether bad'; they had looked for men who were 'noble' — high of caste and concerned about honour. This ideal continued; commanding officers still looked for men with a high sense of their own honour and the honour of the regiment. But it was modified a little after the Mutiny; another figure becomes increasingly familiar in the romances of the second half of the nineteenth century, the simple and unquestioning native servant, movingly faithful. The men who carried Livingstone's dead body hundreds of miles down to the coast were an example in real life. In India after the Mutiny there was good reason to put fidelity high among the virtues of a soldier and simplicity, too, came to be admired. In this tradition of simplicity, the Gurkha was ideal, burning with the one ambition of being a good soldier and no more. Gurkhas would drill each other in their spare time; they wanted only to be led against an enemy, no matter who. But 'nobility' as well as 'simplicity' was still prized highly and officers idealized their men. The drawings of Major Lovett, for example, show the men of the Indian Army as ideal types of male physical beauty; the trooper or private is like a young Bacchus or Michelangelo's David — sometimes with just a hint of the advertisements of firms who hire out formal clothes for weddings; the old subadar is like Jupiter or Moses. Increasingly the word used of the Indian soldier is not sepoy — *sipahi*, the army man — but *jawan*, which means a heroic or martial young man.

Just as the seeds of the Mutiny go back thirty years, so the seeds of the reconstruction run back at least as far as the Sikh Wars. The beginnings of the new army were already in existence before the Mutiny. Two last scenes from the Mutiny will make two points which complement each other, the sharpness of the distinction British officers drew between their old servants and their new and the narrow line that in fact divided the rebellious from the faithful.

The first incident is noted in his diary by Russell of *The Times*. It was after the final relief of Lucknow and the remaining mutineers were being hunted into the jungles that lie at the foot of the Himalayas. A number had taken refuge in a strong place which they had desperately defended, but it had been assaulted with a courage even fiercer than theirs and now it had been taken. The defenders hoped for no quarter; most of them were fighting to the last. One party, however, had given up the contest and the man who told Russell the story perceived them crouching upon a flat roof, hoping to escape notice. When they knew they were seen, they offered to surrender. He ordered them to come down from the roof; as is usual in India, there was a narrow outside staircase and down this they came one by one. He ordered each man to lay his belt, pouch and musket on the ground. There were fifty-seven of them. 'I fell them in against a wall and told some Sikhs who were handy to polish them off. This they did immediately, shooting and bayoneting them, so that, altogether, they were disposed of in a couple of minutes.'

The second incident concerns Skinner's Horse, a regiment which had been formed by Captain James Skinner in 1803 from men enlisted by the French adventurer Perron in the service of Scindia; they came over to the British after Lake's victory at Delhi. At the outbreak of the Mutiny, they were the 1st Bengal Irregular Cavalry. They were at Multan, under the command of Captain Neville Chamberlain, and the general situation at Multan was of a kind with which we have grown familiar. Apart from Skinner's Horse, there were two regiments of Bengal Native Infantry and a battery of native horse-gunners; no European troops except fifty artillerymen. The senior officer in the station had thirty-four years' service and was quite unfit for duty but he was ready to let Chamberlain take the initiative and virtually command the station. It was a dangerous responsibility to assume. There was reason to suppose that the infantry and artillery would prove no more reliable here than they had elsewhere and Chamberlain decided that he must get help from another station and disarm them. He sent for help; there was no hope of British troops but the 1st Punjab Cavalry and the 2nd Punjab Infantry were ordered to march. Until they arrived, he must rely implicitly on his own men, Skinner's Horse; he told them he trusted them and he showed it by the tasks he gave them to do. Skinner's had always recruited near Delhi; their men were counted Hindustanis by the Punjabis. They were Hindustani Muslims, Rajputs and Jats and the people known to the army as Ranghars, that is, Muslims who claim Rajput origin. They did not come from Oudh but were of just the same class as the Bengal Regular Cavalry such as the 3rd with whom the trouble had started at Meerut. They differed mainly in having only three picked British officers to a regiment. Their native officers were therefore much more used to taking responsibility; they had to command their squadrons and troops.

At this anxious juncture, the native officer commanding the squadron of Ranghars came to Chamberlain and asked for a private interview. He was unhappy because something had given the Ranghars the impression that the captain did not trust them as completely as he trusted the other squadrons. Chamberlain heard him out, then sent his orderly to the bank, with a note requesting the banker to send him a sword he had deposited for safe custody. It was a jewelled sword, valuable to anyone, but doubly so to Chamberlain because, as everyone in the regiment knew, it had been given him by a close friend who had captured it in battle in Sind. He handed this sword to Shaidad Khan, the ressaidar* of the Ranghar squadron. 'Give me this back', he said, 'when this war is over.' The ressaidar's eyes filled with tears; he knelt and touched the captain's knees. Nothing but death could sever the bond between them.

Skinner's were loyal throughout the Mutiny and became the senior regiment of Indian cavalry. One good officer by one gesture — vivid, emotional, generous — could turn the scale. But it is time to look at the kind of questions that were discussed concerning the new army.

2. The New Model: Views and Opinions

A Committee — one of great distinction — met in 1858 in London to hear evidence on the points which had to be settled before the army in India could be reorganized. The same points, in slightly more detail, were sent to India and many officers, civil and military, were asked to give their opinions. On some of these points there was almost complete unanimity and some are not of interest from the point of view of this book. We need not spend long, for instance, on the Company's Europeans. There was an end of Company rule and the Crown had taken over, but some thought that the Queen should enlist in England certain regiments solely for service in India. The main argument in favour of this was that the officers would understand the country but the majority view was that the disadvantages of having in India two armies enlisted in Britain on different terms of service outweighed this. It was agreed that from now on the only British cavalry or infantry in India should be part of the Royal army, enlisted for service anywhere in the world. So there was an end of the Company's Europeans, who became the 101st to the 106th Foot. There was a little trouble, because the men complained that as free-born Englishmen they could not be switched from one allegiance to another; they should be discharged

---

* The ressaidar was intermediate between the risaldar and the jemadar. The rank became obsolete soon after this, leaving risaldars for cavalry and subadars for infantry. Jemadars were common to both.

from the Company's service and allowed to earn a bounty by re-enlisting with the Queen. This was known in the press as 'The White Mutiny', but it was settled without much difficulty.

There was much discussion about the size of the army needed for India and the proportions of British to Indian troops. A hundred years later, a committee of this kind, trained in Staff College methods, would have begun by defining the threats likely to arise, and assessing the forces needed to deal with them. But there was not much of this in 1858; most of the witnesses gave their figures without any reasons and a surprising number said they had never given the matter any considera-tion. The Committee thought that the strength of the forces in India would vary but that there should be about 80,000 Europeans, of whom 50,000 would be in Northern India, with 15,000 in each of the two southern Presidencies. This was a high figure, double that present at the beginning of 1857, higher than most of the witnesses had suggested; the Committee do not say how they arrived at it. In fact in 1863 there were 62,000 British troops and by 1907 there were 74,000; there had been no startling variations above or below either figure.

As to proportion, hardly anyone thought that it was possible to do without an Indian army at all. To hold India with British troops alone would be far too expensive and it would be impossible to recruit the numbers that would be needed. Those were two nice knock-down arguments which anyone could understand and which almost everyone accepted. But there was a school of thought, vigorous and influential if not numerous, which went much further. If we could hold India only by a foreign army of occupation, we had no business there at all. So argued Sir Bartle Frere, who had been Chief Commissioner of Sind, was a member of Lord Canning's Executive Council, and went on to be Governor of Bombay. Our rule, he believed, was only justified if there was a large measure of consent. We must rely on Indian officials and an Indian army. It followed that the British troops in India were there, not to hold down Indian soldiers and overawe them, but to help them. Indian troops must be trusted if they were to be any use at all. They could not be *half*-trusted. They must be armed with the most efficient weapons available, just as British soldiers must. To give them weapons inferior to the British soldier—muskets instead of rifles, as many witnesses suggested—was to underline mistrust and make it clear that the British were there to overawe them. And it was inefficient and wasteful. 'Why have two sepoys with muskets (or three with clubs) when one with a rifle can do what is needed better? If sepoys are incurably untrustworthy—which I do not believe—why have three traitors instead of one?' There should be better weapons and better organization for Indian troops—'though it is as much as a man's reputation for sanity is worth to urge this truth at present.' British troops should be concentrated in large stations, with much better barracks and amenities, kept lively and interested by camps of exercise, and regarded as what would later be called a strategic reserve.

There was some military support for these views, but almost all witnesses before the Committee clearly did express mistrust. Very few thought that the proportion of British to Indian troops should be as low as one to four; it had been more like one to nine in 1856. The Committee finally recommended one to three for Madras and Bombay, one to two for Bengal and the north, which on the basis of the 80,000 they recommended for British troops would have given a total of 190,000 Indian. In fact, the figures in 1863, when the reorganization was complete, were 62,000 British and 125,000 Indian, one to a little more than two. This proportion was generally borne in mind until 1914. In spite of Frere's views, there was a good deal of support in 1858 for the idea of inferior weapons for the Indian army, and the new Lee-Enfield rifle was only slowly introduced. It did not reach the Madras Army till 1870. Almost without exception the witnesses considered that gunners should all be European, though there might be Indian drivers and lascars to clean the guns. As we have seen, from earliest times there had been supporters of this idea in London. The Committee accepted these views and, from 1861 until the period of reconstruction as a national army, there were no Indian gunners except with mountain batteries, whose guns were carried on mules.

It had been suggested that 'other colonial troops' should be employed as soldiers in India, but for this there was not much support, though not all would have put their view so vigorously as a pamphleteer who wrote that it was 'out of the question to impose upon India an army of Africans'. It would be 'humiliating and disgusting' to Indians and 'putting in the hands of the most untameable and treacherous beings upon the earth the arms which we dare not trust in the hands of our own Asiatic subjects'. The Committee were unanimously against it. They were also agreed that in future all units of the Indian army should enlist for service anywhere; there could be no more pleading that caste forbade a journey by sea. Uniform should be simpler and more comfortable and promotion must be by selection from the most efficient; there must be no more subadars of seventy. To all these points there was virtually no alternative opinion expressed.

The most controversial questions were the composition of the new army and the number of British officers. Many witnesses thought that in future caste should play no part, though they sometimes added rather inconsistently that there should be no Brahmans. Few thought much of a proposal that there should be one, or even two, companies of Europeans to a battalion of Indian infantry; most thought British and Indian should be in separate battalions but that a brigade ought to include both British and Indian. As to the different castes, religions and 'nationalities' of India, there was much disagreement; the Committee came down on the side of as much variety as possible and thought the 'different nationalities and castes should be mixed promiscuously through each regiment'. But a good many of their witnesses took what was surely the more practical view, that at least the squadron or company must be homogeneous. In fact, as it worked out, the regiments which survived were generally picked on the basis of their past records, and kept as far as they could to their old traditions, with results that were illogical. Most regiments took several classes but each company was of one class only; several regiments, however, were homogeneous, taking one class throughout—Marathas, Sikhs, Dogras, Garhwalis and of course Gurkhas. Battalions of one class became more popular as the century wore on.

As to officers, there were before the Mutiny two kinds of units, regular and irregular. The irregular had fewer British officers, in some cases only three. The praises of the irregular system had been loudly proclaimed for some years before the Mutiny by a remarkable man, John Jacob, who had himself commanded an irregular cavalry regiment —later, two regiments—of a rather special kind; both, by general consent, were very good indeed. Jacob's views were put forward in a stream of pamphlets, letters to the press and articles in journals; they are worth spending some time on, because they form a coherent whole, a philosophy of the army in India. He had, for years before the Mutiny, criticized the Bengal Army and 1857 showed that much of his criticism was justified.

Jacob had one superb argument to support his case. When the Mutiny broke out, he was himself in Persia with the force under Sir James Outram. His two regiments, the 1st and 2nd Scinde Irregular Horse, were in Sind. He had taken command of the first of these regiments when it was four years old, organized and trained it on his own system, and raised a second regiment on the same principles. The men were most of them Hindustanis, from Delhi and the western part of what was to be the United Provinces, of the same classes as those in the regular cavalry regiments; he frankly expressed a preference for the Hindustani Muslim over Sikhs, Pathans, Punjabi Muslims, or anyone. His men were cousins and brothers of the mutineers—men who were fighting the Government or being executed as traitors; they were continually pressed to join them but not a man showed the least sign, not a man deserted. Why was this? Because of the principles of their training, he replied; he was not there himself but throughout the two regiments everyone thoroughly understood the system.

The first thing was that there must be a minimum of British officers and they must be hand-picked. He had begun with three British officers for the first regiment: himself, a second-in-command and an adjutant; when he raised the second, he needed only two more, as he commanded both—five British for sixteen hundred Indians. This meant that the Indian or native officers must be given real responsibility and trusted. They genuinely replaced British officers; they were often in command of outposts a hundred miles from headquarters, and for this purpose were in his view better than junior British officers. It followed, of course, that they too were picked for their energy and efficiency; his system could never have worked if the officers were automatically promoted for seniority as in the Bengal Regular Cavalry.

It was essential that the right spirit should run through the whole regiment. A commander should treat his native officers as gentlemen. 'You should show all the men that you respect and regard them as *men*; you should get them to respect themselves and feel proud of themselves—and then you will be loved, respected, almost adored.' It was part of this system that all power should be in the hands of the commanding officer, who should recruit, promote and punish. There should be no formal courts martial; a committee of five native officers should inquire into any case and report on it with their recommendations. They might, and often did, recommend dismissal; this was a severe punishment, because of the dishonour, and an admirable way of keeping up standards. There would be no supervision of such committees, no formal procedure, no rules of evidence. Above all there should be no appeal from the commanding officer's decision to a distant and impersonal court, who might teach the men that they could flout their commander with impunity.

All this had been possible in the case of the Scinde Irregular Horse because they had not usually been under the Commander-in-Chief either of Bombay or Bengal, but directly under the control of the Chief Commissioner for Sind, Sir Bartle Frere. Frere was a firm believer in giving power to the man on the spot and holding him responsible for the result. He did not think a district officer should have his authority questioned within his own district and he applied the same principle to the commanding officer of the Scinde Horse. The regiment had to be efficient; he relied on it to protect the people of the plains against marauders from the hills.

There can be no doubt that Jacob had built up in the Scinde Irregular Horse a magnificent instrument for the main purpose for which it was meant—the control of the frontier. Their watchwords were instant readiness for action and immediate pursuit of raiders from the mountains. When news reached an outpost that a party of Baluch tribesmen had carried off some camels, Durga Singh, the officer in charge of the post, started at once in pursuit. He had fifteen troopers but the tribesmen had a long start and it was a hard ride of thirty miles before he came up with them. By that time there were only two troopers and a Baluch guide still with him. The enemy were some forty strong and the guide urged him to turn back. But Durga Singh replied that he could not show his face to Major Jacob if after coming in sight of the robbers he went back without killing some of them. It was a matter of honour. He and his two troopers attacked the enemy and killed or disabled fifteen before they were killed themselves.

Jacob argued that his men were 'irregular' only in having few British officers and in owning their own horses. Their discipline was as exact as at the Horse Guards, and they had proved in the Sikh War that they were not mere police; at the battle of Gujerat, 243 troopers of the regiment had charged '4,000 of the best men of Afghanistan, the élite of Dost Mohammad's army, splendid men on splendid horses', and the Afghans had been 'overthrown, beaten to pieces, and driven from the field with tremendous loss'. The Scinde Irregular Horse were dressed in loose, comfortable clothes, suited to the habits of the men and to the climate; they were armed with the best weapons procurable, which they owned themselves. They could move at a moment; asked one morning in 1845 when his regiment would be ready to march to the Punjab, Jacob replied: 'Immediately!' and did leave that evening. He had marched 220 miles before the first regular regiment of cavalry or infantry was ready to start, fifteen days later. This was because of the regiment's organization as a self-contained silladar unit.

Originally, it will be remembered, the silladar had ridden in with, say, fifty followers, feudal retainers, tenants of his land perhaps, men whom he mounted and armed. They were his bargirs and he was a kind of military contractor who agreed to provide fifty troopers at so much a head. 'Silladar' had come to mean something rather different by the middle of the nineteenth century; in most irregular cavalry, there were so many 'places' or berths in the regiment, usually eight hundred, which were known as *asamis*. For each 'place' the Government would pay a fixed sum every month. This would be drawn by the holder of the place, who might be a man in the regiment, or an old soldier who had retired, or his widow, or even a money-lender, to whom the widow had sold it; if the holder of the place was not a soldier in the regiment, he would pay a bargir, provide him with a horse and arms and keep a small profit for himself. But the holder of a place might ride the horse himself; a native officer would often own several places, mounting as bargirs his sons or nephews. The system provided a trooper for between a third and a half of what he would cost in a regular regiment.

Jacob modified this in several respects. He would have no places owned from outside the regiment. If a silladar died, his horse and the place would be sold separately, within the regiment, and his heir would get the proceeds. Both must be paid for in cash; there must be no debts. No officer or man was in any circumstances permitted to be in debt; a silladar in debt would be discharged at once. But it was not in the best interests of the regiment that each man should own and manage his own horse. It was better, Jacob thought, that there should be a good many men owning three or four places. A man with three places could mount two cousins or younger brothers as bargirs and could afford to keep a groom, a grass-cutter and a camel or one or two ponies to carry the baggage; a three-horse silladar with his two bargirs and their servants made 'a very comfortable little family', completely self-contained and ready to move at a moment's notice. There must be no wheeled vehicles, no hired animals. If a horse was killed in action, compensation would be paid by the Government, but if a horse died of natural causes compensation would be paid from a regimental fund, but not the full value. Everything was done to encourage individual care and a sense of responsibility; if a horse had a sore back, a man must walk till it was fit, and pay a fine into the bargain.

All this Jacob had preached for years and, long before the Mutiny, he had denounced the Bengal Army in the most outspoken terms; officers and men alike were in debt, promotion was by seniority, native officers were too old and were given no responsibility; the normal condition of the Bengal Army was what anyone from the Bombay Army would regard as a state of mutiny. To Jacob, the Articles of War were anathema; they encouraged a soldier to think of rights against his commanding officer, whom he was thus led to picture as someone who might try to harm him. This might be all very well for British troops, who were brought up to think of themselves as having some share in their Government, but would not do for 'the Oriental, who *insists* on being governed ... he considers being forced to govern himself the greatest oppression ... He expects to be ruled and to be ruled well—if not he will perhaps rebel and destroy his bad rulers ... but he will merely set up another tyrant who will perhaps rule better than the last.' Native soldiers must therefore look on their commander as their absolute prince. 'One active, energetic, right-feeling and right-thinking English gentleman can, even when alone, infuse an excellent spirit into thousands of these Eastern soldiers, till they will follow him anywhere ... and feel the greatest pride in acting in his absence as they know he would wish them to do if present.' But if there are thirty British officers instead of one, 'the native officer finds himself of no importance and the sepoy becomes a lifeless automaton.' Men should not see their European officers engaged in frivolous or vicious pursuits; they should hold them in proper respect. The officers should therefore be carefully picked, specially chosen for service with native troops; 'natives should never be associated with any English but gentlemen.' But treated properly they could be made as good, true and faithful soldiers as any in the world.

Jacob, like so many of that period, was a man of immense force of character, adored by subordinates, followed by a devoted band of faithful friends, but prolific also in enemies. Frere was a man of wider vision but he admired Jacob and accepted many of his ideas on military matters. Each influenced the other, and there was a Sind school of thought on how the army should be reorganized. Merewether, who succeeded Jacob in command of the Scinde Horse, put Jacob's case vigorously to the Reorganization Committee in London; some of the pamphlets, not only Jacob's own, repeat very similar opinions. When Frere argues that railways have changed the problems of Indian defence and British troops should be concentrated in healthy stations as a strategic reserve, one may guess that these are opinions he has formed after discussion with Jacob; Jacob perhaps had acquired from Frere his conviction that India must be held by 'moral force'. India, said Jacob, can be held 'not by English bone and muscle, but by mind ... a moderate number of cultivated English gentlemen, rather than ... a multitude of rude soldiers'. And Merewether before the Committee in London argued on just the same lines: 'It was the neglect of the proper use of moral power that rendered the application of physical force necessary.' Officers should be given increased powers so that the men looked up to them as their benefactors, their leaders in everything. There should be a commanding officer, a second-in-command, an adjutant and a surgeon—no other British officer. And Bartle Frere writes in a masterly minute: 'What you cannot effect by force of arms, you must secure by sound policy and good government—and no government can be good which depends solely on a military superiority which requires to be constantly exerted and exhibited in view.' Indian soldiers you must 'treat as men, with feelings, passions and prejudices which may be developed and worked on for good or for evil. Treat them like this and they will be like their officers, brave zealous and loyal soldiers, or careless idle mercenary and discontented drones ... you must not treat them as mere machines or animals, obeying some invariable instinct of caste or race.' To Frere it was axiomatic that there was 'nothing but our own mismanagement to prevent Natives of India being as good soldiers and as loyal to us, their foreign masters, as they have ever been.' And he was equally positive that 'a mixed force of Natives and Europeans combined is absolutely more efficient than any purely European force' that could be maintained at the same expense.

Such were the views of the Sind school and though orthodoxy did not wholly accept them it was very considerably influenced. The Committee were convinced that the irregular system was the best for native cavalry but that infantry should be mainly regular, with some irregular. The first weakness in Jacob's system of having only three British officers was that it demanded officers who neither married nor took leave; they were expected to spend their private income on the regiment, to which they were dedicated. This is not a good recipe for a whole army. And though three officers to a regiment might be admirable for guarding the Sind frontier, it was not really a practical proposition in war. After Chillianwallah, H.M. 24th Foot laid the bodies of thirteen officers and the Regimental Sergeant-Major dead on their mess table. How would the Scinde Horse function when their three officers were dead? Their Indian officers had no experience of commanding anything more than a squadron. As for the silladari system, that too was not really suitable for a war outside India.

What is remarkable is that in the atmosphere of the period the irregular system, which was based on trust and responsibility, should have had so good a hearing, and that such ideas as introducing African troops should have been so firmly rejected. A collection of letters published in London newspapers and signed 'Caubulee' by 'a military officer of 32 years experience in India' was reprinted as a pamphlet in 1857. It represents the opinions of many English at the time. The writer believes that English women were publicly tortured in the streets of Delhi and that 'this was systematically done to insult and degrade us. My blood courses like boiling lava through my veins as I write ... Have we been weighed in the balance and found wanting? ... The swarthy demons of India must give account to the God whom they have insulted and defied.'

Fortunately blood of a more comfortable consistency and a more temperate heat began to flow in most veins before the reorganization was completed in 1863.

3. The New Model: How it Worked Out

There was no root-and-branch abolition of all that had gone before; the English are inveterate patchers and that is not their way. They built on what survived. The two southern armies had stood fast; Bombay and Madras men pointed out that in the last twenty years they had often been urged to conform to the Bengal pattern and that if they had done so we should have lost India. It might therefore have been expected that after the Mutiny, there would have been a swing to the south—more recruiting in the south, and the adoption of the southern principle of mixing men in the ranks and playing caste down. In fact, the opposite took place; there was a swing to the north as a recruiting-ground and *more* attention was paid to class and caste, as a factor in recruiting though not as an excuse for special treatment. These were tendencies already in being before the Mutiny; the loyalty of the Madras Army in the Mutiny delayed what might otherwise have happened sooner but could not arrest it altogether. Similarly, the Mutiny delayed, but could not halt, the amalgamation of the three armies. A point often raised in the long discussion was that there should really be one Commander-in-Chief, not three, and under him not three but four armies, or, perhaps better, Commands, Bengal being split into the Army of the Indus and the Army of the Ganges. At the end of the century this came about; it was delayed by the Mutiny, because it was felt that British strength lay in keeping the three armies separate. There was merit, it was said, in watertight compartments.

It was agreed then that for the present the Bombay and Madras Armies should remain substantially as they were. It would be folly at this moment to change what had stood the test. But the Bengal Army was radically reorganized, step by step. All the regular cavalry regiments of the Bengal Army had mutinied and they now ceased to exist. Eight irregular regiments from before the Mutiny survived and in 1861 became the first eight regiments of Bengal Cavalry, led by Skinner's Horse. To these were added eleven regiments raised during the Mutiny. The infantry of the line were headed by eighteen old regiments of Bengal Native Infantry; the senior of these was the old 21st, which had survived at Peshawar, and the next senior was the old 31st, which will be remembered from Bhurtpore. The 19th to the 45th were most of them, but not all, regiments raised in the Punjab during the Mutiny. There were also the Gurkha regiments, now numbered separately, and the Punjab Irregular Force, which was not part of the Bengal Army and was not ordinarily under the orders of the Commander-in-Chief but under the Lieutenant-Governor of the Punjab. The Punjab Force was quite a formidable army of five cavalry regiments and nine infantry battalions with four mountain batteries. But this does not end the story. There was the Hyderabad contingent of four regiments and six battalions, and there were odd irregular local corps formed for special purposes. Some had been raised among a local tribe or people of aboriginals and had been meant to keep their cousins and brothers in order and give the young men employment. One such regiment was described by Kipling and given the name of Chinn's Irregular Bhil Levies; the men were 'small dark and blackish, clothed in rifle-green with black leather trimmings; and friends called them the Wuddars.' Sometimes a corps of this kind eventually became police or the need for it disappeared and it was disbanded. Others became regular troops; this, for instance, was the beginning of several Gurkha regiments, such as the Assam Sebundy Corps, raised as very irregular semi-military police, which became eventually the 8th Gurkha Rifles.

Another local corps which later became regular was the Central India Horse, formed by the amalgamation of various emergency units raised during the Mutiny and active in the pursuit of Tantia Topi; it was kept in being after the Mutiny to clear Central India of dacoits and keep open the Trunk Road from Bombay to Delhi.

Even before the Mutiny, the ways of the Bengal Army would have seemed strange to an outsider, but its reorganization afterwards would have seemed almost as bizarre to a Prussian officer who studied the Army List in 1862. It was a Gothic cathedral of an army; it had been gutted by fire and rebuilt, not on some orderly and logical concept, but by making use of what would still safely stand up; the columns and arches of an older style were built into the new fabric. The cavalry were all on the irregular model, though not all on the pattern of the Scinde Horse. The infantry, however, were at first of two kinds; the eighteen old Bengal regiments of the line had been renumbered but not reorganized, and were still officered in the old way. But the new regiments, the 19th to the 45th, had been irregular from the start. In 1863 all were reorganized in accordance with Jacob's ideas, somewhat modified.

A battalion or regiment from 1863 onwards would have seven British officers, not three as in the Scinde Horse or twenty-three as in the old line regiments. They would include the commanding officer, second-in-command, adjutant and four others, who would *not* be company or troop commanders; Indian officers would command companies and troops. An infantry battalion normally consisted of eight companies and a cavalry regiment of six troops; the cavalry troops were paired in squadrons. Thus officers were meant for supervision and not for direct command of anything smaller than a battalion or regiment, though they might command a wing of half a battalion or some such force temporarily detached. And British officers were not regimental but were all on one General List. This was the Indian Staff Corps—rather strangely named by modern ideas, since it included all British officers, who were posted to it direct from Sandhurst. Addiscombe was closed in 1861. From this General List, officers were posted to appointments, either regimental or staff in the ordinary sense of the word, including the many miscellaneous posts which in the past had taken men away from their regiments. The regimental posts were staff appointments; it could no longer be the case that half the officers were away from the regiments on special appointments nor could those who stayed with the regiment feel that they were the failures nobody else wanted; they had been specially selected for service with a native corps. The General List was another idea of the Jacob school; 'Select, select, select!' wrote one of the Sind pamphleteers. The commanding officer was given greater powers, as in the old irregular system. The officers with mountain batteries were specially chosen from the Royal Artillery, those with Sappers and Miners from the Royal Engineers. There were no longer any British N.C.O.s with cavalry or infantry; they survived only in the Sapper battalions. Jacob's ideal of 'no English but gentlemen in contact with native troops' was in a fair way to be realized.

How different from the early days of the Madras Army, when differences of class and colour were recognized but taken for granted, and when a good sergeant might hope for a commission with a native battalion! In the later days of Queen Victoria the English, without much consciousness of what they were doing, were building up an imperial ruling class of public-school boys, trained on the classics, cold baths and bodily exercise. They had the knack of dealing with the uneducated English and with all the peoples of the Empire; they were hard with themselves and they knew how to get the best from others by trusting them and giving them responsibility within a framework of discipline and by a manner which combined the outwardly genial with the inwardly firm. They were trained for this skill and in their personal lives were to be as brave and hardy as the Spartans and as disciplined as the Romans — though, at least in the army and in India, with rather less emphasis on Athenian virtues. Since getting the best from others was their special skill, they were likely to feel that others could not exercise it — and they tended to become specialists in the *mystique* of dealing with one particular kind of person, Sikhs or Marathas or British other ranks. But expert knowledge was made human by real affection and warmth and a boyishness that made a strong link with the *jawans* of the New Model.

Jacob was full of references to 'old Cromwell' and his New Model Army which had made the 'best cavalry in the world'; there was a puritan element in the absolute concentration on duty which he expected of his officers. Let us look by contrast at another irregular corps, perhaps more famous than any, no less devoted to duty but with a distinguishable outlook. The Guides did not in fact become a normal part of the Commander-in-Chief's army until the end of the century; they were raised with a special role and special objects, yet they seem, looking back, to sum up the classical period of the later nineteenth century, when the Indian Army were Soldiers of the Queen. The idea was not new; there had been a Corps of Guides in the Madras Army as far back as 1787. It was meant to make maps for military purposes and to provide intelligence; the men were to be one hundred Brahmans 'or of some good caste'; they were to be remunerated by a piece of land yielding twenty-four star pagodas (about £12) a year, to them and their heirs, and were to be ready to serve when required. They were reduced in numbers only four years later and their role changed to surveying, pure and simple; the *harkaras* or guides and spies used by

Wellesley do not seem to have been organized as a corps. Napoleon also had a corps of Guides. But the famous corps owed their origin to Henry Lawrence.

When Henry Lawrence was first in the Punjab in 1846, he proposed a corps whose task would be to procure intelligence and act as guides to troops in the field; the men should be chosen for their fidelity and organized for mobility and their clothes should be loose, comfortable and designed for efficiency. The corps was formed with Lt Harry Lumsden in command—there was no other British officer—with one troop of cavalry and two companies of infantry. From the start scarlet was laid aside; their uniform was dust-coloured or khaki. They did not reject drill or discipline, but the emphasis was on individual initiative and intelligence, and 'while still in the hands of the drill sergeant' they were taken to the frontier and exercised in semi-hostile country. At this stage, between the two Sikh Wars, the Punjab had not been annexed and Henry Lawrence was administering it in the name of the Sikh Durbar, in effect as guardian of the minor heir of Ranjit Singh; the duties that fell to the Guides were therefore very mixed, sometimes only the collection of land revenue. But Lumsden seems never to have lost sight of the objects Henry Lawrence had had in mind; his men were to be soldiers, good soldiers, better than any others, with intelligence as a special additional function. They were used, just before the beginning of the Second Sikh War, as detectives to get information of the suspected plots of the Maharani, and later, as soldiers, to escort her into exile.

When war actually broke out, the Guides had already expanded considerably and soon distinguished themselves in action; they were near Multan when a man galloped into their camp with news that a small raiding party of the enemy, some twenty troopers, had succeeded in cutting out some camels with supplies for the British forces. There was no British officer present; Risaldar Fateh Khan gave the order to mount and ride in pursuit with all the men he could raise, about seventy. But instead of coming up with a small party of skirmishers driving home some captured camels, he found in his way the bulk of the Sikh cavalry, twelve hundred men. They too had been misled by false intelligence and had come out from Multan in the hope of intercepting a convoy of treasure on its way to the British camp. But they had missed it and were leisurely returning when they found themselves charged with lance and sword by Fateh Khan and seventy troopers of the Guides. They were taken by surprise and perhaps they supposed he was the advance guard of a larger force. The Guides cut their way through them; Fateh Khan halted them—not always easy with cavalry—wheeled, charged again, a second time pulled up, turned, got his men together and charged for the third time. But this time the Sikhs broke and fled and were pursued to the gates of Multan.

But their special spirit, what made the Guides different from others, is better illustrated by the tale of Gorindghar. This was a strong fort near Amritsar, held during the Second Sikh War by the Sikhs. It lay on the line of communication between Ambala and Lahore and it was therefore important to get possession of it. A strong force was dispatched against it, but with some anxiety; a fort of this kind, well supplied with guns, might hold out a long time, and troops were urgently wanted with the main army. In advance of this force marched Subadar Rasul Khan with 140 Guides infantry; he was incidentally the brother of the Fateh Khan who had distinguished himself at Multan. His orders were to find out all he could about the fort, its guns, stocks of food and ammunition, the character of its commandant, the numbers and morale of its garrison. It has to be remembered that this war was a rather chaotic affair, in many ways typical of civil war. The Guides had lately been in the service of the Sikh Durbar but the Durbar was now the enemy. The ward had risen in insurrection against the guardian. All over the country there were parties of soldiers disbanded from the former Sikh armies marching to join the forces of the insurrection, while other bodies of men were in arms to defend the property of a landlord or to despoil a neighbour.

Rasul Khan and his men arrived before the fort as dawn was breaking; he was confident that he was a good twenty-four hours ahead of the main force. His men did not look at all like British troops; there was no scarlet or pipeclay, their loose khaki clothes had seen a good deal of service. He had carefully removed every badge that could have given them away and three men had been chosen for a special service; they were bound and under guard. He marched boldly up to the gate of the fort and called for the Commandant; he explained that he was taking three prisoners to the Sikh headquarters, men for whom a reward had been offered. He would like to put them in the cells for twenty-four hours; he and his men would camp outside. But—he added, with a grin to remove offence—he did not want the Commandant of the fort to make off with those valuable prisoners and get the reward! Perhaps he might be permitted to put a sentry of his own on the cells!

He seems to have established a cheerful back-slapping relationship with the Sikh Commandant; there had always been Muslims in the Sikh service and he managed easily to pass as an old warrior of the First Sikh War. His men worked on the same lines; they hung about round the gate, cooking their food, making themselves comfortable, gossiping with the garrison, picking up all the information that they could. Towards nightfall Rasul Khan, still in his part as a blunt old fellow-warrior, pointed out to the Commandant that the guard on the gate was very weak—only one sentry and two reliefs with an N.C.O. in charge; he generously offered to provide an extra sentry with reliefs.

He now had two sentries inside—and since it was obviously undesirable to keep opening the gates at night, he suggested that the reliefs for the two sentries with an N.C.O. in charge should sleep inside. This too the unsuspecting Commandant agreed to; he had after all a thousand men in the fort. But Rasul Khan now had ten, and towards dawn the two sentries of the Guides fell on the unfortunate Sikh sentry; they released the three prisoners, overpowered the Sikh reliefs while they were asleep, opened the gates and let in their comrades. Soon after first light, when the British force came in sight of the fort, a Union Jack was already flying above the ramparts. Rasul Khan and his 140 men had taken a fort with seventy guns and made a thousand men their prisoners. No British force need be tied up in a costly siege. And there was a daredevil humour about the whole affair that must have appealed enormously to Lumsden.

The Guides' famous march to the siege of Delhi has already been mentioned. Their strength by this time was 600; their casualties by the end of the siege were 350 and their British officers—there were now three —had been four times replaced, one having been six times wounded. When they marched back from Delhi to Peshawar, the whole garrison paraded to meet them, the gunners fired a royal salute and the massed bands played while cavalry and infantry came to the salute.

Intense pride in the regiment and its honour, devotion to officers who were part of that honour, readiness to go anywhere and do any-thing—those were the ingredients in the spirit of this regiment. When Wigram Battye was killed in the Second Afghan War, the Guides would not let ambulance men carry back his body; only his own comrades, troopers of his own regiment, could do that. And there is a startling story of an occasion when John Lawrence, always blunt and sometimes rough of tongue, had uttered some sharp sentence to Lumsden on parade. Lawrence was then Lieutenant-Governor of the Punjab and thus the ultimate authority for the Punjab Frontier Force. The regiment knew what had happened. Lumsden himself felt it acutely at the time but knew Lawrence too well to let such a matter rankle long; the regi-ment, however, were less forgiving. That evening, last thing at night, Lumsden's orderly came to tell him how deeply he and his comrades felt it. It was not suitable that anyone—Governor or no Governor— should speak in such a way to the Colonel of the Guides. The Governor was to leave next morning for Peshawar but the orderly and his friends thought that he should not arrive; they would intercept him on the way and make clean the honour of the regiment.

This, no doubt, was an extreme example of devotion, but then Lumsden was one of those men, like Nicholson and Jacob, who do inspire such feelings. Lumsden, however, was not deified as Nicholson had been; he managed to direct personal loyalties to the regiment. The spirit survived his departure and it was seventeen years after he left that the Guides displayed it in their most famous adventure. This was at Kabul in 1879. In policy, the Second Afghan War was not much less ill-advised than the First, but it was much better managed. There was no gout among the generals and they were nearer fifty years of age than seventy. All that need here be said is that one of the main matters in dispute was whether there should be a permanent British representative at Kabul; with the Afghans, it was an obsession that this would eventually mean British annexation. The Amir Sher Ali knew that it was as much as his life and throne were worth to agree to such a proposal. The first stages of the war were a brilliant success; the Afghans were everywhere driven back, Kabul was occupied, the Amir Sher Ali fled and conveniently died. One of his sons, Yakub Khan, was found who was ready to agree that there should be a British Resident and that the Afghans should deal with no foreign power but Britain; he was placed on the throne. Sir Louis Cavagnari took up the post as Resident, with an escort of twenty-five Guides cavalry and fifty-two Guides infantry.

The new amir could hardly be popular; he owed his throne to foreign bayonets, he had agreed to foreign demands. He must have wanted some Afghan support and it is hard to suppose that he did not try to convince the Afghan chiefs that he was only waiting for a suitable moment to break his engagements with the British and get rid of the Resident. But the degree of his complicity in what followed need not concern us. The Afghan regiments in Kabul had been defeated recently and had perhaps had enough of the war; they were transferred and replaced by regiments from the west who had all the self-confidence of inexperience. As the new men marched into Kabul, they shouted slogans and demonstrated the fierce resentment at a foreign presence which was widespread among the Afghans. They were owed several months' arrears of pay which they perhaps supposed would be paid on reaching the capital. A few days after their arrival they were offered, not the full amount, but one month's pay only. This was the signal for a mutiny, which may or may not have been intended; it needed only one man to suggest that loot could be found at the Residency and the mass of Afghan soldiery poured in that direction. They were soon joined by many from the town.

Cavagnari had one civil assistant, Jenkyns; the Guides were commanded by Lt Walter Hamilton, who had already won the V.C., and there was a surgeon, Kelly. The first attack came about eight in the morning, when Cavagnari was just back from his morning ride. The Residency was not a defensible position but a mere cluster of bungalows and huts. A few shots were fired; the mob was sufficiently organized to perceive that it could not simply overrun the quarters and take what it wanted without fighting. There was a brief lull while they went to fetch weapons and ammunition. Hamilton used it to concentrate his men on the main building. Cavagnari tried to send a message to the amir, claiming the protection due to a guest because he was there under treaty. Two messengers were killed; the third eventually reached the amir, but by that time he had not the power to intervene if he had the will. The messenger was confined, ostensibly for his safety, but eventually escaped and reached India; he was the only inhabitant of the Residency to survive that day. By mid morning, about ten o'clock, the fight had been raging some time; the defenders had made a first sortie to drive back the assailants and clear a space around the main Residency building; Cavagnari had been killed in this charge.

The attackers now fell back to the mud wall which made the boundary of the Residency and used this as an encircling parapet. They assaulted the main building with ladders and obtained a footing on the roof and even inside but they were driven back. About mid afternoon the assailants brought up two guns with which they opened fire. But they fired only two shots; Hamilton led a second sortie and captured the guns. His men slewed them round and began to pull them back but they had not the numbers or the muscular strength to pull both guns and defend themselves at the same time. They had to leave them and get back to the Residency. Kelly was killed in this sortie. The guns were turned again and fired a second time and again Hamilton charged and captured them and again failed to bring them back. Jenkyns was killed this time. Most of the building was now in flames, but Hamilton rallied the survivors in the *hammam*, the bath, which was of brick and partly underground. Here he planned yet another sortie; this time they would bring back one gun only, while he faced the mob. Then they would try again for the second. Again they took the guns and began to pull one back. Hamilton stood single-handed to defend them but this time he was killed and the enemy recaptured the gun a third time.

Now there were no English left. All day, the Afghans had shouted to the Guides to leave the English; they had no quarrel with them and would let them go free. The offer was now made again. Jemadar Jewand Singh was in command. There was a pause and he consulted the survivors, of whom not much more than a dozen remained. Perhaps they did not put much faith in Afghan promises. Perhaps their one thought was the honour of the Guides. They were in the heat of action and there would be no long debate. What is known is that they made up their minds quickly and came out to die. They charged for the last time. An eye-witness, an old soldier, saw them fight to the last; Jewand Singh killed eight men before he was killed. Not a man of the Guides survived. Their defence had lasted twelve hours and six hundred of the enemy lay dead around them.

4. The Great Game

The new army had one thing in common with the old, a concern for honour, and even that was not seen quite as the old army had seen it. But in almost every other way the differences were striking, not only in organization but in the kind of warfare for which the men were trained. The old army in Madras had been expected to fight battles of the eighteenth-century kind, pitting rock-like infantry against elephants and cavalry, wheeling and marching in pipeclayed lines and pouring in volleys of musketry at close range. They had assaulted forts on precipitous crags, chased recalcitrant polygars and robber chiefs through almost impenetrable jungles, sailed to Java, Manila, Singapore, China, Egypt, Mauritius. The old Bengal infantry had been similar; they had marched with Lake against Scindia's French-trained legions and with Gough against the Sikhs and still it was a warfare of pitched battles and volleys at two hundred yards range. To keep in line and load quickly were the essence of a soldier's technique. The scene had been the plains of India and the enemy generally envisaged had been Indian armies.

But by 1861 a change had come about which was exactly what the sepoys had obscurely feared. There were no more enemies within India; there was the North-West Frontier and the Frontier tribes and beyond that Central Asia and the advancing Russians. In the discussions about the new army, the threat is not exactly defined but it is clearly implicit in much of the argument. The forces in India must be strong enough to deal by themselves with any internal trouble, with Frontier tribes, and with Afghanistan, Persia or any other Asiatic neighbour; further, they must be able to hold a Russian invasion till help came. This remained the task of the Indian Army until the Second World War; with the one modification that the twentieth century Russia alternated confusingly between the two roles of ally and principal threat. But in the nineteenth century no one doubted that the major threat meant Russia.

In London, Russia often seemed more important than in Calcutta; 'in England they are fidgety about this border beyond all reason,' Dalhousie had written. They could not forget that two thousand miles had once lain between the Russian frontier and the English on the coast of Coromandel, while by the 1880s the two Empires were divided only by Afghanistan. Step by step, they had moved forward; engulfing one Indian prince, one Asian khan, after another; if either made a last mouthful of Afghanistan, it would be an immediate threat to the other. It was argued — and indeed widely accepted — that from a narrowly military point of view it would be wiser to let the Russians rather than ourselves contend with the inhospitable mountains of Afghanistan and meet an invasion near our own frontier, though there was a good deal of difference as to just where. A Russian invading army was no more likely than a British to find the Afghans friendly. But it would be a different matter if the Russians could establish sufficient diplomatic influence in Kabul to build up a friendly base and from that launch an attack on Peshawar.

Here of course the political considerations came in. A Russian army emerging tattered and haggard from the passes, with the wolves tearing at its coat-tails, would be no great temptation to the disaffected in India; it would be very different if the Russians came with the blessing of the amir, promising, however implausibly, the restoration of Islam and a semi-independent khanate linked with Central Asia. Not even the most sanguine Victorian could contemplate with much confidence a long defensive war in India. With a great land-mass to defend, it may be an effective strategy to fall back, to let the enemy extend himself and grow weaker as he advances. Russia had proved this against Napoleon and was to prove it again against Hitler. But India was another matter; it was ruled by foreigners and the inhabitants on the whole consented to that rule so long as it was successful. There could be no tough inner resilience to such an empire; it could hardly survive a slow rearguard action and a stand at Panipat. The Russians must therefore be kept out of Afghanistan—this was a constant principle of British foreign policy in London, but the Tories put more emphasis than the Whigs on active steps to keep them out.

To Commanders-in-Chief and Viceroys, these considerations were important and by no means remote. To regimental officers, they lay in the background and the tribes were the reality. The amir in Kabul had never exercised any administrative control over the border tribes; they managed their own affairs, they called no man master. An essential part of their economy and their tradition was to prey upon the plains, whether by trade or at times by merely looting. The harsh soil of the rocky valleys and the wind-swept tops provided the barest necessities of life; for anything more—a wife, a horse, a rifle—a man must either go down into Hindustan with a caravan and hope to come back with a full purse or he must raid across the border for camels or cattle or ransom. There had been no settled boundary when the British took the Punjab from the Sikhs; no one could say where the Punjab ended or tribal land began, nor at what point the amir's authority began to carry weight. Some tribes were vaguely the amir's, some were not; in the broadest sense, there was a no man's land where knife and bullet spoke the law. Nearly fifty years later, in 1894, the Durand Line was drawn between tribal territory and the amir's; that became the international frontier and the tribesmen acquired a legal status; they became 'British protected persons'. Long before this, the British administrative frontier had been fixed; that was the line up to which British law was in operation; on the east side, revenue was collected, there were police and roads and schools. Beyond there were only the tribes, whom we did not profess to administer.

This is not the place to discuss in any detail the many controversies about the Frontier, its administration and its defence. There was a complicated criss-crossing of arguments; finance, strategy and politics all suggested different answers. Jacob, needless to say, believed that the methods he had successfully applied in Sind would work just as well in the north; human nature, he argued, did not change at the boundary between Sind and the Punjab. Perhaps not, but tribal structure did change; in a Baluch tribe there was a chief known as the *tomandar* who had some hope that the tribesmen would obey him, but the *maliks* of the Mahsuds were no more than spokesmen for their sections. Again, John Lawrence was a 'close frontier' man; he was convinced that there must be no interference with Afghanistan and the least possible with the tribes. The administration in the north began in a far more guarded spirit than in the south, where Jacob's men had standing orders to follow a thief across the border and bring the crime home, if possible to the men who did it, failing that to the tomandar. But in the north, in Lawrence's time, the Deputy Commissioner was forbidden to cross the border without permission; the tribe as a whole was held corporately responsible for any outrage—which meant that if the tribe would not yield to diplomatic pressure and pay compensation, usually reckoned in rifles, an expedition must be mounted against them and they must be punished.

Thus from the Mutiny until Independence the Indian Army was confronted with a strip of wild and mountainous territory, some four hundred miles long and about a hundred wide, in which law in the ordinary sense of the word was not administered, in which every man was armed and into which they might be required to penetrate with orders to capture an outlaw, to force a tribe to come to terms, or to punish, which usually meant destroying villages. There were changes in policy, from John Lawrence's 'masterly inactivity' to the 'conciliatory intervention' of Lord Lytton. There were advances; Pishin, Zhob, the Kurram became British administered territory; troops were pushed forward to Wana; aircraft modified the technique of control. But basically the problem was unaltered; the finances of India did not permit, it was held, the immense expenses involved in 'pacification'—the building of roads and schools, the collection of revenue—to all of which resistance would have been bitter. Nor was finance the only reason against such an attempt to coerce wild folk into civilization; the Nagas, after Independence, were to show an Indian Government how bitterly tribal peoples may resent the imposition of modern ways.

On the other hand, it was not possible to disclaim all responsibility; raids that went unpunished would simply have led to more raids. No one could find any alternative to the system of treating tribal territory as a national park or game reserve, within which the tribes could prowl like tigers, getting their living in their own tigerish way. So long as they stayed within bounds they were subsidized, but, if they came out, they must live decorously or pay the price. The policy had two main defects. In the first place, punishment for any breach of this very loose control was more expensive to the Government of India than to the tribes. They were utterly reckless of life, they could assemble in a few hours and disperse as quickly; neither movement nor supply caused them any problems. Secondly — and this was more important — it was a barren policy. The relationship between troops and tribes was one of punishers and punished; it could hardly develop into more. It led nowhere. To some extent, it was redeemed by personal qualities on both sides, but the only argument in its favour was the greater strength of the arguments against any other course.

The little wars of the Frontier which arose from this system were the staple fare of the Indian Army for the Victorian period. And what could be more different from the wars of Frederick the Great and the tactics of Waterloo! Terrible country, harsh, fierce, and jagged; rocky peak, serrated ridge, dry icy upland, stony breathless valley that pens up the heat; a marksman behind every rock; a war of sniping and ambush and long marches at night, occasionally the rush of yelling fanatics sworn to die for the faith of Mohammed. In Madras the British troops had been pitted against ten, twenty or thirty times their numbers; here on the Frontier, it might be the other way round; the enemy were sometimes outnumbered and the greater skill in mountain warfare was sometimes with them. But the extraordinary part about these wars is the spirit in which they are fought; death is real enough, exhaustion, hunger, thirst and above all courage, but across this harsh and bitter landscape will flash suddenly a jagged lightning-streak of humour. It is a game — a contest with rules in which men kill without compunction and will die in order to win, in which kinship and friendship count less than winning — but in which there is no malice when the whistle blows and the game is over. And the transfer of an important player may be arranged at half-time while the lemons are being sucked.

This odd spirit grew over the years, as the Pathan tribesmen and the British on the Frontier came to know each other better. Each side defended its own interests but the players admired the same things — courage above all, loyalty to the side on which a man happened to be fighting at the moment, personal honour. Frontier officers were a rather special breed of the British and they were sometimes almost converted to the Pathan's sense of honour and usually to his sense of humour; it did not often happen the other way round. The same kind of stories recur whenever people talk about the Frontier; they remember, for instance, the Zakka Khel men in 1908 crowding round Roos-Keppel, once their political agent, when the expedition against them was successful and the fighting over. 'Did we fight well?' they asked and he replied: 'I wouldn't have shaken hands with you if you hadn't.' They recall the tribesman who has been in the army but is now engaged in sniping at his old friends and trying to kill them. They too are trying to kill him, but they are firing low and he does not like to see good ammunition wasted, so he stands up from behind his rock and signals them to raise their sights as though he were on a rifle-range. Those are the kind of things they remember.

No sooner was the army reorganized after the Mutiny than it was faced with one of these small Frontier campaigns. Behind the murderous chivalry of border war, there was a smouldering core of religious fanaticism and a determination to keep foreigners out of the hills; a focal point for the first was a community who were known as 'the Hindustani fanatics' and who were exactly that. They had come from Hindustan and they admitted no compromise or toleration in respect of their faith; their intransigence was at the roots of the Umbeyla campaign, but diplomatic clumsiness brought in on the side of the fanatics tribesmen who were slighted because the troops had entered their hills without proper warning. There was some very hard fighting, one outlying position known as the Crag Picket being taken and retaken three times. But even now the characteristic note of the Great Game is sounded. Sylvester, surgeon with Probyn's Horse, mentions a soldier of the Guides who 'recognized his old father in the enemy's breastwork and immediately took a shot at him.' And Lord Roberts, noting that the Pathans and Gurkhas fighting for the British were at home on the hillside, adds that the enemy would joke with them, saying: 'We don't want you—where are the red turban men and the white folk? They are better sport.' This meant the 14th Sikhs—the Ferozepore Sikhs, later the 1st/11th Sikhs—and the 101st Foot—once the Company's First Bengal Fusiliers. Roberts goes on to say that there were no desertions, although 'all the native regiments except the Gurkhas and the Punjab Pioneers had amongst them members of the tribes we were fighting and many of our soldiers were even closely related to some of the hostile tribesmen. On one occasion a young sepoy recognized his own father among the dead.' Why were there no desertions? 'When the religious cry is raised, pay, pensions, Order of Merit, count for nothing, only personal loyalty to the officer whom he has praised to his family.'

That judgment is perhaps too simple. It was not only personal loyalty to an officer; honour was involved in loyalty to the side, to the salt. Younghusband has a story of a young Afridi in the Guides whose own village was to be destroyed. He was torn by the two loyalties; he hesitatingly decided in favour of the regiment. But severe temptation suddenly assailed him. He was sentry on a dark night; his own village was near and his companion sentry, who happened to be a Gurkha, asked him to hold his rifle while he fetched something from his tent. Two rifles! And the dark night! He was a very young soldier and it was too much. The Gurkha came back to find he had gone. Horrified, he ran to report his negligence and the Afridi's crime. The Commanding Officer—it was after Lumsden's time—summoned all the men in the regiment who belonged to that section of the Afridis and told them what had happened. There were seventeen; he told them to take off their uniform and not show their faces again till they brought back those two rifles. It was a bare chance; he thought they might be back in two days perhaps. But it was two whole years before they were back with the two rifles. What had happened they would not say. What blood-feuds had been started, what bones left to bleach on the hillside, no one ever knew.

As for the transfer at half-time, the Guides again provide a classical example. Lumsden was pursuing Dilawar Khan, a famous outlaw, the hero of a dozen raids, a man on whose head the Government had set two thousand rupees. It occurred to Lumsden that Dilawar Khan— a man quite without fear and unrivalled at finding his way through difficult country at night—would be very useful in the Guides. He sent him a safe-conduct, asking him to come and talk. Dilawar Khan came and, after some chat about how nearly he had been caught on such an occasion and how cleverly he had given the soldiers the slip on another, Lumsden pointed out that sooner or later he would catch him and then he would hang him. Why not surrender now and join the Guides? Dilawar laughed loud and long at so absurd an idea. But he said he would think it over and six weeks later he came in to enlist. The two thousand rupees was still on his head and he had no safe-conduct, but he trusted Lumsden. He said later that he had meant to learn what he could and then desert—back to his old life but with much more under-standing of what the soldiers were likely to do. But something caught him and he stayed on. He said it was because the officers were so straight —a word which means much the same in Hindustani, Pashtu and English. He became a subadar and eventually died while on a secret and very dangerous mission—but that is another story.

Thus a man in the new army was an individual. He must be able to move on the hill and take cover, stalk his enemy, lie still and patient, shoot straight and quick. It was not enough to stand rigidly in a line. It would have seemed very strange to Sita Ram; the old kind of sepoy was right to think he might not be so valuable in this kind of world. But it is time to sum up what had happened by 1863, and no one can do it better than Lord Roberts, who had come out as a subaltern in the Company's artillery in 1852 and had won the Victoria Cross five years later. He spent most of his early service as an A.D.C. or in the Quarter-master-General's department and from his earliest days he had thought about how the army could increase its efficiency and how the soldier's life could be improved. He became a legend in the British Army and the Indian alike, because he was direct, uncomplicated and brave and because he put his duty to the State and to the men under his command before his own comfort and convenience. His was not a far-reaching or wide-ranging mind. There was nothing of the prophet about him; he did not see far into the future or preach any startling doctrines. But he did often get his way because he did not make enemies. Everyone spoke well of him. No one could be a better representative of the way his fellow-officers looked at the army as it stood after the Mutiny.

The outstanding facts, he wrote, looking back after he left India, were that the number of British troops had been nearly doubled, while the number of Indian troops had been reduced. At the same time, improved communication and greater mobility made a smaller number of men more effective. Could there be another Mutiny? Not if we kept the proportion of British to Indian troops at one to two and maintained discipline; not if we chose for the higher posts men who were neither too old nor ignorant of the country; not if we guarded against the dangers of dogmatism and centralization, by which he meant that we must give power and responsibility to the man on the spot; not, finally, if we made the civil administration firm, strong, tolerant and sympathe-tic, if we gained the confidence of the people and convinced them that we had the determination and the ability to maintain our supremacy.

No one could accuse Roberts of being a sentimentalist. The army of his vision had to provide the nucleus of force on which British rule in India depended. But he saw clearly the point about moral force made by Bartle Frere and Jacob and, indeed, by everyone who had thought about the subject, back to Malcolm and Munro; an army of two hundred thousand men could not hold an Empire of three hundred million unless most of the subjects acquiesced in the Government's rule; a contented peasantry was worth many divisions. To think of a national army would have been to take one step more, but for that no one was yet ready.

XIV

The Martial Classes

1. The Changes of Sixty Years

There was a new army by 1863. It changed in several ways between that date and 1922, when there was a thorough reorganization, but the changes of these intervening years were on the whole consistent in direction; they were moves towards the shape that then emerged. It took the shock of the First World War to bring men to the point of completing what they had secretly felt ought to be done. Those earlier moves can really best be understood if we go forward in time, look briefly at the lessons of the First World War and describe in essence the reorganization that followed.

The Indian Army sent an Army Corps to France in that crucial first period of 1914 when earth's foundations fled. They too followed their mercenary calling; they too took their pay and died; to their part in stopping the first onslaught of the German armies, to their achievements, their valour, and the difficulties they had to contend with, we shall return. But one thing became abundantly clear. An army based on individual units of less than a thousand strong was not suited to modern war. A battalion might come out of the line at a quarter of the strength it went in; it might lose all its British officers. It had gone in with four companies; each company would consist of Punjabi Muslims, or of Sikhs, or of Rajputs, or of Dogras, or of some other class, the men in each company speaking one language and eating the same food; one of the links that bound the companies together was artificially created, the strong corporate spirit of the regiment, built up over years; another was the personal influence of officers the men knew. In the maelstrom of France, how could such a battalion be created anew? Where could be found a vast superhuman machine that would spit out a Rajput for every vacant place in a Rajput company, a Dogra for every Dogra? It would have to find officers who spoke Pashtu or Punjabi or Marathi as well as Hindustani, who understood the peculiar traditions of regiments of the most diverse origins. It simply could not be done. A half-company of Jats would be mixed with a half-company of

Sikhs; officers were posted who could not understand what their men said, let alone what they thought or held dear. To a certain extent these were difficulties even for British battalions; they were linked in pairs in the Cardwell system and based on strong local ties; they were designed for small wars in a vast colonial empire. Tynesiders did not always understand men from Devon. But the Indian Army was still almost without national feeling, divided by religion, region, language and caste. The reorganization of 1922 did not attempt to overcome these differences, but tried to build on their basis a system of recruiting and reinforcement that could keep units up to strength in war without sacrificing the individual traditions of each regiment.

The solution was to join battalions together, ideally in a group of six, of which one was a training battalion for recruits and kept the regimental records of the whole group. It was essential that all six battalions should have the same class composition; it was desirable that they should have some common traditions. Thus, for example, six battalions of the old Bombay Army were now linked into one regiment, the 5th Mahratta Light Infantry. The first two of these battalions had been at Seedaseer* since when for a century and a half they had kept Seedaseer Day with ceremonial parades and sports and feasting. The first of these two battalions for most of its life had been the 3rd of the Bombay line; the other had been the 5th. As the 5th, they had acquired the nickname of the 'Black Fifth', the *Kāli Pānchwin*, a title in which they had gloried and which they compared with that of the Black Watch. The facings to their uniform were black as early as 1812. It would be tedious, and beside the point, to continue the catalogue, battalion by battalion. But it should be added that although Lord Roberts, as we shall see, had recorded a poor opinion of Marathas as a class, they had strikingly vindicated their worth as soldiers in Mesopotamia and Palestine, and one of the battalions of this regiment had in 1921 been honoured with the title Royal; it became the 5th Royal Battalion, 5th Mahratta Light Infantry. The tenth battalion in every group was the training battalion and housed the regimental records.

There were twenty such groups or regiments of Indian infantry in 1922. There had to be some compromise about grouping them in accordance with their past traditions, but on the whole it was possible. Thus the 11th Sikh Regiment included two Sikh regiments raised in 1846 after the First Sikh War, the Ferozepur and Ludhiana Sikhs; Rattray's Sikhs, raised in 1856; and three other Sikh regiments raised later in the century as the tide swung more and more in favour of this class. The 6th Rajputana Rifles were six regiments of the Bombay

* See page 134.

Army who had usually recruited some Rajputs from Rajputana; three of them—Wellesley's Rifles, Outram's Rifles and Napier's Rifles—had been distinguished as rifle regiments. The 12th Frontier Force Regiments shared much common history, as the first four active battalions had been raised in the Punjab as the Frontier Force Brigade, while the fifth was the Guides Infantry, also part of the Frontier Force. The battalions kept as much as they could of their own individuality but shared a training battalion from which all their recruits were drawn. In war, the training battalion could send reinforcements to any of the five active battalions and could raise a sixth, seventh and eighth battalion if need be.

That was the general pattern. It was still very different from the great continental armies, in which individuals and battalions were mere numbers, interchangeable and indistinguishable units. And there were still further changes between 1922 and 1939: the 3rd Madras Regiment was disbanded, the 4th and the 9th were amalgamated. Substantially, however, the 1922 reorganization provided the framework which lasted till Independence, and it was the crown or summit of the minor changes which took place after 1863. Thus in 1886 most battalions had been loosely linked in groups of three, of which one could provide drafts for the other two. But they had no common training battalion and reinforcements to one could only be at the expense of another; they could not be regarded as one regiment. The amalgamation of the three Presidency Armies had taken place step by step, the most important date being 1895, when the Commanders-in-Chief for Bombay and Madras disappeared. But it was not till 1902 that the old numbering disappeared. In 1901, for example, there were at least seven infantry battalions known, with various differences, as the Second. Our old friends of Bhurtpore, once the 31st, were now the 2nd (Queen's Own) Rajput Light Infantry, the second of the Bengal line. But there was also the 2nd Gurkha Regiment, the 2nd Sikh Infantry, the 2nd Punjab Infantry, the 2nd Madras Infantry, the 2nd Infantry (Hyderabad Contingent), the 2nd Bombay Infantry. All except the Gurkhas were now given numbers which ran consecutively, the 2nd Sikh Infantry for instance becoming the 52nd and the 2nd Bombay the 102nd.

These were changes only of names or numbers. Two other tendencies were more important. The old controversy about the right number of British officers was still not dead. Jacob, the most extreme champion of the irregular ideal, had thought three enough for a unit; the reorganization of 1863 compromised at seven, with Indian officers commanding squadrons and companies. But this principle was gradually abandoned; the number of officers was raised to nine, and when four double companies took the place of eight companies, they were commanded by British officers. The term 'Indian Staff Corps' lasted till 1903, when officers were posted from Sandhurst to the Indian Army and wrote 'Indian Army' after their names. By 1914, the establishment of British officers had been raised to twelve and Indian officers were normally in command of platoons not companies. Their importance had receded at each step since 1863.

Still more marked was the trend towards fewer classes. In 1863 an infantry battalion consisted of eight companies; in 1900 there were four double companies and by 1922 there were four companies. It will be remembered that the Bombay Army had prided itself on taking little account of caste, but when the armies were amalgamated the Kāli Pānchwin (the 'Black Fifth') had eight caste companies, a company each of Rajputs, Dekhani Mahrattas, Konkani Mahrattas, Bedars, Pardesis, Sikhs, Konkani Muslims and Dekhani Muslims. By 1903 this fantastic arrangement was simplified to four double companies, two of Dekhani Mahrattas, one of Konkani Mahrattas and one of Dekhani Muslims. After 1922, their class composition read simply 'Mahrattas'.

That is an extreme example of the length to which the passion for distinct groups had gone and of a simplification which in itself was sensible. In that battalion, eight classes had been reduced within ten years to three. But while the Rajputs and Sikhs whom the Black Fifth had lost were still recruited in large numbers to other regiments, three classes that they had taken had disappeared from the Army List altogether. For sixty years, the list of classes recruited was growing smaller and more selective. This was due in part to a purely military preference for large men rather than small, for men accustomed to extremes of temperature and easy to train, in short, for the 'best' men a commanding officer could find for his purpose, judged by standards similar to those he applied when choosing horses or mules. Height, weight, conformation and disposition—all these would be taken into account. Just as he might prefer Arab horses or Kathiawari or Australian, he would prefer men of one region, speech and religion. But underlying that military choice lay the mental division of Indians into the 'good' and the 'bad' or unreliable. This again was reinforced by a current of opinion about race and heredity that flowed through the Western world in the latter part of the century. 'All is race,' sighed a character in one of Disraeli's novels, and for about sixty years this opinion grew steadily. It enabled Western Europeans to feel that their startling material success was inevitable, because it was due to inborn qualities. There was no need to feel guilty; it was the survival of the fittest, part of the plan of nature that men should be different and that the strongest should rule.

Lord Roberts would not have expressed himself in such language as that. He observed what he saw and drew simple conclusions. He spoke for many of his contemporaries and most officers would have agreed with him.

2. Lord Roberts and his Views

Lord Roberts had long maintained that there should be one Commander-in-Chief in India with four Commands. He had made his proposals on paper in 1879 but, though there was a good deal of agreement in principle, it took sixteen years to put them into effect. It was therefore somewhat ironic that in 1880 he should have been appointed Commander-in-Chief of the Madras Army. His impressions can best be expressed in his own words.

'I made long tours in order to acquaint myself with the needs and capabilities of the Madras Army. I tried hard to discover in them those fighting qualities which had distinguished their forefathers during the wars of the last and the beginning of the present century. But long years of peace and the security and prosperity attending it had evidently had upon them, as they always seem to have upon Asiatics, a softening and deteriorating effect; and I was forced to the conclusion that the ancient military spirit had died in them as it had died in the ordinary Hindostani of Bengal and the Mahratta of Bombay, and that they could no longer with safety be pitted against warlike races or employed outside the limits of Southern India … It was with extreme reluctance that I formed this opinion.'

There can surely be little doubt, after reading this passage, that Lord Roberts went to Madras with a strong expectation of finding what in fact he found, that the Madras Army was not as efficient for war as the northern army reconstituted after the Mutiny. He did, however, recognize as 'a brilliant exception' the Madras Sappers and Miners, who were 'a most useful, efficient body of men'. He noted also that 'Madrassies, as a rule are more intelligent and better educated than the fighting races of Northern India' and drew the conclusion that they might make Sappers or Pioneers though not infantry; he therefore converted two regiments of infantry to Pioneers. But there was, surely, another conclusion that might have been drawn. Madrasis in the eighteenth century had not as a rule been noticeably skilful as soldiers until trained by French and British officers. That the Madrasis of the Sappers were better soldiers than others might therefore suggest a difference in the officers who trained them. And indeed there was a difference.

The officers of the Madras Sappers were volunteers, seconded from the Royal Engineers; they had seen service elsewhere, they had prospects elsewhere; most of them were vigorous and ambitious men who came for the opportunity of widening their experience and making a mark. But infantry officers came to the Madras Army for life, with a fixed time-scale of promotion, and much less likelihood of seeing active service than in the British service or in the Bengal Army. Battalions of the Bengal Army were seldom away from the Frontier long; officers and men alike were kept constantly on their toes by field-days with real bullets. There was action, excitement, responsibility; the seat of government was close, it was easier to catch the eye, the chance of a good appointment was far better. Would it be surprising then to find a higher proportion of good officers in the Bengal Army? Would one not expect in the Madras Army—now an almost stagnant back-water—rather more officers who deserved Bartle Frere's description of 'idle mercenary drones'? And surely Frere's point, that the men would be what their officers were, was at least as likely to be true as the hereditary degeneration of a whole people? The climate of Madras is certainly enervating to Europeans but Madrasis have lived in it for many thousands of years. Sylvester, Roberts's contemporary, surgeon with a cavalry regiment and a highly critical observer of Indian character and customs, wrote of the Madras Sappers: 'Neither could anyone, after seeing these men work under a broiling sun, doubt their vast superiority in physical endurance over the sepoys of Bengal and Bombay. Nothing daunted their cheerful disposition.'

Roberts went to Madras as Commander-in-Chief in 1880, and in 1885 became Commander-in-Chief of the Bengal Army, with super-visory powers over the other two; he did not leave India till 1893. 'From the time I became C. in C. Madras until I left India the question of how to render the army … as perfect a fighting-machine as … possible … caused me most anxious thought,' he wrote, and no one can doubt the sincerity of his beliefs nor the vigour with which he pursued them. 'The first step', he continued, 'was to substitute men of the more warlike and hardy races for the Hindustani sepoys of Bengal, the Tamils and Telagus of Madras and the so-called Mahrattas of Bombay.' But he met difficulties. His views were not always accepted because of 'the theory of equilibrium between the armies of the three Presidencies' and because of an 'ignorance that was only too universal with respect to the characteristics of the different races, which encouraged the erroneous belief that one Native was as good as another for purposes of war.'

The insistence on 'equilibrium' was, he argued, out of date; once, no doubt, it had been 'prudent to guard against a predominance of soldiers of any one creed or nationality, but with British troops nearly doubled and the Native army reduced by more than a third, with all the forts and arsenals protected and nearly the whole of the Artillery manned by British soldiers, with railway and telegraph communications from one end of India to the other, the risk of internal trouble greatly diminished and the possibility of external complications daily more apparent ... it became essential to have in our native army men who might confidently be trusted to take their share in fighting against a European foe.'

It is really inescapable to go on quoting Roberts because he does so accurately represent the prevailing view, in opposition to the view expressed by Frere and Jacob—and later by Auchinleck—that training and officers were of such importance that they could give military value to the most unlikely material. 'In the British Army,' Roberts wrote, 'the superiority of one regiment over another is mainly a matter of training; the same courage and military instinct are inherent in English, Scotch and Irish alike, but no comparison can be made between the martial value of a regiment recruited amongst the Gurkhas of Nepal or the warlike races of northern India and of one recruited among the effeminate races of the South ... I was in despair at not being able to get people to see the matter with my eyes.' Still, he managed to get his way in detail and step by step. 'Several companies and regiments composed of doubtful material were disbanded ... and men of well-known fighting castes entertained instead. Class regiments were formed, as being more congenial to the men and more conducive to esprit de corps ... recruiting was made the business of specially selected officers who understood Native character.'

The term 'Native', incidentally—with the connotation it had gradually acquired of a mysterious alien folk incomprehensible to Europeans and essentially treacherous—had been officially discarded in 1885. The term 'Indian officers' replaced 'native officers' and in the course of the next few years the official titles of units were changed to eliminate a word which had become offensive. For example, the 1st Bengal Native Infantry (which as the 21st had survived at Peshawar in 1857 and thus become 'as rare as the dodo') became the 1st Brahman Infantry. But of course Lord Roberts was not alone in using the term in writing and conversation.

'Native officers (he wrote) can never take the place of British officers ... Eastern races, however brave and accustomed to war, do not possess the qualities that go to make good leaders of men ... I have known many natives whose gallantry and devotion could not be surpassed but I have never known one who would not have looked to the youngest British officer for support in time of difficulty and danger ... I have a thorough belief in and admiration for Gurkhas, Sikhs, Dogras, Rajputs, Jats and select Mahommedans ... I thoroughly appreciate their soldierly qualities; brigaded with British troops I would be proud to lead them against any European enemy ... but we cannot expect them to do with less leading than our own soldiers require.'

Nine British officers out of ten thought as Roberts did, perhaps more. He vastly increased the efficiency of the Indian army; perhaps, if he had had his way, he would have made it even more efficient—for the moment. He put his faith in roads, railways and swift movement rather than fortifications, and here he was surely far-sighted. Strategic railways, improved transport with emphasis on the mule and the light cart instead of the camel and the elephant, a higher standard of marksmanship—these were some of his contributions. Simple, honest, brave, he put his duty before anything else and was loved by both British and Indian troops. No one could have written more generously of the men under his command at Kandahar: 'I looked on them all, Native as well as British, as my valued friends ... never was a Commander better served ... a grand spirit of camaraderie pervaded all ranks ... all were eager to close with the enemy.' He did much to curb drunkenness among British troops; he worked for better nursing, better accommodation, for a more humane and dignified life for both British and Indian. He set a pattern for the British officer for eighty years.

But surely he was less than fair to Indian officers when he held it against them that they turned to a British officer for support in time of difficulty. They had been taught to do just that; they were subordinates. They might indeed have been blamed if they had not. It was the commission that gave the authority; the colour of the skin was only the sign. 'Thou hast seen a farmer's dog bark at a beggar? ... There thou might'st behold the great image of authority,' said King Lear, perceiving that the dog had behind him the farmer and the farmer's men with their pitchforks. It was quite another matter in the Second World War, when Indians held the King's Commission and as officers won decorations for valour alongside British comrades. Roberts was shown to have been wrong about the Maratha in the First World War and about the Madrasi in the Second. What he pictured was an Indian Army of 150,000 men superbly efficient for frontier war, able in a major war to hold a Russian enemy till help came and to expand in war to perhaps double its peace-time size. That was as much as anyone then foresaw and a soldier can hardly be blamed for not being a prophet. Probably Roberts would never have won either the Victoria Cross or the Field-Marshal's baton if he had had the imagination to foresee an independent India and a national army.

In short, he was a practical man and his views were those of his own generation and not of eighty years later. But his virtues lent them weight; the canon of the martial races was chanted as an incantation— Sikhs! Gurkhas! Jats! Pathans!—long after the First World War, at a time when there was no excuse for so restricted a vision. As late as 1933, for instance, Lt-Gen. Sir George MacMunn, in his book *The Martial Races of India*, wrote: 'The mass of the people of India have neither martial aptitude nor physical courage.' This, he continues, is the effect of 'prolonged years of varying religions ... of early marriage, of premature brides, and juvenile eroticism, of a thousand years of malaria and hookworm ... and the deteriorating effect of aeons of tropical sun on races that were once white and lived in uplands and on cool steppes.' Of three hundred and fifty million people, he continued, there were only thirty-five million who qualified as belonging to the martial races and of these only three million were males between twenty and thirty-five years of age. It was from these three millions that volunteers had been found for the Indian Army in the First World War. Half of them had come voluntarily to the colours. But if it were not for the British officer and the British soldier the martial races would 'once more eat up the peoples of the South.' This, of course, led him to a political conclusion which in Lord Roberts's time hardly anyone troubled to discuss.

The idea that some people will make soldiers and some will not is of course much older than the British. It is implicit in the Hindu caste system; no raja would have paid the money-lender or the trader castes to bear arms. But it was the British who, after the Mutiny, step by step, formulated and codified the principle, turning what had been a matter of practical choice into a dogma proclaimed with theological rancour. Such an opinion, held by the rulers of a country, is likely to have a cumulative effect; if you recruit fewer Madrasis because you think poorly of them, fewer will think of the army as a career. In areas intensively recruited, it will be a common ambition in the village to pass the recruiting officer's test; it will be like getting a place in a university, the family will be congratulated, friends will rejoice. That was how it was in the 1930s in Garhwal, a single district which in peace provided four battalions of infantry as well as men for sappers, the supply corps and other ancillaries. But it will be very different where opportunities have grown fewer and fewer till men have forgotten to think of a life in the army.

Let us look at the effect this doctrine had on the infantry of the old Madras Army. Let us disregard regiments that disappeared in the early days and also those raised for a special purpose, as for the Mutiny, and disbanded when the special need was over. Let us take the fifty-two battalions of the Madras line as they stood after the reorganization of 1824. All stood fast throughout the Mutiny and were still in existence in 1860. Twelve battalions were disbanded between 1862 and 1864. Eight battalions were disbanded in 1882, one in 1891, three between 1902 and 1904, two in 1907 and four in 1922. Four were renumbered in 1902 and grouped together as the 3rd Madras Regiment in 1922 but disbanded one by one between 1923 and 1928. Three were converted from infantry to Pioneers, but disbanded with all other Pioneers in 1933.

Fifteen were converted to Punjabi regiments. Five of these fifteen went
to the 1st Punjab Regiment, five to the 2nd and five to the 8th. Thus
not one regiment of infantry remained which recruited in Madras. This
remained the case until the Madras Regiment was revived by Auchinleck
in the Second World War (see note, page 361).

3. The Specialists

By the end of the century the procedure for recruiting was much the
same for all regiments. A commanding officer was permitted to recruit
men only from the class or classes prescribed by Army Headquarters.
Sometimes the whole regiment or battalion was of one class; sometimes
he had three classes, each squadron or company being of one class
only. Within this broad classification, he might to a considerable
extent consult his own preference. Thus, if he had a company of
Rajputs which by the end of the season would be short of its establishment by twenty men, he would tell the recruiting officer for Rajputs
that he wanted twenty recruits and would prefer them to belong to
certain sub-castes and to come from certain areas. The recruiting
officer would give advice about which areas were likely to prove
fruitful and between them they would eventually settle where a recruiting party from the regiment should operate and the sub-classes it
should try to find. An Indian officer or a senior N.C.O. of the regiment
would be chosen to command the party, which, if twenty recruits were
required, would probably consist of about six recruiters, working in
pairs. When a pair of recruiters had persuaded a suitable young man to
volunteer, they would bring him to the recruiting officer, who would
either reject him or confirm his suitability and arrange for a medical
examination.

'Suitability' meant physical fitness and something else not easy to
define; the ideal recruit would be high-spirited and intelligent, independent but respectful, straightforward, honest, manly—and if all
these qualities could hardly be revealed at a glance, still a good
recruiting officer could form an opinion as to whether they were
likely to develop. He would want to see a boy who was a 'good stamp
of Rajput recruit'; he ought to conform as far as possible to the un-
written specification for the breed. The recruiting officer had a mental
picture of the perfect Rajput or the perfect Sikh; it was a Platonic
ideal, laid up in heaven, but if it had been expressed in words it would
have been faintly reminiscent of the requirements laid down to guide
judges in the show-ring: a broad brow, a firm jaw, a clear eye, an
alert expression. Nor was that all; someone in the village, preferably
the headman or collector of land revenue—this would differ according

to the region—must certify that the boy had a good character and came of a good family and that he did really belong to the caste, class and sub-class he claimed. A cavalry recruit must also be able to invest the sum needed for his 'place' in the silladari regiment and for his horse. It was all very different from the recruiting sergeant's pint in the pub and the Queen's shilling of rural England.

The initiative lay with the regiment. The regiment stated its requirements and sent the recruiting party. The commander of the recruiting party must belong to the class, sub-class and district from which he hoped to get recruits. He would go to his own village first; it was natural that he should want to see his family and this was not at all discouraged. The commander of the party would usually have been allowed some say in choosing his recruiters and they too would be of the same class, sub-class and neighbourhood and would go to their own villages first. Since the Colonel would specify the sub-class which he thought made the best soldiers and would send recruiters of the type he wanted—since recruiters would naturally bring men of their own kin or 'brotherhood' and of the kind they thought would please the Colonel—the network would inevitably be drawn closer and closer, each company tending to be linked together by close ties of blood, caste and religion. This had always been so, but the process became even more marked with the growing emphasis on class, with the class companies and the class regiments.

The recruiting officer for Rajputs—to continue with one class for the moment—would be a major or a captain, and would be helped by an assistant recruiting officer—in some cases by two. The assistant would be a subaltern who would be appointed for a short tenure of only six months, thus providing for the regiments who recruited that class a steady flow of young officers who had seen something of recruiting and of the villages their men came from. There rubbed off on these young men something of the specialized skill which the recruiting officer himself acquired and in which he gloried. Much of this knowledge and experience was embodied in a series of Handbooks for Officers of the Indian Army. These were usually written by recruiting officers and periodically brought up-to-date by their successors; they were meant not only to help recruiting but to give officers some knowledge of their men. They all follow much the same pattern, sketching the history of the group—Sikhs, Dogras, Rajputs, Hindustani Muslims or whoever it may be—and describing their religion, their customs at marriage, birth and death, their principal festivals and fasts, above all their divisions into class and sub-class and their ideas of social and religious precedence.

Social anthropology was then in its infancy, but some recruiting officers would surely have made excellent anthropologists and, as it is, their handbooks provide a starting-point that a modern anthropologist would find useful. Let us look at one as a sample, and let us start with Captain R. W. Falcon's *Handbook on Sikhs.*

Falcon gives a brief history of the Sikhs, laying emphasis on the purely religious character of early Sikhism. The first of the Ten Gurus or teachers was a holy man, teaching a reformed and purified form of Hinduism. He was a follower of Kabir, the weaver poet who had once been a Muslim, and called himself the child of both Ram and Allah.* It was only with Guru Govind Singh, the tenth and last of the Ten Sikh Teachers, that Sikhism became a military order as well as a religion and Falcon emphasizes the fact that a Sikh in the full sense is not born but becomes a Sikh only when he is initiated by the ceremony known as the *pahul* or gate; there is thus always a tendency to lapse or slip back into Hinduism, simply by apathy, by failing to undergo the *pahul*. And again, even within the formal fold, for those who have passed the gate, there is always a Hinduizing tendency. Hinduism absorbs foreign influences and its complexities creep back even when its own children have tried to purify it. Caste is repugnant to the teaching of either Christianity or Islam but there are nevertheless Muslim castes and Christian castes. It is not surprising then that there should be castes among the Sikhs, for whom the repudiation of caste is a basic doctrine and one of the reasons for their existence. They even go so far as to invite the blessing of Brahmans on their weddings. Falcon suggests that if it had not been for the army the Sikhs would after the end of Ranjit Singh's empire have become once more an unimportant sect of Hindus—and this was an opinion held even by some Sikhs themselves at least until the time of partition and Independence.

Most Sikhs—particularly in the army—are descended from Hindus who were Jats by caste before their conversion; in the time of Govind Singh, the Jats of half a district at a time would go through the *pahul* and join the order. The handbook contains therefore an account of the Jat people, who among the Hindus are not reckoned among the higher castes such as Brahman and Rajput; their widows may remarry and they do not wear the sacred thread. They are landowners, ranking high among the castes who may actually handle a plough, patient and enduring cultivators, stubborn and courageous, assertive of personal and individual freedom. They make good soldiers—and the Jat who is also a Sikh is better still.

'The new creed has added a more ardent military spirit ... (writes Falcon). The Sikh is a fighting man and his fine qualities are best shown in the army, which is his natural profession. Hardy, brave and of intelligence; too slow to understand when he is beaten; obedient to

* Kabir's verses, soaked in the consciousness of one divine light, are familiar to many English readers in Robert Bridges's anthology, *The Spirit of Man.*

discipline; attached to his officers; and careless of caste prohibitions, he is unsurpassed as a soldier in the East and takes the first place as a thoroughly reliable, useful soldier. The Sikh is always the same, ever genial, good-tempered and uncomplaining; as steady under fire as he is eager for a charge ... when well and sufficiently led he is the equal of any troops in the world and superior to any with whom he is likely to come into contact.'

Although all Sikhs are, in a sense, brothers, there are important distinctions to be understood and these Falcon carefully records. First, there are those whose ancestors were once Jats and those whose ancestors belonged to other Hindu divisions. Those whose ancestors belonged to the menial groups outside caste are still separate. It is true that after the Ninth Guru was killed by the Muslims, three scavengers carried his body away and that Guru Govind Singh welcomed them and their descendants into Sikhism and named them Sikhs by Religion—Mazhabi Sikhs. But the name, Falcon insists, properly applies only to descendants of those three; he clearly regrets that it has now been appropriated by all converted scavengers—and a Jat Sikh cannot eat with those whose grandfathers were untouchables. They are not suitable for an ordinary Sikh regiment.

These broad divisions are only a beginning; there are many more respectable Hindu castes of which some have been converted to Sikhism, but a Jat Sikh may marry none of them. A Jat, whether Sikh or no, must marry a Jat—but not a Jat of the same sub-caste as himself. Falcon gives a list of eighteen Jat sub-castes which are predominantly Sikh; he calls them tribes, but this word does not convey the right impression in English. Their link is only that they imagine themselves to have some degree of common ancestry which forces them to marry outside their group. There are also many more sub-castes which are Jat but not predominantly Sikh. Each of the principal eighteen is again divided into *mūhins* or sub-sub-castes—clans or septs in Indian army language—and it is felt to be almost incestuous to marry within the sub-sub-caste. And overlying this division by caste are two other intricate networks of distinction. There is region and village; a Jat Sikh must not marry from his own village or an immediately neighbouring village, but should on the other hand keep within the region. Among the army Sikhs, there is an important division between the region known as Mānjhā and that known as Mālwā; they are separated by the river Sutlej. This division is historical as well as geographical because the Sutlej was once the boundary of Ranjit Singh's empire and the Sikh chiefs on the south-eastern bank were protected allies of the British at the time of the Sikh Wars. And then again, before Ranjit Singh emerged, in the struggles against the Mughals and Afghans, the Sikh leaders had been loosely linked together in groups and known as *misl*. There were twelve of these and a friend might call them divisions in a guerrilla or partisan army, while the Mughals no doubt called them by harsher names—gangs of terrorists, bandits or rebels. They survive today in the personal names of some Sikhs.

To Falcon, it was clearly of fascinating interest to record the names of seventy-nine of the eighty-four sub-sub-castes into which the Sandhu sub-caste of Jat Sikhs was said to be subdivided. To have found the missing five would have given him, one feels, the same kind of pleasure that a stamp-collector would feel on completing a set of rare stamps with a triangle or penny blacks. None the less, he is firm in his opinion that 'qualities such as hardiness, boldness, independence of spirit ... qualities useful for soldiering, appertain much more to districts than to tribes or even religions.' However, 'tribe is of some value because value as a military Sikh is hereditary' and 'one must count as the best Sikh tribes those that supplied converts in the time of Guru Govind Singh.' 'A good Sikh district is one where there are a majority of Sikhs'; where there are only a few, they will be 'weakened by marrying Hindu wives' or 'through the weakening influence of their surroundings'. He does not mention the point made in the last section that where only a few recruits are taken, a boy is less likely to think of the army as a career. He goes on to supply lists not only of 'tribes', 'clans' and 'septs', with their characteristics, but also of districts and the subdivisions of a district, graded for the purpose of recruiting as Very Good, Good, Fair, Poor, Bad and Very Bad. His grading takes into consideration both the quantity and quality of the Sikhs to be found there. If the land is too fertile, the inhabitants become 'immersed in the drudgery of cultivation'; some areas are 'unhealthy and malarious', others 'too far East; the characteristics of the people being less of the Punjabi and more of the Hindustani type.' Again, 'this district is too far South to be desirable.' 'The cultivation of sugar-cane to any great extent seems to me to give a softer character to the cultivator.' 'The Sikhs of this area are of a softer type—their Sikhism is very diluted by Hinduism.' 'Sikhs in this area require very careful recruiting ...' 'the best of this district are to be found along the banks of the river ...' So the catalogue continues. In conclusion, Falcon notes, 'though I recommend judicious recruiting from certain other Sikh castes as well as the Jat, both because there is good material available and because it is liable to harm Sikhism if military service is made the exclusive right of Jat Sikhs ... still the Jat must ever be the main source for recruits as he far and away outnumbers the other castes and possesses as a class qualities which no other caste can claim.'

Clearly Falcon has come to think of Sikhism as something he wants to see preserved for its own sake as well as for its part in producing material for the army. He has become a kind of honorary Sikh himself and this was at once a strength and a weakness of the system—an immense strength to the battalion, but a danger to the army because it made for the sharp specialization that proved such a problem when the Indian Army went to war in France and Mesopotamia.

Falcon urges regimental officers to accompany recruiting parties if they can; a British officer can be a great help to a recruiting party, he will get to know more about his men, and it should easily be possible to get some shooting. Indeed, Falcon's notes on subdivisions include information on likely ground for snipe and partridge as well as for recruits. 'Wherever you go in the Manjha,' he adds, 'you will be delighted with the fine stamp of Sikh met with and with the friendly welcome and ungrudging hospitality.'

To deal with other classes at the same length would be tedious; there is a good deal of repetition and the same points emerge. Lt-Col. Eden Vansittart, writing of Gurkhas, is equally confident that they are natural soldiers—'bold, enduring, faithful, frank, very independent and self-reliant. They despise the natives of India and look up to and fraternize with Europeans.' And he quotes Brian Hodgson, who, contrasting the Gurkhas with the Rajputs and Brahmans of the Bengal line, had written as early as 1832: 'These Highland soldiers, who despatch their meal in half an hour and satisfy the ceremonial law merely by washing their hands and face ... before cooking, laugh at the pharisaical rigour of the Sipahis, who must bathe from head to foot and make *puja* before they can begin to dress their dinner, must eat nearly naked in the coldest weather and cannot be in marching trim in less than three hours ... they are by far the best soldiers in Asia.' Yet though Vansittart, like everyone else, praises the Gurkhas for their freedom from the prejudices of caste, he is no less interested than Falcon in their divisions into groups which he lists with minute care.

Magars (pronounced 'Muggers') and Gurungs, he says, are by common consent the *beau idéal* of what a Gurkha soldier should be. These two groups are 'the basic Mongolian peasant of Central Nepal'. The Gurungs are slightly less Hinduized than the Magars, yet even the Gurungs are divided into the Four Castes and the Sixteen Castes. The Four Castes are the aristocracy and when travelling in their own country men of the Sixteen Castes will carry the load of a man from the Four Castes. It is said that a Gurung Colonel of the Nepalese Army offered his daughter's weight in gold to any man of the Four Castes who would marry her—and a poor man came forward. But a hastily summoned council of the Four Castes threw him out and reduced him to one of the Sixteen Castes, so the marriage fell through. Vansittart's experience was embodied in the handbook of 1895, and to this part of it the revising editor in 1915 has added a revealing footnote: 'I am afraid this is dying out a little and the Four Castes and the Sixteen Castes are getting mixed up.'

Vansittart, like Falcon, gives a long list of 'tribes' and 'clans'. From one area, there is a likelihood of young men of a certain group presenting themselves for recruitment as Magars—but they are not really Magars at all, though their mother may be a Magar. They are properly known as Matwala Khas. Men of this group should be recruited with great caution; though 'excellent results have been obtained, the greater proportion are coarse-bred and undesirable.' It is important that the N.C.O. sent in charge of a recruiting-party should be able to distinguish between the 'coarse-bred lad of good physique but undesirable as a recruit and the clean-bred lad who only requires good food, free gymnastics and so on to turn him into a first-class fighting man.' Seven of the ten Gurkha regiments—each of two battalions—take Magars and Gurungs from the central region; the 7th and 10th take Limbus and Rais from eastern Nepal, the 9th take men of two groups from the west who are of higher caste, somewhat taller, more Hinduized. The editor of 1915 clearly feels uneasy about over-recruiting in central Nepal; he calculates that there are only 900,000 males of the fighting castes in all Nepal, giving 200,000 of military age. The British Government recruits 25,000 in peace for the army and military police, apart from those that the Nepalese Government want for their own army. He seems to imply that the net should be thrown a little wider.

Falcon is certain that Sikhs are the best, Vansittart is just as confident about Gurkhas. Other recruiting officers, though enthusiastic for their own special kind of man, are a little more defensive. Captain Bingley, writing of Rajputs, tells of the traditional valour of Rajput warriors and rehearses some of the past glories of the old Company's army; he recalls the story of the Queen's Own Rajputs (once the 31st) at Bhurtpore; remembers Nott's praise of his 'beautiful sepoy regiments' when they first went to Kandahar. 'Our troops carried the enemy's position in gallant style; it was the finest thing I ever saw. Those 8,000 Afghans could not stand our 1,200 men for an hour.' He goes on that the system of class regiments has given a 'great impetus to the *esprit de race*. To each regiment is now entrusted the military reputation of the class which it represents.' Rajputs, he continues, are 'soldiers by tradition and taught by their religion to regard the profession of arms as their legitimate occupation … they form a military caste which should hold its own and bear favourable comparison with the most warlike of the races now serving under our colours.' 'Hold its own'—that is the extent of his claim.

Like his colleagues, he goes into immense detail over sub-castes and sub-sub-castes; this is necessary because 'Fighting capacity depends not only on race but also on hereditary instinct and social status,

therefore it is essential that every effort should be made to obtain the
very best men of that class which a regiment may enlist ... Men of good
class will not enlist unless their own class be represented in the regiment.'
So if you have a good tradition all will be well — but on the contrary,
if you have 'native officers who as regards race and breeding are not
altogether desirable, they will naturally bring into the regiment
men of their own kind' and a ring will be formed that will be a powerful
deterrent to the good class. The 'country Rajput is a straightforward,
guileless, honest, gentlemanly fellow and his manners betray him.'
But outsiders try to pass themselves off as what they are not and it is
important to make quite sure of a man's every particular. Against
some 'clans' or sub-castes Bingley puts a note to warn the unsuspecting:
'Undesirable; of spurious descent and practice widow remarriage'
'Rajputs of fallen grade who permit widow remarriage' 'Undesirable;
cunning and treacherous clan' 'Turbulent and troublesome race of
spurious descent'.

A jealous, sometimes an anxious, enthusiasm for the good name of one
particular class; a minute concern with the details of social precedence
and an almost obsequious readiness to recognize the men's social
prejudices — these are the marks of the recruiting officer. He admires
his men, just as they are; he does not want them different. 'Dogras' was
the term generally used of the Rajputs from the foothills of the
Himalayas north of the Punjab. They have none of the Mongolian
look of hillmen from further east and their caste system is much the
same as for Rajputs from the plains. The handbook for Dogras lists 420
subdivisions usually recruited and ranks them in four grades according
to their own estimation. All four grades are mixed in Dogra companies
— in spite of the damning fact that the lower grades allow their widows
to remarry. But recruiting should not go beyond these limits. There are
Jats living in these same hills, who were 'formerly more or less freely
enlisted ... but now castes are so clearly defined and well-known they
find it increasingly difficult ... They are sturdy and of better physique
than Dogra Rajputs, and officers ... speak highly of their discipline,
courage and soldierly fitness; but when mixed in the same company as
Dogra Rajputs they suffer somewhat as the Dogra Rajput does not
consider them on the same social plane.' Physical fitness is not enough;
the recruit must be socially acceptable as well.

It is depressing to turn from the handbooks for groups that are
highly esteemed to those that are not. Jacob, it will be remembered,
thought Hindustani Muslims made the best soldiers in India and
greatly preferred them to Pathans or Afghans. But the handbook for
1914 dismisses nearly all Muslims from east of the Jumna, who had
once made the bulk of the Company's cavalry and a substantial
element in the infantry. 'Original Muslims' — that is, those whose

ancestors came into India from Persia or Afghanistan as Muslims—generally 'live in cities and owing to a life of ease and to inbreeding are an effete race.' 'Town Muslims are not suitable for the army, being possessed of all kinds of vices.' Those who do not live in towns are mostly 'spurious', that is to say, not what they profess to be. Rohillas, for example, whose cavalry had swept over half India in the eighteenth century, 'are an untrustworthy and useless class and a degenerate race.' The best Muslims are converted Rajputs and the best of these come from west of the Jumna, where 'they are much superior in quality to the Eastern Rajput.' This is due to the fact that the western Rajput 'retains in all their strictness the same rules as to exogamy and clans in which marriage may take place as his Hindu fellow-clansmen, thus preserving the purity of the race.'

The handbook for Marathas follows the familiar pattern, giving much detailed information about festivals and rituals for birth, marriage and death, making the same careful distinctions and warning recruiting-parties of people who may try to pass themselves off as Marathas. But Betham's edition of 1908 ends on a note that is quite new.

'As a class (he writes), the Marathas possess great military qualities. They are quiet, orderly, amenable to discipline, clean, intelligent, determined and well-behaved. These qualities have not yet been recognized at their true worth. Judged by the races from the north, they are not a showy race of men; they do not go in for picturesque dress, they are quiet in demeanour and small in stature, they are not warlike in appearance and are noticeable for ... want of swagger. For want of these qualities, they have been judged unwarlike. Whatever they have been called on to do, they have done. What other class in India have fought as the Marathas have, except perhaps the Sikhs? Yet they have been given very little opportunity of showing their worth on active service. The popular cry is for nothing but Sikhs, Pathans and Punjabi Muslims, yet Marathas are equally as good. It is hard that they should be misjudged without fair trial.' On this point, Mesopotamia was to prove Betham right and Roberts wrong.

4. Divide and Rule

In the time between the two world wars, when the dispute about the pace of political progress was at its height, the Indian National Congress constantly threw at the British the imputation that they seized on every opportunity to foment division between Indians. This is not the place to discuss that general charge at any length. Undoubtedly, some Englishmen—perhaps most—felt a certain satisfaction at signs of disunity. But in the political field they had little need to manufacture them;

rather, it was they who had brought the first glimpse of unity and it was talk of their departure, coupled with the inevitable processes of the democracy they had introduced, that made rifts so wide and so dangerous. One branch of this charge is, however, central to this book. Did the army deliberately foster the concept of the martial classes in order to preserve a political hold on India? Was this part of a general policy of dividing in order to rule?

Undoubtedly the Bombay and Madras Armies were kept in being long after any military justification for them existed because of the theory of 'watertight compartments'; two compartments would keep the ship afloat even if one out of three sprang a leak. This was a political concept and it was based on the idea of dividing and ruling. Its result was that until 1895 the army was kept on a broader base than efficiency alone would have dictated. But it was the soldiers, and particularly Roberts, who regarded the watertight compartment idea as obsolete and defeated it. It was for military efficiency that Roberts believed he was fighting when he cut down Madrasi recruitment and concentrated on the peoples of the north. He thought the 'divide and rule' idea could be ignored and he was the champion of class regiments, which had once been thought dangerous. The army he aimed at creating had too narrow a base for modern war; still less could it be said to represent the nation. But it would be unfair to charge Roberts and those who thought as he did with deep political motives. They were military technicians concerned with physical efficiency in a limited kind of war.

At this point it becomes clear that the charge, if it is directed at the army, is put the wrong way round. What the military authorities wanted to do was to *concentrate* and rule. What, one may ask, would have been the right course for a quite unscrupulous Machiavelli determined to *divide* and rule India? Would he have been more afraid of the army or of the people? If it was at the army that he looked with anxiety—as British authorities undoubtedly did in 1860—he would have recruited as many classes to the army as possible and kept them apart. This, as we have seen, happened only to a limited extent. The Bombay and Madras Armies were preserved longer than they would otherwise have been; the military trend was to concentrate. But if Machiavelli was afraid of the people and calculated that he could keep the army faithful, then he might try to build up an army as distinct as possible from the bulk of the nation. This in fact was much nearer to what did happen. We did build up an army quite out of sympathy with the middle class that was just beginning to grow.

It was therefore with a certain glee that officers recorded the contempt of the Gurkha for the inhabitant of India, the dislike of the Sikh for the Easterner. When the recruiting officer lovingly notes the 'clans' and 'septs' of the Rajputs or the Jats and the importance of taking only the best, he believes that he is picking only the best because he wants his men to have self-confidence and swagger and panache and to avoid the trouble that arises from having misfits in the ranks. This, not some obscure plot to divide and rule, is his conscious motive. But he also greatly enjoys the exercise of his specialized skill; *he* knows, as hardly anyone else does, the difference between the Gurkha who is a genuine Magar and the Matwala Khas who is only pretending to be a Magar. He is also pleased to find that the principle of rank, so essential to military organization, is so widespread and exists as it were naturally in the structure of society. He is pleased too to find that these men, on whom his life may depend, are so irrevocably and hereditarily different from the great mass of the population of whom he knows so much less and whom he cannot help but distrust. In fact, his exact record of every distinction he can find turns out to be a stationary picture of a social structure that is really in movement, changing and melting. That it should move in any way is bound to be a disappointment to him — just when he had got everything labelled and in order! In his obsession with social precedence, breeding and heredity, he represents the British upper middle class of the period — and perhaps goes a little further than most. They lived in a society in which class distinctions were greatly to their advantage, but it was a society already threatened by doctrines of equality. They had to find reasons for the privileges they enjoyed and it soothed them to feel that they were different by birth and heredity from the men in the ranks and that this principle ran through all societies as well as their own.

The army's concentration on fewer and fewer classes gave India value for money if her wars were to be frontier wars only. But even from a strictly military point of view, it did not look far enough ahead and provide a wide enough base for recruitment. It did provide a political weapon which could probably have been used with success against the urban and politically conscious classes, even as late as the 'thirties of the twentieth century. But such a weapon would only have been effective if there had been the political will to use it with absolute ruthlessness. This there never was and the weapon was eventually transferred to the hands of the political classes, who did not make the startling changes that might have been expected. It is true that in the 'thirties the concentration of military power in the hands of 'the martial classes' was used as an argument for keeping British officers and British political control. MacMunn, for instance, as we have seen, thought that without British control the martial peoples of the north would 'eat up' the south — and views of this kind were constantly expressed in clubs and messes. But they were already out of date; the days of Genghiz Khan and Tamerlane are past, and they did not in the end prevail with Parliament.

In fact, there were two separate aspects to the charge of 'divide and rule' made against the army. It was felt that recruitment should have had a broader base — and also that the army was out of touch with the nation. In the first there was much substance, even from a purely military point of view; but concentration on a few classes did not divide the men once they were in the army; on the contrary, they often acquired a sense of comradeship. The second was true. The army *was* out of touch with the nation and its political leaders, but in the long run it is doubtful whether this should be regarded as a reproach. That the army was not political was of value to India in 1947 and has been ever since.

NOTE (see page 350)

Fate of 52 battalions numbered in 1824 as Madras Native Infantry 1–52.

Disbanded between 1862 and 1864:   18, 42, 43, 44, 45, 46, 47, 48, 49, 50, 51, 52.
Disbanded 1882:   34, 35, 36, 37, 38, 39, 40, 41.
Disbanded 1891:   10.
Disbanded 1902–4:   5, 8, 11.
Disbanded 1907:   17, 25.
Disbanded 1922:   3, 20, 23, 28.

Became the
Third Madras Regt. 1922: ⎫
Disbanded 1923–8:   ⎬   13, 15, 19, 26.
Converted to Pioneers around 1880: ⎫
Disbanded 1933:   ⎬   1, 4, 21.

Converted to Punjabis 1902–4 and grouped in 1922 as:
First Punjab Regt.   1922:   2, 6, 16, 22, 24.
Second Punjab Regt. 1922:   7, 9, 12, 14, 27.
Eighth Punjab Regt. 1922:   29, 30, 31, 32, 33.

XV

Her Majesty's Servants

1. A Military Order

We have become used, in the twentieth century, to the idea of vast armies of conscripts. We have read the memoirs of the peaceful citizen hastily trained for war; we know something of his boredom, his disgust at squalor, his flashes of intense fear, his animal satisfaction at being still alive, and also of his moods of wonder at the folly of organized killing. We have shared with many temporary soldiers that sharp moment of surprise—prolonged in consciousness, instantaneous by the clock—that a man so like myself should be trying to kill *me*, that *I* should be killing this young man, so like myself, whose face shows such astonishment. But these are the emotions of amateurs; there is little of this in the memoirs of soldiers of the Queen in the long stretch from the Mutiny to the Kaiser's war. They are professionals; courage is their essential quality and it is taken for granted that they have overcome fear and the dislike of killing.

That half-century covered the heyday of British Imperial rule. Add a half-century at the beginning, when the idea was growing, another quarter-century at the end, when it was dying, and you have more than a century during which the British polished and brought to perfection a considerable social achievement. They created an Imperial class, servants of the Queen and of the Empire, rulers of the subject peoples and of about nine-tenths of their fellow-countrymen. We of course are concerned with one section only of that class, the soldiers, and in particular with those who went to the Indian Army, but the whole class had much in common. Let us look first at all officers of the army, whether of the British service or the Indian and particularly in that central period from the Mutiny to the First World War.

It was an Imperial class, not a caste. In the first place, it was not quite hereditary. The Chief of the Imperial General Staff in the First World War, Field-Marshal Sir W. Robertson, had risen from the ranks. He had to overcome great difficulties; he refused the offer of a commission the first time it was made because he knew he could not live in the officers' mess on a subaltern's pay of £120 a year. But by iron self-control, abstinence and hard work, he did at last achieve this career. That was the extreme example; he went all the way in one lifetime. There were many others whose parents had perhaps made money in business and who obtained entry to the military class by going to the right kind of school. And it was possible to fall out of the class; there were gentlemen-rankers, as in Kipling's verses:

> Gentlemen-rankers out on the spree,
> Damned from here to Eternity.
> God ha' mercy on such as we …

The class was also not at all like a caste in being extremely competitive; esteem within the class depended on a whole set of factors. Birth and money were not enough by themselves. From a good house in a good school a good all-rounder might hope to go to a good regiment, but at every stage he was expected to contribute to that excellence. He must help to make his house, his squadron, his regiment, the best. This meant something more than high standards in house matches and examinations, on the rifle-range and the parade-ground; it meant tone, it meant good form, qualities not easy to define.

Membership of the class was not quite hereditary, but to be born into it was undoubtedly useful. If your father and grandfather had been in the Queen's service, there would be many friends ready to give a young man a chance and it was permissible to write to them for advice and to apply for employment wherever military experience could be gained. A campaign on the Frontier, war in the Sudan, offered a chance of distinction — perhaps a brevet or step in rank, perhaps a mention in dispatches, certainly experience of fighting — and a flood of applications from eager young officers would reach the Military Secretary. The memoirs and biographies of those who reached high rank all tell the same story: you had to push to get there, but it would not be good form to push too hard. The young Winston Churchill left his regiment in a dull garrison station and contrived to see fighting at Omdurman and also with the Malakand Field Force. The term 'to wangle' did not come into general use till 1914, but the art was well understood, and it was not discreditable to pull strings in order to get to the front. But in this, as in all things, some discretion was needed. There were some who thought Churchill *had* gone rather far — but no doubt they were jealous.

Whether you were picked from two or three hundred applicants for a post at the front would depend on general reputation. It certainly did no harm to be the son of someone who perhaps long ago had chosen the Commander-in-Chief for just such a post; it was a help to have been an A.D.C., to have been to the Staff College, to have met officers in high positions. But no single qualification was enough in itself; to get far, a man must be judged to be efficient at what he undertook, and he must be neither a mug nor a bounder. The positive side of this was to be a good fellow; Birdwood was a superlatively good fellow, liked by everyone, but it was not a term that would have been applied to Kitchener, who achieved a good deal without it.

A 'mug', wrote Younghusband, was 'a brother officer who neither rode nor shot nor played games, who drank water at Mess, went to bed early and swotted at algebra, fortifications or French.' He was unlikely to be rich and perhaps he was not born into the class; whatever the reason, it was a fatal reputation to acquire. The typical successful soldier—Smith-Dorrien, Rawlinson—records with delight his successes at polo and racing while at the Staff College; to be Master of the Drag, drive four-in-hand, beat the Aldershot Command at polo, win a point-to-point were as important as to pass out high. You must not be a slacker; you must get through your work and it must be thorough; nothing was more fatal than to be labelled showy or superficial. But you must not be *seen* to work hard; to swot was the sign of a mug.

This was partly a reaction against the early opposition to having a Staff College at all. When the college was instituted, it was thought suitable only for 'mugs' and in India graduates from the college were for some time regarded with suspicion. When they held a dinner in Simla, one senior officer comforted himself in a speech with the reflection that he need not feel abashed, since no one from the Commander-in-Chief down to the rank of colonel had P.S.C. (passed Staff College) after his name. But by the 'nineties this was changing, and 'the best bloods and best all-round men began to compete,' says Younghusband.

Of course, not all officers were ambitious for high command and it was only a minority who thought of the Staff College. Some no doubt were idle and frivolous for most of the time, but to most officers there was a certain inner core of dedication. Their life on the surface might seem mainly a matter of sport and enjoyment but they were liable to become instantly serious about the excellence of their regiment. And it was a point of honour to which there could be no exception that everyone, officer or man, British or Indian, was eager for active service. For the officer it might mean distinction, for the British soldier it meant escape from deadly boredom; for the Indian soldier it meant that he had two rupees a month more to send his family. But these do not wholly explain the enthusiasm; at the rumour of active service, the men 'cheered lustily ... the Majors smiled with sober joy and the sub-alterns waltzed in pairs down the Mess-room,' wrote Kipling, and there is plenty of evidence that this was the spirit. Perhaps in part it was because they knew that this was what was expected of them; almost certainly it was due to a pugnacity that was never far from the surface, a delight in the mere idea of fighting and a firm belief that to fight was the mark of true manhood. This was as true of British soldiers as of Sikhs, Rajputs and Gurkhas. And probably there was a deeper sense of dedication and honour: 'This is what we are *for*; this is our proper task.' Much of this died in the mud of Flanders. After Passchendaele not many men said they wanted to go to the front.

That is to anticipate; let us go back to the Victorian heyday. There were essentials of right conduct that an officer must observe, but also an elaborate code of behaviour that was a matter of subtle distinctions. A man should, and indeed must, believe that 'there is no regiment like ours; never by word, sign or deed, may he let those in other regiments know that this is what he thinks.' He must learn to drink a good deal, enough to make him do silly and amusing things, but not enough to become boastful or quarrelsome, still less lecherous or insensible, enough in short to be merry but not drunk. He might get a little in debt, but not hopelessly. Mistakes due to ignorance would be corrected, sometimes gently, sometimes less gently. A young subaltern was deputed for a big ceremonial parade as an additional aide-de-camp to a royal personage; as the great lady's carriage rolled past his own regiment, he was heard to say to a lady-in-waiting: 'This is my regiment.' That evening Colonel Western, who recalled the occasion many years later, happened to visit his mess and found him receiving instruction from his brother-subalterns; he was writing out in a clear round hand over and over again: 'This is the regiment to which I have the honour to belong.'

In a good regimental mess, wrote Younghusband, corners were generally rubbed off; 'the prig ceases to be priggish, the cad to be caddish ... The untamable bounder quietly disappears from Her Majesty's service.' The newly joined will soon be taught the unspeakable vulgarity of offering a man a drink in the ante-room of his own mess; he will soon learn that he should call captains by their surname, never by a nickname, while majors in the mess should be addressed as 'Major', without a surname. As to what constitutes an untamable bounder, Younghusband again has a tale to the point. At Viceregal Lodge in Simla, an officer—from a departmental corps, one is glad to note, not a regiment—went to the buffet to get his partner a drink and, being kept waiting for a moment or two, began to abuse the *khidmatgar*, that is, waiter. The Military Secretary to the Viceroy, Lord William Beresford, was within earshot and came up to him. 'That man', he said, 'is the Viceroy's private servant; this is the Viceroy's house and you come here as his guest. But it is clearly no place for you and unless you are gone in five minutes I shall kick you out. And you will not come here again.'

Neither caste nor class conveys quite the right impression, because both ignore the element of dedication. To be an officer and a gentleman meant joining a military order, in some ways not unlike a monastic order, with a code of virtues admired by all, and a subsidiary canon of polite behaviour. No man between the Mutiny and the First World War was more loved than Lord Roberts and when he died the main virtues of the code were set out in Rawlinson's order of the day to the Fourth Corps in France. Rawlinson spoke of 'the Commander-in-Chief whose first and last thought was always for the rank and file' and of his 'courage, modesty, devotion to duty and self-denial ... it is for us to imitate him.' There is nothing unusual, to an English ear, about these words; indeed, they are so trite that it is hard to feel their meaning. But these were the essential virtues of the military order and some of them are unusual. Courage came first and without that nothing else counted; a later generation would often heighten a story by the admission: 'I was in a blue funk,' but not the Victorian professional. Fear must not be mentioned. Modesty came next to courage and this was something that not all armies have valued. But in the military order we are thinking of, it held a high place; it was an essential ingredient in good form. To boast or show off was the first thing a subaltern must learn he should never do; it was the mark of a bounder. Devotion to duty came next and with it self-denial, which again is not always thought of as a military virtue. But it meant self-denial in war, putting duty before life, putting the welfare of the troops under a man's command before his own comfort, putting a wounded comrade before himself.

To compare the military brotherhood with the monastic will seem to some far-fetched. Much of the soldier's higher code of conduct came into operation only in war; in peace, provided he observed the lesser canon of polite behaviour, his life was often an easy one. But *hardiness* was admired, in the sense of being able to live simply when it was needed, and although life in a mess was not exactly abstemious it became more so. 'When I first joined the Army, forty-five years ago, the consumption of wine and spirits in a mess was treble and quadruple what it now is. Competitions and tournaments have helped to check the drinking spirit ... they demand absolute physical fitness,' wrote Colonel Western in 1922. On the other hand, he notes wistfully that when he was a boy at Cheltenham, hacking was permitted; you were allowed to kick a boy on the shins to make him leave the ball. 'I don't understand why hacking has been so universally abolished; it did no particular harm and made boys more hardy.'

Self-denial, in one aspect, meant unselfishness to a comrade. By the nature of his profession, a soldier must exclude the enemy from those to whom he extends practical good will; he is bound to be more inclined even than most men to distinguish between 'people like us', who are good, and enemies, who are bad. For the British soldier, in Victorian times, the enemy was usually a different colour from himself and came from a different culture with a different code of behaviour. The Frontier tribesman, for example, finished off enemy wounded and mutilated enemy dead; it was therefore with considerable gusto that 'punishment' was inflicted on tribesmen when hostilities were in progress. A cavalry charge was rare on the Frontier but did sometimes take place. 'The most joyous moment for a cavalry soldier, to be let loose in a glorious charge! ...' wrote Younghusband, describing such an occasion. 'Some of our men lost their turbans ... A Sikh, with hair long as a woman's streaming in the wind, bending low and hard forward, yelling like a fiend and bringing his curved sword down on all and sundry with a soft whistling drawing cut is like a demon of dark dreams.' There was no more mercy for those fleeing enemies than they would have shown themselves.

Hardness to an enemy, unselfishness to a comrade, was part of the code. But who is my comrade? To the British private soldier, who shared only some aspects of his officer's code, a comrade was usually defined narrowly; it is considered 'more excusable to "win" or "borrow" things belonging to men of other companies than things belonging to men of one's own company ... and ... to pinch something belonging to another battalion ... is considered a good joke ... But no man worth anything steals from a comrade.' This is Frank Richards, the Old Soldier Sahib, whose account of life in India in the ranks is brilliant. For the officer, of course, theft was always inexcusable except from the enemy in war; 'when one thinks nothing of taking a man's life one gets careless about relieving him of less important possessions.' For the officer, a comrade was more widely defined; in war it meant 'anyone on my side'; in peace it might mean 'anyone in my regiment', or it might mean 'anyone who has joined the military order and keeps its rules', or in other words, anyone whom he could regard as an officer and a gentleman.

Self-denial did not mean mortification of the flesh in the monastic sense. But it did often mean putting duty, or the good name of the regiment, before personal inclination. This was particularly the case in respect of marriage. Subalterns must not marry and a man would not get his captaincy till he was into his thirties, perhaps not till he was past thirty-five. Other military societies—Spartans and Zulus, for example—have made their soldiers postpone the begetting of heirs till they were mature and have regarded family life as an interference with military duty, but it was a strange custom to prescribe sterility until half a lifetime had passed. And what meanwhile did the subalterns do? In the Company's time, officers had kept Indian mistresses, but this was, as we have seen, less and less frequent in the twenty years before

the Mutiny and by the 'sixties—except in Burma—it meant social
ostracism. Silence on the whole subject was the Victorian rule and it is
hard to generalize with certainty, but Kipling's stories suggest that,
although a civilian might occasionally keep a mistress in the native
city, it had to be done with extreme care and he dared confide in no
one. It would be much more difficult for a subaltern to arrange anything
of the kind and keep it secret; his life was far too public. What he might
do when away from his unit was another matter, but most colonels
would want to know how a subaltern spent his leave. To go shooting
mountain sheep in Kashmir was approved, but a subaltern would be
asking for trouble if he proposed to spend two months on leave in
Mussoorie—a hill station supposed to be frequented by Eurasian girls
hoping to make a good match.

In the 1930s I recall a cavalry officer describing his experiences
while showing some Polish officers round India. 'And what', they
asked him when they had seen the regiment on parade and in stables
and on the hockey-field, 'do you do about sex?'

'I hardly expect you to believe me,' he replied, 'but we don't do
anything about it.' They were too polite to say so, but he did not think
they did believe him. In fact, however, it was true. Yeats-Brown, who
joined his regiment in 1905, writes of his early months: 'My life was as
sexless as any monk's at this time ... what is good for the Roman
priest is good (I suppose) for the Indian Cavalry subaltern, who has
work to do (like the priest) which he could scarcely perform if hampered by family ties.' But sex and family ties do not always go together
and Yeats-Brown does not seem very sure of the advantages of celibacy.
Soon afterwards he took leave to Peshawar in order to learn Pashtu
and there he clearly did not behave quite like a monk. But, in fact, he
had stated the official attitude.

When Kitchener was Commander-in-Chief, he more than once
addressed commanding officers on the best means of checking venereal
disease and he also wrote a memorandum addressed directly to British
troops. The primary causes leading to impurity and disease were drink
and idleness. A commanding officer, he told them, should encourage
his men to lead a good healthy life, mentally and physically. He should
foster a love of games and outdoor sports; he should see that his men
have plenty to do. Officers should 'prevent impurity by advice and
influence, setting an example of self-restraint.' And to the men he
referred to 'the trials and temptations of the hot weather, when time
often hangs heavily' and continued that none the less 'men should
exert their powers of self-restraint and avoid any excess in liquor ...
Unless pride in their corps ... keeps men from this danger [i.e., venereal
disease], they must be prepared to see other regiments chosen for
active service ... No soldier who is unable to exercise due restraint in

these matters can expect to be entrusted with command over his comrades ... Every man can, by self-control, restrain the indulgence of these imprudent and reckless impulses that so often lead men astray ... What would your mothers, your sisters and your friends at home think of you?'

These are remarkable words from a Commander-in-Chief, unlikely, one imagines, to find many parallels among the orders of French or Prussian generals. They were quite unrealistic. Kitchener mentions the fact that there had once been brothels officially maintained by the Government and that the system had been discontinued owing to public opinion in England. But in fact, at the very time when Kitchener addressed his exhortation to the troops, there were brothels in Agra and Meerut, and no doubt in many other stations, self-supporting, though with a backing from regimental funds, inspected by medical officers, and protected by military police from any visitors but British troops. It could truthfully be said in the House of Commons that the Government did not support anything of the kind; it was a matter for commanding officers. But such regimental brothels are described in detail by Frank Richards, who says they were used by all but a very few men, because it was generally believed to be bad for a man's health to abstain altogether in a hot climate. Nearly all men went with prostitutes, said Richards, 'but would sooner have died than married one of them.' None the less, a rough chivalry towards women was almost universal. Even in the Mutiny, when Indian males were attacked with such indiscriminate ferocity, women were generally treated as neutrals, and in frontier warfare, too, this was the rule.

But though Kitchener's words give little indication of how other ranks behaved, they are evidence of how officers were supposed to behave. It was, of course, much easier for officers than for men to find interesting employment for mind and body; the obsession with games grew steadily as the century progressed and officers were now all convinced that in a hot climate exercise was essential, preferably violent exercise and preferably twice a day. If there was no parade before breakfast, it was best to school polo-ponies or gallop after a drag or a jackal; in the evening there would be polo or racquets or hockey. And a good deal of energy was also worked off in ragging; games after dinner in the mess on guest nights were apt to take violent forms. One party might build a human platform like a rugger-scrum and another would try to break it by launching their heaviest men in a succession of flying leaps on to their backs. Or there might be a moonlight steeplechase ending with the winner riding through the anteroom to the mess table. Endless absurd and often dangerous projects would present themselves as desirable and amusing to high-spirited youth and so long as everyone was on parade at 6.30 next morning few questions would be asked. Not long might be spent in bed but sleep would be heavy and immediate.

Behind the shooting-parties and the balls, the polo tournaments and races, there was tension in Victorian India. Life was so competitive and so many boys were far from home with no one to confide in. Sometimes a lonely man would take to drink; there were suicides among subalterns who had got too deep in debt, murders among other ranks over some trivial slight or over bullying that had gone too far, when self-respect had been outraged too long and could only be restored by the shock of violence. Heat and loneliness, sexual privation and a sense of guilt, the sharp contrast of dry biting sun by day and often icy searing nights—these built up a pressure that for most could be released by games and the vigorous bodily life of camp and saddle and physical fatigue. But it was a special kind of life that made for close ties with those who shared it, a sharp sense of differences from those who did not.

Not quite a caste, something more than a class, not exactly a military order—the officers of the Victorian army were a society set apart. To be enrolled among them meant, for those who were going to stay, a long apprenticeship with no home of one's own and, when eventually family life was permitted, the prospect of long separations, of instant readiness for war. To a certain temperament, the surrender of personal choice is attractive; this applied in varying degrees to both officers and men, British and Indian. But, a soldier's surrender is intermittent; for most of the time, it is nothing like so complete as a monk's. Further, it brought many compensations, in public esteem, in the certainty of belonging to a privileged group and yet of being under orders. It set its stamp on a man; Younghusband has a story of an officer in England ordering a first-class railway ticket at the special rate to which officers were entitled. 'How do I know you're an officer?' said a pert Cockney voice. 'Look!' was the superb reply, as the officer lowered his chiselled features and glossy whiskers to the level of the booking-clerk's window. And there was no more argument.

But the arrogance of class, the champagne and the polo, the gorgeous full dress, the gold lace and aiguillettes, must be left behind at a moment's notice. And in war, the superlative qualities were courage and self-denial, of which neither officers nor privates, neither British nor Indian, had a monopoly. It was the knowledge of this essential dedication that sustained the military order and held it together. Let us end this section with the story of one Indian soldier, a Dogra sepoy, who won the Victoria Cross when that decoration was belatedly opened to Indians. It was in the First World War, after an attack on Turkish trenches had been repulsed with heavy loss. Sepoy Lalla found a major of his own battalion, wounded and unable to move, about a hundred and fifty yards from the Turkish wire, completely exposed to enemy fire. Lalla managed to drag him to a shallow depression, only a few inches deep but enough to provide some cover from rifle fire. Here he gave him first aid and patched up his wound. That done, he crawled out of cover and one by one dragged four of his comrades to this oasis of inadequate protection. Then he heard a voice, which he recognized as that of the Adjutant, calling for help. It was clear that the voice came from much closer to the Turkish trenches and from ground that was wholly exposed. The major ordered him not to go but he disobeyed the order and went. The Adjutant died of his wounds but before he died he dictated an account of what had happened. He had been hit and had lain in great agony, unable to crawl; an officer of the Black Watch had tried to get to him but had been killed; another sepoy had tried and been killed. Then Lalla appeared, gave him such first aid as he could, put his coat over him and lay between him and the enemy till dusk fell, when he slipped away explaining that he was going to find stretcher-bearers. After a little he came back, managed to get the Adjutant on his back and crawled to where the stretcher-bearers were. Then he went back and brought in the major and his four comrades.

That could only have happened in a service in which the men recognized in their officers a dedication that demanded from them too a response no less total.

2. The Indian Service

What sort of men made up the Imperial class and why did some of them choose India as their field of service? There was a generally accepted belief about this, often expressed in memoirs; like most such orthodoxies, it contains only a part of the truth. It is stated in his *Sabre and Saddle* by Colonel E. A. W. Stotherd; he thought that officers of the army in his boyhood were the product of a social system which, in the 1930s, he saw as already passing. They had been the younger sons of country squires, brought up to shoot and ride and enjoy the open air; they joined the army because it gave them that kind of life and the prospect of adventure and a sense of service. Some of them were attracted to India because the pay was a little better and expenses less, because the sport was excellent, and because there was a better chance of active service. 'A very good type of man', he went on, 'is attracted to the Indian services,' which is very important because 'natives of every class are extremely quick at sizing up a man and will respect and do anything for one they decide is what they call a pukka sahib.'

The conviction that all Indians shared their own views about class was always dear to British hearts. As to the social background of army

officers, Stotherd is right only of some. There were more who admired
the life of a country gentleman than were actually born to it. Some
were the sons of army officers who had spent their lives in the service;
some were the sons of the Indian Civil Service. Some were sons of the
vicarage, grandsons of the manor. Some came from entirely outside the
Imperial class. As to the choice between service in the British Army or in
India with Indian troops, there were several influences at work and pay
was certainly one of them. In 1862 the pay of a subaltern in the British
Army was reckoned at £95 and his minimum expenses at £157 annually.
These were official estimates by the War Office and it would not have
been pleasant to live on those minimum expenses; indeed, few regiments
would have been prepared to accept a newly commissioned officer
who could not find from his private pocket at least as much as his pay,
often two or three times as much. In some regiments, the amount
needed was much higher, and this continued until 1914. There were
contributions to the band, to the entertainment of guests in the mess
and in some stations to balls and race-meetings. Different uniforms
were required for full dress, mess-kit and parade order and all were
expensive, while an officer must buy his own chargers. This was apart
from private expenditure in the mess if he was to keep up with others
of his rank. In a cavalry regiment or such an infantry regiment as the
60th, the Rifle Brigade or the Durham Light Infantry, a man would be
expected to hunt or play polo. When Robertson was first offered a
commission in 1884, he refused it because a subaltern's pay was then
£120 a year while the regiment expected an officer to have at least
£300 a year of his own. This was the 16th Lancers and it would have
been less in some infantry regiments but as a troop sergeant-major he
did not feel he could go to infantry. Richards in 1905 speaks of a subaltern in the Royal Welch Fusiliers who actually confided in a private
soldier the loneliness he felt because he had only £200 a year of his own.
This was in India, where pay was more and expenses less. General
Twiss, who left Sandhurst in 1897, says that at that time, in general
terms, cavalry regiments, the Guards and the 60th required a man to
have at least £500 a year and British infantry of the line at least £100,
while in the Indian Army private means were not needed. But this was
not so of Indian cavalry, nor of all infantry regiments.

In the end, Robertson did accept a commission with a transfer to a
regiment in India. Here he was just able to manage until by constant
hard work he won a staff appointment but he notes laconically: 'It was
not altogether agreeable to be seen drinking water at mess when others
were drinking champagne.' Here we should be clear; pay for a British
subaltern with a British regiment in India was better than in Britain
by a proportion not absolutely constant but usually around 20 per
cent; in the Indian Army, for those who made India a career, it was

about 50 per cent better. Twiss as a subaltern in the Indian Army had £200 a year.

But it was not only financial reasons that influenced choices. Smith-Dorrien, of the British service, had been seconded to the Egyptian Army, where there was action, responsibility and quick promotion; none the less, he left Egypt for the Staff College because he 'wanted to become an up-to-date modern soldier, which he could not do by pre-historic warfare with dervishes.' On leaving the Staff College in 1888 he applied for employment in India, because he thought the life pleasant, because the standard of soldiering was 'high and practical' and only lastly because he had 'spent all his ready money and a bit more.' At least until the South African War, the view seems to have been general that India provided better military experience than Britain or Ireland. ('Oh, what fun it was, racing, dancing and hunting!' writes Smith-Dorrien of his earliest days at Dublin.) But army organization was very backward. There was no General Staff till 1906, and at the outbreak of the South African War there was not even one division in Britain organized as a striking force ready to move overseas.

Rawlinson visited France and Germany while at the Staff College in 1893 and noted that 'The Germans are miles ahead of the French in organization, equipment and training, and both are miles ahead of us. Our battalions are just as good as theirs ... but there we end ... India is better, but not good enough.' Organization in India did not really improve till Kitchener completed the work Roberts had begun, but the chances of active service were distinctly better. Something very like active service was permanent on the Frontier, flaring up occasionally into minor campaigns; Indian regiments belonging to the Punjab Irregular Frontier Force — 'Piffers' they were called — were certain of some Frontier experience and British infantry in India — not cavalry — stood a fair chance, at least a fifth of the infantry at any one time being in the north-west. The routine of the Frontier accustomed men to bullets and to taking cover, to guards and sentry duty which had real purpose, to night marches and sniping; it was all on a small scale by continental standards but it was infinitely superior to a field-day at Aldershot. And, leaving the Frontier aside, expeditions and campaigns from India during the half-century were fairly frequent.

There was the Abyssinian expedition of 1868 — wholly successful in its object and followed by immediate withdrawal; there were three expeditions to China. Then there was the Third Burmese War, a swift campaign followed by three years of a 'subaltern's war' in which small bodies — often companies or platoons — of British or Indian troops pursued in thick jungle Burmese parties whom they regarded as dacoits, or armed robbers, but who might also be looked on as the remnants of patriotic resistance. There were the Second Afghan War and several larger-scale Frontier campaigns, of which the most serious, the Malakand affair, kept the equivalent of four divisions busy for a year; there were expeditions to Aden and to Somaliland, several to the Persian Gulf, to the Lushai Hills, to Sikkim and Tibet. An officer of the British service might have gone with his regiment to Egypt, to Ashanti, to Zululand, to the Sudan, but, unless he was on the staff or his regiment was in India, his opportunities would have been fewer than in India. Winston Churchill put the point strongly; he had taken leave from his own regiment, the 3rd Hussars, which was vegetating in Southern India, and managed to get himself appointed a war correspondent in order to see the Malakand campaign. He complained that British cavalry was regarded as too expensive to risk on the Frontier, and thought this a mean, penny-wise policy; it might be far more expensive to send an inexperienced regiment into a major war. And he offers some personal advice:

'For a young man who wants to enjoy himself, to spend a few years agreeably in a military companionship ... the British cavalry will be suited ... To the youth who means to make himself a professional soldier, an expert in war, a specialist in practical tactics, who desires a hard life of adventure and a true comradeship in arms, I would recommend the choice of some regiment on the frontier, like those fine ones I have seen, the Guides and the 10th Bengal Lancers.' (This was Hodson's Horse.)

Either a light purse or an eager ambition might then be part of the reason for choosing the Indian rather than the British service. But it would be misleading to draw a hard and fast line, suggesting that poor men went to India and rich to the British service or that ambitious men went to India and idle did not. There was a good deal of overlapping. In both services there was a gradation; in both cavalry was more expensive than infantry, and in both services and both arms there were more expensive regiments and less. Family tradition counted in both and it would be easy to underestimate something which few mentioned, because it was hard to express, the element of romance. Temple bells and spicy scents meant something even before Kipling. In both, the regiments which expected their officers to have more private means usually had more applicants and sharper competition; they would also be quicker to get rid of a man they did not think came up to their standards. Sometimes he would feel lonely and on his own motion apply for transfer to another regiment or to a departmental corps; sometimes, it would be necessary for the Colonel to have a quiet talk with him. But it might take time. Western has a tale of a Piffer regiment under orders for active service to whom an unknown captain was posted without warning. They were horrified when they saw him; he was far too fat to keep up with them on the hills. They would have to detail

half a company to act as escort. Their efforts to get rid of him were
unavailing and he went to war with them but did not last long. He
took cover behind a stone that would have been quite big enough for a
lean, hungry Piffer, but his rump protruded and an Afridi sniper
nicked it with a bullet.

After South Africa Kitchener had asked to be Commander-in-Chief
in India. But his experience was almost entirely Egyptian, and when at
last he was appointed he asked advice of Birdwood, who, in spite of
belonging to Probyn's Horse, had been on his staff both in the Omdurman campaign and in South Africa. He asked that the Indian Army
should be explained to him. When he had heard it all, he said: 'I see.
You really have no Indian Army with esprit de corps as such. You have
a number of small armies ... each probably thinking itself superior to
the rest.' This of course was after Lord Robert's amalgamation of the
three Presidency Armies in 1895. What Kitchener meant was that there
were still Gurkhas, Piffers, the Hyderabad Contingent, a group of
former Bombay regiments, a group of Madras regiments and two quite
distinct elements, from before the Mutiny and after, among the
regiments that were called 'Bengal Native Infantry'. It was still very
much a Gothic cathedral of an army. 'What he would have thought of
the old system of Presidency Armies I cannot imagine,' added Birdwood. As we have seen, one of Kitchener's first reforms was to re-
number regiments consecutively and link them together; we shall
come back to the more important part of his plan, the organization in
peace of divisions which had trained together and were ready to move
away in war under a commander they knew. Perhaps there was more
unity than Kitchener perceived; certainly his renumbering did not
end the differences in regimental spirit. The Indian Army was, after all,
the child of the British and the British had been called by a continental
observer 'a loose federation of regiments'. Perhaps the differences can
best be illustrated by a closer look at two regiments which were markedly
different in their traditions.

3. Two Regiments

To say exactly when the Central India Horse began is like deciding on
the source of a river; several tributaries came together and one source
had had before the Mutiny a long existence of a kind peculiarly Indian,
more often engaged in persuading recalcitrant villages to pay their
revenue than in soldiering proper. But it was in the Mutiny that the
three main tributaries—Mayne's Horse, Beatson's Horse and Meade's
Horse—first came to be heard of; all three took part in many minor
expeditions in Central India, sometimes against petty chiefs who had

tried to take advantage of the general chaos to cast off their allegiance and refuse to pay revenue, sometimes against robber gangs or parties of mutineers. All three were bodies of irregular horse ready to fight mutineers. One of them eventually captured Tantia Topi. All three had been raised in the jungles of Central India — 'inaccessible regions ... the haunt of tigers and dacoits' — and, after several changes, they had settled down in 1861 as two linked regiments with two permanent headquarters 130 miles apart. It was their duty to keep order in Central India and to protect the Grand Trunk Road from Bombay to Delhi. The two regiments had one commanding officer, and this was an enviable post, not perhaps for a man who meant to be Commander-in-Chief, but for a man who enjoyed shooting tigers, an occasional brush with dacoits and some political work. It was pleasant to command two regiments of horse without much routine; each regiment had a second-in-command who did most of the commanding officer's work, and in any case, since they were irregular silladari regiments, routine was kept to a minimum. The commandant was also Political Assistant in charge of a number of small states, which had to be visited from time to time; it was his job to see that they did not lapse into dacoity* or oppress their subjects unduly and if he was good at this kind of relationship, the longer he stayed the more his advice would be sought. So men were glad to get the appointment; three of the early commandants were V.C.s and several were heroes of the Mutiny. Daly, for instance, had fought at Multan and Gujerat in the Sikh Wars, commanded the Guides on their famous march to Delhi and later commanded Hodson's Horse; other commandants were Sam Browne of Sam Browne's Horse, Watson of Watson's Horse and Probyn of Probyn's Horse.

'Silladari' by this time had come to mean something a little different from Jacob's day. The man who had no stake in the regimental funds and rode another man's horse — the bargir — became more and more rare and was abolished altogether in 1871. Now every man in the regiment rode his own horse. A trooper was expected to put down at least Rs. 200 and the regiment would lend him Rs. 150, which he would pay back in instalments. With this stake, he bought his own horse and equipment from regimental stocks and sold them back when he left. The men were linked in pairs and each pair owned a pony and a small tent and hired a *syce* (groom) or grass-cutter. The regiment could march at an hour's notice and after a day in the saddle meet at an agreed camp, where, if they were lucky, each pair would find the tent and syce and a pile of forage. The Government provided only carbines and ammunition. On large manœuvres, Lord Birdwood wrote later, elaborate

* Dacoity under the Indian Penal Code is robbery with violence or the threat of violence committed by a gang of five or more persons. But the gang might be of many hundreds.

previous arrangements were needed for British cavalry, but the silladari regiments could do everything for themselves and move at a moment's notice.

Thus the regiment was a joint-stock company, with a strong co-operative element, almost a family business; family links among the men were strong, and among officers too son often followed father. It was not entirely a legend that the latest joined subaltern might be greeted by the risaldar-major who had been his father's orderly and had held him in his arms as a baby. The silladar trooper drew thirty-two rupees a month when Birdwood joined, four times the pay of a private in the infantry, and about half what it would have cost the Government to keep a regular trooper. He was sure of something when he left the regiment and spoke with contempt of anyone who was not a silladar; 'naked he comes, naked he goes,'* they said of such a man, echoing the Anglican burial service. The officers at first were few; Beatson's Horse had a commandant, a second-in-command, an adjutant and a doctor. Later, there was one extra who was called a doing-duty officer, squadrons and troops still being commanded by Indian officers. As in other regiments, the number of British officers crept up, and the status of Indian officers was correspondingly reduced. But all Indian cavalry, and perhaps particularly the Central India Horse, clung with jealousy to the irregular tradition; they allowed their Indian officers all the responsibility they could, claiming that this had the double advantage of giving the British officer plenty of time for shooting and polo and encouraging in the Indian officer initiative and power of command.

This regiment prided itself on keeping close touch with its men, but not with that anxious paternalism into which some infantry regiments fell. Their historian says this arose naturally from their 'peculiar situation alone in the jungles'. 'The men were with us in all our doings ... and told us much about themselves ... on the polo ground or in the shooting camp they were wont to discuss all sorts of matters, even politics, with a frankness that would have astonished officers of most other regiments ... it is fair to express doubt whether officers of any other corps formed so close a touch.' That claim would certainly have been disputed, but it is a fact that few regimental histories, except perhaps the Guides', have so many reminiscences of Indian veterans, characters sometimes as eccentric even as the commandant's. One of the earliest was Barmadin, who in early days played a big part in the capture of a celebrated dacoit. The dacoit's party greatly outnumbered the soldiers, but they brought him back, the British officer winning a V.C., Barmadin the Indian Order of Merit. Though illiterate, he became a risaldar, or squadron commander; he was a Brahman and

* '*Nangā ātā, nangā jātā.*'

would touch neither wine nor meat but was known to be not only one of the bravest but quite the strongest man in the regiment. 'A favourite trick of his was to get two or three subalterns to hold on with all their strength to his ears, when he would shake them off as a horse shakes off a fly' — an exercise which calls up an engaging picture of relations between British and Indian officers.

It was long a tradition to hold a regimental shooting-party in April and May, interrupted by a return to the station for one day on May 1st, when every officer, man, horse and syce must be counted or his absence explained — a kind of check for audit. For the rest of these months, as many officers as possible went to the shooting camp. There were usually five or six guns present, two or three being guests; the usual bag was about twenty-five tigers, five or six lions, a few panthers or bears. On one occasion, a senior general came to inspect this unusual regiment. They entertained him in the mess and next day came the inspection, which after formal movements on the parade-ground was to take the form of an operation against an imaginary enemy in open country. The commandant posted a line of vedettes, then galloped back to the general, saluted and reported: 'The enemy has been located in a bush on the side of that hill, sir. I propose to attack.' He handed the general a spear and galloped off; the enemy was a panther, which after a brisk and dangerous gallop through broken country was speared by the colonel.

The Central India Horse admired reckless daring, were inclined to parade a light-hearted dislike of red tape and pipeclay, frequently showed an interest in Indian states and the ways of the country, achieved startling success at polo. In the increasing military professionalism of the century, when so many fell by the way, a regiment who had been brought up to hunt tigers and dacoits might have been expected to stand in danger of disappearing. But they had a succession of distinguished commandants with an ability to get the ear of the influential — and who could ever think of reducing a regiment which twice won the Indian cavalry tournament three times in succession?

'Hindu Horse! They think more of their polo cups than of their battle-honours!' This remark was made to me by a bigoted infantryman from a corps of great distinction. He had forgotten a Prussian writer's warning to his fellow-countrymen, that they should not underestimate the fox-hunting, polo-playing British officer. In two world wars, the Central India Horse, at whom that reproach might have been aimed with some justice in 1912, proved the point of the remark; in particular, they adapted themselves with extraordinary skill to motorized war in the Western Desert. They do not exactly represent Indian cavalry, providing rather an extreme example of tendencies shared by most cavalry regiments. It would be tedious for the general reader, and undue self-indulgence for the writer, to dwell on the long and varied history of Skinner's Yellowboys, the senior regiment of cavalry, and of Gardner's Horse, the 2nd Lancers, or on the distinctions of Hodson's Horse, Probyn's, Watson's, the group raised in the Punjab during the Mutiny; of the Frontier group, Sam Browne's, Prince Albert Victor's Own and the Guides; of the group from the Madras Army; of the Deccan Horse, from the Nizam's Contingent; and of the Bombay group, which included the 13th Lancers, the Scinde Horse and the Poona Horse. Each cherished its own traditions; they were magnificently different in their full dress, apricot yellow, blue and silver, blue and scarlet, scarlet and gold; but they had something in common. All prided themselves on the cavalry spirit—but it was the cavalry spirit with a touch of added zest and gaiety that came from their irregular ancestry. What the cavalry spirit meant was dash, elan, swagger, readiness to engage the enemy at once without counting the cost. The added touch is harder to identify; perhaps it was in a higher degree that peculiarly English affectation of achieving excellence without being seen to try very hard and of not being a specialist. It embraced an affection for eccentricity, as of the commanding officer who would not allow his men to march in step when dismounted because it was foreign to the cavalry spirit. In an Indian cavalry regiment, you were quite likely to find a man who painted in water-colours or wrote short stories in his spare time. You would find too that Indian officers took more responsibility than was usual in the infantry, that officers and men shared a common interest in their horses and that there survived, even after the silladari system came to an end, a comradeship of a rather special kind, a readiness to laugh at the same jokes as the men, a feeling that the regiment was a family affair.

'Gurkhas! Not one of them can talk five minutes without starting to tell you about: "My little men".' This, needless to say, was a cavalryman's gibe and the truth behind it was that in all the twenty Gurkha battalions the officers were filled with an intense pride in their men. If some Gurkha officers did talk of their men a good deal—sometimes with a kind of wonder, as of a young mother whose first-born really is the infant prodigy she had supposed, almost with the first twinge of surprise of a hen who has hatched out ducklings—it was mainly because they really were such admirable soldiers. It was perhaps also because they were so very different from their officers. Peasants from tiny holdings in the remote hills where even the cart is unknown, their view of life was as different as could be from the Victorian English, and even from the small landowners who went to silladari cavalry. And yet they developed the warmest affection for their officers and for British other ranks as well. But let us look briefly at the history of one Gurkha regiment.

The 2nd Gurkhas, as we may as well call them from the start, like the 1st and 3rd, were raised in 1815 before the Nepalese War had ended. Peace seemed in sight and some Gurkhas left the Nepalese forces and came over to the Company; they were joined by some men—not properly Gurkhas—from the districts that Nepal had overrun in the last twenty years. When the war flared up again, the commanding officer of the 2nd—it was then called the Sirmoor Battalion—reported that they were ready to march against Nepal, but they were not put to that test. They did go to the Maratha War in 1817, but did not get the opportunity to distinguish themselves particularly. They were soon back in Dehra Dun, which from the beginning they had made their headquarters, employed from time to time in subduing robber chiefs, and in one of these expeditions earned a distinction which fifty years later they were permitted to commemorate by a ram's head on their appointments. The chief they were hunting took refuge in a strong fort; the Gurkhas had no artillery and were outnumbered; they had to get in quickly, so they improvised a ram from a tree they cut down and trimmed with their kukris, brought it up to the gate of the fort under heavy fire and forced an entry. Soon afterwards they were at the second siege of Bhurtpore, where they won their first battle honour. But it was in the Sikh Wars, in particular at Aliwal and Sobraon, that they sprang into fame; at Sobraon, where their casualties on one day were one in four of the whole battalion, they attacked the centre of the Sikhs' strongly entrenched position and only fought their way in at the fourth assault. Sir Hugh Gough wrote that he had particularly noticed their 'determined hardihood and bravery'. 'Soldiers of small stature but indomitable spirit,' he continued, 'they vied in ardent courage with the grenadiers of our own nation.'

They were still an irregular corps. At first they had only three British officers, a commandant, an adjutant and a doctor to ten companies of Gurkhas; at Sobraon they were commanded by a captain, killed at the head of his men. It is not surprising that, in spite of Sobraon, there was some suspicion in 1857 when they joined the force marching to Delhi under General Barnard. They were the first Asian troops, they had very few British officers. But, as we have seen, they were present at Badli-ki-Serai, the first engagement before Delhi, advanced to the Ridge, and took up their position in the key post on the extreme right at the Hindu Rao's House. On that evening of June 8th the whole British force was exhausted by heat, but, when a large force of rebels advanced from the city, Reid led out his Gurkhas and two companies of the 60th Rifles and drove the enemy back. They had fought two engagements and had been sixteen hours under arms when they got back to their post; they were cheered by the British troops and from that moment they were accepted as comrades by all. They held

their post for 3 months and 8 days during which they sustained and
defeated 26 attacks. Companies of the 60th and the Guides held the
post alongside them, but were relieved after a week, taking turn about;
only the 2nd were under fire morning, noon and night for the whole of
the siege. They were 490 strong at the beginning and lost 327 in killed
and wounded.

From this time on, the battalion was famous. They were given the
privilege of carrying colours, which as irregulars they had not done;
they were given the privilege of a third colour, inscribed 'Delhi'. They
became a rifle regiment. They had formed a close friendship, officers
and men alike, with the 60th Rifles, and now, with the warm support
of the 60th, they petitioned that their private soldiers might be known
as riflemen not sepoys and that their clothing might be as like that of the
60th as possible. All this was granted. But rifle regiments do not carry
colours, so their blood-stained and shot-ridden colours were laid up —
to be brought out again and paraded nearly fifty years later in the
streets of London at the coronation of King Edward VII. Instead of
colours, they received from Queen Victoria a truncheon, a six-foot
staff of bronze and silver, surmounted by a crown supported by three
Gurkha soldiers. This takes the place of colours; when a recruit takes the
oath, he touches it and salutes. When the Princess of Wales, later to be
Queen Mary, visited the regiment in March 1906, she asked to see the
truncheon and took it in her hands to read the inscription. The Gurkha
officers standing by were delighted. 'Full of value before, now greater
virtue has gone into it,' they are reported to have said. But that is to
anticipate.

On an earlier royal visit, in 1876, the Prince of Wales, who was to
become Edward VII, inspected the 60th Rifles and the 2nd Gurkhas
together on the Ridge at Delhi. The 2nd became the Prince of Wales's
Own, and it was not an empty title; the Prince continued to take a
personal interest in the corps. They continued their friendship with the
60th Rifles, who presented them with a silver statuette of a rifleman of
the 60th with a rifleman of the 2nd; later they formed a similar friendship with the Gordon Highlanders. They were brigaded during the
Second Afghan War with the 92nd Highlanders, later the 2nd Battalion
of the Gordon Highlanders, and together attacked the centre of the
Afghan position at the battle of Kandahar, breaking their line and
capturing their guns in a charge that decided the day. Here an observer
heard a Gurkha shout: 'This gun belongs to the Second Gurkhas —
Prince of Wales!' and stuff his cap in the muzzle as a mark of possession.
The friendship with the 2nd Battalion of the Gordons was repeated
with the 1st Battalion (once the 75th) in another frontier campaign in
1897. Here again the 2nd Gurkhas led in a frontal attack on a carefully
prepared position; the tribesmen had built stone breastworks with

loopholes along the crest of a ridge near Dargai and held their fire till it could be most effective. The Gurkhas' casualties were sixty-eight in a few minutes, a big share of the brigade's losses. They were brigaded with the Gordons, Derbys and Dorsets, but it was with the Gordons that their links were specially warm. The Gordons brought down their wounded for them when they were ordered to a duty which prevented their doing it themselves. One night when there were 18 degrees of frost, the 2nd Gurkhas reached camp just before midnight, after fighting a rearguard action all day, to find the Gordons had put up their tents for them. At the end of the campaign, when the train carrying the 2nd Gurkhas went through Rawalpindi, the Gordons came down to the station to say goodbye to them. And later they too gave them a silver statuette of a Gurkha and a Gordon Highlander standing side by side. In the South African War, the 2nd Gurkhas volunteered every man a day's pay for the widows and orphans of the Gordons and the 60th.

The friendship of Gurkhas and British troops goes back as far as the second siege of Bhurtpore, where an observer noted the 'extreme good fellowship and kindly feeling' with which they regarded each other. 'A six-foot-two grenadier of the 59th would offer a cheroot to the little Gurkha ... the latter would take it from him with a grin' and the grenadier would stoop to let him light it from his own. 'The Gurkhas are patted on the back and called prime chaps'; the Gurkhas, after the assault, told their officers: 'The English are brave as lions; they are splendid sepoys and very nearly equal to us.' And Lord Roberts mentions the special friendship in the Second Afghan War between the 72nd Highlanders and the 5th Gurkhas and in particular an occasion in October 1879 when the Highlanders insisted on giving the Gurkhas their greatcoats for the night.

That campaign of 1897 had been severe, the 2nd at one stage being reduced to only 240 effective men. A letter from the Prince of Wales congratulated them on not merely maintaining their reputation but adding to it. It would be out of place here to mention the other expeditions of this regiment, not only to the North-West Frontier, but to the North-East—twice to the Lushai Hills and once to Manipur. Enough has been said to underline the difference in spirit of two regiments, one determined to rival the Guards in military professionalism, the other to display the cavalry spirit and to enjoy life between battles. But concern with honour was common to all.

There is a story of Kipling's, 'In the Presence', which is based on fact and makes the point exactly. It was the custom that four Indian officers should spend the summer on duty in London as Orderly Officers to the Sovereign. When King Edward VII died, one of the King's Indian Orderly Officers came from the 2nd Gurkhas, one from the 3rd

Gurkhas and two from the 39th Garhwal Rifles, who had been raised as the 2nd Battalion of the 3rd Gurkhas. These four asked that they should be allowed to mount guard at the lying-in-state. A soldier stood, motionless and with bowed head, at each corner of the catafalque. Three were Grenadier Guards, the fourth a Gurkha officer. The guards were at first relieved every hour but the men came off duty exhausted by the rigid immobility and distressed by a nervous twitching of the eyes; they had to watch the feet of the crowds walking by, step by step, in twos. It was arranged that the British guard should be relieved every half-hour; even so, they found the vigil an ordeal and each Grenadier did it only once; there were plenty to draw on. But the Indian Army had only these four and they agreed that they would stand guard each for a full hour, with three hours off. They could not in that short interval cook but took water and a little parched grain. They did not want much food. The time drew near when the coffin was to be moved to Windsor and it was decided that all wreaths of flowers should go there in advance. The four decided that they must themselves take to Windsor the wreath bought on behalf of the Indian Army—and there must be a fitting escort. Three would go and one would stand guard. The youngest took the watch for four hours at a stretch, while eight British guards were mounted and relieved. When the coffin had gone to Windsor, they ate and slept, and after a time their eyes ceased to twitch and they no longer saw feet trudging interminably past.

King George V sent a portrait of his father to Subadar-Major Santbir Gurung with a message: 'In memory of your vigil' and his own signature. It hung in the mess of the 2nd Gurkhas. But the vigil was kept, as Kipling says, for the honour of all the armies of India.*

4. Officers and Men

We have looked at two regiments, one being like all irregular cavalry regiments only more so, the other being like all Gurkha regiments only more so. The Gurkhas formed eventually ten regiments of two battalions each; they liked to feel that they played a part similar to that of the ten battalions of Foot Guards and spoke of themselves as the Gurkha Brigade. The 1st, 2nd and 3rd were raised on the western borders of Nepal, during or immediately after the Nepalese War; the 6th, 9th and 8th, which were not far behind them in seniority, were at first local levies, more like military police, and associated with Assam

* They are all Gurkhas in Kipling's story, but actually they were Subadar Baij Sing Rawat and Subadar Bude Sing Negi of the 39th Garhwal Rifles, Subadar Santbir Gurung of the 2nd Gurkha Rifles and Subadar Singbir Ghale of the 3rd Gurkha Rifles.

and the North-East Frontier. The 4th and 5th were raised at the time of the Mutiny, while the 7th and 10th and a number of second battalions date from the period under Roberts and Kitchener when Madras soldiers were being replaced by men from the north. All these regiments, as we have seen, grew increasingly particular about the kind of Gurkhas they recruited, but until the 'seventies, when they were allowed to send recruiting-parties into Nepal, they took hillmen from the Himalayan districts which the Nepalese had overrun before their defeat. Many of those who won fame for the 2nd Gurkhas at Delhi were in fact Garhwalis, a point mentioned by Colonel Shakespear in his history of the 2nd Gurkhas; he draws attention to the number of Garhwalis among those who were awarded the Order of Merit for Delhi. In 1887, as distinctions became sharper, the 2nd Battalion of the 3rd Gurkhas was raised, Garhwalis being drafted to it from other battalions and their places filled by Nepalese. Three years later this battalion was renamed the Garhwali Regiment and they became the 39th Garhwal Rifles in 1901, when their second battalion was raised. They continued to wear the Gurkha type of uniform and to carry the kukri.

It is an injustice to many other regiments not to linger on their history in the same way. It would be pleasant in particular to dwell on those infantry regiments which bore the name of some hero of the past — Wellesley's and Outram's in the Bombay service, Coke's and Wilde's in the Punjab Frontier Force — and on the extra zest which that association gave to their pride in their history and their determination to live up to the distinction of their past. It would be pleasant too to spend time on the special atmosphere of the Piffer regiments. But the diversity of the Indian Army has been stressed enough. Two general points stand out from the regimental histories. One is the growth of competitiveness; in the intervals of peace, success in the divisional hockey tournament, in the assault-at-arms or on the rifle range becomes more and more important. By the twentieth century, the note of the school magazine begins to be heard; 'meanwhile, the battalion was making a name for itself at hockey,' writes one of them; old boys in retirement will read with delight that the battalion has won the divisional shield for hockey three years running or in China defeated German, Japanese and Russian teams on the rifle range.

Of course, games were not really an end in themselves; they were played for bodily fitness and to encourage pride in the regiment, while musketry was a direct preparation for war. Indeed, most writers on the First World War agree that it was excellence with the rifle that saved the British Expeditionary Force in 1914; not so many remember that it was Roberts in India whose enthusiasm began a cult of the rifle that spread to England. Kitchener carried the competitive spirit further; he started an elaborate competition for excellence in all aspects of training and discipline: guard-mounting and moving in the presence of an enemy across country as well as performance with the rifle. In spite of his remark to Birdwood about armies each thinking themselves better than the others, Kitchener did more than anyone to encourage that very belief in battalions. How strong it was! And it was installed in the breast of every man. I remember in the 'thirties seeing a man of the 2nd Battalion, 12th Frontier Force Regiment resting by the side of a hill path; he was on his way back from leave and it was a twenty-mile walk and a 5,000-foot climb from railhead. 'Tired?' I asked him, not intending to tease him but merely to start a conversation. He sprang to his feet as though bitten by a snake. 'The 2nd/12th can never be tired!' he said indignantly. They had been the 2nd Regiment of the Frontier Brigade, later known as the Hill Regiment of Sikhs and later the 52nd Sikhs, and certainly were prodigious marchers.

Another point stands out from the descriptions of campaigns on the Frontier; in the judgments about the excellence of different regiments, the dividing line is between experience and the lack of it. In the early wars of the Company, it was taken for granted that the British were the stormtroops and the Indian would be used in support; it is not so now. Smith-Dorrien of the 95th, later the Sherwood Foresters, notes with pride that, when his men had been on the Frontier some time, a man from a newly arrived regiment said: 'The Derbys are as nippy as the Gurkhas!' Stotherd speaks of 'the Gordons, Sikhs, Gurkhas, Punjabis, all exceptionally fine fighting regiments', in contrast with newly arrived and inexperienced British regiments. Winston Churchill, who will not be accused of bias in favour of things Indian, remarks that the arrangements of Frontier Force regiments are excellent; 'they always have lances and bullets for an enemy, sandwiches and "pegs" for a friend'; and again, discussing the short-service system for British troops, he suggests that man for man they do not compare very favourably with experienced Indian frontier regiments. 'They are on average boys of twenty-one or twenty-two competing with Sikhs and Gurkhas of thirty,' he writes. It would be fatal, he thought, if they were seen to be inferior, and all that saved them from this was that they were generally one step ahead in the rifle they were armed with. In the course of twenty years the Enfield rifle had given place to the Snider, the Snider to the Martini-Henry and this to the Lee-Metford; each in turn was quicker to load, and fired a smaller bullet with a higher velocity and longer range. Until the Kitchener period, the new weapon usually reached Indian troops later than British, partly as a heritage of the Mutiny, partly for reasons of economy. But it is the use of troops that makes the point; for a frontal assault, a march round a flank, a rearguard action, it is the most experienced troops that are chosen and more often than not they come from the Indian Army.

Thus Britons of the imperial class had built up a strange partnership; they had turned schoolmasters, their pupils being young men of certain hardy peasant stocks and of certain fierce tribes, of whom they had made a highly efficient professional army. It was based on the concept of honour—the honour of the regiment and of the 'class' and the personal honour of a man who must respect himself and stand in honour before his comrades in the village and the army. But it stood or fell by the relationship of officers and men, who were linked together by enthusiasms that sometimes seem strangely boyish. Officers had often simply carried on the processes to which they had been subject at school, learning from their seniors what they passed on to their juniors. The company took the place of the house, the regiment of the school. They went on with cricket and hockey and football just as they had when they were prefects in their last year at school. New boys were now called recruits. The substance of some of the training was different, but the spirit was much the same.

It was an extremely successful experiment. Its influence was felt from Ethiopia to Hong Kong, from Lhasa to Singapore. Quite a small force was usually enough. Persia, whose King of Kings had once ruled the world, withdrew from Herat in 1857 and apologized for past affronts within five months of the declaration of war and dispatch of a force from India to the Persian Gulf. The Ethiopian expedition again was wholly successful. It is no part of the purpose of this book to discuss British imperial policy. Some aspects of it were morally indefensible, in particular forcing China to buy opium. But the broad effect is unassailable. Whether you like it or not, the Pax Britannica was a reality. For about a century, from Waterloo until 1914, the Indian Ocean, the Arabian Sea, the Bay of Bengal and the South China Sea were dominated by the Royal Navy; no great armament could cross those seas. And the land-masses whose shores those waters washed were all within reach of a small disciplined force which could be escorted from India by the Navy. Such a force could impose its will quickly wherever there was a nucleus of authority on which to act. This was a state of affairs making for stability and on the whole for peace and it would not have been possible without a reservoir of troops in India.

It would be hard to apportion between Britain and India the benefits of this system of defence. For one thing, it would be out of place to discuss here the total results for India of British rule. But internal peace and freedom from invasion are generally held to be benefits and these were secured for India for an unusually long period. On the other hand, Britain derived two clear benefits, the training of British soldiers and the ability to enforce her policies in the Indian Ocean. It was a settled convention that India should pay 'for her own defence'. But where could India's defence be said to begin and end? One military leader—

Lord Wolseley, once Sir Garnet—thought the best defence of India would be an expedition to the Black Sea and a landing that would threaten the lines of communication from Moscow to Meshed and Samarkand—a project that seemed visionary to Roberts and indeed to anyone who looked at the map. But no one questioned the view that defence is seldom best achieved by sitting quiet behind walls and that a diversion might be effective. In 1878, when the Russian threat seemed particularly likely to result in war, Disraeli and Lord Lytton, then Viceroy, moved Indian troops to Malta and Cyprus. It was a game of imperial chess in which India was the king—the object to be defended— but the Indian Army was also part of the apparatus of attack, say a rook and a knight, the queen being the Royal Navy. The move succeeded and both Britain and India benefited. At the time, hardly any Victorian doubted that the British could govern India much better than anyone else and that British rule was for India's good. Therefore the defence of India and British imperial policy were really inseparable; Hong Kong and Constantinople lay on the outer rim of the fortress's defences. India was the jewel for which the whole Empire existed and equally the pillar by which it was sustained.

A rough working arrangement was achieved. India paid for all troops in India; in the two world wars, Britain paid for all military expenditure above the peace-time level. But around that simple theme there were many complications; India paid, for instance, a share of the cost of training and pensioning British soldiers and eventually, after a long struggle, won a compensating grant for the value to British soldiers of training on the Frontier.

What did a sepoy in, say, the Ferozepore Sikhs or the Jat Regiment think of all this? Certainly, very little about imperial strategy or finance. Nor can he be supposed to have thought much, at this period, about the justice of the cause for which he fought. His only principle, an officer once told me, is 'There's the enemy!'* Of course, it was important to him that his family should get their remittances and himself his pay, but these were the basic conditions of service; once these were satisfied, where did his allegiance lie? It is easy to know what his officers thought about this, impossible to get any direct evidence from the mouth of the sepoy himself. There is no Sita Ram for this period. Most officers would have agreed with Sir George Younghusband that personal contact was what counted. The Indian soldier, he thought, bears a distant allegiance to the King, as a great and far-off god, but his real personal loyalty is to *his* Sahib, the commanding officer of his regiment, his squadron or company commander. There is hardly a book of memoirs from the Indian Army that does not stress this point. The young Birdwood, for instance was out in the country for some days with

* *'Dushman hai!'*

his squadron, travelling very light and sleeping in the open. One night it came on to rain—and winter rain in Northern India can be very chilling. But he woke warm and dry; three men's cloaks had been laid over him. 'You are *our* Sahib,' they said when he protested; 'it is our duty to look after you.'

But personal devotion to an officer is clearly not the whole story; it does not account for the behaviour of the Guides at Kabul or of a hundred other acts. In 1897, for example, 200 men of Rattray's Sikhs (later the 3rd Battalion, 11th Sikh Regiment) defended the fort of Chakdara successfully for six days against continual attacks by thousands of tribesmen, suffering heavy losses and extreme fatigue. One man, Sepoy Prem Singh, used every day 'to come out through the porthole of the tower, establish his heliograph and under a terrible fire from short range flash urgent messages to the main force. The extreme danger, the delicacy of the operation of obtaining connection with a helio, the time consumed, the composure required, these things combined to make the action as brave as any which these or other pages record.' The words are Winston Churchill's and he goes on to wish the Victoria Cross had been open to Indian troops. Such behaviour can hardly be put down directly to personal devotion to an officer; it suggests rather a feeling that honour demands courage and the exact performance of duty.

The performance of duty did not go unrewarded. There was an ancient tradition in India of rewarding soldiers by a grant of land. Until the end of the eighteenth century land was still uncultivated; there were also areas temporarily depopulated by famine or plague where such grants could be made, while the Mughals never hesitated to reward their servants by grants over the heads of existing cultivators, who continued to plough but with less chance of keeping much of the produce. As the nineteenth century advanced, population increased, famine was more often successfully dealt with, and pressure on the land in most of India increased until there was really no means of rewarding a soldier by a grant of land except at someone else's expense. And it was the keystone of British policy to establish a peasantry who felt their rights in land to be secure.

But the Punjab was an exception to this. Here immense stretches of land previously desert were made fertile by irrigation. And here colonies were established, colonies in the Roman sense, whole districts or subdivisions of small farmers, many of whom had served in the Indian Army or whose fathers or brothers or sons had been killed or wounded or had won distinction. It was a policy that convinced soldiers that this was a good Government to serve. It brought soldiers, and particularly Punjabis, together, emphasized their sense of difference from the rest of India, set them apart as the friends and servants of the Raj.

There was still no clash of loyalties between military duty and the spirit of national independence. Most British officers believed that it would be many years before India could be a nation; India was, they would say, a sub-continent of enormously different tribes, languages and peoples; there are 300 million Indians, 'for 298 million of whom the best system of government is the paternal ... one clean-bred perfectly honest and unbribable Englishman standing under a tree and according to his lights ... deciding cases on commonsense lines.' In contrast, 'the unsuccessful lawyers sometimes write and preach rank treason ... and represent nobody but themselves' and are in short 'poisonous polluters'. What exactly the Victorians meant by 'clean-bred' is hard to determine, but it is clearly in contrast with 'poisonous polluters'. This again is Younghusband and many others use much the same language.

At this point, the writer usually goes on to draw a further comparison with the good sepoy or the faithful Indian. It is extraordinary how often the name recurs of Sir Partab Singh, brother of the Maharaja of Jodhpur, 'a man whose name spells chivalry and all that is highest and noblest in the human race'. Thus wrote Smith-Dorrien, who adds that all Englishmen admired 'his bravery, his adroitness at every form of sport and especially pigsticking and polo and his wonderful stories, so modestly and picturesquely told'. Indeed, Sir Partab summed up the Englishman's idea of what an Indian should be: brave, courteous, dignified, handsome, manly—and devoted to Queen Victoria. Sir Walter Lawrence, whom, by a simple but effective gesture traditional among Rajputs, Sir Partab made his adopted brother, has written a most attractive account of him; no one can doubt that each felt affection and respect for the other. Towards the end of that account come these words: 'And here was Sir Partab, my brother by adoption, the great and courteous Rajput gentleman, telling me with terrible truthfulness that now he had only two things to live for, to fall leading a charge of cavalry against the foes of the King Emperor ... and to wipe out the Moslems from India.' Sir Partab was the ideal whom every good officer wished his risaldars or subadars to resemble; his first ambition was wholly admirable, his second to be tolerantly deprecated. It was wrong, but it was none the less one of the facts of life—and not altogether inconvenient.

Sir Partab's feeling for the Queen was essentially religious; he wore the brooch she had given him, with her portrait set in pearls, as an ikon (says Sir Walter) and after her death sat in meditation for two hours beneath her statue in a church. He had met her, he had known the best of English society in its heyday; he saw much to admire. To the Indian soldier the sovereign was far more shadowy; what he experienced in the army was a system of justice much less unpredictable than any to which he had been subjected before; what he saw was the colonel and the squadron or company commander. Any attempt to assess what he thought about them is based on what he wanted them to think and they wanted him to believe. There is a further bias, because in this period the man who sits down to write memoirs of army life has usually enjoyed an amiable ability to get on well with his comrades; there must have been black sheep whose names are not remembered. But the impression remains of a genuine liking on both sides.

About the middle of the century, officers begin more and more often to express their admiration for the Northerner and from the Mutiny onwards this is at the expense of the Hindustani. Sylvester, a man who spoke in very harsh terms of the old Bengal Army, speaks for many others when he records his pleasure at joining Probyn's Horse, with its Sikhs and Afghans: 'Every man had a bronzed hearty expression and a frank honesty of face which besides his stalwart figure, proclaimed at once how much he differed from the native of Hindostan.' 'In the days before the Great War,' wrote Stotherd sadly from retirement, 'there were many natives of India who were loyal trusty men and all of us had friends among them and liked that class.' Men have on the whole a tendency to like those who like them and there is no reason to doubt that in this case the feeling was generally mutual.

Just as it would be misleading to imagine a widespread national consciousness, it would be wrong to read back into Victorian and Edwardian times a resentment at inequality that is a feature of our own. Both Britain and India were societies based on class, highly stratified, and most people took this for granted. British privates and Indian sepoys alike accepted without serious question the wide differences that existed between the treatment of officers and men. Frank Richards in *Old Soldier Sahib* speaks of it with a wry recognition that this is something that exists and cannot be changed. Indeed, he thinks no battalion in the British Army had better officers than his; they were landed gentry from North Wales, Shropshire and the Welsh Border, with private means above the average for infantry of the line, interested, like their men, in sport, 'strict disciplinarians ... but far from treating us with contempt. The case was one of mutual trust in military matters and matters of sport but no social contact.' The Indian soldier had even further to go than the British before the democratic and egalitarian awakening that today is universal. He took it for granted that in any society there were great differences in social level; some men were leaders by birth, others were destined to be led. He felt neither envy nor discontent when he saw the mess dining-room, with its glittering silver statuettes and its gold centrepiece; the Persian carpets, the swords and pictures on the walls, the heads of oryx and ibex from the Hindu Kush, the great horns of bison, the snarling tigers and snow leopards. On the contrary, he was proud that his sahibs should be rich and should have expensive rifles and polo-ponies, provided only that they were 'far from treating him with contempt'; he was impressed that on the march, on manoeuvres and at war they should share the privations, the exhaustion and the danger. Rajput, Sikh, Gurkha or Pathan, the *jawan*, the young man, was as a rule by social background, by religion and upbringing, ripe for devotion to a leader and now he found one—someone utterly remote from himself in training, education and outlook, someone whom he could never aspire to equal, to whom he could never be a rival, but who nevertheless taught him, looked after him, played games with him, shared his enthusiasms. Just because the officer was remote, because there was no social contact, the jawan could give him a loyalty that accepted differences and did not ask questions. And he certainly did not resent paternalism, neither minute care for his well-being nor even the manner that sometimes went with it, the jocular, teasing manner of an uncle with a favourite nephew. 'This man', I was told in a Gurkha mess 'is wonderful at imitating a jackal; go outside the mess tent, Prem Bahadur, and make a noise like a jackal.' But Prem Bahadur was shy in the presence of a stranger.

It was the cardinal belief of British officers that their men would 'go through thick and thin for an officer they had decided was the right kind.' They would follow him to the death—and very often they did. Something in each responded to the other; each had his own code of honour and admired the other's. An engaging fidelity met an attractive and often surprisingly selfless leadership. A Spaniard turned American, George Santayana, is the unexpected source for a comment on the imperial class at its best. 'Never', he wrote, 'since the heroic days of Greece has the world had such a sweet, just, boyish master.' And never had master such response.

No doubt there was much beneath the surface. In the close-knit community of an Indian village, a subtle web of relationships is continually manipulated for personal advantage, for power, for prestige, and sometimes—it often seems—for sheer love of the game of intrigue and for pleasure in the skill required to manoeuvre the pieces. Can it be supposed that in the army these arts were wholly forgotten? 'In war, under stress, there is no one like the Sikh; work him almost to death and he is magnificent. But relax, give him leisure and a chance to recuperate, and he will start to intrigue—Jat against Khattri, Manjha against Malwa or village against village—he will find some way of making allies and enemies and trying to get promotion or favour.' So spoke a British officer from a Sikh regiment and in some degree it is true of all. But the mask of discipline overlay all this, the smooth face of a justice which tried to base itself on efficiency and seniority not kinship. The mask of discipline forced such manoeuvres into hiding; this surely is the basis of morality and society. What man is there who does not harbour within his bosom both a Jekyll and a Hyde? The bonds of society, military discipline, the criminal law, may require compliance with a code as coarsely framed as an income-tax return or a sociologist's questionnaire. An inner integrity may require something more exacting. But in either case, a mask goes on, and a man with any pretensions to decency will try to hide his lust, anger and greed, the distaste for his neighbour which sometimes clouds his benevolence. Which is *real*? The behaviour seen by the world or the impulses that have gone into hiding? No one can say; the question is meaningless. Both exist, and without the mask, the world is a scene of chaos and violence.

5. Kitchener and Curzon

Between the South African War and 1914 the Indian military scene was dominated by Kitchener, just as Roberts had dominated the 'nineties. The object of both was to make the army fit for war, but their characters could hardly have been more different. 'It would be difficult', Younghusband wrote, 'for an honest admirer of Lord Roberts to be an equally honest admirer of Lord Kitchener'; and one sees exactly what he means. Kitchener was essentially an autocrat; he made no attempt to conceal his dislike of politicians and from the time of his successful Egyptian campaign onwards he found it increasingly difficult to work in a team. He did not really operate as Chief of Staff under Roberts in South Africa and when he became Commander-in-Chief himself sent his Chief of Staff away on independent missions as much as he could. In Egypt he refused to keep copies of telegrams, preferring to rely on his memory. He refused appointments at the War Office, however exalted, saying he would rather sweep a crossing, the truth being that he knew that he would there have to accommodate his views to the Cabinet and other departments of State. In short, he was a commander who believed in personal command. And since he had a remarkable grasp of detail, he made his own methods work.

But he was a much more complex character than these points would suggest. He never married and revealed himself to few, but in the close circle of his personal staff he was ready to listen, to learn and to modify his views. His passion for flowers, for china, for interior decoration and landscape gardening were apt to surprise those who knew only the general; he disliked wasting time on continual social engagements, but when he entertained, everything must be perfect and he would personally inspect the flowers, the menu and the table arrangements. And yet this feminine perfectionism was married in him to something elemental and titanic; Curzon, who never understood Kitchener's point of view in the dispute with himself, did perceive this element of size in the man; in the course of their quarrel, he wrote that Kitchener was 'like a caged lion, dashing his bruised and lacerated head against the bars', and ten days later he wrote: 'He stands aloof and alone, a molten mass of devouring energy and burning ambition.' When he wrote that, Curzon was confident he had won a battle which he had really lost, but though he mistook the situation he had some understanding of the man he had to deal with.

The two in fact resembled each other in ambition, in determination and in mastery of detail but not much else. Curzon was an aristocrat by birth and conviction, intellectually one of the most unswerving authoritarians that ever walked. His sense of his high office was matched only by his sense of duty; nothing was too much trouble but nothing could be left to anyone else, because no one could be trusted to do it so well as Lord Curzon himself. This was the outward man; personally he was deeply dependent on his first wife and never quite recovered from her death. He was aware of the devastating acidity with which he habitually dealt with the ignorant and ill-considered opinions of others and daily resolved to be more charitable. But in this resolve he suffered a daily defeat; he simply could not forbear from tearing to pieces the shallow and inept opinions which were daily expressed to him. He was a kind man at heart; that is, he wished to be kind, but the brilliance of his intellect would not allow him. He saw his work in the light of an imaginative vision; he saw the greatest Empire in the world, the Empire of Asoka and Akbar, the Viceroy its glittering apex, Maharajas in pearls and diamonds in obedient ranks, ancient splendours taking new life in the new glory of the British Crown. Its glory was more splendid than those that had gone before because it was based on justice and benevolence. The army was the instrument by which the mighty fabric was sustained but it must come, taut yet supple, ready to the hand of the sovereign's representative. It must never fall below the heights of perfect conduct demanded by justice.

Lord Curzon made himself extremely unpopular with the army, in particular with British troops in India, before the dispute with Kitchener arose. There can be little doubt that at this period most British troops felt both contempt and dislike for Indians in general; they had been brought up on stories of the Mutiny, and the Indians with whom they came in contact, the hangers-on round cantonments, hawkers and pimps, were not people to inspire respect. Soldiers made few distinctions; they saw a nation of hawkers and pimps. Frank Richards speaks again and again of a kind of casual brutality of outlook; cuffs and kicks were the way to get service and unless there were plenty of cuffs and kicks the natives would get cheeky. There were several 'incidents' and Lord Curzon made it clear that he thought they should be dealt with severely; he wanted justice but he contrived to give British troops the impression that for him they were always in the wrong. Richards says that they felt it was no longer safe to go on shooting-parties; they might be attacked by villagers and if they defended themselves the Viceroy would insist that they should be punished.

The Viceroy, of course, was right in principle. Soldiers ought to treat all civilians as human beings with rights and responsibilities. But it is not easy to change attitudes. He could no doubt have made some improvement if he had consulted the Commander-in-Chief and worked through him and his officers. But he had not the knack of getting people to work *with* him and he alienated officers as well as men by acid, sarcastic comment. He was right—it must be said again—in principle, frequently unwise in method. The climax came when a drunken frolic at midnight ended in the death of an Indian cook. There was an inconclusive court martial and the accused was acquitted. No doubt facts were concealed and lies were told; perhaps not enough effort was made to get at the truth. The general who forwarded the proceedings accompanied them with comments and a summary which Smith-Dorrien, then Adjutant-General, thought missed the point and were ill-advised. Curzon dealt with this in 'a nice little minute covering some sixty or seventy sides of foolscap in the Viceroy's own hand-writing simply rending the general in question and tearing him limb from limb'. 'As an example of powerful expression in perfect language, of hard-hitting and savage invective, of laborious scrutiny and biting metaphor, I cannot imagine a more perfect model,' wrote Smith-Dorrien, 'but as a summing up by a ruler who could not be answered back, it did not commend itself to me.' Since there could be no conviction, Curzon insisted that the whole regiment should be punished, and this produced a surge of feeling against the Viceroy among British officials and particularly military officers and their wives. It was openly expressed by the spectators at the Coronation Durbar—the Curzona-tion, as it was called. This was something without precedent in British India.

Curzon's unpopularity was part of the background to Kitchener's arrival, but it was not all. The convention had already been established that the Commander-in-Chief should come alternately from the Indian and from the British service. Sir William Lockhart, of the Indian service, had died in office in 1900. Kitchener was the obvious successor but was busy in South Africa; Sir Power Palmer, an Indian cavalryman, was given the acting appointment, and, as the South African War dragged on, he held it for three years and a half. He was thus in a weak position and he appears to have been an amiable and accommodating man, ill-equipped to deal with so masterful a Viceroy

as Lord Curzon; he resigned himself to keeping the seat warm for
Kitchener, but did not sit idle. He introduced several measures which
were frustrated. Smith-Dorrien writes that he was 'snubbed on every
possible occasion' and 'the tone of the minutes on his recommendations
was hurtful and trying.'

The Indian Army, once ahead of the British, had fallen behind
since the South African War. It had been a war in which Indian
troops, and particularly Indian cavalry, could have been used to
great advantage. But it was a period when the rule of Europeans was
almost world-wide and in most parts of the world it did not depend on
numbers but on the aura of invincibility. To raise 'native' troops in
South Africa to fight the Boers might have showed them the way to
fight the British too; it was agreed that it should be a 'white man's
war'. Indian troops had been moved to the Mediterranean in order to
fight, or at least threaten, the Russians and it could not be argued that
they would never be used against a white enemy. It was only on the
quite illogical ground that all 'natives' must be lumped together that
there could be any reason for not using them against the Boers; it was
out of respect for the prejudice we shared with our enemies that they
were left behind, not for any reason internal to India.

The lessons of the war had therefore still to be applied to the Indian
Army and Roberts had sent Smith-Dorrien to India as Adjutant-
General for that purpose. There was no General Staff and of course no
Chief of the General Staff; the Adjutant-General was at that time the
senior staff officer to the Commander-in-Chief. But after a few months
Smith-Dorrien asked Palmer for permission to resign his post; he felt no
progress was possible. This was partly because of the Viceroy's obstinate
determination that on every military point he would make up his own
mind rather than take advice, partly because the arrangements for
obtaining the Viceroy's approval were at best cumbrous and could
only be made to work at all in an atmosphere of determined goodwill.
Palmer begged him not to resign; he agreed to postpone his departure
until after Kitchener's arrival, but only on condition that he was
allowed to go to London and put the whole case before Kitchener and
Roberts. This he did, apparently without Curzon's knowledge;
Kitchener therefore arrived in India fully briefed on the difficulties that
Palmer and Smith-Dorrien had been meeting and already convinced
that he, and he alone, should be the Viceroy's military adviser.

The system to which he objected, and which was to be the outward
cause of the dispute, had grown up partly as a matter of convenience
when there were three armies and three Commanders-in-Chief. The
Viceroy needed one military adviser and one who would be always by
his side. A Commander-in-Chief necessarily spent a great deal of his
time inspecting troops away from headquarters, and it was therefore

convenient that there should be an Army Member of the Viceroy's Council who was not a Commander-in-Chief. There was also a constitutional point. In the United Kingdom, the Commander-in-Chief, often a member of the Royal Family, was quite separate from the Secretary of State for War. The latter shared with his colleagues in the Cabinet responsibility to Parliament for military policy. The Commander-in-Chief was in theory a military technician, responsible for carrying out the wishes of the Government; he was in an especially strong position through his relationship with the Sovereign but Parliament held the purse-strings and in the last resort he could only carry out Parliament's will. He was like an architect building a house for a wealthy client.

In India, the Viceroy as Governor-General ruled on behalf of Parliament. He had an Executive Council and most important decisions were taken in Council, but he could overrule his Council. Each member of Council had a department under him which sent out the instructions of the Government of India; these letters might be signed by a young man with only five or six years' service but they were legally decisions of the Governor-General-in-Council; whoever signed the letter had either taken the approval of the man next over him or judged that it fell within the range of agreed policy. In the case of, say, the Home Department, all was clear; there was a chain of responsibility from Under-Secretary up to Deputy Secretary, thence to Secretary and thence to the Home Member. Each acted on behalf of the Government. It seemed therefore logical that there should be an Army Member and an Army Department on just the same lines—and the place of the Commander-in-Chief might, therefore, on purely constitutional grounds, have been expected to be outside the Viceroy's Council, just as the Commander-in-Chief in England was outside the Cabinet. Here too, from the point of view of constitutional propriety, he should have been the supreme technician carrying out the policy of the Governor-General-in-Council, responsible to the Army Member and through him to the Viceroy and to Parliament.

But this would never have done for India, which was a pyramid of officials; no one but the Viceroy could be over the head of the Commander-in-Chief. Throughout India these two were known as the Lord of the Realm and the Lord of War.* India had been won by the sword; Clive was not forgotten. So, though there was an Army Member, he was a soldier and *junior* to the Commander-in-Chief. Both had seats on the Council, but while, outside the Council Chamber, the Chief bulked in everyone's mind far higher than the Army Member, the latter had officially an enormous advantage. The Commander-in-Chief

* *Mulki Lāt* and *Jangi Lāt. Lāt* is the English word 'Lord'; *mulk* and *jang* are Persian nouns turned into adjectives.

could give a military order but for anything that needed the sanction of the Government of India he must go cap-in-hand to the Army Member, his junior, who might put it to the Viceroy with a recommendation that it should be turned down. To make things worse, part of the military machine — ordnance, the supply of stores, tents, food, ammunition, mules, horses, carts — came directly under the Army Member.

Once again, it will make things clearer if we look forward to the 'thirties, when I joined the Army Department as an Under-Secretary. The division of the military machine between supply services and fighting services, obviously indefensible, had vanished. The Commander-in-Chief had no longer to ask someone else for small arms ammunition. Ordnance factories were under his own hand. Nor were there two military members of Council. The Commander-in-Chief had by this time two functions: he was Defence Member of the Viceroy's Council — a colleague and adviser on defence and the politics of defence — and also Commander-in-Chief, the supreme technician. As Member, he was advised by the Secretary to the Government in the Defence Department, an officer of the Indian Civil Service, who also had access to the Viceroy; as Commander-in-Chief, by the Chief of the General Staff and three other Principal Staff Officers, the Adjutant-General, the Quartermaster-General and the Master-General of the Ordnance. There was also a senior officer of the Indian Civil Service as Finance Adviser, Military Finance, who had a direct responsibility to the Finance Member of the Viceroy's Council. Any proposal which needed the approval of the Government was worked out by the military staff in the first place and discussed with the financial representatives and then came to the Army Department for approval. Clearly it was a system which required tact and a readiness to co-operate; it did in fact work because both chains of authority met in one man and the Commander-in-Chief generally remembered to distinguish between his two roles; if he did not, he was reminded by the Secretary, for whom he always had a respect.

The system which Kitchener found, though slow and cumbrous, had also generally been made to work, mainly because those at the top had been determined it should. But lately the Viceroy's acid sarcasm had created in the Army Department a contempt for suggestions from the Commander-in-Chief; a carefully considered proposal, which had the Commander-in-Chief's approval, would be turned down, after long delay, by a curt note that the Government of India did not approve, sometimes signed only by a captain on the Army Member's staff. Delays had grown more and more outrageous. An example is quoted of a request for small arms ammunition taking eleven months before it was complied with — and then only in part. Within three months of his arrival, Kitchener sent the Viceroy a memorandum stating that the

dual control of the army would be fatal in war; he wanted the Army
Member and the Commander-in-Chief united in one person and the
supply system to come under military control.

Everything in the background just sketched would suggest that a
head-on collision was inevitable. The only grounds for hope that it might
be peacefully resolved were that Curzon had genuinely wanted
Kitchener to come to India; he believed that the military machine
needed complete overhaul. 'I see absurd and uncontrolled expenditure;
I observe a lack of method and system; I detect slackness and jobbery ...
I lament a want of fibre and tone,' he had written—and he thought
Kitchener was the man to deal with all these evils. What he wholly
failed to understand was the strength of Kitchener's support in England.
Kitchener had been a popular hero after Omdurman and Khartoum;
he had won a second hero's welcome after the South African War. It
is easy in the 1970s to forget the hysterical enthusiasm which was
lavished, in the heyday of jingoism, on a successful soldier; neither
football stars nor popular singers have quite so wide an appeal today.
Kitchener was a political asset to any Government and if he were to
resign it would mean a heavy loss of votes. This was not true of Curzon,
an intellectual and an aristocrat with no popular appeal. This Curzon
never grasped; he was confident of his own position as the most
brilliant of the Viceroys and also quite confident that the advantages of
having a separate Army Member would be clear to Kitchener with
more experience. He asked him to wait till he had watched the system
working for a year.

Kitchener agreed and flung himself with enormous energy into his
work of reorganization. His scheme for renumbering regiments consecutively and weeding out the least efficient, largely designed by
Birdwood, we have already looked at. More important was his organization of divisions. The principles were simple. The army's task was war;
keeping the peace was essentially for the police, soldiers being used for
internal security only as a last resort. The first task was to calculate
how many troops were needed for this purpose; the rest must be ready
for war. They must be organized in peace in divisions and brigades, the
formations in which they would go to war, and they must be trained by
the man who would command them in war. War was still visualized
as on the North-West Frontier and since there were two ways into
Afghanistan—one by Peshawar and the Khyber, one by Quetta and
Kandahar—the divisions should be placed in echelon, behind one
another, like the steps of two ladders, near the two lines of communication, one from Calcutta through Lucknow to Peshawar and one from
Bombay through Mhow to Quetta. Each line made an Army Command,
a Northern and a Southern. Thus there would be nine divisions in the
field force, all ready to march—while under the old scheme, there had

been only four, which would still have had to be assembled and given a commander and staff when war was declared. Army Commanders, under Kitchener's scheme, must not waste their energy on administration, but must concentrate on training; their staff should be small and they should be always on tour. Divisions—five in the Northern Command, four in the Southern—should send their administrative problems direct to Army Headquarters.

This was radical and far-reaching; troops had been distributed in the 'sixties with the Mutiny in mind; in 1904 the arrangement looked higgledy-piggledy. The plan met with Curzon's general approval and the details began to be worked out and put into effect; had it not been for this, it would not have been possible to send troops from India to France in 1914. There was, however, a weakness in the plan, due to Kitchener's obsession with his own success in the campaign of Omdurman. He believed an Army Commander should be freed from administrative detail—but administration, however wearisome, is inescapable and must be done somewhere. By freeing his Army Commanders he placed a heavier burden on the divisions and the flow of work from them to Army Headquarters was too much; this was one reason for the administrative breakdown in Mesopotamia.

With this exception, the scheme was brilliant; it was enough, if nothing else had been done, to earn posterity's gratitude. Kitchener was also responsible for the Staff College at Quetta; this was run on similar lines to Camberley, with some British service staff and some pupils at Quetta, some Indian at Camberley. The Staff College unquestionably helped India to absorb the lessons of South Africa and to acquire some readiness for war on quite a different scale from the Frontier campaigns. Equally important, perhaps, was Kitchener's firm and frequently repeated opinion that the Mutiny must be forgotten. Weapons must be identical for British and Indian troops, but it must be recognized that their supply problems were different. There would therefore be administrative advantage in brigading British battalions with British, Indian with Indian; thus there would be one British brigade and two Indian in a division. In modern war their differing virtues could best be used in brigades—the stolid lack of imagination and the parade-ground precision of British troops, who never know when they are beaten, being contrasted with the mobility of the Indian troops, who will move easily over ground the British would find formidable. This idea, briefly adopted, was abandoned until Slim returned to it in Burma; more fruitful was his approach to the problem of higher commissions for Indians. He was cautious, seeing British prejudice as the objection, but he was in favour of a beginning with Military Colleges.

Having launched his redeployment of the army so as to provide a field force of nine divisions, Kitchener came back to his attack on what he saw quite simply as divided control. 'In war, the system must break down and unless it is deliberately intended to court disaster ... through divided counsels, divided authority and divided responsibility ... it must be abolished.' He was determined to carry his point or resign his command. Throughout the whole dispute, neither party was able to see the other's point of view. To Curzon, the constitutional aspect was paramount. Soldiers should be outside the governmental system; for English constitutional thought, this had been a dogma since the time of Cromwell. The Viceroy, representing Crown and Parliament, must have the last word on military policy and he must have advice that was independent of the main military machine. His argument would really have been stronger if his Army Member had been a civilian; to take advice on the Chief's proposals from another soldier, who was his junior, was surely to open the way to confusion.

Had Curzon realized that the Cabinet would prefer his resignation to Kitchener's—a possibility which does not seem to have occurred to him—he might have been wise to stick to his constitutional point and to offer to transfer all the executive functions of the Army Department to the Commander-in-Chief. He would then have been on strong ground and would have deprived Kitchener of the absolutely unanswerable point that a fighting force must not be divided from its transport and supplies. He might then have obtained as Army Member a civilian colleague who would have made himself master of all the Commander-in-Chief's proposals at an early stage and who could have helped the Chief to a full understanding of the financial and political implications. This Kitchener might well have accepted. But Curzon thought his own case unanswerable, and was helped in this illusion by several minor triumphs of dialectic. Much bitterness was added because on one occasion Kitchener said he had not seen a paper which was in fact on the file, several inches deep. Curzon's infallible eye detected it and he drew attention to the error in his usual scathing terms. He could not believe that anyone could have failed to delve to the bottom. Kitchener took it that he had been charged with a lie, and momentarily regretted a change in manners which prevented his calling Curzon out. Thus Warren Hastings preserved the distinction of being the only Governor-General to fight a duel with a member of his Council.

The drama proceeded, a stage being reached when the Viceroy's staff and the Chief's were not on speaking terms. At last the matter was taken in Council, the Viceroy's views being expressed in one of his long brilliant minutes, crushing every opinion on the other side. Kitchener refused to speak; he read a brief note recording his dissent and repeated that he must resign if he did not have his way. All the rest of the Council voted with the Viceroy and it was then that Curzon wrote of Kitchener as a molten mass, alone and defeated. The affair seemed to be over and Curzon victorious. But the Secretary of State dramatically reversed the situation, proposing a 'compromise' which in fact gave Kitchener most of what he wanted; a shred of the old system remained — to save Curzon's face — in the shape of a civilian Supply Member, who continued some degree of divided control, but had no right to advise on military matters. Curzon was deeply wounded but said he would accept if he might choose his own man as Supply Member. But again he was rebuffed and in the end it was he who resigned. The Supply Member did not last long after Curzon went; Kitchener had won on all points. Curzon's successor, Lord Hardinge, worked amicably with Kitchener, who intended to succeed him and very nearly did.

The drama of the dispute overshadows the period; the size of the two contendants, the uncompromising vigour of their views, the violence of their passions, obscure its historical importance. Kitchener's greatest contribution to readiness for war, his reorganization of the army in India in fighting formations, did not depend on his victory, but there can be little doubt that the Indian fighting forces in 1914 would have been far less effective if he had been defeated. On the other hand, Curzon's partial defeat on the constitutional point held a threat for the future of independent India. A Defence Minister who is also Commander-in-Chief is a formidable figure in a young democracy; fortunately the ghost of Cromwell had walked so long and shed such fear in the hearts of all English Parliamentarians that the leaders of independent India, who had learnt their democracy in England, did not allow the dual role to survive.

It is something of a paradox that Roberts, who had never forgotten the Mutiny and who was so firmly opposed to commissions for Indians, should have been so warm a character in his personal relations and have inspired such affection among Indian troops. Kitchener, who knew no Indian language, never won their hearts and though he insisted that the Mutiny should be forgotten, this was rather in the interest of a smooth-running machine than for any appreciation of Indian capabilities or feelings. The Indian Army was still a network of human relationships but every step towards readiness for war made units a little more interchangeable, a little more mechanical.

Thus 1914 approached and the end of the Pax Britannica. There were rumblings in the distance, warnings of what was to come, signs of active discontent among the civil population, still confined to a few, still mainly urban and middle-class; there was a groundswell of feeling, both in Britain and in India, that change must come, that India must find means of governing herself, that Indians must themselves take the high posts that were so far reserved for the British. But the clash of loyalties that this would bring so far hardly existed for the Indian Army. Muslims had sometimes known it when fighting tribesmen on the Frontier; for the others, so far there had been no enemy with whom they could feel any fellowship. The ties of the regiment, of comradeship with each other, of trust in their officers, were still supreme.

Part V
Under Which King . . . ?

XVI

Change on Two Fronts

In 1914 the Indian Army consisted of about 150,000 men; it was highly professional and extremely efficient for its limited purposes, of which the most obvious was keeping the peace on the North-West Frontier. About a fifth of its strength was cavalry, which still meant horses; its transport was based on mules. It was armed with rifles, not quite up to date. Aircraft were unknown; it had virtually no artillery. It increased tenfold in numbers in the First World War and went back to its old strength between the wars. By 1945 there were 2,500,000 men on its books. Its men had learnt to fight in thick jungle as well as in mountain and desert; they had become adept in trench warfare, they drove tanks and armoured carriers, there were machine-gun battalions, close support battalions and artillery of all kinds; they relied on trucks and Jeeps more than on mules; they had been trained in amphibious operations from ships, and in parachute-jumping; they had learned to live on rations dropped from aircraft.

So far, much the same might be said of the British Army. In 1914 its men too were still, by contrast with continental armies, long-service professionals; they were still armed mainly with the rifle and mainly supplied by mule; cavalry still meant horses. More of them than of the Indian Army could read and write, more came from backgrounds in which machines played a part. But, from a narrowly military point of view, the differences were marginal. In a wider sense, however, if the whole background of each army is taken into account—in relation to the State it served and to the society to which its soldiers belonged—then in the course of those thirty years the Indian Army had had to face stresses for which there was no counterpart in Britain. Its men had had to adjust themselves to change on two fronts.

In Britain the nation was embodied in the State and loyalty to the State was almost universal; treason was the blackest of crimes. In India there were ties to religious faith, to the family, to the caste-group, to the village, not yet to the nation. But there was another, not the least strong, for which there is no exact word in English. It is a personal relationship, implying service and devotion on one side, on the other the duty to feed and protect. Something like it once existed in Britain;

Highlanders looked to their clan chief for protection and gave him their devotion in much this way; the kempery-men of a Saxon or Danish leader would have understood it. 'Feudal' does not exactly express it, because it need not be service for land. It is personal and often hereditary; it was strong until lately throughout Northern India, perhaps stronger in Rajputana than anywhere else. It was never stated in so many words, but it arose when one man in effect said to another: 'I am your man; I shall serve you in any way you command and you will protect me against everyone else.' It ran through Indian life; when peasants left the village they carried it with them and usually transferred their allegiance to some new authority. If a man entered Government service, he still looked to a patron to whom he would give loyalty and from whom he would expect help and protection.

This combination of loyalty and expectation was strong in the Indian Army. The recruit brought it with him from the village and gave his allegiance to the regiment, to the army, perhaps especially to a single officer, perhaps to all the officers of the regiment; eventually, but, in a remote and shadowy way, to the sovereign. It was something officers and men both understood without words. It knit them in a close bond, from which the rest of the world was excluded. To be disloyal was to be a *badmash*, a 'bad character'. For a soldier, disloyalty was treason, the worst of all offences. For him, there was no half-way house; he must give total obedience, total loyalty, total devotion. Even in the world outside the army, where it was expected that men should intrigue for power and wealth, the soldier classed them in two simple categories, those who were faithful to their allegiance and those who were not — the rebellious, who were thieves or murderers or dacoits. It was like that in the stories they had heard in the village under the pipal tree; kings were good if they dealt firmly with rebels, rebels were bad by definition. Politics meant fidelity or the reverse to the raja or sultan; it was part of the tradition of Hindu and Muslim alike.

Think, then, how hard it was for a soldier to understand a world in which rebels — men who actually preached disobedience to the Government and were very properly put in jail for it — were taken out of jail and welcomed at the Viceroy's House. And it was even more perplexing when there was a provincial Government made up from the Indian National Congress, people who waved a flag that was white, green and orange instead of red, white and blue. It was hard to explain. I was District Officer in Garhwal when Congress came into power in the United Provinces in 1937. For me, it was not difficult because I had gone to India believing that power would gradually be handed over; it was a stage on the way. But I could not explain this to Honorary Lieutenant and Subadar-Major Makar Sing Kunwar, who had led a platoon in France at Neuve Chapelle, who had won the Order of

British India. He had been the confidant and adviser of many colonels; he must have known the men who spent that long vigil by the catafalque of Edward VII. He was an old man, widely loved and respected. He sat at home now and read the sacred books of his people and guided the affairs of the pensioners of fifty villages. He saw politics in the simplest terms. 'Why', he asked, 'has the Government allowed these "bad characters" of Congress to have power?' There was only one Government as far as he was concerned; Lucknow was subordinate to Delhi and Delhi to London, but it was one chain of command, as from regiment to brigade and division. I told him we had had a Labour Government in England and it had worked quite well; in fact, no one had noticed much difference and the Labour politicians had learnt a great deal. But even that was hard to explain; he pictured Ramsay MacDonald and Ernest Bevin as coolies. Dominion Status was neither one thing nor the other; if it meant those bad men in Congress, he did not like it. 'I don't like it,' he said, over and over again, in his rather nursery Hindustani.

Some of his British officers found it almost as difficult. One of them, travelling in the hills to visit old pensioners and to look at recruits, wrote to me of one of the most humiliating days of his life. He had seen a group of schoolchildren with Congress flags coming towards him along the narrow mule-track and had been so embarrassed that he turned off the track and hid from them in the one-room office of the District Board. But they thought this funny, surrounded the building and laughed at him. He could no more understand than old Makru that there might be democratic processes in India and a new Government which might wish for independence. It was the flag that disturbed him; to wave it was disloyalty, which was treason and anathema.

It is not to be supposed that for the rank and file this divergence of loyalties was an anxiety all the time. With the regiment, everyone was too busy with training and games and inter-company competitions to sit and think; loyalty here was simple. It was when they went on leave that they were puzzled. For the new kind of Indian officer it was another matter. In 1914 there had been virtually no Indian officers above platoon commander; between the wars, a beginning was made with Indian officers who would replace British. They were at first trained at Sandhurst and later at Dehra Dun. By 1939 they were becoming majors; by 1945 there was a sprinkling of brigadiers and colonels and majors in every battalion. For them it was much harder to get away from the problem. To them we shall come back later.

It will be convenient here to remember in outline the political background. In 1909 there were reforms, instituted by John Morley as Secretary of State and Lord Minto as Viceroy, which today seem far from radical but to the English in India at the time seemed revolutionary. There was a growing nationalism in the towns and among the educated, a frustration, a feeling that British rule had become stifling, oppressive and unnatural. But this had as yet hardly touched the villages or the landowners, particularly in the north and west, while even among professed nationalists there were still very mixed feelings towards Britain. A very small minority were bitter and uncompromising. Most had acquired from their English education a reverence for the idea of Parliamentary government; they understood Mill and Gladstone and Morley; often they had an affection for English literature, sometimes for some British schoolmaster or lecturer. As a rule, they were so far from rebelling against British principles that they wanted to apply them more consistently. They could not see why democracy should stop at Dover; they wanted India, like Canada and Australia, to share in the devolution of power. They disliked what they had heard of Prussian rigidity, of German doctrines of the super-man and the master-race; in 1914, some had sufficient faith in British generosity to believe that help in time of trouble would be recognized when peace came. Gandhi offered his services and raised a Field Ambulance Corps; Gokhale thought that the Indian Army would in the end do more to help India's progress than any number of Royal Commissions.

Among the princes, Sir Partab of Jodhpur—the perfect Rajput, every Englishman's ideal of what a prince should be—rejoiced at the thought of leading his Lancers in a cavalry charge and dying in battle. Others of the princely order no doubt mingled a similar chivalrous gallantry with a feeling, like that of the politicians, that this was the moment to show that their goodwill was worth having. The Maharaja of Rewa offered his troops, his territory, his private jewels and ended simply: 'What order has my King for me?' In a long telegram of September 7th, 1914, Lord Hardinge, the Viceroy, gave London details of the offers of help and sympathy received. Seven hundred princes offered their services in various forms; some wanted to send their troopers, many, like Sir Partab and his nephew, the Maharaja, to go with them; others offered a camel corps or a hospital ship. And from British India came hundreds of letters, resolutions, telegrams, pledging support. They were from bodies representing every kind of opinion; they included, for example, the Provincial Congress Committee of the United Provinces, the All-India Muslim League, and the Khalsa Diwan, which is the national synod of the Sikhs. The Indian Legislative Council—the embryonic Parliament of India which since 1909 had been 'a miniature popular assembly'—passed a resolution expressing 'unswerving loyalty and enthusiastic devotion to the King Emperor', pledging 'unflinching support', recording their belief that the people of India would wish to share in the heavy financial burden of the war, and asking the Government of India to take this view into consideration.

The substance of this telegram received publicity in Britain and was

backed by hard facts; Britain sent four infantry divisions to France in
1914, India sent two. To the part played by that force we shall return;
small though it was in comparison to the German armies, it provided
just the margin that saved France from being totally overrun as in 1940.
And India's part in it evoked in Britain a response which should not
be forgotten in the light of the ignoble hesitations that followed. John
Buchan's *History of the War*, which first appeared in fortnightly parts, as
an almost contemporary document, conveys exactly the exhilarating
atmosphere of enthusiasm. The Germans, he wrote, had calculated
that the British were so lost in commercial greed and the love of wealth
that they would not fight, but, if they did, the Empire would rise
against them. But they were wrong on both counts. 'By the gift of
liberty we had made the conquered our equals and our allies and the
very men we had fought and beaten became in our extremity our
passionate defenders ... The response of the Empire is a landmark in
our history, far greater perhaps than the war which was its cause ...
No man can read without emotion of those early days in August, when
from every quarter of the globe there poured in appeals for the right to
share in our struggle.' Buchan speaks of Canada and South Africa
and goes on: 'But it was the performance of India which took the world
by surprise and thrilled every British heart ... The British Empire
had revealed itself at last as ... a union based not upon statute and
officialdom but upon the eternal simplicities of the human heart.'

Brave words! And brave old world that knew such happy faith!
But for Muslims this honeymoon atmosphere was disturbed when
Turkey came into the war in October. The Sultan of Turkey had been
the Khalif of Islam, the successor to the Prophet, and an Indian villager
could hardly be expected to know that power had passed from the
Sultan to a committee of Young Turks who scorned Islam. Later in the
war, the Sharif of Mecca, the guardian of the Holy Places, proclaimed
a holy war against the infidel rulers of Turkey—the committee of Young
Turks—but that was not till 1917 and in the meantime Indian Muslims
—and particularly the uninformed—appeared an easy target for propaganda. In fact not much reached them and with certain exceptions
it was disregarded.

But there was another stress, more widely spread. It had always been
understood that India could not use against Russia the tactics Russia
had used against Napoleon and was to use against Hitler. The loyalty of
her millions was passive; the civil population could hardly be expected
to display the passionate endurance of the Russians. And this was
bound to apply in a lesser degree to any long war which the British
began with a series of defeats. This was the case both in 1914 and 1939.
Again, it is instructive to look at John Buchan's summary of the situation after the first year of war and his second summary after the second.

They were written at the time, and in both he is forced to admit that, at first glance, all the advantage seemed to rest with Germany. To justify his confidence in ultimate victory, he has to appeal to slow, mounting pressures, economic and financial, to the gathering concentration of British manpower and output of munitions, arguments much less likely to appeal to simple folk than the occupation of Belgium, Serbia, Montenegro, Russian Poland and part of France. Weariness of war was part of the war; a stubborn determination to endure anything rather than give in was what each side hoped to preserve in its own people and destroy in the enemy's. India was more liable to weariness than Britain; only at second-hand was it her quarrel. That is not to say that weariness had affected the troops; on the contrary, in the last rounds, in Palestine and Turkey, they had a confidence in their superiority to the enemy which they could hardly feel in 1914, when they were not only outnumbered but hopelessly under-equipped and lacking in artillery support.

Whose fault was that? In the chapter that follows we shall look at the spirit in which Indian soldiers faced the almost unbelievable months of the first winter in France. That must be seen against a simple point which cannot be made too often. In the spring of 1914 His Majesty's Government in London had again endorsed the established definition of India's responsibility. The Indian Army was not asked to maintain any forces beyond those needed to protect India against attack by any neighbouring power and to delay attack by a first-class power until help could come from England. This was a matter on which London was adamant and it arose from parsimony; the men at the Treasury were not prepared to pay for a reserve held in India and they knew they would have to pay if the War Office admitted that in fact the Indian Army and the British troops in India included an Imperial reserve. In Australia and Canada there was no lack of goodwill, but there was no standing army to send; they had to raise and train troops. They had relied on the reserves kept in Britain and in India to tide them over the first months of war. India alone could spare forces at once for an Imperial emergency. The war underlined the hollowness of the arguments used by the War Office and Treasury; there *was* a reserve in India which ought to have been equipped and paid for by Britain in peace.

In almost every regimental history, in almost every book of reminiscences, the charge recurs that it was the Government of India that was the skinflint. But in fact, although the Government of India maintained forces larger than were really needed for purely Indian purposes, they rightly equipped them for those purposes only. India has always been a desperately poor country; the peasant lives near the border of starvation. It was the policy of the Government to tax him as lightly as possible and it followed that to be careful with military resources was right for India; it was from Britain that a more generous foresight should have come.*

Despite these strains, it is broadly true that throughout the First World War, India persevered in the course on which the Legislative Council had resolved in 1914. The troops sent to France were two infantry divisions, two cavalry divisions and four field artillery brigades; a mixed force was sent to East Africa and a brigade, later increased to a division, to the head of the Persian Gulf. Six infantry brigades and a cavalry brigade went to Egypt. This was in 1914; the total was 23,500 British troops and 78,000 Indian. All but nine of the regular British battalions were sent away, being replaced by territorial battalions which were untrained, had obsolete rifles and no machine-guns. The force left in India was quite inadequate to fulfil its peace-time task. At one time there were only 15,000 British troops in India.

By the end of the war, Indian troops had fought in France and Belgium, in Gallipoli, Salonika and Palestine, in Egypt and the Sudan, in Mesopotamia, at Aden and in the Red Sea, in Somaliland, the Cameroons and East Africa, in North-West Persia and Kurdistan, in Trans-Caspia, in the Persian Gulf, and in North China. The troops sent out from India before November 1918 were 1,302,394; by the end of the war, India was providing rations for a million men. The total of Indian combatants sent to France was 138,000; to Mesopotamia 675,000; to Egypt 144,000. Those were the three main fields. Political India on the whole trusted and waited, believing that India's contribution must be recognized when the war was won, that India would then take a place among the nations beside Canada, Australia and New Zealand. But India was bitterly disappointed, as will be seen.

That is the background to the story that follows. No one can read of the doings of men in these years without horror at the folly and cruelty of war, without wonder at the courage, endurance and self-sacrifice that men displayed. The Indian Army, once it was properly trained and equipped, showed that its troops could equal any in the world. And its record proved once again the supreme importance, even in a war in which equipment played a part so much greater than ever before, of the subtle and intangible bond which holds men together in a determination not to be defeated.

* As explained before, it was agreed that during the war India should pay no more than her peace-time budget; the excess fell on Great Britain. But India made a voluntary contribution of £100 million.

XVII

The First World War

---

1. France and Flanders

The two Indian infantry divisions which went to France were the 3rd Lahore Division and the 7th Meerut Division. They arrived at Marseille at the end of September and were enthusiastically welcomed by the French. They were given a new pattern of rifle and within a month — in some cases only a fortnight — were in the firing line.

The situation was desperately critical. The Germans had aimed not at taking Paris but at enveloping the Allied left in a vast encircling movement and destroying the French and British Armies. But their advance had been slowed down from the start by stubborn resistance and at last it had been stopped and turned at the Marne; by the skin of their teeth the French and British had staved off utter disaster. Then had come the race to the sea; each great mass of soldiers extended its length northwards, trying to overlap the enemy's flank and encircle it. Neither succeeded; both reached the sea at Nieuwpoort. The Germans had planned for a quick victory; they were far better prepared for war than anyone else and they knew that with every month after the opening stages the Allies would train more men, make more shells, catch up with them. Their immediate need was a victory in the west that would let them throw everything against Russia. They determined to pierce the line that had now reached the sea and they flung all they could into assaults on four sections — the coastal strip, Ypres, La Bassée and Arras. It was at Ypres and La Bassée that the defence was mainly British. And again, and yet again, it was by the skin of our teeth that disaster was staved off.

The war had begun in August and every day since then had been a crisis. The British II Corps had been fighting continuously and was exhausted; the Indian Corps relieved them and held for three months the sector which includes Neuve Chapelle and La Bassée, to which they came back in March 1915 for the Neuve Chapelle offensive. But it was not really as tidy as that. Cavalry had been used to plug the gaps. For years the delusion persisted that one day the lines of trenches would be broken and the lances and sabres would pour through, but for the moment the horses were picketed miles to the rear and their riders went into the line to grapple with German infantry in the mud. Some units of the Lahore Division were first used to stop holes in that already improvised cavalry stopping. This was in the Ypres sector.

The Indians were trained soldiers, but they had been trained almost entirely for the Frontier. Snipers' bullets, the charge of fanatical tribesmen, the ambush in a lonely pass, a murderous rush on a dark night—of these they had much experience. Cold and heat, long marches, hunger and thirst—with these they were familiar. But the cold they had known had usually been dry and biting; now they must face continuous damp cold in trenches that were always wet and often deep in water, while they met heavy high-explosive shells, machine-guns, mortars, gas and liquid fire. They had no bombs or grenades, no searchlights, only two machine-guns to a battalion; till Christmas, many of them were still in khaki drill. Even more bewildering, to an army in which personal ties had played so great a part, were the results of replacing casualties. They had left India with reserves of ten per cent, but whole companies were wiped out; battalions came out of the line at a quarter their strength. Drafts from India included reservists who were too old and quite unfit; drafts from other battalions might not speak the same language or eat the same food. Above all, British officers could never be replaced; their successors had not grown up with the men and had to learn their language and their ways. There were usually twelve British officers with a battalion when it reached Marseille; in some battalions none survived with the regiment at the end of a year in France, in many only one or two were left.

Yet the men fought like heroes. Hear the evidence of one of their enemies, a letter from a German soldier printed in the *Frankfurter Zeitung*:

'Today for the first time we had to fight against the Indians and the devil knows those brown rascals are not to be underrated. At first we spoke with contempt of the Indians. Today we learned to look on them in a different light—the devil knows what the English had put into those fellows ... With a fearful shouting thousands of those brown forms rushed upon us ... At a hundred metres we opened a destructive fire which mowed down hundreds but in spite of that the others advanced ... in no time they were in our trenches and truly those brown enemies were not to be despised. With butt ends, bayonets, swords and daggers we fought each other and we had bitter hard work.'

What the English had put into those fellows—discipline, technical mastery—was less important than something of their own which they had helped them to develop. The King Emperor sent a message to his Indian troops in France, which must have been drafted in its first form by someone who knew them. It would be surprising if Lord Roberts had had no hand in its final form. It embodies very clearly the ideals which the best British officers expected to find in the best Indian soldiers — pride in themselves and in their own honour.

'You are the descendants of men who have been great rulers and great warriors ... ' ran the King's message. 'You will recall the glories of your race ... Hindu and Muslim will be fighting side by side with British soldiers and our gallant French allies ... You will be the first Indian soldiers of the King Emperor who will have the honour of showing in Europe that the sons of India have lost none of their ancient martial instincts ... In battle you will remember that your religions enjoin on you that to give your life doing your duty is your highest reward ... From mosques and temples prayers are ascending to the God of all ... You will fight for your King Emperor and your faith, so that history will record the doings of India's sons and your children will proudly tell of the deeds of their fathers ... '

Thus they were encouraged in competitive pugnacity; Sikhs and Dogras were to compete with Pathans and Punjabi Muslims; all were to show themselves as good as French or British. And it was at home, in the village, in the mouths of their children, that their honour would live.

This is not a military history and I shall make no attempt to give even an abridged account of all the events of that year. The British in the autumn of 1914 held about one-tenth of the Allied line, the Indians about one-third of the British sector. That was the scale, numerically considered, and still looking at it numerically, it was such a near-run thing that if there had been one corps less, it is hard to see how the Germans could have failed to pierce the line. The memoirs, and above all the regimental histories, of those days bring to mind another saying of Wellington's after Waterloo: 'I know nothing of the services of particular regiments; there was glory enough for all.' But it is only by looking at the particular that a picture can be drawn of how men behaved. Let us therefore look at some incidents in those early months, taken from the doings of some battalions. It would be easy to pick many more. There are literally hundreds of citations for honours and sometimes, reading the bleak official words, it is hard to see why this man won the Victoria Cross and another the Indian Distinguished Service Medal. No man won either without the highest courage but the supreme award sometimes went to the man as the symbol for his unit, and to the unit because of a consistent record, rather than one heroic occasion. But, since we must choose, the Victoria Cross may serve as a guide and help us to pick certain regiments.

The first Indian unit to attack the enemy, and one of the first two to go into the line, was the 129th Baluchis, later the 4th Battalion, 10th

Baluch Regiment. They were part of the Lahore Division, who reached Marseille at the end of September and on October 23rd were pushed into the line under command of Allenby's British Cavalry Corps near Ypres. At that time the trenches were not continuous and enemy parties might insert themselves between our units at night without being detected. In many places the water table was so high that a trench began to fill when barely a foot deep and it was hard without sandbags to pile up a bullet-proof parapet. The wounded were sometimes drowned on their stretchers in the communication trenches. It was desperate defensive fighting; there were days when everyone seized what weapons he could find; troopers of the Household Cavalry, cooks, sweepers, grooms, struggled grimly to keep the Germans out. It was a matter of principle to counter-attack when the enemy's assault died away. On October 26th the Baluchis were ordered to counter-attack and made some progress. Captain Hampe-Vincent fell mortally wounded. Lance-Naik Nek Amal went out under fire to look after him, found he could not bring him in single-handed, went back to fetch a sepoy, a second time went out and with the sepoy's help brought him back.

Soon after this, orders were received for the whole line to fall back. This was in the face of greatly superior numbers, the British line being so thin that there were many gaps in it. A squadron of the 1st Life Guards and another of the 2nd Life Guards were cut off, surrounded and eventually wiped out in hand-to-hand fighting. A company of the 57th (Wilde's) Rifles met a similar fate, the order to retire having reached them too late. On October 31st the Baluchis were engaged all day in very heavy and confused fighting. In the course of this, the two machine-guns of the battalion were cut off; their crews continued to fight until all were shot or bayoneted. One man, Sepoy Khuda Dad Khan, left for dead by the Germans, recovered sufficiently to crawl back and rejoin the battalion. He was awarded the Victoria Cross, being the first Indian to receive that honour. The other machine-gunners of this party were given posthumous awards of the Indian Order of Merit and the Indian Distinguished Service Medal.

Alongside the Baluchis in this first encounter were Wilde's Rifles. They had been raised in 1849 after the Sikh War from disbanded Sikh soldiers and were part of the Punjab Irregular Frontier Force. In 1914 they were the 57th, but still Wilde's Rifles; they were to become the 4th Battalion, 13th Frontier Force Rifles. They had one company each of Sikhs, Dogras, Pathans and Punjabi Muslims. They went through the same eight days of confused fighting as the Baluchis, desperately struggling against far greater numbers of Germans, far better equipped. They were divided into two halves, the Pathan and Dogra companies being actually the first Indian troops to go into the line in France. On their first day Sepoy Usman Khan was hit by rifle fire but refused to leave the firing line; he was hit again but again insisted that he must go on firing; only when hit a third time by a shell splinter would he consent to be carried back. He was awarded the I.D.S.M.

The Dogra company met the full force of a German attack on the 31st. Both British officers with this company being out of action, one dead and one unconscious, Jemadar Ram Singh was left in charge, refusing to retire until the British cavalry on their flank should do so. Ram Singh survived, but no one else of this party. Jemadar Kapur Singh fought till he had no choice but death or surrender and shot himself with his last cartridge. This half of Wilde's now had no British officer; Subadar-Major Arsla Khan collected the remnant and charged the enemy with the bayonet, but being heavily outnumbered was pushed back, and succeeded in withdrawing with the few men left to him.

Meanwhile the other half of the battalion had been engaged in fierce hand-to-hand fighting. Havildar Gagna, in peace a famous gymnast, killed five Germans with his bayonet before it broke. He picked up a sword and continued to fight with this until he collapsed with six wounds. That trench was lost but recovered by a bayonet charge, made by a squadron of the 5th Dragoon Guards and a company of Wilde's, who found Gagna still alive. On the morning of November 1st Major Swift went up to the front line with about a hundred men whom he believed to be all that were left of Wilde's. But he found about another hundred, mostly of the Sikh company, who had held on all night against all attacks, although the Germans were past them on both flanks. In the course of seventy-two hours the battalion's casualties were six British officers and four Indian, 274 other ranks.

Wilde's were in the line till Christmas, but they were now organized as two companies instead of four. They were then withdrawn, rested, reorganized and reinforced; they were brought up to a strength of 11 British and 18 Indian officers and 657 other ranks. They were back in the line in February but were not in heavy fighting till April, when they were again in the Ypres salient. They were sent to repair the breaches the Germans had made by their first use of gas. They were ordered to counter-attack on a front of 180 yards but the artillery support was ineffective and the Germans were ready for them. As they came to the top of a slight ridge, they were met by heavy fire from machine-guns and artillery. Three British officers were killed and four wounded; six Indian officers were casualties. A cloud of poison gas rolled towards them; the men of course had no gas masks. The quartermaster brought up some tins of chloride of lime; the men wet the ends of their turbans, dipped them in this and tried to cover their mouths and noses. Jemadar Mir Dast rallied all the men he could find, among them some who had been slightly gassed and were beginning to recover. With these men he held on to the position they had reached until ordered to retire; in the course of the retirement he helped to bring in eight wounded British and Indian officers, although himself wounded. He was the fourth Indian to win the Victoria Cross.

Closely linked with Wilde's in tradition and history were Vaughan's Rifles, in 1914 the 58th, later the 5th Battalion, 13th Frontier Force Rifles. This battalion was brigaded with the 2nd Battalion of the Black Watch, and the two units acquired a lasting respect and friendship for each other. Sir Arthur Wauchope, who at that time commanded the Black Watch, wrote to their colonel when they left France: 'A year's experience had taught our men that there was no regiment who ever served in the brigade they would as soon have as the 58th to come to their aid ... I write in haste, Colonel, but I write with such feeling I cannot write with clearness.' He recalled an occasion when the Black Watch found their flank exposed; two companies of the 58th advanced to cover it — 'and a fine sight it was', wrote Wauchope, 'to see the 58th pushing forward, driving all before them.' They had landed in France with 14 British officers; in a year they had lost 21 officers killed and 12 wounded. Casualties of Indian officers were 31, of the rank and file 1,511.

Vaughan's, too, had many stories of gallantry and devotion for which there is no room, but one is of a special significance. A patrol went out near the enemy trenches. Wauchope incidentally recorded his belief that a mixed party of Highlanders and Pathans was the best possible combination for this kind of work. One man, Naik Jehan Dad Khan, a Yusufzai Pathan, was separated from the party and was close to the enemy's lines when he was illuminated by the full glare of a German searchlight. He at once rose to his feet and walked towards the German trenches, salaaming profoundly. They dubiously let him into their trench. With vigorous gestures he conveyed that he was a Muslim, that he hated the English, whose throats he would like to cut, and that there were fifteen or twenty more like him. Several officers came to question him; eventually they fed him and sent him back, on the understanding, clearly stated in signs, that he would bring over his party of deserters the following night. He told the story to his British officers with peals of laughter, and gave them a good deal of useful information about the layout of the enemy trenches and the badges and numbers of the men who had questioned him. He was at once promoted havildar, but was killed before the end of 1914.*

* There is a slightly different version of how this episode began but it does not affect the point. And very much the same thing happened in June 1915 to Naik Ayub Khan of the 129th Baluchis. He brought back very useful information, was promoted jemadar and survived.

Jehan Dad told the Germans that he was a Muslim. This suggests that he knew of the propaganda the Germans had addressed to Muslims when Turkey came into the war. It would be odd if it were merely a coincidence that it was from this regiment, whose record in battle was so magnificent, that there occurred one of the very few cases of desertion to the enemy during the year when the Indians were in France. In March 1915, three months after the death of Jehan Dad, Jemadar Mir Mast with fourteen Afridi Pathans deserted. He was the brother of Mir Dast who had won the V.C. with the 57th and he too had previously shown himself an exceptionally gallant and useful officer. The incident was never explained, except that the party included a havildar whom his officers had begun to regard as a trouble-maker.

Let us turn to the Garhwalis, who had not been famous before the war either as a class or as a regiment. As we have seen, they had once been enlisted as Gurkhas and had done well in Gurkha regiments; since they had been treated as a separate class they had had few opportunities to show what they could do. The 1st and 2nd Battalions, with the 2nd/3rd Gurkhas, all stationed at Lansdowne, on the border of the Garhwal District, were brigaded with the 2nd Leicesters to make the Garhwal Brigade. This brigade won three of the five V.C.s awarded to Indians in France. The Garhwalis formed a close friendship with the Leicesters which survived long after the war. Their record in France was uniformly good. 'They never had a bad show and so kept their original morale and prestige,' wrote the Colonel of the Leicesters in his introduction to one account of their year in France. 'They were definitely not an advertising regiment, but we were soon to learn what sort of stuff we had alongside of us. They tackled their job very quickly and seemed to shake down to the strange conditions of fighting and climate much sooner than most Indian Units ... they never lost their form though they had a full share of casualties.' Sir James Willcocks, the Corps Commander, wrote: 'The 1st and 2nd Battalions both ... did splendidly on every occasion on which they were engaged ... the Garhwalis suddenly sprang into the very front rank of our best fighting men ... nothing could have been better than their élan and discipline.' The whole regiment, not merely a battalion, was later awarded the title Royal.

They landed at Marseille on October 13th and on the 29th were in the trenches in the Neuve Chapelle–La Bassée area. Five men were hit the first night, during the relief. The trenches were very shallow, hardly deep enough to cover a man kneeling; they started digging at once and, having no sandbags, used timber from ruined houses in the village behind them to improve the trenches. They were always at work on the trenches and every visitor who came congratulated them on what they had done. They had a long spell, twenty days without relief; they worked at night, often bare-

legged in icy water, to clear ditches and get the water away. Twenty
years later, at home in Garhwal, men showed me feet without toes.
The men were 'marvellously steady under shell fire'. They were terribly
short of everything; they had at first no bombs and the supporting
battery was limited to eighteen shells a day. The 2nd Battalion had
1,100 yards of trench to hold with six hundred men; the German
front line was only 50 yards away. There were days of severe shelling
by the enemy, notably on November 5th, and a few casualties even on
the best days. On the 9th a party from both battalions brought off a
most successful night attack, crawling right up to the enemy trenches
before jumping in with loud yells. Some live prisoners were taken but
perhaps the main value was the moral effect. The Germans had run —
and in those days it was rare to see their backs.

The Garhwalis were relieved on November 18th but back in the line
near Festubert on the 23rd. The Germans were attacking with great
vigour and they had taken a section of trench which the 1st Battalion and
the Leicesters were ordered to recapture. The Garhwalis' commanding
officer believed that a frontal assault would mean very heavy casualties
and probably be unsuccessful; he obtained permission to use any
method he chose. The tactics used 'made history', wrote the Colonel
of the Leicesters, but the main credit for the plan must go to an engineer
officer, Lt Robson. 'It was a bitterly cold night,' wrote Colonel Gordon
of the Leicesters; 'we got into the trench, but the Garhwalis did better'
—they took it in flank and then 'bombed their way along the whole
length, capturing over a hundred prisoners, and this became the
standard practice.' In this affair, Naik Darwan Sing Negi was foremost
in the attack on each successive bay of the trench and although twice
wounded in the head and once in the arm continued fighting till the
struggle was over, when his company commander saw that he was
streaming with blood from head to foot. His was the second Victoria
Cross for an Indian soldier.*

The 2nd Battalion's great day came at Neuve Chapelle on March
10th, 1915. This was the first great British offensive and great hopes
were entertained of its result. The plan was to put down on the enemy
front line such a concentration of fire that resistance would be virtually
impossible. The Garhwal Brigade were to go through to the fourth line
of German trenches and the Dehra Dun Brigade were then to go through
them and go on. Ladders were provided to help the men out of the
trenches for the assault but Colonel Drake-Brockman, commanding
the 2nd Battalion Garhwalis on the left, was not happy about the delay
this would cause; he discovered a fold of dead ground in front of our

* The fire trenches were never straight; every few yards there was a traverse built
across and a man going along the trench must make four right-angle turns to get
into the next bay.

own trenches and by 05.15 he had his two assault companies concealed here. There they lay still until the bombardment began at 07.30. Nothing like that concentration of fire had ever been known before. From miles behind, guns were putting shells on that narrow strip, 18-pounder field guns, 15-inch howitzers, everything we had. It lasted 35 minutes; as it lifted and moved on to the German communications the 2nd Garhwalis scrambled to their feet and were in the first trench before the surviving Germans could get to the parapet. That first trench they took without casualties; it was more difficult as they went on, but nothing would stop them and soon they were in the fourth line of trenches. It was here that Rifleman Gobar Sing Negi, on the extreme left of the brigade, his platoon commander being killed, took command of his platoon. There was a gap between them and the British troops on their left and this section of trench was full of Germans. Gobar Sing led his platoon to close the gap; they met a most determined resistance but bombed each bay and he was the first round each traverse with the bayonet. He was awarded a posthumous V.C., the third of the five. Two Garhwali officers from the 2nd Battalion won the Military Cross on this day, one other rank the Order of British India and two the Indian Order of Merit.

The Leicesters and the 2nd/3rd Gurkhas also reached the fourth line of trenches, but the 1st Battalion of the Garhwalis had very heavy losses, having worked too far to their right and come up against German trenches untouched by our bombardment. Despite their losses, the assault party carried a section of the German trenches but they were cut off from the Leicesters by a long stretch of German trench strongly held. They had no British officers surviving, but Subadar Kedar Sing Rawat took command and held the position until support reached them. The first battalion that day lost seven British officers killed and five wounded and soon after this the two battalions were amalgamated. But before the end of the war there were four active battalions.

It is a temptation to dwell on the doings of the whole brigade at Neuve Chapelle but it must be rejected, except for one incident which is irresistible. The 2nd Battalion of the 3rd Gurkhas were the first into the village of Neuve Chapelle. Rifleman Gane Gurung noticed heavy fire coming from one house and on his own initiative entered it alone, by some unrecorded means forced eight Germans to surrender and drove them out at the point of his bayonet—one small man driving eight large men. He was greeted with cheers by the Rifle Brigade, who had meanwhile entered the village.

The fifth Indian V.C. was from this regiment. At Loos, in September 1915, the 2nd/3rd Gurkhas had been ordered to attack a position where the wire proved to be uncut and enfiladed by machine-guns. They had terrible losses; only one small party got into the enemy trench and were all killed. One man, Rifleman Kulbir Thapa, although wounded, somehow got through the German wire and beyond the trench. Here he found a wounded private of the Leicesters. This man begged Kulbir to leave him but he refused and stayed with him all that day and the following night. The next day there was mist and Kulbir managed to get this man over the trench and through the German wire without being seen. He left him concealed in a shell-hole, and went back twice into the wire to fetch out wounded Gurkhas. He finally brought the British soldier into our lines, carrying him most of the way under fire, the mist having now lifted. This was not done in hot blood, in the passion of battle; it was sustained and unselfish heroism over forty-eight hours during which he had no one to rely on but himself. As a single act, it must surely rank the highest of all.

Neuve Chapelle proved that it was possible to take the first four lines of German trenches. The Garhwal Brigade was in Neuve Chapelle by 09.30. But the Dehra Dun Brigade did not get the order to move till 16.00 — and the organization of a wave of fresh troops who could succeed in exploiting first success remained a problem never solved, either by the Germans or ourselves. The Indian infantry left France at the end of the year; they were wanted elsewhere and it seemed more natural that they should contend with heat and thirst than with cold and mud. The cavalry stayed on, still hoping for the day when they would gallop through a gap in the lines. Like the British cavalry, they had fought in the trenches as infantry, and they too had splendid deeds to their credit. But their real day was to come in Palestine.

Two pictures of Indian non-combatants in France are indelible. One is of two stretcher-bearers carrying a wounded man. One was badly hit by shrapnel; he was just able to say: 'Put him down gently' and having done that collapsed. The other is told by George Younghusband; it was dark, they had been fighting for twenty-four hours and had had no food or drink since early morning of the day before. The ground was soaking wet, with water standing in pools; there was pouring rain and an icy wind. There were still bursts of heavy firing and it was dangerous to move or light a cigarette but there was nothing for it but to stay where they were till morning. And then, miraculously, there was old Kadir Dad, his Indian servant, with whisky, water, a tumbler, biscuits and a deck-chair; he had somehow groped his way in the dark through shell and rifle fire to bring these comforts.

2. The Other Side

Sixty years later, the picture sketched in the last section may be greeted with scepticism. These were peasants, someone may say, who enlisted because grinding poverty and shortage of land forced them to seize any means of earning money; once in the ranks they were drugged with food and exercise and physical well-being; discipline and fear of the consequences kept them on course and they fought because they had no alternative; it takes courage and initiative to desert. But it is sheer self-deception to talk about honour and to suppose these men gave a thought to the King.

There is a basis of truth in such a criticism, but it is not the whole truth. Recruiting officers preferred men who were hardy—and that meant that they came from areas where it was difficult to get a living and land was usually short. But it was not true that they were forced to come by poverty; in Garhwal—which I know much better than any other recruiting-ground—there was a shortage of land and also of cash, though this was much less compelling in the parts of the district near the permanent snows from which the most admired recruits came. Here, and to some extent throughout the district, people lived largely by barter and needed cash mainly for weddings; there was no shortage of food. There was a push from poverty but it was not compelling. But there was also a positive pull to the regiment that was at least as strong. It was a matter of pride to a boy and his family to get into the regiment; in peace men came on leave with tales of a life they had enjoyed and they were sad to go on pension. Recruiting continued in war with men competing for places, and by the end of the war about one in six of those of the right age and caste from this district were in the army.

Once there, it is true up to a point that inertia would keep a man going. A private in the American Civil War remarked: 'Between the physical fear of going forward and the moral fear of turning back, there is a predicament of exceptional awkwardness.' The fact remains that in some armies of the First World War—even national armies—a breaking-point was reached when whole battalions would desert or mutiny. The Indians in France surely faced a greater psychological strain than French or British troops; they were not fighting to defend their homes and they could not go on short leave. Yet they never broke and, what was more, again and again they gave more than it was reasonable to expect of mercenaries. No mere inertia moved Kulbir Thapa or Gobar Sing.

It is hard to be sure what Indian soldiers thought of it all, but there was at Boulogne a censor's office for the letters to and from Indian troops. Those from units in the field were censored from a purely military point of view by their company officers, as of course the letters of British troops were. The Boulogne office had also a political function: it was on the look-out for material sent to Indian troops with the deliberate intention of disturbing their allegiance, and also for

THE FIRST WORLD WAR

letters from soldiers which might have unintended results in India. Hardly any seditious material was sent *to* troops. The censor was extremely sensitive about any letters which might give the impression in India that the religion of the troops was being tampered with and he would not, for instance, permit them to write to their friends in India on headed writing-paper supplied by the Y.M.C.A. because it carried the word 'Christian'. He wrote a weekly report to the India Office and also a report on his year's work; extracts from the letters were translated and accompany his reports.

His reports are increasingly concerned with letters from the wounded in hospital in England. The number of letters increased steadily and the Chief Censor — Capt. E. B. Howell, later Sir Evelyn, of the Political Service — believed that at first the soldiers in Brighton hospitals did not know their mail was being censored, though in some hospitals they clearly did. On January 9th, 1915, he reports: 'On the whole, the Indians in England appear to be wonderfully cheerful and stouthearted but there are naturally many exceptions who write despondent and depressed letters.' A week later the impression is still the same: 'The English country and people, the excellence of the arrangements made for the comfort of the Indian wounded, and the kindness of the King and Queen on the occasion of their visit to Brighton are all mentioned over and over again in terms of the warmest admiration.' But there is a deterioration before long. 'Grumbling is still almost entirely absent and there is never any hint of resentment or anti-British feeling ... most appreciative references to the excellence of the arrangements in the English hospitals are still very common ... But ... the number of letters written by men who have given way to despair has increased' and there is a 'melancholy impression of a fatalistic resignation to a fate that is regarded as speedy and inevitable ... Despair is exceptional, resignation common.' Depression, Howell points out, is usual in convalescence, and some of it is due to the relaxed discipline of hospital and lack of occupation, to distance from home and friends, to the English winter. But part is due to the dismay at realizing they will have to face again the horrors of the trenches. References to this become more frequent and soon Howell writes: 'Indian opinion regards the man who has been to the trenches and there wounded as having very amply discharged his duty ... the return of wounded to the firing-line is something unprecedented in Indian experience ... But there is nothing which can be construed as disaffection.' There are, however, many letters in which the writers urge relations not to enlist and 'no attempt has been made to suppress these'.

By the end of February 1915 he thinks they begin to know their letters are censored; by April it is well known. Letters continue to be 'doleful' and 'the men generally think it unfair to have to go back'.

But some extracts will give the flavour and supplement Howell's reports, which hardly mention the positive expressions of loyalty he takes for granted. A Sub-Assistant-Surgeon in the Punjab writes to a relation in the Sikh Pioneers at Brighton: 'Keep your thoughts fixed on the Almighty and show your loyalty to the Government and to George V. It is every man's duty to fulfil his obligations towards God by rendering the dues of loyalty to his King ... even if he must yield his life.' And a sepoy in the 29th Punjabis in Africa writes to a relation in the 47th Sikhs in Brighton: 'You who are serving in France have a fine chance ... Do your duty bravely for your King, God bless him, and sacrifice your lives for him if need be.' A Jat expresses the general feeling on first arrival in hospital: 'The inhabitants are very amiable and kind, so much so that our own people could not be kinder ... The food and clothes and buildings are very fine ... Everything is such as one would not see even in a dream ... It is as if one were in the next world ... The King and Queen talked with us a long time ... I have never been so happy in all my life as I am here.' But a Dogra, the class Howell thought the most liable to depression, perhaps in convalescence and approaching release from hospital, wrote: 'There is no counting the losses and no hope of peace and none of either side giving way. The world is being ruined ... Up till now only the troops from India have withstood the enemy and held their ground ... The dead bodies lie like stones in the bed of a river [He means of course a Himalayan river of which the bed is entirely stones] ... Pray only to God saying "O Lord make peace" ... Save that, there is nothing.'

A Garhwali writes: 'I have no confidence in being able to escape death.' But another Garhwali tells his friends: 'Our regiment has made a great name for itself and its bravery has been spread abroad ... ' A Punjabi Muslim says: 'No one has any hope of survival ... only those who have lost a leg or an arm or an eye will see the Punjab again.' Another Punjabi Muslim writes: 'On no account allow my brothers Gulzar Khan and Sher Zaman to enlist.' A Dogra in hospital echoes the advice of one of the greatest of the Hindu scriptures when he writes to his brother in France: 'We must all die one day, so I tell you that it is your duty to go into battle and fight ... I too have put away all thoughts for my life.' And a Rajput writes: 'A Rajput could not in all his life find a better opportunity than this of displaying the virtue of his sword.'

These are representative extracts; they are of course various and contradictory, but so are the feelings of men, and perhaps that Dogra who found things so hopeless would have been in another mood a month later. Horror at the scale and savagery of the war is recurrent: it is not a war as we have understood it before, it is the end of the world. They are spoiling the world. Strange rumours sometimes circulated in the hospitals, some of them absurd enough; it is said, one letter runs, that the Germans have captured our King and offered to return him for one lakh of rupees—£7,500—and we have paid the money but they have not returned him. There is no good word for the Germans and the Kaiser is sometimes compared to Rawan, the king of the demons in one of the great Hindu epics. There is no trace of disaffection, Howell repeats, though he does detect a beginning of 'Indian nationalism'. But all he means by this is that there begins to be a common feeling of being Indian, not at all surprising so far from home; it is expressed in such a phrase as 'Greetings to all Indians with you.' Such a feeling had not yet found any political expression; there was no idea among the troops of Indian independence.

Altogether, the censor's reports give the impression that Indian troops at this time were far more like the men their officers supposed them to be than anyone sixty years later would imagine. Today we take nationalism for granted and can hardly believe there were people who did not want to be independent; in 1914 the idea of loyalty to a King or Emperor was accepted morality among Indians and their British officers. Of course the mails were slow and pay did not always reach relations promptly but the only real grievance was the unfairness of sending wounded men back to the trenches. Sir Walter Lawrence, who was in charge of the Indian hospitals, makes just the same point; the men always spoke with great appreciation of the kindness they received and of the care taken not to violate religious scruples about food. But they told him that to send them back to the trenches was *zulm*, which literally means 'tyranny' and in Indian usage is sometimes much what a British soldier would call 'a bit hard'. This attitude played some part in the decision to move the Indian Corps from France.

There was not much else to ruffle a censor's brow except a barely visible ripple among the Pathans and particularly the Afridis. It became known to the British in the summer of 1915, that, with a perspicacity they did not always show, the Germans had simply returned Jemadar Mir Mast and his party (from Vaughan's Rifles) to the Frontier; they came from tribal areas beyond the administrative line. It was also learnt that some men from the 129th, previously thought to be prisoners, had reached their homes on the Frontier and that there had been a few Afridi deserters from the 40th Pathans; this was thought to be due to a personal military grievance about promotion. Afridis could hardly be expected to show much loyalty to the King; they would probably be sniping at British troops within a year or two of going on pension and at home in their tribe they owed allegiance to no man, living in an anarchic paradise ruled by the bullet and the blood-feud. The wonder is that there were so few. Rumours had reached the hospitals of the mutiny at Singapore of the 5th Light Infantry. But in general the commander of the Indian Corps had much less reason to be disturbed than French commanders on the Aisne in 1917 or Italian, Russian and Austrian commanders at various periods.

The mutiny at Singapore had the classic ingredients of every Indian mutiny—ineffective officers, disruptive influence from outside, a military grievance. The 5th Light Infantry had been raised in 1803 and had been awarded the distinction of being Light Infantry in 1842. They were then the 42nd and carried as battle honours 'Cabul 1842' and the great battles of the Sikh Wars. The regiment had survived the Mutiny, after which it was renumbered the 5th. It was unusual in being entirely Muslim, mostly Ranghars from Delhi and the eastern Punjab, Delhi Pathans and some Baluchis. The commanding officer had been until recently a major in the battalion, commanding one of the double companies. The previous commanding officer had officially expressed doubt as to his fitness for command, reporting that he was unpopular with his brother-officers and that he inspired little respect among the men. He had been sent away from the battalion for three months for special report and at the end of that time pronounced fit for command. After this it would surely have been wise to give him the chance to start afresh elsewhere, but he was sent back to command the 5th. He thought some of his brother-officers had entered into a cabal to keep him out of command and let this be known. He slighted British officers in the presence of the men, while at least three British officers had openly showed their contempt and dislike for him, a feeling the others managed to conceal.

In these circumstances it is not surprising that there was faction and intrigue among the Indian officers. This centred on the expected promotion to commissioned rank of an ambitious colour-havildar. The whole battalion took sides and when this man was not promoted one faction was left bitter and disappointed. And there were outside influences at work. There was a mosque near by, to which some of the men went on Fridays, where a Maulvi regularly preached that Turkey was the seat of the Khalifa of Islam and no Muslim should fight against Turkey. There was a camp for German prisoners of war where the men acted as sentries; the prisoners managed to communicate with the sentries and convinced them that Germany was winning and Britain suffering repeated defeats. The men seem to have believed that the Germans were Muslims, no doubt confusing them with Turks. Two of the Indian officers were spreading pro-Turkish stories.

Things came to a head through the total lack of understanding between officers and men. It was known that the battalion would soon be moving; orders were expected daily. The officers hoped that they would go to Mesopotamia and fight the Turks; they hoped perhaps that their differences would then disappear and that the regiment would have a chance to distinguish itself. They confidently assumed that the men felt just as they did. Orders came at last; they were to sail almost at once, but for Hong Kong, at which the officers were bitterly disappointed. The move was announced to the men by the Brigadier at a farewell parade; he praised their past services and gave them his good wishes but entirely failed to tell them where they were going. They thought it was to fight the Turks and that evening the greater part of four companies out of eight mutinied, opening fire on guards, murdering several officers and trying to release the prisoners of war. But the Germans were so frightened of the mutineers that they asked for British troops to protect them. The mutiny was quickly suppressed, but more than two hundred men were brought to a court martial. There was a somewhat similar affair at Bombay involving some Muslims of the 130th King George's Own Baluchis.

Thus there can be no doubt that from the entry of Turkey into the war Muslim troops were liable to be under strain, particularly of course if there was a weakness among the officers. But in a mixed regiment and with good officers it hardly came to the surface. If the commanding officer was outstanding and had a good team, he could transform into excellence a unit that might otherwise have been average. The Garhwalis owed some of the high reputation they won in France to Drake-Brockman. 'When the officers', he wrote, 'know their work, show themselves good men to follow, know the character and dispositions of their men and gain their confidence, a firm and rigid discipline can always be maintained.' 'You must be just but strict,' he insisted, and his discipline was long remembered. The men must be kept occupied. Billets must be kept spotlessly clean—and he records that the C.O. of a Guards Battalion wrote specially to congratulate him on the billets he had handed over—and a period of rest must be used for training, drill, cleaning up and general rehabilitation. Back in the trenches, there must be constant work on improving them and the men must keep themselves as clean as they can; smart men will take a pride in themselves and idle men will have time to get frightened or depressed. In his portrait, he has the look of a man hard with himself and hard with others. He cannot have been easy to live with but his forethought and thorough reconnaissance saved many casualties.

It was good officers, who had grown up with their units, who gave them the stability which carried them through four years of war. And to such leaders troops responded and gave their best.

3. Mesopotamia: Wide-Angle Lens

It had been agreed, as we have seen, that the task of India in Imperial defence was strictly limited. India was to be strong enough to deal by herself with Afghanistan or Persia; if attacked by Russia, she must be able to hold on till help came from Britain. This was the traditional view, turned upside down in 1914, when India sent substantial help to France. The Persian Gulf and the Suez Canal were nearer home and far more what India had been expected to defend; the Canal was a vital link with Britain, while control of the Gulf had been regarded as essential to trade with India since we had fought the Portuguese there in the seventeenth century. Now oil had added to the Gulf's importance and it had been demonstrated that quite a small force landed at the head of the Gulf was enough to prevent Persian hostility. There was another point. Germany had visions of a sphere of influence stretching down through the Balkans and Turkey to Aleppo, Baghdad and Basra. It was unquestionably a part of Germany's aims to cause unrest in India, and there is some evidence for believing — as the British at the time certainly believed — that Germany had dreams of a Mesopotamian colony where German engineers would make the desert blossom like the rose.

All these were good reasons in war-time for placing forces at the head of the Gulf. As for the Canal, to defend it was as obvious a move for us as to attack it was for the Germans and Turks. Looked at another way, Turkey was essentially the land-mass of Anatolia, with a small extension into the Balkans and an Arabian empire to the south. To attack Turkey there were four routes. The first was by a direct thrust at Constantinople from the sea by the Dardanelles and Gallipoli; the second, an approach from Egypt by the coast of Palestine to Jerusalem, Damascus and Aleppo; the third, from Basra by the Tigris to Baghdad and thence to Aleppo; the fourth, from Russia by the Caucasus. Fronts were opened on each of these routes; indeed, they may be looked on as sectors of one front, interrupted by great intervening masses of mountain and desert. Turkey, lying at the centre, appeared to have the advantage of being able to transfer troops quickly from one sector to another, but poor communications made it less of an advantage than it appeared.

This is not a history of the war nor does it attempt to record all the doings of the Indian Army. In the Gallipoli affair, the 29th Indian Infantry Brigade was the only body of troops to reach the summit of the ridge and gaze down on the waters of the Dardanelles. Seeing the dash of the 6th Gurkhas, Lt William Slim, then a subaltern in a territorial battalion, decided that day to apply to join them and thus set his foot on the way to becoming a field-marshal and Chief of the Imperial General Staff. But there was only that one Indian brigade. In the second sector of this vast circular front — Egypt and Palestine — for the first year of the war we were on the defensive, protecting the Canal. Indian troops were essential in this not very dramatic phase. In the middle

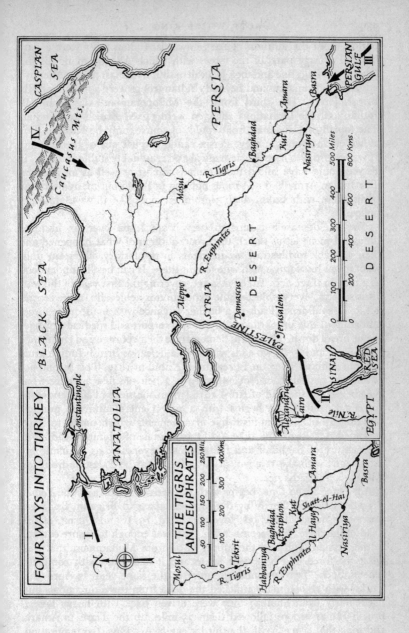

FOUR WAYS INTO TURKEY

period, from the autumn of 1915 onwards, Indian units were a part, but not a large part, of the forces with which Allenby made his first advance in Palestine and took Jerusalem. But in the last phase, Allenby's advance to Damascus and beyond, Indian troops were a majority of the British forces. The third front, the Mesopotamian, was essentially Indian; all the formations engaged were mixed British and Indian. The fourth or Caucasian front could, of course, only be Russian. But, as we circle round Turkey, Persia cannot be left out of the account. It was essential to keep Persia neutral and reasonably stable; anarchy in Persia would have suited the Germans almost as well as an alliance. The Indian Army had no serious fighting in Persia but many units had spells there with tasks which were often more like those of military police.

The Mesopotamia campaign drew from India over six hundred thousand men; let us sketch the broad outlines of what happened and then go back to illustrate by incidents in the history of certain units what it was like for the men who fought there. It can best be understood as a play in three acts. In the first act, covering the first year of the war, all is success; every object of the expedition is achieved. In the second act, over-confidence leads to a further advance with inadequate forces and without due preparation; supplies, transport and medical arrangements break down. The troops demonstrate their courage and endurance to no avail and Act Two ends with such a defeat as British Indian arms had not suffered since the retreat from Kabul in 1842. This second act covers the period from November 1915, when the first advance from Kut began, to the end of April 1916, when the siege of Kut ended in surrender. Act Three begins with a new General and the gradual building up of the administrative arrangements which ought to have preceded Act Two. This, like Act One, is a tale of triumph, leading to the capture of Baghdad and the advance beyond it; its dramatic interest ends with the removal of large forces to the Palestine front for Allenby's final advance.

Act One, Scene One, begins with the arrival at Basra of the Poona Brigade, followed shortly by the Ahmadnagar and Belgaum Brigades. Basra was in our hands on November 23rd, 1914, and Qurna, at the head of the delta, by December 9th. This was enough to ensure control of the Persian Gulf and the supply of oil from Mohammerah; it was what the force had been sent to do and it had done with complete success. Scene Two continues the story in the same vein; in April, the Turks, with 18,000 men, attacked the delta from three directions, but particularly from Shaiba; they were driven back with heavy losses; British Indian troops followed them 75 miles up the Tigris to Amara and took that place. With the third scene of Act One, the temptation theme begins to be heard; why not go a little farther? The Tigris and

Euphrates approach each other at Baghdad, then meander in diverging beds until they converge at Basra. But from Kut, about 150 miles up the Tigris from Amara, there is a stream called the Shatt el Hai which carries water from the Tigris to the Euphrates at Nasiriyeh, making a triangle of which the Turks held two angles. It was possible to picture the Turks at Kut dispatching a force down the Shatt el Hai to Nasiriyeh and thence to Basra. There were therefore arguments, though not very strong ones, for possessing ourselves of Nasiriyeh and Kut. So we pushed on and took Nasiriyeh on July 25th, 1915, and Kut in a battle which covered September 28th and 29th, 1915. The Turks were out-generalled and outfought in a brilliant engagement in which the 117th Mahrattas particularly distinguished themselves. Now we had the three angles of the triangle and it was time to stop. On November 2nd, 1915, Mr Asquith, the British Prime Minister, said in the House of Commons: 'I do not think that in the whole course of the war there has been a series of operations more carefully contrived, more brilliantly conducted, and with a better prospect of final success.' Those last three ominous words meant Baghdad.

That is the end of Act One. In the opening scene of Act Two, the temptation theme is played fortissimo. Mr Asquith was eager for a resounding success; everyone had heard of Baghdad, the city of the Arabian Nights, and the news that it had fallen would reassure a British public who knew that Gallipoli had been a failure and had learnt of the Gallipoli casualties with an angry feeling that the management of the war was callous and incompetent. In India, too, it would be good that people should hear of a success. But there was no strategic reason for immediacy in the advance on Baghdad and the very fact that made it politically important carried with it a military consequence which was ignored. The folding up of the Gallipoli front released Turkish troops — and the veterans of Gallipoli were the pick of the Turkish army. The troops in Baghdad and Mosul at the outbreak of war had been partly Arab and of much lower quality than those the Mosul Command was now getting as reinforcements. Further, with every step taken from the base at Basra the problems of supply increased for the British, while the Turks of course would be falling back towards their base and shortening their supply-lines. There was then no railway from Basra to Baghdad and the river was full of shifting sandbanks. There were no accurate maps and little reliable information as to where water was to be found in the dry season. An army almost wholly dependent on animal transport could venture away from the river only after very careful preparation or with reliable local knowledge — and the Iraqi Arabs seem to have had no aims but the plunder of the defeated, whether Turkish or British. The country in the summer months is one of the hottest in the world, rivalling even Upper Sind; it is cold in winter and heavy rains usually begin to fall at the end of December, when floods follow and the country becomes almost impassable. The best campaigning season is thus very short—October to December. The troops had been at war for a year with no opportunity for genuine recreation or retraining but they had done everything they had been asked. They were battle-weary but in reasonably good spirits, more weary of the climate than of battle.

All these were reasons for postponing a further advance until 1916. Major-General Townshend, the Force Commander, a skilful soldier, as his capture of Kut had shown, and usually an optimistic man, was doubtful whether his forces were strong enough to take Baghdad, but Lt-Gen. Sir J. Nixon, who commanded all the troops in Mesopotamia, was confident they were and was backed by the Viceroy, Lord Hardinge and the Commander-in-Chief in India. The Cabinet in London unquestionably approved. An Allenby or a Maude would perhaps have insisted that he must have time to build up supply and transport—but there was no one with the authority, the courage and the foresight to insist.

The decision was taken. Townshend moved forward and on October 23rd he outflanked and defeated a Turkish force at Aziziye, half-way to Baghdad. By November 12th he was within 30 miles of Baghdad—that is to say, by river more than 500 miles from Basra—and within seven miles of a strong Turkish position at Ctesiphon. He had now to meet the Turkish reinforcements from Gallipoli. He had only one division, about 12,000 strong. Full of confidence—like Lake before Bharatpur—he attacked on November 22nd a prepared position held by 20,000 Turkish infantry and took the first line of trenches. It was a great feat of arms but the kind of victory which spells the beginning of defeat. He had lost 4,500 men, more than a third of his force, and he could not face another battle; he ordered a retreat. He had to make forced marches; arrangements for the wounded were primitive and inadequate; if a man fell out, he was liable to be murdered, stripped and mutilated. By December 3rd the exhausted column was back at Kut and here Townshend decided to stand. The Tigris at this point makes a loop and Kut lies on a peninsula some two miles long, with the river on three sides. The pursuing Turks now greatly outnumbered Townshend's force, but he believed that help would soon come from the south. Two Indian divisions from France, the 3rd (Lahore) and the 7th (Meerut), had been in Egypt but were now on their way to Mesopotamia. They were hurried up the river as soon as they arrived, but a supply-line that had been inadequate for one division was no better for two. The rains had come, with icy north winds from the mountains; much of the country was flooded and the Turks were in strong defensive positions. Kut was besieged and all attempts to reach it failed. Townshend's force held out till April 29th; after 150 days, most of it on half-rations, they had eaten the last day's supplies and they surrendered.

That was the end of Act Two. Act Three began in August 1916 with the appointment of Sir Stanley Maude to the Mesopotamian command and the steady improvement of administration. Mesopotamia had some months earlier come under the direct control of the War Office and as so often before—and as it was to be so often again—everything for want of which the first attempt had failed now began to arrive. When Maude's advance began, there was a sufficient flow of men and material to the front and, though there was some very hard fighting, Kut was taken in February and Baghdad on March 11th, 1917. The summer was spent in retraining and refitting and there was even leave to India. The advance was resumed at the end of September. By November 5th, after several actions conducted with skill and determination, Tekrit was occupied. This is almost half-way from Baghdad to Mosul, and once again it was a question of whether to push on.

This is the moment to pause and look at the other side of the hill. The Turks had naturally been dispirited by the loss of Baghdad and attached great importance to recovering it; the Germans, now that Russia was virtually out of the war, spared some troops and a distinguished General, Falkenhayn, to help the Turks. Falkenhayn was building up at Aleppo a new Turkish army, with considerable German stiffening; this was known by the Turks as Yilderim, or 'the Thunderbolt'. It was meant for Baghdad and Maude expected it to advance at some stage to Mosul. But Jemal, the Turkish Governor in Syria, was convinced that it was the Palestine front which ought to be reinforced. From Egypt, General Murray had been cautiously feeling his way forward across the Sinai desert and had secured a foothold on the coast of Palestine which was supplied from Egypt by a railway and a piped supply of water. He had made two attempts, in March and April 1917, to push up through the coastal strip of Southern Palestine and had twice been stopped. These were the first and second battles of Gaza. In June 1917 Allenby had come to take command in Palestine; the Prime Minister, Mr Lloyd George, had told him the British nation would like Jerusalem as a Christmas present and promised reinforcements. Jemal was right in thinking he was in danger and Falkenhayn at once perceived that if he were to move Yilderim forward to Mosul and there become locked in battle with Maude, he would be in serious danger from Allenby. It would be better to launch his thunderbolt in Palestine. But he had to convince the Turkish Government and this was a slow business. They were bent on Baghdad. In fact, there was so much delay that the thunderbolt was still at Aleppo when Allenby's campaign began.

This helps to explain the end of Act Three in Mesopotamia. Maude

died of cholera at Tekrit in November 1917 but even if he had lived
the decision must still have been to go on the defensive in Mesopotamia.
It was all Lloyd George could do to get the agreement of our Allies to
his reinforcing the Palestine front; Haig and Sir William Robertson
opposed his plans with all the vigour they could, believing that all our
effort should go to France. We could not have mounted two big offensives, one between Tekrit and Mosul and a second in Palestine, and if
the choice had to be made, Palestine was obviously to be preferred.
The supply-line from Egypt was shorter and could be supplemented by
sea. After Maude's death, the process of transferring Indian troops to
Palestine began; it was enormously accelerated in March 1918 when the
last great German offensive broke in France, when the British line was
stretched back in a great bow forty miles long and twenty miles deep,
when once again things in France looked as desperate as in 1914.
Allenby sent 60,000 British troops to France and they were replaced
by Indian for his second great offensive, which in the autumn of 1918
reached Damascus and beyond and gave Turkey the final blow.

4. Mesopotamia: Closer Focus

Let us take another lens and shift our gaze from the sweep of strategy
to the doings of individual units. Of the regiments which in 1922 became the First Punjab Regiment, four battalions were engaged in
Mesopotamia. They had all been Madras regiments, going back to the
earliest days of the Company's Army; the 1st Battalion, 1st Punjab
Regiment—as it became in 1922—had been formed in 1759 from
independent companies and had then been the 3rd Coast Battalion.
It had become the 62nd Punjabis in 1903 and was known by that name
in Mesopotamia. The other three were then the 66th, 76th and 82nd
Punjabis. But let us call these four units the 1st, 2nd, 3rd and 5th
Battalions of the First Punjab Regiment. Both the 2nd and 3rd came to
Basra in the spring of 1915 and took a part in repelling the Turkish
attack of April. Both were at Ctesiphon, the victory which was the
beginning of defeat. Broadly, this battle was an attempt to repeat
the plan Townshend had so far found successful—a direct attack on the
key-point in the enemy's position accompanied by a sweep round a
flank. But it is not easy to outflank an enemy of greater strength than
one's own. The 2nd Battalion, with the 117th Mahrattas (later the 5th
Royal Battalion), the 2nd Battalion of the 7th Gurkhas and two companies of the 4th/14th Punjabis, formed the assaulting force for the
attack on the key position. They forced their way into this strong point,
the 2nd/1st hacking down the posts supporting the wire with *dahs*,
heavy choppers brought from Burma; they broke the Turkish second

line and pressed on, only to be recalled when well ahead of it. Successive Turkish counter-attacks at last drove them back to the Turkish first line. The battalion had 242 casualties, about half its strength on that day. Of twelve British officers, all were hit, but two, wounded in the hand and arm, were able to remain at duty. The 3rd Battalion was part of the encircling force but it came up against extremely heavy resistance in the Turkish second line and was eventually ordered to withdraw; its losses were 289.

There followed the retreat. The river was the main line of supply and the progress of shipping was slow owing to its winding course and to frequent sandbanks from which barges had to be refloated. To cover the shipping, counter-attacks were sometimes necessary. For the final stages, Townshend pressed on by forced marches, hoping to shake off the enemy and win time to prepare for his stand at Kut. 'The troops were very tired,' says the official historian, ' ... the force stumbled on, only half awake ... all ranks were thankful to lie down and sleep on the road in column as they were. But even sleep was difficult, as the cold was intense and there was no food.' Kut was reached on December 3rd and the official history records: 'For over twelve days, General Townshend's force — largely composed of young soldiers — had been fighting, march-ing, or working continually, frequently without sufficient food or water and deprived of sleep. This forty-four-mile march ... carried out in thirty-six hours was therefore a severe test' and must arouse admiration. But it was of course only the prelude to the siege of a hundred and fifty days. In that narrow loop of the Tigris, two miles long by a mile wide, flat and featureless, some of it below the level of the river, sani-tation was a serious problem and it was hard to construct trenches. The Turks were active and never let the garrison rest; they made a number of full-scale assaults; there was daily shelling and the troops in reserve from the front line were under shell-fire while at work on trenches and ditches. Rations were reduced from January 20th; by March 7th the allowance per man was ten ounces of barley flour and four ounces of parched barley grain. This was soon reduced but horse-meat was added. By the end of the siege, the daily ration was four ounces of flour and nine of horse or mule. Indian troops at first often refused horse or mule and by the time they were persuaded to eat it they were sometimes too weak to obtain much benefit. Men fainted at work and some died of the weakness resulting from semi-starvation. But there was no lack of fighting spirit. Subadar Akbar Khan, of the 2nd/1st Punjabis, hit in the knee early in the siege, rejoined after a month in hospital, was hit in the other leg, rejoined a second time, was knocked senseless by a bomb from an aeroplane which killed the men on either side of him, and rejoined a third time, permanently deaf in one ear.

The 3rd Battalion shared the hardships of the siege; their casualties during the siege were 171 out of 320; 101 died in captivity. But the nature of the Mesopotamia campaign is even more vividly illustrated by the total needed to replace casualties from April 1915, when they landed, till November, just before Ctesiphon. In that seven months this battalion had absorbed drafts totalling 1,600 men, nearly twice its original strength.

The 1st and 5th Battalions of the 1st Punjabis were in the force which tried to relieve Kut. The 1st arrived at Basra on the last day of 1915, having been in Egypt and Aden; they were at once sent forward and took part in the attack on the Turkish positions at Shaikh Saad some thirty miles short of Kut, on January 7th. It is impossible here to detail all the expensive and ineffective attempts to relieve Kut which continued from January 7th to well into April. They cost 23,500 casualties. The Turks, as at Gallipoli, were attacked in prepared positions; from mid January rain was falling and much of the country was flooded. A description of the aftermath of one such attack will be enough; it took place on January 21st. The area was completely flat, there was no cover at all, and the troops came under heavy rifle and shell fire as soon as they left the trenches. They established a line about 250 yards short of the Turkish position, but could get no farther. The losses of the 1st Battalion that day were 372; the losses of the whole force were 2,740.

'The sufferings of the wounded', wrote Major Evans, 'were horrible. Men lay out all night in icy rain, dying from exposure because the medical personnel—heroic in its efforts—was hopelessly inadequate... In the morning many sepoys were found dead without a mark upon them; others were picked up and were slowly jolted, petrified and sodden with freezing mud, in springless carts to dressing-stations which for hours had been nothing better than a shambles. Still later men arrived at Amara with wounds which for eight days had remained untended ... putrefying, gangrenous and full of maggots.' In many cases, the field ambulances were still on their way from France.

The 5th Battalion arrived in Mesopotamia rather later than the 1st and joined them for the operations in March and April 1916. They learnt that Kut had fallen and that their efforts had been in vain. But conditions did not improve; on the contrary, the months that followed immediately on the fall of Kut were some of the worst of the campaign, though rather from sickness and heat than from enemy action. With this battalion was a diarist, Major Davson, whose jottings give some idea of what men endured.

'April 30th 1916 ... we are now in another lot of first-line trenches. Heat is appalling and only just begun. Flies bite hard and are in thousands. Cholera has started ... We lie and gasp all day ... Food now is disgusting; we exist on bully beef—fly-blown—and stale bread ... But I am very fit ... I do not eat much ... May 10th ... Meals are practically an impossibility on account of the flies ... May 14th ... A good deal of cholera at the back ... May 20th–22nd: The most awful march ... We marched at 04.00 a.m. One water-bottle per officer and man was the allowance and no more. En route men fell like flies. More than 1000 collapsed from heat and lack of water ... men simply crumpled up. They looked as if they had been shot. The last two or three miles I was carrying one man's rifle and pulling another along by the arm ... I collected my strongest men and we kicked, cajoled and pulled men along. Anything to get them in. One felt an awful brute, letting a man have it in the ribs as hard as one could, but it was a case of getting them in or leaving them out to have their throats cut by Arabs, to mutilation. Young sepoys were stumbling along blindly, calling out "*Mai, mai!*" ("Mother, mother!") ... As it is I have lost four men. I am afraid I shall never see them again ...

'July 1st. There is an enormous wastage through sickness ... scurvy and jaundice, both of which might be avoided if rationing arrangements were better ... July 19th. We muster 800 ... The rate of sickness is appalling: 18 today, nearly all jaundice and scurvy. Lack of green food. I wonder if my system, being accustomed to very little, stands it better than others ... We have sent 175 to hospital in 19 days.' And three weeks later, on August 11th he notes: 'Scurvy has now reduced us to 250 men. We are now eating a green shrub which only camels eat in India and the juice of which natives use for taking stains out of clothes.'

In September Davson finds 'the weather a little cooler at last,' though in tents it is over 120° during the day. By January 30th, 1917, he is writing in a very different spirit. The battalion, having marched for twelve hours, from 16.00 till 04.30 next morning, was told it was to assault enemy trenches at 10.40 hrs. 'We hopped the parapet at 10.40 and they say we looked as if on parade. We didn't run but walked in quick time up to the enemy trench which we took and kept.' And on February 23rd 'The advance was the most magnificent thing I have ever seen. We advanced in quick time, no rushing, over 3000 yards of flat ground with no cover. It took us 35 minutes and we had the enemy main position in our hands.' He records casualties among various officers and goes on that though there was shell fire nearly all the casualties were from machine-gun fire on the right flank. 'We went through three belts of it. Whole platoons dropped but we went on steadily... Only two British officers left and three Indian, instead of eight and fifteen. For the third time in a year we have lost half the regiment in one swoop. I am awfully proud of my company ... My greatcoat changed hands four times. My orderly was carrying it first. He was hit and threw it to another man and so on. My Mahomedans made it a point of honour that my greatcoat must get in.'

The battalion's losses for that month were 9 British and 12 Indian officers, 489 rank and file. Davson writes: 'The thing that stands out is the magnificent conduct all through of the Regiment. I suppose the price paid is not too high.' He lists the officers who have been killed and comments: 'A long list. A more charming crowd to serve with and a better lot of officers I shall not again meet.'

The record of another group of battalions who in 1922 became one regiment illustrates in perhaps a more representative way the part the Indian Army played in the war. The 2nd Punjab Regiment was composed, like the 1st, of units from the old Madras Army. In 1914 they were the 67th, 69th, 72nd, 74th and 87th Punjabis, but again we will refer to them as battalions of the 2nd. The 1st Battalion lost two companies at Kut, was re-formed on the basis of the other two and took part in Maude's operations and the taking of Baghdad. The 3rd Battalion — we shall come back to the 2nd — was on the North-West Frontier for most of the war, engaging in various skirmishes with Mohmands and other tribesmen, and at the same time training recruits and sending drafts overseas. But in March 1918 this battalion went to Palestine, replacing a battalion of the Somerset Light Infantry who went to France. The 4th was at the taking of Tien-Tsin, the German colony in north China; then for some time in Hong Kong and later on the Frontier, from both stations sending numerous drafts to other battalions, and then moving as a whole to Egypt and Palestine in 1918. The 5th too was steadily milked for other units until the last phase in Mesopotamia. This battalion was abroad as part of the occupying forces till 1921.

It was almost inevitable, so long as Kitchener's organization continued, that some battalions should be used to receive and train recruits and dispatch drafts while others were active in the field. This group of regiments were particularly liable to be milked since they took, in various combinations, the basic Indian Army mixture — Punjabi Muslims, Sikhs and Dogras. The 2nd Battalion, however, had an active role from the outbreak of war. After six months defending the Suez Canal they went to France, where they fought alongside the Black Watch and Vaughan's Rifles in the Bareilly Brigade at Neuve Chapelle and Loos. Then they went back to Egypt and eventually to the Aden Field Force. Here there was a minor front with the Turks which lasted till the Turkish surrender; there were many engagements which never rose to the level of a battle. One of these illustrates the comradeship which grew up between men of different faiths. There was a Turkish force at Lahej some thirty miles from Aden and it was the duty of the Aden Field Force to keep them on the alert by patrols and minor attacks and so prevent their being diverted elsewhere. On September 11th 1917, one such patrol, consisting of thirty men of the 2nd Battalion and a few other details, commanded by Lieutenant O'Shea, met an enemy

party about a hundred strong. O'Shea was hit early in the action but
would not give up command. He fought till he judged it necessary to
order a retreat. The senior N.C.O., Naik Fazal Ahmad, who saw that
O'Shea was much more severely wounded than he knew, refused to
obey the order and took command himself. With the help of Lance-
Naik Sher Mohammad he got O'Shea under cover and continued the
fight. O'Shea died of his wound; Fazal Ahmad was hit and died; Sher
Mohammad was hit and the enemy overran the position where the
bodies of O'Shea and Fazal Ahmad lay. But Lance-Naik Prabhu
Singh took charge, rallied the men, led a spirited counter-attack and
recovered the two bodies. They were Irish, Muslim, Sikh—but between them was an overriding loyalty to each other.

It will be remembered that Lord Roberts had been of the opinion
that the Marathas, though their cavalry had once overrun India, no
longer made soldiers who could compete with men from the north.
But they survived his opinion, as the Madras regiments did not, and in
Mesopotamia they distinguished themselves particularly. On April
28th, 1916, an article in the *Civil and Military Gazette* of Lahore made
the point that 'one of the surprises of the war has been the Maratha.'
In this war, the writer continued, 'the less conspicuous types have
made good. In France we were always hearing of the Garhwalis, in
Mesopotamia it is the Marathas. Three battalions, the 103rd, 110th
and 117th Mahrattas, were all present at the battle which gave us Kut;
they fought three consecutive engagements in 48 hours, without any
water but what they carried.' The 117th with the Dorsets broke through
the enemy wire and stormed the Turkish trenches; they were led by the
Subadar-Major, all British officers being dead. The 117th at the end of
the war were awarded the title Royal and became eventually the 5th
Royal Battalion of the 5th Mahratta Regiment. But the others had done
almost as well. 'The praises of the regiment ring from Basra to Kut.
The men fought like tigers ... Some Gurkhas turned out to cheer us and
the Corps Commander congratulated a British regiment on being
brigaded with us!' So wrote the Commanding Officer of the 105th
(later the 2nd Battalion), who came to Mesopotamia after the others,
in 1916. During the later advance this battalion was showered with
Hindi pamphlets, telling them that England was starving and would
soon be unable to feed and clothe them. The Indian officers wrote out a
reply which they wanted to have dropped on the enemy. Part of it ran:
'We have never been fed and clothed so well but prisoners taken from
you are in rags ... We will never cease to fight for the King Emperor
Jarj Panjam [George V] until the evil Kaiser is utterly trodden into the
mud, as was the ten-headed demon Rawan by Ramchandarji.' It is
hard to know what Turks or Germans would have made of that.

Let us look only at two more units and record of each only one incident. The 9th Bhopal Infantry was an odd survival; it was raised originally in Bhopal as a state unit and reconstituted after the Mutiny as a regular battalion of the line. There was no other battalion linked with it by history and tradition and in 1914 it had no linked unit with the same class composition. Eventually, in 1922, it became the 4th Battalion, 16th Punjabis, but from 1914 to 1919 the Bo-Peeps (as they liked to call themselves) were odd man out and had special difficulties over reinforcements. But they had a very active war. They went to France with the Lahore Division as part of the Ferozepur Brigade; they fought at Festubert and Neuve Chapelle and were inspected on November 23rd by the Prince of Wales in falling snow while still wearing khaki drill. After that first frightful three months they were built up again into a new regiment early in 1915 only to be gassed in the German attacks of April 1915, again rebuilt and in more fighting in France in May. They spent six months patrolling the Suez Canal and in December 1915 went to Mesopotamia and straight into the operations for the relief of Kut. In the course of these operations, during an attack on a Turkish entrenched position, the commanding officer, Colonel Thomas, was hit and fell within 200 yards of the Turkish lines. There was no cover. Sepoy Chatta Singh went forward to Thomas's help, bandaged him and covered him with his own body while digging cover for them both. Thomas's leg was shattered and he was in great pain; Chatta Singh stayed with him till night when he brought him in. He was awarded the Victoria Cross.

And let us take a glance at one specially revealing incident which concerned the 2nd Battalion, 13th Frontier Rifles (in 1914 the 56th). They had been in Egypt and Aden and they too had come to Mesopotamia for the relief of Kut. They too were at the operations beginning at the Sheikh Saad positions on January 7th. They were in two severe actions. On January 7th the four companies had to leave the trenches company by company in succession. The Sikh company and the Punjabi Mohammedans went first; they were met by a withering fire but went forward in rushes with great discipline and gallantry. The Dogra and Pathan companies had to watch this and then get up and attack. They 'showed less dash' than the first two companies. All their officers were wounded and the attack failed. They appear afterwards to have reproached themselves bitterly. On January 13th, six days later, the Dogra company led the attack and about 800 yards from the enemy position met very heavy gun and rifle fire. But nothing would stop them. An eye-witness, commanding the Sikh company, wrote:

'I have never seen individual men behave so well. Seventy yards short of the Wadi was a ditch. The Turkish bank of the Wadi was much higher, giving them a wonderful field of fire to the ditch. I saw men in that deadly seventy yards get up singly and make a dash forward until killed. Not one here and there but man after man and not by order of any leader. Anyone who has once gone to ground ... knows the courage required to get up and go on even if a leader calls for a party of chaps to dash forward together. I have never seen such heroism. They did it to redeem the name of their clan which they thought had been besmirched — I thought quite unjustifiably.'

To redeem the name of their clan; to make clean their honour — that was why they did it, like the Rajputs at Bharatpur and the Guides at Kabul.

5. Not In Vain

To dwell on Allenby's advance of September 1918, the battle of Megiddo, would really add nothing to the purpose of this book. It was one of the most complete victories of the war, even more decisive than Tannenberg or Caporetto, though not on so vast a scale. Two Turkish Armies, VII and VIII, were surrounded and most of them forced to surrender. The Turkish IV Army did not last much longer. As in Allenby's first offensive, the third Battle of Gaza, the enemy was convinced, by a masterly use of deception, that the real attack would come at a point where in fact there would be only a feint. In both cases, the real attack came where a feint was expected and in both cases it made a gap through which cavalry could be poured to sweep behind the enemy's rear. But at Megiddo this sweep was far more successful and virtually ended Turkish resistance. The battle was a masterpiece of careful planning and preparation; when it was first planned, there had been British troops available, but these were withdrawn for France and replaced by Indian, first by the 3rd and 7th Divisions and later by individual Indian battalions. Many of them were inexperienced and needed some further training, but the whole plan would have had to be abandoned without them. This was the last battle in which horsed cavalry played a big part; in fact there were four cavalry divisions and they were central to the plan. Half the cavalry for this breakthrough were from Australia and New Zealand; the other half consisted of Indian cavalry, usually with one British Yeomanry regiment to a brigade.

But to linger on pictures of the 2nd Royal Lancers (Gardner's Horse) trotting into the plain of Armageddon and, on another occasion, taking a Turkish trench at the gallop, would throw no further light on the fidelity, the courage and endurance already demonstrated. It is not when things are going well that men waver in loyalty. Since mention has been made of the desertion of a group of Afridis in France, it should be said that the remaining Afridis of Vaughan's Rifles were drafted to East Africa before that battalion went to Palestine, where it arrived in time for the third battle of Gaza. A faint question mark hung over the Pathans throughout the war but the Punjabi Muslims were steady as a rock.

East Africa again was a campaign in which the Indian part was essential, but it was a side-show, and one in which the Indian Army units were engaged in a game to which they were accustomed: a colonial war, with small numbers, long marches, an elusive enemy. It is time to go on to the period between the wars, when nationalism began to grow vigorously throughout India and when a recruit sometimes found that ideas accepted in his village were treason in the army, while what he was taught in the army might be regarded as a betrayal of the national cause when he went on leave. But we cannot leave the First World War without recording one conclusion about the Mesopotamia campaign.

It was a mistake to go on from Kut in the autumn of 1915; it would, as it turned out, have been much better to wait a year but it is easier to see that now than it was at the time. The responsibility for such a mistake seldom rests entirely with one man; in this case, Townshend, Nixon, the Viceroy, the Prime Minister—all have some share in what went wrong. Once the first mistake had been made and Ctesiphon had proved that we had overreached our strength, it was inevitable that great risks should have been taken to save Townshend from surrender. These further disasters, the casualties incurred in the operations to relieve Kut, the deaths in hospital, all flowed from the first mistake. But the scurvy, the dysentery, the jaundice and cholera of the summer of 1916 could surely have been prevented. They were due to mismanagement: lack of medical staff and material, lack of proper food. And for this too the responsibility is mixed. Various scapegoats were found; no doubt some of it was due to Kitchener's having centralized too much of the administrative responsibility for his divisions in Army Headquarters. But surely it goes back further than that. Much of it must rest with the War Office and the Treasury in Whitehall, and with the Secretaries of State for India who had acquiesced in their views. Between them, these three departments had contrived a system by which India in peace kept a larger army than was justified by purely Indian reasons. But no one would admit it; there was a fiction that the army was for local purposes only and since India was a poor country her army was trained, equipped and organized for local purposes. An expedition overseas of one or two divisions was what India was supposed to be capable of mounting. And in spite of having sent an army corps and a cavalry division to France, India was able to execute with brilliant success the first stage of the Mesopotamia campaign, which might be regarded as a local purpose. But to take Baghdad was more than local, and surely, when the decision to go on from Kut was taken, the War Office became morally responsible for ensuring that this front was as well supplied as any other.

No one can think of the carnage of this war without horror. But in the case of the Indian deaths there is a special question to be asked, grim but wry. In every English village, there was built after the war a memorial with an inscription to the memory of the dead. The survivors thought they knew why these men had died. It was to defend their homes and ultimately to make possible a more peaceful and civilized world. This last was illusion—but it was their belief and it was recorded in suitable words. In India, there were no such village memorials, only one great arch in Delhi, erected and inscribed by the British.* Why did their kin in the villages think these men had died? There are also memorials to them in the regimental histories, written, of course, by their officers. And surely there is something ironic and a trifle empty in the thought with which they often commemorate the dead. 'May those left behind rest in peace', wrote one such officer on leaving Mesopotamia, 'in the assurance that their sacrifice was not in vain and the example they set inspired their successors to win fresh laurels for the regiment.' 'They have given their lives nobly', wrote another, 'to perpetuate the name of the regiment and to prove beyond all question the fighting qualities of the Marathas.'

To die for one's country or to save the life of a leader or a comrade is a noble end. To die for the regiment is not very different if the regiment is part of the national tradition. But in India's case the regiment was not part of the national tradition and the time was not far off when the allegiance of the regiment would be transferred from the King Emperor to the President of India. Perhaps an uneasy and as yet hardly conscious presentiment of the coming divorce induced officers to shrink from saying that these men had died for their King or their Country. They said instead that they had died for the regiment, which thus became an end in itself, an idol demanding men's blood. But surely what they had really died for was honour—the good name in the world of their kin and clan and village, their own good name among those who knew them, and last of all personal honour, that vindication of integrity which is involved in faithful perseverance in a path once chosen.

* After the publication of this book, a correspondent told me that in 1946 he had gone to the village of Nakka Khurd on the Frontier to stay with his Pathan orderly. There he had seen a War Memorial inscribed with the names of the men from that village who had died in the First World War. It had been their own idea; they had built it themselves. But they had asked the Commissioner what it should look like and he had drawn it for them—and there it stood, strangely English. That was an exception—but how different everything in that letter sounds from what a younger generation has been led to expect! The officer going to stay in the village as his orderly's guest, the villagers deciding to commemorate their dead and asking the Commissioner's advice!

XVIII

Between the Wars

1. Insulation versus Incitement

To read any political account of India between the wars is to picture a scene of constant turmoil and agitation, one campaign of civil disobedience succeeding another, national leaders moving in and out of gaol, delegations going to London for Round-Table Conferences — a long, intricate and confused succession of events in which the one constant is the will of national leaders for some form of independence. After this, to read the regimental histories is to blink in astonishment; we seem to have gone back to 1910. The infantry regiments record the prowess of their regimental hockey teams, the cavalry their successes at polo. Commanding officers retire or are promoted; the regiment puts on a beautifully rehearsed musical ride at the Delhi Horse Show or sends a contingent to London for the Coronation; the Commander-in-Chief presents new colours and speaks of the glorious traditions of the regiment and the spirit which is unchanged from one generation to another. There is some fighting in Waziristan and some battalions have the unpleasant experience of being posted to Bengal. But there is only the most occasional mention of political events and hardly a hint that there might be any strain on the loyalties of sepoy or sowar.

Question, on the other hand, a score or so of Englishmen about their own experiences and you will find that neither of these impressions is exactly confirmed. The sense of strain and opposition was there, but it was intermittent; there were areas of apparent calm, but there were usually undercurrents beneath the surface, below the placid succession of proclamation parades, race-weeks and polo tournaments. There was a struggle in progress for the minds of the great inarticulate mass of the Indian peasantry. And it was a struggle in which both parties, judged forty years later, can be seen to have had aims of which they were not fully aware at the time and which were to some extent in conflict with those they professed.

The peasants of India, as of most other countries, were sceptical of innovation; they did not expect much comfort in this life or much consideration from townsfolk or the rich; they were frequently pessimistic about human efforts to change the human condition. They distrusted all outsiders; to the English, they expressed their suspicion of Indian townsfolk, to whom no doubt they were equally scathing about the English. It was not easy to persuade them to try a new kind of seed, a new plough or an expensive fertilizer. The margin between survival and starvation was too narrow to take risks. And it was not very much easier to persuade them to take part in a widespread political movement based on general principles. Indian nationalism was still hardly born. The task of Indian nationalist leaders was thus at the same time to excite and to unify. And the causes in which they believed did not particularly appeal to the peasants, who were four-fifths of the population.

The contradiction at the heart of Indian nationalism was that the reasons for change were Western reasons. There was a burning need for reform of the ancient Indian social system. The rigidity of caste and the humiliation of the untouchables who were beyond caste cried out for sweeping change; the position of women — their segregation behind the purdah, their early marriages, their lack of education — came second only to caste. The princely states were strongholds of absolute feudalism and arbitrary power; even in the provinces of British India large areas were ruled in much the same way as the states by great landowners whose ancestors had long ago established a claim to British gratitude. All these remnants of an ancient past were detestable to Indian leaders who had been trained in the politics of Bentham, Mill and Gladstone. But they were not of much interest to the peasants, while it was on these same liberal principles that the English based the reasons *they* found for their instinctive resistance to the transfer of power. They must look after the untouchables, the Muslims, the princes, who would otherwise be crushed out of existence by an irresistible majority led by the best educated — that is to say, Brahmans and money-lenders. The peasant must be protected because he was helpless; who but the English had protected him and taught him to expect justice? And just as the nationalist leaders were sure that none but they could carry out the reforms which liberal principles so urgently demanded, the English were sure that none but they would ensure that respect for the rights of individuals which the same principles guaranteed. Thus there was a contradiction in the attitude of both; the nationalists invoked Western principles to destroy their own Indian form of society, while the English sought excuses for denying to their fellow-subjects freedom to govern themselves — something that they had boasted was the corner-stone of their constitution.

On the highest political level, both parties expressed their aims in the same terms, and the conflict was therefore seen as one of timing and method; in practice, in the district, the opposition was simple and direct. The nationalist sought to excite, to stimulate, to stir up; he wanted to arouse the peasants from their age-long toleration of their position in the social structure. But the district officer did not want the peasants aroused; he knew that there would be trouble; sooner or later, they would start killing each other—or perhaps someone else. His first aim was to avoid a disturbance in his district; he would have preferred the peasants to be insulated against the winds of change. Often he recognized philosophically that this was impossible, but still he wanted as much insulation as he could get.

The soldier—the British officer—was almost bound to take a more absolute view. There could be no more or less, no half and half, about the loyalty of the army. The Indian Army had always been insulated against politics; that insulation must continue. Even if there were ever to be an independent Dominion of India, 'politics' must be eschewed; the army must be the servant of the State, in the Duke of Wellington's great tradition. Few perceived that when the struggle is between Whig and Tory, politics has one meaning, but quite another when the question is whether your country shall be ruled by your fellow-countrymen or by foreigners. Most officers felt rather that the need to keep out of politics was even more important when politics meant sedition. The men in the ranks must be preserved from every corrupting taint. In fact most officers took an unconscious decision that they would see no politics, hear no politics, think no politics. And the men behaved accordingly. There was a conspiracy to keep a stiff upper lip and behave as though loyalty to anyone but the King Emperor simply could not arise.

The conspiracy was extraordinarily successful. It lasted for the quarter-century from the end of the First World War till the eve of Independence. With a few exceptions, the rank and file of the army were insulated from changes in the life of the nation; they fought with conspicuous gallantry and fidelity in Italy and in the recovery of Burma; Hindu, Sikh and Muslim worked together in the army as comrades when hatred was growing in the nation. There is, however, something brittle about an allegiance which depends on insulation and this was shown in the story of the Indian National Army, which came into being among those taken prisoner by the Japanese, a story to which we shall come back later. Still, for this period and within limits, the policy of insulation worked. To write about it is necessarily to enter into the realms of surmise; what the Indian soldier thought is even more closely hidden than it had been in the time of Sita Ram. Something can be deduced from his behaviour and what his officers thought he thought—but since there was so clear a resolution on their part to shut their eyes, it is unlikely that he opened his mind freely to them. It is guesswork to say that it was an artificial insulation, but soldiers cannot have been wholly unaware of what was going on. They obediently, and on the whole contentedly, put it out of their minds when they were with the regiments; they put in its place the company's success at hockey or on the rifle range. But to understand how improbable it is that they never gave national politics a thought, let us look briefly at the course of events and the politics of the recruiting areas.

2. Non-co-operation, Civil Disobedience and Partition

In 1915 the Indian National Congress had passed a resolution which they had asked might be conveyed to the Indian troops fighting in Europe. 'This Congress', it ran, 'rejoices to place on record the deep sense of gratitude and pride in the heroic conduct of the Indian troops whose deeds of valour and conspicuous humanity and chivalry in the Great War are winning the respect of civilized mankind for the Mother Country and resolves to send a message of hearty and affectionate greetings to them and their comrades in arms, with fervent prayers for their well-being and success.' Nationalist India still hoped that the devotion of the Indian Army would lead to some dramatic recognition. But the war dragged on; the disaster of Kut and subsequent mismanagement added to the feeling of disillusion and impatience. And when it came, recognition was not exactly dramatic. Edwin Montagu, as Secretary of State, announced on August 17th, 1917, that the aim of the British Government was 'the increasing association of Indians in every branch of the administration and the gradual development of self-governing institutions with a view to the progressive realization of responsible government in India as an integral part of the Empire.' The words were carefully chosen; they had to be acceptable to conservatives and liberals alike. It was an achievement to have won so much — but they do not carry the ring of warmth or spontaneity. They were followed by the Montagu–Chelmsford Report, which appeared in July 1918, recommending steps in the direction of these aims. But, again, they were cautious steps; in the provinces, but not at the centre, there were to be ministers for such subjects as education and local government but the backbone subjects — finance, law and order — would still be administered by the Governor. The progress made would be reviewed in ten years' time, by a committee of the British Parliament, and there would be further steps if the review was judged satisfactory — but again, the judge was to be the British Parliament.

Ten years is a long time to an impatient reformer and it was irksome that even then the British should be the sole judges of success. The

proposals would have seemed cautious and disappointing even to the
moderates who had managed Congress in 1915, but their day was done.
They had been outflanked from the left and the more militant group
now in control had no inclination to curb the disappointment which
most of their supporters felt. To aggravate the impatience and sense of
betrayal, it was not until March 1921 that the new constitution was
inaugurated, and by that time two events had taken place which
alienated Indian opinion deeply. In 1919 the Government of India
passed the Rowlatt Acts, giving them very wide power to act against
persons judged guilty of sedition. The Acts were passed against the
votes of every non-official in the Legislative Council. They were never
used, but they were felt as a slap in the face for a people who had
supposed their services in the war would be acclaimed with superlatives and rewarded by trust. But worse was to follow. At Amritsar on
April 13th, 1919, General Dyer ordered a party of Gurkhas to open
fire on a crowd who had gathered to hold a meeting in defiance of
orders. The meeting was in an open space surrounded by buildings to
which the only entrance was held by the troops; the crowd could not
disperse. Dyer continued to fire until he had killed 379 persons and
wounded over 1,200; what made even this slaughter more appalling
was that he said afterwards that he had determined to administer a
lesson that would have an effect throughout India. In this he succeeded,
though not in the way he had meant. Instead of ending opposition to
the Government, he intensified hostility; he dealt a wound to relations
between British and Indians that has never been healed. Dyer was
officially censured but many English people noisily approved of him.
And for the purpose of this book it is important that his massacre
happened at Amritsar, the heart of the Sikh religion.

The Rowlatt Acts, Amritsar, the delay in introducing the new constitution, the terms of the constitution itself—all produced the tense
angry atmosphere in which Gandhi launched the non-co-operation
campaign of 1921. The idea was quite simple; the machine of Indian
government only worked because Indians helped to work it. If they
simply refused, it would stop. Not enough refused and in the end the
public tired of it; the Government, in a sense, won. But their victory
left the country sullen and disappointed, and something irreversible
had happened. Since Joan of Arc—'*la belle Lorraine, Qu'anglois brulèrent
en Rouen*'—no one had been more adept than Gandhi at perceiving
intuitively what had to be done and finding reasons for it afterwards.
He knew—without putting it in words even to himself—that neither
liberal reforms nor even an Indian nation were causes that would
rouse the villagers. They might be roused for a local cause, but if his
appeal was to be universal, it must appeal to something deeper. He
must strike a religious note; he must speak in the key, not of orthodoxy,

but of ancient Hindu feeling. And therefore, year by year, as the struggle swayed to and fro, the Hindu flavour of the movement convinced more and more Muslims that it was not for them.

The Simon Report reviewed the constitution two years before it was necessary—which was regarded in London as a concession. But the commissioners who signed it were all British; they had to be, because it was a Parliamentary Commission. This seemed mere pedantry to the nationalists, who found it intolerable that not one Indian should take part in deliberations that were to settle their fate. Gandhi launched his civil disobedience campaign, and civil disobedience was more positive than non-co-operation. It meant breaking the law on a massive scale and filling the prisons till they would hold no more. That campaign too failed in a sense; it was easy to excite a village mob to a sudden burst of violence, impossible to sustain for long periods the steady determination required for peaceful disobedience. Apathy won again, but again it was a sullen apathy and the tide was mounting. Edwin Montagu had been on the side of the nationalists in seeing that 'the placid pathetic contentment of the masses is not the soil on which Indian nationhood will grow.' He went further and believed that 'in deliberately disturbing it, we are working for India's highest good.' He was quite right; the old order had depended on the resigned acceptance of a society which was regarded as unchangeable. But Montagu's difficulty resembled Gandhi's. If the villagers did not want to be stirred up, still less did district officers or military officers want to stir them. There was a conflict between high policy and all that the services had been trained to aim at. The district officers could not insulate their charges; there was still general apathy but an awareness of things political was growing. By the 'thirties 'placid pathetic contentment' was in general a thing of the past. But the army was still insulated against the new spirit.

3. The Recruiting Grounds

We need not attempt to follow the differences within the nationalist movement, except those of particular interest to the army. The Khilāfat* movement, in support of the Khalif of Islam, had, as we have seen, caused some anxiety about Muslim soldiers in the First World War; it died away when the Sultan of Turkey was deposed in 1923.

---

* In Arabic the meaning of the root of this word is 'to succeed or follow' and the Khalif is the Successor of the Prophet. But the phrase 'in succession' came to mean 'by contrast' or 'in opposition'—a bitter comment on the history of many Mohammedan dynasties—and to everyone in Northern India the most familiar word from this root means 'against'. Many village Muslims must have supposed the movement was *against* the Government.

But the Punjab, the army's main recruiting-ground, was far from being a political backwater. The western parts were predominantly Muslim, the eastern Sikh or Hindu, but there was no clear-cut dividing line. In the province as a whole, the Muslims were in a majority, being about 57 per cent of the population, but the Sikhs had once ruled the Punjab and were still an active, intelligent and often aggressive community. Their rule was not remembered with affection by the Muslims. And it was with the express purpose of fighting Muslim intolerance that the Sikhs had become a military order three centuries ago. To Sikhs and Muslims alike it was intolerable to contemplate living under a Government composed entirely of the other community.

From 1921 onwards the provincial Government was becoming more and more important; to most villagers it mattered more than the Government of India at the Centre. And in the Punjab it was the object of successive Governors to prevent a clear-cut political division between Muslims on the one hand and Sikhs and Hindus on the other. The Hindus included Jats in the south-east and Dogras in the north, all men who made good soldiers and were recruited to the army, men whose hostility might easily flare up in violence. Until the end of the Second World War it was possible to keep in power a Unionist Government in which Muslim, Sikh and Hindu interests were represented. It was a Government which sought to maintain unity and the established order against divisive forces. But these were strong, and growing in strength. There was the vigorous sect of Akali Sikhs, who in the 'twenties were militantly anti-British. Meanwhile the Muslim League, an all-India party with at first little hold in the Punjab, moved steadily towards the separation of Hindu from Muslim India and in the end to the idea of Pakistan as a separate sovereign State. To the Muslim League, the Unionist Party in the Punjab must be an enemy. At one time the League argued that the whole of the Punjab, because of its Muslim majority, must go to Pakistan. This would have been resisted to the death by the Sikhs. As Muslim support swung from the Unionists to the Muslim League, communal feeling grew more and more bitter until, finally, just that situation was reached which the Governors had sought to avoid — a division into parties on purely communal lines. It was only in the last years before Independence that Pakistan became a live issue, but long before that, when the question was not one of sovereignty but of a self-governing province, Sikhs and Muslims were alike resolved that they would never live under the exclusive domination of the other. Can it be supposed that no one talked about this in the villages where the recruits grew up?

The Frontier Province was also a recruiting-ground. This was overwhelmingly Muslim. But perhaps because the Muslim League at first hardly existed in the Punjab, the nationalists sought another ally and after the collapse of the Khilāfat movement saw in Congress the principal opponent of the Government and therefore a friend. It was an incongruous alliance, since the Frontier people generally despised Hindus, had no use for liberal principles and regarded non-violence as a creed for milksops. But it provided a people naturally turbulent with a banner under which they could enlist in order to indulge in opposition to the Government which was as much sport as politics. The militant wing of the Frontier Congress was called the Redshirt movement; they paraded and marched and held meetings and on the Frontier such activities were always dangerous.

The only other recruiting-grounds of any importance were Bombay and the United Provinces, both Congress strongholds. Bombay provided the six battalions of Marathas; the U.P., apart from some men for the Indian Hospital Corps, the Indian Army Service Corps and other ancillary troops, sent to the fighting units some Jats and Muslims from the western districts and four battalions of Garhwalis. I have dwelt on the splendid record of these men in the First World War and used my personal knowledge to illustrate how difficult they found it to understand what was happening when there was a Congress Government for the province. And they better than anyone show how impossible it was to insulate the recruiting areas.

Garhwal had long been insulated by nature. Its hills rise straight up from the plains and there was only one motorable road and that went only a few miles into the district to Lansdowne, the cantonment of the Garhwalis and the 2nd/3rd Gurkhas. All the rest of the district, right up to the perpetual snows, could be reached only on foot or by mule. The people were simple and law-abiding; there were no regular police and no need for them. The battalions had usually been thought of as just as dependable as Gurkhas. When there was the likelihood of riots, they were interchangeable with Gurkhas or British troops. But in 1930 one of their battalions refused duty at Peshawar.

The men had been on duty in Peshawar city, facing an excited mob of Redshirts hurling bricks and soda-water bottles and trying to break their lines. They had been in close physical contact with hostile Pathans who used clubs and sticks and they had not been allowed to retaliate. Next day two platoons refused to get into the buses that were to take them to the city for more of this kind of thing. There was uncertainty later about how many had really known what was happening; some of them had signed a paper asking to be discharged but said that they had been told it was a petition for an increased ration of rum. The Court of Inquiry found that the trouble was confined to these two platoons and that the behaviour of the troops in the city had been entirely in accordance with their orders; indeed, they had been complimented by the G.O.C. for their steadiness. But they had been mishandled; it was a breach of a general principle to bring troops into such close physical contact with a violent and hostile crowd. The N.C.O.s of these two platoons were sentenced to various terms of imprisonment,* the rifle-men of the two platoons were dismissed. The Court found that there had been no direct subversive influence at work.

Now on every occasion when there was trouble in the Indian Army, from the earliest days of the Company till the incident at Singapore in 1915, there have been present in some degree the three classical factors —ineffective officers, a general political unease or some general grievance in the villages, and a direct military grievance as the imme-diate spark. In this regiment the officers were remarkable for the interest they took in their men. On this occasion, however, by a rare combina-tion of circumstances, a fine commanding officer had recently finished his time and gone to a staff appointment; his second-in-command and another experienced officer were on leave in England, while a third had just left for a temporary staff appointment. Another of the company commanders, one who had spent all his service with the regiment, was hit on the head by a brick and taken unconscious to hospital during the riot in Peshawar. That was five of the most experienced; the establish-ment was twelve. The new commanding officer had not had time to make much impact; he had only just come from a regiment that had recently been disbanded and he was removed immediately after this incident. His acting second-in-command was also new to the regiment; Garhwalis usually knew their officers by nicknames and they had already come to know this man as 'Perhaps Sahib'.† The Garhwalis had shown in France that Garhwali officers could take responsibility when their British officers were killed but it was worse to be com-manded by unknown and indecisive officers. On the day in question the subadar commanding one of the two platoons affected was punished, as he thought unjustly; he resented the punishment and was later proved to have engineered the incident as a protest.

Thus we have two of the classical ingredients—strange officers in whom the men had no confidence, and a personal military grievance resented as an injustice. As to the third, no evidence was found of direct subversion—no political agitator had got at the men. But can it really be supposed that there was not, deep in the men's minds, some consciousness of coming change, of a new Indian nationalism, some confusion as to where their loyalty really ought to lie? The simple faith of such a man as old Makar Sing would hold them while they were in

---

* A havildar, the last of these men, was released after serving his sentence in 1938 or 1939, when I was in charge of the district. By that time there was no doubt about his politics.

† 'Shayyad Sahib'. *Shayyad* means literally 'it may be' and is not a word which ought to occur in military orders.

the regiment and in contact with British officers. But they went on leave and heard rumours and must have had twinges of doubt. And when they had no trusted officer to whom they could turn, such doubts might recur.

It remains to add that in 1937 the district by a large majority voted for two Congress candidates whose simple platform was to reduce the taxes and spend more money locally. Most of the district believed passionately that a road ought to be built into the district, whatever the engineering difficulties and expense, and they wanted representatives who would put their case with passion — not Government pensioners. They were voting for spokesmen; there was little idea that there would be a change of Government. But it is hard to convey the confusion of mind that arose among people who for hundreds of years had thought of government as personal and authoritative. There was still not a village in the district where they would not welcome the Deputy Commissioner, listen to him respectfully, and ask for his help.

Nowhere, then, is it reasonable to suppose that the recruiting-grounds could be altogether insulated from nationalism. Nor was it possible to picture the recruit as belonging to a dissenting minority which was actively loyal; there was really no alternative creed in which one could expect him to have a strong emotional commitment. To fight for one's king as a religious duty had still been an ideal in 1914; it could hardly be as strong a generation later. But there was still an incentive to belong to the regiment, to have money in one's pocket to spend, to send money home, to come home on leave, smart and shining with health, full of news of the great world. And once in the regiment, insulation was usually complete. There was so much to do and they were so well; they surrendered happily to discipline and good food and company sports and they forgot all about the puzzling talk in the village.

4. The King's Commission

When Lord Rawlinson came to India as Commander-in-Chief in 1919 he was faced by more problems than any Commander-in-Chief since the years after the Mutiny. What was more, he had to justify expenditure to a Government beginning to be responsive to a public opinion, if a somewhat narrow one. Of the problems confronting him, there are some we have anticipated. The grouping of battalions into regiments with training battalions we have already dealt with and also the position of the Commander-in-Chief as the Viceroy's sole military adviser. The Chief's formal position remained essentially as Kitchener had left it; he was both Commander-in-Chief and the Defence Member of the Viceroy's Council. Nor was there much change in regard to the Frontier.

Rawlinson had inherited from Roberts and from his father, who had held high office in India, a belief in a moderate forward policy; roads were less expensive than military expeditions and roads would in the end civilize and pacify the tribes. 'Shutting them up only tempts them to break out.' He eventually obtained approval for a garrison at Razmak, well into the hills. But the Frontier was still much as Roberts had known it; there was still the belt of tribal territory, unadministered, between Afghanistan and the British administered districts; the tribes still periodically defied the Government and had to be punished. 'Air blockade' became a new weapon in the Government's armoury, but it could only be used after warning notices had first been dropped, and, even without that humane precaution, bombardment from the air is not very effective in sparsely inhabited mountainous country. The Frontier was still a training-ground for troops.

One problem, however, was new. In 1918 it had been announced that in future the King's Commission would be open to Indians and that ten places a year would be reserved for Indians at Sandhurst. They were to be in every way on a footing with British officers and were posted in the same way, doing a year's training with a British battalion on leaving Sandhurst and then going to an Indian Army regiment. The young officer usually expressed a choice and if there was a vacancy in the regiment he was interviewed and the regiment might agree to accept him. No difficulty had so far arisen over this. But there was much uneasiness, widely expressed. Rawlinson mentions it more than once in his letters and diaries. 'People are frightened,' he wrote; 'old officers say they won't send their sons out to serve under natives ... Are we going to find a sufficient number of Partabs and Ranjis to act as leaders?' He meant of course Sir Partab of Jodhpur and Ranjitsinjhi, the England cricketer. And again, in his diary, he expressed his doubts more fully:

'If rushed, the supply of British officers will dry up long before India is in any degree ready to do without them ... Will we ever get a young educated Indian to lead a charge of veteran Sikhs against a *sangar* [stone emplacement for riflemen] held by Mahsuds and, if he did, would the Sikhs follow him? Will we ever get the sons of the landowners of the fighting races, who are brought up to despise the Babu ... sufficiently educated to be trusted with the lives of men in modern war? ... It will take at least two, and probably three, generations to produce Indian officers of the right kind in sufficient numbers.'

These were the fears of most British officers. How far this contempt for 'the Babu' was their own feeling, perceived by their men and echoed back to them, is a matter on which there can be no certainty, but of their own opinions there can be no doubt. The fear that British officers 'of the right kind' would not come forward was strong in the 'twenties and it was to meet this that the 'eight units scheme' was devised. The scheme was announced on February 17th, 1923; the essence of it was that two cavalry regiments and six infantry battalions should be 'Indianized' as a first step; Indians with the King's Commission in other units should be encouraged to transfer to them and no new British officers would be posted there. This, it was said officially, would give Indians 'a fair chance' to show that such units could be just as efficient as those with British officers.

But there can be no doubt that it was primarily a solution of the difficulty of 'serving under natives.' The idea of special 'Indianizing' units is mentioned early in Rawlinson's diaries; it is taken for granted, as not needing discussion, by the Indianization Committee of 1922. This was a committee of staff officers at Army Headquarters set up by the Commander-in-Chief to 'frame a progressive policy, working up by degrees to final Indianization'. The principle of 'Indianization' had been accepted and it was not their duty to comment on that. As to how it could be done, they rejected as unworkable a suggestion by the Legislative Assembly·that one-quarter of the commissions should be offered to Indians in the first year, the proportion going up by 2½ per cent every year; this would have taken thirty years to Indianize the *intake*, not the whole body of officers. They thought it far better to proceed in three stages, each of 14 years. To begin with, twenty battalions of infantry, seven regiments of cavalry, and artillery units in proportion, should be chosen and to these no British officers would be posted; this would require 81 Indian commissions a year. After 14 years, in Phase II, forty battalions of infantry and another seven of cavalry would be added to the list; in Phase III all units would be in process of Indianizing, and by year 42 of the scheme (which would be 1967) every unit in the Indian Army would have Indian officers from top to bottom. But no British officer would have had to serve in a unit commanded by someone commissioned under this scheme.

The new officers would hold King's Commissions but in His Majesty's *Indian* Land Forces only—and here they would resemble Canadian officers or Australian. The commission then being granted to those from Sandhurst, whether British or Indian, was in the Land Forces (not the Indian Land Forces) and carried command over both British and Indian troops. There would no longer be any need for Viceroy's Commissioned Officers—the old subadars and jemadars. Special arrangements would be needed to educate and train the youngest and brightest of them for the new kind of commission; the older would waste out but perhaps some of their sons could be commissioned.

This was an honest attempt to work out the implications of a policy of which the committee themselves probably disapproved. It is noteworthy for its unquestioning acceptance of the idea of segregated units and for the time thought necessary to complete the process. But in

fact the report proved a dead letter; after discussion with the War
Office, the India Office proposed that a beginning should be made with
four units only. Now nobody thought the British officer's fear of serving
under an Indian was quite the sort of reason for segregated units that
ought to be given in public. The official reason was that only by this
means could we be sure that a unit officered by Indians was thoroughly
efficient. Considering the whole operation as a scientific experiment, this
could not be proved until there were Indian lieutenant-colonels in
command of regiments; this would occur in twenty-six years' time. If
the experiment took so long and was confined to four units it was hard
to see when the process would be complete. It cannot really be regarded
as an honest attempt to implement the policy; it meant that the War
Office refused to take seriously the proclamation of 1918 and put up a
token proposal as a way of shelving the question. Rawlinson saw the
absurdity and persuaded the India Office to agree to eight units.

Lord Rawlinson deserved well of India in many ways. He reduced
the military budget from 82 crores* in 1921 to 56 in 1925; the number
of British troops was reduced from 75,000 to 57,000 and the Indian
Army from 159,000 to 140,000 — with, he believed, a considerable
increase in efficiency. He wrote: 'The Home Government has introduced the Reforms and must face the consequences, which means
trust ... We must either trust and go on to Dominion self-government
or go back to ... ruling India by the sword.' And in the last speech
before his sudden death he laid an emphasis on education for the army
which really spelt an end to the old system of insulation. 'For the modern
battle we want men of education who can get the maximum value
from scientific weapons.'

But it is no use pretending that the eight units scheme was anything
but unpopular. It was not much better than four. Indian 'public
opinion' meant of course only a small number of India's millions and,
even of that limited public, few had any detailed knowledge of things
military. But it did not take much knowledge to see that the real reason
for segregated units was dislike for serving under a 'native' — and the
reason publicly given was not much less wounding, while it seemed to
postpone completion of the process indefinitely. No one could disguise
the fact that most Englishmen believed that hardly any Indians were
really good enough to lead Indian troops.

The belief ought really to be put in a different way. What almost
every British officer believed was that only the British public-school
system could produce the right kind of officer and only the right kind of
officer could give Indian troops the leadership they needed. The public-
school system, it was believed, made a boy independent; he left home
early and had to look after himself. He learnt to believe that there was

* A crore of rupees was about £750,000.

something praiseworthy about enduring hardship without complaint. He was taught to own up to a fault and take the punishment without bearing a grudge. He put a high value on physical health and on success at games; he learnt to exercise authority when he was only thirteen, then at a new school went back to the bottom of the ladder and had to work up it again. He had therefore learned both to obey and command before he arrived at Sandhurst. He had learnt that to command he must be just and impartial and must put the comfort and safety of those under his command before his own.

Unless he had been to the Prince of Wales Royal Indian Military College at Dehra Dun—which was run on public-school lines—an Indian boy had had none of these advantages. Few Indian schools at that time paid much attention to games or physical fitness and discipline was sometimes lax, sometimes brutal and arbitrary. He had perhaps never been long away from home before he went to a foreign country and at Sandhurst was plunged into a course that was deliberately designed to be exacting, both physically and mentally.

The results of the first few years were reviewed in 1923 by another A.H.Q. committee which was to report on the Progress of Indianization. It was appointed by the Commander-in-Chief a few months after the announcement of the eight units scheme. It began by laying great stress on the impartiality of British officers between different classes of Indian soldiers; this they could never hope for from Indians. It acknowledged the courage of Indian trooops but pointed out that throughout the war no Indian had risen from the ranks to high command—a point that was grossly unfair, since Indians had not been eligible for the King's Commission till 1918. The committee went on, with more justice, to argue that the army in India had been reduced to an absolute minimum and that every unit must therefore be highly efficient. No risks must be taken and every unit must be interchangeable and fit for war.

Officers of the British service often inclined to the logical view that, if the Indian Army was to be officered entirely by Indians, they should be on exactly the same footing as British officers serving with British regiments in their own country. British officers of the Indian Army served away from home all their lives and it was reasonable that they should have extra pay, but Indians in their own country did not need this. Nor did they need an intermediate class of officer with a Viceroy's Commission to interpret the men's wishes to them; they should start by commanding a platoon and work up from that, like a British subaltern. This of course would incidentally delay by a few years the stage when they actually supplanted British officers. And it seemed to follow that they should have a Canadian type of commission, in the Indian Land Forces only.

The Progress of Indianization Committee rejected this view firmly.

It would never do to have two classes of officer in the same unit on different rates of pay and with different kinds of King's Commission. Further, the prospect of promotion to a Viceroy's Commission was a very important inducement in recruiting. They therefore believed that Indians who held the King's Commission must be what were later called 'Brindians'. They must resemble British officers—and, what is more, British officers from public schools—in every respect except the accident of birth. Nothing else would do; there must be no lowering of standards. No risks could be taken; efficiency must be maintained.

It is hard to quarrel with this reasoning without questioning the one basic assumption on which it all hung: that the only standard of excellence for an officer was that accepted by the Rifle Brigade or the 60th Rifles, the Guides or Probyn's Horse. This standard included an implication peculiarly British, that certain moral qualities were linked with class and could not be acquired in one generation. An officer was judged by social as well as professional standards by delicate distinctions in behaviour difficult to define in writing and hard for a foreigner to learn. It was puzzling to explain how it was that the French and American armies seemed able to manage with officers who had not been to public schools. But this difficulty, touched on by a later body, the Indian Sandhurst Committee, was shrugged aside and no one ever mentioned the fact that in 'modern war', when requirements are so high, no one had thought it necessary to keep up these social standards. The assumption reigned supreme: everyone accepted it.

And how could the Commandant at Sandhurst and the commanding officers of regiments administer any standards but those they knew? They must either be told to keep up their standards or be told to lower them and let cadets pass out of Sandhurst for the Indian Army who would not have passed if they had been British. No Indian politician would have asked for that. What was difficult to explain to Indian parents and politicians was that cadets were not judged only on examination results or only on athletic achievements, both of which are measurable; they had to reach a standard in these subjects and in drill, but it was more important to get a good opinion for such intangible qualities as leadership, an even temperament, the ability to put up with horseplay and leg-pulling without loss of temper, cheerfulness, quickness to obey, initiative and self-reliance; above all—and hardest of all to define—'pulling one's weight'. And obedience must not be slavish but tempered by initiative. The boy must learn to be a brother-officer as well as a junior, linked in a common bond of honourable behaviour. In all these, the Indian boy who had not been to the Prince of Wales Royal Indian Military College at Dehra Dun really was at a disadvantage.

How difficult some of them found it can be seen from the reports on them by the company commanders and the Commandant at Sandhurst. These give the impression that the reporting officers had resolved to be fair and at the same time to keep up standards but were sometimes confronted by a young man outside their experience. Sometimes a cadet who made an unfavourable impression in his first term improved and got his commission eventually; the reports suggest that company commanders did not close their minds against a cadet without giving him the opportunity to mend—but nothing could alter the fact that they were judging boys who were not English by English standards in respect of qualities hard to measure. Here are some samples:

Cadet A: Company Commander: 'Has worked well and his conduct is good. But he is rather dull and lacking in personality and I do not consider him up to the standard of the other cadets under my command.' Commandant: 'I agree. I do not consider that this cadet is of the right type to make an officer.' (Removed.)

Cadet B: 'Nervous and undeveloped. Tries hard but shows no signs of making a leader and is much below the standard of his class in intelligence.' (Removed.)

Cadet C: 'Leadership undeveloped. Ability below average. But has done well and developed very satisfactorily during his 18 months at Sandhurst. Keen and hard working though handicapped by poor knowledge of English.' (Commissioned.)

Cadet D: 'Takes trouble with his work but is handicapped by limited knowledge of English causing poor results. Lacks power of command due to nervousness and self-consciousness. He will require time before he reaches the necessary standard. I think he will eventually be all right but he is very backward.' (He improved steadily and was commissioned.)

Cadet E: 'Average of Indian Cadets. Works hard and always does his best, though handicapped by indifferent English. A good manner and temperament. Plays games well: a plucky footballer. Should do well.'

Cadet F: In his first term, this cadet was 'sadly handicapped by a strange tongue.' But in his final report he has 'a very nice personality. Tries hard and should make a good officer.'

Cadet G: Was at first reported on as inclined to argue and sulk if corrected. But later: 'He tries hard and always does his best. Writes better English than the average Indian Gentlemen Cadet and knows his books but is inclined to stick to them slavishly. Appears to have quite overcome his sulky temper ... '

Cadet H: 'Ability above average. Conduct very good. Intelligent and hard working. A good type and has done well.' And the Commandant notes: 'A very good type of Indian Cadet. Keen both at work and play. Very intelligent and shows great promise.' (He became Commander-in-Chief!)

Cadet J: 'Has tried hard but is not the type and does not appear to have it in him to make an officer.'

These reports do not give an impression of unfairness. But the results reported by the Progress of Indianization Committee were certainly disappointing. Of the first twenty-five Indian cadets admitted to Sandhurst, ten had failed to reach the standard for passing out, two had died, two resigned, one had been deprived of his commission and ten had passed. Five of these were already with regiments of the Indian Army, and four of them refused to transfer to Indianized units; the committee understood that the other five who had passed out of Sandhurst and were training with British units were likely to resign their commissions rather than go to such units. The committee thought this could only mean either that they did not wish to serve under Indians or that they were afraid of taking responsibility without British officers to back them up. This again was most unfair; they might also object to going to a unit which was socially segregated and which in the circumstances of the time was bound to be regarded as socially, if in no other way, inferior. They might have special family reasons for preferring other units.

One may think of pressures from several directions converging to mould this new kind of Indian officer. From the British side, at the highest level there was a conviction that India must eventually be a self-governing dominion with officers of her own, but this was tempered at a lower level by a distaste for the whole business and the conviction that if Indians were to be officers they must be just like British officers. On the Indian nationalist side, there was an intense desire to see the army officered by Indians as soon as possible, but this was still generally accompanied by a feeling that on this kind of thing the British really did know best and their kind of officer was the best kind to have. With a diffidence that was very far from being revolutionary, Indian leaders strangely, indeed rather touchingly, accepted the whole British concept of an officer, complete not only with technical standards but with social shibboleths such as not wearing brown shoes with a dark suit and not mentioning a woman's name in the mess. And then there were the parents of these young officers-to-be. The father, no doubt, was socially ambitious but deeply disturbed by the cost and had an eye to the boy's future if at any stage he should fail to overcome the obstacles in his path; the mother would often be saddened and bewildered by all the processes that were necessary to turn her little son into a hard-faced, shiny sahib with a stiff upper lip, impervious to pain and discomfort, resolute in understatement, grimly repressive of emotion and of those tremulous heartfelt disclosures which a mother hopes to share with the youth as he grows.

And what of the young man himself? An Indian boy's home if he belonged to the middle classes was likely to be a good deal more permissive in general atmosphere than a British boy's at that time, though in other respects more rigid. He would probably have been expected to show more outward respect to his father, but to have counted on a more continuous indulgence from his mother. Unless he had been to one of the few boarding schools, the tyranny of his schoolfellows' opinion would have made less impact on him and the first shock of homesickness would coincide with the shock of a new country and an entirely new concept of education. Such a boy would have to get used to a new kind of food, which he usually found insipid and disagreeable, to new clothes, which felt thick and clumsy, and a language in which even if he was fluent he was sure to miss shades of meaning and which sometimes he misunderstood. Even if he came from a quite humble middle-class home he would have had servants to do everything for him; now suddenly he must polish boots and equipment to mirror-like perfection, spending at least an hour a day on menial tasks which he had always considered degrading. The sum total of strangeness would have been overpowering even if he had not been brought up in an atmosphere in which the British were the lords of creation and Indians their subject people. Sandhurst was described by the Indian Sandhurst Committee as an ordeal and if in the case of the ordinary British boy, that was perhaps too strong a word, for an Indian it was hardly strong enough.

Nor was the ordeal over when he had passed out. There was a year in India with a British battalion in which he must command a platoon of British troops and live in the mess with young British officers. Here he must learn the strange nuances of British military behaviour, the narrow tight-rope between being offensively bumptious and insignificantly dull. How hard for an Indian, used to making his points by expansive overstatement, to learn that this was not the thing and that he must instead get his effects by off-hand understatements perfectly timed to catch the attention! He must also keep up with his contemporaries without getting into serious debt. It was no longer approved to be seriously in debt—but almost everyone talked as though an overdraft was normal and in most messes to be too careful of one's money was regarded with scorn. In the British regiment some of the subalterns would have private means, and even those who had no regular income would have parents who had perhaps started them off in India with a gun and a pony, a saddle or a silk dressing-gown, cuff-links, a dinner-jacket—touches which softened the edges of life in a mess on a subaltern's pay. And this would be so in the Indian Army regiment which followed. This kind of help was much less common with Indian parents, most of whom thought that once he had passed out of Sand-hurst, a young man should at least be able to live on his pay, as he would be expected to do in any civil profession.

The temptation to spend would be great; we have glimpsed Robert-son, the future field-marshal, sipping water while everyone else drank champagne, but he was already a mature man and one of unusual character. The temptation to make up for newness and ignorance by generous display was there for the young British officer, but surely it would be stronger for the Indian; the strain of the whole situation was so continuous that he must often have longed to purchase cheap approval from someone—if not in the mess, at least in the bazaar. And credit seemed to have no limits; tradesmen in India were usually in hot competition with each other and if a subaltern or a newly joined assistant magistrate ran up a bill, they would not worry him until six months had passed. And even then they would not begin to press hard.

Perhaps the young officer would have gone to his Indian Army regiment before it began to come to light that there were several bills outstanding. Of course, the moment one creditor began to press, the eagles would gather. If it reached the Colonel's ears he would send for the young man and give him a talking-to. The severity with which he looked on what had happened would vary very much, but, whether he was fatherly or grimly unsympathetic, he would always demand a list of debts. The boy would falter out the grisly figures one by one and the Colonel's frown would deepen till a point was reached when the boy dared not go on. 'Are you sure that is all?' he would be asked. And perhaps he would remember one more. And then his spirit would fail and he would say there were no more. Then the Colonel would calculate how much he could afford to pay every month and would take the bills over and start seeing them paid. But of course there were some more and of course they would come to light. Then the Colonel's face would set like flint. The boy had lied to him and concealed debts he knew he had. It was a dishonourable act. He would never make an officer. And, after much discussion, out he would go.

This sometimes happened to British boys as well as to Indian. But it was surely more excusable in the case of an Indian and several went in just this way. None the less, there were those who survived. They had indeed been tried in the fire, hammered and beaten out, honed to a sharp edge.

It may be argued that all this was necessary. Indian soldiers had been trained to follow a certain kind of officer and would not, it might be said, have made such magnificent soldiers as they did with any other kind of leader; if the process of turning Indian officers into British involved some hardship for individuals it was all for the sake of the regiment and for the new army of the future. But the question persists: how did the French and the Russians get soldiers to follow officers who had no hesitation about showing off, who wore brown shoes and openly talked about women and who, in short, behaved like thumping cads?

The truth is that, with no national bond between officers and men, the Indian Army depended on the concept of honour in both officer and man. That his debts must be paid, that his word was as good as his bond, that he was frank and straightforward with his brother-officers was an essential part of an officer's code of conduct. It was a kind of religion, and there are few religions in which a moral code is not accompanied by distinguishing marks of behaviour, dress or diet which have little to do with its philosophical core. Black shoes with a blue suit marked the gentleman who paid his debts and was looked up to by his men because he respected their honour as they respected his. They were like the Sikh's turban, the Muslim's concern about pork and the Hindu's concern about beef.

Rigidity about accepting everything British was more marked in the early or Sandhurst stages than later. The appointment of the Indian Sandhurst Committee was a turning-point. That committee found that results at Sandhurst were still poor; of the first 83 places filled at Sandhurst the percentage of failures was 30 compared with only 3 per cent for British boys. The members of the Indian Sandhurst Committee were nearly all Indian politicians, under the chairmanship of Sir Andrew Skeen, Chief of the General Staff; they included Mr Jinnah and Pandit Moti Lal Nehru (though the latter resigned before the report), figures of world-wide reputation, and Sir Jogendra Singh, the Sikh Minister of Agriculture in the Punjab. They of course were quite free from the subconscious desire to delay the whole policy which had been so manifest in the report of the Progress Committee. But they do not appear to have questioned the British certainty that the right kind of officer must have been to a public school or something like it. They were sure that plenty of boys of the right kind existed if they could be found and persuaded to come forward. They would have liked to see a widespread network of Indian public schools, like the P.W.R.I.M. College at Dehra Dun; 'Dehra Dun is an easy first and the rest nowhere,' the Commandant of the Staff College had told them. Clearly that was not something that could happen as it were overnight, but they saw two measures which more than any others could overcome the lack of such schools.

The more obvious was that there should be an equivalent of Sand-hurst in India but that it would give three years to training instead of eighteen months; here there would be time to encourage in a cadet qualities that had been neglected during his school education. But, what was even more important, the committee perceived that the operation was on too narrow a front. Ten places a year, from a population of over three hundred million! And the method of selection involved a formidable succession of hurdles—an interview with the Deputy Commissioner, another with the Commissioner, another with the Governor and then one with a Board in Delhi—even before the examination. After all this there was the high rate of failure at Sandhurst—and what was open to a young man who had failed to pass out of Sandhurst? After all the expense, both of his time and his parents' money, he must start again, at a university, with the prospect of very acute competition for a job even if he obtained a degree. Unemployment among the educated was already an acute anxiety to Indian middle-class parents. Even the eight units scheme was experimental; how could parents encourage their sons to take such risks? It was the official view that there could be no expansion until a better supply of candidates was forthcoming, but surely it should be the other way round; a better supply could hardly be expected until a bolder attempt was made to give the new policy something more than a token beginning. It was of the first importance therefore to abandon the eight units scheme and substitute a substantial and progressive programme of Indianization, which must include artillery and the air arm.

The committee proposed to increase the places at Sandhurst from ten to twenty at once, with a further annual increase of four till 1933, when the Indian Sandhurst would open with 33 places a year and an initial capacity of a hundred, expanding by 12 places after three years. Twenty places a year for Indians would still be open at Sandhurst and there would also be vacancies at Woolwich for gunners and at Cranwell for air cadets. Under this scheme, half the young officers coming to the Indian Army would be Indian by 1945 and by that time the first Indians from Sandhurst would be getting command. Some members of the committee thought this too slow but all agreed that by 1938, five years after the beginning of the Indian Sandhurst, the progress of the scheme should be reviewed. A much higher proportion of the cost of training all these young officers should be met by the State, as in Canada and France, and not by the parents. The preference for soldiers' sons, which had so far been the rule, should now be the exception; boys from the professional classes should have exactly the same chances as those from the land-owning and military.

Few commissions of inquiry see their plans adopted exactly; the Indian Sandhurst Committee was on the whole fortunate. The Indian Military Academy was set up, sited like the P.W.R.I.M. College at Dehra Dun; by 1938 its output was 56 officers a year, but no Indians now went to Sandhurst. The eight units scheme was superseded by a plan for Indianizing three cavalry regiments and twelve infantry battalions, but one feature to which Indians had objected remained. The new Indian officers were not mixed with British throughout the Indian Army but all went to the selected units; they were commissioned in the Indian Land Forces, which automatically gave them command over Indian troops, while over British troops in India they had power of command by a special order of the Commander-in-Chief, which excluded the power of punishment. They were paid on the scale of British officers in Britain, but with some help in their early days, a second lieutenant having his mess bill reduced by forty rupees a month. This looked forward to an eventual dominion army in which there would be no competition with British officers who were receiving higher pay as compensation for being away from Britain. The Viceroy's Commissioned Officer would gradually be replaced by warrant officers, as in the British Army.

Thus, a beginning had been made on a course of action that was perfectly logical. The old Indian Army had special features peculiar to its own development and history. Because the higher officers spoke a different language and came from a different culture and religion, there had been an intermediate class of officer which would now disappear; it was logical that the Indian Commissioned Officer in India should receive pay at the same rate as the British officer in Britain. Why saddle the new dominion with rates of pay meant to compensate men for lifelong exile? But the fact remained that if two young men came to the Indian Army at the same time, they might have different rates of pay—and feelings are seldom logical.

Nevertheless this was a big step forward, and the foundation of the Indian Military Academy at Dehra Dun was of the first importance. It was opened by Sir Philip Chetwode on December 10th, 1932, and on the walls were inscribed words which formed the keynote of what he said to the first cadets: 'The safety, honour and welfare of your country come first, always and every time. The honour, welfare and comfort of the men you command come next. Your own ease, comfort and safety come last, always and every time.' The choice for the first Commandant was singularly happy, one of those rare decisions which could not have been bettered. Brigadier Lionel Peter Collins, a Gurkha officer, was a man with the gift of inspiring affection in everyone who knew him. No one can define the quality which produces this result, but it seems most often to accompany a kind of repose or restfulness, which comes from an inner self-confidence which has no need for display. Collins had this quality of quietness and modesty. As a leader, he expected the best of men and to an extraordinary degree they gave it him; this is a recipe that is singularly effective with Indian young men who respond with ready warmth to encouragement and trust. His company commanders gave him their affection as readily as the cadets and that the atmosphere was different from Sandhurst is suggested by the fact that the cadets referred to Mrs Collins as their 'mommadant'. They remember the I.M.A. Dehra Dun as an inspiring place, while Sandhurst had generally been a searching ordeal. It was clearly the right decision to send all cadets to Dehra Dun and not (as the committee had proposed) to continue places at Sandhurst at the same time. There really could have been no clearer indication than the I.M.A. that Britain did not mean to stay in India for ever.

5. Goodbye to All That

In the time between the two world wars, there was, then, a largely subconscious psychological plan for the Indian Army, summed up in the single word 'Insulation'—insulation against the forces of nationalism. But the trouble about a subconscious plan is that it does not always take into account all the forces working in the opposite direction. How could insulation of the rank and file continue indefinitely after the introduction of Indian officers from the educated middle classes, however effectively they had been anglicized? And how could it persist in the face of technical advance—all that was comprised in the ugly words 'modernization' and 'mechanization'? There had been a time when a recruit was looked on with disfavour if he could read or write. By 1939 war had become a highly technical business and the soldier—as Lord Rawlinson had forecast—had to be able to handle complicated scientific equipment; he had to have some education—indeed, from the beginning of the decade the army deliberately set about educating him—and sooner or later he was bound to read the newspapers and open his mind to a wide variety of influences. The point need not be laboured and we need not go through the details of reorganization and re-equipment. But there are odd and revealing resemblances between the two processes—the introduction of Indian officers and the substitution of tanks for horses. Both were opposed by conservative forces which seldom deployed their full strength in public. Both therefore moved slowly, with compromises and half-measures delaying progress. Part of the opposition in both cases arose from the British social system of the nineteenth century, with its emphasis on the country gentleman and on a world of which the horse was to some extent a symbol.

In Britain, affection for the horse and all it stood for perhaps delayed mechanization but not for long; the disaster of conversion to tanks was characteristically tempered by permitting cavalry officers to keep two chargers on the strength. India in social change was usually a little behind Britain. Also the reign of the horse was stronger, because horses were still used as a means of transport and were less obviously obsolete than in Britain, while Indian cavalry had played an essential part in Allenby's victories. Three Commanders-in-Chief in succession — Birdwood, Chetwode, Cassells — were cavalrymen and could not refuse sympathy to those who saw in the horse much more than a means of getting about. Like fagging and the public-school system, the horse was very good for the character. Another potent factor in delay was penury; the initial cost of modern equipment was frightening to a poor country.

In spite of all this, the spectre drew closer. There were even soldiers so keen on their profession that they were eager to hurry on a process which made the army more efficient, if less appealing to a gentleman. Indeed, there were some who reacted very sharply to the cult of the horse, taking it to be a kind of idolatry, a whoring after false gods, hating as vigorously as the others loved. There were infantry regiments in which a young man who wanted to spend money on horses was as much disapproved of as if he had wanted to marry at twenty-two. But all this became irrelevant as the 'thirties moved on. After about 1936, no one who looked at the international scene closely could fail to see that the danger of war was growing; only an irrational optimism — of which of course there was plenty — could hope that the spectre would go away. From the autumn of 1938 it was clear that we had won a period in which to prepare; from now on, change at a speed previously unimagined began to transform the essentially conservative machine of the Indian Army.

Lord Chatfield's committee came in 1938 to discuss the whole question of Indian defence and defence expenditure. It reported in the spring of 1939. As far as the army was concerned, Lord Chatfield's conclusion had largely been anticipated by the Modernization Committee, which met in October 1938 under the chairmanship of Major-General Auchinleck. The substance of its report was that the army in India (that is, the Indian Army and the British troops) ought to be modernized. The greater efficiency that followed could mean a reduction in the number of units, giving a yearly saving of 2·36 crores of rupees (about £1·8 million), but only if the Government spent 28 crores (about £21 million) on capital equipment. This was a return of over 8½ per cent on the investment, and need involve no burden on the Indian taxpayer. The surplus units — two British cavalry regiments, five British infantry and five Indian infantry battalions — could be held in India as an imperial reserve if the British Government would pay for them. But the process would need four or five years — and we know, though the committee did not, that so much time would not be available.

A year later the 1939 plan for modernizing the army in India showed in the peace establishment two British cavalry regiments with light tanks, and of Indian cavalry four light tank regiments, four armoured regiments, six motor regiments and two still horsed. There were 37 British and 82 Indian battalions of infantry, excluding four Indian infantry battalions overseas, in Hong Kong and Malaya. It was asserted once more, in that fatal year 1939, that the responsibility of the Government of India was local defence only; that meant internal security and the frontiers of India, until local forces were reinforced by Imperial. The troops for the defence of India were allotted specific functions: Frontier Defence, Internal Security, Coast Defence, Air Defence and General Reserve. Infantry was now divided into those battalions which had fully mechanized first-line transport and those which still relied on mules and packs, but with eight trucks to a battalion. Battalions had been reorganized internally; there was a headquarters company consisting of a signals platoon, a support platoon with light machine-guns and 15-cwt trucks, and an administration platoon; there were four rifle companies, each with three platoons of three sections; a battalion had 44 light machine-guns, 4 mortars and 6 anti-tank rifles. An Indian battalion still had 12 King's Commissioned Officers and 17 Viceroy's Commissioned Officers; British or Indian, a battalion's establishment was 662 of all ranks.

This was better than 1914 but it is clear from the regimental histories that some of it was on paper only. The Auchinleck committee had contemplated four or five years for modernization and Britain too was feverishly trying to catch up; the equipment was not available. And a curious reversal of roles now took place. In the 1920s and early 1930s, the very highest authorities were convinced of the need to train Indian officers and to modernize the army, while there was an instinctive, often subconscious, conservatism amounting sometimes to hostility at regimental level. Now, at least from 1938, it began to be the other way round. Young cavalry officers began to be excited about tanks and to realize they must sell their polo ponies; colonels were eager to get the equipment and be among the first to take their regiments to war. But His Majesty's Government in London did not think Indian troops would be needed much in this war. When war broke out, the Commander-in-Chief asked London what help was needed and offered to train forces for service abroad. He received a chilling negative; India could help with certain supplies but it was unlikely that troops would be needed. The Financial Adviser at Army Headquarters had continually to reiterate this slogan. As in the First World War, Britain had agreed to meet the bill for any excess in defence expenditure above the level that had been thought necessary for India in peace. The Financial Adviser was Britain's agent to watch what happened and could not be generous at Britain's expense against Britain's express orders. But the Adjutant-General repeated the words as not merely official doctrine but his personal view. 'We shall not be required to send troops abroad.' All through what came to be called the 'phoney war', from September 1939 until the fall of France in the summer of 1940, the atmosphere at Army Headquarters was repressive from above; there were eager young officers frustrated and irritated by the negatives of their seniors — all traceable back to London.

This, however, is to anticipate. Though mechanization came even later in India than in Britain, it was one more change in the life of the rank and file. Not that there was reluctance from that quarter. A trooper, asked his views on mechanization, replied: 'On Sunday, I pat my tank and tell it to sit still. I do not have to take it to be fed and watered five times a day.' And it cannot be supposed that infantry anywhere had any complaints about travelling by truck instead of walking. None the less, so much was new that if anyone had had time to think it would surely have been unsettling. It was not much to fall in by threes instead of twos; to learn the intricacies of a petrol engine by itself was no great matter. But there was so much that was new — Bren guns, Sten guns, light machine-guns, signalling apparatus both telephone and wireless, carriers, trucks, mortars — that to a boy not long from the bullock, the plough and the cart the effect must have been dizzying.

New weapons increased the battalion's firepower and so fewer troops were needed. The number of Indian troops in 1939 was about two-thirds of that in 1914 and the reduction in British troops was proportionately greater. Firepower is what counts in war and in war one battalion with trucks and machine-guns may be able to do as much as two with rifles and mules. It is not quite the same in the case of troops for internal security. They are there as a deterrent; if they have to fire at all, it is a failure. The object is prevention and a battalion with rifles on the spot may be more effective than one with machine-guns and armoured cars a hundred miles away. It is therefore remarkable that during a period of almost continuous political unrest it should have been possible to make such considerable reductions in the number of troops, and, particularly, a more than proportionate reduction in the number of British troops. The explanation is twofold. The danger feared had imperceptibly changed; and the Indian Army was far more wholeheartedly trusted. Kitchener had said that the Mutiny should be forgotten; he began and everyone continued to put faith in the new, insulated, Northern, Indian Army. Meanwhile, the political scene had changed dramatically; now that some form of self-government was clearly on the way, the likelihood of a widespread armed rising against the British, though never entirely dismissed, was not in the forefront of men's

minds. Internal Security in practice had come to mean primarily the
prevention of riots between Hindu, Muslim and Sikh.

For twenty years India had appeared in the world's press to be in
ceaseless turmoil. That during those twenty years there had been a
steady reduction in the number of troops for 'local purposes' is one
of the paradoxes of history. It was partly due to the success with which
the insulation of the Indian Army had been maintained. It was still
loyal to its officers, its colours, its traditions. But it was not a loyalty
that could conceivably be maintained much longer; there was no positive ideal or symbol to which appeal could be made in the face of
growing Indian nationalism. Specialized equipment and the need for
education meant that the simple boy from the plough who had never
heard of politics would not last much longer; the new kind of Indian
officer from the middle classes was bound to tire in time of drinking
the King Emperor's health every night.

The outbreak of war in 1939 was the beginning of the end. One
perhaps rather trivial scene may stand for many, as the symbol of
something that was over. The 19th Lancers were the last regiment of
horsed cavalry — except of course the Viceroy's Bodyguard. They kept
their horses till November 1940, when they held the last parade with
horses. Their commanding officer addressed the regiment, recalling its
good name and reputation, expressing confidence that the spirit of the
regiment would go on. But 'let us remember', he added, 'how much of
our good name we owe to our horses. For the last time — "Make much
of your horses!" ' And with that familiar cavalry command the parade,
and an epoch, ended.

XIX

The Second World War: Defeat

1. Strategy: the Central Bastion

The Second World War was fought on the most gigantic scale; the front stretched from Archangel and the North Cape, by way of Norway and Britain in a vast sweep through the North Atlantic, through North Africa, Egypt, Syria, Iraq and Persia to India, through Burma, Malaya, Singapore and Australia to the enormous distances of the Pacific. India was the central bastion of this encircling crescent—though hardly anyone at the time, either in Britain or in India, realized that it *was* the centre; it did not *feel* like the centre because so many vital supplies came from the tips of the crescent. Of the four great battle-areas—Western Europe, the Middle East, South-East Asia and the Pacific—two could not have been sustained without India. For the Middle East and still more for South-East Asia, India was a base, a storehouse, a springboard and a recruiting-ground.

As long as men have any interest in history, there will be controversy about this war. Was it wise, from the point of view either of justice or expediency, to devote so much effort to the bombing of Germany, to drop the bomb on Hiroshima, to proclaim that there could be no terms but unconditional surrender? The expeditions to Norway and Greece, the invasion of Italy as opposed to Southern France—on these and a dozen questions as momentous, controversy will continue. The drama of the titanic struggle is heightened by the size of the great armies, by the rapidity of their movements, by the shattering completeness of national collapse, the lightning alternations of defeat and victory. The burden of decision in each combatant country was placed on a small group of tired men under heavy strain; thousands upon thousands of lives rested on their decisions. Indeed, they believed—and surely they were right—that the lives of hundreds of thousands yet unborn would be influenced by what they did.

These are considerations that lie beyond the scope of this book's main purpose. But they form the back-cloth to the last act, a scene like the storm in Lear, darkness lit by jagged cracks of lightning, with human misery and folly in the foreground. Never was the central question about the Indian Army so dramatically posed, nor, surely, so ironically answered. With every reason to doubt the possibility of British victory, in the teeth of Indian politicians who demanded that the British should quit India, the fighting units of the Indian Army were not only faithful to their colours but again and again displayed heroic valour. Politically unawakened though they were, dumbly loyal to their foreign and yet friendly and familiar officers, their victory brought independence within two years. Their defeat would have postponed indefinitely anything worth calling independence. They were called traitors to the national cause yet they achieved its objects; the nationalist politicians inherited a kingdom they would have lost if their own plans had been successful.

Both the strategic and the political background must be sketched, in the simplest, most diagrammatic form, if we are to understand this paradox. And, first, what was the war about? Why were the Middle East and Burma important for the defence of Britain? The main aims of both Germany and Japan can be stated simply. Both wanted room to expand. Both were intensely vigorous nations under centralized autocratic rule, each was determined to establish by military force a wide-reaching empire and a still wider sphere of influence. No doubt they had additional aims; Germany wanted revenge on France, Japan a more subtle racial revenge for the arrogance of Europeans in the nineteenth century. Their eyes were on two great mastodons, Russia and China. Indeed, Japan was already at war with China, burrowing and gnawing into that great mass of flesh, and it was the support of the United States for China that was the immediate occasion for Pearl Harbour.

It was the German plan to knock out France and then turn on Russia, from whom vast areas would be bitten off and annexed, while the Balkans, Turkey and the Middle East would become a sphere of influence. Britain, it was thought, would not fight. But Britain did fight and would not yield. Hitler, confronted by this obstinate and irrelevant check to his plans and by the abortion of a hasty and ill-prepared invasion, impatiently turned back to his main object and attacked Russia. Like Napoleon, he underestimated sea-power and the vast distances, the bitter winter of Russia, the stubborn enduring courage of the Russians. By the time Japan and the United States were in the war, the contest had taken the shape represented in the diagram opposite.

Russia and China may be thought of as two herds of buffalo defending themselves against two packs of wolves, one from the east and one from the west, with an encircling line of conservationists, who hope to preserve the buffaloes and destroy the wolves. Here the metaphor breaks down, because buffaloes carry their defensive equipment with them,

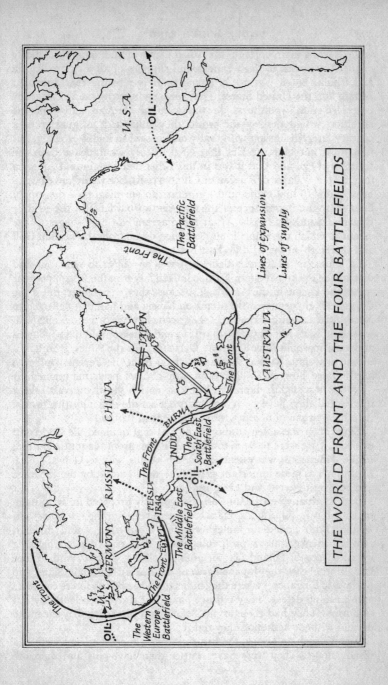

THE WORLD FRONT AND THE FOUR BATTLEFIELDS

The Pacific Battlefield

The Front

Lines of Expansion
Lines of supply

U.S.A.

OIL

JAPAN

CHINA

RUSSIA

GERMANY

U.K.

OIL

The Front

The Western Europe Battlefield

EGYPT

PERSIA

IRAQ

The Middle East Battlefield

INDIA

BURMA

The Front

OIL

The South East Battlefield

AUSTRALIA

The Front

while it was a main object of the Allied Chiefs of Staff, and particularly of the Americans, to get weapons and supplies of all kinds to Russia and China. But it was not of course entirely altruism that animated Britain and the United States. They meant to destroy the wolves; they perceived that wolfishness on the scale of German and Japanese ambition would destroy the world they inhabited. A quarter of a century later, disillusion with that world has set in and is growing, but that must not blur the fact that Nazi victory would have been the triumph of evil and that it was in this belief that Britain and America fought. The collapse of Russian or Chinese resistance would have been a heavy blow to that cause, and—to return to our diagram—the supply lines show the importance of the two central battlefields, the Middle East and South-East Asia. What the diagram can only suggest is the extent to which the whole front depended on oil from the Persian Gulf and therefore on the Middle East battlefield.

Of course in all four battlefields it was an object to wear out and destroy the enemy. Western Europe bulked larger in the British popular mind, the Pacific in the American, because they were closer. But if the Germans had postponed the attack on Russia and had first deflected to North Africa a tenth of the forces they needed for the drive to Stalingrad, we should have lost Egypt; Syria, Iraq and Persia would have followed and then it would have been the Germans, not the Allies, who had a second way into Russia. And without oil from the Persian Gulf it is hard to see how the whole front would have been maintained. A diagram in a slightly more realistic convention shows the vast salient that would then have been lost and suggests the difficulty that would then have arisen of holding India, the central bastion.

Egypt then was a key position in a front that spanned the world and essential if we were to be in touch with Russia from the south. Burma, to the Americans, was essentially a step on the way to China; to the British, it was more important as the first step in defeating the Japanese and recovering what had been lost.

Both Germany and Japan were meticulously prepared for war; men, tanks, aircraft, ships, guns, plans—all were ready to the last screw and button. Both hoped for quick crushing blows that would make it possible to negotiate a profitable peace. Both scored overwhelming initial successes. Poland fell; Belgium, Holland, Norway and France fell. In the east the Japanese swept southward through Siam and Malaya to Singapore, where they inflicted on the British forces complete and crushing defeat. They did not pause but drove us relentlessly out of Burma. They had thought out beforehand just what they meant to do and without hesitation they did it.

Against such an attack, the British, French and Americans were at a disadvantage. They were haves rather than have-nots and therefore

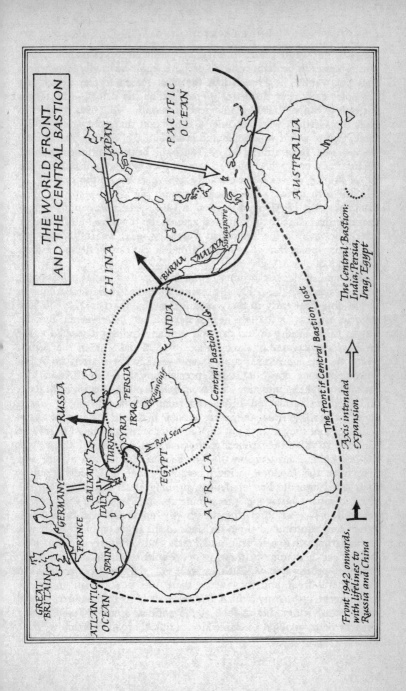

THE WORLD FRONT
AND THE CENTRAL BASTION

GREAT BRITAIN

GERMANY

RUSSIA

FRANCE

BALKANS

ITALY

SPAIN

ATLANTIC OCEAN

TURKEY

SYRIA

IRAQ

PERSIA

Red Sea

EGYPT

Persian Gulf

AFRICA

Central Bastion

INDIA

BURMA

MALAYA

Singapore

CHINA

JAPAN

PACIFIC OCEAN

AUSTRALIA

The front if Central Bastion lost

The Central Bastion:
India, Persia,
Iraq, Egypt

Axis intended
expansion

Front 1942 onwards,
with lifelines to
Russia and China

they had not wanted war. And it is very difficult to persuade a nation that professes to be democratic to prepare whole-heartedly for a war it does not want. The French had the most reason to fear attack but psychologically were no better prepared than the British—and it was not only weapons but psychological preparation that was needed to meet the German war machine, a conviction that war would really come, that to win it would demand every ounce of courage and energy we possessed. But until the fall of France the British continued to think of Hitler as a bogy who would go away if they took no notice. From the fall of France, it was almost exactly two years before the turn of the tide in North Africa, when Auchinleck and the Eighth Army stopped Rommel at the El Alamein position in July 1942. It was another eighteen months before the tide turned against the Japanese and they were utterly defeated in the Arakan in February 1944. To India, this was the turning-point that was close and real and it came after more than four years of defeat.

It is against the background of this long spell of initial defeats that we must consider the political situation in India. India sent troops to the Middle East early in the war and they took part in Wavell's first victories against the Italians at Sidi Barrani and in Abyssinia. But the war in Libya swung to and fro, and to many Indians it seemed as far away as France, one of those remote professional wars of the British which hardly concerned them. Japan was another matter, an Asian power, pressing towards India, proclaiming a Greater Asian Co-Prosperity Sphere, inflicting shattering defeats on the British in Malaya and then in Burma, on India's doorstep. To the British, it was a cherished tradition that they were at their best with their backs to the wall and that they always lost the first battle. Indians could hardly be expected to share their robust confidence that they would always win the last fight. They were in the war because Britain was at war and here were the Japanese, within bombing-range of Calcutta, sailing their ships into the Bay of Bengal, pressing closer and closer up the coast towards Chittagong, threatening Assam. India was in danger— yet India never withdrew the superb 4th Indian Division from North Africa and contributed three divisions to the invasion of Italy; it was Indian troops that held Iraq and Persia and very largely Syria. Had India been a dominion, these troops would surely have been withdrawn to protect Bengal. But they were not; they held key positions in the general front and meanwhile there was built up in India the magnificent 14th Army, which, in the words of its commander, turned defeat into victory. Let us look at the political scene in India during the war years, giving it the same kind of quick, broad look that we have given to the strategic.

2. Politics: Disarray and Division

At the outbreak of war, there were Congress Governments in eight out of eleven of India's provinces. The 1935 Act for the Government of India had put into operation the first stage of a Federation and the provinces were now far more powerful and autonomous bodies than they had once been. All provincial subjects were now allotted to ministers, who formed a cabinet and were responsible to an elected assembly. The ministers were inexperienced and there were few who had not made rash promises to the electorate which they were unable to keep. There can be little doubt that there were some who felt that a period out of office might be no bad thing; it would provide an interval for reflection before starting again with a clean slate, or, perhaps better, with a slate on which the deficits and mistakes could once again be blamed on someone else. That apart, there were mixed feelings in the Congress hierarchy. Not many would make the explicit statement that England's extremity was India's opportunity; such cynical realism was not the tone Congress favoured. The Congress creed was rather a mixture of the Gladstonian and the Gandhian, highly moral, combining liberal democracy with occasional genuflexions to non-violence and pantheism. Nothing could be more abhorrent to Congress than the Nazi brand of authoritarian racism. Skilfully managed, Congress might have been induced to declare sympathy for Britain and to offer support, but they might not have gone so far as declaring war.

Nor was every Englishman with knowledge of India convinced that Congress backing would have been much help. It could hardly have been whole-hearted; it would have been bound to involve delays, arguments, discussion; far better, some would have argued, to go back to the old system of bureaucratic administration till the war was over and then resume the political debate. To American observers on the other hand it seemed self-evident that to have the good will of Congress would be better than not to have it. But however those opposed views might have been weighed against each other in India or Washington, Whitehall characteristically acted on a correct legal view of the constitution — which in effect was a quibble. India was not yet a dominion; in the stage of development so far reached, India was automatically at war when Britain was at war. Therefore — without discussion or debate — the Viceroy proclaimed a state of war. To many Indians this seemed to advertise that India was a mere dependency, and the eight Congress Governments seized the opportunity to resign. Three Governments offered support; they were Sind and Bengal, which were Muslim League, and the Punjab, which combined Sikhs, Muslims and Hindus.

There were few educated Indians who had not at some time valued some aspect of the British connection. Gandhi wept at the thought of

Westminster Abbey destroyed by bombs. But India's own national independence was what most Indians put first and as the war dragged on it was increasingly difficult to see how it could best be achieved. British victory seemed remote and it is not surprising that Gandhi should have regarded a British offer of dominion status at the end of the war as 'a post-dated cheque on a failing bank'. This was 'the Cripps offer' made in the spring of 1942. Congress rejected it partly because it gave a chance of secession to provinces with a Muslim majority and partly because it did not immediately give full legal independence. By August 1942 so strong was the belief of Congress that Britain could not win that they launched a campaign with the slogan 'Quit India', accompanied by attempts to disrupt the main lines of communication from Bombay to Burma. The leaders were arrested before the movement got under way; the rebellion was abortive and it was afterwards denied that a rebellion had really been intended. But the words of the leaders were for once unambiguous; 'After all,' said Gandhi, 'this is open rebellion.' And if the incidents which followed were spontaneous, it is a singular coincidence that they should have been so clearly related to lines of communication.

Gandhi was the prophet of the national movement, the voice that could reach the heart of the villagers. His colleagues did not always share his views: certainly, some of them were dubious about his pacifism in its most extreme form. They may have shared his opinion that it was the British presence that brought Japan to the gates of India; they can hardly have seriously accepted the belief he sometimes appeared to hold, that the Japanese soldier would lay down his rifle and bayonet if confronted by unflinching non-violence. Perhaps they calculated that with China, Burma, Malaya and the Dutch East Indies, Japan would have enough to digest without India. However that may be, the effect of their gamble was from their point of view more unfortunate than they can have realized at the time. They had backed the wrong horse and had lost, but they knew they could emerge from prison and resume discussions with the British. What they cannot have foreseen is that by the time that happened the Muslim League would be much stronger and its expectations vastly increased. By the end of the war, nothing but an independent Pakistan was enough for Jinnah and the Muslim League; the Congress hope of inheriting an undivided India had disappeared.

The details of the conflict are not our concern here. What is important for us is that, throughout the war, the main Indian political parties were far more concerned about the constitutional future and about independence from Britain than they were about the war. It was far more Britain's war than theirs; their business was the kind of India they were going to manage when it was over. And their aims were increasingly divergent and irreconcilable. Congress wanted a united India and a strong centre; the Muslim League a divided India, a weak centre, at last a separate State. Congress claimed to be a national body, speaking for the whole of India, not merely a party speaking only for its own supporters. Emphatically, it was not Hindu; it believed in a secular State. In the same transcendental spirit, the League claimed to represent every Muslim and would not recognize the fact that there were Congress Muslims; they would not allow Congress to nominate a Muslim as their own representative in any attempt at compromise. They were a nation already and every Muslim was a national or a traitor. Tempers grew harder; for one side to make the least gesture towards compromise was only the signal for the other to demand more. And whatever truce or settlement — or panting intermission of hostilities — might be reached between Hindus and Muslims, the Sikhs were bound to suffer.

This was the background against which the Indian Army expanded to twelve times its peace-time strength, learnt to use complicated modern equipment and trained itself in new kinds of warfare until its battalions could take on and defeat Germans and Japanese on level terms.

3. North Africa

Let us sketch the course of events in the war as they affected India and Indian troops. There were Indian troops already in Egypt at the outbreak of war with Germany — the nucleus of what was to become the 4th Indian Division — but the intentions of Italy were not yet known; there were no German formations in North Africa but large Italian forces in Libya and in Abyssinia. There was therefore a time of waiting. This was the stage of 'the phoney war'; Poland had fallen by Blitzkrieg, the lightning war, but for France and Britain it was still the Sitzkrieg — stationary war, sea and air engagements, a half-hearted hope that economic stringency in Germany would lead to a peace by negotiation. Then came the Blitzkrieg again and within six weeks Norway, Denmark, Holland, Belgium and France had fallen. Italy now declared war on France and Britain. Italy does not appear in the diagrams shown in the first section of this chapter; Italians were not wolves. Mussolini cast them for the ignoble part of jackal but his people showed little enthusiasm for the role. Their military record throughout the war was not impressive; they were no more responsive to the blustering of their fire-eating national leader than Indian troops to the pacifism of theirs. But their entry transformed the situation in the Middle East, where General Wavell had a total of less than 85,000 men, widely distributed, to hold Egypt, the Sudan, Kenya, Somaliland, Aden and Palestine, confronting five times their numbers—more than 200,000 Italian troops in Libya and as many again in Abyssinia. He attacked these two armies in succession, first establishing a moral ascendancy by hit-and-run raids and constant aggressive patrols which led the enemy to believe his numbers were as great as theirs. In December 1940—with the 7th Armoured Division and one tank regiment, the 4th Indian Infantry Division and two infantry brigades, only 31,000 men all told—he drove through the centre of the line of forts carefully constructed by the Italians, swung round, assaulted them from the rear and took them. Between December 7th, 1940, and February 7th, 1941, the desert force of never more than two divisions destroyed ten Italian divisions; they captured 130,000 prisoners, 400 tanks and 1,240 guns for a loss of 500 killed, 1,373 wounded and 55 missing; they swept forward five hundred miles to Benghazi.

This was the first taste of success in a war which so far had brought nothing but disaster. For the troops concerned, it was their introduction to a quite new kind of war. There were few obstructions and vast open spaces. The men were in tanks, trucks and armoured carriers; so long as they had petrol, water and ammunition, they could move almost anywhere between the two defensive positions, El Alamein in the east and El Agheila in the west. These were narrow defiles round which vehicles could not pass. Nowhere else could a strong flank be established. By air, these two positions were six hundred miles apart and in between there was a war of manœuvre. In some ways it resembled naval warfare, though the resemblance could be, and often was, exaggerated. Lines of communication were still important but it was far less a matter of fronts and flanks than any war known to history before.

Speed, firepower, protective armour, reliability, were the qualities men required of their vehicles; they learnt to make use of speed if they had no armour. The Central India Horse, for instance, with trucks but no armour, developed great skill in operations behind the enemy lines in which one of their many objects was to lure enemy tanks into positions where they could be knocked out by our own 25-pounders. It was a war that demanded courage, of course, but also to a high degree quick thought, leadership, initiative and skill in framing and communicating orders. It was a war for young men and professional soldiers, and, in these opening stages, troops of the Indian Army were highly professional. Up to battalion level, even up to brigade, this was a war that suited them. But the higher command, at corps and army level, had still a great deal to learn about control of the battle once it was joined.

In that first round against the Italians, the 4th Indian Division developed a self-confidence they never lost. They were pulled out at the end of January and moved to the Abyssinian front, where another lightning campaign against greatly superior forces was equally success-ful. Abyssinia was conquered and restored to the Emperor Haile Selassie; the Duke of Aosta, who had commanded 220,000 men, surrendered unconditionally. The 4th and 5th Indian Divisions— which had made the northern arm of a gigantic pincer movement from points a thousand miles apart—had met some stubborn resistance, particularly at the great mountain position of Keren which the Italians had thought impregnable. But the country, with its jagged rocks, cliffs and gullies, was like enough to the Frontier; the 4th and 5th Divisions knew each other and could talk in clear over the radio in a jargon which would deceive the most learned Italian interpreter. 'Bumbeaten', for example, was immediately intelligible as 'Asmara', *mara* being the Hindustani for 'struck' or 'beaten'. The leadership was swift, incisive, well concerted; everyone, rifleman or sepoy, was quite sure that man for man he was a better soldier than any Italian. By May 1941 the 4th Indian Division was back in North Africa and throughout the war it served in this theatre with great distinction. But while it had been in Abyssinia, the pendulum of desert war had swung the other way.

Obviously it was desirable to press on after the great victories of December, January and February. But tanks are even less able than men to run indefinitely; after a time, they must go into the workshops for maintenance. The 7th Armoured Division had shot its bolt by the time it reached Benghazi. Loss of impetus was always a factor in the desert war; since no strong flanks could be formed nearer than the defile of El Agheila or El Alamein at either end, victory usually meant advance over enormous distances, and unless the victors had consider-able reserves their impetus was bound to diminish. If the defeated could obtain reinforcements, particularly of tanks, a counter-attack could be launched and the pendulum would swing back. Two hundred years before, in those first wars on the Carnatic coast, there had been a similiar alternation of victory and defeat—but in that case the perishable article had been the French or British troops, who came, like tanks, a few hundreds at a time and wore out quickly—and usually beyond the help of any workshop. But while it had then been thought that British troops were always needed as a stiffening to Indian, it was a question now of tanks and infantry; no one thought there was a better infantry division than the 4th Indian.

But in the case of this first swing, other factors had operated as well as the loss of impetus. Germany had overrun Rumania and Bulgaria and attacked Yugoslavia and Greece. General Wavell had by now been reinforced but, instead of being allowed to use his reinforcements profitably in North Africa, he was ordered to send help to Greece. Nearly 60,000 men with vehicles and equipment were dispatched on an expedition for which from a military point of view there could be no hope of success.* About two-thirds of the men were eventually with-drawn in the classic British style of Corunna and Dunkirk, but with the loss of their heavy equipment. Meanwhile Hitler had sent Rommel with a German armoured division to stiffen the defeated Italians and —to make things still worse—the R.A.F. were so much reduced in strength by the expedition to Greece that they could not protect the port of Benghazi from German air attack and it became unusable by shipping. This moved the British source of nourishment two hundred miles east to Tobruk.

It would be impossible in a book of this size to deal with all the operations in which Indian troops took part in the Middle East and South-East Asia. Since events in the Middle East are better known to most readers—and since the part played by Indians was proportion-ately smaller—it seems best to deal with the Middle East in very broad outline and to move on to South-East Asia, where the battlefield and the base were so intimately linked and the proportion of Indian troops so much higher. But one incident should be mentioned at this stage because the writers of the official history of the Indian armed forces have attached so much importance to it.

Rommel attacked on March 31st, 1941, concentrating his air attack on petrol stores and petrol-carrying vehicles. Benghazi was lost and the British forces began to fall back towards Tobruk. Since Benghazi had become unusable, they had become dependent on petrol landed at Tobruk and moved forward to stores in the desert. The most important of these was at Msus, half-way from the El Agheila position to Tobruk. Being—wrongly—informed of the approach of a German armoured column, someone hastily destroyed this store, and the 3rd Armoured Brigade of the British 2nd Armoured Division, comprising most of the armour available, came there for fuel but found none. This brigade was now so short of petrol that it could not manoeuvre and was captured. It therefore failed to arrive at Meikili, where it ought to have met the 3rd Indian Motor Brigade and the 9th Australian Division and where it had been hoped to halt, or at least delay, Rommel's advance.

The 3rd Indian Motor Brigade, consisting of the 2nd Royal Lancers, the 11th Prince Albert Victor's Own Cavalry and the 18th Lancers, was not yet either equipped or trained for desert warfare. Two of the regiments had given up their horses only six months before; none of them had any armour; all had had to supply drafts of trained men to other units; they were 40 per cent below strength in light machine-guns and each regiment had *one* anti-tank rifle instead of forty-two. But, in this crisis, they were ordered forward to Meikili, which they were to hold till joined by the 2nd Armoured Division and the 9th Australian Division. As we have seen, the 3rd Armoured Brigade of the 2nd Armoured Division was captured and its signals broke down even

* There is an important correction to the view here expressed in Appendix 2.

before that; the Australian division was eventually ordered to move straight to Tobruk. The 3rd Indian Motor Brigade were joined by the 2nd Australian Anti-Tank Regiment and some elements of the 2nd Armoured Division, including M Battery R.H.A. (Anti-Tank), but they still had virtually no armour. And they did not know that the main forces due at the rendezvous were not coming. They lay across Rommel's route and his armoured formations came into contact with them on the morning of April 6th and attacked them. Three times at intervals over the next forty-eight hours German officers came to them with white flags and called on them to surrender; the third message came from Rommel personally. After each refusal, the Germans put in attacks, but they did not bypass the position. Perhaps Rommel did not realize how weak the brigade were; perhaps he was already short of petrol and ammunition. However that may be, he was delayed at Meikili for forty-eight hours, until the evening of April 7th, by which time the 9th Australian Division was in Tobruk. The 3rd Indian Motor Brigade eventually broke out; its headquarters and other elements were captured but a considerable part of the Prince Albert Victor's Own Cavalry and the 2nd Lancers got away, Major Rajendrasinhji of the 2nd Lancers capturing 300 prisoners on the way home and winning the first D.S.O. to be awarded to an Indian Sandhurst-trained officer.

The Indian official historians rightly emphasize the importance of Wavell's decision to hold Tobruk and Rommel's several failures to break into the beleaguered fortress that this port became. They argue that this affected the whole course of the war and that, had Rommel not been checked on April 6th and 7th at Meikili, the Germans would have got to Tobruk before the Australians and cut them off. 'Having lost Tobruk, they lost Egypt and North Africa and for that matter even Sicily and Italy in an inexorable chain of sequences,' they write, and again: 'if the march of events ... between 4th and 8th April, 1941, had not been interrupted or deflected by the 3rd Indian Motor Brigade, the Axis had a fair chance of reaching Alexandria before Alamein was even thought of.' About such far-reaching consequences there can be no certainty, but Tobruk was of great importance and the gallant stand of these ill-equipped and ill-prepared cavalry regiments did help the Australians to get there before the Germans.

Here we must leave North Africa, where the battle was to ebb and flow between El Agheila and El Alamein until the Axis was finally defeated in Italy. The 5th Indian Division came back to North Africa from Abyssinia in July 1941 and the 10th came from Iraq in May 1942; there were never less than two Indian divisions in the North African field. It was a war that suited that free use of individual initiative which British training encouraged in the junior officer and something in the dry, stimulating air of the desert seemed to bring out the best in the combination of British and Indian. In the advance through Italy the 4th, 8th and 10th Indian Infantry Divisions took part; they were in some of the most severe fighting, at the crossing of the Sangro and the Senio, at Cassino and the Liri Valley, at the Gothic lines. They met and defeated crack German troops from Parachute and Panzer Regiments. But we must for the moment leave them and return to India.

4. Iraq, Persia, Malaya

In the spring of 1941 and—as it later appeared—in preparation for the attack on Russia that was coming in June, the Germans intensified attempts to obtain political control of Iraq and Persia. In Iraq—since the First World War a British mandate, now independent but linked with Britain by treaty—they were successful in promoting a *coup d'état* which put in power one Rashid Ali, who was entirely in the Axis camp. The Regent fled in a British aircraft. As Rashid Ali took one tentative step after another, it was clear that Iraq would soon be lost; this would break the front between India and the Middle East and would seriously threaten the supply of oil from the Persian Gulf which was essential to both India and the Middle East Command.

In what followed, the initiative came from India. The Viceroy, Lord Linlithgow, and the Commander-in-Chief, Sir Claude Auchinleck, pressed for prompt military intervention; London and the Middle East Command were more cautious, fearing political reaction in the Arab world if we went a step beyond our treaty rights. There can be no serious doubt now that the bold course was the right one. Had we waited longer it would have been too late; Iraq and Persia would have gone the way of Rumania and Bulgaria; Syria—whose Governor had opted for Vichy—would have been far more difficult to recover; Turkey could hardly have held out; and we should have lost the southern supply line to Russia, though the importance of this was still in the future. In the end, India's views were accepted; strong pressure was brought to bear on Rashid Ali to permit the fullest exercise of our treaty rights and indeed something more. A friend would not have boggled; Rashid Ali boggled aggressively and pointedly. Eventually he attacked the airfield at Habbaniya near Baghdad, which was controlled by the R.A.F. under the treaty; the R.A.F., however, successfully defended it until the arrival of troops. This time Rashid Ali fled, the Regent returned and resumed his government; Iraq was saved. It was achieved largely by troops from India and even more by pressure from India.

Less than two months later Germany declared war on Russia. The importance of Persia now became obvious and a course of events followed that was similar to that in Iraq. Indian troops moved in; there was virtually no opposition and for the rest of the war they acted in Persia as a kind of military police. The political effects in India of the attack on Russia were more complicated. To the British, Russia had been the traditional danger, the rival empire expanding dangerously in Asia. But in the twentieth century Russia for a few uneasy years became an ally; then with the Bolshevik revolution she resumed her more accustomed role as bogy. Now again Russia was a British ally. If this was a little confusing to the average Englishman, it was still more difficult for Indian politicians. Before 1917 Russia had been another imperialist power and probably worse than the British; from 1917 on, as a declared foe of imperialism, Russia had seemed to embody a vague promise. But in 1939 Russia's pact with Hitler and brutal treatment of Poland and Finland came as a sharp disillusion to the rather sentimental liberalism of most Congressmen. Russia was now exposed as cynical, power-hungry, no better than Nazi Germany. Then Germany's attack made Russia a victim, and therefore an object of sympathy—but on the other hand an ally of Britain and one who showed not the least concern for the political future of India. Congress had decided against support for the war and they could not feel any warmth for Russia. For Indian Communists, however, the turn of events meant a much more startling reversal; Russia could do no wrong and they were suddenly on the same side as the British. They began to preach support for the war effort. This angered Congress and affected the relations of the Communists with Congress for many years to come; it also posed a problem to British authorities concerned with security.

But the Japanese attack on Pearl Harbour on December 7th, 1941, brought India far more intimately into the war. A force from India was already in Malaya and was immediately attacked. It was without armour and the enemy had complete superiority in the air. Even worse than the lack of equipment was the lack of concerted plan or decisive control. Malaya is the southern half of a narrow peninsula seven hundred and fifty miles long. The northern half, a long narrow isthmus, is Thai territory. Much the best military plan for the defence of Malaya involved a breach of Thai neutrality. If that was to be rejected for political reasons, at least a decision was needed to adopt the second best plan. But when on December 8th the Japanese landed in Thailand and crossed the border into Malaya, no decision had been taken.

At the southern tip of the peninsula lay the naval base of Singapore, then supposed to be the strongest in the world. Sixty million pounds had recently been spent on it. It looked out to sea but it was not from the sea that the attack came. We had lost command of the sea; the

Prince of Wales and the *Repulse* had been sunk by aircraft.* But the enemy used command of the sea to supplement his land attack by continual landings on the coast. No one had really believed that a modern army could approach Singapore by land; the roads were rudimentary, the jungle thick. Neither British nor Indian troops had been trained or equipped for fighting of the kind they now encountered. On the one hand, they were without the powerful modern armament needed to stop tanks, of which the Japanese had plenty; on the other, they had not been trained to move rapidly through the jungle on a light scale of equipment. They were tied by motor vehicles and their supply arrangements to the few roads. Their opponents, on the other hand, outnumbered them—overall, about three to two, but at any given spot usually in a far higher proportion—knew exactly what they meant to do and were trained to do it. They expected to move away from roads in lightly equipped, self-contained parties, carrying rice and ammunition for a few days in light metal carts. Their tactical plan conformed always to the same pattern. Their infantry would engage any force they met by a frontal holding attack, not pushed home, while a subsidiary force would move off the road through the jungle and establish a road-block behind the enemy. Or they would make a fresh landing behind our positions. To troops used to receiving supplies by road from the rear, this was a very disturbing manœuvre; for centuries, soldiers had regarded their flanks and rear as something they must protect, if necessary by refusing a flank—that is, bending the line back—or retiring. Now they were outflanked before they knew it; they believed they were surrounded and must extricate themselves and, in order to retreat, they had to fight their way back against strong defensive positions. Further, the Japanese were so admirably prepared for this campaign that they were able to relieve their front-line advancing troops with fresh formations every thirty-six hours.

It is dispiriting to read the regimental histories. Notes from the story of one battalion will give some idea of what it felt like and how surprisingly long it was before these tactics produced a sense of hopelessness. The 5th Battalion of the 2nd Punjab Regiment had gone to Malaya before the outbreak of war. It was part of the 12th Brigade of the 11th Indian Division, but the brigade, when it met the Japanese, consisted of only two battalions, the 5th/2nd Punjabis and the Argylls. They quickly realized that they were up against first-class troops, very well trained and armed, and that the enemy had complete command of the sea and air. They were immediately outflanked and had to retire; none the less, their first encounter was a success; they checked the Japanese at a river crossing and inflicted heavy casualties. This, however, was the prelude to a long, steady withdrawal, still perfectly orderly; they withdrew in alternate moves with the Argylls in the face of greatly

* See Appendix 2.

superior strength. In spite of the continuous retreat, which meant that they could not bring in their wounded, the 'men's morale was still extremely high' and they felt that 'man for man they had the measure of their formidable enemy.' They were highly commended in orders. But the men were very tired and there could be no rest. They were continually bombed by Japanese planes; no British were to be seen.

On Christmas Day Sepoy Shiv Ram, a Dogra, volunteered to cycle in civilian clothes through the screen of Japanese patrols and get information. He understood the penalty if he was caught; this was before it was known that the Japanese frequently treated any prisoner in the same way as a spy. Shiv Ram carried out his mission successfully in spite of meeting two Japanese patrols; he went again and was able to indicate the exact time and place of a Japanese attack, which was repulsed with heavy loss. He was awarded the Indian Order of Merit. December 26th was 'an exhilarating day', with much success, although the men were very tired and still retreating. Next day there was a very heavy attack and the battalion was ordered to retire through the Argylls sooner than had been expected. The orders did not reach one platoon commanded by Jemadar Mohammad Hassan, who held his ground till he realized that the battalion had gone. He was called on to surrender but ignored the summons, fought his way out and rejoined the battalion with some men from another unit he had found on the way. He won the Military Cross.

Day after day, there was no rest and little time for food. At last, after three weeks of this, on December 30th and 31st came two full nights' rest. The men were much restored, but were at once ordered to the coast to deal with a fresh Japanese landing. They checked a Japanese turning movement, drove them off a bridge and burnt it. Under continual heavy air attacks, they were again ordered to withdraw, again leap-frogging through the Argylls. Again the brigade formed the rear-guard, covering the withdrawal of the division, constantly in action, constantly under air attack. Again, there was no sleep for night after night; the men were swaying on their feet. On January 7th, C and D Companies were cut off from brigade headquarters in a fierce attack by tanks. They had succeeded in blowing up four tanks with mines and one more they had stopped with anti-tank rifles, but these weapons, still quite new to the Indian Army, were quite inadequate for the purpose and already obsolete. Thirty more tanks followed. It was men against machines—and the enemy were still able to bring up fresh infantry every thirty-six hours and launch them against troops who were utterly exhausted, outnumbered, outweaponed, outorganized, outplanned.

On January 27th, after seven weeks fighting, there were 80 survivors of the battalion. They were joined to fresh drafts recently arrived from

India and to remnants of other units to form a new battalion. This had hardly begun training when it was called on to take part in the final defence of Singapore and surrendered with 70,000 British, Australian and Indian troops on February 14th. Two hundred and eighty of this renewed battalion died in captivity. The battalion had been raised in 1798 in the Madras Presidency and had become the 27th Madras Native Infantry in 1824, the 87th Punjabis in 1903. It was a run-of-the-mill Indian Army regiment, enlisting Punjabi Muslims, Sikhs and Dogras.

5. Burma Lost

There followed the Japanese invasion of Burma and a further succession of defeats. There were no formed divisions in Burma. The number of troops was less than the equivalent of two divisions; their training was poor and they were ill-equipped; in the north some Chinese troops, even worse equipped than the British and mostly of very poor morale. The frontier of Burma with Thailand is about nine hundred miles long and quite indefensible but the approaches to Rangoon might have been defended, if only anyone had given to the danger which now arose one-tenth of the thought devoted in the previous century to the North-West Frontier. But it had been assumed by the British without any question that Burma, surrounded by mountains on the east, north and west, could only be invaded as we had invaded it ourselves, from the south and by sea. And since it was axiomatic that we had command of the sea, there was really no need to bother about the defence of Burma and no one ever had.

Again, a diagram will simplify the map and make clear certain essential points about Burma. There were no modern means of communication with India except by sea — no railways, no metalled all-weather roads. There were only three routes into India by land. One ran from Rangoon to a point some hundred miles inland from Akyab, which is virtually an island. From a point some fifty miles north of Akyab on the coast an indifferent road ran to Chittagong in India. There were boats and jungle tracks between the two points, 150 miles apart. Four hundred miles to the north there was a way through the mountains* by Tamu to Imphal and Kohima and thence to Dimapur on the Bengal–Assam railway line. Two hundred miles farther, another way through the mountains led from Myitkyina† to Ledo, also on the

---

* The phrase 'way through the mountains' is deliberately vague. All three land routes were very rudimentary when the war began, but improved later.

† The pronunciation of this name is indicated, more or less, by the rhyme:

> There was a young lady of Myitkyina
> Who desired an affair with Lord Kitchener . . .

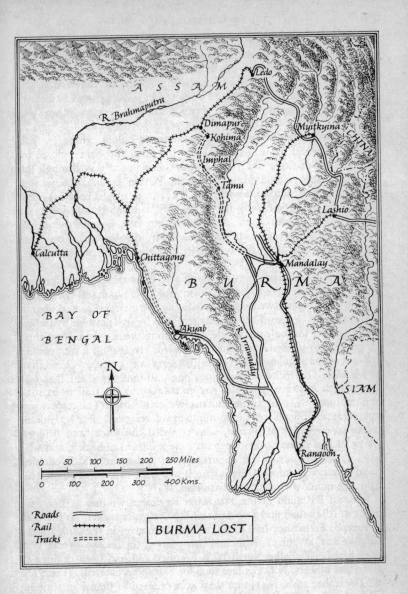

ASSAM

R Brahmaputra

Ledo

Dimapur
Kohima

Myitkyina

CHINA

Imphal

Tamu

Lashio

Calcutta

Chittagong

Mandalay

B U R M A

BAY OF

BENGAL

Akyab

R Irrawaddy

SIAM

N

Rangoon

| 0 | 50 | 100 | 150 | 200 | 250 Miles |

| 0 | 100 | 200 | 300 | 400 Kms. |

Roads
Rail
Tracks

BURMA LOST

Assam railway. On the east, there is a way through the mountains from Lashio to China and in the years immediately before the war this had been developed, to become the 'Burma Road' from Lashio to Chungking. The Burma Road was of such importance to China that the Japanese had demanded it should be closed in July 1941 and had made British and American refusal an occasion for war. To close it now was one of their aims.

Thus Burma can be thought of as a box, an oblong rectangle, with the southern end open to the sea, and the other three sides closed by mountains. But there is a frontier with China and a way through the mountains into China from the north. Within Burma, the railway runs from Rangoon to Myitkyina; for our purpose, broadly north and south. The great river, the Irrawaddy, runs north and south the roads run north and south. And outside the box, beyond the mountains in India to the west, the great river, the Brahmaputra, runs north and south, the railway system and the roads run north and south.

Rangoon was abandoned on March 7th. Now the Japanese pressed north. Their aims were to cut the Burma Road and to defeat the British. They were completely successful, repeating the tactics they had used in Malaya, hooking round behind any strong defensive position by impossible marches through the jungle, establishing themselves behind their enemy so that he found himself surrounded, keeping up a tremendous impetus of continual assault. The British were even worse prepared than in Malaya; General Slim mentions one anti-tank regiment that was armed with Austrian ·77 millimetre guns taken by the Italians in 1918 and captured by us from the Italians in North Africa. The retreat was made more difficult by large numbers of refugees, mostly Indians trying to escape from Burma, who crowded the tracks and bridges, whose lack of sanitary arrangements were a hazard to health, and who gave Japanese parties the opportunity of a disguise which enabled them to spread confusion. But again it will help to look at the retreat from the point of view of one battalion.

The 1st Battalion of the 11th Sikh Regiment we met as Brasyer's Sikhs at Allahabad and Lucknow eighty-five years earlier. As the 14th Ferozepor Sikhs they had distinguished themselves in the 29th Indian Brigade at Gallipoli. For the first two years of the Second World War they had been on the North-West Frontier and had been drained of their best officers, N.C.O.s and men for battalions overseas. It was not till December 29th, 1941, that they were ordered to Jhansi for training with the 63rd Brigade, which was going overseas. Hardly anyone, officer or man, had seen a three-inch or a two-inch mortar, a Bren gun, an anti-tank rifle, a radio set or an armoured carrier; there was not enough of such equipment for troops on the Frontier. Six days before the move they had to send away another draft; one British officer, two Viceroy's Commissioned Officers and a hundred men. On arrival at Jhansi, they were told they would have six months to train, but within a few days were suddenly ordered to mobilize by February 1st. They were made up to full strength by a draft of 400 recruits, mostly with only five months' service; they had to form specialized groups—an anti-tank platoon, an anti-aircraft platoon, a mortar platoon, a Pioneer platoon—to supply drivers for brigade and battalion headquarters; above all, to provide signallers. Their rifle companies were left with 'inexperienced officers, untried N.C.O.s and recruits'. There were not more than twenty trained men to a company. Within a fortnight they were on the way to Burma; they unpacked their new weapons in the ship and fired them over the stern as their only practice. They were soon in action; they were bombed and shelled, had to retreat again and again without any opportunity for rests, and were under great strain and badly shaken when they were ordered to charge the Japanese with the bayonet. This they did successfully, driving them off their ground, but they were too inexperienced to maintain cohesion after the charge. 'Only B Company managed to maintain any organized control.' The others were 'all mixed up and did not know what they were supposed to do.' The battalion had marched and fought and fought again with practically no food or sleep for four days. Now they snatched three days in which they could rest, clean up, reorganize and do some training. 'The men soon recovered and their wonderful spirit gradually returned. They were all firmly determined that the chaos of the past would not be repeated and it never was.'

It has to be recorded that in those first terrible days 2 V.C.O.s and 24 men surrendered and deserted. There were very few cases of this kind. This desertion, and that first relapse into chaos, must be mentioned because they are the prelude to a remarkable recovery. There cannot be many cases of a raw battalion, plunged almost without training into a disastrous retreat, improving steadily in the course of the retreat and emerging with such credit as to enhance a previously high reputation. They were part of the 17th Indian Division and this division soon found itself retiring through the dry belt of Burma, outnumbered—they believed by about seven to one—and continually outflanked. It was decided to guard the road by platoon posts, to be established on either side of the road along which the main body was marching. These posts of course had to move on as soon as the main body had passed, and manning them was very tiring work, involving much movement at the double through rough country. It was 'beyond the capabilities of the British and Gurkha battalions, which were almost exhausted', and it therefore fell to the three Indian battalions to provide these posts. They were the 1st/11th Sikhs, the 4th/12th Frontier Force

Regiment and the 2nd/13th Frontier Rifles, who in one day covered the division's march of 29 miles, through country overpoweringly hot and dusty and without water, under constant attack by enemy aircraft. The 1st/11th Sikhs were singled out for compliment by the corps and divisional commanders for their skill and devotion on this day. They had made good under stress; we shall meet them again in the Arakan, the country between Akyab and Chittagong, when the tide turned.

It would be monotonous to recount the experiences of other battalions in this long retreat, of which an observer has said that it was 'less disorderly than that to Corunna, better controlled than that from Mons ... far more prolonged, difficult and dangerous than either.'

It will be best to let Slim, the Commander of the Burma Corps, complete the picture. But first one unforgettable and characteristic glimpse of the Corps Commander himself. In the confusion of the retreat, he had gone forward to find the headquarters of one of the brigades and found himself alone in an open space, where, crouching behind every little mound and bush, were men of the 7th Gurkhas, whom he had once commanded. 'A lot of stuff was coming over' and a salvo of mortars fell in the clearing. 'Not liking it a bit, I continued to walk forward. Then from behind a bush that offered scant cover to his bulky figure rose my old friend the Subadar-Major of the 7th Gurkhas, his face creased in a huge grin which almost hid his twinkling almond eyes. He stood there and shook with laughter at me. I asked him coldly what he was laughing at, and he replied that it was very funny to see the General Sahib wandering along there by himself and not knowing what to do!' General Slim says that only a Gurkha would have stood up and laughed at him, but he was of course a Gurkha himself, and it may be that some other officers—devoted to their Sikhs, their Jats, or their Punjabi Muslims—would have similar stories. But let us hear General Slim's account of the end of the campaign. On 12th May, the monsoon

'burst in full fury ... From then on the retreat was sheer misery. Ploughing their way up slopes, over a track inches deep in slippery mud, soaked to the skin, rotten with fever, ill-fed and shivering as the air grew cooler, the troops went on, hour after hour, day after day. Their only rest at night was to lie on the sodden ground under the dripping trees, without even a blanket to cover them ... On the last day of that nine-hundred-mile retreat I ... watched the rearguard march into India. All of them, British, Indian and Gurkha, were gaunt and ragged as scarecrows. Yet ... they still carried their arms and kept their ranks, they were still recognizable as fighting units. They might look like scarecrows but they looked like soldiers too.'

XX

The Second World War: Victory

1. The Stage for Victory

The first campaign in Burma came to an end partly because even the Japanese were beginning to exhaust their impetus, partly because of the mountain barrier that lay between the two parallel systems of communication in India and in Burma, and partly because of the monsoon. In Burma the wind begins to blow from the south-east, bringing heavy rain, early in May; it continues for four or five months. As one moves west and north in India, the rain comes later and is less intense. In Upper Burma and Assam the rain is torrential and it not only slows up the movement of troops, still more of tanks and heavy vehicles, but it makes it impossible to construct temporary landing-strips for aircraft or to use any that have not been built to all-weather standards. Since air cover was essential, the monsoon thus dictated a close season and a campaigning season for any major offensive. But there might be a dubious hard-won advantage to the side which defied these limitations.

Few of the public, either in Britain or India, were aware of the magnitude of the dangers from which the monsoon had for the moment saved us. We have seen the state of the 1st/11th Sikhs when they were pushed into Burma. They went in as recruits; they came out soldiers but scarecrows. After the losses in Malaya and Burma, with troops still abroad in the Middle East, Iraq and Persia, no trained soldiers were left in India, only tattered remnants who often needed time in hospital, and always needed rest, retraining, new equipment. We had lost command of the sea; in April 1942 the Japanese sailed into the Bay of Bengal and sank a hundred ships. They raided Ceylon, both Trincomalee and Colombo, with carrier-borne aircraft; the R.A.F. in Ceylon were left after that raid with no aircraft that could take the air.

One vivid personal memory for me summarizes the situation. It was a hot June evening in Delhi. The offices were closing. Field-Marshal Wavell came into the Chief of the General Staff's office before going back to his house; he stood, square and dogged, before the map of Burma, gazing at it, his hands behind him.

'Think how stretched *they* must be!' he said. 'This is the moment to hit the Japs if only we could! If I had one division in India fit to fight I'd go for them now!' But he had not.

We had eight anti-aircraft guns in India and the Chiefs of Staff Committee debated whether to put two in each major post or whether to keep them all together and make a show.

It is hard to convey to anyone who thinks in European terms what a task it was to drive the Japanese from Burma. The military side of it was bad enough; we had lost command of the sea and to get in by land involved the appalling problems of the mountain barrier and the parallel lines of communication; Dimapur was on a single-line metre-gauge railway and everything must go up the Assam railway. To advance into Burma from Imphal, with a base at Dimapur, pushing the Japanese back towards a base at Rangoon, was a staff college nightmare. We had also to build up a new army. And politically, the majority party was, as we have seen, sullen and disaffected, while administratively an underdeveloped sub-continent of 400 million people had to be turned into a vast industrial base.

India's defences had all faced west and had been based on the axiom that we should command the sea. In the first two years of the war India had sent westward a quarter of a million troops — more than Great Britain had sent to the Middle East. India had sent to North Africa pipe-lines, railway rolling-stock, locomotives and 1,200 miles of railway line. India's own lines had been torn up and sent to North Africa. Now India's gaze had suddenly been wrenched eastward. Troops trained for open warfare in the sandy waterless desert must suddenly be taught to creep through sodden, steaming jungles on the slopes of razor-edged ridges. To get supplies to China and keep China in the war became a first demand; since the Burma Road had gone, that meant flying supplies to China across the Himalayas, 'over the hump', at heights that were then unusual. For that, airfields must be built in the north-east corner of Assam; the stores to be flown and the petrol to fly them with had to be transported to that remote corner, where the rainfall was the highest in the world. Everything had to go there on India's Victorian railway system, admirably designed for transporting enormous numbers of people slowly and uncomfortably but very cheaply. It was a most efficient railway system for its purpose; it actually paid its way. But it was not designed for the strain it must now take.

By the end of the war, the capacity of the Bengal–Assam railway system was multiplied by four. In the one year 1944 Indian railways carried 96 million passengers 36,000 million miles. Two hundred fully equipped operational airfields had been built, as well as seven huge bases, with runways over a mile long, for the big American planes carrying stores to China. Hundreds of miles of roads and pipe-lines had been constructed; the capacity of the ports had been multiplied many times; four hundred million garments had been supplied to the forces and fifty million pairs of boots. Aircraft had been assembled, minesweepers built, parachutes cut and sewn and finished; the steel-yards turned out railway bridges, armour-piercing steel, bullet-proof steel; India made surgical instruments, cranes, floating docks. No doubt all these ought to have been made in India before. But they had not been; owing to the war, they were; after the war, independent India was equipped for all these enterprises and many more.

The Indian Army expanded from 189,000 in 1939 to 2,500,000 in 1945; at the same time, a force of eight million men were employed for special tasks required by the defence services, five million in war in-dustries and an extra million to meet the strain on the railways. This was the background to operational planning; every move had to be considered in relation to what the railways could carry, what the ports could take, what the ships could bring. Much shipping had been lost by enemy action and, since it must go round by the Cape, each in-dividual ship spent longer on each voyage. There was never enough shipping. Far away, on the other side of the world, Churchill and Roosevelt would agree that supplies must get to China and that Burma must be retaken by a given date. The Chiefs of Staff in London would elaborate and ask India what resources would be needed. The reply from India would specify, item by item, a long list of stores but explain that these could be handled by India's ports and railways only if they came in regular monthly amounts, in a specified order, and that the Prime Minister's date could not be met unless the consignments started at once. If they did not, we should miss the monsoon and a year's delay would result. This would be ignored; no shipping would be allotted, no consignments would arrive. At last, one of the Prime Minister's stimulating telegrams would be dispatched, upbraiding India for hesitancy and half-heartedness, demanding bricks without straw, cutting through knots, brushing aside difficulties, suggesting that all these elaborate stores were not needed for fighting the Japanese. Why did India need landing-craft? Surely it would be possible to land against Japanese opposition from sampans or barges, which could be found locally? Surely it need not take more than a few days to train men to get in and out of boats? Surely nobody need mind a little rain? He reverted continually to a purely emotional belief that Japanese shells and bullets were in some way less lethal than German; the aggressive spirit was all that was really needed to defeat them.

Certainly the requirements of a modern army were formidable. They inspired one of the planners to a song to the tune of 'Widdecombe Fair', of which the refrain ran:

> With your field butcheries, field bakeries, docks
>   operating companies, bulk issue depots, field
>   transfusion units, R.A.F. servicing parties,
>   mobile X-ray units
>   and Cattle Stock Sections and all!
>   and Cattle Stock Sections and all!

All the same, an army cannot fight well for long unless it is well fed
and its health is good; long distances, tropical disease and climate do
not reduce—as the Prime Minister sometimes appeared to think—
they increase the need for care and preparation. There is high praise in
Churchill's book for the care with which the Duke of Marlborough
prepared his march to the Danube; it was not done in a day. But then
he had chosen his Prime Minister—which no British general has done
since—and he was not harried by impatient allies. It was the view of
most far-sighted officers in Delhi in the summer of 1942 that a full
year would be needed for preparation and that only after the monsoon
of 1943 would it be possible to mount a victorious offensive. This
proved to be the case.

One example will show the difference that preparation could make.
In 1943 for every man admitted to hospital with wounds there had been
one hundred and twenty from tropical diseases. By 1945 the rate had
dropped to ten men sick for one battle casualty and in the last six
weeks of the war to six for one. That kind of improvement was achieved
in almost every aspect of military supply and care for the troops; indeed, in one all-important respect—cover by operational aircraft and
supply by air—the improvement cannot be measured because these
had simply not existed during the retreat.

Another ditty composed by the planners, and incidentally quoted
by General Slim, sums up one aspect of the period of preparation for
victory:

> Plan followed plan in swift procession,
> Commanders went, commanders came;
> While telegrams in quick succession
> Arrived to douse or fan the flame.

A complicated system of command was devised which made the
India Command under General Auchinleck a gigantic base, a training
and recruiting ground, while the operational command, and the difficult political task of harnessing into one team American and British
aims and methods, was given to Admiral Lord Louis Mountbatten as
Supreme Allied Commander. He brought to it a youthful enthusiasm,
a zest, an energy, a power of winning sympathy, that were of incal-

culable value; he had the confidence of the Prime Minister and of the President of the United States and this helped to bring supplies, particularly in the vital matter of aircraft. Behind all this continuec the steady grind of administrative building. After the monsoon of 1943 the building began to take shape and there was a base from which victory could be launched. But that is to go forward in the narrative, which has been brought up only to the end of the retreat from Burma in the summer of 1942.

It was hard to accept the long delay, and there were two good reasons for attacking the Japanese, even before we were ready. The first was Wavell's conviction that the enemy had stretched out too far and should be hit before he had time to recover and consolidate. The second was the need to show our allies that we wanted to fight, and to convince the troops that they could beat the Japanese. It was for these reasons that two preliminary offensives were launched. One was in the Arakan, beyond Chittagong and towards Akyab. This attack by the Indian 14th Division was in itself a failure; not enough attention had been paid to Japanese tactics and the lessons to be learnt from them. We made frontal assaults on prepared positions; when the troops were exhausted the Japanese counter-attacked in the familiar form by a hook behind our positions and forced us to retire. We ended where we started, but after heavy losses in men and vehicles. As an offensive, the operation had failed. It is arguable that it postponed the Japanese plan for the conquest of India and destruction of the route to China which they launched after the next monsoon; it kept them busy for one campaigning season. But perhaps General Slim's reflections on the campaign were the most fruitful result. They formed the basis for victory.

The second offensive of this period had far-reaching consequences of another kind. Wavell had a great belief in the value of disruptive operations behind the enemy lines, whether by local guerrillas or by long-range penetration groups. He had been impressed by Orde Wingate's success as a guerrilla leader in Abyssinia and in February 1943 he formed and dispatched into the heart of Burma the 77th Indian Infantry Brigade to operate under Wingate in a number of dispersed columns. These columns reached the centre of the communications system and cut the railway to Myitkyina in several places. They were thoroughly trained to move through jungle without depending on a line of communication; they were trained to live on what they had and on what could be dropped to them from the air; they were trained to fight in the jungle. They succeeded in cutting the railway—but more important than the material damage was the fact they had fought and won. They prepared the road for victory by teaching everyone else a great deal about training. They ended the feeling that the Japanese had some special jungle magic which made them unbeatable.

2. The Beginning of Victory

After the Arakan offensive of the spring of 1943, General Slim sat down
to think out what had gone wrong and how it could be put right. Much
of what was needed was administrative; we must have better equipment
and better medical arrangements. Something has been said about this
already. But equipment would be no use without an improvement in
training and in the will to win. He had been struck by the skill of the
Japanese in attack, the confidence and daring of their plans; how could
the tables be turned? Would they be as confident when we called the
tune and set the pace? A good deal suggested that they would not.
The men under his command—British, Indian, Gurkha—must be
trained to win, must be convinced that they were in the right and must
believe that they *would* win.

He has set out in his book *Defeat Into Victory* the results of his thinking.
First, British and Indian soldiers must be trained to move in the jungle
themselves and to look on Japanese tactics in quite a different way.
When the Japanese hooked behind and established a defensive position,
they must see this as a chance to surround the Japanese. They must
stand fast and their supplies must come by air; fresh troops must move
up and attack the Japanese outflanking party. They would have a good
chance of destroying it, because the Japanese were habitually so sure of
victory that they took with them on these flanking expeditions supplies
for a few days only. We must not fling troops direct into all-out attacks
on a narrow front, but do just what the Japanese had done: hold the
enemy in front and work round a flank ourselves. And in all this, the
first step was to learn to patrol in the jungle—'boldly, widely, cunningly
and offensively'.

This was the essence of the change in training and tactics. As to the
will to win, Slim set down, in the brisk language of a military appreciation, what was necessary to build it up. He put his points under three
headings—spiritual, intellectual and material, in that order. Under
'spiritual', which most people would have called moral, the essential
point was that 'There must be a great and noble object.' To a more
complex man or a weaker man, this might have presented problems;
some of his troops were Hindu, some Muslim, some Sikh, some Christian, some agnostic; they spoke many different languages, while in
India, the homeland of more than half, the three main communities
were becoming more and more hostile to each other, more and more
resentful of British leadership. But his was a singularly integrated
character and on profound matters his views were simple. There was
no problem for him; there *was* a great and noble object. All that was
necessary was to state it. He wrote later:

'If ever an army fought in a just cause, we did. We coveted no man's country; we wished to impose no form of government on any nation. We fought for the clean, the decent, the free things of life, for the right to live our lives in our own way, as others could live theirs, to worship God in what faith we chose, to be free in body and mind and for our children to be free. We fought only because the powers of evil had attacked these things.'

This was something he believed without question but it was not being said and it had to be said. That was the moral side. Intellectually, the troops must be convinced that they could win and — to end with the material aspect — they must get the best equipment they could and must be well looked after. He went round saying these things — 'I became more like a parliamentary candidate than a general,' he wrote — but he also *did* a great deal about them. An important part of his view was that there should be a number of minor offensives in which we had overwhelming strength. Above all, he believed in offensive patrols, to find out what the enemy was doing and where he was, to rob him of sleep and keep him on the jump, to show our men that he could be frightened and that man for man they could beat him.

But let us look at the second Arakan campaign; this was the moment when the tide turned against the Japanese by land. It will be remembered that the Burmese road-system reaches a point about a hundred miles inland from Akyab, while the Indian coast road to Chittagong starts about fifty miles north of Akyab at Ramu. The Mayu peninsula is a tongue, with its root at Ramu and its tip at Akyab. The sea lies on the west side, the Mayu river on the east; down the middle runs the Mayu range of mountains, which are not very high, but are extremely difficult to cross or to move in. They are precipitous, thick with jungle, cut by creeks, some steep-sided and fast-running, some muddy and sluggish, all obstacles to progress. One all-weather road, sixteen miles long, connected neither with the Burmese nor with the Indian system, crossed the range from Maungdaw on the coast to Buthidaung on the Mayu River. This was held by the Japanese.

The campaign with which we are now concerned took place in the piece of country north of this road. A map which includes the relevant points need be only twelve miles square, though two points which on the map are twelve miles apart may be several hours apart on the ground. Picture then a square, twelve miles each way, with Maungdaw in the bottom left-hand corner and Buthidaung in the bottom right-hand corner. Between them runs the one all-weather road, held by the Japanese, who had built behind it three immensely strong defensive positions with tunnels deep in the hill-side. Half-way up the map, there is a track across the Mayu range, which it crosses by the Ngakye-dauk Pass, known to British troops as the 'Okeydoke' Pass. This track we held. In the top right-hand corner is Taung Bazar, and from Taung

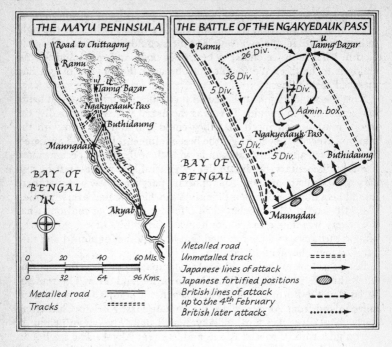

Bazar to Buthidaung there is the river, with tracks along its banks. All the central part of the map is mountain and jungle, crossed only by tracks and footpaths. The aim of the British offensive was to take the metalled road and the Japanese positions—almost fortresses—behind it. The 5th Indian Division was to advance along the coast and take Maungdaw. The 7th Indian Division would advance on the east of the range, engage the enemy along the front and then hook round behind Buthidaung and take it from the rear; then the two divisions would turn inwards and reduce the three great fortresses in the centre.

The bare outline of what happened can be stated simply and shortly, but this involves gross simplification of complicated events, which at the time, to many of those concerned, seemed confusing in the extreme. The offensive began on the night between November 30th and December, 1st, 1943. Good progress was made by both the 5th and the 7th

Division, though with much hard fighting; they pushed forward step by step and established themselves close to the road and the main Japanese fortified positions. The 5th Division took Maungdaw; the 7th was by the end of January preparing for its hook round behind Buthidaung.

But the Japanese also had a plan. They meant to wait till the 5th and 7th Divisions were locked in an attack on their immensely strong positions on the road, then to hook round behind them in their usual way to Taung Bazar, then to drive across the hills to the sea, cutting the coastal track and the flow of supplies to the 5th Division, curving round sharply behind the 7th Division. These two divisions would be surrounded and destroyed and the Japanese forces would then advance on Chittagong and into India. This would draw all British reserves to the Akyab–Chittagong area. When these were committed, the main thrust would come in the north, up the Tamu–Imphal–Kohima route and into Assam. The airfields in the north-east supplying China would be taken, India would be invaded and there would be no reserves left to meet the march on Delhi. We should here briefly note a matter to which we shall return, that with the Japanese was Subhas Chandra Bose, once an extreme radical of the Congress Party, now proclaimed as Netaji, the Führer, the Leader, at the head of the Indian National Army, composed partly of civilians of Indian birth from Malaya, partly of prisoners of war who had defected. He expected, and the Japanese hoped, that there would be a general rising when he led them into India.

This was the Japanese plan and on February 4th, 1944, they began to put it into execution. Their attack swept round in a curve and took Taung Bazar, then drove south towards the Ngakyedauk Pass and west towards the sea where they cut the track behind 5th Division. They overran the operational headquarters of the 7th Division, of which the remnants fell back to the administrative box near the pass. But for once everything was ready for just this. The 7th Division was surrounded but it stood fast; it was supplied by air, and the 26th Division was launched against the Japanese rear on the east of the mountains, the 36th on the west. It was the Japanese outflanking force that was surrounded. Their plan had allowed ten days for the destruction of the 7th Division; they had no time to spare and attacked with intense ferocity, particularly the administrative box, full of mules, petrol, hospital stores—a vulnerable target under constant shell-fire for days. But it held; as in France twenty-six years before, cooks, clerks, hospital orderlies lent a hand. And they were well supplied by air. The tenth day passed and Japanese supplies began to run out. Ten days later, by February 24th, the battle was won; the encircling force was destroyed. They would not surrender. They had to be killed one by one. One part of this encircling force had consisted of 7,000 men, of whom 5,000 bodies were counted.

The ferocity of this fighting was grim and personal. Once the Japanese broke into the 7th Division's administrative box and took the hospital; they killed the patients on the beds and shot the doctors; they made the orderlies carry their own wounded back and then killed them in cold blood. That put an edge on the savagery that men brought to a bayonet charge. A Sikh company of the 4th/14th Punjabis found the body of a comrade who had been taken prisoner by the Japanese the previous day and beheaded; they 'went completely berserk,' discarded their fire plan, went in with the bayonet and put the Japanese to rout.

Well before the main battle began, battalions had been carrying out the offensive patrols that Slim had wanted, had found that there was nothing the Japanese could do that they could not, had built up a cheerful confidence that they could beat him. On Christmas Eve some Indian troops were listening to a Japanese broadcast which announced that Bose and his Indian National Army would be in Delhi in ten days' time; a Punjabi soldier who had just been on leave and had suffered from the congested railway system called out: 'Not if they go by train they won't!' — the kind of joke traditionally associated with British troops. A platoon of the 1st/11th Sikhs, being surrounded and in a place to which it would not be easy to bring help, was asked by radio how long they thought they could hold out without supplies. The jemadar commanding replied: 'Without food, six days. Without ammunition, as long as you like; we have bayonets!' There is often a touch of the Gascon about the Sikh. In fact, the 4th/14th Punjabis got through to them with both food and ammunition within two days. When the war was over, and Japanese impressions could be pieced together, it was found that on many occasions quite small bodies of troops had successfully made the Japanese think they were far stronger than they were; at the beginning of this campaign for example, A Company of the 1st/11th Sikhs made the Japanese think they were a full battalion and, towards the end of it, A Company of the 5th/16th Punjabis, defending two small features known by the British as Spit and Polish, did just the same.

We saw the 1st/11th Sikhs — once, long ago, Brasyer's — go into Burma recruits and come out scarecrows but soldiers. Now they were veterans. One incident will show them in action and illustrate the nature of the fighting. After the Japanese hook had been defeated, the 7th Division resumed its offensive, of which the next step was to take Buthidaung. During the attack on India Hill, a feature near Buthidaung, on March 12th, 1944, Naik Nand Singh was leading his section towards a Japanese position. His was the leading section of the leading platoon of C Company. India Hill was a knife-edged ridge covered with jungle and the exact layout of the Japanese position could not be seen. In fact, it was held by about forty Japanese, placed singly in holes or in trenches that took two men each. There was only one way to get near the position, by a narrow track; as Nand Singh's section reached the crest they came under heavy rifle and machine-gun fire and every man but Nand Singh fell. But he went straight at the nearest trench and though hit by a fragment of grenade he sprang into the trench and bayoneted both occupants. There was another trench of the same kind close by and Nand Singh jumped out of his trench and dashed towards it. He was hit again and knocked down but he got up and hurled himself into the second trench, killing the two occupants of that too. He went on and took a third trench. The rest of the platoon then moved up and took the position, killing 37 of the 40 men holding it. Nand Singh won the V.C.

The second Arakan campaign ended with the Japanese driven from the metalled road and from the three formidable fortresses they had built there. The campaign was not of great strategic importance but it was a rehearsal of what was to come and it was the first taste of victory.

3. Burma Regained

The Japanese too had a plan. And, despite defeat in the first phase of it, they stuck to it—rigidly, stubbornly, as was their custom. They had meant their counter-attack in the Arakan at best to lead into India, at worst to draw all British reserves to the south and prepare the way for their attack on Imphal. In fact, the opposite occurred; their defeat in the south—and Allied command of the air—made it possible for Slim to withdraw forces from the south and use them in the north; the 5th and 7th Indian Divisions were pulled out of Arakan and moved, mainly by air, to the new battle in the Imphal area.

Slim, thinking things out after the first Arakan campaign, had tried to picture the use he would make of the new, confident, well-trained army which he meant to create. With such an army, with plenty of transport aircraft, and with fighter aircraft to keep the Japanese out of the skies, the best situation he could imagine would arise from a big Japanese offensive in their usual style. This would give him the chance to beat them before he went into Burma. How could he lure them into making such an attack? But he did not have to lure them. During the last months of 1943 they built up their forces in Burma to double what they had been. In February they launched the Arakan offensive and captured papers revealed their whole intention. On March 15th, 1944, according to plan, they launched the Imphal offensive. This was on the usual Japanese lines, and differed from its little brother, the Arakan offensive, only because of the peculiar nature of the Imphal front. Arakan had been more like a textbook battle; the British lines of communication ran south, the Japanese north, the opposing fronts lay east and west at right angles to the communications. But the line of communications to Imphal ran north-eastward from Calcutta by the Bengal–Assam railway, roughly parallel with the boundary between Burma and India, then east from Dimapur by road to Kohima, thence south to Imphal and Tamu. From Kohima to Tamu, it was parallel to the tactical front; the Japanese were on the Chindwin, only forty miles away. Thus the line of supply was like a shepherd's crook or reversed fish-hook and if the Japanese could cut it at Kohima—the top of the crook—everything from that point to the tip should fall into their hands. There was a good deal to fall. In the Imphal plain, a comparatively level island in the mountains, there had been constructed a vast forward base for the reconquest of Burma. If the three divisions holding Imphal could be surrounded and destroyed and the base captured, the road to India would be open.

This was the decisive battle. In the Pacific, things were going against

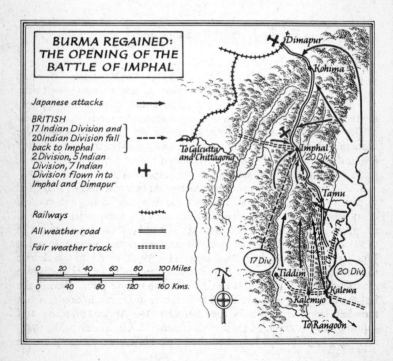

BURMA REGAINED:
THE OPENING OF THE
BATTLE OF IMPHAL

Japanese attacks

BRITISH
17 Indian Division and
20 Indian Division fall
back to Imphal
2 Division, 5 Indian
Division, 7 Indian
Division flown in to
Imphal and Dimapur

Railways

All weather road

Fair weather track

0   20   40   60   80   100 Miles
0   40   80   120   160 Kms.

Dimapur
Kohima
To Calcutta and Chittagong
Imphal
20 Div
Tamu
Chindwin R.
17 Div.
Tiddim
20 Div.
Kalewa
Kalemyo
To Rangoon
N

the Japanese, but if they could break through into Assam the line would be cut to China and Chiang Kai-shek would make a separate peace; India would fall into their hands and then they could go to the peace table and negotiate.

Imphal was defended by IV Corps, two of whose three divisions, the 17th and 20th Indian Divisions, were forward in the areas of Tiddim and Kalewa. The 23rd Indian Division was in reserve at Imphal. With considerable moral courage—he was fortunate in not being in direct communication with the Prime Minister—Slim decided to withdraw the 17th and 20th Divisions to the Imphal plain. 'I was tired of fighting the Japanese when they had a good line of communications behind them and I had an execrable one. This time I would reverse the procedure.' In the Imphal plain, it would be they who attacked prepared positions—and with time against them, because they would soon be impossibly short of supplies. They gambled on capturing our supplies before the monsoon broke.

That was how it was planned. But it did not work out exactly according to plan. We knew how strong the Japanese were and almost exactly what they were going to do; the forecast was a little out only on the timing and on the strength the enemy could deploy against Kohima. But that little was important. The Japanese offensive began before the 17th Division had moved back; the Japanese attacked the 17th Division in front and hooked round behind as usual; the division had to fight its way back against heavy opposition, while part of the 23rd Division from Imphal had to move down the road to Tiddim to attack the Japanese road-block from the other side. The 20th Division too had no easy march back. In the end, both reached the Imphal plain intact, having inflicted heavier losses on the Japanese than they had sustained. But this left IV Corps with no reserves and Imphal itself was now under direct attack from the east. Here it was touch and go—and not just for a few days but for week after week. As for Kohima, the enemy moved towards it faster and in greater strength than had been expected. Slim characteristically remarks that, like many generals before him, he was saved from the consequence of his mistakes by the stubborn valour of his troops and the mistakes of his enemy. The newly formed Assam Regiment, in the first battle of its career, met the main weight of the enemy advance on Kohima and 'put up a magnificent resistance, held doggedly to one position after another against overwhelming odds, and in spite of heavy casualties ... never lost cohesion. The delay the Assam Regiment imposed on the 31st Japanese Division at this stage was invaluable.' But eventually this screen was pushed back and the 'very miscellaneous garrison' at Kohima faced 'fifteen thousand ravening Japanese' closing in on them. Fortunately the enemy commander appears to have been an exceptionally rigid and stupid man.

He had been ordered to take Kohima, so he flung his troops at it again and again, while if he had left it he could have taken Dimapur, a far greater prize which was far less defensible.

It was touch and go everywhere. A few days one way or the other would have made all the difference. Imphal was surrounded; and enemy attacks from every angle were held—but only just held; much of Kohima was in enemy hands; Dimapur lay almost defenceless. Then the reinforcements began to arrive. The 5th Indian Division was flown from the Arakan, two brigades to Imphal and one to Dimapur, all three going almost straight from their aircraft into battle. The 2nd British Division was flown in from South India and the 7th Indian direct from operations in the Arakan. The move of the 5th Division began in mid March; the 7th began to move early in April. The battle raged throughout April; the most acute danger passed at Kohima with the arrival of the 161st Indian Infantry Brigade—part of the 5th Division —but things still hung in the balance, there and on every front.

The general scene is admirably described by Slim himself. 'The prolonged and hard-fought battle ... swayed back and forth through great stretches of wild country; one day its focal point was a hill named on no map; the next a miserable unpronounceable village a hundred miles away. Columns, brigades, divisions, marched and counter-marched, met in bloody clashes, and reeled apart, weaving a confused pattern hard to unravel.' Yet one can see a pattern, several times repeated, never exactly the same, but recurring like a motif in a Persian carpet. There is a centre, like the fiery nucleus of a star, which is a British position. Swirling round it and savagely attacking it are the Japanese and moving up to assail them are fresh British forces from outside. That was the pattern at Kohima, at Imphal, again and again at smaller positions—like a series of Catherine-wheels, whirling and flaming, but striving inwards but not outwards. By the middle of April, Slim felt that 'our original pattern for the battle was reasserting itself.' The phase of attrition was beginning; the reinforcements were coming in. The 2nd Division came to the defence of Dimapur; the 161st Brigade of the 7th Division moved forward to the final relief of Kohima and on April 18th at last broke through, the 1st/1st Punjabis being the first to enter and taking over part of the defences from the exhausted garrison. But it was typical of the ferocity of this war and of Japanese stubbornness in defence that it was not till mid May that Kohima itself was in our hands and not till June that we were in the Naga village that overlooks it from a mile away.

On every trail and footpath leading to Imphal the Japanese continued fanatical onslaughts right through April and May. It was only in June that it began to be clear that though, as always, Japanese soldiers fought as long as they could move, their supplies were exhausted, they were starving and dying of hunger and control over formations was coming to an end. Japanese were now found dead of starvation with grass in their mouths. They had gambled on getting into Imphal. There was no pause; the fighting went on. The hills were cleared of them, though the monsoon was now raging. The results of the monsoon were noted in the diary of one brigade: 'Hill tracks are ... either so slippery that men can hardly walk or knee-deep in mud ... Half a company took ten hours to carry two stretcher-cases four miles. A party of men without packs took seven hours to cover five miles.' None the less, the pursuit went on through the monsoon.

This battle did not end the war in Burma. Much fighting of intense ferocity was still to come. But from now on there could be no doubt that we were winning and that the total defeat of the Japanese was only a matter of time. Slim summed up the results; five Japanese divisions had been destroyed as fighting formations—the 15th, 18th, 31st, 33rd and 55th—while more than two others had been badly mauled. Fifty thousand Japanese had been killed and perhaps twenty-five thousand wounded. Only six hundred prisoners had been taken and most of those only because they were too weak to move. The nature of Japanese resistance can best be illustrated by one example, which took place after this battle, near Meiktila. A Japanese force attacked by tanks had run out of mines but had aircraft bombs; the commander had holes dug where he expected tanks and in each put a man with a bomb between his knees and orders to detonate it when a tank passed over his head. As Slim remarked: 'If five hundred Japanese were ordered to hold a position, we had to kill four hundred and ninety-five before it was ours—and then the last five killed themselves.'

This was the kind of enemy against whom the mere mercenaries of the Indian Army had to fight. Twenty-seven V.C.s were awarded in Burma of which twenty went to the Indian Army. No less than three of these were earned by one battalion, the 2nd/5th Royal Gurkha Rifles who were part of the 17th Division. Once again, it is hard to choose between so many acts of valour; once again, it sometimes appears that deeds of equal courage received less glittering rewards—but then how can such qualities be measured? But there is one Victoria Cross that seems to stand out even among these many instances of an unbelievable forgetfulness of self. It took place after the Imphal battle, but the nature of the fighting had not changed; the Japanese were still fiercely attacking.

In February 1945 a battle second in importance only to Imphal took place for Meiktila, a central spot in the Burmese system of communications. It was the task of the 20th Indian Division to cross the Irrawaddy well to the north of this battle area and give the impression that theirs was the main attack. They crossed the river and established a bridgehead; the Japanese reacted savagely and tried to drive them out of it. The 14th Battalion, 13th Frontier Force Rifles—a war-time unit raised in April 1941—was engaged from February 13th to 20th, 1945, in very hard fighting in defence of this bridgehead. On the night of the 16th–17th, the enemy attacks mounted to a crescendo. Platoons and sections were frequently isolated; the assaults on the position held by C Company were particularly fierce. The company was under constant heavy fire from mortars, grenades and machine-guns, and repelled frequent charges with the bayonet. The forward observation party, who had been directing artillery support—one British officer and four British other ranks—were all killed and no more artillery support was possible. Jemadar Prakash Singh, a Dogra, commanding one platoon, was hit in both ankles; the Company Commander ordered Lt H. H. Khan to take over command from him. But Khan too was hit and Prakash resumed command, dragging himself from section to section on hands and knees. The Company Commander came back to the sector and found him propped up by his batman, who was also wounded, firing the platoon two-inch mortar, of which all the crew were killed, shouting encouragement to the men and directing their fire. When no ammunition was left for the mortar, he crawled round the position collecting ammunition from the killed and wounded and re-distributing it. The Bren gun section being all casualties, Prakash took over their sector and worked the gun single-handed. Since he could not stand up in the trench, he had to expose himself outside it. He was again wounded in both legs, above the knees. Both his legs were now quite useless, but he hauled himself about by his arms only, encouraging and regrouping what was left of his platoon. They stopped another fierce Japanese charge. Prakash was hit again in the right leg, he was getting weak from loss of blood but went on encouraging his men. Fighting was hand-to-hand again and Prakash shouted the Dogra war-cry so loudly that the whole of C Company took it up and drove the enemy from the position. Prakash was hit again in the chest by a fragment of a grenade. His Company Commander reached the platoon again and knelt beside him. He told him not to worry; he could look after himself—and with those words he died, at half past two in the morning of February 17th, 1945.

4. The New Army and its Leaders

In the eighteenth century, the Sultan of Mysore had said that if he had troops who fought like English soldiers, he would treat them like hunting-leopards, bringing them to the battle in litters so that they would not be fatigued, and loosing them at their prey when they were close. And though the English in India had never done quite that, they certainly had looked on their British soldiers as shock troops, the spearhead of the assault, while Indian battalions had at first often been auxiliaries or moppers-up. This was due to a belief in the innate superiority of the British soldier as a fighting man; then after the Mutiny came distrust, and Indians must always be brigaded with British troops, usually two Indian battalions to one British. Kitchener had thought this out of date and had argued that it would be much easier to feed brigades that were wholly British or wholly Indian; he also thought that used in this way their good qualities could supplement each other. Slim went back to Kitchener's idea and in Burma towards the end brigaded Indian with Indian and British with British. Not only were they easier to supply, but he thought they fought better like that.

Gone were the days when it had been supposed that the example of British troops was needed to fire Indians to valour. British battalions in Burma were generally under strength and Slim thought they had sometimes been reinforced from other units to such an extent that they had lost much of their old regimental spirit. After Imphal, he wrote, 'divisional commanders were now calling for Indian battalions in place of British.' In comparison with British troops, Slim thought the Asian fighting man — and here he was putting together Indian, Gurkha and Japanese — 'is at least equally brave, usually more careless of death, less encumbered by mental doubts or humanitarian sentiment, not so moved by slaughter and mutilation' — in fact, more like the British soldier had been in the eighteenth century. He thought that it was only in education and technical skill that white troops now had any advantage. To win against Asians, they must be better trained, better disciplined and better led. Slim ends his thoughts on this subject with the words: 'My Indian divisions after 1943 were among the best in the world. They would go anywhere, do anything, go on doing it and do it on very little.'

Much of this was due to two men, Slim himself, and Auchinleck. Slim, as we have seen, had given much thought to bringing the 14th Army to a high pitch of training and of morale. His success in this was due to his qualities as a man and as an outstanding representative of the Indian Army officer. He had been lucky, in more ways than one; any soldier who reaches high command is lucky, because a bullet might have ended his career at any stage, and Slim had been in Gallipoli and Mesopotamia in the First World War. Again, for a British general, it is not usually an advantage to be near the top at the outbreak of a major war. Slim had had a brigade in Abyssinia and only came to the top when equipment began to be available. And there was always someone between him and the Prime Minister. But of course luck was not enough. His crossing of the Irrawaddy was a remarkable feat of arms by any standard, but his success as a general was not so much because he was a brilliant tactician or strategist as because of his moral and human qualities. He was a complete man, an integrated character, following a straightforward course with modesty, courage, energy and resource. 'God helps those who help themselves' was his constant cry; when he was told there were no more silk parachutes to be had, he thought that it must be possible to make them out of jute, and managed to arrange that it was. This kind of resourcefulness and adaptability he showed again and again; 'in more generous theatres,' he notes, 'it was thought proper to allow 400 tons a day to supply a division', but the 14th Army got the figure down to 120.

Orthodox in one respect, Slim was convinced that the main effort must be to beat the enemy in the field and he thought that the immense effort directed to opening Stilwell's Ledo road to China would have been better used in strengthening the 14th Army's line of communications and enabling it to get sooner to Rangoon. Similarly, while he recognized the value of Wingate's first long-range penetration behind the enemy lines, he thought the cost of the second too high; it amounted to a dissipation of force that would have been better used directly against the enemy in the main battle. These are two matters on which there will no doubt long be controversy. But rigidly orthodox he was far from being; on the contrary, he was a master of improvisation, constantly impressing on his officers the need for personal initiative. They must 'shoot a goal when the referee isn't looking.' It is significant that he several times speaks of one of his divisional commanders as an artist, in one case as 'conducting an orchestra'. There is an attractive glimpse of Slim 'hearing through all this noise and the clatter of men clearing a battle-field a strange sound—singing.' He went towards it and eventually found General Pete Rees, commanding the 19th Indian Infantry Division, 'surrounded by a group of Assamese soldiers whom he was vigorously leading in the singing of Welsh missionary hymns. The fact that he sang in Welsh and they in Khasi only added to the harmony. I looked on admiringly. My generals had character. Their men knew them and they knew their men.' It is a glimpse that tells one something of both men. Another attractive picture comes from much earlier in the story, at the end of the retreat. When he said goodbye to his troops in the Burma Corps, he wrote: 'To be cheered by troops whom you have led to victory is grand and exhilarating. To be cheered by the gaunt remnants of those whom you have led only in defeat, withdrawal and disaster is infinitely moving—and humbling.'

Something in Slim's tenacity, humour and modesty endeared him to the men under his command; they knew he was genuine; there was no window-dressing; they understood him and trusted him. They called him 'Uncle Bill'. But if he had built up the 14th Army's morale, the

Indian Army as a whole owed as much to Auchinleck. He had been unlucky compared with Slim; he had already been marked for high command when war broke out and he became the Prime Minister's special find—only to suffer the sudden eclipse of a seraglio favourite. He was a more complex character than Slim, less easy to know; he had grown slowly in mental stature, having been not at all precocious as a junior; he had first distinguished himself as a major with the 1st/1st Punjabis in Mesopotamia and during the 'thirties had begun to be recognized as the Indian Army's coming man. He was a dedicated soldier, his thoughts never far from his profession. But they were wide-ranging, going far beyond the merely military in the narrowest sense. His chairmanship of the Modernization Committee has already been mentioned, but it was not only in wanting to make the army a modern efficient mechanized force that he was far-seeing. A man dedicated to his profession is often extrovert and insensitive but this was far from being the case with Auchinleck. Though he was no politician, in the sense of seeking political backing to his own advantage, he was con-scious as few soldiers—indeed, as few Englishmen—were of the emotional importance of nationalism, not only in politics but in every aspect of Indian middle-class life. He had a deep understanding of Indian soldiers but also—and this was rare—of the Indian middle classes and he felt an instinctive sympathy with them in the humiliation which the British sometimes unconsciously inflicted on them.

He understood, for example, that however logical it might be to pay Indian officers when in India in the same way as British officers when in Britain, in practice it meant a discrimination that was bound to be felt as humiliating. This was still more true of the segregation of Indian officers in 'Indianizing' units and it is due to Auchinleck that this was abandoned. Now all Indian Army units (except Gurkha battalions) took both British and Indian officers. Their pay was now equal and there was no longer any question of their replacing the old Viceroy's Commissioned Officers, the subadars and jemadars who had been raised from the ranks. Having started the war with just over 1,000 Indian officers, the Indian Army ended with 15,740—three times the total peace establishment, British and Indian, of the mid 'thirties. This was an incalculable asset after Independence and the two dominions owed it to Auchinleck.

In the regimental histories there are traditional photographs, the subadar-major sitting by the colonel's side in the centre of the row who have chairs, flanked by the majors and senior captains. At their feet, cross-legged on the ground, sit the junior British subalterns, inter-spersed with the jemadars just commissioned. Behind the chairs are two rows of British and Indian officers, the 'middle-piece' officers. You can tell at a glance, often by different headgear as well as complexion, who is who. But after the war, when formal groups were taken again, or during the war, in snapshots of officers having breakfast in a trench or scanning the country through binoculars, you see that now there are three kinds of officers. Some of the 'British officers' in the old sense are now Indian, perhaps a third; by 1944 there are Indian battalion commanders. The regimental histories record their gallantry and initiative and there are special tributes to some specially loved. Major Ghulam Qadir, of the 1st/17th Dogras, for example, killed near Imphal, is mentioned in the regimental history as 'a most gallant leader. A Pathan in a Hindu battalion, the Dogras would have followed him anywhere; an amiable and attractive personality with a natural sense of humour, he was essentially a soldier and an absolutely first-class one at that.'

There are many such entries, and those who have memories of the kind of companionship that this implies owe it to Auchinleck, for it could hardly have occurred under the old system. Auchinleck also widely extended the class composition of the Indian Army, reversing the trend towards the 'martial classes', returning to Madras and Behar as recruiting-grounds and taking men from castes such as Chamars, who are traditionally leather-workers and often land-less agricultural labourers. In this and other matters, he showed a sensitivity to Indian criticism that no other Commander-in-Chief had shown. He invited elected members of the legislature to join a com-mittee which toured military installations, training-centres and the like, was given talks by senior officers, and in fact went through a kind of short course in all those defence matters which Indian political leaders were apt to complain had been kept from them in a sealed book. Few of them had any family connections with the army; they had none of the links which in Europe give almost every family some idea of what army life is like. What they had gleaned by parliamentary questions had generally been sparse; it had been the tendency not so much to withhold information as to volunteer no more than literally and exactly what was asked. The results, meagre in themselves, had often been misinterpreted through a mixture of ignorance and suspicion. Now they were really being told what happened; information was being volun-teered. Many of them told me how deeply they were impressed.

Auchinleck's appeal to Indian soldiers was of another kind and again it was quite different from Slim's. Slim appealed to all soldiers, British, Indian or Gurkha, because he was one of themselves. But of Auchinleck, no one felt exactly that. He was quite different from themselves, but Indian soldiers felt at once that they would do anything at his com-mand. He had only to walk on to the parade-ground to give them the feeling that they were his men. It was a personal link. They were conscious of his authority. They needed his leadership. Perhaps also they were obscurely aware that this essentially lonely man needed them. He cared for them not merely as part of his command, but because their loyalty was important to him. Loyalty was something he gave freely to others—sometimes indeed, too freely and not wisely, and this had been one of the causes of his misfortunes in North Africa. And because he gave loyalty so freely, he needed loyalty from others.

5. Clashes of Loyalty

It was Auchinleck as Commander-in-Chief in India who trained, supplied and forwarded the troops to the 14th Army in Burma, to the three Indian divisions in Italy and to the garrisons in Iraq and Persia. The extraordinary paradox still held good; political India seethed with controversy about the future, refused to co-operate, even tried briefly to sabotage telegraph and railway lines. But the Indian Army was unaffected; recruiting was good; never had it been so trusted, never had it repaid trust so superbly. There was the special case of those captured in Malaya, to which we shall presently return, but hardly a sign of disaffection in the fighting units. There were some Sikhs who deserted in Burma, already mentioned; there was a picket of the Gwalior Lancers—not part of the regular Indian Army but of the Indian State Forces—which went over to the enemy on February 4th, 1944, at the beginning of the Japanese counter-offensive in the Arakan; there was the mutiny of the Sikh squadron of the Central India Horse at Bombay in 1940. Those are the failures that have come to my knowledge.

The case of the C.I.H. squadron has all the classic ingredients. This regiment had had a particularly distinguished succession of commanding officers but the regiment had been unfortunate in their last, who had recently been invalided from the service and had been lucky to be so treated. It was a tradition in all cavalry regiments to rely heavily on the risaldars and jemadars, the Viceroy's Commissioned Officers, and this tradition worked well if the commanding officer was of high quality. But in this case an inefficient commander had just been succeeded by a newcomer, an excellent man but from another regiment, and the officers did not know that some men of the Sikh squadron had been in touch during the past few months, while stationed in Meerut, with an organization known as the Kirti Lehar—the 'Peasant Movement'—preaching an incendiary peasant communism.

Of all the peoples of India, the Sikhs were at this moment perhaps the most inflammable. They were prosperous by Indian standards; their lands were fertile and they did not subdivide them indefinitely but sent their younger brothers to the army or to the police in Hong Kong or Singapore, to drive taxis in Calcutta, to work as electricians or carpenters in Kenya. They were better educated than most peasant communities; like the Scottish peasantry they were a people of their book. Such people cannot be insulated; it is among the thriving, the go-ahead, the intelligent, not among the destitute, the lacklustre and the hopeless, that radical doctrines take hold. The Sikhs had once ruled the Punjab; those days had gone but, since the Mutiny, their relationship with the British had been a special one because of their contribution to the army. It was a military alliance, essentially a marriage of convenience, and there had always been the substantial Akali element who had condemned it as irreligious. If the British alliance was to come to an end, the Sikhs must look for something else. Change was in the air. The claim for Pakistan was not yet taken seriously and they did not know that their homeland might be divided, but if there was to be independence they might again rule the Punjab—or they might find themselves in a Punjab with a Muslim majority. The Sikh nation therefore was uneasy; the Sikhs were conscious of politics to a higher degree than any other element in the Indian Army.

When the Central India Horse was ordered overseas, the men entrained without any unusual signs, but at Bombay there was an unexpected delay; they were shunted into a siding and kept there for a day and a night, during which the four Sikhs who had been really infected by the Kirti Lehar propaganda had their chance. Two-thirds of the Sikh squadron refused to go overseas. Their officers reasoned with them but nothing would shake them; the regiment sailed without them and a squadron of Dogras was sent later to take their place. The regiment distinguished itself in North Africa and in Italy as the reconnaissance regiment of the 4th Indian Division; the mutinous Sikhs went before a court martial and the leaders were transported to the Andamans where they fell into Japanese hands. In a linked regiment, the 19th Lancers, the Sikh squadron unanimously petitioned to take the place of the C.I.H. squadron.

The men made prisoner in Malaya were of course in far larger numbers. The surrender came after weeks of retreat; they had seen the Japanese masters of the British by land, sea and air. Their British officers were taken away from them as soon as they had surrendered. The Japanese in general despised prisoners and they did not allow themselves to be taken prisoner; their normal treatment of prisoners was therefore by British standards harsh. This, however, was a special case; some 85,000 prisoners had been captured of whom nearly 60,000 were Indian and they clearly might be useful. On these the Japanese soon began to work. Let us consider first the rank and file. They were told that the British were everywhere defeated and the war virtually finished. The truth was bad enough and of that they knew something;

what they were told as prisoners was a good deal worse than the truth. They were offered the immediate inducement of better treatment if they would co-operate in the Greater Asia Co-prosperity Sphere and they were threatened with increasingly bad treatment if they did not. Nor was it only threats. 'Harsh methods of persuasion were used, including severe corporal punishment, and the Bidadari "Concentration Camp" ... became a place of terror the mere threat of which could often induce a man to volunteer.' Several thousand were very early shipped to Japanese labour gangs in the South Pacific. And if men looked further ahead—what kind of India could they hope to go back to if the British were really finished? Would it be ruled by Congress or the Japanese? In either case their prospects seemed bad. Indeed, would they ever get back at all if they persisted? Why should the Japanese bother to take them back? They would be despised serfs, condemned to labour at degrading tasks in frightful conditions until they died. Many must have simply weighed an oath to a power that was defunct against the prospect of again being soldiers, of drawing pay again, of having a chance of getting home. So they signed on and swore a new oath, this time to an Indian Government-in-exile of which the head was eventually Subhas Chandra Bose.

Perhaps in the end the degree of credulity was the dividing factor. They had no means of checking what they were told and, if they believed it, it must have seemed a vain scruple to persevere in loyalty to a vanished empire. The wonder is rather that so many did refuse to believe. Many stuck to their oath, perhaps to some irrational faith that the British always did win in the end, perhaps to the memory of an officer, perhaps to a steadfast personal integrity, perhaps to a deep religious conviction. Personal influence of course played a large part; sometimes almost the whole of a battalion stood firm, sometimes almost a whole battalion went over. Hardly any Gurkhas went over; most of the 3rd Cavalry stood fast, and this can be put down to the example of two commissioned Indian officers who were not, like the British officers, separated from the men and told them that they did not believe what the Japanese said, that they meant to stand to their allegiance and that the men must do the same. These two, Captain Hari Badhwar and Captain Dhargalkar, were confined for weeks in an iron cage in which they could neither stretch out nor stand upright. Badhwar's leadership so much impressed a battalion of the 2nd Gurkhas who were imprisoned with him that they petitioned that he should be made an honorary officer of their regiment. Many Indian officers and Viceroy's Commissioned Officers who would not co-operate were transferred to an 'Officers' Separation Camp' where every kind of pressure was put on them. Captain Durrani was tortured by the Japanese for many days but refused to give the information they wanted. After the war he was awarded the George Cross.

But it would be a mistake to suggest that all those who joined the Indian National Army did so to escape coercion. Mohan Singh, the first leader, was undoubtedly a man whose nationalist sentiments had been growing for some time; he acted from conviction in starting the I.N.A. and, when he found that the Japanese had no intention of treating him as an independent ally, attempted to dissolve it and paid the penalty of arrest and imprisonment. Subhas Chandra Bose, who took his place, was a man of burning enthusiasm. He was absolutely convinced that India would only become independent if she took her freedom by force; he had perfect confidence in his own ability to manage both Germans and Japanese; he was sure they would treat him with the deference due to a friendly Head of State and would respect India's independence. What he wanted to believe, he believed, and here he was naive, not to say gullible. But he was utterly sincere and he proclaimed his doctrine with tireless energy and devotion. He was arrogant, cocksure, ruthless, quite without humour; he saw everything in stark terms of right or wrong, good or bad; there was no hesitation or indecision. All this made him a most effective orator. As Hugh Toye, his biographer, points out, complete certainty of outlook and the sharp contrast of opposites are often satisfying to a soldier, and in Germany, where there is no reliable evidence of physical coercion, Bose did win volunteers from prisoners of war for his first attempt at an army. His theme was nationalism and the motherland; it was heady, emotional stuff; he poured scorn and contempt on those who had been toadies of the British—and, in any case, the British were everywhere defeated. He recruited enough men to form three battalions, but Rommel would not have them in North Africa and they were never used in battle; the impetus left the movement when Bose went to the East.

Here it was another story. The Germans had hesitated for various reasons about raising the standard of a general revolt in India; the Japanese were much less cautious. Bose formed the Provisional Government of Free India with himself as Head of State and Leader. He recruited Indian civilians in Malaya as well as prisoners of war. The Japanese were quite prepared to use Bose's men as infiltrators and spies, but they were distrustful of their military value and at first proposed that they should be split up into parties for political warfare, one of which should be attached to each Japanese formation. Bose would have none of this. They must be kept together; they must fight to free India; they must lead the triumphant armies that would be greeted as heroes by the people of India, who would rise as one man at the sight of them. The Japanese were of course too realistic to use as a military spearhead formations that were very imperfectly trained, quite untried in battle and extremely short of qualified officers. And it must have entered their calculations that men who had once changed sides might do so again.

There was a compromise. Some small parties were attached to Japanese formations for political warfare but the I.N.A. were used as military formations, two weak divisions being sent to Burma. But the Japanese never regarded them as front-line troops and their military value was slight. A Major Misra of the I.N.A. subverted an outpost of the Gwalior Lancers, as already mentioned, near Taung Bazar in the hook of February 4th, 1944; this incident, however, was of no great consequence. Slim remarks drily that the chief contribution the I.N.A. made to either side in the Burma War was considerably later, when the 89th Indian Infantry Brigade had met with various mishaps in their attempt to get across the Irrawaddy by night. They had only country boats, heavy and clumsy, without engines, and to try again by daylight, in a swift-running stream, in the face of what might be strong opposition, would be madness. It seemed they must lose a vital twenty-four hours, when a small boat appeared with a white flag and two 'Jiffs'—that is, Japanese-Indian forces, Bose's men. They reported that the Japanese had moved upstream, believing no doubt that the British movements were a feint, and had left the beach defended only by the I.N.A., who wished to surrender. This proved to be the case. But it should be added that on a number of occasions I.N.A. parties did make themselves useful to the Japanese by shouting contradictory orders; a few small parties fought with courage.

As formations, however, they were negligible. The 1st I.N.A. Division went to the Imphal battle six thousand strong; 715 men deserted and 800 surrendered, 400 were killed in action, about 1,500 died of disease and starvation. About 2,600 returned to rest-stations in September, of whom 2,000 had to be admitted to hospital. This Bose attributed entirely to the Japanese failure to supply or support his men properly, but it is clear that, while they shared the privations of the Japanese defeat, they cracked far more easily than the Japanese. This is not surprising. Bose's utterances show that he believed revolutionary fervour and a passionate love for the motherland would make up for lack of training, leaders and equipment. His men went forward believing that the Indian troops would join them at once; they had only to cry '*Jai Hind!*' ('Victory to India!') to be greeted as comrades. They were greeted instead with bullets; they soon found that they were regarded as traitors by their former comrades, who were full of confidence and were winning the battle. The effect was shattering. They had forfeited their honour as soldiers on false pretences; they had sold themselves to the devil and he had bilked. Revolutionary fervour was confined to Bose's highest commanders, to the men inspired by close and continuous contact with himself. It diminished rapidly with diminishing rank, while inexperience was abysmal. His divisional commanders were captains, his brigadiers were lieutenants, his colonels and majors at the best subadars and jemadars who had never commanded more than a platoon; some came straight from the ranks.

From Imphal onward the story was, from Bose's point of view, one of increasing shame. Desertions grew more and more frequent; 'the Jiffs had little stomach for the fight and fled or surrendered,' wrote Slim of an encounter soon after the crossing of the Irrawaddy; and again, 'the I.N.A. had no wish to fight.' Slim turned south after the crossing of the Irrawaddy and the great battle of Meiktila. Now he began his race for Rangoon and on the way, 'The 1st Division of the Indian National Army was encountered. It surrendered *en masse*, with its commander, 150 officers and over three thousand men.' Bose had already issued general orders that every member of the I.N.A., whatever his rank, was entitled to arrest any other member, whatever *his* rank, if he behaved in a cowardly way, or to shoot him if he acted in a treacherous way. That order would indicate how completely the I.N.A. had crumbled, even if all British eye-witnesses did not stress the contempt in which the Indian Army held them. Indeed, Slim remarks: 'Our Indian and Gurkha troops were at times not too ready to let them surrender and orders had to be issued to give them a kinder welcome.'

This brings us to the question of how they should have been treated. They came in, starving and in rags, defeated and demoralized. Most of them were bitterly ashamed because they had been false to their allegiance, not from conviction but simply as the easy course. In retrospect, it was often said by British officers that they should have been 'dealt with on the spot'. But what exactly did that mean? Legally, all had been guilty of 'waging war against the King Emperor', an offence punishable with death. But no responsible British commander could have ordered the mass executions of several thousand men; on grounds of humanity and justice, of world opinion, of political expediency, it was unthinkable. Slim and his commanders had enough to do in the middle of the battle without thinking out complicated matters of policy by which the political future would clearly be affected. There were very different degrees of guilt which could not be sorted out easily or quickly. And finally, Slim was an operational commander, under the control of South-East-Asia Command, which was an Allied Command. This was a matter for India, and it was to India they were sent back.

Consider the matter first from the point of view of justice, taking the law for the moment at its face value. There were some prisoners of war who had joined the I.N.A. as a means of escape and with the intention of coming back to the British as soon as possible. Opportunities were not always forthcoming and intentions are not easy to prove, but there were such men; they were legally innocent and eventually they were classified 'white' and continued in service. The great majority—70 or 80 per cent—had been credulous about false information, had believed that the British, to whom they had given allegiance, were out of the war, and had believed that what they were doing was the only chance they had of getting home. Such men were legally guilty but in most cases a court would have taken into account extenuating circumstances. Men of this category deserted from the Japanese when they got the chance and were later classified 'grey'. Finally, there were those who clearly knew what they were doing and did their utmost to bring about a Japanese victory, either on a simple calculation of immediate self-interest or because they were captivated by Bose's eloquence. Such men were classified 'black'. Surely no one will argue that all these should have been treated alike, and the classifications were only established after long interrogation and checking which was not possible till the war was ended.

But shake the kaleidoscope and black turns white. How far did the legal position hold good in the circumstances? 'Waging war against the King Emperor' was an offence punishable by death under the Indian Penal Code but Bose rejected the King Emperor's sovereignty and regarded himself as the head of a free Government in exile, like General de Gaulle. He believed he was fighting a just war in a legitimate cause, and some of those classed as 'black' accepted his view. Everyone knew that, at the end of the war, it was intended that India should have some form of freedom; no one thought that leaders of Congress in India who had tried to interfere with the war effort should be shot. In strict law, there was no question that the I.N.A. were rebels, not prisoners of war, but the circumstances were paradoxical. The British were fighting for the freedom to give India freedom; Bose was fighting to take the freedom which they were going to give. In three years' time everyone would be shouting '*Jai Hind!*' Would it really have been wise to treat them strictly as rebels?

There had always been Indian officers whose feelings were contradictory; even those who were most convinced that they had been right to go to Sandhurst and enter the King's service saw it as a way to serve the independent India of the future, which would need trained officers. There were few who had never felt some twinge of doubt as to whether they were on the right side. Such doubts are easy to brush aside when pay is coming in and life is comfortable, not so easy when to reject them means privation and possibly torture; it is a heroic spirit who will face martyrdom for a cause he does not believe in. At the end of the war, when the whole truth was known, many of the loyal Indian officers who would be the backbone of India's new army felt some sympathy with those who had followed Bose.

That however was still in the future in late 1944 and early 1945, when a victorious army was sweeping through Burma under the Union Jack. Its soldiers had sworn allegiance to the King Emperor. They were winning. There was not much doubt or hesitation in their minds; they had no time for traitors. But within three years they had to be transformed into the soldiers of a new dominion, which would need fidelity, stubborn loyalty and military honour. How could those standards be preserved? To exonerate the I.N.A. completely would leave the new army with a disrespect for those essential virtues; to wipe out dishonour in blood might leave it a heritage of political feud. Bose was living; no one knew in 1944 that he would die in an aircraft accident at the moment of Japan's defeat. What would be his position in the India that was to come? And what would be his attitude to an army that had summarily executed his most devoted followers?

Enough has been said to show that it was not easy to apply on the field of battle a rule of thumb that would have been either just or politic. The prisoners were sent back to India and there it was decided in 1944 that the political issues involved were so important that action should be postponed till the end of the war. The I.N.A. should for the time being be treated as prisoners of war, and their existence should remain secret from the public. In the meantime, they should be encouraged to surrender and told they would not be shot. The impression that this would be their immediate fate had been strong among them. One of the I.N.A. officers who had surrendered said: 'The feeling that they will be shot if caught is so strong that it produces a state of hopelessness [made up of] a loathing for the Japanese, a desire to return home and a fear of being shot if they do.' Leaflets were scattered from the air and they began to come in.

By the late summer of 1945 it was clear that the war would soon be over and that the existence of the I.N.A. could not be kept secret much longer. Nor could a decision be postponed as to their treatment. It was agreed, without any serious alternative being proposed, that two principles must be preserved. Such offences as desertion and waging war against the State must not be treated as of no account; on the other hand, there must be no mass executions. The men would be graded as already described; the 'whites' would be reinstated, the 'greys' dismissed, the 'blacks' brought to trial. The latter would in most cases be found guilty and might be sentenced to death but the sentence would be commuted to one of imprisonment for various terms, unless the offender had borne some very special responsibility or had been found guilty not only of desertion and waging war but of some such offence as torture or murder. One officer named Burhan ud Din was alleged to have ordered two men who had been caught trying to desert to be hung up by their arms and flogged by a whole battalion, every man in turn filing past and striking them. When they were taken down, one was dead.

When this policy was announced, the Indian press and most Indian politicians regarded it as moderate and merciful. The war had just ended, the fear of Japanese air attack had gone, there was a brief mood of relaxation. But it did not last. Within a few weeks, a wave of hysteria swept over the press and the vocal public, which the leaders of Congress made no attempt to stem. Privately, many leaders expressed grave doubts; they saw the danger to the army of independent India which they hoped to control. But in public they would only pledge themselves to the cause of the I.N.A. A stage was reached when no evidence of coercion or brutality would be believed; the I.N.A. was a national army and its heroic deeds, largely imaginary, became an article of faith. Not a voice was to be heard from the Indian public in condemnation of soldiers who violated their oath; there was nothing but praise for those who had 'fought for the motherland'. Political leaders who had not been inside a law court for years competed for the privilege of defending the first three of the I.N.A. to be tried.

Two tactical errors were committed by the British. Burhan ud Din, who had had a man flogged to death, was to have been tried first, but his case was postponed at the last minute for a technical reason. The first men who were tried were charged with nothing that did not follow from the initial step of waging war. Once a man had decided on that, it would be his duty to shoot a former comrade on the British side or to confirm the sentence of a court martial on a man trying to desert.

The other error was that Auchinleck had been so confident that Indian opinion would repudiate Burhan ud Din that he decided against the remote place proposed for the first trial and chose one to which the public could have free access. But the place chosen was the Red Fort in Delhi, the former seat of the Mughal Emperor; it had been the symbol of imperial rule at the time of the Mutiny and to recover the Red Fort had been one of the slogans Bose had used. The maladroit choice was interpreted as a deliberate taunt. At the time both mistakes aggravated the wave of hysterical nationalism. In retrospect it seems doubtful whether they made much difference.

Faced with this surge of emotion, Auchinleck as Commander-in-Chief took a decision which demanded great courage. He first made up his mind that the overriding object was 'to maintain the reliability, stability, and efficiency of the Indian Army for the future, whatever Government may be set up in India'. The second pillar of his thinking was that every Indian, including the loyal officers of the Indian Army, was now a nationalist—and ought to be. He could not be a good Indian without wanting Indian independence. On this basis, Auchinleck tried to think forward; he had to weigh the consequences, in the state of public opinion at that time, of proceeding with rigour against men found guilty of waging war against the King Emperor. India was very near independence and if one of the last acts of the imperial power was to punish men for casting off an allegiance which the State was on the point of relinquishing, it would leave a legacy of hatred and was likely to produce an immediate outbreak of violence. Such an outbreak might result, he believed, in 'active and widespread disaffection in the army, especially among the Indian officers and the educated Indian rank and file'. He therefore decided in the case of the first three trials to confirm the finding of guilt, to confirm the sentence of cashiering, but to show clemency in respect of the sentence of transportation for life, which he remitted. This was to act as he believed a Dominion Government would have acted; it demanded great courage because to the majority of British officers it seemed a negation of justice and a betrayal of those who had stood fast.

It was more than that. The trial had become a symbol of India's determination to manage her own affairs. Whatever the rights and wrongs, whatever the facts, Indians were determined that Britain should not as a last act punish these men who had professed to be fighting for India. The trial and its outcome were seen as a defeat for Britain and convinced India that independence was at last really in sight. The decision therefore took a special kind of courage of a high order. It was greeted with relief throughout India and the leaders of the political parties, having ridden with the storm, proceeded to forget the I.N.A. as quickly as they could. But the I.N.A. would not have been forgotten if its heroes had been made martyrs, or if Bose had lived.

6. The Fruits of Victory

Victory over the Japanese was won by the Indian Army and within two years victory brought independence. But it brought also partition. The leaders of Congress and the Muslim League could not agree and at last the British Government had to force the pace, end the discussion and go, leaving two mutually hostile dominions. A power which has held the balance magisterially between conflicting interests cannot go without releasing pent-up forces; no imposed solution will last and an agreed solution—one to which both whole-heartedly agree—is hardly possible because each of the contestants overestimates its own strength. That at least was the case in India, where Muslims had once been rulers and were fiercely convinced they could rule again, while Hindus and Sikhs were equally determined that they should not.

The effect of partition on the Indian Army was tragic. Its fidelity had lasted so long because the army had been insulated against politics but clearly that could continue no longer. Technical needs and education had undermined insulation; since the I.N.A. trials, every soldier had become aware of the clash of loyalties and the pull of nationalism. The trials had brought a gradual process to a sharp point. That the Indian Army of the last two hundred years should not continue as before was inevitable. What was tragic was that it must now serve not one new State but two. It must be divided. What was worse, the grounds for partition denied something that had been essential to the old army and was one of its finer elements.

In the whole great empire of undivided India there had been no better example of co-operation between communities. Squadrons and companies were rivals on the rifle-range or the hockey-ground, each determined to do better than the other, but they were comrades too. In the month of Ramazan, when from dawn till sunset Muslims must abstain from food and, what is much worse, from water, Sikhs and Hindus would ask permission to undertake their duties. They had come to each other's support on a hundred battlefields. But the basis of partition was that Muslims and Hindus could not live together.

It was ironic that the last task entrusted to the Indian Army was to keep the peace on the border between the two new dominions. The area involved was 37,500 square miles—larger than Ireland, North and South—and the population was more than fifteen million, rather more than half Muslim. The task was entrusted to Major-General Pete Rees, who was given the equivalent of about two divisions with which to help the civil administration. The divisions were composed of mixed regiments and battalions which had not yet been divided, though they would be soon. On the night of 14th–15th August, 1947, British rule would end and the two new dominions would come into being. The boundary between them, not yet announced, would divide this area in two, leaving many Sikhs in Pakistan and many Muslims in India. The Punjab Boundary Force was responsible to Auchinleck, who was the Supreme Commander of the forces of both dominions; he was responsible to a Joint Defence Council of high authorities from each dominion.

Men seldom foresee the exact consequences of their actions. But they must, even if vaguely and obscurely, visualize a set of circumstances in which those consequences will take place. The high authorities of the Joint Defence Council must have supposed that on August 15th life on either side of the boundary would be much the same as on August 14th; men would go peacefully to work in their fields, women would grind the corn, cook the meals, scour the brass vessels. They perhaps supposed that Muslim policemen in India and Sikh policemen in Pakistan would carry on their work dutifully until midnight, resuming the next day in a new district on the other side of the border or at least waiting peacefully till told to move. If things had been like that, the Punjab Boundary Force would have had a possible task. It could have acted as military forces had often acted in the past, moving to focal points where trouble had arisen or was threatened, keeping order till calm was restored and people began confidently to go about their business.

But things were not at all like that. In every district, the civil administration was mixed from top to bottom. Neither policemen nor tax-collectors are popular in any society—and a Sikh who had been a policeman in a mainly Muslim district in a Muslim dominion would face a future as unenviable as the Muslim's on the Hindu side of the border. In every district, magistrates, police, civil officials of all kinds, were eager to be on the right side of the border when partition came. But both parties entertained till the last minute extravagant hopes that the boundary would be drawn on a line far more to their advantage than any impartial person could think possible. The last Governor of the undivided Punjab, Sir Evan Jenkins, had gloomily forecast that at the critical moment the whole civil administration would be on the way somewhere else and this was what happened. There was a general post among officials, Hindus and Sikhs going east, Muslims going west.

Nor was it easier for peasants to contemplate living on the wrong side of the line. There had been fearful slaughter in the Punjab in March; both communities wanted revenge and there can be no doubt that both were preparing for it. They wanted revenge—but they wanted more than that. Each wanted to make quite sure of a majority in his own area and the quickest way to get it was to kill the other side. There was a rush of refugees, long columns from either side leaving their lands and houses, taking what they could carry, migrating with a cart and a pair of bullocks, the cooking-pots and the bedding.

Partition came on August 15th; the actual line of the boundary was announced on the 17th. The Punjab exploded; it was no case of isolated incidents. It was civil war, accompanied by complete breakdown of the civil administration. Armed bands made for the lines of refugees and slaughtered, raped and robbed. The forces of communal hatred, once loosed, are usually reinforced by men whose sole purpose is loot and this was now the case. But the main purpose was to kill. Refugee trains were stopped or derailed; the passengers were killed. Trains ran into Lahore and Delhi loaded with the dead. When a line of bullock-carts or a train was too well protected by an army escort, the gangs turned away and made for villages where they could kill without interference.

The task given the boundary force was hopeless. Order can be restored by military force if disorder is limited in space and time. If there are places where rioting is expected, the army can go there, but if people are killing each other in every village there is little they can do. And people must believe that order and the rule of law will some day come again. When that is what they expect, a small force of soldiers and police can exercise an influence far beyond their physical presence. There was no such belief now. A neutral force answerable to neither dominion could exercise authority only over the area it could cover by its fire. It would not be there for ever and whatever it did could be challenged by the leaders of the two dominions. A platoon in every village might have kept the peace but there were fifteen thousand villages and only three hundred platoons. The task required not two divisions but a hundred.

Rees was a man of infectious optimism and enormous energy; on August 17th he wrote to Auchinleck that without his force the slaughter and terror 'would have been desperate and completely out of control,' that they were keeping down the worst of it, that his men were 'standing firm and rock-like as the united Indian Army always has when called on.' But by August 25th he had to report that, although there had not yet been any actual conflict between Muslim and non-Muslim troops, the atmosphere within the force was explosive and any small incident might provoke fighting. The press on both sides attacked the force and its commander, while politicians on both sides were bitterly hostile because it could not carry out an impossible task. Auchinleck realized that the situation was hopeless and asked the two dominions to assume responsibility each on their own side of the border. Both agreed and the force ceased to exist on September 1st.

During the short period of its existence, the men in that force had been under a strain hard to imagine. Their officers would be leaving in a few weeks' time; their battalions would be divided. Their countries were being wrenched apart; their own homes might be in danger. They saw villages burnt, the bodies of women who had been raped and cut to pieces or burnt alive. These were their own people; they too were Punjabis and lived in villages as the refugees had done; they did not know what was happening in their own villages. Discipline and tradition held, but only just; they protected people of both sides, they repelled attacks from both sides, by men armed sometimes with Bren guns and mortars. But discipline and tradition could not have held much longer. They were to be divided and they were obeying officers who were already ghosts.

Some regiments had already been divided. By the end of October, all were to be allotted to one or the other of the two dominions. Regiments all of one class — Marathas, Sikhs, Dogras, Garhwalis — went to India; but there were no regiments wholly Muslim and these must be divided. The 19th Lancers, for instance, went to Pakistan with their

Muslim squadron, receiving Muslim squadrons in exchange from the Poona Horse and the Central India Horse, while their Sikhs went to Skinner's Horse and their Jats to the C.I.H. This regiment was at Peshawar and their regimental history describes the murderous hatred felt there for Sikhs and the difficulty they had in getting their Sikhs to India—protected by their Muslim comrades. So it was with other mixed regiments and battalions; the 1st Punjabis went to Pakistan. 'With great sorrow and amidst moving scenes, the several battalions of the Regiment bade farewell to their Hindu and Sikh brothers in arms,' the Sikhs going to the Sikh Regiment, the Rajputs to the Rajputana Rifles. Some speak of 'heart-rending scenes' and tears as these farewells took place. The Muslim historian of the 1st Punjabis writes of the Indian Army: 'What had taken two hundred years to build was dismembered in three months.'

The Gurkha battalions were a special case, because they were re-cruited from the independent kingdom of Nepal. The arrangement depended on a treaty with the British and was re-negotiated amicably between the new Dominion of India, Nepal and Britain. There had been twenty battalions of Gurkhas in peace, linked in ten regiments of two battalions each. During the war, extra battalions had been raised in each regiment; these were now disbanded, leaving the original twenty. It was agreed that they should be divided, six regiments of two battalions each going to India, four of two battalions each going to Britain. The 5th Royal Gurkhas were a Frontier Force regiment, whose permanent headquarters, like that of the 6th Gurkhas, had been at Abbottabad; this being in Pakistan, they had to leave, and received, in July 1947, orders to move—after 95 years—at a fortnight's notice. It is pleasant to record that the two regiments were given an official civic farewell and that the Abbottabad Municipal Committee passed a resolution recording 'their deep appreciation of the services of the Gurkha regiments ... to the country' and adding: 'The general behaviour of the Gurkha sepoy in his private capacity while dealing with the public has always been exemplary and perfectly gentlemanly.' As the historian of this regiment remarks: 'It is not easy or pleasant to break associations of such long standing but neither is it easy to be sentimental or nostalgic when doing two or three things at a time and doing them for twenty-four hours in the day.'

That was a great mercy. An old soldier once told me that when he first came home to his village he thought only of the regiment. He remembered the games and the companionship and the happiness of a life in which there were no worries and yet a sense of purpose. 'My heart would beat', he said—and he showed with his hand how quickly it would flutter in his breast—'when I heard that one of our old officers was coming on tour and I would hurry to meet him and talk about old times.' But now he had settled down in the village, he thought about the crops and his children, that eagerness had dulled. So it would be one day with all those who now hurried with an ache in the heartstrings through a multitude of tasks.

XXI

Valedictory: One Word More

No one who has persevered through this patchwork of memories and glimpses can doubt that the difference between a bad army and a good is not only a matter of equipment but also of something in the human spirit. Mere enthusiasm is not enough; fervour must be controlled, trained and guided. In the Indian Army two hundred years had built up a tradition and a relationship of a most unusual kind. Was there, in 1947, any hope that some of that tradition would survive?

A break with the past often seems at the time more complete than history will concede. Fortescue ended his monumental history when purchase was abolished for officers and service for soldiers was reduced from twenty-one years to seven; this, he felt, was 'the knell of the old British Army' but few can now remember when it occurred. It is, however, no illusion that something vital changed in 1947. Soldiers cling to the minutiae of tradition; in the British Army, regiments cherish the tradition of a badge, a special button, a flash or a hackle worn to commemorate a royal visit or some feat of gallantry. The regiments of India and Pakistan have cherished many such details. Long after partition I heard the drums and pipes of Punjabi regiments beat the retreat in the Shalimar Gardens at Lahore. The pipe banners bore the armorial devices of British officers long forgotten — stags' heads and castles, crowns and roses. The white spats shone with pipeclay. They wheeled and marched, the drum-major tossed his baton with all the old swagger and precision. For such things — the outward and visible signs of regimental tradition — the two new armies have shown a wise respect.

Nor have they forgotten their old officers. They greet them with genuine pleasure, crowd round them with memories, give them a special reception in the mess, load them with garlands, pour copious libations. Their portraits still hang in the mess, their exploits are recorded in the histories. The old comradeship is remembered, but it can be only a memory. Those officers have gone; new ones have taken their place. What of present realities? How far does anything remain that distinguished this army? What of fidelity to an impossible cause? What of respect for the civil population? Will the new soldiers rival the gentlemanly Gurkhas of Abbottabad? Will they keep aloof from politics, in the sense valued by the English since Cromwell and hallowed since Wellington?

To answer these questions would mean going beyond the scope of this book and writing another. But on one of them a suggestion may be hazarded. A quarter of a century has passed since Independence and the judgement is made in retrospect, but a sufficiently intelligent observer should have been able to foresee that Pakistan would find it more difficult than India to keep the army out of politics. Pakistan was from its foundation an Islamic State; in Islam, there is traditionally no division between Church and State, no distinction of priest from husband and father, of citizen from soldier. All earthly power is delegated from the Almighty and it is indivisible. It is hard for a Muslim to regard life as divided into separate functions and to believe that his particular function is properly exercised if he is merely a good soldier. But the division of function is an essential part of Hinduism, and, though India after partition was supposed to be a secular State, its thought and the structure of its society are still deeply Hindu. It was traditionally the Brahman who was counsellor and the Rajput who was warrior; the new officers become in a modified form a new occupational caste and they perform their proper function outside politics.

That points to one of the secrets of success in the Indian Army of undivided India. It fitted something in the traditional structure of Indian life. It provided a framework of discipline and organization within which the links of family and caste could play their part. The British, like the Muslims before them, gave ground to Hinduism; they were subtly infected by the caste system — cavalry regiments at one time made a return showing the caste of their horses. The idea of martial classes was a part of Hinduism long before Muslim came or British. The British gave way to it, they came to accept it, and they systematized and regularized it so that it became more rigid than ever before. But they did not invent it, nor was it without a foundation in fact. If a man has been brought up to believe that he and his ancestors for generations before him are warriors proud of their courage, if he has been taught that cowardice is the ultimate disgrace, he is more likely to be a good soldier than a man who has been brought up to believe he is the lowest of the low, disgraced for sins in a past life, doomed in this life merely to suffer. Such men can be brave, as the Mahars showed at Koregaum, as the untouchables of the Madras Sappers showed on scores of battlefields. But they have no ready-made stock of pugnacity waiting to be harnessed. Sikhs and Pathans, like the Irish, had exactly that; they would fight each other if there was no one else to fight. It was quicker and easier to make them into soldiers, and, if an army is going to be small, it must be good.

The Indian Army was kept small for financial reasons. India has always been a poor country and in the classical Victorian period it was a policy to keep taxes as low as possible. Low taxes meant a small army — 75,000 British and 150,000 Indian to a population of 350 million — and that meant picking men who could easily be trained to be good soldiers, men who understood before they came to the colours the concepts of military honour: courage, fidelity to comrades, pride in a man's body and his skill at arms, pride in himself and in his regiment, his caste and clan. If it was to be small, it must be good; that it was so small proved that it was good. It proved also the extent to which the people of India accepted British rule as something permanent and inevitable.

The relationship of British officer and Indian soldier was something that grew both from the Indian social scene and from the British. On the Indian side, there was the deep and ancient tradition of allegiance to a superior, with the obligation of protection on one side and devoted service on the other. Closely linked with this were the twin ideas of fidelity to the salt one has eaten and the treachery of ingratitude to salt. It was not hard for the recruit, coming from his village at eighteen or nineteen, to transfer this traditional allegiance to a sympathetic British officer or to the idea of the regiment. And if handled with understanding, the allegiance would become a passionate devotion — which might, very occasionally, if rejected or betrayed, turn to a sudden and hysterical hatred.

This was on the Indian side; but allegiance could not have been given so often and so freely if there had been nothing on the British side to make it worth giving. And here, as we have seen, the British developed an imperial class, men trained as officers, and taught to devote their lives to a double service, of the State and of the men they commanded. Of course some failed to live up to the ideal, but in the high Victorian period — when an Indian regiment still had very few British officers, when everyone was known to everyone else — it was impossible to reject it altogether. And while the tone of one regiment differed very much from another, in most there would be found some officers who paid the ideal a good deal more than lip-service, while surprisingly often there would be at least one officer who was a hero to all his men. They would laugh over the legends of his eccentricities and glory in tales of his daring, but above all they knew that their interests were close to his heart. The whole Victorian achievement owes a debt to those soldiers, schoolmasters, and dons at universities — famous men, renowned for their power, giving counsel by their understanding — who eschewed the love of women and devoted themselves wholly to the instruction and encouragement of young men. Their devotion was usually Platonic and idyllic; it gave the young a companionship that was hardly possible with parents, a wisdom they could not expect from their contemporaries. There is a touch of this devotion in all the great Victorian schoolmasters, in many of the best regimental officers. It is to be seen in the idealization of their men that is so marked a feature of the Indian Army in its classical period. It answered to the allegiance and the devotion which the soldier found for his officer.

When nationalism began to grow, the Indian soldier of the British period was called by compatriots a mercenary — a mere 'rice soldier'. But a British army once made 'mercenary' a term of honour in British ears. And if it means that cash was all that mattered to him, it is rubbish. Men work in factories for cash but they do not die for the honour of the factory. Consider the last Victoria Cross to be mentioned in this book. It was awarded to Rifleman Thaman Gurung of the 5th Royal Gurkhas for his behaviour in Italy on November 11th, 1944. His platoon had advanced into a position on the crest of a ridge which was swept by German machine-gun fire. They had some cover but could not move without showing themselves and probably being annihilated. The company commander ordered them to fall back. But there was no covering fire available and without covering fire they could not move without the certainty of very heavy losses. Rifleman Thaman Gurung ran forward on to the skyline, poured burst after burst of tommy-gun fire into the German trenches and threw two grenades, giving the platoon the covering fire it needed for one section to get back. But it was not enough to get the whole platoon back and he ran forward to the skyline a second time, throwing grenades he had collected and giving two sections the chance to get back. On both occasions he was under heavy fire at short range and it is hard to see how he survived. But he got back to the position, where one section remained. He then took the section's Bren gun, ran a third time to the crest of the ridge and again fired burst after burst at the enemy positions. He had emptied two magazines and the last section was well on its way to safety when he was killed.

That was deliberate self-sacrifice. It is true it was done in the heat of action, when the blood was up and the heart high. But it was not simply unbridled pugnacity, the courage of a brave animal determined to fight; it was done to make the retreat of his comrades possible, and three times he exposed himself to what each time seemed certain death. That kind of disciplined valour can only arise when a man has made a habit of courage. It has become second nature because he has ruled out the idea of cowardice. It has become a matter of honour with him to be a good soldier; he may be only a boy, simple and uneducated, but his is a high form of the same regard for honour that makes a surgeon use his best skill to save life or any man use to the best whatever skill he has, with the plough, the pen or the brush. The soldier seals his devotion to his craft with his life. He may by chance also win honour in the eyes of other men, but not in the highest degree unless his concern is with his own honour, with his own determination to perform his proper function to his own best ability. This is a central virtue of Hinduism and it is close enough to what is best in Islam and in Christianity to have made it possible for men of these three faiths to live and work and die together.

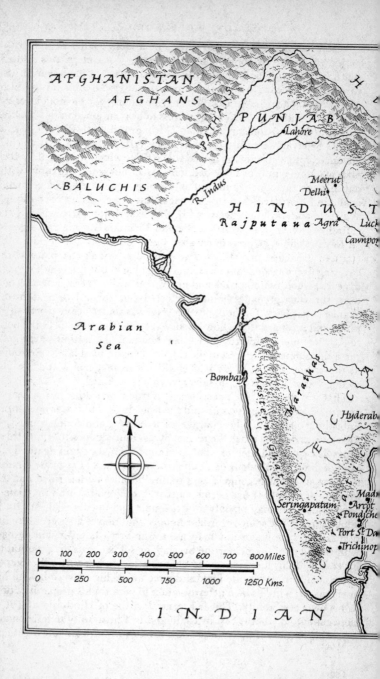

AFGHANISTAN

AFGHANS

PATHANS

BALUCHIS

PUNJAB

•Lahore

R. Indus

Meerut
Delhi•

HINDUST

Rajputana Agra

Luck

Cawnpo

Arabian

Sea

Bombay

Western Ghats

Marathas

Hyderab

D

Seringapatam

Mad

Arcot
•Pondiche

Fort St Da

•Trichinop

N

| 0 | 100 | 200 | 300 | 400 | 500 | 600 | 700 | 800 Miles |

| 0 | 250 | 500 | 750 | 1000 | 1250 Kms. |

INDIAN

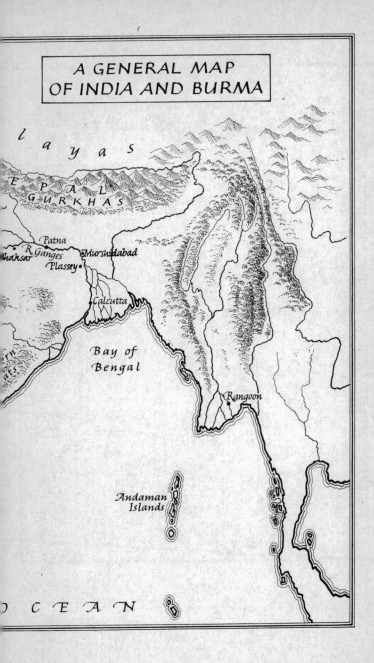

A GENERAL MAP
OF INDIA AND BURMA

l a y a s

E P A L
G U R K H A S

Patna
R. Ganges
Buxar
Murshidabad
Plassey

Calcutta

Bay of
Bengal

Rangoon

rn
ats

Andaman
Islands

O C E A N

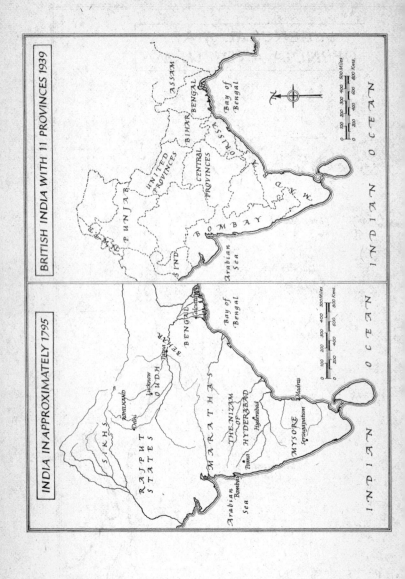

INDIA IN APPROXIMATELY 1795

BRITISH INDIA WITH 11 PROVINCES 1939

Appendix 1

It may be helpful to note the main reorganizations of the Indian Army which involved changing the names of units. There were many lesser reorganizations within the unit, for example, the change from eight companies to four. There were also many more changes of name than are here shown; for the expert, these are detailed in the Marquess of Cambridge's *Notes on the Armies of India*.

1796

In all three armies, pairs of battalions were joined in regiments, with one list of officers. There was a colonel for the regiment and forty-four British officers, twenty-two to each battalion. For example, the 4th Battalion, raised in Bengal in 1758, became the 1st Battalion, 2nd Regiment, Bengal Native Infantry. In the Madras Army, the 3rd Battalion Coast Sepoys, raised in 1759, became the 1st Battalion, 2nd Madras Native Infantry.

1824

In all three armies, the battalions again became separate, each with twenty-two officers in a separate list. In Bengal the 1st/2nd became the 5th Regiment B.N.I. and the 2nd/15th became the 31st. In Madras the 1st/2nd became the 2nd Madras N.I.

1860, 1861, 1863

Several changes took place after the Mutiny; these are summarized in Chapter XIII.

The Bengal line now began with the former 21st, which became the 1st. The former 31st became the 2nd, the former 43rd the 6th Bengal Light Infantry, and so on, those which had not mutinied being retained. The 14th Bengal Native Infantry in 1861 were the Ferozepore Sikhs, (Brasyer's Sikhs), and from this point on the numbers refer to regiments raised after the Sikh Wars or in the Punjab during the Mutiny. Until 1903 the list is chaotic, as the Punjab Irregular Frontier Force is numbered separately, as are the Gurkhas (though the 3rd Gurkhas were once the 18th Bengal N.I. and the 9th Gurkhas were the 9th B.N.I.) and the Hyderabad Contingent. The fate of Madras regiments has been shown in the note to Chapter XIV. Bombay regiments on the whole kept their numbers between 1824 and 1903. Officers were now at first seven to a battalion, raised to nine and step by step to twelve.

1895

The three armies were amalgamated but few changes made in designation.

1903

Lord Kitchener's reorganization. All battalions except the Gurkhas were renumbered consecutively, though as far as possible they kept a number with which they had some association. Thus the 2nd Infantry of the Hill Brigade in the Punjab Frontier Force became the 52nd Sikhs, the 4th Sikh Infantry became the 54th Sikhs, the 5th Bombay Light Infantry became the 105th Mahratta Light Infantry, and the 2nd (Grenadier) Regiment of the Bombay N.I. became the 102nd (P.W.O.) Grenadiers.

1922

The last major reorganization before Independence grouped battalions into regiments of usually five or six active battalions and a training battalion. There were still twelve officers to a unit.

Appendix 2

Notes to pp. 482 and 486.

p. 482

This passage in the first edition was based on the information then available to me. The view that there was no hope of success had been put to me verbally by a number of officers and I thought that General Wavell had been overruled for political reasons. But I have since learnt that General Wavell believed that the military prospects were favourable and that his view was decisive. I therefore apologize for the implication that the Prime Minister disregarded his opinion.

p. 486

It has been pointed out to me that plans for the defence of Singapore were made when the French still held Indo-China. The fall of France changed the whole position and we were then too heavily engaged in the rest of the world to be able to reinforce Malaya on anything like the scale required. The Chiefs of Staff recognized that in these circumstances Singapore could not be successfully defended against a massive attack by land. But it still does not appear that adequate thought had been given locally to the best way of delaying the Japanese advance.

Notes and Sources

I decided against numbers in the text partly because they are distracting to the general reader and partly because much of this book is not attributable to a specific source but to personal experience and general reading. The following notes give the main sources for each chapter and there follows a list of books which should give a sufficient indication of where they are to be found. It is nothing like a complete bibliography, which would need a second volume.

It is impossible to be consistent about the spelling of Indian names without appearing pedantic. Our ancestors wrote 'Lucknow', rhyming with 'tuck' and 'cow'; in a modern phonetic system we should write 'Lakhnao'. 'Maratha' is the modern spelling but the six regular Maratha battalions were 'Mahratta' till 1947. 'Meerut' should really be 'Merath'; and so on. I have kept the traditional British spelling for well-known places and, except in the footnotes, avoided diacritical marks except for an occasional long *a*. But in Hindustani there are four phonetically distinct letters for which we have only *t*, four for *d*, four for *r*, and an even greater variety of gutturals, so it is not surprising that there is some confusion.

I am very grateful for the help I have received from the staff of the London Library and the India Office Library and particularly from A. J. Farrington and Mrs Mildred Archer of the latter. I also thank Mrs Prudence West for her typing and Mr James Atkins for his re-arrangement of the notes and list of books and his sympathetic reading of the text.

I: Ruffle of Drums
Fortescue; Wilson; Cadell; Rafter; Cambridge, *Notes*; Sen, *Marathas*; Moon, *Hastings*; Kaye, *Sepoy War*; Hervey.

II: French and English
Malleson, *Dupleix*; Dodwell; Wilson; Orme; Malcolm; Forrest; Irvine; Malleson, *Clive*; *Siyyar-ul-Muntaqerin*.

The siege of Arcot is described with verve and eloquence in Macaulay's essay on Clive; I have tried to reconstruct it in *The Founders*. There is a story, told by Malcolm and repeated by Macaulay and often since, about sepoys at the siege of Arcot. When the garrison was reduced to a daily ration of a handful of rice for each man, the sepoys begged that their share might be given to their British comrades, who were so much less used to starvation. Enough for them would be the water in which the rice had been boiled. Unfortunately there is a letter from Clive in Arcot to the Madras Council in which he says that there is no shortage of rice; fatigue, not famine, is the danger. Wilson, the historian of the Madras Army, believes that the incident occurred in one of the many sieges which took place in the next few years. The story, being handed on by word of mouth, would easily be transferred from some lesser-known affair to Arcot; it is entirely typical, he adds, of the Madras sepoy.

III: Elephants and Cavalry: The Indian Model
I have relied heavily on Irvine and on Sen, *Marathas*. See also Gleig; Cambridge, *War*; *Arthashastra*. I use Platts' *Dictionary of Urdu and Classical Hindi*.

IV: Rock-like Infantry: The British Model
For the first section of this chapter, see C. T. Atkinson's article on Infantry in the 1911 edition of the *Encyclopedia Britannica*; also Fortescue; G. M. Trevelyan, *The Age of Queen Anne*; Churchill, *Marlborough*; various books about Wellington and the Peninsular War. For Chapter IV generally, Blacker; Dodwell; Wilson; Orme; Cambridge, *War*.

V: Crisis Upon Crisis
On the revolution in Bengal, see Orme; Scrafton; *Siyyar*; Williams; Barat; Broome; Rafter; Trotter; Thorn; Fortescue. On estimates of expenses, see the Hammond's *Town Labourer* and *Country Labourers*. My own *Year of Decision* has some remarks on such estimates in Africa.

VI: An Army in Being
Dodwell; Longford; Edwardes and Merivale; Cadell; Fortescue; Thorn; Creighton; Jackson; *Oxford History*; Garwood. 'A tiger's horrid meal' comes from Rafter; the recipe for cholera from Hervey. For golandaz and guns, see Wilson and Broome; for horse gunners, Hughes; for Sitabaldi, Wilson, Rafter, Jackson; for Kirkee, Cotton; for sappers, Wilson and *Record of Service*. On caste in North India, I have given a much longer explanation in *Patterns of Dominance*; on caste in South India my main authorities are Dubois and Béteille.

The story of the 1st/7th Rajputs was told me many years ago by Lt-Gen. Sir Ernest Wood of that regiment; it is repeated in Jackson and in Bingley, but the earliest written version I have found is in the *Asiatic Register* of 1839. There are some slight discrepancies that I cannot reconcile but they do not affect the point. The story of the five brothers after Assaye is told by Malcolm and repeated by Fortescue and others;

it relates to the 1st/8th Madras Native Infantry of that period who were disbanded in 1902 and not to Wellesley's Rifles (the 1st/16th Rajputana Rifles) who were at that time the 2nd/2nd Bombay Native Infantry.

VII: Generals
For Coote, see Wilks; Sheppard; Wilson. For Wellesley, see Garwood; Longford; Bryant; Weller; Wilson; Cambridge, *Notes*; Thorn; Qureshi; Malleson, *Battles*. (The Marquess of Cambridge's *Notes* have been invaluable throughout.)

VIII: Officers
1. Shore; *Deficiency*; Hervey; Emma Roberts; Sleeman, *Discipline*; Stocqueler; Bellew. 'Burjoor Sing' (Barjur Singh) is mentioned in Creighton.
2. Sleeman, *Discipline*; Briggs; Emma Roberts; Bellew; Atkinson, *Curry*; Meadows Taylor; *Blue Pamphlet*. 'Simlah and the nice young men' from *Deficiency*.
3. Stocqueler.
4. Bevan; Bellew; Hervey. For Napier's and Elphinstone's comments, and deserters to the French, see Cadell; for Wellesley on the Bombay Army, see Garwood; for the lieutenant of 14 and the Company's junior officers, see Wilson.
5. Emma Roberts; Munro; Sleeman, *Journey*; Sleeman, *Rambles*. Bentinck's minute is conveniently accessible in Boulger but a new Life is needed. I have altered the order of some words in the minute to make the meaning clear. Metcalfe is quoted in Boulger, but see Kaye, *Metcalfe*.

IX: Men
1. Sleeman, *Discipline*; dictionary meanings of *iqbal* and *raunaq* from Platts. My conversation in 1957 has appeared in the *Listener*; there is much personal experience in this chapter.

Amiya Barat has collected much valuable material but does not explain why men joined the service. She overestimates the sums paid to domestic servants and does not know how little cash there is in a village on a subsistence economy. Her use of figures is sometimes misleading, but she is sensitive about people's feelings.

The ruse at Bhurtpore is in Creighton.
2. Sita Ram (Lunt's edn); Brasyer; Laverack; Hervey.

X: Gathering Darkness
1. Mackinnon; Sale; Sita Ram; Trotter; Colvin; *Cambridge History*; Eden. But there is a considerable literature on the First Afghan War.
2. Kaye, *Sepoy War*; Lambrick; Barat.

3. Fauja Singh; Khushwant Singh; Kaye, *Metcalfe*; Thompson, *Metcalfe*; Edwardes and Merivale; Brasyer; Pearman.

4. The pattern of mutiny is discussed in *The Founders*. See also Kaye, *Sepoy War*; Barat; Wilson; Fortescue; Rafter; Broome. The 'old native officer' occurs in T. C. Robertson: *Political Incidents of the First Burmese War*, quoted in Kaye.

XI: Fear and its Causes
Kaye, *Sepoy War*; Sen, *1857*; *Oxford History*; Sleeman, *Journey*; Sleeman, *Rambles*; Edwardes and Merivale; Laverack; Metcalfe; *Narrative of the Mutiny at Bolarum*. See also the article on Rifles in the *Encyclopedia Britannica* (11th edn.)

Almost every biography or book of memoirs touches on the threat to property and to religion, the growing intolerance of Indian custom. One of the states which Dalhousie proposed to annex was called Udaipur, but it was not the famous state of Rajputana but a much smaller state far to the east.

XII: The Storm Breaks
1. Kaye, *Sepoy War*; Sen, *1857*. It is not clear how Mangal Pande obtained a sword.

2. Kaye, *Sepoy War*; Sen, *1857*; Gough. But there are many accounts of May 10th. It is interesting that Gough, writing from memory, doubles the sentences on the 85 troopers of the 3rd; he must have felt at the time that they were too severe.

3. Quotations are from Kaye unless otherwise stated. It is Sen who points out the inconsistency of treating Delhi as a captured city and the enemy as rebels. See also Metcalfe; Trevelyan, *Competition-wallah*; Thompson, *Medal*; Smith; Roberts, *Forty-One*. But the sources for the Mutiny are endless.

4. Kaye, *Sepoy War*; Sen, *1857*; Russell; Holmes; Trevelyan, *Cawnpore*; Trevelyan, *Competition-wallah*; Metcalfe.

5. Kaye, *Sepoy War*; Wilson; Cadell; *Record of Service*. For the episode of 'The Lincolnshire Poacher', see Qureshi. 'Extinct as the Dodo' is Macmunn—but by seniority the 21st ought to have been on the right of the line.

XIII: The New Army
1. Russell; Roberts, *Forty-One*.

2. *Reorganization Comm.*; *Letter 235*; Frere; Jacob, *Answers*; Campbell; *Crisis in India*; *Five Letters*; Jacob, *Tracts*; Pelly; Jacob, *Present Condition*; Jacob, *Silladar*; Napier.

3. Younghusband, *Guides*. 'Chinn's Irregular Bhil Levies' appear in 'The Tomb of His Ancestors'.

4. Martineau; Younghusband, *Guides*; Roberts, *Forty-One*. Sylvester has many reminiscences about the Frontier.

XIV: The Martial Classes
1. Personal knowledge; the Indian Army List; Cambridge, *Notes*.
2. Roberts, *Forty-One*; Cambridge, *Notes*; Wilson.
3. Falcon; Bingley, *Sikhs*; Vansittart, *Gurkhas*; Bingley, *Rajputs*; Bingley, *Dogras*; Betham, *Marathas*.

XV: Her Majesty's Servants
1. Churchill; Magnus; Arthur; Smith-Dorrien; Robertson; Birdwood, *Khaki*; Birdwood, *Time*; Maurice; Wavell; Younghusband, *Memories*; Stotherd; Western; Richards; Yeats-Brown; personal conversation.
2. Stotherd; Robertson: Birdwood, *Khaki*; Arthur; Western; Churchill.
3. Watson; Filose; Shakespear.
4. As 1; also Lawrence; Sylvester. The quotation from George Santayana is to be found in the *Oxford Book of Prose*.
5. Arthur; Magnus; Ronaldshay; personal knowledge.

XVI: Change on Two Fronts
Buchan; *Oxford History*; *India's Contribution*; personal experience.

XVII: The First World War
1. Buchan; Merewether and Smith; Willcocks; Condon; Evatt; Drake-Brockman; Younghusband, *Memories*.
2. Censor's Office, Boulogne. For the mutiny at Singapore, see report in India Office Library.
3, 4. Buchan, Qureshi; Condon; Wavell; Evans; Callwell; Betham, *Galley*; Hennell; Lawford and Catto.

XVIII: Between the Wars
Much of this chapter is a summary of what is well known.
1, 2, 3. Deedes (excellent summary of Peshawar mutiny); Moon, *Divide*; personal knowledge.
4, 5. *Indianization Comm.*; *Esher Comm.*; *Indian Sandhurst Comm.*; *Progress Comm.*; *Modernisation Comm.*; *Two Plans*; Pocock; personal information. Reports on Sandhurst cadets are in India Office Library.

XIX: The Second World War: Defeat
Fuller; Slim; *Defeat*; Slim, *Unofficial History*. See also the various official and regimental histories.

XX: The Second World War: Victory
1. Personal knowledge; *India at War*; Fuller.

2, 3. Slim, *Defeat*; Roberts, *Arrow*; Atkinson, *Dogra*; Bamford; Qureshi; Condon; *5th Gurkhas*.
4. Personal knowledge; Slim, *Defeat*; Connell; Young.
5. Filose; personal knowledge; Toye; Connell (who prints Auchinleck's circular to commanding officers about the I.N.A.). My introduction to Toye is more detailed on the I.N.A. than seems proper here.

XXI: Valedictory
5th Gurkhas; Fortescue.

LIST OF BOOKS

The Arthashastra of Kautilya, tr. R. Shamashastry (Mysore 1923)
Arthur, Sir George: *Life of Lord Kitchener* (London 1920)
Atkinson, C. T.: *A History of the 1st Prince of Wales's Own Battalion the Dogra Regiment 1887–1947* (Southampton 1950)
Atkinson, Capt. G. F.: *Curry and Rice* (1856; 2nd edn 1859)
Bamford, Lt-Col. P. G.: *The 1st King George V's Own Battalion the Sikh Regiment 1846–1946* (Aldershot 1948)
Barat, Amiya: *The Bengal Native Infantry: Its Organization and Discipline 1796–1852* (Calcutta 1962)
Bellew, F. J.: *Memoirs of a Griffin* (London 1843)
Béteille, André: *Caste, Class and Power* (University of California 1965)
Betham, Lt-Col. Sir Geoffrey: *Handbooks for the Indian Army: Marathas and Dekhani Musulmans* (1908)
Betham, Lt-Col. Sir Geoffrey, et al.: *The Golden Galley: The Story of the 2nd Punjab Regiment* (Oxford 1956)
Bevan, Major H.: *Thirty Years in India, or A Soldier's Reminiscences 1808–1838* (London 1839)
Bingley, Capt. H.: *Handbook for the Use of Regimental Officers: Rajputs* (Simla 1899)
——*Handbooks for the Indian Army: Dogras* (revised A. B. Longden)
——*Handbooks for the Indian Army: Sikhs* (Simla 1899)
Birdwood, Field Marshal Lord: *In My Time*
——*Khaki and Gown: An Autobiography* (London 1941)
Blacker, Lt-Col. Valentine: *Memoir of the Operation of the British Army in India ... 1817, 1818 and 1819* (London 1821)
The Blue Pamphlet: by an officer once in the Bengal Artillery (London 1858; pamphlet)
Boulger, Demetrius C.: *Lord William Bentinck* (Oxford 1892)
Brasyer, Jeremiah: *The Memoirs of ...* (London 1892)

Briggs, Lt-Gen. John: *A Letter on the Indian Army* (London 1857)

Broome, Capt. Arthur: *History of the Rise and Progress of the Bengal Army* (Calcutta and London 1850)

Bryant, Arthur: *The Great Duke* (London 1871)

Buchan, John: *Nelson's History of the War* (London 1915 onwards.)

Cadell, Sir Patrick: *History of the Bombay Army* (London 1938)

Callwell, C. E.: *Life of General Sir Stanley Maude*

The Cambridge History of India

Cambridge, Marquess of: *Notes on the Armies of India* (Journal of Army Historical Research)

Cambridge, R. O.: *Account of the War in India* (1761)

Campbell, George: *A Scheme for the Government of India* (London 1853; pamphlet)

Churchill, Winston S.: *The Story of the Malakand Field Force* (London 1901)

Colvin, Sir Auckland: *John Russell Colvin* (Oxford 1895)

Condon, W. E. H.: *The Frontier Force Rifles* (Aldershot 1953)

Connell, John: *Auchinleck* (London 1959)

Cotton, J. S.: *Elphinstone* (Oxford 1892)

Creighton, J. N.: *Narrative of the Siege and Capture of Bhurtpore 1825–6* (London 1830)

The Crisis in India: its Causes and Proposed Remedies: by a military officer, signing himself 'Caubulee' (London 1857; pamphlet)

Deedes, Lt-Gen. Sir R.: *Historical Record of the Royal Garhwal Rifles: Volume II* (Dehra Dun 1962)

Deficiency of European Officers in the Army of India: by one of themselves (London 1849)

Dodwell, H.: *Sepoy Recruitment in the Old Madras Army* (Calcutta 1922)

Drake-Brockman, Brig. Gen. D. H.: *The Royal Garhwal Rifles in the Great War* (London 1934)

Dubois, Abbé: *Manners and Customs of the People of India* (London 1817)

Durand, H. M.: *Life of Major General Sir Henry Marion Durand* (London 1885)

Eden, Emily: *Up the Country* (1886; latest reprint 1937)

Edwardes, H. B. and Merivale, H.: *Life of Sir Henry Lawrence* (London 1872)

Evans, Major R.: *A Brief Outline of the Campaign in Mesopotamia 1914–18*

Evatt, Brig. Gen. J.: *Historical Record of the Royal Garhwal Rifles: Volume I* (Aldershot 1922)

Falcon, Capt. R. W.: *Handbook on Sikhs for Regimental Officers* (Allahabad 1896)

Fauja Singh Bajwa: *The Military System of the Sikhs*

Filose, Brigadier A. A.: *The Central India Horse* (vol. II) (London 1956)

Five Letters on Indian Reorganization; to the Editor of the Daily News: by
'C.D.L.' (London 1858; pamphlet)

Forrest, Sir C. W.: *Life of Clive* (1918)

Fortescue, Sir John: *History of the British Army* (London 1910)

Frere, Sir Bartle: *Answers to Letter 235* (Indian Office Library)

Fuller, Maj. Gen. J. F. C.: *The Second World War: A Strategical and
Tactical History* (London 1948)

Garwood, Lt-Col. (ed.): *The Despatches of F.M. The Duke of Wellington ...*
(London 1837)

Gleig, G. R.: *Life of Sir Thomas Munro* (London 1830)

Gough, Gen. Sir Hugh (junior): *Old Memories* (London 1897)

Hennell, Col. Sir Reginald: *A Famous Indian Regiment, The Kali Panchwin*
(London c. 1924)

Hervey, Capt. Albert: *Ten Years in India, or The Life of a Young Officer*
(London 1850)

History of the 5th Gurkha Rifles (vol. II) (Aldershot 1958)

Holmes, T. R. E.: *History of the Indian Mutiny* (1883)

Hough, W.: *Hints Regarding the Reorganization of the Bengal Army* (London
1857)

Hughes, Maj. Gen. B. P.: *The Bengal Horse Artillery 1800–1861* (London
1971)

India at War 1939–1945 (India Office Library Temporary Number 891)

India's Contribution to the Great War (Government of India 1923)

Irvine, William: *The Army of the Indian Moghuls* (London 1903)

Jackson, Major D.: *India's Army* (London 1940)

Jacob, Brig. Gen. John: *Answers to Letter 235* (India Office Library)

——*Papers on Silledar Cavalry* (Bombay 1848)

—— *The Present Condition of the Bengal Native Army* (London 1851)

—— *Tracts on the Native Army of India ...* (1859)

Kaye, Sir John: *Life and Correspondence of Charles Lord Metcalfe* (1854)

Kaye, Sir John and Malleson, Col. G. B.: *History of the Indian Mutiny*
(6 vols.) (London 1897) (a later completion of Kaye's *The Sepoy
War in India*)

Khushwant Singh: *The Sikhs* (1953)

Lambrick, H. T.: *Sir Charles Napier and Sind* (1952)

Laverack, Q.M.-Serg. Alfred: *A Methodist Soldier in the Indian Army*
(London 1874)

Lawford, Lt-Col. J. P. and Catto, Major W. E.: *Solah Punjab: The
History of the 16th Punjab Regiment* (Aldershot 1967)

Lawrence, Sir Walter: *The India We Served* (London 1928)

Letter 235, dated November 25th, 1857, from the Honourable Court of
Directors, setting up a Commission to inquire into the future of the
Army in India, with a series of questions addressed to officers in
India (India Office Library)

Longford, Elizabeth: *Wellington: The Years of the Sword* (London 1969)

Mackinnon, Capt. D. H.: *Military Service and Adventures in the Far East* (London 1849)

Macmunn, Lt-Gen. Sir George: *The Martial Races of India* (London 1932)

Magnus, Philip: *Kitchener* (London 1958)

Malcolm, Sir J.: *Life of Clive* (1836)

Malleson, Col. G. B.: *Clive* (Oxford 1893)

——*The Decisive Battles of India* (1883)

——*Dupleix* (Oxford 1890)

Martineau, John: *Life and Correspondence of Sir Bartle Frere* (London 1895)

Mason, Philip (*see also* Woodruff, Philip): *Patterns of Dominance* (Oxford 1969)

——*Year of Decision* (Oxford 1960)

Maurice, Sir Frederick: *Life of General Lord Rawlinson* (London 1928)

Meadows Taylor, Philip: *The Story of My Life* (1877)

Merewether, Lt-Col. J. W. and Smith, Sir Frederick: *The Indian Corps in France* (London 1919)

Metcalfe, Charles Theophilus (tr.): *Two Native Narratives of the Mutiny in Delhi* (London 1898)

Moon, Penderel: *Divide and Quit* (London 1961)

——*Warren Hastings and British India* (London 1947)

Munro, Sir Thomas: *Disaffection in the Native Army* (1857; pamphlet)

Napier, Sir Charles: *Standing Orders for the Army in Scinde: with rhetorical additions, those drawn up in the Peninsula for the Light Brigade by Robert Craufurd*

Narrative of the Mutiny at Bolarum in September 1855: by an Eye-witness (Edinburgh 1857)

Orme, R.: *History of Military Transactions ... in Indostan* (1803)

The Oxford History of India (Vincent Smith's *History* brought up to date by Percival Spear 1958)

Pearman, Serg. John, ed. Marquess of Anglesey: *Sergeant Pearman's Memoirs* (London 1968)

Pelly, Capt. Lewis (ed.): *The Views and Opinions of Brig. Gen. John Jacob* (London 1858)

Pocock, J. G.: *The Spirit of a Regiment: The History of the 19th Lancers 1921–1947* (1962)

Qureshi, Major Mohammed Ibrahim: *The First Punjabis* (Aldershot 1958)

Rafter, Capt. George: *Our Indian Army* (London 1856)

Rawlinson, H. G.: *Outram's Rifles: A History of the 4th Battalion, 6th Rajputana Rifles* (Oxford 1933)

Record of Service: Queen Victoria's Own Sappers and Miners; and Other Regiments Honoured in 1877

Reports of Censor's Office, Boulogne (India Office Library)

Reports of Government Committees:

    Army in India Committee (chairman Lord Esher) (1919–1920) (Cmd 943)

    Committee on the Indianization of the Indian Army (1922) (I.O.L. Mill. Dept Temp. No. 279)

    Committee ... on the Progress of the Indianization of the Indian Army (June 1923) (I.O.L. Mil. Dept Temp. No. 278)

    Indian Army Reorganization Committee (H.M.S.O., London, 1859)

    Indian Sandhurst Committee (Skeen Committee) (November 1926) (I.O.L. Mil. Dept Temp. No. 309)

    Modernization Committeee (October 1938) (I.O.L. Mil. Temp. No. 570)

Richards, Frank: *Old Soldier Sahib* (London 1936)

Roberts, Emma: *Sketches of Hindustan* (London 1837)

Roberts, Field Marshal Lord, of Kandahar: *Forty-One Years in India* (London 1897)

Roberts, Brig. M. R.: *The Golden Arrow: The Story of the 7th Indian Division* (Aldershot 1952)

Robertson, Sir William: *From Private to Field Marshal* (London 1921)

Ronaldshay, Lord: *The Life of Lord Curzon* (London 1928)

Russell, W. H.: *My Diary in India* (London 1860)

Sale, Florentia: *A Journal of the Disasters in Afghanistan 1841–2* (London 1843)

Scrafton, L.: *Reflections on the Government of Indostan* (London 1763)

Sen, Surendranath: *Eighteen Fifty-Seven* (Delhi 1957)

——*The Military System of the Marathas* (Calcutta 1928)

Shakespear, Col. L. W.: *History of the 2nd King Edward's Own Goorkha Rifles* (Aldershot 1912)

Sheppard, E. W.: *Coote Bahadur: A Life of Lt-Gen. Sir Eyre Coote* (London 1956)

Shore, Sir John: *Correspondence of John, Lord Teignmouth* (vol. II) (London 1843)

Sita Ram (tr. Lt-Col. J. T. Norgate): *From Sepoy to Subedar* (1873; latest reprint, ed. James Lunt, London 1970)

Siyyar-ul-Muntaqerin (Mirza Ghulam Husain, tr. Briggs)

Sleeman, Sir William: *A Journey through the Kingdom of Oudh* (1858)

——*On the Spirit of Military Discipline in the Native Indian Army* (Calcutta 1841; tract)

——*Rambles and Recollections of an Indian Official* (1844)

Slim, Field Marshal Sir William: *Defeat Into Victory* (London 1956)

——*Unofficial History* (London 1959)

Smith, Reginald Bosworth: *Life of Lord Lawrence* (1883)

Smith-Dorrien, Gen. Sir Horace: *Memories of Forty-Eight Years' Service*

Stocqueler, J. H.: *The Old Field Officer ...* (Edinburgh 1853)

Stotherd, Lt-Col. E. A. W.: *Sabre and Saddle* (London 1935)

Sylvester, J. H.: *Cavalry Surgeon* (London 1971)

Thompson, Edward: *Life of Charles Lord Metcalfe* (1937)

——*The Other Side of the Medal* (1925)

Thorn, Major William: *Memoirs of the War in India 1803–1806* (London 1818)

Toye, Hugh: *The Springing Tiger: A Study of Subhas Chandra Bose* (London 1959)

Trevelyan, G. O.: *Cawnpore* (London 1886)

——*The Competition-wallah (*London 1864)

Trotter, L. J.: *Auckland* (Oxford 1893)

Twiss, Maj. Gen. W. L. O.: *Some of My Memories* (1960; privately printed)

Two Plans for Modernizing the Army (1939) (India Office Library Mil. Dept Temp. Nos. 592, 617)

Vansittart, Henry: *Narrative of Transactions in Bengal* (1756)

Vansittart, Lt-Col. Eden: *Handbooks for the Indian Army: Gurkhas* (Calcutta: reprinted (rev. Nicolay) 1915)

Watson, Maj. Gen. W. A.: *The Central India Horse: The Story of a Local Corps* (1930)

Wavell, General Sir Archibald: *Allenby, A Study in Greatness* (London 1940)

Weller, Jac: *Wellington in India* (London 1972)

Western, Col.: *Reminiscences of an Indian Cavalry Officer* (London 1922)

Wilks, Col. Mark: *Historical Sketches of the South of India* (London 1817)

Willcocks, Gen. Sir James: *With the Indians in France* (London 1920)

Williams, Capt. J.: *Bengal Native Infantry 1757–1796* (London 1817)

Wilson, Col. W. J.: *History of the Madras Army* (Madras 1882)

Woodruff, Philip (Philip Mason): *The Men Who Ruled India: Vol. I, The Founders* (London 1953); *Vol. II, The Guardians* (London 1954)

Yeats-Brown, F.: *Bengal Lancer*

Young, Desmond: *Rommel* (London 1950)

Younghusband, Maj. Gen. Sir George: *A Soldier's Memories in Peace and War* (London 1917)

——*The Story of the Guides* (London 1908)

Index

I am very grateful to F. N. Crofts, formerly Indian Civil Service, who has generously made the index

---

Regiments are, as a rule, indexed under the names they bear in the text, with references or cross-references to any other names they may have borne at various times, provided that those names too are in the text. Where, however, a regiment was distinguished by only a numeral (e.g. 10th Foot, 3rd Cavalry) it will be found under a general heading such as 'Bengal Native Infantry' or 'British Infantry Regiments' (for this group the modern names are added in brackets). The Highlanders are also listed together. British regiments have 'H.M.' in front of their names or numbers where there might otherwise be uncertainty about nationality.

pore, 128; in Skinner's Horse, 316, and Sikhism, 352–4; compared with Dogras, 357; recruitment of, 359, 450, 451; love to intrigue, 391; in Punjab, 450; and partition of Army, 526

Java, expedition to, 170, 204, 334

Jawan (young man: hero), 182, 315, 328, 391

Jehan Dad Khan, Naik, 417–18

Jemadars: number in company, 62, 63; sit on courts-martial of sepoys, 66; in cavalry, 141, 144, 317, 513; in Engineers, 147; number in battalion, 173, pay and pension of, 173, 201; long-serving, 173; delegation of work to, 178, prize-money for, 206, in infantry, 317; and redundancy, 455, 511

Jemal, Turkish governor in Syria, 433

Jenkins, Sir Evan, Gov. of Punjab, 524

Jenkins, Sir R., Resident of Nagpur, 142–3

Jenkyns, Mr, 332–3

Jennings, Captain, 100–104

Jennings, Miss, 300

Jerusalem, 428, 430, 433

Jewand Singh, Jemadar, 333

Jhansi (city), United Provinces, 148

Jhansi district, United Provinces, 490, 491

Jhansi State, annexed, 254; Rani of, 254, 255, 297, 304

Jinnah, Dr Mohammed Ali, 463, 478

Jodhpur, Maharaja of, 389

Jogendra Singh, Sir, 463

Joint Defence Council, 523

Juah River, 159, 160–61

judicial courts, sepoys' status in, 206, 257

Juggernaut, temple of, Puri, 168

Jumna, River, 186, 279, 284, 357–8

jungle warfare, 486, 494, 497; training for, 498

justice: administration of, 30; British, 389–390, 393–4, 445

Kabir, Guru, 352

Kabul, Afghanistan, 426: retreat from, 19, 233–5, 430; Company's reputation for invincibility shattered by disastrous retreat from, 131, 162, 219, 225, 247, 313; Russian threat via, 194, 220, 325; Sita Ram and, 207, 209, 223; captured, 221–3; Indian troops at, 227, 269; attack on Residency at, 332–3, 441

Kadir Dad, 421

Kaiser (Wilhelm II) of Germany, 299, 362, 425, 439

Kaitna River, 157, 159, 162

Kali Panchwin ('Black Fifth'), 342, 344; see also Mahratta Light Infantry, 5th (Royal)/5th

Kandahar, Afghanistan, 220, 221, 222, 225, 269, 348, 356, 398

Kandahar, Battle of (1880), 381

Kalewa, Burma, 505

Kapur, Singh, Jemadar, 416

Katwa, Battle of (1763), 99–100, 151

Kautilya, 42, 43, 54, 55

Kaveripak, Battle of (1752), 37

Kaye, Sir John (quoted), 234, 246, 248, 249, 259, 261, 263, 266, 276, 277, 290, 295, 296, 299, 301, 302

Kedar Sing Rawat, Subadar, 420

Kelly, Mr, 332–3

Kenya, 480; Sikhs in, 514

Keren, Abyssinia, 481, Khalsa Diwan, 408

Khan, Lieut. H. H., 508

Khartoum, Sudan, 398

Khatmandu, Nepal, 137

Khattris, 391; see also Banias

Khilafat movement, 449, 451

Khuda Dad, Sepoy, 415

Khyber Pass, 209, 222, 398

Kilpatrick, Major, 86

King's Commissions, for Indians, 348, 454–5, 457, 459–66, 519; King's Commissioned officers, 468

King's Service, 31, 111, 188–9, 194; see also Royal regiments

Kipling, Rudyard, 64, 70, 98, 368, 374; (quoted), 47, 326, 363, 364, 382–3

Kirkee, Bombay, 143

Kirkee, Battle of (1817), 136, 142

Kirti Lehar (Peasant Movement), 513–14

Kitchener, Field-Marshal Lord: character of, 364, 392–3; on venereal disease, 368–9; reorganizes Indian Army, 373, 398–400, 438, 534; becomes Commander-in-Chief, 375, 392, 394–5; prefers recruits from North India, 384; encourages competitiveness, 384–5; dominates Indian Army, 392; and Curzon, 397–8, 400–401; wants the Mutiny forgotten, 401, 469; relies too much on centralization, 442; and the position of Commander-in-Chief, 453; and brigading of troops, 509

Knox, Capt. Richard, 79, 90, 94–5, 100, 106, 107

Kohima, Assam, 488, 501, 505–6

Koregaum, Battle of (1818), 15–17, 21, 144, 529

Kshatriyas, 124

Kulbir Thapa, Rifleman, 421, 422

Kumaon, N.W. Provinces, 137

Kumaon Battalion (3rd Queen Alexandra's Own Gurkha Rifles), 287

Kunwar Singh, 293

Kurdistan, 411

Kurram, the, N.W.F. Province, 336

Kut, Mesopotamia, 430–31, 432–3, 435–6, 438, 439, 440, 442–3

Kutuzov, General, 150

La Bassée, France, 412, 418

La Bourdonnais, Bertrand-François Mahéde, 33–4

Lahej, skirmish at (1917), 438–9

Lahore, Punjab, 283, 290–91, 293, 330, 524, 528

Lahore Division, 3rd, 412, 413, 415, 432, 440

Lake, Gen. Lord, 184, 189, 213, 334: his victorious campaign in Second Maratha War, 19, 128, 135, 141, 146, 162, 180,

MORE ABOUT PENGUINS
AND PELICANS

Penguinews, which appears every month, contains details of all the new books issued by Penguins as they are published. From time to time it is supplemented by *Penguins in Print*, which is our complete list of almost 5,000 titles.

A specimen copy of *Penguinews* will be sent to you free on request. Please write to Dept EP, Penguin Books Ltd, Harmondsworth, Middlesex, for your copy.

In the U.S.A.: For a complete list of books available from Penguins in the United States write to Dept CS, Penguin Books, 625 Madison Avenue, New York, New York 10022.

In Canada: For a complete list of books available from Penguins in Canada write to Penguin Books Canada Ltd, 41 Steelcase Road West, Markham, Ontario.